WHO KNEW? II

WHO KNEW? II

OVER 15,000 TIPS, SECRETS, FACTS AND QUICK FIXES TO MAKE YOUR LIFE EASIER, YOUR HOME CLEANER, AND YOUR FOOD TASTE BETTER—ALL WHILE SAVING TIME AND MONEY

BY JEANNE BOSSOLINA LUBIN AND BRUCE LUBIN

Castle Point Publishing
Hoboken, NJ

DEDICATION

To Jack, Terrence and Aidan, for everything, and to Beth Blackburn and Maureen Lordon, for keeping our engines running.

ACKNOWLEDGEMENTS

We're grateful to our families for putting up with us while we wrote this book, particularly to our three boys for their good humor as we missed more than a few soccer matches, basketball games, and other events. Kids, this isn't the first time your parents will disappoint you—get used to it. Once again, James Tavendale pulled a rabbit out of his hat and has proven to be an indispensable resource. Karen Matsu Greenberg has forgotten more about printing books than we'll ever know, and we're thankful for her for keeping us on track with our schedules. Joy Mangano has been a good friend and inspiration, and we'll always be grateful for her boundless energy, words of encouragement and sound advice. Joanie Rudolph and Andrea Cajuste have guided us through the scary, scary world of shipping, logistics and stickering, and imparted so much information to us that we thought our heads would explode (which we would have cleaned up with club soda and vinegar, naturally). Thanks, ladies, for not laughing at us as we asked a series of dim-bulb questions. The team at Quadrum Solutions have done a remarkable job designing and typesetting this book, and we're still scratching our heads and wondering how they manage to work 27 hours a day. Finally, special thanks to Brian Scevola, who suggested we write this book in the first place, and offered enthusiastic guidance throughout the entire process. Brian, you handled every setback and delay with good humor and patience (and maybe just a little profanity), and for that we're grateful.

CONTENTS

CHAPTER 1
SIMPLE STAIN REMOVERS   11

CHAPTER 2
HOUSEHOLD HEROES   41

CHAPTER 3
ESSENTIAL BEAUTY TIPS   61

CHAPTER 4
MORE TIME- AND MONEY-SAVING TIPS   91

CHAPTER 5
PESTS & PETS   153

CHAPTER 6
WATER, BOOZE & PARTIES

167

CHAPTER 7
IN THE BATH

201

CHAPTER 8
HERBS & VITAMINS FOR HEALTH AND HEALING

209

CHAPTER 9
FRIDGE & FREEZER FACTS

217

CHAPTER 10
SURF & TURF TIPS

231

CHAPTER 11
TURKEY TIPS AND CHICKEN FACTS 285

CHAPTER 12
CHEF'S SECRETS 299

CHAPTER 13
FOR THE BAKER 339

CHAPTER 14
POTATOES, PASTAS & GRAINS 393

CHAPTER 15
SOUPS, STEWS & SEASONINGS 423

CHAPTER 16
CHEESE, EGG & DAIRY 475

CHAPTER 17
FRUIT & VEGGIES 517

CHAPTER 18
AT THE SUPERMARKET OR RESTAURANT 643

CHAPTER 19
IMPORTANT SAFETY TIPS 657

CHAPTER 20
FREE STUFF! 669

SIMPLE STAIN REMOVERS

TEST IT FIRST

Always test a stain remover on an area of the fabric that will not show to be sure how colorfast the fabric is. Allow the product to stand on the area for at least three to five minutes before rinsing it off. If there are any changes in the fabric's color, do not use the remover.

ORDER BY MIDNIGHT TONIGHT!

Don't be taken in by TV commercials and newspaper ads touting cleaners that take any spot or stain out of any fabric. They're often just a combination of a detergent and bleach. Most do work well, but you can make them effectively at home.

FORGET IT

If you wash clothes in cold water, you don't need to purchase a special cold-water detergent. The difference between detergents formulated for hot and cold water washing is insignificant. The only compound that is capable of changing the effectiveness of a detergent is a surfactant, and most detergents have similar amounts. Surfactants actually make the water "wetter" by changing the surface tension, so the water and detergent enter the fibers of the garment more freely.

RUST? TRY LEMON JUICE

Remove rust stains by wetting the spots with lemon juice, then sprinkling with salt. Let the fabric stand in direct sunlight for 30 to 45 minutes.

ONION FOR BURNS AND INK STAINS

Scorch marks will come out if you rub the area with a raw onion and let the onion juice soak in thoroughly—for at least two to three hours—before washing. Try this on ink stains, too.

LEMON WORKS

Lemon extract will remove black scuffmarks from shoes and luggage. So will rubbing alcohol.

SHINE ON

To shine chrome fixtures, dampen them, and then rub them with newspaper. Baby oil and a soft cloth work well, too.

STAIN REMOVAL RULES

- Never wash any fabric before attempting to remove the stain. Washing in a detergent and the heat of the dryer may actually set the stain and make it impossible to remove later.
- Stains on washable fabrics should be treated as soon as possible. Remember, fresh stains will come out more easily than old ones. Items that normally go to the dry cleaner should be taken there as soon as possible. Point out the stain to the dry cleaner, and identify what caused it. Different stains can require very different treatments.

STOCK UP ON THESE

Prompt treatment is the key to stain removal, and it's wise to have the supplies on hand at all times. Listed on the next page are some of the more common items needed for most stain removals. In case you run out of an item, look in this chapter for natural stain removers, as well as tips for using common cleaning products.

BOOM!

Most solvents are highly volatile. Heed all warnings on bottles as to use, storage, and proper disposal of empty containers to prevent disasters.

SPOT BEGONE

When treating a spot, place the cloth with the stain facedown on paper towels, then apply stain remover to the back of the cloth, allowing the stain to be forced to the surface and not back through the fabric. If the stain is stubborn, replace the paper towels frequently.

Cleaning Must Haves	
BLEACHES	Chlorine bleach
	Fabric color remover
	Nonchlorine, all-fabric bleach
MISCELLANEOUS REMOVERS	Ammonia
	Rust-stain remover
	White vinegar
DETERGENTS	Enzyme detergent
	Enzyme presoak
	Liquid detergent
SOLVENTS	Dry-cleaner spot remover
	Nail-polish remover
	Rubbing alcohol
	Turpentine
SOAPS	Laundry detergent
	White bar soap
SUPPLIES	Clean white cloths
	Paper towels

CLUB SODA CURE

Bloodstains can cleaned with cold club soda. Just pour it on and rub with a soft cloth.

VINEGAR, AGAIN

If you suspect the rinse cycle isn't getting all the soap out of your clothes, add 1 cup of white vinegar while they are rinsing. The vinegar will dissolve the alkalinity in detergents as well as give the clothes a pleasant fragrance.

WATCH OUT

If you're using chemicals that give off vapors, work in a well-ventilated location, preferably outside. A mask specifically designed to protect from fumes is necessary so you don't inhale harmful vapors.

LEARN THIS

Caution! Never use a solvent near an open fire or even something that seems as benign as a lit cigarette or an electrical outlet. Nearly all solvents are extremely flammable.

PAY ATTENTION

Some stain removal materials are flammable, while others are poisonous or toxic. Store them safely and use them with care. Never allow chemicals near your face and eyes; wear rubber gloves and safety goggles in case they splash. Wash any spilled chemicals off your hands as soon as possible.

Keep stain removal supplies out of the reach of children. They should be stored in closed containers, ideally their original ones, with childproof lids and in a cool, dry location away from any food products.

NEVER EVER

Never add solvents directly to the washing machine. Always let a solvent-treated fabric dry before washing or putting it into the dryer.

A TOXIC BREW

Never mix stain removal materials, especially ammonia and chlorine bleach.

SAFE CLEANING PRODUCTS

The recipes below are safe when mixed exactly as directed. Varying from these quantities or from these products may be dangerous.

All-Purpose Household Cleaner

Add 1 teaspoon of any liquid soap and 1 teaspoon of trisodium phosphate (TSP) to 1 quart of warm water. This is a great cleaner for most cleaning jobs, including countertops and walls. However, try an area of the wall that will not show before using it, in case your walls are painted with a poor-quality water-based flat paint.

Chlorine Bleach

Best to use a hydrogen peroxide-based bleach.

Degreaser Number 1

To clean you car's engine, use a water-based cleaner that is well diluted (instead of kerosene or turpentine) or a commercial engine degreaser, available in auto-parts stores. Look for labels that say "nonflammable," "nontoxic," or "store at temperatures above freezing." These are water-based products and will do the job.

Degreaser Number 2

For the grill, add 2 tablespoons of TSP to 1 gallon of hot water, or use a scouring pad or steel-wool pad sprinkled with a nonchlorinated scouring cleanser.

Fabric Softener

Fabrics made of from natural fibers do not need fabric softeners; only synthetics do. Add ¼ to ½ cup of baking soda to the wash cycle to soften synthetic fabrics.

Floor Cleaner

For mopping vinyl floors, use ½ cup of white vinegar added to 1 gallon of warm water. For wood floors, damp-mop with a mild liquid soap.

Furniture Polish

Mineral oil may be used, however, most wood surfaces can be cleaned with a damp cloth.

Glass Cleaner

Fill a 3-cup spray bottle with ½ teaspoon of liquid soap, 3 tablespoons of white vinegar and 2 cups of warm water. If the windows are very dirty, use more liquid soap.

Laundry Detergent

Use laundry soap instead of detergent. Baking soda can be used in place of a fabric softener. An alternate would be to use a detergent with no added bleaches or softeners. Bleach should be used in moderation, and only when needed.

Mildew Remover

Scrub the area with baking soda; if very stubborn, scrub with TSP.

Oven Cleaner

Mix 2 tablespoons of baking soda or TSP in 1 gallon of warm water and scrub with a very fine steel wool pad (0000 grade). Rubber gloves should be worn and the area rinsed well. For difficult baked-on areas, try scrubbing with a pumice stone. If this fails, use an oven cleaner with "no caustic fumes" on the label.

WHO KNEW?

Ink stains got you down? Just spray ultra stiff hairspray on the stain and launder as usual.

Scouring Powder

Baking soda will work well in most instances.

Toilet Bowl Cleaner

Use a nonchlorinated scouring powder and a stiff brush. To remove hard-water deposits, pour white vinegar, a mixture of white vinegar and baking soda, or a commercial citric acid-based toilet bowl cleaner into the toilet and allow to sit for several hours or overnight before scrubbing. A fizzy denture tablet works well too!

DON'T FORGET

Washing soda (which can be found in the laundry section of your supermarket) and TSP are caustic and should always be kept out of the reach of children. TSP is a skin irritant—so always wear rubber gloves to protect your hands.

SUEDE STRATEGIES

Water spots can be removed from suede by rubbing lightly with an emery board. If there are grease spots on suede, blot with white vinegar, then brush lightly with a suede brush.

HOW TO REMOVE JUST ABOUT ANYTHING

Remember, even the best enzyme detergent or enzyme presoak product is not capable of removing all types of stains. Grease and highly colored stains may require special pretreatment before laundering. Because many stains require a variety of different treatments and techniques, it is important to identify a stain before trying to remove it. A number of stains may actually be set if the wrong method is used.

The following stains can usually be removed with the recommended methods that are specified. Use these treatments on washable fabrics only. Treat the stain, and then make sure it is gone before drying the fabric. Once it dries, the stain may never come out.

HOW TO REMOVE JUST ABOUT ANYTHING

STAIN	METHOD OF REMOVAL
Alcoholic beverage	Sponge the area with cold water or soak, then sponge again. Launder with oxygen bleach and the hottest water that is safe for the fabric.
Blood	Soak the fabric in cold water as soon as possible. If the stain persists, soak in warm water with a presoak product before laundering. Try club soda.
Candle wax	Scrape off surface wax with a dull knife. Place the item stained side down on paper towels and sponge the remaining stain with dry cleaning solvent. Let dry, and then launder. If traces of color from the wax remains, try soaking it in an enzyme presoak or an oxygen bleach before laundering again. If the stain is still present, launder again using chlorine bleach, if the fabric is chlorine-bleach safe.
Ketchup and tomato products	Remove excess with a dull knife, then soak in cold water 30 minutes before laundering in the hottest water the fabric will stand.
Chewing gum, adhesive tape, rubber cement	First apply ice to the adhesive to harden it. Scrape off as much as you can with a dull knife. Place the item face down on paper towels and sponge with a dry-cleaning solvent.
Chocolate and cocoa	Soak the article in cold water 30 minutes, then launder with oxygen bleach using the hottest water the fabric will stand.
Coffee and tea	Soak in an enzyme presoak or oxygen bleach using the hottest water that is safe for the fabric for 30 minutes, then launder. If the stain is still present, launder again using chlorine bleach if it is safe to do so.
Cosmetics	Dampen stain with water and rub gently with white bar soap, then rinse well and launder.
Crayon	If there are only a few spots they can be treated the same as candle wax. If there are many items that are stained, first wash the items with hot water and laundry soap (e.g., Ivory Snow)—not laundry detergent—and 1 cup baking soda. If the spots remain, have the clothes dry-cleaned.
Deodorants and antiperspirants	Apply white vinegar, then rub and rinse. If the stain remains, saturate the area with rubbing alcohol, rinse, then soak in Biz or an oxygen bleach, and launder. If the stain remains, wash in chlorine bleach if it is safe for the fabric.
Dye transfer	If you have white fabrics that have picked up dye from a colored garment that bled, restore the white by using a fabric color remover. If any of the dye remains, launder using chlorine bleach if it is safe for the fabric.
Egg and meat juice	Remove excess with a dull knife, then soak in cold water 30 minutes. Then launder in oxygen bleach in very hot water.

STAIN	METHOD OF REMOVAL
Fabric softeners	Fabric softener stains usually result from accidental spills and can be removed by rubbing the area with a piece of cloth moistened with bar soap before laundering. You can also try a paste of water and detergent, or a prewash stain remover.
Infant Formula	Soak in warm water, then launder with oxygen bleach in the hottest water that is safe for the fabric.
Fruit and fruit juices	Soak in cold water before laundering.
Grass	The green area should be sponged with denatured alcohol before washing in very hot water and oxygen bleach.
Grease stains	The stained area should be placed facedown on paper towels. Blot with dry cleaning solvent on the back side of the stain, then brush from the center of the stain to the outer edges using a clean white cloth. Moisten the stain with warm water and rub with bar soap or mild liquid detergent, then rinse and launder.
Gum	Rub with ice and carefully remove the gum with a dull knife before laundering.
Ink stains	To remove ball-point pen ink, place the stain face down on paper towels and sponge the back of the stain with dry cleaning solvent. If there is some ink left, try rubbing the area with moistened bar soap, rinse, and then launder. For ink other than ball-point or felt-tip pen ink, try to remove the stain with a dampened cloth and bar soap, rinse, and soak in an enzyme presoak or oxygen bleach using very hot water. If the stain won't come out, try chlorine bleach, if the fabric is safe. Some permanent inks may never be removed. For felt-tip pen ink, rub the area with Fantastik or Mr. Clean, rinse, and repeat if necessary. These stains may be impossible to remove.
Iodine	Rinse the fabric from the underside with cool water, then soak in a solution of fabric color remover, rinse, and launder.
Lipstick	Place so the stain is face down on paper towels, then sponge with dry-cleaning solvent, replacing the paper towels frequently. Moisten the stain with cool water and rub with bar soap, then rinse and launder.
Mildew	The fabric should be laundered using chlorine bleach if it is safe for the fabric. If not, soak it in oxygen bleach before laundering.
Milk	The fabric should be rinsed in cold water as soon as possible, then washed in cold water using a liquid detergent.
Mustard	Moisten the stain with cool water, then rub with bar soap, rinse and launder using a chlorine bleach, if it is safe for the fabric. If not, soak in an enzyme presoak or oxygen detergent using very hot water, then launder. It may take several treatments to remove all of the stain.

STAIN	METHOD OF REMOVAL
Nail polish	Blot up the excess from both sides of the fabric with paper towels. If the fabric can withstand acetone or nail-polish remover, work it in from the inside of the fabric by pressing it in gently with a paper towel.
Paint	Treat the stain while it is still wet; latex, acrylic, and water-based paints cannot be removed once dried. While the paint is wet, rinse in warm water to flush the paint out, then launder. Oil-based paints can be removed with a solvent; your best bet will be to use one recommended on the paint can. If none is mentioned, blot with turpentine, rinse, and rub with bar soap, then launder.
Perspiration	Moisten the stain and rub with bar soap. Be gentle, as perspiration may weaken some fibers, especially silk. Most fabrics should be presoaked in an enzyme presoak or detergent and then laundered in hot water and chlorine bleach, if it is safe to use on the fabric.
Perfume	Same as alcoholic beverages.
Rust	Apply a rust stain remover, rinse, then launder. You can also use a fabric color remover and then launder, or if the stain is really stubborn, dissolve 1 ounce of oxalic-acid crystals (or straight warm rhubarb juice) in 1 gallon of water in a clean plastic container. Soak the garment in this solution until the stain is gone, then rinse and launder. Never use chlorine bleach on rust.
Scorch marks	For washable fabrics, use all-fabric bleach. For non-washables, use hydrogen peroxide.
Shoe polish	Try applying a mixture of 1 part rubbing alcohol and 2 parts of water for colored fabrics and only the straight alcohol for whites. Sponge this on, then launder.
Tar	Rub gently with kerosene until all the tar is dissolved, then wash as usual. Test a small area first to be sure the fabric is color fast.
Tobacco	Moisten the stain and rub with bar soap, then rinse and launder. If the stain persists, try soaking it in an enzyme presoak or oxygen detergent before laundering. As a last resort use chlorine bleach, if it is safe for the fabric.
Urine, vomit, and mucus	Soak the fabric in an enzyme presoak or detergent, then launder using chlorine bleach, if safe for the fabric. If not, use an oxygen bleach with a detergent.
Wine and soft drinks	Soak the fabric with an enzyme presoak or oxygen bleach using very hot water, then launder. Use chlorine bleach if needed and if it is safe for the fabric.

WHO KNEW?

If wax drips on silver candlesticks, simply put them in the freezer. The wax will peel off easily.

A REALLY TOUGH STAIN

Iodine stains can be removed using a mixture of baking soda and water. Allow to remain on for about 30 minutes, and then rub gently.

THRIFTY AND NIFTY

To use less detergent—and save money—put slivers of old soap in a sock with the neck tied. Put the sock into the washer and it won't be necessary to use a full amount of detergent.

STAIN REMOVAL SMARTS

A number of stains can be removed right in your washing machine. Laundry detergents that state that they contain enzymes will provide the best cleaning and stain removal. Enzyme presoak products provide extra cleaning and stain removal for fabrics that may have more difficult stains.

An enzyme detergent or enzyme presoak product should be able to remove the following common stains: blood, gravy, body soils, egg, fruits, milk, chocolate, grass, cream soups, infant formula, baby foods, pudding, vegetables, ice cream, and most other food stains.

CHEAPER AND JUST AS GOOD

To make your own spray starch, purchase a bottle of liquid starch concentrate and mix equal parts of liquid starch and water in a spray bottle.

UNUSED FLOSS IS PREFERRED

When buttons pop off, sew them back on with unwaxed dental floss, which is much stronger than thread.

ZIPPER STUCK?

Rub beeswax on the zipper and the problem is solved.

STORING YOUR STUFF

Empty and wash all stain-removal containers immediately after using them. It is best to store stain removal supplies in their original containers. If you need to transfer them to smaller containers to use, opt for glass containers, because solvents will ruin plastic. Rusty containers should never be used.

THE SHOWER CURTAIN TRICK

Need to remove mildew from a plastic shower curtain? Wash the curtain with two large white bath towels in ½ cup bleach and 1 cup powdered detergent in a washing machine filled with water. To prolong the life of the shower curtain, add 1 cup white vinegar to the rinse cycle.

WITHOUT ORDER, WE HAVE CHAOS

Your clothes will get cleaner if you turn the washer on while it's empty, add the detergent, and let the detergent dissolve and mix with the water before you add the laundry. Putting detergent onto clothes that are still dry can cause dyes to fade.

THESE COLORS DON'T RUN...THANKS TO *SALT*?

Washing colored material for the first time can be risky unless you wash it in salt first. Really. Add ¼ to ½ cup salt to the wash water (about 1 teaspoon per gallon of water). The colors will not run.

NO MORE IRONING

Banish wrinkles easily by removing clothes from the dryer the second it stops. Fold or hang them up immediately.

TOOTHPASTE? MOLASSES?

Get this—you can get rid of grass stains with toothpaste. Scrub it into the fabric with a toothbrush before washing. Or rub the stain with molasses and let stand overnight, then wash with regular dish soap by itself. If all else fails, try methyl alcohol, but be sure the garment is colorfast.

NICE AND EASY

Wash woolen garments with great care, since wool fibers are very weak when wet. Don't pull, stretch, or wring out the garment. Instead, roll it in a towel and squeeze the excess water out, and then dry flat.

IF YOU HAVE KIDS, READ ON

To remove dirt from difficult areas like shirt or blouse collars, mix $1/3$ cup water, $1/3$ cup of liquid detergent, and $1/3$ cup ammonia in a spray bottle. Rubbing shampoo into the area can also do the job. Just be sure you never mix ammonia with bleach.

INSIDE OUT

To keep corduroy garments from retaining lint, wash them inside out. This also will keep acrylic sweaters from pilling.

AND PRESTO! THE BURN IS GONE

If you scorch a garment when ironing, cover the scorch mark with a vinegar-dampened cloth, then iron with a warm iron (not too hot). Scorch marks on cotton, however, tend to remove better with hydrogen peroxide.

YUCK

Petroleum jelly will remove tar from clothing; just rub it in until the tar is gone. Remove the jelly with any type of spray-and-wash product.

WHO KNEW?

The best way to polish copper is to rub it with ketchup and let it stand for an hour. Rinse off the ketchup with hot water, and buff to an incredible shine.

WETNESS HELPS

Do you use a thimble to sew or sort papers? If you wet your finger before you put the thimble on, you'll create suction so the thimble stays put.

SWEATER STRETCHED?

If cuffs or necklines of woolen sweaters are stretched out of shape, dip them in hot water and dry with a blow dryer.

BID ADIEU TO OIL STAINS

Cleaning oil spots off the driveway is difficult, and the cleaners can be quite expensive. Instead, sprinkle baking soda over the stains, then rub with a wet scrub brush with hot water. The baking soda breaks apart oil particles, so with a little elbow grease you can have your driveway sparkling in no time.

DON'T FORGET TO BLAME THE KIDS

Candle wax on tablecloths? Remove it by rubbing with an ice cube and then scraping with a dull knife.

SHAVING YOUR SWEATER

A pilling problem with your sweater? A disposable razor does a wonderful job of removing small pills from sweaters.

ANOTHER GREAT STAIN REMOVER

If you have non-greasy stains on washable fabrics, an excellent spot remover can be made using 2 parts of water to 1 part of rubbing alcohol. Test for colorfastness by applying to an inconspicuous area first.

GOOD TIP OR FREAKISHLY ODD? YOU MAKE THE CALL

To clean stuffed animals, just place them in a cloth bag or pillowcase, add baking soda or cornmeal, and shake.

?? WHO KNEW?

Ah, vinegar. To remove smoke from your clothes, fill the bath with hot water and add 1 cup of white vinegar. Then just hang the clothes above the steaming water—and the smoke smell will be gone!

WHO KNEW?

A great way to clean tarnished silverware is to line a pan with aluminum foil (shiny side up). Fill with 1 tablespoon of baking soda per 2 cups of water, and give your silverware a bath. Your silver will shine!

STAIN CUTTERS

To remove coffee stains or wine stains from a favorite garment, stretch the garment over a bowl, cover the stain with salt, and pour boiling water over the stain from a height of one to two feet. (The gravity helps). Of course, always test first that the garment can withstand hot water (unlike, say, cashmere). If the stain still remains, soak with a laundry solvent and launder as usual.

LESS IS MORE

Your clothes will get cleaner if you don't overload the washer. They need to be able to move freely during the different cycles.

GET RID OF THE YELLOW

Yellowed fabrics can be restored to white and even old, unknown stains can be removed by soaking the fabrics in an enzyme presoak before laundering.

BLAME THE FABRIC SOFTENER

Does it seem as though your clothes get greasy stains on them in the laundry? It may not be your imagination. One cause: adding undiluted fabric softener. Always dilute it, because it can cause stains that look greasy. Remove these stains by pretreating the fabric with a paste made of water and detergent, or with a prewash stain remover.

ANOTHER REASON TO HATE IRONING

Tap water contains impurities and minerals that will ruin your iron over time. Always use distilled water when filling your iron.

THE DUMB GUM

If your kid gets gum stuck on his shirt or the carpet, fill a plastic bag with ice and apply to the stain for 10–15 minutes. The gum will get cold, then shrink and harden, which makes it easy to peel off.

TRUST US ON THIS ONE

A tip for the thrifty (and clever): Always remove buttons before discarding a garment. They will come in handy later.

SALT TALK

Clean silk flowers easily by placing them, bloom end down, in a plastic bag with 2 tablespoons of salt. Hold onto the stems and close the bag, then shake vigorously. Salt tends to attract the dust.

FETCH THE STARCH

Your pot-holders will look fresh if you spray them with starch very often. Starch repels grease, so the pot-holders will stay unstained.

DIDN'T LUCY AND ETHEL DO THAT ONCE?

Adding too much soap to the washing machine can cause bubbles to overflow, and it won't get the clothes any cleaner than if you used the correct amount. If you add too much, pour in 2 tablespoons of white vinegar or a capful of fabric softener to neutralize some of the soap.

NEVER FADE AWAY

To prevent jeans from fading, soak them in 1 cup white vinegar and 2 quarts of water for one hour before you wash them for the first time.

STICKY IRON?

Sprinkle some salt on a piece of waxed paper and iron away.

WHO KNEW?

There's no need to buy expensive dish washing detergent. Use the cheapest brand you can find, add a few tablespoons of white vinegar to the water, and your dishes will shine. The same is true for dishwashers—just buy the least expensive detergent, and add in some white vinegar to the machine.

ZAP THE SAP!

Tree sap is one of the hazards of summer, but you can remove it easily from your car with butter or margarine. Really. Just rub on the sap with a soft cloth, and it should come right off.

FOR CLEANER SHADES

Smudges and stains on your window shades? Lay the shades on a table or countertop and rub the spots with an art-gum eraser.

BE A BUTTER FINGER

The easiest way to remove sticky tree sap from your hands is with butter. Or margarine. Really.

STAYING DARK

Two tricks for keeping dark clothes dark: Wash them inside out, and air dry them; if you dry them outside, keep them inside out or dry them out of direct sunlight. Rubbing darks against other clothes as well as the insides of the washer and dryer will fade them fast.

NEVER LOSE A BUTTON AGAIN

Dab a small amount of clear nail polish in the center of every button on a new garment. This seals the threads and makes them last longer.

REALLY, WHAT ARE PIPE CLEANERS FOR?

Dip a pipe cleaner in white vinegar and use it to clean the holes in an iron after it is completely cool. Just make sure the iron is unplugged!

WHO KNEW?

Toothpaste removes stubborn black marks on linoleum or vinyl flooring.

TELL THE KIDS

Shoelaces are more likely to stay tied if you dampen them before tying.

WORKS BETTER THAN BLEACH

To get the whitest whites, add a cup of dishwasher detergent with the laundry detergent. This even whitens sweat socks.

SHARPEN YOUR NUMBER TWOS

Sticky zipper? Just rub it with a lead pencil. The graphite in the pencil does the trick.

DESPERATE TIMES

In a pinch, a button can be reattached with the wire from a twist tie. Just tear the paper off each side of the tie.

HELPS AVOID SHRINKING, TOO

If you wash slipcovers, put them back on your furniture while the covers are still damp. Not only will the slipcovers be easier to get on, but they will also not need to be ironed.

FOR A STIFFER SNEAKER

After you wash cotton sneakers, spray them with spray starch to help them resist stains in the future.

THOSE DAMNED SLUBS

Don't use a terry cloth towel to cover silk before ironing—the slubs (Merriam-Webster's Collegiate Dictionary entry: *n (1851): a soft thick uneven section in a yarn or thread*) in the towel will "pock" the silk. Use a pillowcase or cotton knit shirt instead.

A TIP FROM MAMIE EISENHOWER

If you are the sort who has lace doilies, well, what can we say? They can be hand washed in sour milk for best results.

A BLOODY GOOD SOLUTION

Bloodstains can be incredibly difficult to remove. If the blood is fresh, make a paste of water and talcum, cornstarch, or cornmeal and apply it to the stain. Let it dry, and then brush it off. If you have a powdered meat tenderizer, cover the stains with that and cool water. Sponge it off with more cool water after about a half hour.

CHEER UP CHROME

Oven rings made of chrome often become sticky. Shine them up with a paste of vinegar and cream of tartar.

DRY YOUR TONGUE

To dry the insides of shoes or sneakers quickly, try placing the blower end of the vacuum cleaner hose inside.

SOMETHING TO REMEMBER

Glass cleaner makes an excellent spot remover if you need something clean in a hurry. Make sure the fabric is colorfast.

COLD WORKS BEST

No matter which temperature you choose to wash your clothes, always use a cold-water rinse. It will help the clothes retain their shape and color, and you'll save money and energy by not taxing your water heater.

IT GETS ALL GUNKY SOMETIMES

If the bottom of your iron gets dirty, clean it with a steel-wool soap pad (don't use steel wool if your iron has a nonstick finish). To make it shiny again, just run a piece of waxed paper over it.

WHO KNEW?

Nail polish stains on the floor are impossible to remove, right? Maybe not. Just try shaving cream on a clean cloth—it works like magic.

CAWFEE TAWK

Spilled coffee can be very problematic, particularly if it has milk in it (milk proteins require solutions different from coffee compounds). Here are three methods to remove coffee from fabric or carpet:

- Dip a white cloth in a beaten egg yolk. Rub the yolk into the stain, then rinse with clean water.
- Blot denatured alcohol into the stain, then rinse with water.
- Mix a solution of ½ teaspoon of mild detergent and 2 cups of warm water. Blot this solution into the stain. If the stain remains, blot with a 50-50 solution of white vinegar and water.

    If the inside of your cup is stained, one of these methods should have it looking like new. Be sure to wash the mug thoroughly afterward.

- Mix a paste of coarse salt or baking soda and water; or use a 50-50 mixture of salt and white vinegar. Scrub the mug with this, then rinse well.
- Dissolve a denture cleaning tablet in the mug and let stand overnight.
- For a lot of stained mugs, put them a solution of ½ cup of household bleach and 2 quarts of water. Let the cups stand overnight.

SAVE YOUR SILK

If a clothing label of a silk garment doesn't specify dry-cleaning only, you can wash it by hand. Silk should be hand-washed using cool water with mild liquid soap. Always air dry—never place silk in the dryer—and then iron on the wrong side of the fabric.

AND ALWAYS BLAME THE PERSON TO YOUR LEFT

If you spill wine on a tablecloth, blot up as much as you can as soon as you can with a cloth, then sponge with cool water. If the fabric is not machine washable, cover the stain with a small cloth dampened with a solution of detergent, water, and vinegar, then rinse. Get the cloth to the drycleaner as soon as you can.

SPOT THE BLOT

Remove really tough stains in your pots and pans by filling them with boiling water and adding a denture tablet. Let it sit overnight, and the stain should disappear.

GOOD ALL-ROUNDER

For a cleaner that's ideal for glass and silver, mix together 7 pints of hot water, 3 ½ fl oz. of household ammonia, 3 ½ fl oz. of white vinegar and 7 oz. of bicarbonate of soda together. Store in a tightly sealed bottle.

BAKING SODA TO THE RESCUE

Tea and coffee stains can be removed from your countertop by applying a baking soda paste and rubbing with a warm, damp cloth. If the stain still remains, consider using a drop or two of bleach, but be careful-bleach can fade your countertop along with the stain!

KITCHEN SINK DRAMA

For a spectacular finish, wipe round an aluminum sink with a solution of diluted bleach and pat dry with kitchen paper. Buff with more paper and baby oil for a gleaming sink.

TEA-LEAF TRICK

Fill a stained decanter half-full with warm soapy water to which a few tea-leaves have been added. Let it soak, shaking well at intervals. Empty and rinse thoroughly.

DRINK UP

Don't fret over spilled red wine. Just wet the tablecloth with club soda, and let it stand for 20 minutes before washing.

STAINS ON STONE

Determine whether the stain is water-based (spilled fruit juice) or oil-based (mayonnaise). For water-based stains, pour hot water from the tap onto the stain and leave for a few minutes. Wipe away excess. Blot with paper towels and a heavy weight. Leave overnight. Repeat for oil-based stains but use acetone (don't heat). Again, leave overnight. Repeat as necessary.

SINKING FEELING

If your stainless steel sink is looking a bit dull, rub the surface gently with a scrunched-up ball of newspaper or sprinkle it with baking powder, scrub and rinse off.

OLD IS GOLD

A great way to clean wallpaper is with day-old white bread. You can eliminate fingerprints, light stains, and even ball point ink that way. It's easy to remove tar from the outside of your car this way: Make a paste of baking soda and water, and apply with a soft cloth. Let it dry, then rinse.

BREAD LINE

You can clean slatted blinds with crusts of fresh bread. Just hold the crusts around each slat as you run them along the length. An old paintbrush will also do the same job or use the brush attachment on your vacuum cleaner.

ALL-PURPOSE CLEANER

For a cleaner that's perfect for use on work surfaces and throughout the house, mix 2 heaped tablespoons of bicarbonate of soda with 1 tablespoon white vinegar. Store in an airtight container.

TREAT TIES TENDERLY

Never try to remove a stain on a tie with water or you may create a large watermark that's hard to remove. Blot away excess stains (salad dressing, sauces and gravy are popular ones) with a napkin or clean white cloth. Take it to the dry cleaner as soon as possible: stains set after 24 or 48 hours. Don't attempt to rub the stain out or you could rub color from the fabric, especially if silk.

CLEANER-VINEGAR

There's no need to buy expensive, chemical-filled cleaners for your stainless steel sink. Just mix white vinegar and club soda on a cloth and wipe away. Dry with a clean cloth to eliminate streaks and your sink will shine.

WILY WITH WOOL

Dry-cleaning wool blankets can cost some major money. Save by washing them with mild dishwashing liquid in cold water on the gentle cycle, then air fluff to dry.

HONEY, I SHRUNK THE SWEATER

If you shrink a woolen garment, soak it for 15 minutes in a mixture of ½ cup hair conditioner and 1 gallon lukewarm water, then squeeze out the excess solution. This will help to soften the fibers so you can gently stretch the article back to the original size. Another method is to dissolve 1 ounce Borax in 1 teaspoon hot water, and then add it to 1 gallon warm water. Place the garment in the solution, stretch back to shape, and then rinse it in 1 gallon warm water with 2 tablespoons white vinegar added.

STAIN SOLUTIONS

Marks on light-colored wood can be removed by dipping a cloth in wood cleaner and working with the grain. Buff with a cloth and apply furniture polish. Alternatively, try a mix of 50:50 baking soda and white toothpaste or leave mayonnaise on the stain for an hour. On light carpets and upholstery, wet a cloth in 50:50 water/white vinegar and blot the surface gently.

THE GRIME ELIMINATOR

If your oven is a mess and it's not a self-cleaning model, there's no need to buy the expensive, pungent chemical cleaners. Just apply a paste of baking soda and water (or white vinegar), let it sit for 15 minutes, and wipe with a damp cloth. Baking soda really eliminates grime. You can also make a paste with dishwasher powder for stubborn stains.

ONLY SKIN DEEP

A great way to remove ink from your skin is with a baby wipe. Washing your hands with dish detergent and sugar also does the trick. If you're painting with oil-based paint and it gets on your hands, the only way to remove it is with grotesquely smelly turpentine, right? Wrong. Just wipe olive oil on your hands, and rub with a damp, soapy sponge.

TIPS FOR CLEANING STUBBORN STAINS

To remove coffee stains from inside of a glass coffee pot, add a tablespoon of water, four teaspoons of salt, and a cup or so of crushed ice. Gently swirl until it is clean, then rinse thoroughly. Just make sure the coffee pot is at room temperature before cleaning. The most effective way to remove blueberry stains from clothes is to soak the stain, overnight, in equal parts of milk and white vinegar. Then, launder as usual. There's hope for cleaning hopelessly burned pots: Put enough hot water in the pot to cover the stain, add a tablet or two of denture cleaner, and let it sit overnight. Here's a great tip for you when you get a tomato sauce stain on your favorite shirt: Immediately apply a bit of shaving cream to the stain, and dab it with a damp, warm sponge. Let it dry and launder as usual, and your shirt should look good as new.

FROM YOUR BABY'S VANITY

Bacon grease is one of the hardest stains to remove from your clothes, but if it hasn't dried on, try applying baby powder to the stain. Let it sit for an hour or so, and then wipe off the powder. Removing gasoline stains from clothing can be tricky. The most effective way we know is to apply baby oil to the stain, and launder as usual. Since gasoline is an oil-based product, it takes another oil to pull out the stain and smell.

AMMONIA-MANIA

The easiest way to remove most concrete stains is with ammonia. Just add one cup to a gallon of hot water, and scrub. The stain should come right off.

IT'S NOT JUST FOR HEADACHES

A great way to remove perspiration stains from white shirts is to crush four aspirins into ½ cup of warm water, and apply to the stain. Soak for at least three hours, and launder as usual. If the stain is still there, well, you always need more polishing cloths, right?

HANDLE WITH CARE

Prevent breakages by washing porcelain in a bowl or sink lined with a towel or rubber mat. Fired at high temperatures, porcelain is glass-like, so use a mild solution of dish liquid and warm water. Wipe with a soft cloth and use a soft toothbrush to get to all the nooks and crannies. Rinse well in clean water.

THE SMART PEROXIDE

Hydrogen peroxide removes bloodstains, as well as grass and mustard stains, from virtually any fabric. Just make sure to test the peroxide on a small piece of the fabric first.

CANDLE'S SCANDAL

Removing candle wax from your wood floors is easy if you soften the wax first with a blow dryer, wipe with a paper towel and then clean with white vinegar and water.

ART ATTACK!

If the kids have drawn with crayons on the wall, remove it with a bit of WD-40 spray, which works like a charm. Afterwards, you'll need something to remove the grease—we like a mixture of dishwashing detergent and white vinegar.

THE GREASE CEASE

Forget about buying those expensive cook top cleansers to get rid of cooked-on grease stains. Just wet the stains with water or vinegar, and cover with baking soda. Clean with a damp sponge and buff with a dry, clean cloth, and your cook top will sparkle.

TRY PEROXIDE

If you prefer not to use bleach when doing laundry, substitute 3 tablespoons hydrogen peroxide in the wash load.

IS THAT WHAT THEY CALL "A SPOT OF TEA?"

Remove tea stains from tablecloths with glycerin. Let it sit overnight before washing. Glycerin, which is available at pharmacies, is a wonder for softening old stains before laundering.

VINEGAR DESCALER

Cover the element of your kettle with a solution of half cold water, half distilled vinegar. Leave for a couple of hours then rinse the liquid and discard.

THE BROWN BAG SOLUTION

Candle wax is difficult yet not impossible to remove. Just cover the stain with a brown paper bag, and iron with a warm iron. The wax should transfer to the bag.

ERASER: THE STAIN CHASER

The easiest way to clean smudges off aluminum blinds is with a pencil eraser. Dust comes off with a few swipes of a fabric softener sheet.

WINE

An effective way to remove stubborn red wine spills from carpets is with a dab of foaming shaving cream. And consider switching to vodka to really eliminate the problem in the future.

START COOL, THEN HOT

Always start your ironing with silk, rayon, and other delicate fabrics that require a cool temperature, before the iron heats up.

BREEZY CLEANING

The easiest way to remove smells and stains from a thermos is by filling it with hot water and ½ cup of baking soda, and let it sit overnight. In the morning, just rinse well and it should be good as new. Perspiration stains are difficult to remove, but not impossible. Try soaking the offending shirt in a solution of water, white vinegar and laundry detergent for one hour, then launder as usual. If you get a pen mark on your favorite leather chair, don't panic. Just blot the stain with milk until the ink disappears, and wipe it clean with a damp sponge.

IF YOU'VE GIVEN UP HOPE OF EVER REMOVING STUCK ON FOOD IN YOUR POTS AND PANS, HELP IS ON THE WAY—IN THE FORM OF A FABRIC SOFTENER SHEET

Just cover the stain with hot water, and float a fabric softener sheet in it. Leave overnight, and in the morning, the food should wipe off easily.

BECAUSE SHRINKAGE MAY OCCUR

To minimize shrinking, wash blue jeans in cold water, dry them on medium heat for only 10 minutes, and then air dry them the rest of the way.

SPREAD THE BREAD

The easiest way to remove dirt and other stains from your walls with a piece of balled up white bread. Really.

THE SPRAY PREY

To remove ink stains from a garment, spray a liberal amount of hairspray on the stain, let it dry, then launder as usual.

STAIN NOSTALGIA?

To get red wine out of carpeting, forget about pouring white wine on the stain. Instead, blot as much as you can with a paper towel, then sprinkle a mixture of salt and baking soda on the spot, and cover with a hot, damp towel. After an hour run a vacuum over it, and the stain should be history.

HOUSEHOLD HEROES

chapter 2

WHO KNEW?

To keep soaped steel wool pads from rusting, just store them in a zipped plastic bag in the freezer.

CRYSTAL CLEAN

Use a paste of lemon juice and baking powder to remove small stains from crystal. Treat tougher stains by placing 2 teaspoons of uncooked rice inside the crystal piece, add water and swirl it.

RING AROUND THE TOILET

The ring around a toilet bowl is caused when dirt accumulates and becomes embedded in minerals in the hard water. A mild acid will easily remove the stains. Oxalic acid is one of the most common and least expensive; it is available in a powder or flake form. In some instances, a cola that contains phosphoric acid and has gone flat will also do the job.

IT'S STILL A DISGUSTING JOB

If your oven is not self-cleaning, here's a way to get the gunk off without a lot of scrubbing: Set a small bowl with ½ cup of ammonia on the center rack, close the oven, and let stand overnight. The next day, open the oven and let it air for 30 minutes in a well-ventilated kitchen. Wipe up the mess with warm, damp paper towels.

HOW REVOLTING

Hair spray is basically a resin dissolved in a volatile solvent or alcohol. When you spray it on your hair, the solvent evaporates rapidly, leaving a thin layer of plastic. Don't believe it? Try this experiment: Coat a mirror with a thick layer of hair spray and let it dry for a minute or two. You should be able to peel off the layer in one thin sheet.

CLOGGED SHOWER HEAD?

No more. Just unscrew it and submerge in white vinegar overnight, and the clogs disappear. It you can't unscrew it, fill a small, sturdy bag with vinegar and attach to the shower head with duct tape.

LOSING THE SMELL

The smell of new carpets can be overpowering, but take heart: The smell will dissipate over time. The fumes are caused by oils added to plastic during manufacturing. Most of the oils are absorbed by the plastic; you smell those that are left on the surface. Over time, oils come to the surface of the plastic, but they are not strong enough to produce fumes.

LET THE CANDLE HANDLE

Sealing the cracks around your doors and windows not only keeps the cold out, it cuts down on the dust in your house dramatically. Consider rubbing a white candle on your windowsills to eliminate even more dust from coming inside.

BOTTOMS UP

If you suffer from stomach irritation when you take aspirin or other analgesics, be sure to take them with a full glass of water. Stomach irritation is usually the result of too little water when taking the product.

CEASE THE CREASE

Creases in the hems of your pants can be removed with white vinegar. Just sponge a little on with a damp sponge, and press with a warm iron.

SORRY TO BE A BUZZKILL

Those tablets you place in the toilet tank are not a substitute for a thorough scrubbing. They're designed to help keep the bowl clean, but they won't clean a bowl that's already dirty.

THE PAINT ERASE

After painting your window trim, there's no need to use a dangerous razor blade to remove any paint that may have spilled on the glass. Instead, remove the paint safely and easily with a pen eraser. If the paint has dried, or is old, dab on some nail polish remover, wait a bit, and erase.

LEAVE THE JUMPER CABLES IN THE GARAGE

Car engine won't start? It may not be the battery. Cold temperatures can turn motor oil into a thick sludge, so the battery has to work harder to turn the engine over. If you live in colder climates, look for a higher amp battery, or use an electric blanket (one made for cars, not a household blanket), which will keep the motor oil from becoming a semisolid.

NEWS ABOUT NEWS!

A great way to clean your barbeque grill is with wet newspaper. After cooking, just place it on a warm grill for one hour with the lid closed. You'll be amazed to see how easily the grime comes off!

NOT FOR THE TYPO

Use typewriter correction fluid to cover nicks and chips on ceramic sinks and tiles, and white refrigerators as well. It does a great job covering small scratches, too.

CAN COLA HELP?

Antiemetics control the gag reflex, which comes into play when you're nauseated. But in most instances, cola syrups that contain sugar and phosphates are every bit as effective. Most pharmacies sell cola syrup; ask your pharmacist. Regular or diet colas will not work—just cola syrup.

LET'S NOT SKIMP IN THIS AREA

When it comes to toilet tissue, most people have no trouble telling a better (often more expensive) brand. All toilet tissues are made from purified wood pulp, but the better brands also include skin softeners; lesser quality products do not go through any softening process. Colored toilet paper contains traces of metals that produce the different colors. People with very sensitive skin may experience a reaction from the colored papers.

WHO KNEW?

If the screws in your eyeglasses keep loosening, just put a drop of clear nail polish on the screw after retightening.

FOR ALL YOUR FANS

Oven fans are magnets for grease. The simplest way to clean that revolting mess is to pop out the fan filter, and run it through your dishwasher on the top shelf.

ICE AIN'T NICE

Most windshield deicers work fairly well, but the thicker the ice, the longer it will take to melt. Deicers are similar to antifreeze, though they tend to be much more expensive. An inexpensive yet effective solution: Fill the windshield washer fluid reservoir with a mixture of 1 part antifreeze, 4½ parts alcohol, and 4½ parts water. Never pour hot water on your windshield. The glass may expand from the heat and then contract as it cools, causing the windshield to crack.

A PERSONAL ORGANIZER

You'll never waste time looking for tweezers, nail clippers or small scissors again if you attach a magnetic strip inside your medicine cabinet door.

SERIOUS STUFF

Commercial drain cleaners can be made from very dangerous, volatile chemicals. Be sure to follow the manufacturer's instructions to the letter when using these products.

VASE SPARKLER

When washing vases with narrow necks, add a little uncooked rice to the water, and your vases will sparkle.

DOWN THE DRAIN

For a clogged drain try this first: Remove all standing water so you can access the drain. First pour 1 cup of baking soda, then 1 cup of table salt, and then ½ cup of white vinegar into the clogged drain; these will start dissolving any organic matter and grease immediately. Let stand for 5 minutes, then flush 1 to 2 quarts of boiling water down the drain.

TOP BRASS

Apply non-gel toothpaste (a mild abrasive) on a soft cloth to door fittings then rub the brass. Use a fresh cloth to wipe clean. No further treatment is required for lacquered brass – otherwise protect with a light coating of olive or lemon oil.

ELIMINATE THE DRIP

Prepare a solution of 2 tablespoons of salt per candle in just enough water to cover the candles. Let the candles soak in the salt water for 2 to 3 hours, and then rinse them, let dry, and wait at least 24 hours before you use them. The salt water hardens the wax, which makes it burn slower and more cleanly, reducing the chance of drips onto linens or furniture.

WHO KNEW?

Need to wash your sheer curtains but hate the thought of ironing them afterwards? Simply dissolve a packet of clear gelatin in the final rinse when laundering, and hang them up damp afterwards. The gelatin removes almost all of the wrinkles.

ROLL YOUR OWN

The best way to clean dusty lampshades is to run a rolling lint remover over them.

REMEMBER WHEN?

Way back when, Ivory soap sank. In 1930, an employee fell asleep on the job instead of watching the machinery and stopping the mixer at the appropriate time. Air was incorporated into the soap, which provided the buoyancy necessary for floating. Rather than discard the batch, the company marketed the flotation as a bonus, and consumers bought it.

THE HOTTER THE BETTER

When you wash dishes, be sure to use hot water. It activates the detergent better than cold water, and it's more effective at rinsing off the soap.

ALCOHOL HELPS

Isopropyl alcohol belongs in the bathroom for more than first-aid purposes. It cleans the bathtub caulking, and it shines chrome and glass.

NEED TO EASY WAY TO CLEAN YOUR OVEN?

Try this: Pour a cup or two of ammonia into an aluminum pan and place in the oven overnight, then wipe with a damp sponge. You might still have to use an abrasive cleaner or soaped steel wool afterwards, but the ammonia will have loosened the baked-on food considerably.

WHO KNEW?

To clean a stained glass vase, fill it with water and drop in a fizzing antacid tablet.

NO SLIP-UPS

Never use soap on stone floors: it cannot be absorbed and makes them slippery. Instead clean with 1 ¾ pints water to 2 tablespoons washing soda powder.

STEAM AWAY SMOKE

To remove the smoke smell from clothes after a night out, add a cup of vinegar to a bathtub of hot water. Hang the clothes above the steam.

WATER BATH

The most effective way to get rid of sand and grit from clams is to soak them in water with a bit of cornmeal stirred in. It irritates the clams and they expel the sand while trying to eliminate the cornmeal.

There's no need to buy expensive detergent for hand washing delicates. Instead, just wash them in equal parts of baking soda and warm water.

GET IN THE GROOVE

Hand-wash cut-glass crystal individually in warm soapy water and use a toothbrush to get into all the grooves. Rinse in warm water with lemon juice for extra shine and dry with a linen tea towel.

THE BEST WAY TO CLEAN GROUT

Make an inexpensive yet very effective grout cleaner by mixing ¼ cup chlorine bleach with 2 tablespoons phosphate-based liquid floor cleaner, ¾ cup rubbing alcohol, and 1 cup plus 2 tablespoons water in a plastic spray bottle.

PERFECTLY PRESERVED

Clean the inside of brass preserving pans with a paste made from vinegar and kitchen salt. Wash and rinse thoroughly before cooking; dry well. Metal polish may be used on the outside but never use this inside any pan intended for cooking.

THE FIZZ IS MAGIC

The easiest way to eliminate the odors and stains from a thermos? Fill the container with hot water and drop in a denture-cleaning tablet, and then let stand overnight. Baking soda will also work, but not as well.

COUCH CLEANER

A quick and easy way of freshening up your sofa is to sprinkle a little baking soda beneath the cushions. The baking soda draws in the odour. Leave for at least 15 minutes then vacuum away.

MORE THAN YOU NEED TO KNOW ABOUT ODORS

Baking soda is inorganic, which simply means that it is not produced from living matter. Household odors are composed of organic oils, and they get stuck in the inorganic powder, which neutralizes them.

MAKE IT EASY

A simple way to a clean oven is to place a bowl of water inside. Heat on a high temperature for 20 minutes to loosen dirt and grease. Wipe the condensation with a cloth or paper towel and use a cloth to smear a thin paste of bicarbonate of soda and water on enamel linings which dries to a protective layer that absorbs greasy soiling and makes it easier to clean next time.

REDUCE CALCIUM DEPOSITS

Add 1–2 tablespoons washing soda to the detergent drawer of your washing machine. You'll also reduce the amount of commercial powder needed by 30 percent.

GLEAMING GLASS

For glass that stays clean and static-free, add one tablespoon of cornflour to about 2 pints of lukewarm water. Wet a rag, squeeze away excess water and wipe down the glass. Because the rag is less static, dust and debris build up less frequently.

WHAT IF YOUR NONSTICK PAN STICKS?

For the most part, plastic-coated pots are easy to keep clean, but they do stain, and over time grease and oil may build up. If this occurs it will adversely affect the efficiency of the nonstick surface. To clean, mix 2 tablespoons baking soda, ½ cup white vinegar, and 1 cup water in the pot, set on the stove, and boil for about 10 minutes. Wash the pot, then rub vegetable oil on the surface of the plastic coating to re-season it.

THE TOOTHPASTE SOLUTION

A terrific way to hang posters in your kid's room is with white toothpaste. Just put a drop on the back of each corner, and press to the wall, and watch it stick—without marring the wall with pinholes.

FOR THE DRIEST CRAYONS

If the kids have been playing and you later discover crayon marks inside the dryer, don't despair. Soften marks by running the machine on empty for five minutes. Then wipe with a cloth and warm soapy water.

CRAYON MARKS

Caught the kids crayoning on their bedroom walls? Dip a damp rag into baking soda and with a little elbow grease the stain will be removed. White spirit can be used on vinyl and gloss but not emulsion (latex) walls.

OFFICIALLY YOURS

Organize your office with ice cube trays. Keep thumbtacks, paper clips, small binder clips, and other essentials from rattling around in your desk by storing them in their very own compartments.

A FOOD MARK?

You can use a single strand of raw spaghetti to mark your page in a cookbook while you prepare dinner.

INVOLVE THE DISSOLVE

To keep your tub and sinks unclogged, pour one half cup of baking soda and a cup of boiling water down the drain, followed by a cup of white vinegar. Let the mixture sit overnight, and it will dissolve most hair and other buildup in your pipe drains. Repeat once a month.

SCARY STUFF

Most aerosol oven cleaners contain lye, also found in drain cleaners. When you spray lye on burned fats and carbohydrates, it converts them to soap that can be wiped off with a damp cloth. If possible, choose one of the newer oven cleaners that use organic salts—they're less noxious. Whichever type you use, make sure that your kitchen is well ventilated or the cleaner fumes may burn the lining of your mouth and throat.

A PRIMER PRIMER

Paint primers are usually colorless or white, so you might wonder if you need them. They serve many functions: Primers seal the surface to be painted, so paint does not soak in. Colored primers hide colors already on the wall that may bleed through; they can also lessen the appearance of an uneven paint job. If you're painting metal, primers can help prevent corrosion; they also help paint adhere better.

BURNT FOOD BE GONE

A great way to remove burnt food from pans is to sprinkle baking soda, salt and dish detergent into the pan, cover with water, and boil for an hour. Then just wipe up the (former) stain!

THE GOOD LEMON

Clean brass and copper easily with half a lemon dipped in salt. Rinse with cold water.

YOU GOTTA HAVE IT

Petroleum jelly, the most popular of which is Vaseline, is a must for every medicine chest. It seals off the skin and protects it from surface damage, especially from irritations and mild abrasions.

CURE SCORCH MARKS

If you iron on a very high setting, you run the risk of scorch marks. If the affected item is 100 per cent cotton, soak the scorched area in pure, freshly squeezed lemon juice. Rinse out thoroughly in warm water and leave outside to bleach naturally in the sunlight.

IF CHIPS MAR YOUR GOOD GLASSES OR CHINA, DON'T WORRY

A few gentle strokes of an emery board can smooth out minor chips.

THE INVISIBLE GUIDE

When arranging flowers, use transparent tape across the mouth of the vase in a grid to make an invisible guide.

VACUUM OFF THE ODORS

To rid your house of pet or cooking smells, add a cotton ball soaked in vanilla or lavender to your vacuum cleaner bag, and vacuum away. It's an effective way to rid your home of the offensive odor—by creating a nice scent instead.

The sugar content in Vidalia and other onions makes them spoil quickly if they are stored closely together. The solution? Store your onions in a clean but old pair of pantyhose, making knots in the legs so the onions can't touch. Yes, it's freaky, but it works!

SHINE YOUR LEATHER SHOES WITH VEGETABLE OIL

First, dampen a cloth and wipe away any dirt, then put a few drops of oil on a clean, soft cloth and rub into your shoes. They'll shine like new, as the oil removes the scuffmarks.

NOT SURE IF YOUR THERE'S ANY GAS LEFT IN YOUR GRILL'S TANK?

Just boil water and pour over the side of the tank. The area where the tank is warm indicates it's empty and coolness indicates there's propane inside.

USE UNCOOKED RICE TO CLEAN YOUR COFFEE GRINDER

Simply mill a handful of rice as you normally do to your coffee beans. The chopped rice cleans out the stuck coffee grounds and oils, and absorbs the stale odors to boot. Afterwards, throw away the rice, wipe the grinder clean…and brew fresh coffee.

OR WEAR NOTHING AT ALL

So you're confused by the difference between perfume, cologne, and eau de toilette? The main variant is the concentration of the compounds that are responsible for the aroma of each of these products. Perfumes are produced with the highest concentrations, and that is why they last longer. (Hint: Before you apply perfume, dab a bit of petroleum jelly on those areas; the perfume will last twice as long.) Colognes contain less of the same compound and more fillers, and eau de toilette, or toilet water, is just diluted cologne. Here's another thing worth knowing when you're browsing the perfume counter: The cost of a perfume has more to do with its advertising and marketing expenses than the cost of its ingredients.

THE ART OF HANGING

To hang lightweight artwork that's not in a heavy frame, there's
no need to buy picture wire. Dental floss will do the trick.

SEAL IT!

A great way to seal the end of a frayed shoelace is with
transparent tape. A drop of clear nail polish also works.

THE QUICKEST WAY TO CLEAN UP THE BATHROOM

Just apply a touch of baby shampoo to a wet sponge and clean
your sink, fixtures, tiles and bathtub. It cuts through oily
residue, and smells good, too.

REHABILITATE A PAIR OF OLD SCISSORS WITH THESE SIMPLE TIPS

Remove the rust by applying a paste of salt and lemon juice,
and rub it thoroughly with a dry cloth. Then, sharpen the
scissors by cutting a piece of steel wool or aluminum foil 20
times or so.

WEIRD BUT TRUE

If your knife is rusty, use it to chop up a few onions, and the rust will disappear.

If you've misplaced your measuring cups, use an ice cream scoop. The typical
scoop holds exactly one-third cup.

If you've lost your ruler, grab a dollar bill. It's exactly six and a quarter inches long.

THE FINISHING TOUCH

Repair scratches in your wood furniture with shoe polish. A crayon also works. Just wipe off any excess wax with a credit card edge, and buff with a cotton cloth.

THE MULTI-PURPOSE BOTTLE

Make your own funnel by cutting an empty, clean bleach bottle in half. Use the half with the handle to scoop up fertilizer or clean up the litter box.

THE PEEL FEEL

A self-cleaning oven can leave an odor after it's done its work. Eliminate the lingering smell by baking orange peels in a 350 degrees oven for half an hour after the cleaning cycle is over.

A CLEAN INVESTMENT

Invest in good quality entrance mats, both outside your door and inside. Disgustingly, they can capture more than a pound of dirt per square foot.

CLEANING GLASS SHOWER DOORS CAN BE A STREAKY MESS, RIGHT?

Eliminate the water spots and streaks by wiping the doors with fabric softener sheets. You'll be amazed how effective they are.

A DOSE OF ADVICE

A great way to clean your coffee maker is to fill it with hot water (not cold), drop in a denture-cleaning tablet, and brew. Just make sure you rinse it thoroughly afterwards.

PENCIL MIGHTIER THAN A SWORD

Squeaky door hinges can be fixed with a pencil. Just rub the point over the hinge. Pencils contain graphite, which is an effective lubricant. It also works on stubborn house keys, too.

PUFF UP!

On sticky summer nights, cool down by sprinkling a little baby powder between your sheets before retiring for the night.

SAVES NINE...

The easiest way to thread a needle is to spray the end of the thread with a bit of hair spray beforehand.

USE OLD SOCKS

Wear a pair of old socks on your hands when dusting. It's efficient (you're using both hands), cheap (remember, these are old socks) and you can wash and reuse them, too.

A CANDLE IN THE WINDOW

If your windows or desk drawers are stuck, simply run a candle or white soap on the runners and the problem should be solved.

AN EYE-CATCHING FACT

Cleaning your mirrors or eyeglasses with shaving cream will keep them from fogging. Weird but true!

BE PREPARED

Prepare for those Valentine's Day flowers by cleaning your cloudy vases. Just pour a little white vinegar and uncooked rice in the vase, swish it around, and watch the clouds disappear.

A STRING OF TRUTH

Use dental floss when making a popcorn garland for the holidays. It's stronger than regular string and less likely to break when you wrap it around the tree.

WEIRD BUT EFFECTIVE

After cleaning your car's wheels, spray them with a light coat of vegetable oil. Next time you clean them, the brake dust that has accumulated will wipe off easily.

DUSTERMINATOR

Eliminate dirt and scratches from your favorite CDs with (nongel) toothpaste. Really. Gently rub the toothpaste on the CD with a damp, soft cloth, and wipe with another damp cloth, and listen to your favorite song again, without any skipping.

TANGLE-FREE

If the cables in your office are a tangled mess of computer, fax machine, printer and telephone wires, get a coiled telephone cord and run the wires through it. The coils will keep everything together neatly. You can also use a few of the cardboard tubes from paper towels instead of a telephone cord.

USE A BIT OF BLEACH

Humidifiers often are hotbeds of bacteria—which means that you may be filling the air with germs as well as moisture. Add a drop or two of chlorine bleach for every gallon of water when you refill the humidifier to help keep bacteria at bay.

THE SMARTER MARKER

Always keep a black magic marker handy. You can use it to eliminate scary red eyes on favorite photographs, and to fill in scratches and scuffs on black shoes and furniture.

THE FIZZ FIGHT

If your clothes are extra greasy, add a can of lemon-lime or cola soda to your washing machine along with detergent. The acid in the soda breaks down the oil in the greasy clothes, and your wash will sparkle.

A CLEARER THOUGHT

Clear nail polish can be helpful in a variety of ways: Use a drop to hold the thread of your buttons secure, and try a drop on the screws in your eyeglasses if they tend to come loose. You can also paint loose screws in doorknobs with the polish, which acts as an adhesive to keep the screws in place.

MAKE THE PANS SMILE

The best way to clean cast iron pans is to cover any stain with a paste of cream of tartar and white vinegar. Apply liberally, let it sit, and scrub with a damp, soft cloth.

KEEP YOUR FIZZLE IN

The refrigerator is a good place to store many chemicals such as hydrogen peroxide. It will stay active for a longer period. Nail polish is another chemical that likes the cold. It will last longer if you keep it in the refrigerator, but bring it to room temperature before your manicure.

TOOTHPASTE FILLS THE CAVITY...OF THE WALLS

A great way to cover up small holes in your white walls is with white toothpaste. It really works!

FORGET IT

Most bathtub cleaners advertise that they contain powerful disinfectants that will kill bacteria as well as clean off the soap scum and dirt residue. While they do contain disinfectants, the chemicals are only effective for a matter of hours, and then the bacteria come right back. The grout cleaner in the beginning of this chapter is just as effective as most commercial bathtub cleaners.

A PENCIL PEELER

The kids are back in school, and you've thought of everything they need—except a pencil sharpener. Avoid a homework-time freak out by using a potato peeler instead.

SQUEAK TWEAK

Eliminate squeaky floorboards by sprinkling a little talcum powder on the floor. May we suggest you do this before sneaking home late from last night's holiday party?

WHO KNEW?

The easiest way to clean the gunk and dust between your computer keys is with transparent tape. Just slide a 2-inch strip between the rows of your keyboard, and the adhesive will pick up any debris.

ESSENTIAL
BEAUTY TIPS

chapter **3**

WHO KNEW?

Models know the easiest (and cheapest) way to remove makeup is with a fresh baby wipe. Now you know, too.

COVER UP AGE SPOTS

To keep skin in an even tone you need to cover up birthmarks, sun damage, and age spots with a combination of foundation and concealer, using one or two shades blended together.

BACK TO NORMAL

If your hair has changed color from swimming in a chlorinated pool, crush a dozen or so aspirins in a cup or two of warm water, and work through your hair. Let it sit for about 15 minutes, and your original hair color should return.

DETOX WHILE YOU SLEEP

Release bad toxins through your feet while you do nothing at all but sleep. Sticky patches are available that contain a special mixture of tourmaline, eucalyptus, and bamboo vinegar are placed on the soles of the feet to draw out impurities by morning.

KEEPING IT LIGHT

Summer beauty requires a lighter touch. To keep your skin tone looking fresh and even, throw away your foundation and just use a tinted moisturizer with at least SPF 15 to cover the occasional blemish and give protection from the sun.

PEP UP TIRED EYES

For very dark circles or hollow eyes, use a strong concealer and blend it little at a time with a concealer brush. Work by 'tapping' the concealer into the area rather than rubbing it into the skin.

FILLING IN OVERPLUCKED BROWS

Bald patches can be filled in by brushing the brows upwards and then filling in the sparse area with shadow powder that's a shade lighter than your natural brow color. Finish by pencilling over the area with a pencil color that matches your brow color, using short, hairlike strokes.

LESS SHADOW, BETTER RESULTS

Use eye shadows sparingly, as eyelids become wrinkled and hooded as we age, and a heavy-handed application shadow will lie in creases along the wrinkles.

FROST FEAR

If the brisk winter air gives you a bothersome windburn, simply apply petroleum jelly liberally to your face or chapped lips for instant relief.

BANISH BAGS

Lack of sleep is the primary cause of dark circles under the eyes. A quick-fix remedy is to apply a light-reflecting foundation in sequin-sized blobs under the eye. Use the index finger to blend gently into this very delicate skin.

TAMING CURLY BROWS

A little dab of petroleum jelly – or lip gloss in a pinch – can help train curly hairs into a sleek, sophisticated line. Alternatively, use a little hairspray sprayed on your eye brush to smooth them into place.

NO MORE ROUGH LIPS

Rough, un-kissable lips should be treated with a natural exfoliating rub made from finely ground brown sugar and sesame oil. Scuff this delicious mixture gently over lips to remove dead and flaky skin. Finish by applying petroleum jelly.

MAKE TEETH WHITER

Choose your lipstick color carefully; shades of purple or blue-based pinks can make teeth look whiter, while orangey browns will make them look yellowish.

LIGHT TRICK LIPS

To give the illusion of a fuller upper lip, dab a tiny touch of pale iridescent sheen in the centre of the lips. This will highlight your cupid's bow making it appear bigger than it is.

HOT HONEY HAIR

Give your hair and scalp a treat with an organic honey and olive oil conditioner. Mix equal parts together and warm in the microwave, then apply to clean, towel-dried hair, and wrap in a warm towel for 20 minutes. This will leave hair smooth, ultra-soft and shiny.

CHECK LABELS FOR ALCOHOL

Some hair products contain alcohol which can make hair dryer than normal. If hair is colored it tends to make it dull and less vibrant. So look carefully at the list of ingredients and avoid this ingredient.

TEA TREATMENT

Greasy hair will benefit from a weekly treatment of cold peppermint tea, poured over the hair after washing. It will also make your hair smell fresh and minty for 24 hours.

THREAD VEINS ON CHEEKS

Horse chestnut cream is said to strengthen the tiny red veins that appear on the cheeks and nose when skin becomes thinner and loses some of its collagen. It's also available in tablet form to help boost general blood circulation in the skin.

BREATHE DEEP

Make your replenishing night cream more effective by taking five deep breaths to boost levels of oxygen to the skin before smoothing on your cream.

KITCHEN SKIN BRIGHTENER

Dull and sallow skin will benefit from equal measurements of lemon juice and milk mixed together and worked gently into a clean face with a soft bristled cosmetic brush. Leave it on for 5 minutes before rinsing off for brighter, tingly skin.

SWEET AS HONEY

Once a week apply a honey face mask for 30 minutes. It is nourishing for the skin, and will leave your skin soft and supple. Simply apply honey straight from the jar on to skin that has been moistened with warm water. Rinse off with warm water, then splash with cold water to close pores.

NO MORE DANDRUFF

You don't have to buy expensive shampoos if dandruff is a problem. After shampooing as you normally do, massage two tablespoons of lemon juice into your hair, and rinse with water. Then rinse your hair with one tablespoon of lemon juice mixed into a cup of water. Do this every day for a week or so, and your dandruff should be gone.

TWO MINUTE FACE-LIFT

A simple egg white and lemon juice face mask that you whip up in the kitchen has a tightening effect on the skin, and will leave your skin feeling fresh and glowing.

Treat skin discoloration, such as freckles and age spots, with Kojic acid, discovered in Japan in 1989 and derived from fungi. It is gentle on the skin and rebalances discolored skin by penetrating upper skin layers to inhibit uneven pigment formation. Results can be seen after four to six weeks. Vitamin A and mulberry extract are other ingredients that have pigment-leveling properties.

GIVE IT A REST

Moisturizer seals in more than moisture – It stops oil escaping from the skin and can cause spots in those prone to breakouts. Occasionally give yourself a break from night-time creams to allow your skin to breathe and regulate it normally.

FRESH-FACED GLOW

If you mix a tiny blob of exfoliating cream with your night-time cleanser, you will have a fabulous fresh face that looks smooth and glowing the following morning, with the impurities drawn out.

BEWARE OF OVERCLEANSING

Over cleansing is a major cause of sensitive skin, as it strips the skin's underlying layers of its natural protective properties. Make sure you use a cleanser that's right for your skin type and don't overdo it.

FRESHEN UP

If skin looks dull and stressed, spritz on chilled rose water to instantly revitalize and freshen up. Follow this with moisturising rose facial oil massaged in to the skin with small circular movements, to boost circulation and promote a healthy glow.

MOISTURIZE BEFORE MAKE-UP

Apply moisturizer before you put on your make-up because it will give the skin a healthy, plumped-up look. Wait for 5–10 minutes and then apply your make-up over the moisturizer.

NON-ABRASIVE RETEXTURIZING

Don't be tempted to use a body scrub on the delicate skin of your face. Good-quality face exfoliators use calibrated diamond-shaped crystals for precision removal of dead skin cells from the epidermal layer. Body scrubs contain larger, rougher granules that will irritate and inflame sensitive faces.

BE FRANK ABOUT AGING

Frankincense is thought to have some anti-aging effects by plumping up the skin and forming a protective barrier against further damage and stress. Find it in specialist creams and salon treatments.

NIGHT REPAIR WORK

The skin repairs itself most effectively between the hours of 1 am and 3 am, so products aimed at addressing blemishes and eruptions will be more effective overnight. Use an acid-based night-time skin care product after cleansing to exfoliate the outer layers of skin and hydrate the deeper layers.

GIVE UP SMOKING

In smokers, skin looks sallow as a result of poor circulation, and the action of drawing on the cigarette causes lines to be etched around the mouth. To reduce these signs of aging, give up smoking if you're still doing it, and avoid smoky environments.

GET SMOOTH WITH SOY

Soy proteins can help make skin temporarily smoother by improving firmness and elasticity if applied regularly. Look for them as ingredients in new hi-tech face creams.

WHO KNEW?

Papaya contains the papain enzyme, a natural, nonabrasive botanical that dissolves dead skin cells, which makes it a great ingredient for face masks and exfoliations. It deeply cleanses without stripping, leaving dull skin smoother and more refined.

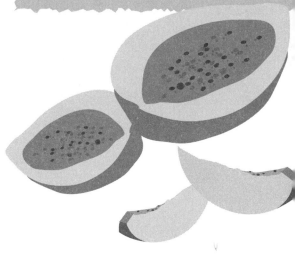

FORGET THE BOTOX... GRAB THE BANANAS

Make an all-natural (and inexpensive) moisturizing face mask like this: Just mash up a few bananas into a paste, and smooth on your face and neck. Let it set (20 minutes should do it) then rinse with cold water. Your skin will look and feel softer.

MAKE TIME FOR MASSAGE

When you apply conditioner, give yourself a slow fingertip scalp massage. Using gentle circular motions and a reasonable amount of pressure pushing down onto the scalp, you will boost blood circulation around the follicle and stimulate re-growth.

HERBAL TREATMENT

Reduce puffy or swollen eyes with a green tea compress. Dip cotton wool into the green tea, drain off excess moisture, and then dab gently around the eye area. This will help to tighten the skin around the eyes.

GIVE SKIN A FEAST

Skin is the last organ to get the benefits of the good things you eat, so often there's precious little nourishment left, even if your diet is fantastic. Choose face treatments which are high in essential minerals such as calcium, magnesium, and zinc to give it a boost.

ESSENTIAL EYE CARE

The skin around our eyes has a tendency to get fine lines and wrinkles because there are no oil glands in the skin directly beneath and above your eyes. You should always use a cream designed just for that area to keep skin moisturized. Put four drops of cream under each eye from below the pupil to the outer corner at crow's-feet and pat into place.

SUPER SHINE

For extra shiny hair, finish your final rinse with a blast of the most freezing cold water you can bear. It closes the hair cuticles so that light bounces off them, resulting in super-shiny locks.

GET HELP FROM AHA

Alpha-hydroxy acids (AHAs), found in many anti-aging products, are organic chemicals derived from fruit-bearing plants, hence they're often called 'fruit acids.' Thought to help generate new collagen, making skin firmer and plumper, they also dissolve the 'glue' that binds dead cells, allowing the old ones to be washed or cleansed away and revealing younger cells.

CONDITION WITH CARE

Some leave-in conditioners are unsuitable for fine hair. They coat the hair to protect it, but they can weigh it down and make it dull and greasy and very difficult to style. Wash-out conditioners generally suit all hair types better.

SOOTHE EYES WITH CUCUMBER

Place a slice of cucumber on each eyelid for 10–15 minutes to allow the high water and mineral content of the cucumber to be absorbed into your delicate eye skin.

SHAPELY BROWS

To determine exactly where your brow should begin, imagine a vertical line or hold a make-up pencil straight alongside one nostril. Where the pencil lands by your brow is where it should begin. To work out where the brow should end, imagine a line from the outside of your nostril to the outer corner of your eye, extending out to your brow.

WHERE DO YOU STORE PERFUME?

Perfume is very volatile—the fragrance breaks down rapidly when exposed to heat and air. If you're not going to use the entire bottle within thirty days, store it in the refrigerator to extend its life.

JUST A LITTLE BIT WILL DO

Do you find your perfume fading after a few hours? To make it last longer, rub a small amount of petroleum jelly onto your skin before you start dabbing on the perfume.

GOES GREAT WITH A MARGARITA

Alleviate dry skin by mashing ½ of an avocado and spreading it thickly on your face. Wait for 20 minutes, and then wash off with warm water.

WHO KNEW?

Headaches magically disappear if you rub ½ of a fresh lime on your forehead. Try it—the throbbing will be gone.

FORGET THE EXPENSIVE TREATMENTS

To restore the natural acid balance to your skin, pour ½ cup of apple-cider vinegar into a basin of warm water. Splash it on your face, and then allow it to dry before removing with a towel.

BECAUSE EVERY LITTLE BIT HELPS

If you want to make a bar of soap last longer, unwrap it before you use it and let it dry out.

A LITTLE DAB WON'T DO YA

The American Dental Association counsels against brushing your teeth with only baking soda. It has not been shown to have any preventive effect on periodontal disease. If you like the taste or feel of baking soda, use a baking soda toothpaste.

LOW FAT AND HELPFUL

To combat puffy eyes, place slices of cucumber on them. Cucumbers have a mild anti-inflammatory action. Parsley seeds also work. To make a compress, mix 1 tablespoon parsley seeds with 1 cup of boiling water, then let it cool. Soak a washcloth in the liquid, wring it out and fold it in thirds length-wise to make a compress. Lie down and place it over your eyes.

HOMEMADE BUBBLES

To make your own bubble bath, try placing soap slivers in a mesh drawstring bag. Attach the bag to the tap while the water is running. Place herbs in the bag for a fragrance treat.

TRY EXPLAINING THIS TO YOUR FRIENDS

Believe it or not, freezing panty hose can keep them from running. Before wearing them for the first time, stick them in the freezer overnight; this will strengthen the fibers. Weird but true!

BURN RELIEF

For bad sunburn, apply a paste of baking soda and water. Or, sponge the sunburned skin with apple-cider vinegar.

WHO KNEW?

To remove garden stains from your hands, add about ½ teaspoon of sugar to the soap lather before you wash your hands. You will be amazed how easily the stains will come off.

QUICK TIPPLE

Stainless steel can be quickly and easily cleaned with vodka. Place a little on a sponge or paper towel and wipe. Your taps (faucets) will soon be sparkling again so pour yourself a glass to celebrate!

VODKA

SUN-SENSITIVE PERFUME

Avoid wearing fragrance that contains alcohol when sunbathing as it makes skin photosensitive, and can result in dryness, burning and pigmentation. The eau de toilette version of your favorite perfume will usually have a lower alcohol content.

CLOUDY DAY DAMAGE

Don't make the mistake of thinking your skin to be safe from sun damage when the weather is overcast. Up to 80% of UV light can pass though cloud cover, so you still need protection on gray days and when sitting under a beach umbrella. Wear a daily moisturizer with SPF even when the sky is cloudy.

OR GO TO LAS VEGAS, WHERE THEY MAGICALLY FALL OFF

If you are unable to remove a ring from your finger, run your hands under very cold water for a few seconds.

HALT THE SHRINKING PROCESS

A strong straight back is key to keeping the height you had at 20. After the age of 40 we shrink by 1 cm ($^2/_5$ in) every 10 years, so practise lying on your tummy with arms outstretched in front of you, and gently raise one arm till the count of 10 as you breathe out. Repeat 8 times with both arms.

GET INTO A ROUTINE

A regular bedtime schedule will help your body to expect sleep at the same time each day. Spend quiet time relaxing in a warm bath infused with a few drops of essential lavender oil to soothe the mind and body and encourage regenerative sleep.

PROTECT YOUR GUMS

Not only is gum disease unattractive and painful, it has also been linked with other more serious problems like strokes and heart disease. Eating a diet as low in refined sugars as possible helps.

WEIGHT TRAIN FOR BONE STRENGTH

Using free weights a couple of times a week for all-over strength training will significantly increase bone mineral density in the spine, which will help to stop the vertebrae from collapsing and decrease your chances of shrinkage.

MINIMIZE NECK DAMAGE

Don't neglect to nourish your neck with a rich emollient night cream every evening before bedtime. The area from the collarbones up to the jaw line often becomes prematurely wrinkled because the skin here is thinner and more vulnerable than that on your face.

DITCH A DOUBLE CHIN

Get rid of your double chin by using a slightly darker shade of powder or foundation under your chin, which will make it appear to recede. Blend towards the back of the jaw-line to add definition.

WHO KNEW?

Playing with your pet is known to reduce blood pressure, improve your mood, and reduce stress. It been proven to work with all pets: dogs, cats, hamsters—everything but dust bunnies.

CHOKER CRISIS

Women over a certain age should avoid wearing delicate chokers, as this will only draw attention to the neck area. Instead choose a pendant necklace that forms a V-shape, and draws the eye upwards.

SHOW OFF AN ATTRACTIVE BACK

Instead of choosing to show a creepy cleavage, find a dress with a high slash neck that has a low sweep, or V-neck at the back. Skin on the back has usually had far less exposure than on the front and doesn't age nearly as much.

TUMMY TRICKS

Many women end up with an extra roll of 'spread' around their tummy, but can still look good in trousers if they choose flat-fronted ones with a side zip that don't add any bulk at the front.

HEAVY UPPER ARMS

Choose a three-quarter-length sleeve top to camouflage flabby upper arms, and leave your elegant wrists and well-manicured hands on show.

SINGLE-BREASTED IS BEST

As gravity takes its toll, and a layer of middle-aged spread appears around the core body, it's time to kiss good bye to all double-breasted jackets. Always choose single-breasted coats, as two sets of buttons make the body appear wider.

A-LINES FOR A BETTER BOTTOM

If your derrière is on the large size, stay clear of flouncy fashion statements like the puffball or tulip skirt, which both have too much volume. Buy an A-line skirt the most flattering shape to cover up your figure flaw.

HIDE AWAY FROM HIGH-WAISTERS

Look for jeans and trousers that are low waisted, or sit between the hips and the waist. High-waisted pants that clamp the middle tummy can highlight a lack of waist and accentuate any middle-aged spread. Even on the slim they can push out abdominal flesh to create rolls of flab.

THROW OUT THE CARGO PANTS

Slouchy combat pants with huge saddlebag pockets add extra inches to your thighs and hips, so dump them in the charity box unless you have the physique of a supermodel.

THE RIGHT FIT

Research has shown that 80% of women wear the wrong bra size. A good-fitting bra should be supportive and uplifting as well as being sexy, so get professional help in measuring and choosing the correct size.

EASY LEG LENTHENER

Add a little extra length to legs by always wearing trousers that cover the top of your shoe and skim the floor.

WHO KNEW?

The easiest way to remove a splinter? Just put a drop of white glue all over the splinter, let it dry, and then peel off the dried glue. The splinter usually sticks to the skin.

FIT YOUR BRA TO YOUR CLOTHES

When you are buying a bra, consider the clothes you will be wearing with it and bring them along if necessary. This is the only way you'll be sure that the bra fits the clothes. Keep an eye out for T-shirt bras, plunging bras and labels that give an indication of the purpose the bra is made for.

UPLIFT YOUR LOOK

One of the narrowest areas on a woman's body is across the ribs, just beneath the bust-line, yet sagging breasts can hide this area and make your figure look dumpier and more middle-aged than it really is. Choosing a well-fitted bra with good uplift will help make the line from rib to hip look more elongated and shapely.

LYCRA ALERT!

Don't be tempted to squeeze yourself into a bra that is too small, thinking that it will give you a greater cleavage, or choose smaller undies than you normally wear believing that you will look even slimmer. Blobby rolls of flesh will be pushed out and on show – defeating the point of the controlled silhouette.

HELP FOR BIG BOTTOMS

Sexy undies come in all shapes and sizes, but if you have a full peachy bottom, don't overexpose it with a G-string. Instead choose bigger 1950s-style stretch shorts made in lacy lycra and sheer.

PURGE YOUR WARDROBE

Make a date to try on all your existing clothes in front of a full-length mirror. Assess yourself honestly and chuck out everything that is unworn, old-fashioned, stained or simply too small. Everything that's left should make you feel fabulous when you put it on.

EMBRACE YOUR CURVINESS

Celebrate your womanly body by wearing clothes that show it off, bias-cut dresses, fitted waistlines and pencil skirts will suit you much better than trying to cover up under a loose kaftan. Wrap dresses are particularly good for the curvy figure.

A HINT OF FLESH

Keeping arms and décolletage lightly covered with lace, chiffon or sheer organza keeps you from revealing too much flesh in the sexiest way possible.

NO MORE TENTS

Fitted clothes are always preferable to shapeless oversized tents. Baggy clothes just hang from your widest point, do nothing to define your good points (everybody has one good asset) and make you look bigger. Elastic waistbands don't work under any circumstances.

HOT STUFF

Even if you don't consider yourself to be in good shape and well-toned, remember: confidence is everything. If you walk into a room like you think you own it, other people will think so, too.

WIND WARNING

In summer a combination of strong winds on a sandy beach can cause as much damage as the sun, so occasionally use a good 'leave-in conditioner' on your hair for the day. Choose one that contains Vitamin B5, which will nourish and protect your hair from beach damage.

BE WHITER AND BRIGHTER

Years of drinking coffee and tea and smoking cigarettes will leave your teeth yellow and stained. In addition to regular brushing, try mixing baking powder and lemon juice together, and gently massage it into teeth and gums for a natural way to whiten your teeth.

CHOOSE DAYLIGHT TO MAKE-UP

Always apply daytime make-up in the daylight, as your skin will change with the season. Set up a magnifying mirror near a window with a good source of natural light, and make sure that shading is properly blended for the most natural-looking face.

BARELY THERE

Most people use far more foundation than they need. Simply dot it onto cheeks, forehead and nose and blend thoroughly. Don't be afraid to leave some areas bare.

LOOK AT THE OVERALL PICTURE

Some women look great with trendy, spiky, shorter hairstyles and can wear them into their seventies with great aplomb, whereas others in their twenties wouldn't be able to carry the look off. The key is to consider not only the quality and texture of your hair but also your bone structure, as well as your build, personality, and dress sense – for a look to work well all these factors need to be in tune.

LET THERE BE LIGHT

If you lose a contact lens, turn off the lights and turn on a flashlight. The lens will reflect the light.

BREAK BAD HABITS

Any repetitive movement such as chewing gum, frowning or sucking on a cigarette will lead to the development of fine lines. Over time micro-tears will appear in the skin resulting in collagen-damaging inflammation. The physical act of smoking causes you to squint, and exaggerates wrinkles around the eyes. It also relies on the repetitive action of pursing your lips: every time you suck in, the small wrinkles around your mouth will become bigger.

STRAWBERRIES AND GLEAM

An inexpensive way to brighten teeth is to mash up a couple of strawberries and turn them into a paste to use as normal with a toothbrush. The malic acid in the fruit will help lighten your teeth.

WHO KNEW?

The age at which you start to go gray and by how much is largely a matter of genetics, but there are other contributing factors. A 1996 British Medical Journal study reported that smokers are four times more likely to go gray at a young age.

PREVENTION IS THE BEST CURE

Breakages and poor condition are some of the reasons hair thins, so take steps to prevent hair loss by restricting the use of blow-dryers – extreme heat can break down the proteins in hair and so can straighteners or chemical treatments such as perms and coloring. The more you abuse your hair, the more risk there is of long-term damage.

TAN FOR HEALTHY-LOOKING HANDS

Hands are one of the areas that show the most signs of aging but they can look a lot better with a little light-colored self-tan. This can be a tricky area to work on, so use your fingertips to lightly stroke and blend well, then use a facial wipe to clean the palms.

REMEDY SCARECROW HAIR

A week of sun, salt water and chlorine will all play havoc with your hair, so spend one day with your hair covered in an intensive conditioner, slicked back and covered with a fashionable scarf. This eight-hour treatment will restore hair to pre-vacation condition.

THIN ON TOP

Hair naturally thins out as part of the aging process, as the number of follicles capable of growing hairs gradually declines. A straight parting with hair that just hangs down from it will emphasize the problem, so ask your stylist to create a style that incorporates color and texture.

DON'T FORGET YOUR CLEAVAGE

If you're wearing a low-cut dress remember to blend a light covering of foundation down from your neck and onto your chest, to give skin an even color and smooth appearance. Always dust with a light covering of translucent powder to avoid getting foundation on your clothes.

IMPROVE LEGS WITH BIRCH OIL

Combat ugly cellulite with regular massage. Diet and exercise are all known to help reduce the lumpy orange-peel skin that appears at the top of the thigh and on the bottom, but massage using a plant-based cream like birch oil helps too by improving blood and lymph circulation, and releasing trapped toxins.

30-SECOND SKIN REVIVER

Place a fresh hand towel into steaming hot water (not boiling) and then cover your entire face with it for 30 seconds. Use the flannel to buff the T zone area, chin, nose and forehead, and then splash freezing cold water all over your face to leave pores tight and tingling.

OVERNIGHT HYDRATION

During the night the skin rests and repairs itself after the stresses of the day. Use a humidifier or place a damp towel over your radiator at night to replace moisture in the air and keep the skin hydrated. This helps to humidify the air around you, and reduces excessive water loss from the skin.

THE DO-NOTHING FACELIFT

Retrain your face muscles to assume their correct, relaxed and natural appearance with stick-on 'Frownies'. Designed to be worn overnight on the forehead and between the brows, they work to smoothen underlying facial muscles and so reduce expression lines, leaving younger-looking skin. You can also use adhesive or Scotch tape instead of expensive alternatives.

PERFECT SLEEPING POSTURE

Sleeping curled up on your side in the fetal position will create wrinkles and creases on the side of your face where the skin is at its thinnest. Try to sleep on your back at night (and avoid rolling over to dribble into the pillow), if you want to wake up with a smooth and crease-free face.

WHO KNEW?

The best way to care for a pearl (or coral) necklace is to wear it regularly – oils in your skin add a gentle luster. After wearing, wipe with a chamois to remove traces of perspiration that can damage the surface. Wash in water and very mild soap then wipe with a soft cloth. Lay on moist kitchen paper to dry.

MAKE YOUR OWN

For a super-smoothing skin exfoliant, massage a handful of Epsom salts with a tablespoon of olive oil over wet skin to cleanse, exfoliate and soften the rough spots. Rinse off well for a polished finish.

DON'T BE AFRAID OF THE PEARLS

A single string of small pearls and miniscule pearl studs will always have a somewhat regal look about them. If you like pearls but feel old wearing them, try several strings all at once, like Coco Chanel, or find expensive fakes with larger chunky-sized stones, which looks more modern. Pearls are brilliant for making skin appear more luminescent.

AMBER LIGHT

Wipe amber jewelry with a soft cloth wrung out in warm soapy water. Dry at once (water makes amber cloudy). A wiping of sweet almond oil will remove grease marks.

CROWN JEWELS

Polish costume jewelry by dropping two Alka Seltzer tablets into a glass of water. Immerse for about five minutes and pat dry on kitchen paper.

GENTLY DOES IT

Occasionally wipe gold and platinum with the softest of clean chamois. Ordinary cloths may hold grit that could damage the surface. Gold plate should be treated with tender care or the thin layer may rub off with excessive polishing.

MAGNIFICENT MARCASITE

Bring back the magic of marcasite by polishing it with a soft brush and then buff with a chamois – it should never be washed.

PRECIOUS & SEMI-PRECIOUS

Gentle detergent and water plus a soft cloth can clean rubies, amethysts, citrines, sapphires, turquoise and garnets.

PURE & SIMPLE

Since turquoise and opals are porous stones, never immerse them in water. Instead polish with a soft, dry chamois and clean claws with a soft bristle brush.

SOFT TOUCH

Emeralds are softer than other precious stones and can chip easily. Wash carefully in a warm solution of washing-up liquid.

WOBBLY CHIN BE GONE

A quick-fix facial toner that can be repeated 20 times a day wherever you are is to push your lips tight together and make a wide grimace. Hold for 3 seconds and repeat, to contract lower facial muscles and tighten a wobbly chin.

HIDE YOUR NOSE

To slim down a wide nose, use highlighter and blend a soft line down the centre of the nose, then add a contour shade (a darker powder or non-shimmery bronzer) to the outside of the nose and blend them together.

WHO KNEW?

Revive hairbrushes and combs by soaking them in a pot of warm water and 1 tablespoon of baking soda or ammonia.

KEEP HANDS HIDDEN

Wrinkled hands are the biggest telltale sign of aging. Exposed to the elements nearly all the time, they take quite a battering so cover up and protect them wherever possible. Use rubber gloves to wash dishes and gardening gloves when working outside.

TIGHTEN UP FACIAL MUSCLES

Like a wobbly tummy, facial muscles need to be exercised on a regular basis to stop them becoming loose and flabby. A routine that takes just 10 minutes a day, and which can be done anywhere – on the bus, in the car or watching TV – will tighten up lazy skin.

PINCH TO RELIEVE STRESS

Many people hold stress in the area between the brows and in time vertical stress lines will develop here. When you feel your brow knit together with concentration or stress, take a moment to pinch the muscle here, working from the centre of the brow along the brow-line in each direction with a thumb and bent forefinger.

WAKE UP YOUR FACE

In the morning the face can look pale and puffy because of the natural nocturnal slow-down in the body. When putting on your moisturizer, take the opportunity to gently massage all the muscles in the face to waken up the lymphatic system and jump start the circulation.

PARISIAN CHIC

Stylish French women know that however beautifully made up your face is, a saggy wrinkled neck will always give away your age. Learn how to keep it covered up with a silk scarf tied in a variety of clever styles.

BRUSH-UP

Invest in good-quality make-up brushes as these will make application easier, faster and more polished-looking. Brushes should always have bristles that feel soft against the skin. It's important to wash them at least every three months with a mild liquid soap.

HANDS HATE WATER

Because the skin there is thin and endlessly ravaged by the elements, keep your hands dry as much as possible. Water left on hands will evaporate leaving them dried up and red. Use a hand cream that contains lanolin.

WAKE UP TO FABULOUS HANDS

Once a month cover your hands in thick nourishing cream, and slip them into soft cotton gloves for the night. In the morning all the cream will have been absorbed leaving hands smoother and softer. It is also helpful to keep a regular supply of hand cream on the bedside table to remind you to apply it before you sleep.

GOOD FOOT HEALTH

Nine out of ten women suffer from corns, calluses or bunions at some point in their life and nine out of ten wear shoes that are too small. To prevent problems with your feet, ensure your shoes are the correct size and never wear the same ones two days in a row. Too-tight shoes can eventually cause such debilitating conditions as hammer toes and bone spurs.

ALWAYS REPLACE MOISTURE

Baths and showers always rob skin of its moisture, even if you use a very gentle body wash. Always use body oil or a specially formulated body lotion after bathing to replace lost moisture and keep skin hydrated.

A BUFF TOO FAR

Nude nails that are clean, shiny and buffed are preferable to a single coat of chipped polish, but only buff nails once a week. Over-buffing weakens the nails by taking away the top layer, and making them more porous.

CHOOSE MILD SOAP

If you wash your hands as often as you should during the course of 24 hours, make sure you are using a good-quality soap with natural ingredients like lemon or oatmeal. Cheap soaps leave hands dry and chapped.

NATURAL SALT SCRUBS

For an invigorating body scrub grab a handful of luxury salt granules, such as 'Fleur de Sel', and mix them with a tablespoon of good-quality almond oil. Massage gently over rough skin, paying particular attention to knees and elbows, then rinse off with warm water.

SALT

OIL

DAILY BODY BRUSHING

Get into the habit of body brushing every day to slough off dead skin cells, boost circulation and encourage new regeneration. Skin will look smoother as better circulation helps disperse fatty deposits.

SHORT SHOWERS

A combination of water that is too hot, and washing your face and body with soap will dissolve the skin's natural moisture balance, so keep your daily shower short and water temperature moderate if you want to avoid dry skin.

SWEAT OUT TOXINS

Make your bath time work for you by adding 1 lb. of Epsom bath salts to the water. Epsom salts are made from the mineral magnesium sulfate, which draws toxins from the body, sedates the nervous system and relaxes tired muscles.

THREE MINUTES WITH A LOOFAH

Dry-brush your skin with a natural loofah first thing in the morning. You will feel the benefits as the accelerated blood flow invigorates you and sets your skin tingling – a great start to the day.

HEAVY HAIR SHADOWS SKIN

A thick and solid curtain of glossy hair can overwhelm the face and make skin look dull and tired. Shorter layers, cut through from underneath, are needed to give movement around the face and let light shine through.

GET INTO A ROUTINE

A regular bedtime schedule will help your body to expect sleep at the same time each day. Spend quiet time relaxing in a warm bath infused with a few drops of essential lavender oil to soothe the mind and body and encourage regenerative sleep.

LEG CHECK

The most common place to develop a malignant melanoma is on your legs, so make sure you check them regularly for freckles or moles that have changed shape or are seeping blood. Don't be tempted to sunbathe without sun protection on your legs because you want to get them brown.

WHEN YOUR HANDS ARE REALLY FILTHY

Laundry detergent makes an excellent hand cleaner for very dirty hands. To freshen your feet, rub a few fresh lemon slices over them.

A LONG BOB

If you want to disguise, or draw attention away from, crow's-feet, try a feathered cut or one that falls naturally forward around the side. Avoid scraping your hair back off your face.

BANANAS TO THE RESCUE

A simple way to help bruises fade fast is with a banana peel. Yep, you heard it right: Just apply a piece of banana peel, flesh side down, to the bruise, cover with a bandage, and leave on overnight. By the morning, the bruise will have faded.

WHO KNEW?

Sun damage affects all of your body, not just the face. Always remember to cover your hands with an SPF 20 when you spend time in the sun to avoid photo-aging wrinkles and liver spots, the telltale signs of aging.

GREAT LENGTHS

Hair products containing copper peptides have already shown a remarkable ability to increase growth. The mineral is thought to increase thickness and reduce brittleness in hair.

It's important to keep 'tweaking' your hairstyle, and not to become trapped in a style that suited you when you were a teenager. Sometimes the best way to change your style, is to try a new stylist or go to a salon that has a different approach than your usual one. All it takes is for someone to see you in a slightly new way.

AVOID SMOKY AREAS

Stay out of places such as bars and clubs where you will be exposed to other people's smoke. Some researchers believe that exposure to cigarette smoke in a confined area is as bad for your skin as the sun's ultraviolet rays. The smoke has a drying effect on the skin's surface plus it restricts blood vessels, so reducing blood flow and depleting oxygen. Even passive smoking will deplete vitamin C, a key ingredient for keeping skin plump and moist.

SMOKING DAMAGES YOUR HAIR

Smoking is very damaging as it affects the take-up of vitamin C and constricts the blood vessels, which means fewer of the nutrients needed for hair growth will be retained by the body. Stop smoking and you will see instant results.

FLATTERING CUTS

Make your haircut work for you. Choose a hairstyle that has a side fringe (bangs) rather than a straight-across fringe, and a length that falls just below the chin if you want to cover a wrinkled forehead and sagging jaw.

THE PERFECT LENGTH

The most flattering and youthful hair length, post 40, is just below the chin to cover the jaw line. This length works on nearly all women and the hair can swing above the shoulder.

COMB, DON'T BRUSH

When hair is damp or wet it is much weaker and more easily damaged. Always treat wet hair carefully and use a wide-toothed comb to straighten out tangles, and never a brush, which will create split ends.

CHEAP AND EFFECTIVE

For an inexpensive bath oil, mix some sunflower oil with either crushed lavender or rose petals. Let it stand for a few days before using it.

THE BEST SORE THROAT REMEDY WE KNOW

Fill a shot glass with honey, and warm it in the microwave for about 10 seconds. Add ¼ teaspoon of cinnamon to it, stir, and drink. Repeat this few times a day. In three days, you'll feel much better!

LESS IS MORE

If your resolution is to lose weight, here's a simple way to start: Switch from 2 percent to skim milk. If you drink just one glass a day, you'll save nearly 32 grams of fat per week!

KEEP ASPIRIN HANDY

To remove hard calluses from your feet, try this old-fashioned but effective remedy: Grind a few aspirins into a paste with equal parts of lemon juice and water. Apply it to the calluses, and then wrap your feet in a hot towel, cover in a plastic bag, and stay off your feet for 30 minutes. When you unwrap your feet, the calluses should be ready to be filed off with a pumice stone.

OATMEAL TO THE RESCUE

Believe it or not, you can help relieve arthritis pain with oatmeal. Just mix two cups of oatmeal with one cup of water, warm it in the microwave, and apply to the affected area.

SOFTER FEET—PRESTO

Kind of gross but effective: For the softest feet imaginable, apply a thick layer of petroleum jelly to your feet, cover it with clean, white, cotton socks, and leave on overnight.

WHO KNEW?

White vinegar heals bruises! Soak a cotton ball in vinegar, and apply to the bruise for an hour. It will reduce the blueness of the bruise and speed up the healing process..

MORE TIME- AND MONEY-SAVING TIPS

chapter

A ROUND-THE-CLOCK WATER SUPPLY

To water your houseplants while away on vacation, poke a small hole in the side of a plastic bottle, fill it with water, and place it in the soil next to your plant. The slow drip keeps the plants watered slowly but continuously.

CLEANING ASHES FROM THE FIREPLACE?

Coat the fireplace with wet coffee grounds beforehand. Sweeping out the fireplace will be easier, and less dust will escape and will not dirty your room.

PETROLEUM PRIMER

Painting doors? It's easier to get paint off hinges if you coat them lightly with petroleum jelly before you start.

GAME, SET, PAINT

Cut a tennis ball in half, and then cut a thin slot in the bottom. Slide it, open side toward the bristles, over the brush handle to catch the drips. A small paper plate works, too.

AVOID DRIPPING PAINT

Notch a few holes along the rim of your paint can. The paint that you wipe off the brush will go back into the can instead of running down the outside.

JUST DON'T EAT IT AFTERWARDS

To remove a broken light bulb from the socket, turn off the electricity or unplug the lamp, and then push half of a raw potato or small apple into the broken bulb base. Turn it to unscrew the base.

DID YOU EVER WONDER HOW TO CLEAN YOUR RANGE'S FILTER?

To give the charcoal filter in your range hood a new lease on life, set it in a 450°F oven for 30 minutes—but clean the frame completely first. Any grease on the frame may catch on fire or smoke up the house.

BECAUSE YOU'LL NEVER REMEMBER IF YOU DON'T

Always dip a three-by-five-inch index card into your paint can and write down the details to make it easier to match at a later date.

THE CASE OF THE SLIPPERY PIN

If a pin or needle will not penetrate an article, stick the pin into a bar of soap to make it nice and slippery.

A SHARPER IDEA

There's no need to replace your sewing machine needle if it's become dull. Simply stitch through a piece of sandpaper a few times and it will be sharp again.

THE RAINBOW CONNECTION

To add color to a campfire, soak pinecones in a solution of 1 quart of water and 1 cup of baking soda. Let them dry for a few days before tossing them into the flames.

PING PONG...POP!

Dented ping-pong balls can be revived by submerging them in very hot water for about 20 minutes. The air inside the ball will expand enough to pop out the dents.

A GREAT SAFETY TIP

Microwave doors may become misaligned, especially if you pull down on them when opening them. They can leak radiation and should be checked periodically with a small, inexpensive detector, which can be purchased in any hardware store.

WHO KNEW?

An easy way to sharpen scissors is to fold a piece of aluminum foil nine or ten times, then cut through it several times.

WHO KNEW?

Cleaning agents can leave a thin film on mirrors. Brighten mirrors by rubbing them with a cloth dampened with alcohol.

WIND UNWIND

Remember this tip for when you take down your Christmas tree: Always wrap the lights around the outside of a cardboard tube (from a roll of paper towels) and secure with masking tape. They'll be easy to unwind next year, and you'll never have another nightmarish day of untangling all the lights while the kids wait to decorate the tree.

THE STARBUCKS SOLUTION

If you need to repair a hole in a piece of wood, add a small amount of instant coffee to the Spackle or to a thick paste made from a laundry starch and warm water. The coffee tints the Spackle.

DON'T BE A DORK, USE A CORK

Did you lose the knob of a pot lid? Place a screw with the thread side up in the hole, and then attach a cork to it. (Headline written by Jack, 10, and Luke, 8).

TWIST AND BLOW DRY

Blow-dryer cords can be kept neat using ponytail holders. This will work for any small electrical appliance, of course.

OURS STAYS UP UNTIL FEBRUARY

To extend the life of your Christmas tree for a few days, add a small amount of sugar or Pine Sol to the water.

IT WORKS WAY BETTER

Hanging wallpaper? Use a paint roller instead of a sponge to smooth it out.

FEED YOUR FERN

Banana skins and eggshells are excellent natural fertilizers, and the minerals they provide are not readily found in many fertilizers. Flat club soda also makes an excellent fertilizer. To perk up colors, give your plants a sip or two occasionally.

THE ODD EVEN SYSTEM

When painting steps, paint every other one. When those are dry, go back and paint the rest. This way, you'll still be able to use the stairs—but only if you're careful.

AIDAN, THIS IS FOR YOU, BECAUSE SOMETIMES YOU SURE DO STINK

Drop a few charcoal briquettes into the baby's diaper pail (under the liner). You'll be amazed at what you *don't* smell. (Headline written by Terrence, 7)

HERE'S ANOTHER ONE FOR YOU, AIDAN

A great way to remove crayon stains from walls is with a spray of WD-40. Any dish detergent then removes all traces of the lubricant. (Another headline from Terrence!)

IMAGINE WHAT IT DOES TO YOUR STOMACH

If you're having a problem removing a rusty nut or bolt, put a few drops of ammonia or hydrogen peroxide on it, and let it stand for 30 minutes. You can also just cover them with a cola soda for the same results.

MEOW

If you run out of salt or sand to keep ice at bay on your walkway, try kitty litter.

SALT SEDATION

If you're having trouble sleeping, but wary of popping a pill, try this instead: At bedtime drink a glass of water, then let a pinch of salt dissolve on your tongue. (Just make sure the salt doesn't touch the roof of your mouth). Studies show the combination of salt and water can induce a deep sleep.

TIMING IS EVERYTHING

When cutting flowers from your garden, be sure to cut them only in the late evening or early morning. Have a bucket of water with you and use very sharp shears. After you cut the flowers, immediately submerge the stems in the water, and cut them again on the diagonal. The stems will then take in water and not air, and the blooms will last longer.

THIS DOESN'T MEAN YOU CAN WALK ON THE TABLE

Linoleum or vinyl floor tiles are excellent for covering picnic tabletops. Linoleum can also be used instead of contact paper on kitchen shelves. It will last longer and is easier to keep clean.

YET ANOTHER USE FOR PAPER TOWEL TUBES

To avoid tangled electrical cords, fold them up and store in paper towel tubes. Label which appliance each tube goes to. Works great for storing Christmas tree lights, too.

ISN'T THIS A GREAT TIP?

Windows will open and close more easily if you rub a bar of soap across the track occasionally.

BECAUSE "RUST" IS A FOUR LETTER WORD

If you place a few mothballs, a piece of chalk, or a piece of charcoal in your toolbox, you will never have any rust on your tools.

SAW SAFETY

Use a split piece of old garden hose to cover saw blades when storing them in the tool shed or workshop.

BECAUSE WE ALL SAVE OLD COFFEE CANS, RIGHT?

Here's another use for them: If you need to use a ladder on soft earth, set the legs inside the empty cans so that they won't sink in from your weight.

DON'T WASTE MONEY ON EXPENSIVE COVERS

No space to bring outdoor furniture inside in bad weather? Protect lawn chairs and tables by covering them with large plastic bags.

OR ATTACK IT WITH A PARING KNIFE

Keep paved areas looking spiffy with this trick. To remove unwanted grass or weeds from sidewalk and driveway cracks, squirt them with a solution of 1-gallon vinegar, 1-cup salt, and 8 drops liquid detergent.

DRY SOIL DOESN'T GET IT DONE

When transplanting, always use moistened soil and peat moss to help retain the moisture.

IF YOU REALLY HAVE TIME ON YOUR HANDS

If you want your plant's leaves to shine, wipe them with glycerin, or clean the leaves with a cotton ball dipped in milk or mineral oil.

UNLESS YOU USE A COASTER

Never place a clay pot on wooden furniture. Water will seep through and can damage the wood finish.

A PRESERVATIVE WON'T WORK

Organize your favorite recipes in a photo album with clear sleeves that let you see the front and back. The plastic protects the recipes from spills and stains.

WHO KNEW?

The fastest way to clean a paintbrush is to put ½ cup liquid fabric softener in a gallon of water, and vigorously swirl the brush in it for 20 seconds.

YOUR NEW YEAR'S DAY TIP

Once your head stops pounding and it's time to clean up last night's broken Champagne glasses, try this: Dampen a piece of white bread, and dab on the glass fragments. It's much more effective than using a broom. And next time, don't drink so much.

TOO BAD IT DOESN'T WORK ON THE KIDS

If you are going a long vacation and are unable to find someone to care for your plants, try placing a large container of water near your plants. Then place long pieces of yarn in the water, laying the ends of the strands across the stalks of the plants. It will keep the plants moist until you return.

THAT'S AN *UNUSED* FILTER, OF COURSE

If you are going to repot a plant, put a small coffee filter on the bottom of the new pot to keep the soil from leaking out.

GRAVEL GETS IT DONE

To keep mud from spattering when you water plants in window boxes (or when it rains hard), top the soil with a one-half-inch layer of gravel.

WE USE "FRAMPTON COMES ALIVE"

Broken cassette tapes make excellent ties for plants; and old ice cube trays make excellent herb starters.

JUST TAKE THEM OFF FIRST

Nylon stockings or panty hose make excellent storage holders for plant bulbs. Air is able to circulate which helps avoid mold. Store in a cool, dry location.

WHO KNEW?

Styrofoam foam cups make excellent plant starters and are easy to break apart when it's time to plant the garden.

WEIRD BUT IT WORKS

You'll distribute sand or salt in a thin, even layer on ice if you use a lawn seeder or fertilizer spreader.

SAVE THE PLANTS

Place a few short, heavy stakes in your garden to stop the garden hose from rolling over the plants when you drag the hose around.

WHAT'S BLACK AND WHITE AND WARM ALL OVER?

If you're a seed, the answer is newspaper. Seeds need warmth, but not light, to germinate, so if you place newspaper (black and white only) over newly sown area, it will keep the seeds warm and block out the light.

I HATE GRASS

Well, not really, but lilac bushes do. They'll flower better if you keep a 16-24 inch circle around their base free from grass. Lime and manure are great fertilizers for lilacs.

WOODEN HANDLE HELP

Maintain the wooden handles on your garden tools by applying a thin coat of linseed oil. Remember, use it sparingly; a little goes a long way.

COILED, NOT FOLDED

Believe it or not, your garden house will last twice as long if you store it coiled, rather than folding it. Try coiling it around a bucket, and remember it's easy to work with when it's not cold outside.

WHO KNEW?

The easiest way to clean plastic or resin patio furniture? Just toss them in the swimming pool before going to bed, and in the morning they'll be good as new.

THERE HAS TO BE SOME USE FOR THAT ANNOYING STUFF

The packing popcorn used for shipping works better than pebbles in the bottom of flowerpots. They don't add much excess weight, and are efficient at retaining water.

COME ON HOME

Bring potted plants inside before the first freeze. Place them in a warm, sunny location.

YET ANOTHER USE FOR PANTY HOSE

Cut narrow strips of panty hose and use to tie up plants. It works better than plastic ties, because the panty hose expands as the plant grows.

REMEMBER THIS ON VALENTINE'S DAY

There are quite a few ways to prolong the life of fresh flowers: you can either mix 2 tablespoons of white vinegar and 2 tablespoons of sugar in a quart of water; or ½ cup of baking soda in a quart of water. Both do the trick.

AND IT'S CHEAPER THAN WD-40, TOO

Squeaky door and cabinet hinges, as well as sticky locks, benefit from a light spritz with a nonstick cooking spray.

NOT TOO MUCH OFF THE TOP

Try and keep your lawn about 3 inches high. By keeping the grass a bit higher, it keeps weeds from getting direct sunlight.

WHO KNEW?

To clean dirty windows or your car's windshield, mix a tablespoon of cornstarch to about ½ gallon of warm water, and dry with a soft cloth. It's amazing how quickly the dirt is removed—and no streaking, either!

SAVE THOSE ORANGE AND GRAPEFRUIT HALVES...

...Because they make great containers for starting seeds. Just fill them with soil and seeds, and plant. After the seeds germinate the holders will decompose, leaving nutrients in the ground.

FALL, NOT SPRING

Plant your new lawn in the fall, not the spring. It should be planted when you expect at least six weeks of 50-70 degree weather.

KEEPING IT CLEAN

If you place masking tape on the rim of paint can before pouring the paint out, you can remove the tape later and the rim will be clean.

BECAUSE WE ALL HATE PAINT WITH LUMPS

If you have lumps in your paint can, cut a piece of screen just under the size of the can and let it settle to the bottom. It'll carry the lumps with it.

I'D HATE TO SEE THEIR ARTERIES

A small amount of fat drippings placed at the base of a rose bush will keep it healthier and make it bloom more frequently.

LADIES, HERE'S HOW TO FIND A REAL STUD

No stud finder? Try this. Hold a compass level with the floor and at a right angle to the wall, and then slowly move the compass along the surface of the wall. When the needle moves, that's where you will find a stud.

WHO KNEW?

To repair small holes in window screens, cover them with a few of layers of clear nail polish.

NAIL ENAMEL

WHO KNEW?

Slice old wine corks into thin disks, and glue them to the feet of your heavy furniture. It's a great way to protect your floors, and makes moving the furniture a bit easier.

JUST DON'T WEAR THEM AFTERWARDS

If you're sanding wood and want to know when it's smooth enough, use the panty hose test: Slip an old nylon stocking over your hand and run it over the wood. You'll have no trouble finding the slightest rough spot.

THE VARNISHED TRUTH

Air bubbles in varnish can be brushed out while the varnish is still wet. If you notice them when it's dry, gently buff them out with very fine steel wool.

OPEN THE TAP

You can keep your water lines from freezing during a cold snap by leaving one of the taps running very slightly. If you have a two-story house, open a tap on the first floor.

WHITE SOAP UNDER YOUR NAILS HELPS, TOO

Slather on a heavy layer of hand moisturizer before painting or doing other dirty chores. It will prevent dirt and paint from seeping into your skin and make personal cleanup easier.

THE DOLLAR RULES

If you just need a ballpark measurement, a dollar bill is just more than six inches long. Its actual dimensions: $6\frac{1}{8}$ by $2\frac{5}{8}$ inches.

SLOWER IS BETTER

Stir varnish thoroughly from the bottom of the can, but don't stir vigorously. Stirring can create air bubbles, which can ruin a smooth finish.

THE SMELL IS GREAT

To restore the aroma (and moth-repelling properties) to cedar blocks or a cedar chest, rub the wood lightly with fine sandpaper.

FLOUR POWER

If you are painting old woodwork and need to patch small holes, fill them with flour and the paint. It will harden and will not be noticeable.

STICKY DRAWERS?

Wooden drawers with wooden runners will glide smoothly if you rub a candle along the tops of the runners.

NO NEED TO CLEAN

If you want to avoid cleaning a paint roller, wrap it in foil or in a plastic bag and place in the refrigerator. This will keep the roller moist and usable for a few days.

THE BLOW DRYER HELPS

If your pipes are frozen but have not burst, use a blow dryer to thaw them. As always, though, take care that the appliance doesn't get wet.

KEEP IT TOGETHER

Lightweight materials that need to be glued together are easily held in place with spring clothespins.

GOOD GROOMING IS A MUST

To soften a hardened paint brush, soak it in full-strength white vinegar and then clean it with a comb.

WHO KNEW?

The easiest way to remember the exact paint you're using is to write the information under an outlet cover when you're painting. When it's time to touch up months later, you'll thank us!

If you want to mow your lawn while the grass is wet, try spraying the blades with vegetable oil, and the grass won't stick!

GREASE SPOTS ON THE WALL?

If grease spots are still visible on the wall after removing wallpaper, apply a coat of clear varnish to the spots. The grease won't soak through to the new wallpaper.

THINK ABOUT IT

To keep a partially used can of paint fresh longer, blow up a balloon until it is about the size of the space in the can; then put it in the can and cover. It will reduce the amount of air in the can and keep paint from drying.

WATER AND SUN DO THE TRICK

Caning can loosen on chairs, but it can be tightened. Apply very hot water to the underside, then dry the chair in direct sunlight.

IS THAT WHY IT'S CALLED A "FROSTY ONE?"

To temporarily "frost" a bathroom window, mix a solution of 1 cup beer and 4 tablespoons Epsom salts. Then paint the mixture on the window. The paint will wash off easily.

AND YOUR HANDS WILL SHINE

Enamel or oil paint can be removed from your hands easily. Rub with floor paste wax, and then wash with soap and water.

GET RID OF THE SKIN

To prevent a skin from forming on top of the paint, place a piece of waxed paper the size of the opening on top of the paint.

IT'S NOT JUST FOR SALADS ANYMORE

After cleaning a paintbrush, rub a few drops of vegetable oil into the bristles to keep them soft.

NO MORE YELLOWING

If you add 7 to 10 drops of black paint to each quart of white paint, it will keep the white from yellowing over time.

A GREAT EXCUSE FOR PUTTING IT OFF

If you allow wood to "weather" before you apply a stain, the stain will last years longer. It's a case where patience pays off.

TAPING BEFORE TAPPING

To prevent plaster walls from cracking when driving in a nail, place a small piece of tape over the spot before hammering in the nail.

ZAP!

Never hang lights on a metal fence, even if the lights are approved for outdoor use. There is the hazard of electric shock.

WHAT A WAY TO GO

The tried and true method for eliminating cockroaches? Fill a bowl with cheap wine under the sink. The revolting little pests will drink it, get drunk, and drown.

IN A PINCH

A one-liter plastic soda bottle can make an excellent hot-water bottle in an emergency. Just make sure that you wrap it in a hand towel before placing it against your skin.

NEED A QUICK ICE PACK?

Just grab a bag of frozen vegetables from the freezer. It won't leak like a plastic bag filled with ice.

WHO KNEW?

Run a fabric softener sheet across the TV screen, which will eliminate static cling and keep it clean.

SWIMMING POOL SAFETY

They're wonderful on hot summer days, but swimming pools require vigilance—particularly in terms of safety.

In 2005, over 4000 people drowned in their homes; over 1100 were under age fourteen. If you have a swimming pool, a fence should surround it, ideally isolation pool fencing. This is a fence that separates the pool from the house, has gates that close and latch by themselves, and cannot be scaled. Your state may require that you have additional security precautions, such as alarms on doors that lead to the pool. Whether law in your area mandates such safety features, if you have small children or play host to small children on a regular basis, you may wish to install such devices.

- Keep all toys out of the pool area. Remove pool toys and store them out of sight, so small children are not tempted to go in unsupervised.
- Empty small wading pools of water after each use. Children can drown in them, and they are a breeding ground for mosquitoes.
- Whenever children are near water, they require constant adult supervision. Don't take your eyes off them, not even for one second.

If there's a large group of children, the number of adults in the immediate area should always be proportionate to provide adequate attention.

NOT MADE IN THE USA

Imported dinnerware, especially pottery and some types of crystal, may still contain traces of lead and other heavy metals. Acidic foods, like vinegar in salad dressings, lemon juice, or even tomatoes, may be strong enough to release these metals.

Add a big, dry towel to the clothes dryer when drying jeans and other bulky items. It will cut the drying time significantly.

MAKES A REVOLTING DRINK, TOO

To remove an unsightly residue buildup inside a vase or bottle, try a solution of 2 tablespoons salt, enough raw rice to create friction, and 1 cup white vinegar. Cover and shake vigorously.

ANNOYING PROBLEM SOLVED

Transparent decals may be easily removed using a solution of lukewarm water and white vinegar. Place the solution on a sponge and dampen the area thoroughly for a few minutes. If this doesn't work, saturate the decal with straight vinegar and let stand for 15 minutes.

BECAUSE YOUR ELECTRIC CAN OPENER IS REALLY DISGUSTING

To clean your electric can opener, run a piece of paper towel through it. This will pick up the grease and some of the gunk.

A GREAT REASON TO PROCRASTINATE

If the sun is shining on your windows, wait until they are in the shade to wash them. When they dry too fast, they tend to streak.

ISN'T THAT WHAT MARTHA STEWART SMELLS LIKE?

To make your house smell great, simmer apple cider with a cinnamon stick and a few whole cloves. Also add a bit of orange peel, if you like.

COVER UP

If there's a grease fire in a pan, cover the pan with a lid. You'll cut off the oxygen supply and the fire will go out.

GET ARTFUL WITH ARTIFICIAL

To revitalize artificial flowers, pour salt into a large paper bag. Place the flowers inside, heads down, and shake vigorously. The dirt will be transferred to the salt. Perk up paper flowers by applying a steam iron on the lowest setting.

ALCOHOL WORKS

Remove unsightly black soot marks from candles by sponging them with rubbing alcohol.

THE LEMON TRICK

For a brighter shoeshine, place a few drops of lemon juice on your shoes when you are polishing them. Also, a small amount of lemon juice mixed with salt will remove mold and mildew from most surfaces. The juice is just acidic enough to do the job.

OR TOSS THE GLASS OUT

Buff away a nick on the rim of a glass with an emery board. Don't use a nail file or sandpaper; both are too coarse and will scratch the glass.

PEANUT BUTTER IN YOUR HAIR?

One of the best methods of removing chewing gum from a child's hair is to use a small amount of smooth peanut butter.

I LOVE YOU IN LEATHER

To revive the beauty of leather, lightly beat two egg whites, and then apply to the leather with a soft sponge. Allow the egg whites to remain on the leather for three to five minutes, and then wipe it off with a soft cloth dampened with clear warm water. Dry immediately, and buff off any residue.

ADMIT IT, YOUR FRIDGE SOMETIMES STINKS

Besides baking soda, a number of other foods are capable of removing odors. Pour a little vanilla extract into a bottle cap and set in the refrigerator to absorb odors.

WHO KNEW?

If you're painting baseboards or other low areas, just sit on a skateboard so you can roll along as you paint.

PROVING YOU NEVER, EVER HAVE TO THROW AWAY ANYTHING IF YOU DON'T WANT TO

Stale milk will do a great job of cleaning plant leaves. The protein in milk called casein has a mild cleansing effect on the plant cell walls.

DELICIOUS

If you run out of furniture polish, try vegetable oil on wood furniture. A very light coat will help protect the finish, but be sure to rub it in well so that it doesn't leave a residue. Leftover tea and mayonnaise can also be used on wood furniture.

OR JUST DRINK WHITE WINE

If you spill red wine on your carpet, pour salt on the area as soon as possible and watch it absorb the wine almost instantly. Wait until it dries, then vacuum it up. Salt tends to provide a special capillary attraction that will work for most liquids. Baking soda, with its high sodium content, works with wine, too. Salt also works on mud stains.

FORGET IT

Don't bother buying fancy dust cloths that are treated to attract dust! Instead, simply sprinkle a piece of cheesecloth with a few drops of lemon oil. Let the cheesecloth air dry, and it will do just as good a job as an expensive cloth.

GIVE IT A TRY

If you want to make a quick and unique salad dressing, just place a small amount of olive oil and wine vinegar inside an almost-empty ketchup bottle and shake.

WHO KNEW?

Always store cut flowers in the refrigerator when you're leaving the house. They'll stay fresh much longer that way.

WHO KNEW?

Weird but true: Discolored socks will return to their original color if you boil them in a pot of water with a few slices of lemon.

BECAUSE GLUE IS A DRAG TO REMOVE

To remove glue residue on almost any surface, try vegetable oil on a rag. Residue from sticky labels is also a breeze to remove this way. The vegetable oil tends to neutralize the glue's bonds.

SPARKLERS

A 50-50 solution of white vinegar and warm water can easily clean gold jewelry and all gemstones except opals, pearls, and emeralds. (Opals, emeralds, and pearls are too delicate for this type of treatment and should be professionally cleaned.) Dip a soft toothbrush into the solution and brush gently. Hot sudsy water and a bit of ammonia also work. Costume jewelry should be cleaned only with a weak solution of baking soda and water to avoid damaging the glue bonds.

IMPORTANT STUFF

Baking soda is one of the best fire extinguishers. It cuts off the oxygen supply and the flame goes right out. Always keep an open box next to the stove to dump onto grease fires—and *never* use water!

FOR A BETTER BATTERY

The corrosion around your car battery posts can easily be cleaned with a thick solution of baking soda and water. Let it stand for 10 to 15 minutes before washing it off. Baking soda is a mild alkali and will neutralize the weak acid on the battery.

SMILE!

Here's a method of cleaning dentures that works as well as the expensive tablets: Soak them overnight in white vinegar.

WITH THIS RING

Does your wood furniture have white rings left from wet glasses? Remove them with a mixture of 2 tablespoons corn oil and enough salt to make a paste. Apply the paste to the rings and let stand for at least one hour before rubbing the area gently. If the finish on your furniture is very delicate, you can substitute baking soda for the salt (it's less abrasive).

IT'S NUTS

To mask scratches in wood furniture, rub gently with the broken edges of nuts (the insides, not the shells!); the results will surprise you. Just find a nut that matches the color of the wood. The most common ones for this purpose are pecans, walnuts, and hazelnuts.

YOU'LL NEVER DRINK SODA AGAIN

Have a load of greasy clothes? Pour a can of cola into the load along with the detergent. It will really improve the cleaning action of most detergents. Colas contain a weak acid that will help to dissolve the grease. Cola can also be used to clean the rings off toilets. Pour into the bowl, let sit for one hour, and then brush and flush.

HOT MILK

A trick used by antique dealers to hide hairline cracks on china plates or cups is to simmer the piece in milk for 45 minutes. Depending on the size of the crack, casein (which is the protein in the milk) may fill in the crack. If your china is old or fragile, though, this could backfire—heat can cause pieces to expand and crack.

WHO KNEW?

Plastic wrap loves to hug itself. Avoid this by keeping the box in the refrigerator. The cold keeps the wrap from sticking to itself.

WHO KNEW?

Do your shoes smell? Fill a clean sheer stocking with tea leaves, and stuff in your shoes. The smell vanishes in a day or two.

REVOLTING BUT TRUE

Spray vegetable oil on a clean car bumper before a trip to make it easy to remove the bugs when you return.

A GREAT GRATER TIP

Cleaning a cheese grater will never be a problem if you grate a small piece of raw potato before trying to wash it out. Sometimes an old toothbrush also comes in handy for cleaning graters.

NO MORE TARNISHING

Storing sterling silver and silver-plate in an airtight container—or wrapping each piece in plastic wrap—prevents tarnishing.

GREASE IS THE WORD

To clean a really greasy pan, add a few drops of ammonia to the pan with your soapsuds.

CHALK TALK

If you place a small piece of chalk in a silver chest, it will absorb moisture and slow tarnishing. Calcium carbonate (chalk) absorbs moisture from the air very slowly. If you break the chalk up and expose the rough surface, it will be more efficient.

ODOR EATERS

To eliminate refrigerator odors, leave a small cup of fresh coffee grounds on two shelves. Deep-frying a small amount of cinnamon will chase all odors from the home. Another excellent method of removing kitchen odors is to keep a few washed charcoal briquettes in a shallow dish on top of the refrigerator.

A DOUBLE BAGGER

Professional cooks keep small plastic bags nearby in case both hands are covered with dough or food and they need to answer the telephone. Or, you could put your hands in plastic bags before mixing meatloaf or kneading dough.

YUCK

The glue on any type of contact paper will melt if you run a warm iron over it or use a blow dryer on high heat.

FOR A CLEANER CARPET

If you want to sharpen up your carpet colors, try sprinkling a small amount of salt over the carpet before you vacuum. The salt provides a mild abrasive cleaning action that won't hurt the fibers.

RAISE ME UP

An easy method of raising the nap of a carpet after a piece of furniture has matted it down is to let an ice cube melt into the matted area; wait until the next day to vacuum.

KIDS, DON'T TRY THIS AT HOME

Have you ever wondered how to get the last drop of ketchup out of the bottle? All you have to is to hold the neck of the bottle and swing the bottle in a circular motion from your side. Hold on tight!

MAKES SENSE

To use the fewest cooking utensils possible, first measure out all the dry ingredients, then the wet ingredients. This way, you can reuse the measuring spoons or cups with having to rewash and dry them.

WHO KNEW?

Adding just ¼ to ½ cup of baking soda to your wash load makes clothes smell fresh and feel softer.

OR JUST ORDER IN

If you accidentally burn or scorch a food, set the pot or dish into cold water immediately. This will stop the cooking action and minimize the damage. Carefully remove the unburned food—don't scrape—then discard the damaged food. When you reheat the salvaged food, set a fresh piece of white bread on top to remove the burnt odor.

SAVE THOSE WRAPPERS

Save the wrappers from unsalted butter. When you need to grease a pan, simply wipe the pan with them. Don't use wrappers from salted butter, since they may cause foods to stick.

THEN WATCH HOW QUICKLY THEY DUMP IT OUT

Here's an inexpensive solution for children to use when blowing bubbles: Mix 1 tablespoon glycerin with 2 tablespoons a powdered laundry detergent in 1 cup warm water. Any unpainted piece of metal wire can be shaped with a circle on one end to use with the solution. Blowing into the mixture with a straw will make smaller bubbles float into the air. For colored bubbles, add food coloring.

SIPPY CUP 101

If your drinking glasses are slippery, put a wide rubber band around them so that children can get a better grip.

IRON TRICK

A drop of perfume added to the water in your steam iron will give your clothes a great fragrance.

WHO KNEW?

To keep melted ice cream from leaking out of ice cream cones, just drop a marshmallow into the bottom of the cone to act as a plug.

IT WORKS

Too much mayonnaise or salad dressing can ruin a dish. To fix the problem, try adding breadcrumbs to absorb the excess.

A REAL BALL

Almost all soft rubber balls, including tennis balls, can be brought back to life and the bounce returned by leaving the balls in an oven with only the pilot light left on overnight. The heat causes the air inside the ball to expand. Just be sure to remove the balls before you turn the oven on!

MICROWAVE MATTERS

It's wise to check and see whether a dish is microwave safe and will not melt. Just place the container next to a cup half filled with water and turn the microwave on high for about 1½ minutes, or until the water is boiling. If the dish is hot when you touch it, don't cook with it.

THE RICE-IN-SALT TRICK

To keep salt flowing freely in high humidity, add some raw rice to the shaker to absorb the moisture. Rice absorbs moisture very slowly under these conditions and lasts for a long time.

HALLOWEEN HELPER

Duct tape is your friend, especially if it's the day before Halloween and you still haven't made costumes for your kids. Consider making a robot, or Tin Man, with a brown paper bag that has been sliced in the back. Just cover it in rows of duct tape, and cover an old pair of pants with tape as well, and the costume is done.

WHO KNEW?

If your photos are stuck together, you can slowly melt them apart with a blow dryer set on low.

MAKE IT MINERAL OIL...

To keep your blender and mixer in top working order, be sure to lubricate all moving parts with a very light coating of mineral oil (not vegetable oil). This should be done every three months.

...OR MAKE IT VEGETABLE OIL

Before using a measuring cup to measure a sticky liquid, coat the inside with vegetable oil or nonstick cooking spray—the liquid will flow freely.

OR TRY AND PICK THEM APART AND SWEAR A LOT

If your postage stamps are stuck together, place them in the freezer for about 10 minutes. This does not work with self-adhesive stamps.

THE WAXED SOLUTION

If you have a problem with ice-cube trays sticking to the bottom of the shelf, try placing a piece of waxed paper under the tray. Freezing temperatures do not affect waxed paper.

FREEZER FOUL UP

A common problem with icemakers is that they freeze up. Next time this happens, just use the blow dryer to defrost. (For safety's sake, keep the dryer away from any pooling water.) This problem won't occur if you release a few ice cubes every few days.

IT'S MAGIC

The next time you have two drinking glasses stuck together and can't get them apart, try this: Fill the top glass with ice water and then place the bottom one in a few inches of hot tap water in the sink. It should only take a few seconds for them to come unstuck.

WHO KNEW?

Use a five-gallon plastic pail to keep your long extension cords untangled. Just drill a hole near the bottom of the pail large enough for the cord's pronged end to pass through. Coil the cord in the bucket—it comes right out when pulled, and is easy to coil again when you're done.

CUTTING BOARD SMARTS

Butcher-block and wooden cutting boards can harbor bacteria deep down in the cracks and can be difficult to clean. The boards need to be washed with a mild detergent and then dried thoroughly and covered with a light layer of salt to draw any moisture that may have gotten into the crevices. Leave the salt on overnight before scraping it off. The wood can then be treated with a very light coating of mineral oil. Make sure it is only a light coat, because mineral oil may affect the potency of a number of vitamins in fruits and vegetables.

DUH

Here's a chef's secret for keeping a grater clean so you can use it repeatedly without washing: Simply grate the softest items first, then grate the firmer ones.

WASH IT BY HAND

Never put a wooden cutting board into the dishwasher. The high temperatures can damage it.

SAVE WHERE YOU CAN

Dishwasher soap can be expensive. If you want to save money, just purchase the least expensive one and add 2 teaspoons of white vinegar to the dishwasher. You dishes will come out spot-free.

YES YOU CAN

If you've only used part of a can of motor oil, cover the can with a coffee-can lid to keep dust and debris out.

EDIBLE CANDLE HOLDER

Make natural birthday-cake candleholders from small marshmallows. If they are kept refrigerated they will work better.

WHO KNEW?

To remove water from inside your watch face, simply strap the watch to a light bulb, and turn it on for a few minutes.

HOW FRUSTRATING

When you can't open a jar, set it in a bowl with a little hot tap water for a few minutes, and then try again. If it's still stuck, carefully work the pointed tip of a puncture-type can opener under the lid and gently loosen the cap. This should release enough pressure to allow you to open the jar.

A STICKY MESS

Use nail polish remover if you ever glue your fingers together by accident when you're working with a quick-bonding glue or epoxy. If you get stuck working with rubber cement, try lacquer thinner; you may need to let the thinner soak in for a few minutes before gently pulling your fingers apart.

A DUSTY SOLUTION

Always clean dust mops after using them. To avoid making a dust cloud, cover a dry dust mop with a damp paper bag before you shake it out. If your mop has a removable head, put it in a large mesh lingerie bag and toss it into the washer.

THE SPONGE METHOD

Water can collect in umbrella stands. Prevent this by cutting a large sponge to fit in the bottom. Remove it and wring it out as necessary.

NOT ENOUGH REASON TO HAVE A BABY

Do you have a "junk drawer" in your kitchen? Baby food jars are perfect storage containers to keep it tidy. Use them for screws, brads, rubber bands, pushpins and thumbtacks, sugar and artificial sweetener packets, loose change, and anything else small that clutters your life.

BUT YOU KNEW THAT ALREADY

An easy way to keep your earrings together: Thread the posts through buttons, and then attach the backs.

SHINY AND NEW

- Polishing silver is never a neat chore, but an old sock can make it easier. Slip the sock over your hand; use one side to apply the polish and the other to buff it out.
- If you have large silver items that are not used with food, consider having them lacquered by a jeweler to prevent tarnishing. Candelabras, vases, and trophies are good candidates for this treatment.
- Sulfur compounds in the air cause tarnish; keeping your silver in airtight containers, or wrapping it in tarnishproof cloths or paper, will help to keep tarnish at bay.
- Never wrap silver in plastic food wrap, though. It will keep air away, but it can also cause stains and corrosion.
- To remove tarnish from the tines of a fork, coat a piece of cotton string with silver polish and rub between the tines.
- Silver can spot easily if you air dry it. It's better to dry it right away with a lint-free cloth and store it properly.

WHO KNEW?

The easiest way to clean stainless steel appliances is with a touch of baby oil on a soft cloth. Club soda works well, too.

STRAIGHTEN UP

If you're moving a large piece of marble like a tabletop, always transport it upright. If you carry it flat, it can crack under its own weight.

OR SMACK IT WITH YOUR CELL PHONE

If a bee or other stinging insect gets trapped in the car with you, don't swat at it! Instead, pull your car off to the side of the road, open all the windows or doors, and let the critter fly out.

FLOOR MAT S.O.S.

If you get stuck in snow or mud, try using your car floor mat for traction. Or you could keep a blanket in the trunk for the purpose.

THE AH HA! TIP FOR WINTER

If your windshield wipers are smearing the windows, wipe the blades with some rubbing alcohol.

THINK ABOUT IT

Used plastic or coated-paper milk containers can be filled with old candle wax and kept in the car for emergencies. Place a long candle in the center for the wick. It will burn for hours.

JUST DON'T LET THE NEIGHBORS SEE

To prevent the rubber around your car doors from freezing, rub the rubber moldings with vegetable oil.

TRY IT

Steel-wool pads make an excellent white-wall tire cleaner. It's best to use as fine a steel-wool pad as you can find.

LET IT SNOW

Come winter, fill a few old milk cartons with sand or kitty litter and keep them in your car's trunk. If you get stuck, sprinkle the sand on the ice to improve the tires' traction.

UM, FIGURE IT OUT

If you place a sheet of fabric softener under your car seat, it will keep your car smelling fresh.

PILLOW PRESSURE

Reduce stress and tension by resting on a thermal neck pillow that can be heated up in the microwave. The heat generated by the pillow penetrates into the tense neck muscles, soothing away aches and pains and relieving headaches and those oh-so aging frowns.

WARM WELCOME

Create an instant ambience by placing potpourri in glass or leather bowls. Remember to turn it regularly though or it will attract dust. Refresh with essential oils.

UNCLOG YOUR STEAM IRON

Pour equal amounts of vinegar and water into the water holder of the iron. Turn the dial to steam and leave upright for five minutes. Unplug and let the iron cool down. Any loose particles should fall out when you empty the water.

DON'T MIX IT!

Never combine silver and stainless steel cutlery in a dishwasher or the silver will turn black. Black spots will also appear if you allow dishwasher detergent to come into contact with silver. Remove silver cutlery from the dishwasher immediately after the cycle has come to a close and dry at once to avoid stains and pitting from salt residue.

FAMILY SILVER

Stains on silver can be removed by dissolving a little salt in lemon juice. Dip a soft cloth into the mixture and rub the cutlery. Rinse in warm water and finish by buffing to a shine with a chamois.

WHO KNEW?

To clean silk flower arrangements, try a blow dryer set on cool. You can also put the flowers in a paper bag, add some uncooked rice, and shake.

PERFECTLY FOILED

To revitalize tarnished silver cutlery, place a piece of aluminium foil in a plastic bucket. Sprinkle over 3 tablespoons bicarbonate of soda. Put the silver on top and cover with hot water. Leave until the mixture stops bubbling. Rinse and polish with a dry cloth.

TOOTHY SHINE

Place toothpaste on a soft cloth and use it to rub solid silver (not silver-plate) and then rinse it off gently. Don't use whitening toothpaste – it can damage the surface.

UNSEALED WOOD

Preserve the beauty of wood by rubbing the surface with boiled linseed oil. Wipe away the excess with a soft cloth.

HAPPY FEET

Soften leather shoes by rubbing with lemon or castor oil. Help prevent cracking and drying by wiping with olive oil. To wear in new shoes, rub alcohol in at the heels and wear while still-wet. Potato peelings will soften shoes if left in overnight. Treat scuffs by wiping them with the cut edge of a raw potato and then buff with a cloth afterwards.

FACELIFT FOR LEATHER

Give a leather jacket a new lease of life by covering it with a paste of fine white pure clay and water. Add just enough water for a spreading consistency. Work from the bottom of the garment to the top, rubbing it in. Leave to dry and then shake until all the clay has dropped off.

WHO KNEW?

The best way to fluff tired bed pillows is to just put them in the clothes dryer for a few minutes.

DUST TRAP

Wrap a paper towel around the broad end of a kitchen spatula and secure with a rubber band. Use this to reach dust trapped between tubes of a radiator. Spray the kitchen paper with all-purpose cleaner to get rid of sticky spills and stains.

MAGIC AWAY MILDEW

Dust mildewed pages with cornflour, French chalk or talcum powder. Leave inside the closed book for several days then brush it off.

CHOOSE LIFE

To prolong the life of cut flowers, add 2 tablespoons vinegar and 1 teaspoon sugar to the water. An aspirin or two in the water is also reputed to work. In both instances, change the water every few days.

SOUNDS FISHY

If you have an aquarium, save the water each time you change it and use it to water your houseplants. You'll be amazed at the results.

LONG-LASTING BLOOMS

To keep flowers fresh for as long as possible, change the water and trim the stems every day. Crush rose stems at the ends to encourage absorption of water. If you can't change the water every day, place a copper coin in with the flowers. Tulips last longer if you make a series of small holes with a pin down the length of their stems.

WHO KNEW?

If your wooden dresser drawers keep sticking, fix it with a light bulb. Just empty out the drawer and place a safety light (with a 60-watt bulb) inside for 30 minutes. The heat from the light dries up moisture, which is most likely the reason why the drawer was stuck.

COLA CLEANER

Try an old masonry trick to brighten up soot-stained brick. Mix a can of cola with 3 ½ fl oz. all-purpose household cleaner and 7 pints water in a bucket. Sponge onto sooty brick and leave for 15 minutes. Loosen the soot by scrubbing with a stiff-bristled brush. Sponge with clean water. For a stronger solution, add more cola.

PATCH WORK

Here's how to eliminate cigarette burns in your carpet: First, cut away the burn mark. Then, cut a bit of the carpet from an area that's covered (like under a couch) and glue carefully over the burnt spot. Finally, smack the person who dropped the ashes.

THE CARNATION TRICK

Carnations last longer if you place them in carbonated lemonade (not the diet variety) rather than water. Change every four days.

MAKE A SPLASH

Brighten up wooden furniture with a solution of water and vinegar. Soak a clean cloth in the solution and wash the piece all over, leave overnight to dry (with the window open, if you can). Next day apply quality furniture polish and buff away.

PREVENT POLISH BUILD-UP

Excess polish soon builds up and leaves a dull finish on wooden furniture. To remove it, mix together 2 tablespoons white vinegar and 2 tablespoons water. Apply to the surface and wipe off at once.

BECAUSE WHO WANTS MILDEW?

If you have a problem with mildew forming in your refrigerator, just spray the inside walls with vegetable oil.

CURTAIN CALL

When slipping curtains over a metal rod, first place a plastic freezer or sandwich bag over the metal end. This avoids snagging the curtains and they will also go on more easily.

SPRUCE UP SATIN & GLOSS

Clean satin and gloss finishes with a solution made up of 4 fl. oz. white vinegar, 1 oz. washing soda and 1 pint water. Or try 7 oz. ammonia, 1 teaspoon of dish liquid and 7 pints of water mixed together.

THE ICE SPLASH

Try watering your houseplants with ice cubes. That way, the water won't run straight through the plant and you'll avoid a muddy mess.

THE ART START

Store art supplies in a clear, vinyl shoe bag hung from the back of your playroom door. It's a nifty way to hold paints, pens, markers, brushes and more.

BLAST THE GRASS

The easiest way to get rid of the grass that grows in the cracks of sidewalks and patios is with a mixture of salt and baking soda. Just sprinkle it on, and sweep it into the cracks, and the problem should be solved.

WHO KNEW?

Cleaning the dust and debris from behind your refrigerator will help it run more efficiently and save money on electricity, too.

WHO KNEW?

The easiest, and least expensive, way to clean your precious gems is with club soda. Soak your emeralds, diamonds, rubies and sapphires in a glass of it overnight, and they will shine like new in the morning.

THE UPSIDE DOWN TRICK

Always store your paint cans upside down, with a piece of plastic wrap under the lid, after making certain the lid is on tightly. The paint is exposed to less oxygen that way and will last much, much longer.

TOP ON THE LIST

If you can only clean one room before guests arrive, make it the bathroom. It's the only room where your guest will be alone, and possibly snoop around, and a dirty bathroom really is kind of gross.

THE COOLER THE BETTER

The easiest way to remove wax from candlesticks is to simply freeze them and peel the wax off. And remember, if you freeze your candles before lighting, they'll last longer and drip less.

SNOW CALLS

When the forecast calls for ice or snow, place two old bath towels across your windshield. When it's time to drive, simply pull off the towels and you're ready to go!

SHOVEL MARVEL

Shoveling wet, heavy snow is backbreaking job, but made easier with a simple tip: Just coat your shovel with vegetable shortening or car wax, and the snow won't stick. If you're using a snow blower, coat the inside of the chute.

FREEZED MOMENTS

To unstuck stuck photographs, place them in the freezer for ½ hour, and gently break apart with a butter knife.

TRYING TO GET A STUCK RING OFF YOUR FINGER?

I'm telling your wife. Seriously, the best way to slip off a stuck ring is to plunge your hand into ice water, then lubricate the ring with baby oil, and it should slip right off.

SMELL THE ROSES...EVERYDAY

Place fabric softener sheets in your dresser drawers and your clothes, towels, and linens will smell freshly washed, all the time.

DO-IT-THE-RIGHT-WAY

It's time to rake the leaves, and nothing is more frustrating than a plastic trash bag that slips down in the garbage can, right? Rest easy, friends, all you need to do is secure the bag with a bungee cord (or two) and get to work.

A FREEZER TRICK

If your favorite cashmere sweater is looking a little worn, put it in a plastic bag and place it in the freezer for ½ hour. The cold causes the fibers to expand, making your sweater look new again!

WHO KNEW?

Even when you're not using appliances, they still continue to use energy. So pull the plug when you're done with the blender, toaster, food processor, even your television—everything, except those appliances where you need constant power to preserve a special setting.

WHO KNEW?

If you like to channel surf while cooking, place your remote control in a plastic bag or plastic wrap. The buttons will still be visible, and the control will stay clean.

FIZZY CLEANER

Club soda is a terrific way to clean stainless steel sinks, dishwashers, ranges and other appliances. The least expensive club soda works as well as the pricey brands; flat club soda works, too. Add a little flour for really stubborn stains.

GOT A STUCK ZIPPER?

Just rub it with a pencil and let if fly. Got a zipper that won't stay closed? Spray it lightly and carefully with hairspray after zipping up.

BRIGHTEN UP!

A great way to brighten dull diamond jewelry is to fill a small pot with a cup of water and a teaspoon of dishwasher detergent. Add your diamonds, bring the water to a boil, then turn off the heat and let the pot sit until it cools. Once it's cool (but not before) carefully remove your jewelry and rinse.

THE SOAP HOPE

It's time to retrieve your winter sweaters—do they smell like mothballs? Sorry—mothballs work great, but leave a nasty odor. When you're storing your winter clothes next year, put a few leftover soap slivers in a vented plastic bag, and add to your closet or cedar chest instead of mothballs. The soap will keep moths from damaging, and smells fresh too.

NOT FOR YOUR POTATO CHIPS

Your new or recently cleaned drapes will stay crisp and fresh if you spray them with a few light coats of unscented hairspray before hanging them up.

THINK GREEN

When it's time to turn on the heat, be patient. Your house won't heat up any faster if you crank the thermostat way, way, up, but you're likely to forget to turn it down, which can be a huge energy waster.

STATIC STICKS...

One way to remove static cling is to run the long part of a wire hanger over a skirt (or for better results, between your skirt and pantyhose).

PAPER WORK

The school year is over, and you need a place to store the kids' artwork and diplomas. Try rolling them tightly in paper towel tubes, so they won't crease, and label the outside, so you know what's what. The tubes can also be used to store marriage certificates, and other important documents also.

SEE THE SUNNY SIDE

A great way to clean your stainless steel sink and faucet instantly is with aluminum foil. Just crumple it up, and scour with the shiny side.

PRE-CAUTION

Always put outgoing bills in a post office mailbox instead of the mailbox on your front door. A thief could get to your mail before the mailman, and the information provided in your letter could lead to identity theft.

WHO KNEW?

Clean mini blinds by simply throwing them in the bathtub filled with water and white vinegar, or your favorite cleanser. Just give them a good shake, and hang them up wet.

WHO KNEW?

Daffodils are one of our favorite flowers. Just remember not to mix them with other flowers when making an arrangement, as daffodils produce a toxin that kills other flowers.

FRESHEN ECO-WISE

You can make a great homemade air freshener. Just cut an orange in half, remove the pulp, and fill with salt. It's effective, easy—and cheap! To keep the house smelling fresh during the dog days of summer, tape fabric softener sheets on your air conditioner filter (but under the grate). Not only will it impart a nice smell, but also it makes the filter last longer.

STORE "WOOL"

To eliminate moth damage or mildew from your wool sweaters and down jackets, wash the garments before storing, and never keep in a plastic bag or airtight container. Your garments need air, so consider a wicker, cedar or rattan trunk for storage, and avoid hot attics or damp basements.

OPEN UP!

Our favorite way for opening a stubborn jar lid is to cover the top in plastic wrap to create a firm grip. Rubber kitchen gloves or a rubber band works well, too.

FRAGILE

Before hand washing your crystal or fine china, always place a towel in the bottom of the sink to act as a cushion.

REVIVER

An ice cube can help you revive carpet that has been dented by heavy furniture. Just melt the cube on the indentation, and as the moisture sinks in, the fibers will plump up. Then you can just brush the carpet and the dent disappears.

FRAT HOUSE ALERT:

Stale beer is a great way to clean wooden furniture. Dampen a soft, clean cloth, wipe it on, and follow by wiping with a dry cloth.

PETTY SPAGHETTI

If you're out of long matches for the fireplace and need to light a fire, try using a strand of raw spaghetti instead. It's also great for lighting hard-to-reach candles as well.

MIX AND SHINE

There's no need to buy a special cleaner for your wood floors. Simply mix equal parts of vegetable oil and white vinegar in a spray bottle, and apply. Then shine with a clean cloth until the solution is gone, and your floors will shine.

ENVIRONMENTALLY SPEAKING

Save your old egg cartons when you mail your holiday gifts this year. Cut them up and use as packing material—it's cheap and environmentally friendly. Styrofoam popcorn is gross—it clogs our landfills and will outlive all of us.

OBJECT D'ART

A pair of wine bottles, either full or empty, makes great bookends for your shelf.

NEWS YOU CAN USE

The best and most inexpensive way to clean windows (and your windshield) is with ½ cup of cornstarch in a gallon of water. Wipe clean, and dry with crumpled newspaper— you'll be amazed at the results.

USE ICE CUBES

Keep your garbage disposal running properly and odor-free with this simple trick: Just grind a dozen or so ice cubes made from white vinegar once a month. The ice sharpens the blades while the vinegar deodorizes the drain.

CLIPS'S TIPS

To preserve special newspaper clippings, dissolve a Milk of Magnesia tablet in a shallow pan with a quart of club soda, and soak the paper for an hour, then let it lie flat to dry. Afterwards, it's best to keep it in under plastic in a photo album.

STOPPING SPILLAGE

If your kids insist on drinking out of glasses instead of plastic cups, wrap a few rubber bands around the glass. The glass is much less likely to slip out of little hands that way.

RETAIN THE SCENT

If your favorite potpourri loses its scent, it's easy to revive— with vodka. Yep, you read it right. Just pour a little vodka into a spray bottle and spritz the potpourri, mixing it up so each piece is saturated.

A CHILD'S PLAY

If your kids complain that the sandwiches you make in the morning are mushy by lunchtime, then try putting the ketchup (or any condiment) in an empty pill bottle, and put it in their lunch box. They can then season their own sandwich at lunchtime.

EARRING'S DWELLING

Don't throw away the corks when you finish a bottle of wine. Poke stud earrings into it and just toss into your toiletry bag when traveling.

KILL THE SMELL

The easiest way to eliminate the smell of bleach from your hands is to wash them in warm water and toothpaste.

CUT THE "RUST"

It's easy to keep your wet, soaped steel wool pads from rusting. Really. Just wrap them in aluminum foil and store in your freezer.

PLUCK MORE TO GET MORE

If you've got pansies in your window box, take the time to pinch out the early buds. It encourages the flowers to grow, and you'll ultimately get more flowers this way.

LEAVE NO TRACES

If you've got fingerprints or excess polish on your wood furniture, reach for the cornstarch. Sprinkle a little on the furniture and polish with a soft cloth.

THE LINT HINT

Did you ever think there would be a use for dryer lint? There is. To prevent the dirt from falling out of your potted houseplants when you water them, place some dryer lint in the pots, covering the holes. The water will drain out, but the dirt will stay in!

WHO KNEW?

To cover scratches in wood furniture, break a hard nut (peanut, pecan or walnut) open and rub the inside over the scratches. The oil from the nut should cover the scratch.

KEEP MOVING

Move your bed sheets and linens to a top shelf in your bedroom closet from the hallway linen closet. That way, they are closer to where they're actually used, and if you fold them properly, they won't take up much room. In addition, you've now freed up a valuable hallway closet to store something else.

WEATHER READY

The best way to get the wicker for the front porch ready is to blow dry off the loose dirt, then clean with white vinegar and warm salt water, and apply a coat of lemon oil.

A CLEAN CUT

If you need to cut the lawn and the grass is damp, try spraying the mower's blades with vegetable oil before starting. The spray stops the grass from clogging the mower, and you'll have your job done in no time at all.

THE MOVIE CONNECT

A terrific way to tie up young plants in your garden is with old VCR tapes. Just remove a foot or two of tape for the spool, and stretch gently until the tape becomes as thin as string.

SPACED OUT

A great way to store your aluminum foil, plastic wrap, waxed paper and other boxes of wrap is on their ends, in an empty six-pack holder. Then you can put it under your sink, and free up a valuable kitchen drawer.

THE BOX WITH A PURPOSE

It's easy to store packets of sauces and gravies in an empty child's shoebox. The envelopes will stay upright and are easy to read, and the shoebox should fit perfectly on a shelf in your pantry.

THE SUBTLE CLEANER

The blade of your can opener is most likely the dirtiest inch in your kitchen, but easy to clean. Just 'open' a piece of waxed paper, which will clean away the grime while the wax lubricates the blades and wheels.

RUST FREE

Toss a few mothballs in your toolbox to prevent your tools from rusting. If you've got nuts and bolts that are rusted together, just submerge them in cola for a day and they'll come apart easily.

GOOD FOR "SOMETHING"

There's no need to throw out your stinky, old sponges. Just soak them in cold salt water, rinse and they're good to use again.

NO WRINKLES

When packing for your family vacation, place your pants in the bottom of the suitcase, with half of them hanging over the side. Place the rest of your clothes on top, and fold the pants back over on top of the clothes. When you unpack, your pants won't need to be pressed.

NEED SPACE?

If you need more counter space to prepare a big meal, simply open a drawer in your kitchen and cover with a heavy-duty cutting board.

WHO KNEW?

Is your family room floor covered with plastic toys and parts? May we suggest hanging a vinyl shoe bag on the back of your child's bedroom door? It can hold dolls, toy cars, and any other small toys that seem to pile up everywhere.

WHO KNEW?

Use dental floss when making a popcorn garland for the holidays. It's stronger than regular string and less likely to break when you wrap it around the tree.

EXPLORE THE UNEXPLORED

If you living room sofa has a skirt that reaches to the floor, you have storage space you didn't even know of. Underneath the sofa is a great place to store a bin of wrapping paper and accessories, old photo albums and other skinny items you reach for too often.

POWDER-COAT

Before heading to the beach, always pack baby powder. Nothing is more effective at removing sand; so don't forget to douse the kids in it before returning to the car or your home.

HALF-CUT

Cut soaped steel wool pads in half before using them. It's economical, because if the pads rust, you'll only be throwing our half. And as a bonus, it's a great way to sharpen your scissors.

THE COLA DIP

The best way to remove rust from your car's chrome bumper? Just rub the rusted area with a shiny piece of crumpled aluminum foil that has been dipped in cola. I know it sounds crazy, but it works!

A TWISTED STORY

If your sunglasses have gotten completely twisted, don't throw them out. Just turn a blow dryer to high and aim it at your frames. The heat makes the plastic arms flexible enough that you should be able to gently bend them into their original shape.

BUTTON THIS FACT

A great way to organize your earrings is to store them in spare buttons. You'll never lose the backs if you keep them that way.

DUST TRAIL

The trail of dust that your broom leaves behind can be eliminated: Just fill a spray bottle with ¾ cup water and ¼ liquid fabric softener, and spray the broom before sweeping. The spritz makes the broom strands more pliable, and helps it collect dirt more efficiently.

LID-DISASTER

Are plastic lids taking over your kitchen?
We feel your pain, and can offer a solution: Store a dish drainer in your cabinet, and you can file the lids on their sides, in size order. It's really easy to pick the right lid this way!

NO-GRAVITY ZONE

A nonskid rug pad is a terrific liner for your office drawers. The tacky surface prevents paper clips, thumbtacks—everything— from slipping around. It's also works well in your kitchen drawers, too.

THE MAIN MENU

Friday night is take out night, and once again you've lost all the menus, right? The problem is solved if you attach a manila envelope to the inside back cover of your phone book, and stick the menus in there.

A COPY TRICK

Before framing a favorite photograph, cut out the negative and tape it to the back. That way, you won't have to go searching through piles of old negatives if someone wants a copy.

?? WHO KNEW?

The least expensive way to childproof a cabinet is with shower curtain hooks. Just lock a shower curtain hook through the cabinet handles, so they cannot be opened. The good news is, you can easily remove it if company is coming and the toddlers are asleep. The bad news is. some smart kids eventually figure out how to unlock the hook!

CLONE IDENTITY

Never carry your Social Security card in your wallet, because if it's lost or stolen, thieves can use it to access all sorts of information about you. In addition, make a copy of the front and back of each credit card you carry, and store in a safe place at home. That way, you'll be able to cancel those cards quickly if you need to.

POWDER-PLAY

If your playing cards are getting a bit grimy and sticking together, consider placing them in a plastic bag with a few blasts of baby powder and giving it a good shake before dealing the first hand.

CHANGING YOUR SHEETS JUST GOT (A LITTLE BIT) EASIER

Keep all your linen sets together the easy way: Just store your folded sheets into its matching pillowcase.

AVOID SMELLING LIKE A PIG

You'll be amazed at the odors a single fabric softener sheet can absorb. Amazed. Just stick one in your gamey old gym bag, and thank us for the tip next time we talk.

GIFTING OPTIONS

Here's a great shower gift for a bride to be:
Buy a blank hardcover book, add dividers, and create a family cookbook. Just ask the bride and groom's families to provide their favorite, treasured recipes, and you'll have a one of a kind gift.

DON'T SNIP THIS

When pruning your roses or other thorny plants in the garden, hold the branches with a pair of kitchen tongs while you snip and you'll avoid pricking your fingers.

RUMBLE JUMBLE

If your bathroom drawers are a jumbled mess, invest in an inexpensive, plastic silverware tray. It's a great way to organize the little things you've got rattling around in there.

TOUGH CLEANING MADE EASY

A good way to clean the grates on your outdoor grill before the barbequing season begins is to place the grate in the tub, and cover with very hot water and one cup each of ammonia and dishwasher detergent. Cover with old fabric softener sheets and soak overnight. The next day don your rubber gloves, scrub away and watch the grease dissolve.

STAND OUT

Be bold when planting flowers in sunny spots. Pastel colored flowers can look washed out in bright sun, so consider bold reds and oranges for your flowers when planting in full sun.

MAKE IT YOURSELF

You can make your own dehumidifier for the basement and not have to spend a lot to do so. Simply fill a coffee can with charcoal briquettes and punch a few holes in the lid, and place in damp areas. Replace the charcoal once a month as it absorbs the humidity.

WHO KNEW?

Make school-day mornings a little less crazy by preparing a few days' worth of the kids' sandwiches at the same time, and freezing them (without condiments). Each morning, just toss the pre-made sandwich in their lunch boxes, and by lunchtime, the bread will have thawed and become soft and fresh.

EGG-XACTLY

Get a head start on your garden seedlings by starting them indoors in eggshell halves. Let them grow in an egg container, and when it's time to transplant them outdoors, just dig a hole for the shells. Eggshells are a great fertilizer.

ON THE X-Y AXIS

Use horizontal strokes when cleaning the inside of your windows, and vertical strokes for the outside. That way, you can easily see which side has streaks. And remember, if you dry your windows with newspapers, they'll be virtually streak-free.

CHEAP CLEANING

The best and least expensive way to clean ceramic floors is with hot water and white vinegar. Give it a try.

KNOT AGAIN

Is your favorite necklace hopelessly tangled? Just massage a drop or two of baby oil onto the tangle, and use a straight pin to carefully untangle the knot.

FREEZING GUM

The easiest way to remove chewing gum from clothing is to freeze the garment, then crack and scrape the gum off. Launder as usual afterwards.

SMELLS GREAT

Add ¼ cup of scented bath salts during your washing machine's rinse cycle when you're laundering your sheets and other linens. Not only will your sheets smell great, but the salt acts like a starch to keep them extra crisp.

FOR A QUICK BEDROOM UPDATE

Wrap a colorful sheet over a piece of plywood, staple in the back, and use as a headboard.

AN ARM EXTEND

If your spring cleaning involves getting rid of cobwebs in hard to reach places, here's a hint: Untangle a wire hanger, and secure an old, clean sock to the end with a rubber band. Your arms just grew by three feet!

SAVE YOUR MONEY

There's no need to buy special chandelier cleaners. When it's time to tackle this difficult job, use a cloth dripping with a solution of two parts rubbing alcohol and one part hot water. Just slop it on, and don't forget to hang an umbrella upside down from the chandelier to catch the mess.

SPRING CLEANING IS JUST AROUND THE CORNER, FOLKS

Get organized by storing your cleaning products in a vinyl shoe holder, and hang it on the back of your laundry room drawer. It's a great way to save space, a way to remind you of the cleaning storm to come!

FIRST THINGS FIRST

Here's an easy way to start your spring cleaning: Begin with your bed pillows. To make them fluffy and fresh smelling, just place them in the clothes dryer with a fabric softener and two clean tennis balls for a few minutes.

BATHE THE BRUSH

A great way to keep your toothbrush clean is to soak it overnight, every few weeks, in a solution of equal parts of water and baking soda. Rinse well before brushing again.

Plastic grocery bags have a way of multiplying and taking over kitchen drawers, right? A space saving solution is to stuff the bags in an empty tissue box. You'll be amazed how many fit, and you can remove them easily one at a time when your need to.

Tissue Box

THE FRESHER WAY

The easiest way to freshen draperies and heavy bedspreads is to place in your dryer with a damp towel, on the delicate cycle, for one half hour. For extra freshness, hang them outside afterwards if the weather allows.

WATER PROOF

Before the April showers get underway, remember this tip: Line the bottom of your umbrella stand with corkboard to eliminate water from building up there.

SHOWERS OF ADVICE

Throw your shower curtain in the washing machine, with a cup of bleach, half a cup of white vinegar, laundry detergent and a white towel, and run the machine with warm water. Afterwards, just hang the curtain back up to drip dry, and it's clean!

IN THE SHADE

How do you clean your pleated lampshades? If you answered, "not well," try this: Just stroke each pleat from top to bottom with a dry, clean paintbrush.

EASY GLIDE

A tip to quicken your interior painting jobs is to mix a quart of semi gloss latex paint into a gallon of flat latex. The finish won't shine any more than it would with straight flat paint, but the paint will glide on and cover much more easily.

STRAW THEM TOGETHER

You don't have to buy a jewelry organizer to keep your necklaces untangled. Just cut plastic straws in half, thread your necklaces through, and fasten the clasp.

A HOT FIT

The best way to fit a candle into a candlestick is not by lighting the candle and melting wax into the base. A simpler and safer way is to place the base of the candle into hot water, which softens it and makes for a great fit.

WIPE TO SHINE

To clean chrome-plated fixtures in your bathroom instantly, always keep fabric softener sheets handy. Just wipe, and the chrome will sparkle. Rubbing alcohol also does the trick.

HATE THY NEIGHBOR

Remember, it's inefficient if your kitchen has 'hot' appliances next to 'cold' ones. Always make sure your refrigerator is not next to your oven or dishwasher—or the appliances will have to work harder.

WATERING THE GARDEN JUST GOT EASIER

Simply cut a wire hanger into six-inch pieces, bend into an arch, and use to keep your soaker hose in place to water the flowerbeds. Virtually all the dirt found in your home comes from outside, so by cleaning you sidewalks, porch and other outdoor areas, you're actually keeping the inside of your home clean as well.

WHO KNEW?

The best way to remove wallpaper is to fill a spray bottle with boiling water and ½ cup liquid fabric softener. Spray it on the wallpaper, wait a bit, and it will peel off easily.

REBOOT THE BOOT

Keep your boots looking their best by storing them with wine bottles inside. It helps the boots maintain their shape.

TIME TO TAKE DOWN THE HOLIDAY DECORATIONS?

Remember to use old socks or nylons for delicate ornaments, and for extra safety, and then place in disposable plastic cups before storing.

SPATIALLY SPEAKING

More is more when it comes to cabinet space, and that's just what you get if you follow this tip:
Screw in cup holders to the bottom of each cabinet shelf. Think how much space you'll gain if your cups hang from your shelves, rather than lying on them, taking up valuable cabinet space!

A TICKER FOR YOUR STICKER

Is it time to get rid of your 'Gore 2000' bumper sticker? Try this: Set your blow dryer on high and run it back and forth over the sticker, until the adhesive softens. Then, apply a bit of vegetable oil and carefully lift a corner with a credit card, and peel.

WARMER WINTERS

Your ceiling fan should not just be used during the summer months. Just hit the reverse switch and push hot air down into your room on the coldest days of winter, and your room will stay warmer.

COUNT THE INCHES

If you want to hang a heavy mirror or piece of art on a nail in a wall stud but are unsure where the stud is located, remember that studs are normally 16 inches apart, so 17 inches from the corner is where the first stud should be located. Keep doing the math until you find the stud nearest where you want hang your art and hammer away.

FLOOR CLEANER FROM THE KITCHEN SHELF

The best and least expensive way to clean ceramic floors is with hot water and white vinegar. Give it a try.

A CLEARER VIEW

If an ice storm is in the forecast, coat your windshield with a solution of one part water to three parts white vinegar. It will keep your windshield ice-free.

BLOOMING FRESHNESS

Keep your overpriced flowers fresh with this trick: Submerge the stems in hot water, and trim an inch off the ends. Florists sometimes cut flowers in the open air, which allows air into the stems and prevents the flowers from absorbing all the water they need.

USE SOLAR POWER

It's easy—just make sure the trees branches around your window are trimmed, to let the most sunlight in during the winter months.

THE STEAM SOLUTION

If you've let the bathroom go and it now resembles a gas station restroom, turn on the hot water in the shower for 10 minutes with the door closed. The steam will loosen the build up of mildew and mold. Now, get in there and clean.

LUBRICATING HELPS

Add a little petroleum jelly to the rim of your rubber plunger. It helps achieve great suction, so the disgusting job ahead gets a little bit easier.

WHO KNEW?

Always try to keep the soap in your soap dish dry. It will last much longer that way, and let's face it—picking up a soggy piece of soap to wash your hands is a bit on the disgusting side.

If you're sending a get well card to a friend in the hospital, but are not sure how long she will be there, try this: Put your friend's home address as the return address on the envelope. That way, you're certain she'll get the card—at the hospital or once she returns home.

IN A COOL WAY

Winterize your car battery so you don't get stuck in the cold. Pour a can of cola over the battery posts, and let it sit for ½ hour, and wipe clean. Then rub petroleum jelly on the posts before reattaching the battery cables and you should be good to go for the entire winter.

A GREAT WAY TO SAVE MONEY

Here's a terrific tip to use during warm weather: turn your dishwasher off after the rinse cycle is done, open it up, and let your dishes drip dry. You'll save a lot by avoiding the heat drying cycle on your machine.

AVOID DIRT BUILT UP

Before vacuuming, always dust first with a damp cloth. Otherwise, the vacuum will blow the dust every which way.

BRINGING THE HOLIDAY MOOD

To fill your home with a wonderful holiday smell, throw a few cinnamon sticks, orange rinds and cloves in a quart of water, and boil on low. The scent it releases is wonderful.

DELICATE SILVER

Remember to wash your silver as soon as possible after it's had contact with olives, salad dressings, vinegar, and especially eggs or salt. All of these foods can cause your silver to tarnish quickly.

SECURED INFORMATION

Always put outgoing bills in a post office mailbox instead of the mailbox on your front door. A thief could get to your mail before the mailman, and the information provided in your letter could lead to identity theft.

A "DIP"RESSION

To keep your mattress from sagging, it's a good idea to reverse it once a month. If it dips in the middle, place a few folded sheets under the center to even it out.

CUP OF FACT

A cup hook mounted next to the sink is a great way to hold rings, bracelets and watches while you're doing dishes—and it keeps your jewelry from getting dirty or banged up.

BUBBLE-FUN

Here's a great way to keep the kids busy: Make a giant bubble wand by bending a wire hanger into an oval, and create a terrific bubble solution from equal parts of water and liquid dish detergent. Then tell the kids to stay out until dinnertime.

COOLER FACTS

To keep your cooler fresh and odor free, throw in 10-15 charcoal briquettes, close the top, and leave it overnight. In the morning, clean the cooler with soapy water and it will smell like new.

ENERGY SAVERS

Here's a great energy saving tip for cold winter nights: If you have cast iron radiators, tape aluminum foil to a sheet of cardboard (shiny side out) and place behind the radiator. The radiant heat will bounce back into your room instead of being absorbed into the wall.

BRUSH THE BRUSH

Clean your dirty hairbrushes and combs in a quart of warm water with three tablespoons of ammonia added. Let it sit overnight, and they'll be completely clean in the morning. Just remember to rinse them well before using again.

WHO KNEW?

Egg cartons and plastic ice cube trays make great jewelry trays, and they fit inside your dresser drawer.

FULLY CHARGED TIP

Use the tip of a cotton swab dipped in rubbing alcohol to clean the battery contacts on your laptop or cordless phone. If the battery connection is clean, the charge will last for a longer time.

FOIL TO LINE

There's no need to spend your money on disposable paint liners for your roller pan. It's just as easy to line the pan with aluminum foil—and a lot cheaper, too.

SUN STROKED

Don't keep your good wood furniture in direct sunlight, especially during the hot summer. It damages the finish and can bleach the wood.

CUT THE ODOR

When you return home from your summer vacation, throw a few dryer sheets in your suitcases before you put it away. The sheets will prevent any musty odor from developing.

STICK-ME-NOT

To prevent wax from sticking to a candleholder, rub a thin coat of olive oil on the base of the holder before lighting the candle.

CLEANING IRON

The best way to clean the bottom of your iron is to rub it (while cold) with steel wool, then heat it and iron a piece of waxed paper that has been covered in salt. Then run it over an old, clean cloth to remove any remaining wax, and your iron should be good as new.

DO YOU KNOW HOW TO CLEAN A BASEBALL CAP?

We do. Just wash on the top rack of your dishwasher, and remove while it's still wet. Then, put it over a bowl to regain its shape, and dry the cap away from direct sunlight.

BABY CARE FOR YOUR CAR

You can eliminate scratches on the dashboard plastic in your car by rubbing it with a bit of baby oil.

FRESHER FOR LONGER

Cut flowers will stay fresh longer if you drop a sugar cube and penny into the vase water. And don't forget to store your arrangement in the refrigerator each night, too.

THE WHITE ESSENTIAL

The best way to clean houseplants is with milk. (It also kills aphids.) You can also clean the leaves with a cup of baking soda in a gallon of water.

TILE IT TOGETHER

If your vinyl tile has loosened, simply put it back in its original place, lay a piece of aluminum foil over it, and run a hot iron over it. In no time at all, the glue will begin to adhere. Then just stack a few books on top of the tile until the glue hardens again.

WHO KNEW?

If your wall art or hanging mirrors just won't seem to stay straight, try sticking a corn cushion behind each corner of the frame. That will do the trick without damaging the wall at all.

To revive crushed carpet after moving a piece of furniture, place an ice cube on the spot. After it melts, the piles will raise.

COLA VOILA

Dirty toilet? Just fill the bowl with 12 ounces of cola, and watch it dissolve all the stains. Then wonder what your favorite drink does to your stomach. (PS—A denture tablet also cleans the bowl.)

TAP THE CAP

When nailing into plaster to hang pictures or art, always place a piece of transparent tape where the nail will go beforehand. The plaster won't chip if you strike the nail through tape.

THE CASE OF A LOST RING

Mayonnaise eliminates water rings on wooden furniture. Just rub a tiny bit (½ a teaspoon) on the ring with a paper towel and let it sit overnight. In the morning, just wipe with a damp cloth and the ring is gone!

WEATHER READY

It's a good idea to put away all your wicker furniture before the first freeze arrives. Freezing will cause cracking and splitting which unfortunately is impossible to repair.

FOR THE JUNIOR DA VINCIS

Keep the kids busy with homemade finger paints. Start by mixing two cups of cold water with one-quarter cup of cornstarch, then boil until the liquid is as thick as, um, finger paints. Put in small containers, swirl in some food coloring and watch your kitchen get trashed.

WEIRD BUT EFFECTIVE

After cleaning your car's wheels, spray them with a light coat of vegetable oil. The next time you clean them, the brake dust that has accumulated will wipe off easily.

SMOOTHER REPLACE

Before it gets too cold, consider applying a thin layer of petroleum jelly to the threads of all your outdoor light bulbs. It will prevent them from rusting and make it easier to replace when they blow out.

A NEW "DOOR" OF THOUGHT

Here are two great ways to clean your glass shower doors: You can use leftover white wine (shame on you for not finishing it), or wipe them down with fabric softener on a damp cloth. Either way, finish by buffing with a clean, dry cloth.

HAS YOUR FAVORITE SWEATER'S SLEEVES STRETCHED OUT?

Not to worry. Just spray the cuffs with hot water and blow dry, and they should shrink back to their original shape.

AS A REMINDER

Only run the dishwasher or washing machine when it's full, and turn off the water when brushing your teeth or shaving. With a few changes like this, the average household will save nearly $180 per year—and it's the environmentally friendly thing to do.

WHO KNEW?

Keep lingerie bags for laundering each family member's socks. It's an easy way to keep them together, and you won't have to sort them later.

PESTS AND PETS

5

MICE HATE MINT

If you can see the mouse holes, smear a bit of mint toothpaste nearby and the smell will deter them.

HERBS HELP

A number of herbs will ward off crawling insects. The most potent are fresh or dried bay leaves, sage leaves, and cloves. Placing any of these herbs in locations where a problem exists will cause the critters to do an about-face and leave the premises. Ants, roaches, and spiders may be more difficult to get rid of. If the above herbs don't work, try mixing 2 cups borax with an equal amount of sugar in a large container, and sprinkle the mixture in areas that you know the pests frequent. When crawling insects cross a fine powder, it removes the waterproof layer of their bodies, causing water loss and, ultimately, death.

IT'S NOT JUST FOR PESTO

If you have a problem with any type of flying insect, keep a basil plant or two around the house. Keep the plant well watered from the bottom; this will cause it to release additional aroma. Drying the basil leaves and hanging them in small muslin bags will also repel flying insects.

CALL HER "TRAMP"

If you find your pregnant dog searching the garbage for citrus peels, don't get upset; she knows what she's doing. Give your pet a vitamin C supplement three to four weeks before she whelps; the vitamin makes the process easier for her. Even though dogs (unlike humans) produce vitamin C, they tend to use more than they can make during pregnancy.

THE PEPPERMINT SOLUTION

Moles, squirrels, gophers, and rats also hate the aroma of peppermint. If you plant mint around your home chances are you will never see one of these pests for any length of time. Soak a cotton ball with peppermint oil and drop it down a gopher hole. You will never see the varmint again.

CATNIP REPELLENT

For an effective insect repellent, rub fresh catnip leaves over the exposed skin or use extract of catnip.

THE LAVENDER OIL SOLUTION

If you don't keep trashcans and compactors sealed tight, you can end up with a swarm of flies, pronto. But flies are repelled by lavender oil. Soak a sponge with the oil and leave it in a saucer, or saturate a few cotton balls with the oil and toss them into your garbage at the beginning of each week. Other natural repellents that will send flies in the other direction are oil of cloves and wintergreen mint sprigs.

FLEA FLICKER

Fleas can be eliminated from upholstery and carpets by vacuuming with a high-powered vacuum cleaner (ideally with a canister) with a bag that seals well. Remove the bag and dispose of it outside as soon as you finish.

MAN, DO THEY STINK

Keeping deer, antelope, reindeer, and other pesky animals away from your garden and trees is a breeze with eggs that have gone bad. Just break them open (outside of the house) around the area that you want to keep the critters away from. The smell of hydrogen sulfide from rotten eggs is not one of their favorite aromas and is sure to repel them from the areas that you want to keep pest-free.

TRY A LITTLE TENDERNESS

Meat tenderizer can be used to treat an insect bite. Commercial meat tenderizers contain papain, an enzyme from papaya. Moisten a teaspoon of tenderizer with a little water and rub it immediately into the skin. Papain's protein-digestive properties will help to decompose the insect venom.

SAY BYE TO THE FLY

You can eliminate fruit flies if you let your fresh fruit ripen in closed paper bags. After it ripens, store the fruit in the refrigerator.

BECAUSE PETS ARE PEOPLE TOO

Vitamins and minerals are very important to your pet's health. Save the water from steamed or boiled vegetables or liquid from a slow cooker and mix it with your animal's food for additional nutrients.

SO ALWAYS HAVE STALE, CHEAP BEER

Whenever you need to get rid of snails in the yard or garden, pour stale cheap beer in a shallow container just below ground level. Snails are attracted to beer. The beer has a diuretic effect, causing snails to lose vital liquids in a short period, and then die.

NO MORE MOSQUITOES

Citronella oil candles will rid your home of mosquitoes. The smell is pleasant and not at all offensive to humans. Adding a few drops of citronella oil to tall gaslights and placing them around the yard will keep the area clear of not only mosquitoes but also of moths.

SORRY, BUGS

If you place a few drops of liquid detergent in the water you use to clean a plant's leaves, it will keep the bugs off, and if they go into the soil at night, they will die.

BUH BYE BAMBI

Hanging small pieces of a deodorant bar soap on trees (especially fruit trees) will keep the deer away. Or, try a piece of your clothing—deer don't like the smell of humans.

ASPIRIN HELPS

Chigger bites respond to a thick paste of aspirin tablets dissolved in water. The paste should ease the pain and itching.

MEOW

To remove a grease stain from your concrete driveway, rub kitty litter into the stain and let stand for one to two hours before sweeping it up.

NO MORE FLEAS

To ward off fleas from a pet's sleeping area, try sprinkling a few drops of lavender oil in the area. Fleas hate lavender oil.

DARE TO DREAM

Finding a toad in your garden is really good luck. One lonely toad will feast on more than 100 slugs, cutworms, grubs, caterpillars, and assorted beetle larvae every night. If the toad is in top form, it can consume more than 10,000 invaders in three months.

A CLEAN SWEEP

Don't you hate the smashed up insects that seem to cover your car grille in the summer? And isn't it a drag cleaning them off? Try this: spray a light coating of vegetable oil on your grille before screaming down the highway, and the revolting bugs will wipe off easily.

GROSS...BUT IT WORKS!

Smearing petroleum jelly around the base of plant stems will make ants and other crawling insects slide right off, protecting your plants.

WHAT'S MORE DISGUSTING THAN A SLUG?

If you're having problems with slugs eating your flowers, here is a simple solution: Just plant a few cabbage plants in your garden. Slugs go crazy for cabbage, and will make a beeline for it.

TRY PEANUT BUTTER

Mice love the flavor of peanut butter even more than cheese. If you're having problems trapping them with cheese, give peanut butter a try.

PICNIC PEACE

To win the war against ants at your picnic, place the picnic table's legs in old coffee cans filled with water. Your food will stay ant free.

MOSQUITO BITES ARE THE WORST, RIGHT?

Eliminate the itch by applying alcohol and soap. It will make the bites virtually disappear.

CLOVE'S THE WAY

Silverfish are disgusting, down to each and every one of their legs. An effective, natural way to remove them is with whole cloves. Just sprinkle a few in the drawers where you see them.

MOSQUITOES SMARTER THAN ZAPPERS

Studies have proven that electric bug zappers have no effect on mosquitoes. They seem to have a special sense that keeps them away from magnetic fields. Citronella lamps will do the trick.

LOOKS NICE, TOO

If you are going to plant in window boxes, try whitewashing them first. This will deter insects and reduce the risk of dry rot.

INSECT BITES & STINGS

Rub neat lavender essential oil directly onto the sting or mix up a paste of 1 teaspoon baking soda and a little water or vinegar. Apply directly to the sting.

HEAVY PETTING

Forget about using soap and water on your dog's messy paws. It's faster and easier to simply wipe his paws with a baby wipe. It's a great way to remove dirt and mud-before he cuddles up with you on the couch.

SERIAL STINGERS

Unlike bees, wasps can sting again and again. If you spot wasps flying to one spot, look for a nest – which can produce up to 30,000 wasps. Contact your local health authority to remove it without delay. For small numbers, fill a jar with half jam and half water. Cover with paper punctured with holes to attract, trap, and drown them.

HOME CLEAN HOME

The easiest way to clean a fish bowl is to wipe the inside with a cloth soaked in white vinegar. Of course, clean the bowl thoroughly before putting the fish back in.

GIVE FLIES THE BRUSH-OFF

If you prefer not to use chemical fly spray and fly-swatting fills you with horror, invest in a fan. Scientists say that flies' wings are unable to operate in a breeze above 15 km (9 miles) an hour. Open the windows, turn the fan to full power and they'll soon buzz off.

THE CHIRPY TALE

To clean your birdbath of algae, empty the water, and cover it in bleach-soaked paper towels for an hour. Rinse, air dry, fill with fresh water, and watch your feathered friends frolic.

FLEAS BE GONE

Every day add one garlic capsule to your pet's food. This helps prevent roundworm and also deters fleas.

BUG PREVENTION

A great way to eliminate crawling bugs in your kitchen drawers is to crumble a few bay leaves along with basil leaves. Bugs hate them. You should also crumble a few leaves on your windowsills as well.

VEGETABLE OIL CURE

If you want to keep your bird bath full but discourage mosquitoes from laying their eggs in the water, fear not: Simply add a few drops of vegetable oil to the water and the mosquitoes will go elsewhere.

WORRIED ABOUT MOTH EGGS?

Well, who isn't? Just place your woolens in a plastic bag and leave it in the freezer for at least 24 hours to kill the eggs. When you do store the garments, place them in a bag that is as airtight as possible.

BYE BYE MOTHS

Trap moths by mixing 1 part molasses with 2 parts white vinegar and placing the mixture in a bright yellow container. Or make a 10 percent solution of molasses in water and hang it from a tree in a quart jar. Use an old-fashioned clamp jar and keep the lid off.

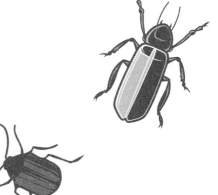

SQUIRREL AWAY

To keep squirrels from stealing from your bird feeder, add a teaspoon of cayenne pepper to your birdseed. The birds like it hot, the squirrels don't, and your problem is solved.

THE GREEN KILL

Nothing is more revolting than roaches, except perhaps the chemicals we use to kill them. Try using this natural pesticide: Make a mixture of equal parts cornstarch and plaster of Paris, and sprinkle it in the cracks where roaches appear. Then stand back, happily, and watch them croak.

SLOSHED!

The tried and true method for eliminating cockroaches is to fill a large bowl with cheap wine, and place it under the sink or wherever you see the revolting little bugs. The pests drink the wine, get drunk, and drown.

FIDO BE GONE

The easiest way to keep the dog or cat off of your good furniture when you're out is to place a piece of aluminum foil on it.

DOESN'T MAKE A NICE SNACK

To rid your house of carpenter ants, just mix up a batch of 4 ounces of cherry or grape jelly in 3 tablespoons of canned cat food and 1 tablespoon of boric acid. Place small amounts in locations that the ants frequent (but keep it away from your cat). They will take the food to the queen and the colony will be eliminated.

COLLECT CONKERS

To prevent moths, place conkers (horse chestnuts) in cupboards and closets. They are easy to find and won't cost you a penny. Store out-of-season clothes in airtight bags or plastic containers to help.

ACCESS DENIED!

Spray your garbage cans with ammonia on a regular basis to keep squirrels and stray dogs from rummaging through the cans.

PARTY POOPERS

Don't let flying bugs ruin your backyard barbeque. Just turn on a few portable fans and aim it at the center of the party, where your guests are. It works great and the party won't stink of bug spray.

PET HAIR ALL OVER THE HOUSE

The easiest way to clean it up is to rub the furniture or carpet with a fresh dryer sheet.

STUFF HAPPENS

If your pet has an accident on the rug, blot it with a paper towel to soak up as much liquid as possible, then spritz it with white vinegar or a mild solution of hot soapy water to remove the odor. However, first test a small, hidden area to make sure the carpet is colorfast.

SPRAY TO ASTRAY

If flies or bees bother you, squirt a little hairspray into the air. They hate it and will go elsewhere.

REPEL AWAY

If you spray rubbing alcohol on your arms and legs, you'll deter mosquitoes from biting you. Another natural repellent is to spray on a mixture of parts water and pure vanilla.

BAG BAIT

If you're squeamish, place a brown paper lunch bag around a baited mousetrap. The mice seem drawn to exploring a small space and all you have to do is close the bag and dispose of it once they've been caught.

THE TOXIC SALT

If you can figure out where ants are entering your house, you can keep them out. Simply sprinkle salt on the their path of entry, and they'll turn around and go elsewhere. Chalk is supposed to have the same effect on ants.

THE FOIL TOIL

If birds are nibbling at your fruit trees, trying hanging long strips of aluminum foil from the branches. It will keep the birds away.

A HAPPY ENDING

Get rid of carpenter ants naturally with this formula: Mix one packet of dry yeast with ½ cup of molasses and a ½ cup of sugar, and spread on a piece of cardboard where you see the pests. This works like catnip for carpenter ants, and they'll all be attached to it, where, happily, they'll get stuck and perish.

A SPOT OF TEA

If you want to keep bugs off your indoor plants, try spraying the plants with a solution of 10 parts weak tea and 1 part ammonia. Try it first on a few leaves to test for damage. An important note of caution: Keep the solution out of reach of children!

CATS HATE HOT SAUCE

If you can't get your cat stop clawing at your woodwork, just rub in a little hot sauce, buff it thoroughly, and your cat will stay clear.

WHO KNEW?

To eliminate fruit flies naturally, fill a spray bottle with water and rubbing alcohol, and spray away. It's about as effective as an insecticide, and you won't poison your family!

THE BEER CURE

It turns out that slugs and snails, those disgusting garden invaders, are a bunch of drunks. If you bury a shoebox lined with aluminum foil and fill it with old beer, in the morning it should be filled with the little beasts, either dead or drunk. Hic.

POWDER DOES IT

A great way to keep cat litter smelling fresh is to mix in a bit of baby powder each time you change the litter.

VISUAL SPLENDOR

To attract birds to your birdbath, just cover the bottom with multi-colored marbles. Are bees a bother while you lounge in the backyard with a cocktail? Keep them from nose-diving into your drink by covering it with aluminum foil, and sticking a straw through the top.

PANTING ANTS

Ants hate peppermint, so if they're in your kitchen drawers, sprinkle in an opened peppermint tea bag, and they'll leave in a hurry. It also works if you open a few bags outside where you see ants.

HAIR REMOVER

A really effective way to pick up cat or dog hair is with rubber dishwashing gloves. Just wipe down all the surfaces, and the hair will stick with the gloves.

WHO KNEW?

Keep a few sticks of wrapped spearmint chewing gum near any open packages of pasta, and they'll never get infested with mealworms.

WATER, BOOZE AND PARTIES

chapter **6**

CRYSTAL CLEAR

Water must be filtered if you want clear ice cubes. In addition, boiling the water before filling the trays allows a number of minerals that cause the cloudiness to dissipate into the air.

WATER WORKS

The human body is dependent on an adequate and healthful water supply. Every bodily function and organ system relies on water. Water assists in digesting foods, transports nutrients to organs, and then cools the body through perspiration, helping to regulate body temperature. Water washes out contaminants through the kidneys in the form of urine. We require about 10 cups of water daily to replace these losses. On average, we get a little over five cups from fluids, about four cups from solid foods, and just over one cup of water is produced by the metabolism.

By weight, the human body is about two-thirds water; a 150-pound adult is about 90 pounds of water. Here's how it breaks down by percentage of water making up tissues, organs, fluids, and bone.

How Much Water?	
BODY PART OR FLUID	PERCENT WATER
Bone	33
Liver	71
Lungs	71 to 84
Heart	72
Kidneys	76
Brain	77.4
Muscle	79
Blood	82
Saliva	94
Perspiration	95

FOR THE HOUSEPLANTS

If you know your house has lead pipes (or if your house is old and you're not sure), play it safe: Always use cold water for cooking, especially when making baby formula, and let the water run for two to three minutes first thing in the morning. The longer water sits in the pipes, and the hotter the water is, the higher the chance it may contain lead.

THIRST QUENCHERS? HA!

Have you ever felt thirstier after you drink a soda? Well, they contain sugar, which the body has to break down—and this is a process which requires water. Additionally, the caffeine in soft drinks acts as a diuretic, which makes you lose fluids. Alcoholic drinks also require one cup of water per drink to metabolize the alcohol.

I DON'T HEART ICE WATER

If you suffer from any form of cardiovascular disease, don't drink ice water. The cold may cause a sudden drop in tissue temperature, resulting in an unnecessary shock to the system. Even if you don't suffer from heart problems, your digestive system functions more efficiently if you drink tepid water (though an occasional glass of ice water won't harm you). Try to avoid drinking water with your meals: It will dilute stomach acids and digestive enzymes.

SORRY, IT'S NOT BEER

If you are really thirsty, the best beverage to drink is water.

A TRICK QUESTION

Are you more likely to become dehydrated in summer or in winter? While it's true that your body loses more water during the summer months, you're more likely to drink more fluids. You still sweat in winter, but it evaporates more quickly because heated rooms are dry, and perspiration is absorbed by clothing. In the winter, we're less conscious of our need for water, so we drink less.

COLORADO, ARE YOU LISTENING?

Where you live affects the amount of water you need to drink. At higher elevations, where the atmospheric pressure is lower and the air is drier, water tends to evaporate faster through your skin. Because the air is thinner, you also tend to breathe more rapidly, thus losing additional moisture through exhalation. If you live in Denver, you need to consume three or four extra glasses of water per day than if you live in do New York.

WHEN YOU'RE REALLY, REALLY THIRSTY

There has been an ongoing debate whether it is better to drink ice water or room-temperature water when you are thirsty. The answer? Drink ice water to quench a raging thirst (of course, read the tip on the bottom of page 169 first)! Ice water will cause your stomach to constrict, thereby forcing the water into the small intestine, where it will be absorbed into the bloodstream faster.

YOU CAN THANK THE LIMESTONE

A number of "natural" beverage makers advertise that their drink contains naturally carbonated water. This water is created underground when the water comes into contact with limestone, resulting in the production of the gas carbon dioxide. The water traps the gas under high pressure underground. Artificially, carbonation is helped along with either phosphoric acid or citric acid in most soft drinks.

WHY ICE FLOATS

When water freezes, the molecules combine loosely, creating air pockets. When water is in its liquid form, these pockets do not exist, making water denser than ice.

TURN IT OFF

If you leave the water running every time you brush your teeth, you will waste about one gallon of water. The average person in the United States uses 80 gallons of water a day.

CLEAN THAT ICE

When ice cubes stay in the freezer tray more than a few days, they tend to pick up odors from other foods. Give ice cubes a quick rinse before using them to avoid altering the flavor of your beverage.

KIDS, DRINK YOUR VEGETABLES

Some fruits and vegetables have a high water content. Carrots are 88 percent water and iceberg lettuce is 96 percent water, for example.

TEA FACTS

- Tea was first grown and served in China. It was originally used to flavor water that tasted flat after boiling for purification. Tea moved from China to Japan and throughout the Far East, and now the island of Sri Lanka leads the world in tea production. Tea is still picked by hand, and a tea picker can pick about 40 pounds of tea leaves daily.
- Pound for pound, tea has much more caffeine than does coffee. However, a pound of tea will brew 150 to 200 cups, while a pound of coffee yields about 48 cups. Brewed tea contains about a third as much caffeine as instant coffee.
- Tea acts as a diuretic and should not be relied upon for providing your daily intake of water.

CLASSIFICATION OF TEAS

All tea comes from an evergreen related to the camellia family.

Black Tea

This is made when the insides of the leaves are exposed to oxygen (that is, they oxidize), which turns them black. The leaves are then dried and allowed to ferment for two to three hours.

Green Tea

This tea is not oxidized—green is the natural color of tea leaves, imparted by chlorophyll. The leaves are steamed, and then rolled and dried. Gunpowder is a Chinese classification for green tea; basket-fired is a Japanese classification.

ICE TRICK

Ice cubes used for iced tea or coffee should be made from tea or coffee, not from water. These beverages tend to become diluted rapidly, because they're often enjoyed on sultry summer days, and this ensures the drinks won't become watered down.

Oolong Tea

This tea is partially fermented and somewhat oxidized. Oolong tea is fermented twice and fired three times. It has a greenish-brown color and is usually sold as Formosa tea; when oolong tea is blended with jasmine tea, it is called Pouchong.

DRAW YOUR OWN CONCLUSIONS

Studies in Shanghai and Japan showed that drinking green tea was effective in protecting against stomach cancer and lowering cholesterol and triglyceride levels. But be cautious about using tea for any medicinal purpose—drinking large amounts may cause problems because of the caffeine or because of the strong binding properties of the polyphenols in tea. Tea's polyphenic antioxidants are being studied for their potential in preventing cancer; the key one is called epigallocatechin-3-gallate. More research needs to be done to determine the exact activities green and black tea perform, as well as to determine how much tea is both safe to drink and beneficial to your health.

I CAN SEE CLEARLY NOW

Cloudiness is common in brewed iced tea but can be prevented easily. Just let the tea cool to room temperature before refrigerating it. If the tea is still cloudy, try adding a small amount of boiling water to it until it clears up. A number of minerals are released when the tea is brewed, which results in the cloudiness.

BREW IT FAST

When coffee beans are ground, a large percentage of their surface is exposed to air, which speeds its deterioration. The longer the ground beans sit, the more carbon dioxide, which contributes to the coffee's body and aroma, is lost. For this reason, coffee beans should be stored in the refrigerator and ground fresh as needed. If you choose to buy the vacuum-packed cans, store them in the refrigerator upside down to preserve the taste and flavor. Why upside down? You reduce the amount of oxygen that had contact with the surface of the coffee, slowing down oxidation.

NOT THAT YOU'VE EVER HAD A HANGOVER

It's a good idea to drink a cup of water for every alcoholic drink you consume. It takes eight ounces of water to metabolize every ounce of alcohol. If you have ever had a hangover, you'll recognize the symptoms of dehydration such as dry mouth, headaches, and an upset stomach.

NOT TOO HOT

Tea experts agree that green teas should be brewed between 180°F and 200°F, oolong teas between 185°F and 205°F, and black teas between 190°F and 210°F. Better quality and more delicate black teas should be brewed at lower temperatures since they tend to release their flavor more readily than do lower quality teas. The higher temperature used to brew lower quality teas seems to stimulate the tea to release its flavor.

OH, THAT CAFFEINE BUZZ

Can't drink coffee but still want caffeine? A cup of English breakfast tea provides you with about 60 milligrams of caffeine—not as much as a cup of coffee, but more than most teas.

THE COFFEE/CALCIUM CONNECTION

Caffeine can leach calcium from bones. If you're a coffee, tea, or soda drinker, be sure you eat enough calcium-rich foods to offset any ill effects.

A CUPPA KONA

The big island of Hawaii is the only location in the United States where coffee is grown. The mineral rich volcanic soil produces Kona coffee, one of the finest and most flavorful coffees in the world.

FOR THE BEST CUP OF COFFEE

Ground coffee oxidizes and loses flavor; it should be used within two to three days for best results. Fresh-roasted beans are usually packed in bags that are not airtight, which allows the carbon monoxide formed during the roasting process to escape. If the carbon monoxide doesn't escape, the coffee will have a poor taste.

If you run out of coffee filters, try using a double layer of white paper towels (don't use paper towels with any printing on them—the inks can be released by the hot water).

Clean your coffeepot regularly, and rinse it well. The slightest hint of soap or scum will alter the taste. Baking soda and hot water work well.

WHO KNEW?

When you keep coffee warm in a coffeepot on a hot plate, it will only stay fresh for about 30 minutes after it is brewed. If your coffee needs to be freshened up, add a pinch of salt to your cup before reheating it.

BURNS YOUR SKIN BUT NOT YOUR MOUTH

There's a simple explanation why you can drink coffee that is hot enough to burn your skin and not your mouth. When you sip a very hot cup of coffee, you suck in cool air. The air lowers the temperature through both convection (air current) and evaporation. Also, saliva partially coats the inside of the mouth, insulating it from very hot liquids.

REDUCING ACIDITY

If you're one of those people who is sensitive to acidity in coffee, here's a tip to reduce the acid level. Just add a pinch of baking soda to the drink. (Use this tip to decrease the acid in other high-acid drinks and foods.)

DOES A HOT DRINK WARM YOU UP?

From a physiological standpoint, hot drinks will not raise your body temperature. Research conducted by the U.S. Army Research Institute of Environmental Medicine showed that you would have to drink one quart of a liquid at 130°F to generate any increase in body temperature. It also stated that it would be difficult to keep that much liquid down. In fact, hot liquids will cause surface blood vessels to dilate; this may make you feel a slight bit warmer but may actually lead to a loss of heat.

OR DON'T DRINK SO MUCH

Coffee will make you more alert and awake, but it will have little effect on making you sober. The quickest way to sober up is to consume a glass of water for each alcoholic drink and to take a multivitamin, multimineral supplement while you are drinking. This will assist the liver in metabolizing the alcohol more efficiently, and it may even reduce the effects of hangover.

DON'T BE BITTER

The best coffee flavor can be yours with freshly ground coffee and naturally soft water. Coffee should never be boiled, which can release the tannins that make it bitter.

IT'S THE TEMPERATURE, NOT THE CAFFEINE, THAT MATTERS

When brewing coffee, the proper temperature is important. When coffee is brewed, the water should be between 200°F and 205°F; after brewing, it should be held between 185°F and 190°F. If the temperature is too low, the coffee grounds will not release adequate flavor compounds, and if it gets too high, tannins are released, affecting the flavor of the coffee. Caffeine has very little to do with the taste of coffee.

FLAT SODA IS A THING OF THE PAST

If you pour a warm soft drink over ice cubes, the gas escapes from the beverage at a faster rate because the ice cubes contain more surface for the gas bubbles to collect on, thus releasing more of the carbon dioxide. This is the reason that warm beverages go flat rapidly, and warm drinks poured over ice go flat even faster. To slow down the process, rinse the ice cubes in cold water for about 10 seconds before adding the soft drink. This will help to eliminate the fizzing, which is when the carbon dioxide escapes.

CAFFEINE

Caffeine is the most widely used behavior-affecting drug in the world. It can be derived from 60 different plant sources, including cocoa beans, cola nuts, tea leaves, and coffee beans.

Caffeine stimulates the central nervous system and is capable of warding off drowsiness and increasing alertness. It also quickens reaction time to both visual and auditory stimuli.

Studies have shown that caffeine does not cause frequent urination in all people, but does cause an acid increase in the stomach after two cups. Chronic heartburn sufferers should avoid coffee completely and limit caffeine from other sources to 300 milligrams per day.

Caffeine Content in Common Foods and Drugs

BEVERAGE	PER 8 OUNCES
Drip coffee	137 mg
Instant coffee	57 mg
Jolt Cola	50 mg
Diet Dr Pepper	41 mg
Mountain Dew	37 mg
Black tea	36 mg
Iced tea	36 mg
Instant tea	31 mg
Coca-Cola	31 mg
Diet Coke	31 mg
Sunkist orange soda	27 mg
Dr Pepper	25 mg
Pepsi-Cola	25 mg
Diet Pepsi	24 mg
Cocoa	4 mg

DRUG	PER TABLET
Vivarin	200 mg
NoDoz	100 mg
Excedrin	65 mg
Vanquish	32 mg
Anacin	32 mg
Midol	32 mg

CHOCOLATE	PER OUNCE
Milk chocolate	6 mg
Semisweet chocolate	20 mg

DUH

Have you noticed that foods marketed to children are becoming more colorful? Kids will purchase blue drinks over any color, and manufacturers are making blue candy, cookies, ice cream, and other foods. Studies performed at the University of Massachusetts showed that younger people "are open to the novelty of unnaturally tinted products" than are a more mature group. It was also discovered that color has an impact on how a food tastes to people.

CAFFEINE, CALCIUM, AND YOU

Recent studies indicate that caffeinated beverages will cause calcium to be excreted in the urine. To replace the calcium losses, try to consume at least 2 tablespoons of milk for each cup of coffee you drink.

AMERICA'S OTHER DRINKING PROBLEM

- In a 24-hour period Coca-Cola is consumed 192 million times in 35 countries around the world.
- Soft drinks account for 25 percent of all sugar consumption in the United States.
- If a child drinks four colas per day, he is taking in the equivalent caffeine in two cups of regular coffee.
- The average American drank almost 55 gallons of soda in 2005.

MAKES A NICE SUMMER TREAT, TOO

Believe it or not, some lemon furniture polishes contain more actual lemon than commercial lemonade drink mixes.

DRINK FAST

Orange juice has a high acid content. If you use frozen concentrate, it will last about a week after it is reconstituted. The nutritional value, especially of the vitamin C, will decrease rapidly, so it's best to consume the juice within three or four days. The oxygen in the water, as well as the aeration when you mix the juice, tends to deplete the vitamin.

DO THE MATH

Most liquor sold in the United States contains 40 percent alcohol, which means that they are 80 proof. The proof figure is always double the percentage of the alcohol content.

AVOID THE COCKTAIL CART

If you suffer from motion sickness, don't have any alcoholic beverage on the plane. It will make things worse.

BEST TO TAKE YOUR VITAMINS

Alcohol impairs the body's ability to absorb, metabolize, and use vitamins A, E, and D. In addition, alcoholics tend to eat less, which may lead to deficiencies in vitamins C and K, as well as calcium, magnesium, iron, and zinc. If you consume more than two alcoholic beverages a day, consider taking a multivitamin, multimineral supplement.

GREAT GRINDING

The size of the grind does make a difference in the taste and level of caffeine in a cup of coffee. Espresso is typically finely ground, and Turkish coffee even finer. Most American coffee is drip grind. This provides the optimum surface area and will brew a rich cup of coffee that is not bitter. However, if you grind your own beans, take care they are not too finely ground. The water will take longer to filter through, which can result in an increase in phenolic acids and bitter tasting coffee.

LISTEN UP, FELLAS

Alcohol has the tendency to increase the excretion of the trace mineral zinc, which is very important to prostate health. Magnesium, another important trace mineral, may also be excreted, which may lead to lowering your resistance to stress.

BRING ON THE FAT

You can slow down the rate that your body absorbs alcohol if you eat while drinking. Eating fatty foods, which take a long time to digest, will slow down the rate of absorption even more.

CAFFEINE TALK

Although caffeine is an addictive drug, cutting back on caffeinated sodas gradually can decrease the likelihood that you'll experience symptoms of withdrawal like severe headaches, nausea, or depression (most of these symptoms are short-lived).

THERE GOES THE VITAMIN

According to information released by the American Cancer Society, consuming alcohol can promote a deficiency in vitamin A.

BUBBLY FACTS

A seventeenth-century French monk named Dom Perignon perfected the process of making Champagne. He manipulated the presses to make a white wine from black grapes, blended wines from several villages for balance, and enhanced the tendency of white wines to keep their sugars, so the wines would referment, and make more bubbles. He also used cork stoppers to keep the bubbles in the bottle.

By law, anything sold as Champagne must come from the region of France by the same name—anything else must be sold as sparkling wine.

Champagnes are best when served between 44°F and 48°F. But never refrigerate Champagne for more than one or two hours before serving. If left in the refrigerator for long periods, the flavor will be poor.

THE CLEARER THE BETTER

Congeners are chemicals in liquor that are by-products of distillation and fermentation. The more congeners a liquor has, the worse the hangover. The safest beverages—that is, those that produce the lowest levels—are gin and vodka (especially Russian vodka). The beverages with the highest levels are bourbon, rum, and Scotch.

IT GOES TO YOUR HEAD

Champagne is produced with a high level of trapped carbon dioxide dissolved in the liquid. The pressure in the bottle is sufficient to keep the carbon dioxide in suspension until the bottle is opened and the pressure immediately drops to room-temperature pressure. The carbon dioxide dissipates and the Champagne goes flat, which will not take very long. The carbon dioxide gas also tends to increase the absorption of alcohol into the bloodstream, allowing you to feel the effects sooner than you would if you were drinking any other type of wine. Wine coolers and spritzers made with carbonated water will give you the same effect.

CHAMPAGNE TASTES

- Brut is the driest, with less than 1.5 percent sugar.
- Extra sec or extra dry is dry; its sugar content is between 1.2 and 2 percent.
- Sec is slightly sweet, with 1.7 to 3.5 percent sugar.
- Demi-sec is sweeter still, with a sugar content of 3.3 to 5 percent.
- Doux is very sweet, with more than 5 percent sugar.
- Demi-sec and doux are considered dessert wines.

WHO KNEW?

The quality of Champagne and sparkling wine can be compromised if the beverage is chilled for too long. Never store it in the refrigerator; it should also only be chilled for a matter of hours.

TIP IT OVER

Wine should be stored on its side to keep the cork damp. If the cork dries out it will shrink; air will pass through, and the wine will deteriorate. Portugal supplies about 80 percent of the corks sold worldwide.

A GREAT RELEASE

Our senses of smell and taste are inextricably linked. When you swirl the wine in the glass, you release its full aroma. Wine may contain 400 different organic molecules, 200 of which have an aroma.

DON'T BLUSH

Blush wines are produced from red grapes from which the juice has had almost no contact with the grape skins. The color will vary depending on the type of grape and whether a small amount of white grape juice is added. These wines are usually best if served chilled but not icy cold.

FORTIFIED WINES

These wines have alcohol added during wine making. The additional alcohol serves to stop the fermentation by killing the yeast. The most common fortified wines are port, sherry, and Marsala.

VINTAGE WINES

These are wines that are produced from grapes grown in a specific year, frequently from a particular vineyard. The year and vineyard are usually stated on the label. A nonvintage wine is made from grapes that were harvested in different years and never has a date on the label.

RULES TO LIVE BY

- Always serve dry wine before sweet and white wine before red.
- If bits of cork fall into the wine, strain the wine into a decanter before pouring it.
- Red wines more than eight years old tend to develop sediment. This is harmless and the wine can be decanted, leaving the sediment behind.

FIRE IT UP

If you are making a flambéed dish and have trouble igniting the brandy, it is probably not hot enough. Some chefs warm the brandy gently before adding it to the food to ensure that it will light. If you heat it too much before adding it to the dish, however, it may ignite too soon.

NOW YOU KNOW WHAT TARTRATES ARE

The crystals you sometimes see on corks are tartrates, which are the by-product of tartaric acid used in wine-making. They are not an indication of an inferior or poorly processed wine, not do they affect the flavor of the wine, and they are not harmful if drunk.

AND DON'T FORGET A LITTLE SIP FOR THE COOK

When cooking with wine, try not to use too much, or the taste may well overpower the dish. Wine should only be used to improve the flavor. If you want to assure that you taste the wine in a recipe, just add it to the recipe about five to seven minutes before completion.

WINE FIRST

If you add wine to a soup or sauce that already contains milk or cream, it may curdle; adding the wine and cooking it briefly before you add the dairy product should help prevent this.

KEEP IT THE SAME

When you cook with wine, you should use the same wine you'll pour with the meal. The flavors will mesh. Avoid "cooking wines" because they are almost always inferior.

LEAVE THE TOAST, KEEP THE WINE

The practice of making a toast originated in seventeenth century England where pieces of spiced toast were placed in a carafe of wine or individual glass to improve the taste. It was polite to eat the toast so as not to offend the host. The toast has since been omitted and just the wine consumed.

CONSTANTLY CHANGING

Wine is composed of water, alcohol, various pigments, esters, some vitamins and minerals, acids, and tannins. It does not remain in a constant state, but is continually changing—even in the bottle. When wines improve in the bottle, they are said to age well; most wines, however, should be drunk within a few years of bottling.

WINE 101

- The best temperature for storing wine is 55°F. White wine should be served between 50°F and 55°F for the best flavor; serve reds at 65°F.

- Wine stored at high temperatures will deteriorate rapidly. White wines are more susceptible to deterioration from heat than are red wines.

- Wine glasses should only be filled between half and two-thirds full—leave room to swirl the wine to release its full flavor and aroma.

SOME SIMPLE GUIDELINES

A number of foods have flavors that clash with those of some wines. Highly acidic dishes, such as those made with vinegar or citrus, can conflict with wine. Egg yolks contain sulfur, which tends to have a negative effect on wine's flavor. Other potentially problematic foods are asparagus, onions, chocolate, tomatoes, pineapples, and artichokes. Here's a guide to temperamental foods and wine to serve with them.

FOOD	WINE
Eggs	Sparkling wine, not too oaky Chardonnay, medium-bodied Pinot Blanc
Asparagus	Sauvignon, Mosel Kabbinett, young Chardonnay, or red Cabernet Franc
Chocolate	Fortified sweet wines such as Málaga, Muscat, 10-year-old tawny Port; liqueurs; youngish Sauternes
Onion tart	Aromatic fruity dry whites from Alsace, or New World Colombard, Sauvignon, or Chardonnay
Tomatoes	Crisp Sauvignon or Vin de Pays des Côtes de Gascone, or a tangy red such as Barbera
Pineapple desserts	Concentrated sweet white with good acidity such as Côteaux du Layon or New Zealand late-harvest Riesling
Artichokes	Tangy white such as a crisp Chardonnay, Hungarian white, New Zealand Sauvignon, or young white Rioja

AND THIS IS A SURPRISE?

It's true: Beer drinking itself is the cause of the beer belly. Across all races and in both genders, beer consumption is consistently and directly linked to higher waist-to-hip-circumference ratios.

DON'T AVOID THE DRAFT

Serious beer drinkers will always order a draft beer over a bottle or can. Because all beer is subject to spoilage, beer that is bottled and canned is pasteurized (which is a form of sterilization). This high-temperature processing causes a loss of flavor, which a discerning beer drinker will notice. Draft beer does not go through the pasteurization process because the kegs are kept cold and are never stored for a period that would allow the microorganisms to alter the flavor or spoil the beer.

SO YOU KNOW

In Europe, the term "light beer" refers to the color of the brew. In the United States, it refers to a beer that is lower in calories.

HEAD OF THE CLASS

The "head retention" on beer is measured by the half-life of the foam—that is, the number of seconds it takes for the volume of the foam to reduce by half. If the head on your beer has a half-life of 110 seconds, it is considered to be very good. The head will last longer if the beer is served in a tall, narrow glass that is scrupulously clean (always be sure to rinse all soap residue off glassware and dry thoroughly). The slightest hint of soap may cause the beer foam to collapse, as well as affect the color.

TRY IT SLIGHTLY WARMER

Beer connoisseurs know: An ice-cold beer might wet your whistle, but it doesn't taste great. In most countries, beer is drunk at what is known as British cellar temperature, or about 55°F. If beer is exposed to light, a chemical change will occur from the intensity of the illumination.

WHO KNEW BEER WAS SO TEMPERAMENTAL?

Cans and bottles of beer should always be stored upright. When beer is allowed to lie on its side more of the beer is exposed to oxygen. Oxidation will take place and the beer will lose its flavor sooner. Also, beer should not be moved from one location in the refrigerator to another since the slightest temperature change will affect the flavor.

I'VE NEVER BEEN HAPPIER

New studies indicate that having one or two drinks a day may reduce the risk of cardiovascular disease. Beer and wine seem to boost the body's natural levels of a clot-dissolving enzyme. Other studies indicate that moderate alcohol consumption— again, one or two drinks a day—may raise the levels of the good cholesterol (HDL) in the bloodstream.

KEEPING YOUR COOL

If you enjoy cold beer, an insulated foam holder will keep the beer close to the original cold temperature for at least 25 to 35 minutes. A glass from the freezer will keep the beer cold for about 10 to 15 minutes longer than a warm glass, but glasses can pick up off odors in the freezer. They can also be uncomfortable to hold, leave water rings from condensation, and can even dilute the beer.

HOW TO COOK WITH BEER

When beer is heated, the alcohol evaporates, leaving the flavoring agents intact. The acids in beer, however, react with certain metals (especially aluminum and iron) to form a dark compound that can cause those pots to discolor. When cooking with beer always use a pot made of stainless steel, glass, or one with an enameled coating. If you like cooking with beer, try using a bock or ale for the best flavor. Light beers do not contribute much flavor to a dish.

FOR THE FASTEST COLD BEER

The best way to chill beer rapidly is to fill a cooler chest with water and ice and plunge the beer into the chest. In about 20 minutes, the beer will be ice cold. Ice water is about 32°F and is, of course, warmer than a 0°F freezer. The ice water, however, absorbs the warmth from the bottles or cans more rapidly and more efficiently than the cold air of the freezer does. Just remember that premium lagers should be served between 42°F and 48°F and ales between 44°F and 52°F, so don't let it get too cold.

FOAM FACTS

The temperature of the beer controls the amount of foam it produces. A cold beer produces less froth than a room-temperature beer.

The Average Percentage of Alcohol in Beers			
BRITISH		**AMERICAN**	
Brown ale	4–5.5%	Light	3.5–4.4%
Mild ale	3.2–4%	Lager	3.8–4.5%
Lager	3.5%	Malt liquor	4.8–5.8%
Stout	4.8%	Pilsner	4.1–4.7%

BOTTLE OR CAN?

Aluminum cans are very thin, and when you hold a can, the heat transfers from your hand to the can, lowering the temperature of the beer. A glass bottle is much thicker. The heat from your hand doesn't penetrate as easily, so the beer stays colder for a somewhat longer period. In addition, aluminum is an excellent conductor of heat; glass is very poor. Whether you buy beer in bottles or cans, connoisseurs recommend that beer always be poured into a glass before serving.

THAT'S RIGHT, BEER AND NO PRETZELS

A 12-ounce serving of American beer contains 150 calories, most of which are from carbohydrates. It also provides at least 10 percent of the daily requirement for folate, niacin, vitamin B6, phosphorus, magnesium, chromium, and selenium. Proteins in the grains are usually removed during the brewing process.

Because beer ranges in alcohol content from 3 to 8 percent, and because the calories can add up quickly, it's wise to drink it in limited amounts. Salty snacks like peanuts, pretzels, and chips should be avoided when drinking beer. Snacks that are high in protein, starch, vitamins, and minerals balance beer's high-sugar content better. Try crackers and cheese, eggs, meat, or unsalted peanuts.

IT'S HARD TO AGE WELL

Unlike wine, beer does not age well and is best consumed as soon as possible. Older beers are inferior in both flavor and overall quality. If beer is not pasteurized, it is best to drink it within a week or two after it is produced. The ideal temperatures for light beers such as lager is 42°F to 48°F, ales and porters should be at 44°F to 52°F.

TYPES OF BEER

Ale

May range in color from light to very dark amber. It has a slightly bitter flavor and is usually stronger than lager beer. Ales are brewed from hops and barley and are slightly higher in alcohol than beer.

Bock

This is German beer that is usually dark and full-bodied. In Germany, bocks are brewed in the springtime. It is slightly sweet and tends to be heavier than lager beers.

SORRY TO BE A BUZZKILL

Alcohol may suppress the immune system. It also reacts adversely with more than 100 medications, and reduces the potency of any vitamin supplements you may be taking. If you have a problem with food allergies, drinking alcohol may intensify any adverse effects.

Fruit Beer

This is made from milder lager or ale; it is flavored with a variety of fruit concentrates.

Lager

This is a light-bodied, pale beer that has a somewhat mellow flavor.

Malt Liquor

This is a hearty, dark beer that has a somewhat bitter flavor and a high alcohol content. Avoid American beverages labeled "malt liquor"—they are inexpensive, sweet beers with high alcohol content. German and British malt liquors are of higher quality.

Pilsner

This is a type of lager. It is pale, with a pronounced flavor of hops, and is almost as bubbly as Champagne. Almost all American beer produced by large commercial breweries is an Americanized pilsner that is neither as hoppy nor as aged as are European pilsners.

Porter

This is a relatively strong, full-bodied dark beer that is quite bitter. Porters are made with roasted malt and tend to be higher in alcohol than lagers typically are.

Stout

This is a very hearty, dark beer, with a pronounced aroma of hops and a flavor that can be quite bitter. Stouts are brewed from a dark-roasted barley, malt, or oats.

Wheat Beer

This is produced from malted wheat. It ranges in color from very pale to dark copper. Its flavor is similar to lager.

KIND OF A CHEESY SOLUTION

Homemade pizzas often lack the crispness of pizzeria pies. Here's one tip that should help: Add the cheese *before* the tomato sauce. Cheese has lower water content than tomatoes do, and the crust won't get as soggy.

PARTY PLANNING

If you have ever wondered how many appetizers each guest will consume, wonder no more. At a cocktail party (no meal served), 10 to 12 nibbles per person is a good estimate. If you're serving dinner, figure four to five mouthfuls. If you are having a wine and cheese gathering, four ounces of cheese per person will suffice. If you're serving a dip and crackers or chips, one cup of dip will serve eight people if you are serving other nibbles (each person will eat about two tablespoons). Four cups of dip will provide about 160 cracker-size servings (each serving being a little over a teaspoon).

DIP TIPS

For an unusual dip holder, use a large green, red, or yellow bell pepper. Remove the top and scrape the pepper clean of ribs and seeds. A scooped-out cucumber or small squash will work as well. Another idea: Hollow out a round loaf of pumpernickel bread and fill the crust with your favorite spinach dip. Cut the bread into cubes and dunk them in the dip.

A COOL IDEA

To keep ice cubes from melting at a party, put them in a bowl, and then set that bowl in a larger one filled with dry ice.

FIRE IT UP

Serving a dessert that's flambéed? Soak sugar cubes briefly in lemon or orange extract that contains alcohol, and then set them on the dessert. Carefully ignite the cubes with a match.

TAKE THAT, MARTHA

For the buffet table, hollow out a melon, orange, or grapefruit and fill it with cut-up fruits and miniature marshmallows. For a more attractive holder, you can scallop the edges, or cut it in the shape of a basket.

USE AN ELECTRIC KNIFE

Slice a loaf of French bread lengthwise, fill with filling of choice, and use an electric knife for easiest slicing.

OR JUST DRINK MORE

Freeze leftover wine in ice cube trays (store the cubes in freezer bags). Use the cubes in wine coolers and any dish that calls for wine.

OR JUST DRINK FASTER

One of the easiest ways to keep a large punch bowl cold is to make large ice cubes in coated paper milk cartons (remove the paper label before using). The larger the ice cube, the slower it melts.

WHO KNEW?

Bringing out the candles for your party? Put them in the freezer the night before, and they'll burn slower and drip less by party time.

DO IT YOURSELF

It's easy to make natural Easter egg dyes. Use grass for green, onionskins for yellow and deep orange, or beets for pink. Add to the water when you boil the eggs. If you plan to eat the eggs, be sure to use plants that haven't been fertilized or treated with pesticides or other chemicals.

YOU'RE IN TROUBLE IF YOU RUN OUT

When you buy ice cubes in the bag, you will get about 10 cubes per pound. The average person at a party will go through 10 to 15 cubes depending on the type of drink.

FASTEST DIP

Here's a great-tasting, super-fast, high-fiber dip: Puree 1 cup of drained cooked white beans with a package of herb-flavored soft cheese.

A SURE FIRE WAY TO RUIN YOUR HOLIDAY

If you're hosting an Easter egg hunt, be sure that no one eats any hard-cooked eggs that have been out of the refrigerator for more than two hours.

WHO KNEW?

Always mail your party invitations on Wednesday, which means they should arrive on Friday or Saturday. People respond quicker to mail received on the weekend—so you'll get your head count worked out sooner!

THE RAINBOW SANDWICH

Color cream cheese with powdered or liquid food coloring to use it as a filling for dainty rolled sandwiches. Try a different color for each layer, and then slice as you would a jellyroll cake.

FOR THE BRITISH READER

Instead of using a pastry shell around the filet when preparing Beef Wellington, try using refrigerated crescent-roll dough. Do not separate the dough into triangles, but keep it one whole piece.

FREEZE 'EM

For children's drinks, freeze red or green maraschino cherries in ice cubes; for adult drinks, freeze cocktail onions or olives in the cubes. Or, freeze lime or lemon rinds in cubes for a nice twist. Inserting toothpicks before freezing makes for easy retrieval.

IF YOU REALLY WANT TO EAT A LION

Surprise the kids with sandwiches in the shape of animals or objects. It's as simple as using animal-shaped cookie cutters.

IT'S LIKE MAGIC

Have you ever had a problem with soda fizzing over the top of an ice-filled glass? The cubes will fizz less if you put them in the glass and rinse them for a few seconds, and then pour out the water. You will have changed the surface tension of the ice, and then the soda won't fizz over.

AND DON'T FORGET LOTS AND LOTS OF BEER

Fifty folks coming for a backyard barbecue? Start with 17 ½ pounds of ground beef for hamburgers and 70 buns; then buy 20 pounds of hot dogs and 100 hot-dog buns. For the traditional side dishes, buy 2 gallons of baked beans, 6 quarts of potato salad, and 10 pounds of cole slaw.

THE HORS D'OEUVRES SOLUTION

To keep meat or cheese hors d'oeuvres moist, cover them with a damp paper towel, then cover loosely with plastic wrap. Many fillings (as well as bread) dry out very quickly.

WHO KNEW?

Keep summer drinks cool without watering them down by freezing grapes and using them in place of ice cubes.

RED WINE EVERY TIME

A natural compound called reservatrol, which is found in the skin of grapes and is present in red wine, is a powerful antioxidant that may protect against cancer and cardiovascular disease, as well as help the body to break down fat. Cheers!

MAKE A MINT

A great post-dinner choice instead of caffeine-rich coffee is a peppermint herbal infusion. Peppermint reduces the more extreme movements of the digestive system, helping to relieve feelings of fullness, nausea and flatulence. It also has antiseptic properties.

NOTHING SAYS 'I LOVE YOU' LIKE FANCY BUTTER

To make fancy butter pats for a party, soften the butter (don't melt it completely), and then put it in a pastry bag with a decorative tip, such as a rosette. Squeeze the butter onto a baking sheet and refrigerate until hard.

BECAUSE WE ALL SHOULD EXPERIENCE A FROSTED GRAPE

Choose some really nice sized grapes, wash them, and dry thoroughly. Dip them in a solution of ½ cup granulated sugar and ½ cup ice water, then freeze. Don't freeze for more than one day for the best results.

PARTY TIME!

For your child's next birthday party, write the invitations on blown-up balloons with a felt marker then deflate and put them in the mail. You kid's guests will have to blow up the balloon to read the invitation.

Planning a big old party tonight, but out of space for your drinks? Just fill the washing machine with ice and your cans and bottles, and you've just created a giant ice bucket. When the party's done and the ice has melted, simply run the spin cycle on the washer to eliminate the water.

FOLLOW THE 80–20 RULE

Drastic food restriction is not the way to a healthier, fitter body. Choose sensible options for 80% of the time, and occasionally relax the rules, when you are eating out or have a special celebration. This way you are more likely to stick to good eating principles, and not feel guilty about having the odd treat.

IF YOU WANT TO KEEP A WINE BOTTLE

If you want to remove a cork stuck inside of a wine bottle, pour a small amount of ammonia into bottle and place it outside for two to three days. The ammonia should dissolve the cork.

HOT OR COLD, BUT NOT IN BETWEEN

At buffets, keep cooked foods either hot or cold, not lukewarm. Hot foods should be kept at 140°F in a warming tray or in a chafing dish. Cold foods should be kept at 40°F or cooler.

WHO KNEW?

If you decide you want to have live entertainment at a party, it might be easier than you think. Often, musicians and singers can be found through a local college, a music school, or a church that is known for its music.

PRE-PARTY PREP

Prior to a big event choose a 'lifting' and lymphatic drainage-based treatment which will improve the appearance of skin tone and reduce puffiness, rather than one that deals with extraction, which is more likely to bring impurities to the surface and may cause your skin to break out.

BRILLIANT BEER

Traditionally beer has always been thought to be good for the hair and the skin. Now we know it is rich in silic acid, the dissolved version of the trace mineral silicon, which is found in the skin, so beer is officially good for you.

SWEET SAVINGS

To save money, purchase solid chocolate bunnies after Easter or Santas after Christmas when they are half price. Store them in the freezer. To use, shave off chocolate with a potato peeler.

FREEZE GRAPES

If you want to keep your wine cool in the glass for drinking on hot summer days, use frozen grapes instead of ice cubes. They'll keep the drink cold and they won't dilute it or change the taste as they thaw. Make sure you wash them before freezing.

BETTER BUTTER

If you would like butterballs, set a melon baller in very hot water for five minutes, then scoop out butter from a 1-pound brick, dropping each ball in a bowl of cold water with ice cubes. Store in the refrigerator.

COCKTAIL HOUR

Always use well-chilled glasses for cocktails. If there's not enough room in the fridge or freezer to chill them for a few minutes, leave to stand with ice inside. Gin and vodka will not freeze so can be stored in the freezer.

WAX WONDER

To remove candle wax from a table or cloth, place some brown paper (not newspaper) over the top and iron it on a low heat. Avoid colored candles on white cloths: the dye is difficult to remove.

IN THE BATH

chapter 7

DESTAIN YOUR LAVATORY

To prolong cleaning effects and to avoid nasty black streaks appearing in the toilet bowl, leave half a cup of vinegar in the lavatory overnight.

LICK LIMESCALE

If your shower head is coated in mineral deposits, here's an effortless way to clean it in two hours or less. Remove and soak for a few hours in a mix of 50/50 water and humidifier cleaner. You need just enough solution to cover the face of the shower head. Rinse well and reattach.

TIME FOR A DRINK

No, not you! Rid glass shower doors and screens of stains and lime scale by wiping them over with a glass of white wine.

BLITZ BATH STAINS

White vinegar is perfect for tough, hard-to-shift stains and its disinfectant properties makes it an amazing all-round cleaner. Remove stubborn bath stains with a 1:5 solution of white vinegar and water.

FLOUR POWER

If your chrome taps (faucets) are less than sparkly, try rubbing them with flour. Rinse and buff with a soft cloth.

CITRUS SCENT

Add a couple of drops of lemon essential oil to the final rinse when cleaning baths. It kills germs and it's deliciously scented, too.

SHOWER CURTAIN PROTECTORS

Avoid leaving a shower curtain bunched up after use, especially in a small bathroom – the steam encourages mildew. If small spots of mildew appear, dab with bicarbonate of soda on a damp cloth. Wash larger areas in hot detergent, rub in lemon juice and dry in the sun, if possible.

WASH & BRUSH UP

Clear soap scum effortlessly away from shower doors by wiping them with a used (dry) dryer sheet. It gets the job done quickly.

CERAMIC CARE

Wipe ceramics regularly with a damp sponge – add a splash of vinegar to the water or use commercial cleaner. Avoid soapy or oily cleaners and never use abrasives – these dull the finish and make glazed tiles more prone to dirt.

CURTAIN CLEANSER

If your shower curtain has seen better days, wash according to the care label but add a cup each of vinegar and bleach to the machine – it will look like new. Remove curtains as soon as the cycle is complete and hang back in position to drip-dry and remove any creases.

QUICK TIPPLE

Stainless steel can be quickly and easily cleaned with vodka. Place a little on a sponge or paper towel and wipe. Your taps (faucets) will soon be sparkling again so pour yourself a glass to celebrate!

VERY VINEGAR

Use vinegar to clean your chrome faucets. The acid helps dissolve grime and brings them up to a beautiful shine. But don't try this on brass taps – or gold!

A PERFUMED BATH?

You can literally bathe in your favorite perfume by making your own scented bath oil. Just add a few drops of perfume to one-quarter of baby oil, shake well, and add to your bath.

BLUE RINSE

Cure blue-green stains on baths and showers caused by water with a high copper content with a paste of equal amounts of cream of tartar and bicarbonate of soda. Rub into the stain, leave for half an hour and rinse well with water. Repeat, if necessary.

PERFECT PORCELAIN

Steel wool and scouring powders will scratch porcelain so rub a freshly cut lemon round the surface to cut through grease and then rinse in running water. Or sprinkle with bicarbonate of soda and rub with a damp sponge. Neutralize with a rinse of vinegar or lemon juice, then rinse with running water.

GROUT-BUSTER

Rid grout of mold and mildew by soaking paper towels in bleach and placing them around the grout (make sure you wear protective gloves for this and open the window first). Leave for at least an hour if not more. Remove the towels and enjoy clean white grout.

BRIGHTEN UP

For tiles that sparkle, sprinkle baking soda, boracic acid, or borax on the surface. Scrub with a plastic mesh scrubber or sponge.

LINGERING LIMESCALE

From time to time rub taps with half a cut lemon. Leave for a few minutes and then wipe and buff dry to get rid of limescale and add a fresh scent to your bathroom.

CUT DOWN ON CLEANING

Apply mineral oil all over shower doors and tiled surfaces. This delays mineral build-up and cuts down on cleaning time.

BOWL BRIGHTENER

Use all-purpose cleaner or sprinkle borax or baking soda in the bowl. Dampen with a little water to make a paste. Scrub with a toilet brush. Alternatively, make a paste from lemon juice and borax. Leave for two hours then scrub thoroughly.

WAX IT ON

Keep your shower tiles cleaner for longer by waxing with car polish after you clean to stop grease and grime from sticking to them.

ADD SPARKLE

To brighten shower heads, soak in vinegar for 20 minutes or brush with vinegar using an old toothbrush. A solution of dish liquid will clean shower screens.

BEAT BLACK STAINS

Lick tough, black stains caused by dampness with a paste made from borax and lemon juice or vinegar. Leave for half an hour, then scrub and rinse away toilets.

MOLD & MILDEW

Moisten a cloth or an old toothbrush with vinegar. Scrub away at the tile grout to remove mildew and mold; this also prevents new growth. Or use a disinfectant solution. Avoid abrasive steel wool.

MIRROR MIRACLE

Make up a solution of equal parts of vinegar and water. Wearing rubber gloves use old newspapers to wipe the surface of the mirror with the mix. Add extra shine by rubbing with a clean blackboard eraser.

COLOR CARE

Wash sets of colored towels at the same time so they fade equally. If towels fade dramatically, return them to the store where you bought them as it is possible that they may be faulty. Use fabric softener just occasionally – too often will coat the towel, making it less absorbent.

CITRUS CLEANER

Clean ceramic tiles the green way by wiping them with the cut side of a lemon. Leave for 15 minutes then polish up with a soft, dry cloth.

DON'T MIX THEM UP!

Never use two different lavatory cleaners at the same time – they may combine to produce explosive or toxic gases. If you want to go green, use vinegar to clean your toilets and its surroundings.

WHO KNEW?

A great and inexpensive way to clean your bathtub's drain is to pour two packets of dry yeast and a pinch of salt down the drain with very hot water for 15 seconds. The yeast reproduces and expands, which breaks up stubborn grime and hair clogs and saves you from calling the plumber.

ON THE SPOT

Steam from a hot shower loosens grime so run the shower beforehand. Try cleaning with 2 ½ fl. oz. dishwasher detergent with 17 fl. oz. warm water mixed in a spray bottle. Wearing rubber gloves, spray liberally on walls then scrub with a sponge.

MAGIC AWAY MOLD

If your shower sprouts mold, wipe down the walls with a solution of 1 teaspoon water softener, 1 tablespoon ammonia and 1 tablespoon vinegar in 7 fl. oz. warm water. Rinse with fresh water and buff dry.

FRAGRANT BLAST

For a quick blast of fragrance, attach a stick-on air freshener to your ceiling fan. Turn the fan on low and you'll be amazed at how effectively the fragrance is circulated.

HERBS AND VITAMINS FOR HEALTH AND HEALING

chapter 8

REJUVENATE WITH C

This multitasking vitamin reaches every cell in the body. Known as ascorbic acid it is vital for collagen production, and as a powerful antioxidant it destroys harmful free radicals that cause premature aging.

GUARD AGAINST HAIR LOSS

Thinning hair that falls out in clumps can come about as a result of a restricted diet. Hair loss from lack of vitamins B, C and iron can be rectified with a diet rich in protein and vegetables. Packed with EFAs (essential fatty acids), flax seeds will make hair thicker and shinier.

FEED NAILS FOR GROWTH

As you age your nails grow at about half the rate they did when you were younger. Feed them by massaging a vitamin-rich oil into the base of the nails every night will encourage growth from the nail bed.

NATURALLY STRONGER

If your hair has become weaker and more brittle with a tendency to break easily, try an infusion of rosemary poured over as a final rinse to strengthen it, or massage some rosemary essential oil (mixed with a carrier oil) onto your scalp to help promote growth and strength.

WHO KNEW?

Vitamin A is a true wonder vitamin. Not only can it soothe and rejuvenate the skin, but it may actually be able to prevent sun damage. Liver, sweet potato, carrots, mangoes, spinach and milk are all great sources of Vitamin A.

GO GREEN

Ditch sweet milky tea in favor of healthy herbal teas without milk and sugar; there are lots of varieties to choose from. Not only is it full of antioxidants, green tea is thought to speed up calorie burning also.

SWALLOW IT EARLY

If you take a daily vitamin supplement, take it with breakfast rather than later in the day, as studies have shown it to be better absorbed earlier in the day. And you should always take supplements with water, which helps absorption.

STAY CALM

The most useful of vitamins for healthy skin, vitamin A has the ability to calm red and blotchy skin and is also thought to visibly reduce lines and wrinkles.

THE NATURAL PROZAC

The herbal supplement St John's Wort can help ease feelings of depression and lift black moods. It is thought to increase the activity and prolong the action of the neurotransmitters serotonin and noradrenalin in a similar way to standard antidepressants, and will need to be taken for a few weeks before it starts working.

PEPPER YOUR DISHES

Why not use a sprinkling of cayenne pepper to help season your sauces? Derived from the plant Capsicum annum, it has been reported to improve circulation and to lower cholesterol. As it's a mild stimulant, it can also be added to hot water with lemon juice as an alternative to coffee.

BREW YOUR OWN

Make yourself a herbal infusion from anise seed (Pimpinella anisum), a member of the parsley family that has a pleasant, liquorice-like flavor and is thought to improve digestion, freshen breath, calm flatulence and nausea, and help to settle coughs.

FLEXI-OIL

If you were given cod liver oil as a child without really knowing why, there is now conclusive evidence that a capsule a day can reduce pain and inflammation in joints, keeping them flexible and supple, as well as proving beneficial for healthy skin, hair and nails.

FLAKY WHITE DANDRUFF

The shiny white scales that separate from the scalp and collect on the hair and shoulders are almost always caused by an impaired general health. Increase your intake of raw foods that are high in enzymes (fruit, vegetables and nuts) and take two dessertspoons of flax oil a day until the condition improves.

SEAWEED REMEDY

To improve the thickness and condition of your hair take a daily sea kelp supplement. This broadly found seaweed comes in several varieties but all are rich in the minerals potassium, calcium, magnesium and iron.

A GOOD CUPPA TEA

Repeated exposure to a daily dose of pollution, stress, cigarette smoke and sunlight ensures we all have to cope with more than 10 million free radical hits a day. Drinking a daily mug of green or white tea can promote antioxidant activity and lower chances of free radical problems. It has also been claimed that if you dunk the tea bag up and down in the water it releases more of its antioxidant capabilities.

GO FOR GINSENG

The root of this plant, which contains ginsenocide, is used as a tonic to strengthen the immune system, increase concentration, boost energy levels and generally revitalize the whole body.

DETOX WITH LEMON

Lemon juice is a great flavor enhancer and mixed with hot water is a really healthy (and detoxifying) alternative to heavily caffeinated hot drinks. Get twice as much juice out of your lemons by heating in the oven or hot water, or by rolling until slightly soft, before squeezing.

MEASURE THE MARIGOLDS

Marigold – mainly listed on cosmetics packages as calendula – is an excellent choice for calming sore, swollen skin and contains natural anti-inflammatory properties which make it great for sensitive skins.

SEARCH OUT SELENIUM

This is a very important antioxidant that works with vitamin E to prohibit free-radical damage to the cell membrane. It is also thought to help prevent cancer, protect against heart and circulatory diseases and promote healthy eyes, skin and hair. Good natural sources include Brazil nuts, kidney, liver and wholemeal bread.

BENEFITS OF POND LIFE

Spirulina is a type of blue-green algae found in most lakes and ponds, and consumed for thousands of years by Mexican Aztecs. It is a very rich source of protein, vitamin B complex, vitamin E and zinc, and is used in many skin-care products to promote healthy skin and hair.

ZINC IT UP

When it comes to skin-boosting minerals zinc is the first choice, as it has a direct effect on the regeneration of skin from the inside out, which can help aging and problem skins. Zinc is mostly found in protein-based foods but vegetarians can find a great source in pumpkin seeds.

A SHOT OF WHEATGRASS

It may taste unusual, but a small glass of wheatgrass is packed with many essential minerals including calcium, magnesium, potassium, iron and sodium as well as vitamins A, B, C and E, all of which are needed for healthy teeth, hair and skin. It's very easy to grow on your own.

GET A FEEL FOR FENNEL

Try adding fennel to roasted vegetable dishes or salads – a member of the parsley family, fennel helps stabilize blood-sugar levels, thus curbing appetite. It also works to relax the muscles of the digestive system, reducing indigestion and wind pains.

KEEP LIVER HEALTHY WITH MILK THISTLE

This herb has lasting benefits for the liver. Trials have proved it can prevent and heal damage to this vital organ and that it also has a significant effect on cirrhosis and chronic hepatitis.

GET CALM WITH MAGNOLIA

A supplement made from magnolia bark extract has been found to relieve anxiety, calm nerves, ward off stress and boost the metabolism. Taken on a regular basis it is believed to lift your mood and general well-being as well as lower levels of cortisol (the stress hormone). High cortisol levels can compromise the immune system and lead to loss of vitality, weight gain and high blood pressure.

ENERGIZE YOUR BODY

A good healthy diet is the single most important way of boosting energy levels. Deficiencies in B vitamins can often be the underlying cause of poor adrenal gland function, which is responsible for energy slumps. Take ginseng and astragalus tea as an afternoon pick-me-up.

DULL HIGHLIGHTS

In between trips to the salon, perk up dull highlights by using a color-enhancing treatment, or adding vitamin E oil capsules to your weekly hair mask, to brighten color and add shine.

HORSE CHESTNUT BENEFITS

Available in creams, tablets and capsules at health food stores and pharmacies, the seeds have long been used as a treatment for varicose veins and hemorrhoids. The horse chestnut contains eosin, which may help lessen the appearance of cellulite by toning the capillaries below the skin.

NOD OFF NATURALLY

The herb valerian has been used in traditional sleep remedies for hundreds of years. It is thought to relieve anxiety and to aid the induction of sleep in a natural and non-addictive way.

IMPROVE MOOD WITH SELENIUM

When US Department of Agriculture (USDA) researchers fed young men a diet that contained 220 mcg of the mineral selenium per day (the average American diet has 40 to 60 mcg), the men reported feeling elated, clearheaded, confident and energetic.

STAY STRONG WITH VITAMIN D

An essential vitamin that requires synthesis from sunlight to turn it into an active form, vitamin D can help with back pain and aching joints, and slow the progression of osteoporosis. It is found in milk and fish such as salmon and sardines so include plenty of these in your diet.

REMEMBER REMEMBER

Scientific analysis has found that the chemicals found in ginkgo bilboa include flavonoids and terpenoids, which mop up free radicals and reduce blood clotting and inflammation. Devotees believe this extract of the maidenhair tree improves memory and concentration.

WHO KNEW?

The right essential oils can help to relieve tension and de-stress. Try lavender, chamomile, geranium, spearmint and peppermint, either added to your bath water for a relaxing soak, or inhaled by placing a few drops on a cotton wool pad.

FRIDGE AND FREEZER FACTS

chapter

9

Does anything stain your plastic storage containers worse than tomato sauce? I think not. Just spray the container with non-stick cooking spray before pouring in the sauce and stains are a thing of the past.

FOOD PRESERVATION

Food can be preserved only if the microorganisms that cause spoilage are destroyed or their growth is controlled. There are a number of methods for doing this: drying, dehydrating, salting, smoking, irradiating, heating, freezing, and using chemical preservatives.

The microorganisms that cause food spoilage are in the water, in the air, and on preparation and storage surfaces. They may be brought home on other foods and may even be in the product itself. In many cases, the contamination is a natural occurrence, such as when salmonella is present in the chicken ovaries. Microorganisms can exist in two forms: First, in colonies that are visible to the naked eye, such as molds on bread, cheese, or fruits and vegetables; second, in small spores that are carried in the air and are for the most part invisible.

- Molds are usually airborne spores or seeds that may alight on food products and start to multiply. They tend to send out feelers or filaments and grow in colonies that may appear in many colors, depending on their food source. Mold spores will move from one food to another, especially among fruits, so it is wise to check all your produce when you bring it home to be sure it is mold-free.
- Yeast is a one-celled fungus that produces enzymes that convert sugars to alcohol and carbon dioxide in a process called fermentation.
- Bacteria are microscopic organisms that need only a small amount of organic material and moisture to grow and multiply. They grow by dividing their cells. When there is no moisture, or if the available moisture is used up, all of these microorganisms will stop growing, and they will dry up and become dormant until moisture is again introduced.

ZERO. GOT IT?

Freezer temperature is critical for maintaining quality of foods. Keep your freezer set at 0°F.

CAN'T FREEZE EVERYTHING

You can freeze any food except canned or preserved food or whole eggs. Some foods, however, do not freeze well. High-fat dairy products like cream and mayonnaise tend to separate when defrosted, and high-water content vegetables such as lettuce and cucumber will go soggy.

THE TIGHTER THE BETTER

The longer a food is frozen, the more nutrients it will lose. Seal all foods to be frozen as tightly as possible to avoid freezer burn and the formation of ice crystals. Ice crystals cause thawed food to become mushy.

TRAVELING WITH FOOD

Transport food in an ice-filled cooler and inside an air-conditioned car, if you're driving, not the trunk. Throw away food that's been in the cooler for more than an hour.

KEEP THESE OUT OF THE COLD

A number of foods, including garlic, onions, shallots, potatoes, and tomatoes, should never be refrigerated because the cold will cause sprouting, loss of flavor, or conversion of their starch to sugar. Garlic, onions, shallots, and potatoes should all be stored in a cool, dark place; tomatoes should be stored at room temperature.

THAWED AND READY TO EAT

If you freeze a sandwich the night before and remove it from the freezer in the morning, it will thaw by lunchtime. (For safety, pack your sandwich in an insulated bag.) If the bread is buttered before freezing, it will not become soggy or absorb any filling. Do not freeze sandwiches that contain jelly, salad dressing, or mayonnaise.

NEGATIVE EFFECTS OF FREEZING FOODS

When food is frozen, ice crystals form and grow, puncturing the cells of the food and absorbing the water; when the food thaws, water that had been in the food is released from the ice crystals. This is the result of osmosis, the process by which a liquid passes through a semi permeable membrane (cell wall) in order to equalize the pressure inside and outside the cell. This occurs in all foods regardless of the method of freezing or the type of wrap. Because the flavor of the food is distributed among all the cells, this causes some of the flavor to be lost. Meats, fruits, and most seafood are more negatively affected by osmosis than are vegetables.

WHO KNEW?

Always fill all the spots in your cupcake tin before baking. If you don't have enough batter, pour 2 tablespoons of water in the unfilled spots. It will extend the life of the tin.

FUN FREEZING FACTS TO KNOW AND SHARE

There are a number of important facts you should know if you wish to freeze foods successfully:

- When preparing most vegetables for freezing, be sure they are blanched, or briefly steamed or boiled. This will lessen the enzymatic activity in the vegetable, and reheating will complete the cooking.

- After blanching, vegetables should be plunged into ice water and drained before freezing.

- Vegetables such as pumpkins, winter squash, and sweet potatoes should be fully cooked before freezing.

- Freezing tends to intensify the flavors of certain foods, such as garlic, peppers, and cloves. Use less in a dish that you will freeze, and when reheating, taste and add more as needed. On the other hand, use more onion than you would otherwise, because freezing tends to cause onion to lose its flavor. Herbs and salt also tend to diminish in flavor, so it's best to add them after freezing, when you're reheating the dish.

- Never use quick-cooking rice in a dish that will be frozen, as it becomes mushy when reheated. Use regular or converted rice.

- Artificial flavorings and sweeteners do not freeze well.

- Don't add toppings to dishes to be frozen; add when serving.

- Freezing causes russet or Idaho potatoes to fall apart; always use red-skinned or potatoes with waxy flesh in dishes that are to be frozen.

- Avoid freezing sauces. Egg-based sauces and those high in fat tend to separate when reheated, and cheese- or milk-based sauces are prone to curdling. Most gravies will thicken considerably when frozen, but they can be thinned when reheated.

- Cool already-cooked foods in the refrigerator before freezing.

WHO KNEW?

Insert paper plates between fine china plates before stacking to prevent scratches.

BLANCH OR STEAM, THEN FREEZE

The enzymes in vegetables, even those previously stored under refrigeration, may remain active and cause changes in the color, texture, and taste when they are frozen. To prevent this from happening, blanch or steam them briefly. The vegetables will not be cooked, but the enzymes will be inactivated. Of course, the enzymes are also important nutrients, and it is always desirable to eat fresh rather than frozen vegetables.

ODOR FREE

One of the best ways to eliminate odors from your refrigerator is to hollow out a grapefruit or orange and fill it with salt, and place in the back of the fridge. Leave it there until the salt gets completely damp, and then throw it out (the fruit, too) and replace.

FILL THE FREEZER

A full freezer works more efficiently than a half-full freezer because the cold in the foods themselves will help to maintain the temperature, saving you considerable money in electricity.

A BUNCH OF BROCCOLI

Broccoli will keep for a couple of weeks if you store it like a bouquet of flowers in the fridge – cut about an inch off the stem and submerge the stem in a bowl or tub of water. Change the water every couple of days and if the base of the stem seems a little slimy, snip the ends off. Broccoli can also be kept in a plastic bag.

AND IT MIGHT JUST STUNT YOUR GROWTH, TOO

The use of smoke to cure foods is one of the oldest methods of preservation, but one that provides a number of risks because of the toxins that may be introduced into the food from the smoke. Smoke may contain as many as 200 different chemical components, including alcohols, acids, phenolic compounds, pyrobenzines, and other carcinogenic chemicals. Many of these toxins are, in fact, the very substances that retard microbial growth, which is why smoking works as a method of preservation. Salt-curing and smoking are frequently used in combination to minimize the oxidation of fats that causes foods to turn rancid. Eaten in moderation, smoked foods should not present problems, but they should never be the mainstay of your diet.

MARGARINE STORAGE

Inside the fridge, margarine quickly absorbs odors from other foods. It should be tightly sealed and will keep 4 to 5 months in the refrigerator or for one year frozen at 0°F.

Freezer Storage Times for Meats at 0°F			
MEAT	MONTHS	MEAT	MONTHS
Bacon, sliced	1	Hot dogs	2
Bacon, unsliced	1	Organ meats	1–2
Beef, roasts	9	Pork, chops	6–9
Beef, steaks	9	Pork, ribs	6–9
Cold cuts	1	Pork, roasts	9
Duck	4–6	Poultry, parts	6–9
Fish, fatty	3	Poultry, whole	6–12
Fish, lean	6	Rabbit	6–9
Goose	4–6	Sausage	2
Ground beef	2–3	Shrimp or shellfish	4–6
Ground pork	2–3	Turkey, whole	6–12
Ham	3	Turkey, parts	3–6

COLD FACTS

- If ice cream thaws it should not be refrozen; bacterial growth is possible if it is.
- Jelly, salad dressing, and mayonnaise do not freeze well.
- The freezer in your refrigerator is not the same as a supermarket freezer.
- The home freezer is best for storing foods for short periods only.
- Foods should be cooled as quickly as possible, and then frozen. This prevents bacterial growth.
- Potatoes in stews or casseroles become mushy when frozen because their cells have a high water content and tend to break down easily. Mashed potatoes, however, freeze well.
- Do not freeze any bakery item with a cream filling because it will become soggy.
- Custard and meringue pies do not freeze well. The custard tends to separate and the meringue becomes tough.
- Waffles and pancakes may be frozen, thawed, and reheated in the toaster.

WHO KNEW?

If your plastic storage containers smell of garlic or onions, wash throughly, and stuff crumpled newspaper before snapping on the lid. In a few days, the smell will be gone.

SEPARATE DRAWERS

Store fruits and vegetables in separate drawers in your fridge. Even when chilled, fruits give off ethylene gas that shortens the shelf life of other fruit and vegetables by causing them to ripen more quickly.

NO NEED TO CRY

Many people object to chopping onions because it makes them cry. Put a stop to regular tears by preparing 20 or so onions at a time – peel and chop them all, then freeze in a plastic bag. Be aware, though, that they may soften and lose a little of their flavor in freezing.

WHO KNEW?

If you're storing cucumber in your fridge and want it to stay fresh, keep it away from apples and tomatoes, which will shorten its life. Cucumber stays fresh for up to a week, then the water content starts to drop.

FREEZER FACE-OFF

The chest freezer, even though its door may be larger that of an upright freezer, will retain its cold setting longer when the door is opened because cold air is heavier than hot air and tends to stay put when the door opens up. The upright freezer tends to release most of its cold air the minute the door is opened.

THE OTHER HALF

If you've used half an eggplant and want to keep the other half fresh, put it in a sealed plastic bag in the fridge and rub the cut side with lemon juice to stop it from browning. Make sure it's kept airtight and it should stay fresh for a couple of days.

WHO KNEW?

To slice meat or poultry thinly, freeze it slightly beforehand and it will cut more easily.

FROST IN TRANSITION

Here's a handy tip for freezing a frosted cake: Put it in the freezer without any wrapping until the frosting has frozen, then cover it in freezer wrap or plastic. This way, the frosting won't stick to the wrapping.

GET OFF YOUR METAL

Don't store food in tin or aluminum cans in the fridge or cupboard as the air can cause metal ions to spread into food (unless they are designed for repeated use, such as with golden syrup). If you only want to use half a can, empty the rest into a bowl or other food container and dispose of or recycle the can straight away.

IS IT TIME TO CLEAN OUT THE REFRIGERATOR?

Don't use chemicals that can linger on your food and produce nasty odors. After emptying the fridge, simply mix a cup of salt in a gallon of hot water and wipe away. Squeeze in the juice of a lemon for a nice scent.

CRISP AND CRUNCH

If you're serving salad in a metal bowl, place it in the freezer for a minute beforehand to make it crisp. Also, never salt your salad until just before serving—it wilts and toughens your greens.

SEAL IT

The longer you leave a fridge door open, the more it will warm up inside. To prevent mold forming on door seals, wipe over from time to time with white vinegar.

ELIMINATE FREEZER BURN FOREVER!

Simply cover the top of your ice cream container with a piece of aluminum foil and place the lid on top. The foil eliminates the moisture that causes the ice to form.

WHO KNEW?

The best way to make sure you don't waste eggs, especially if you cook or bake a lot, is to separate the eggs and freeze whites and yolks separately in a lightly oiled ice-cube tray. When frozen, pop them out and store in separate ziplock bags in the freezer.

HERBAL REMEDY

Place chopped fresh herbs in ice-cube trays. Fill the trays with water and then freeze and use as much as you want in sauces and stews.

ICE IN SOME FLAVOR

Don't worry that freezing your meals will harm them or lessen the flavor – in fact, for dishes such as lasagne and stews freezing can be beneficial as it increases the diffusion of antioxidant-rich herbs and spices.

KEEP YOUR ONIONS

Yellow and brown onions can be kept for a longer time than red ones, as they have a lower sugar content. Store in an open space that's cool and dry, and away from bright light, which can make them bitter. Don't store under the sink or anywhere that may be damp.

BULK UP YOUR BACON

Bacon is a great protein-filled snack, but the mess it creates in the kitchen can put people off cooking it. Try buying in bulk, cooking, cooling, and then freezing. When you want a snack, you can simply microwave a few rashers.

PACK IN THE BOX!

Storing any sort of bread in the refrigerator will dry it out. It's best to place it in an airtight plastic container, and leave at room temperature or freeze it.

FROZEN 'IN TIME'

Cooked wild rice only lasts a week or so in the refrigerator, but four months in the freezer.

ECO-CLEAN

Clean the condenser coils on your refrigerator twice a year, and you'll use less energy while increasing the life of the appliance as well. It's important also to keep your freezer packed—even with bags of ice blocks if necessary—because a full freezer in much more efficient than one which is half empty.

THE ICE TRICK

When you go away on vacation, fill a zip-close plastic bag with a few ice cubes and put it in the freezer. If a power failure occurs while you are away, the ice will melt and refreeze in a solid block, alerting you that your frozen food has been defrosted.

BREAK THE ICE

To defrost a freezer, unplug and place bowls of hot, not boiling, water inside. Use a wooden spoon to scrape ice away. Remove stains with neat bicarbonate of soda on a damp cloth. Wipe clean and dry.

AS NICE AS ICE

The next time you need a quick ice pack, just grab a bag of frozen vegetables from your freezer. It does the trick, and won't leak like a bag filled with ice cubes.

FRIDGE HYGIENE

Store cooked foods above uncooked ones in your fridge. This minimizes the risk of food poisoning caused by drips from uncooked foods. Wrap any food with strong odors and avoid storing them close to dairy foods that may taint. And throw away that slimy lettuce at the back or it could contaminate other foods!

WHO KNEW?

Tupperware stains can be bleached out by strong sunlight. In the summer, put your Tupperware in the garden and leave for several hours in the sun. Alternatively, to remove red stains, apply mustard overnight and then wash well.

COOK IT THROUGH

Contrary to popular belief, freezing doesn't actually kill bacteria or other food microbes, but what it does do is put them in a dormant state so they won't be active or reproducing until the food is thawed again. This is why it's important to cook food thoroughly after defrosting.

FROZEN FOOD CAN BE GOOD FOR YOU

Frozen berries are filled with just as many healthy antioxidants as fresh ones, and in winter they are an excellent source of vitamin C as well as containing small amounts of vitamin A and calcium.

DON'T REPEAT THE REHEAT

If you defrost raw meat and then cook it thoroughly, you can freeze it again, but remember you should never reheat foods more than once. If you want to use a bulky sauce like Bolognese for several meals, reheat individual portions as and when you need them rather than the whole pot.

FROST FRIGHT

Ice cube trays won't stick to your freezer if you place them on a sheet of waxed paper first. And for crystal clear ice cubes, always boil the water first before making the cubes.

RAISE A GLASS

To prevent glasses becoming dusty, place them upside down on shelves. Arrange in order of size so they are easier to find and also to avoid breakages.

GRAPE FULL

Store your grapes in the coldest part of the fridge in a plastic bag. Make sure you wash them well before you serve them to avoid pesticide residues and other toxins, but don't wash them before you refrigerate as this can cause them to rot.

FROSTING "OVER"

Next time you defrost your freezer, make sure you spray it with a thin layer of cooling oil afterwards. That will prevent it from frosting over in the future.

MAKE MINE A DOUBLE

If you are going to freeze any food that has alcohol in it, such as an ice cream or sorbet, remember that alcohol will not freeze like water, and the food may need to be frozen at a lower temperature.

DON'T COVER STRAWBERRIES

The moisture content of fresh strawberries is high, so store them uncovered or loosely covered – since covering the berries can cause them to rot, even when refrigerated.

THEN PUSH THE KIDS OUT THE DOOR

If you don't want to freeze a sandwich, freeze a juice box and pack it in your lunch bag. It will act as an ice pack to keep foods cold but should thaw by lunchtime.

DIRTY AT THE TOP

If the top of your refrigerator is a grimy mess, consider this: After cleaning, just lay an old place-mat on top of it.

FISH FOR SAFETY

Seafood is responsible for a lot of food poisoning, but it's perfectly safe and very healthy if treated correctly. If you can't use it immediately, remove it from its original wrapping and rinse in cold water. Wrap loosely in plastic wrap, store in the coldest part of the refrigerator, and use within 2 days. Store ready-to-eat fish such as smoked mackerel separately from raw fish.

SURF & TURF TIPS

chapter **10**

WHO KNEW?

Always use tongs when turning meat on the grill. A fork will pierce the meat and release some of its natural juices.

ABOUT E. COLI

In the last few years, E. coli has been in the news a lot. E. coli is a bacterium that normally lives in the human intestine, but the fearsome strain, known as E. coli 0157:H7, can pass from contaminated feces to meat during processing; people can also become infected from improperly handled animal or human waste. This strain is capable of causing severe illness or even death.

The bacteria, however, is normally found on the surface of meat, and is killed by searing or cooking it on both sides. When you cook a steak or a roast, the meat is normally cooked on all sides and the risk is eliminated, even if you are eating it at 145°F, or medium-rare.

There is a more significant risk associated with eating ground or raw meat dishes such as hamburgers or steak tartare. Because hamburger is ground beef, any bacteria present on the surface of the meat is mixed in during the grinding process, and if the ground meat is not cooked to an internal temperature of at least 165°F, the bacteria will still be present on the inside.

USDA MEAT GRADING SYSTEM

The United States Department of Agriculture regulates the terms used to describe meat. Only the first three below are retailed. They are:

Prime

Very tender due to higher fat content, well marbled, most expensive. Almost never available in supermarkets—it goes primarily to high-end restaurants and butcher shops.

Choice

Relatively tender and fairly expensive. Meat of this grade is becoming harder to find in supermarkets.

Select

Relatively inexpensive and, therefore, the grade most commonly found in supermarkets. Has less fat and may need some tenderizing.

Commercial

Tougher beef from older cattle. It is mainly used in low-cost frozen dinners and canned-meat products.

Utility, Cutter, and Canner

Usually leftover bits and pieces, used in processed-meat products. Meat of this grade may be very tough.

INSIDE A COW

There are eight major cuts of beef butchered in the United States. They are shank, flank, brisket, chuck, round, rib, plate, and loin. The eight cuts are given a number of additional names that are more recognizable to most consumers. These include sirloin, porterhouse, top round, eye of round, New York, T-bone, and so on, and they are used to explain the way each of the eight major cuts is actually cut up. The tenderness of beef will depend on the location of the cut and the method of cutting. The tougher cuts are taken from the muscles that do more work—neck, shoulder, brisket, and flank—and are also the least expensive.

Brisket Cuts

The brisket is cut from behind a cow's front leg, or it may be cut from the leg itself. Normally a tough cut, brisket should be cooked in liquid for about two to three hours.

Chuck Cuts (Roasts)

These are the toughest cuts. They come from the shoulder. Chuck cuts may need tenderizing and should be braised—that is, cooked over gentle heat in a small amount of liquid.

THE HUBBUB ABOUT RUBS

Applying a rub is a common method of seasoning the surface of meats and poultry. A rub is simply a blend of various herbs and spices that do not penetrate the meat. The rub never blends with the flavor of the meat itself, but it does provide a tasty coating, which usually forms a brown crust of concentrated flavor. Rub on the seasoning before you begin to cook the meat, and let it sit awhile for the coating to take hold.

Flank and Plate Cuts

Most of the time, if the grade is USDA Select, the cuts need to be tenderized. Choice is a much better grade. These cuts are from the abdomen; they are usually sliced in strips and used for stir-frying or stew.

Loin Cuts (Tenderloin)

Cut from behind the ribs, these are the tenderest cuts. They include filet mignon (steaks), fillet of beef (the entire roasts), porterhouse, and New York strip steaks. The loin includes short loin and sirloin.

Rib Cuts (Ribs)

Markets may label these rib steaks, rib roasts, or simply back ribs. For best results, they should be barbecued or cooked slowly in the oven. Adding a sauce or using a marinade can improve the taste.

Round Cuts (Roasts)

Most round cuts are tender and can be cooked in a number of different ways. They include top round, eye of the round, and bottom round. Round cuts can be pot-roasted or spit barbecued.

FAT FREE-FOR-ALL

Beware of the wording on meat packages. If the steak packaging reads "lean," the beef cannot have more than 10 percent fat; "extra lean" cannot have more than 5 percent fat. (Virtually the only red meat with a fat content this low is bison.) "Lean" ground beef is allowed to have as much as 22.5 percent fat by weight.

WHO KNEW?

All meat should stand at room temperature (except organ meats and ground beef) for a few minutes before cooking. This allows it to brown more evenly, cook quicker, and stick less when frying.

BARBECUE SOS

You can actually tenderise tough meat with baking soda. Yep, just rub baking soda all over the meat, refrigerate for a few hours, and rinse well before cooking. For extra tenderising, cover the meat in a sliced kiwi also.

EASY-GREASY

If you wet your hands with cold water before shaping sausage patties, the grease won't stick to your fingers.

MAKING THE GRADE

Lamb is graded Prime, Choice, Utility, or Cull. Prime is sold almost exclusively to restaurants.

FELL FACTS

The fell is a thin, parchment-like membrane that covers the fat on a lamb. It is usually removed from certain cuts, such as lamb chops, before they are marketed, but it is usually left on the larger cuts so they will maintain their shape and retain their juices.

AND THEY SEEMED LIKE SUCH NICE PEOPLE

Supermarkets are using their own wording on meat packages to make you think the meat you are buying is a better grade than it really is. Most of the major chains are buying more Select-grade beef but may call it by a number of fancy names such as "top premium beef," "prime quality cut," "select choice," "market choice," or "premium cut."

WHO KNEW?

The fastest way to make meatballs is to shape the meat mixture into a log and then cut off slices, which then rolls easily into balls.

MEAT MARKET PRIMER

When purchasing a chuck roast, look for the white cartilage near the top of the roast. If you can spot a roast with cartilage showing, you have found the first cut, which will be the most tender. When purchasing an eye of round roast, look for the one that is the same size on both ends; it will be the most tender. When selecting a round steak, however, you should know that the uneven cuts are the ones closest to the sirloin.

IT MAKES SENSE, RIGHT?

When purchasing meats, you should figure the cost per pound and realize that boneless cuts usually cost less per serving. The reason? Because the bone itself contributes weight but not edible meat.

LOOKING GOOD FOR YOUR AGE

Aging allows time for the enzymes in meat to soften the connective tissue so the meat becomes tender. When aging beef, the temperature must be kept between 34°F and 38°F. The meat should not be frozen, because freezing would inactivate the enzymes; too high a temperature, on the other hand, would cause bacterial growth.

LOW-FAT AND DISGUSTING

If you have ever wondered where sweetbreads come from, they are the thymus glands of veal, lamb, and pork. The gland assists young animals in fighting disease, and then atrophies and disappears when they are about six months old. Sweetbreads are a low-fat food, with 3 ounces containing about 2.1 grams, or 19 calories from fat.

IT REALLY WORKS

When storing a cooked roast, place it back into its own juices whenever possible. When reheating sliced meat, try placing it in a casserole dish with lettuce leaves between the slices. The lettuce provides just the right amount of moisture to keep the slices from drying out.

TODAY'S GROSS FACT

Beef and veal kidneys have more than one lobe; lamb and pork kidneys have only one. Kidneys should be firm, not mushy, and pale in color. Before you cook them, be sure to remove the excess fat and membranes.

LOW-PROTEIN DOGS

One of the worst sources of animal protein is from hot dogs. A 3-ounce serving (or about two hot dogs from a 10-per-pound package) contains less protein than an equal weight of any other type of meat. Legally, hot dogs may contain no more than 10 percent water, or a combination of 40 percent fat and added water. If they are labeled "with by-products" or "with variety meats," the hot dogs may consist of not less than 15 percent raw meat by-products like heart, kidney, or liver; these must be named individually in the ingredients label. As much as 3.5 percent of the hot dog may be nonmeat binders and extenders, such as powdered milk, cereal, or isolated soy protein; these too must be named on the ingredients label. Sugar is a very common ingredient in hot dogs but may not be named as such. It may be listed on the label as corn syrup.

AND IT MAKES CLEANUP EASIER, TOO

Roasts will never stick to the bottom of the pan if you just place a few stalks of fresh celery under the meat. This also works well with poultry.

SPRUCING IT UP

When preparing a fatty-looking roast, cut off as much fat as possible before roasting. Be sure to cook the roast on a rack or on thickly sliced vegetables to keep it out of any fat that renders from the meat.

AND WHO WANTS DRIED OUT MEAT LOAF?

When you are preparing meat loaf, try rubbing the top and sides with a small amount of water instead of tomato sauce. This will stop the meat loaf from cracking and drying out as it cooks. The tomato sauce can be added 15 minutes before the meat is fully cooked.

KEEP YOUR MEAT WARM: WORDS TO LIVE BY

Meat gets tougher as it cools on your plate, because the collagen, which has turned to a tender gelatin, thickens. The best way to eliminate this problem is to be sure you serve steak on a warmed or metal plate. After carving a roast, keep it in a warmer or put it back in the oven and leave the door ajar.

KEEP YOUR RIBS COLD

Ribs should always be marinated (in the refrigerator, never on the counter) before cooking. A ready-made barbecue sauce sold at the grocery store works just fine for this. For tender, fall-off-the-bone ribs, be sure to cook them a long time over low heat.

MAKES SENSE

When boiling hot dogs, use a double boiler, and put your hot dog buns in the top to keep them warm.

IS THAT WHAT THEY CALL 'WATER WEIGHT?'

Cured hams are injected with a solution of brine salts, sugar, and nitrites. The weight of the ham will increase with the injection, and if the total weight goes up by 8 percent, the label is able to claim "ham with natural juices." If the weight of the ham increases by more than 10 percent, the label must read "water added."

HAM BONE CONNECTED TO THE ...

To remove a ham bone in an easier way, slit the ham lengthwise down to the bone before placing it in the pan—but leave the bone in the ham. While the ham is baking, the meat will pull away and the bone will come out easily after the ham is cooked.

THIN IS IN

If you want thin ham slices, place the ham in the freezer
for about 20 minutes before you begin slicing.

DESALT HAM WITH GINGER ALE

Because ham is naturally salty, pour a can of ginger ale over it,
and then rub the meaty side with salt at least an hour before
baking it. This will cause the salt water in the meat to come to
the surface, which in the process will reduce the saltiness of
the ham.

MAKIN' BACON

Bacon, like all cured meats, is very high in nitrites. The highest nitrite content is found in the fat,
which means you should choose the leanest bacon you can find.

- Bacon can be prepared in the microwave on a piece of paper towel or under the broiler so the
  fat drips down.

- When you are shopping for a bacon substitute, remember that almost all of these products will
  still contain nitrites. Check the label, and try to find a nitrite-free product.

- Once the package is opened, sliced bacon can be kept in the refrigerator for only one week.

- Never buy bacon that looks slimy; chances are it's not fresh.

LET IT SIT

Stews are usually best prepared a day in advance to allow the flavors to blend—or, as the romantic French say, marry.

NOT THAT YOU'VE EVER BURNT A ROAST

When you burn or scorch a roast, remove it from the pan and cover it with a towel dampened with hot water for about five minutes; this will stop the cooking. Then remove or scrape off any burnt areas with a sharp knife, and put the roast back in the oven to reheat.

HOW REVOLTING

If you're going to buy a canned ham, purchase the largest one you can afford. Most smaller canned hams are made from bits and pieces glued together with gelatin.

SPREAD OUT

Meats may turn grayish in color if they are cooked in too small a pot. Overcrowding tends to generate excess steam—so, for a nice brown crust, give your meat some room to breathe.

SO FORGET ABOUT FREEZING

When any type of fat-containing meat or lunchmeat is refrozen, the fat content may cause the food to become rancid. And this is only one reason why meats should not be refrozen. (In case you need other reasons, the texture of the meat can suffer, and improper thawing can promote bacterial growth.) Leftover cooked meats can be refrigerated safely for four days.

WHO KNEW?

Keep sausages from splitting when cooking them by piercing the skin in one or two places while they are cooking. Rolling them in flour before cooking will reduce shrinkage.

HOW VEAL IS PRODUCED

Veal comes from calves that have been fed a special diet from the day they are weaned until they are slaughtered, which is usually when they are between 16 and 18 weeks old and weigh about 450 pounds. The animals are kept in stalls and are not allowed to exercise, and are fed either with a special milk formula (for milk-fed veal) or one consisting of water, milk solids, fats, and special nutrients for growth. When the calves are about three to four months old, the texture of the meat is perfect for tender veal. The most desirable is the milk-fed veal at three months old. However, the second formula has now become more popular because it produces a calf that is larger at four months, thus providing more meat. Veal is tender and contains about the same amount of fat as beef, though it has more cholesterol. By law, veal producers cannot use hormones.

MORE BAD NEWS

Any type of beef consumed in large quantities may inhibit the absorption of the mineral manganese. This increases the chances of the body losing calcium through the urine—and that's bad for the bones.

SHANKS FOR THE TIP

When purchasing a lamb shank, be sure it weighs at least 3 to 4 pounds. If the shank is any smaller, the percentage of bone will be too high in relation to the amount of meat.

WHO KNEW?

Lamb from New Zealand is best because it is never treated with hormones. Always buy a small leg of lamb because larger legs come from older animals and have a stronger flavor.

IS A RARE STEAK REALLY BLOODY?

No! The blood is drained at slaughterhouses and hardly any ever remains in the meat. There is a pigment called myoglobin in the muscles of all meat that contributes to its reddish color, while blood obtains its color from hemoglobin. Those red juices are for the most part colored by myoglobin, not hemoglobin. For example, beef is redder than pork, because it contains more myoglobin.

TIMING ROASTS

Don't have a roasting chart nearby? Then follow this rule of thumb: Beef roasts will take about 20 minutes for the first pound and about 15 minutes for every pound thereafter. The USDA recommends cooking beef to an internal temperature of at least 145°F.

PRESS FOR DONENESS

An experienced chef rarely uses a thermometer when cooking a steak. Meat has a certain resiliency, and the experienced chef can just press the steak with a finger to tell whether the meat is rare, medium-rare, medium, medium-well, or well done. As meat cooks it loses water, and the more it cooks, the firmer it becomes.

SORRY TO BE SUCH A BUZZKILL

While undercooked burgers may pose a risk of E. coli poisoning, well-done burgers may pose the risk of a potentially harmful carcinogen called heterocyclic aromatic amine (HAA). This compound is formed when meat is cooked to high temperatures. To avoid HAA, try these tips:

- Choose lean cuts of beef. Ask the butcher to remove all the fat from around the edges and put it through the meat grinder twice to break up the remaining fat. Sizzling fat creates smoke, which creates HAA.
- Place the ground beef in a microwave oven on high power for 1 to 3 minutes just before you cook it. HAAs form when browning occurs, and meat that is precooked before going onto the grill reduces the amount of time HAAs have to form.
- Reduce the amount of meat in your burgers by adding mashed black beans or cooked rice and you will have a safer—not to mention delicious—medium-well burger.

FOR A JUICY STEAK

Some backyard cooks think that searing a steak at a high temperature will keep the juices in. Nonsense. Searing *does* cause the browning that creates a good flavor, but it doesn't seal in the juices. A steak cooked slowly and at a lower temperature is more tender and retains more of its juices.

FREEZER FACTS

Chicken has a shorter freezer life than does beef because it has a higher ratio of unsaturated to saturated fat. Unsaturated fats are more easily destroyed by oxidation and thus are more likely to turn rancid. This is because there are more hydrogen sites in unsaturated fat to which oxygen can attach. Beef is high in saturated fat and has almost no open sites.

FOR THE LIVER LOVER

An animal's liver acts as a filtration plant for the body, and toxins may concentrate in its cells. These may include pesticides and heavy metals, depending on the animal's diet. Liver is also extremely high in cholesterol. A 3.5-ounce serving of beef liver contains 390 milligrams of cholesterol, compared with 95 milligrams in an equal amount of hamburger.

GREAT HAMBURGER TIPS

If you are preparing hamburger or meat loaf with very low-fat meat, mix in one well-beaten egg white for every pound of meat. Also, adding a package of instant onion-soup mix will really make a difference. Putting a bit of small-curd cottage cheese or instant potatoes in the center of a meat loaf will keep the meat moist and provide an interesting taste treat.

WHAT WOULD BUGS BUNNY SAY?

The rabbit meat that is from domesticated animals and sold in American markets is all white; this is because the rabbits don't get much time to exercise. European rabbit meat is tougher, because the animals are not farm-raised and get plenty of exercise.

DON'T DITCH THE FAT

It might sound counter-intuitive, but buying fattier meat can actually help you take smaller portions, because (as long as you cut off the fat on your plate) you are likely to eat less. Also, fattier meat generally has a better taste, so it will be more satisfying.

BEEF UP THE DARK

The best-tasting beef should be a dark red color with slightly yellowish fat. If the fat is too white or the meat is bright red, the beef hasn't been hung for long enough and will be lower on taste and tougher. It's better if there's some fat marbled throughout, as this makes it more tender.

ROOM TEMPERATURE HAM

Many times you will see hams on the shelves in the market rather than in the refrigerator case. These hams are actually salt-cured hams, sometimes called country hams. They may have a layer of mold on the skin, which can be scraped off. Salt-cured hams need to soak in water for several hours, and then must be simmered for several more, before being baked. They are much saltier than brine-cured hams and are something of an acquired taste, though their devotees think they're heavenly.

IT WILL ALWAYS BE RED

After ham is cured, it contains nitrite salt. This chemical reacts with the myoglobin in the tissue and changes it into nitrosomyoglobin. This biochemical alteration keeps the meat reddish even when it is cooked on a higher temperature.

A CURE FOR SPLATTERING BACON

If bacon were still produced the old-fashioned way, by curing it slowly and using a dry salt, it would not splatter when cooked. Today's bacon is cured in brine, which speeds up the curing process. The additional liquid from the brine gets released when the bacon is cooked, causing the fat to splatter more. To reduce splattering, use a low heat setting. This will also reduce the number of nitrites that convert into carcinogens, because high heat tends to convert the nitrites faster than does lower heat. You can also soak the bacon in ice-cold water for 2 to 4 minutes, and then dry it well with paper towels before frying it. Also, try sprinkling the bacon with a bit of flour before cooking it, or just put a splatter screen over the pan.

BEEF IT UP

When shopping for beef, choose sirloin or topside as they are the leanest cuts. Sirloin has only 3.8 g fat per 100 g serving and topside 5.2 g, compared to 24.1 g fat for minced (ground) beef. Spend the same amount of money – just buy less of the leaner, more expensive cuts.

INTERNAL TEMPERATURE AND THE COLOR OF MEAT

While you are cooking beef, you can see the color of the meat change: The red pigment myoglobin changes from bright red in a rare steak to brown in a well-done one. The internal temperature of a rare steak is 135°F, medium-rare is 145°F, medium is 160°F, and well done is 170°F.

What is Our Food Composed of?			
MEAT	% WATER	% PROTEIN	% FAT
Beef	60	18	22
Chicken	65	30	5
Fish	70	20	10
Lamb	56	16	28
Pork	42	12	45
Turkey	58	20	20

A SPEEDY SOLUTION

When you are grilling for a crowd and your grill isn't big enough, you can save time by placing a few layers of hamburgers between sheets of foil on a cookie sheet and baking them at 350°F for 15 minutes. You can then finish baking them in only five to 10 minutes. Hot dogs may be done the same way, but bake them only for 10 minutes.

PEE-YEW

The surface of meat can become contaminated with bacteria, spores, and mold because of poor sanitary conditions where the animal was slaughtered and processed. These contaminants break down the surface of the meat, liquefying the carbohydrates and proteins and producing a putrid film. This film produces carbon dioxide and ammonia gases, which result in an offensive odor. The meat may also be discolored by this action on the myoglobin (red pigment), converting it to yellow and green bile pigments. The longer this continues, the more the breakdown progresses, eventually converting the protein in the meat into mercaptans (chemicals that contain a substance related to skunk spray) and hydrogen sulfide, which has a rotten-egg-like smell. Meats must be kept refrigerated and should not remain at room temperature for even short periods.

ALL YOU EVER NEED TO KNOW ABOUT MARINADE

If you have ever wondered why meats turn brown so quickly when they are grilled or cooked in a similar method, the answer is: the marinade. Marinades are high in acids that react with the myoglobin (a muscle pigment) in the meat and turn it brown very quickly.

- The lower the temperature, the slower the marinade will be to cause this reaction, and, incidentally, to tenderize the meat. If you marinate at room temperature, it will take less time than if you do it in the refrigerator. But it's safer to marinate in the refrigerator.

- The acid in most marinades will reduce the meat's capacity for retaining moisture, and the meat may not be as moist as you would expect. This problem is usually offset by the fact that the meat will have a better flavor and may absorb some of the marinade.
- Large pieces of meat should be placed in a large plastic bag and tightly sealed to reduce the amount of marinade required. Smaller foods can be marinated in a glass container with excellent results. Never marinate meat in a metal container because the acid in the marinade may react with the metal to give the food an unpleasant flavor.
- Never baste food with the marinade it was soaked in. Bacteria from the food can contaminate the marinade, and the food may not be cooked for long enough to kill it.
- Always cover food that is marinating, and keep it refrigerated. Also, make sure the food is completely covered with the marinade.

Marinating Times Under Refrigeration	
FOOD	TIME
Fish	20 to 40 minutes
Poultry	3 to 4 hours
Meat*	12 to 24 hours

*If the meat is cut in small pieces, the marinade time should be 2 to 3 hours.

HERE'S HOW TO THAW MEAT

When thawing meat, you want both to minimize any damage from the freezing process and to avoid bacterial contamination. To avoid loss of flavor and reduce the risk of bacterial growth, always thaw meat in the refrigerator. This will require some advance planning. Defrosting in the microwave can partially cook the meat; it will not only cause a loss of flavor but may possibly result in a dried out piece of meat.

KEEP THE FLAVOR

When you refrigerate cooked beef, the flavor changes noticeably. After only a few hours, the fat, which is the main source of flavor, tends to produce an off taste. This off flavor is caused by the heating process, which encourages oxidation of the fat. If you know you'll be having leftovers, avoid cooking the beef in iron or aluminum pots and pans, and do not salt meats until you are ready to eat them.

MOISTER MEATBALLS

If you insert a small piece of cracked ice into the center of your meatballs before browning them, they will be moister. But be careful—you'll need to experiment to make sure the centers don't remain raw. Cut open a meatball and check the doneness of the center to determine the proper browning time.

TASTE THE TABOULLEH

For a fresh and healthy alternative to pasta or rice, make up a bowl of Lebanese taboulleh, which is made from cracked wheat and traditionally contains large amounts of healthy parsley as well as tomato, onion, and extra virgin olive oil.

IS MARBLED STEAK THE BEST?

Those white streaks running through the meat are fat. The fat is a storage depot for energy, and for its meat to be well marbled, an animal must be fed a diet high in rich grains such as corn, which is where we get the old saying that corn-fed beef is best. The fat imparts flavor and provides moisture that helps tenderize the meat. Well-marbled meat indicates that the animal did not exercise a lot, thus the meat will be tender.

WASTE OF RESOURCES

Chickens require only 2 pounds of feed to produce 1 pound of meat. Pigs require about 4 pounds of grain to produce 1 pound of meat, while cows require 8 pounds of grain to produce 1 pound of beef. The latest statistics indicate that there are 1.6 billion cattle worldwide. These cattle consume one-third of all the world's grain, which is not the most efficient use of this food source.

AGAINST THE GRAIN

Meat cut across the grain will be more tender.

WHY ARE CERTAIN CUTS OF BEEF MORE TENDER THAN OTHERS?

There are a number of factors that account for the tenderness of a piece of meat. These include the actual location the meat is cut from and the activity level and age of the animal. The areas of the animal that are the least exercised are typically the most tender. But even if a steak is labeled sirloin—and therefore ought to be tender—the degree of tenderness will depend on which end of the sirloin it was cut from. If it was cut from the short loin end, it will be tenderer than if it was cut from the area closer to the round. Kobe beef cattle from Japan are actually massaged to relax them, since stress and tension may cause muscles to flex and this (a form of exercise) increases the development of connective tissue.

AND WHO WANTS TO EAT AN OLD COW?

Meat should always be thawed in the refrigerator, and then cooked immediately. The color of fresh beef should be bright red, which comes from the muscle pigment. The darker the red, the older the cow. The grayish cast of some beef is from oxidation of the pigments; it is still safe to eat. Beef fat, if fresh, is always white, not yellow.

IT'S PLASTIC WRAP FOR THE FREEZER

When you freeze foods, evaporation continues and fluids are lost. The entire surface of the meat must be protected from this process with a moisture-resistant wrap. The best way to wrap meats for freezing is in plastic wrap covered by a protective freezer paper. This will not eliminate evaporation entirely, but it will reduce the risk of oxidation and rancidity.

THE RAINBOW HAM

Have you ever purchased a ham that has a greenish, glistening sheen? This occasionally occurs when a ham is sliced and the surface is exposed to the effects of oxidation. It is not a sign of spoilage but is caused by the nitrite modification of the iron content of the meat, which tends to produce a biochemical change in the meat's pigmentation.

WHEN SHOULD YOU SEASON A STEAK?

The jury's still out on this one. One authority says to salt before cooking, another equally respected one says to salt after cooking. The salt tends to draw liquid from the meat. The liquid then boils in the pan, and the surface of the meat may not have the desired texture or brown color you desire. The salt does not work its way into the meat to flavor it unless you puncture the meat, which is not recommended since juices escape. If you want the flavor of salt, or of a seasoning that contains salt, the best method is to season both sides of the meat just before serving. Never use ground pepper on any meat that is to be cooked in a pan with dry heat. Pepper tends to become bitter when scorched by the heat of a dry pan.

SALT PEPPER

SLOW AND STEADY MAKES MEAT TENDER

Generally the toughness of beef depends on the level of collagen (a protein substance) in the connective tissue. Slow cooking with moist heat breaks down the collagen and softens the connective tissue. If you cook the meat too long, however, it will actually get tough again as a result of another constituent in the connective tissue called elastin, which does not soften and become tender. The best way to cook meat slowly is in a 325°F oven for a few hours, cooking the meat in liquid. Boiling is not effective nor is slow cooking at 140°F for a long period. Meat tenderizers that actually break down the protein are papain and bromelain.

BURP

The U.S. consumes more hot dogs than the rest of the world combined—28 million in ballparks alone last year.

TO COVER OR UNCOVER, THAT IS THE QUESTION

The two methods normally used for cooking a roast are dry heat (without liquid) or moist heat (with liquid). When the meat is covered, steam is trapped in the pan. Many cooks use this method to prevent the roast from drying out. Dry heat (with the lid off) will brown the outside of the roast, and, if you wish, you can baste it every 15 minutes to provide the desired moisture. This is the method preferred by most chefs. However, if you do roast with a lid and in liquid, you must lower the temperature by 25°F. Roasts should always be cooked on a rack or with stalks of celery placed underneath. If the meat sits in the liquid on the bottom of the pan, the underside of the roast will be mushy.

BIG DIFFERENCE

Saturated fat accounts for only 10 to 25 percent of the total fat in seafood, while it comprises an average of 42 percent of the fat in beef and pork.

IT'S STILL A DISGUSTING JOB

To make scaling a fish easier, rub white vinegar on the scales, and then let the fish sit for about 10 minutes. Put the fish in a large plastic bag (hold it by the tail) to keep the scales from flying all over your kitchen.

STICK WITH SALMON

Salmon is a great protein source because it contains fewer calories than many other protein sources, and it's rich in omega oils that help the development of the brain, heart, skin and joints. For the greatest health benefits, though, it's best to go for wild or organic versions.

CAN THE TUNA

In order to limit your mercury intake, which has been linked to brain damage in unborn babies and is thought to be toxic to adults, don't eat more than two tuna steaks or four medium-sized cans of tuna a week. Tuna, marlin and swordfish have been found to be high in mercury deposits and should be avoided by those who are intending to become pregnant.

WILL FREEZING RAW MEAT MAKE IT SAFE TO EAT RARE?

Unfortunately, freezing will not kill all the bacteria found in meat or chicken, and you will still be at risk if the meat is consumed without having been cooked through. Some microbes survive freezing and will multiply very quickly as meat is thawed.

If you eat your hamburger rare, sear it well on both sides, then grind it in a meat grinder and cook it immediately. Searing will kill any microbes on the outside of the meat.

IT'LL BE ALL WHITE

White fish is an excellent healthy food and although it isn't high in omega-3 oils, it is still a fantastic way to fill up on protein and essential minerals and amino acids without adding fat. Try halibut, skate, sea bass and plaice as well as the usual cod and haddock.

DON'T OVERDO IT

Fish, like meat and poultry, should be marinated in the refrigerator because it decomposes rapidly at temperatures above 60°F. But don't overdo it: Because fish has so little connective tissue, it should never be marinated for longer than an hour or two.

PAY ATTENTION, CLASS

If you stock up on meat, take a few precautions if you'll be freezing it for more than two weeks. Always remove meat from the store packaging and rewrap it in special freezer paper. Chops, cutlets, and hamburger should be freezer-wrapped individually to ensure maximum freshness and convenience.

REDUCE INFLAMMATION

Not only is oily fish great for brain function and skin and organ health, it's also likely to be beneficial if you have an inflammatory type of arthritis (such as rheumatoid, reactive or psoriatic arthritis, or ankylosing spondylitis), as it contains anti-inflammatory essential fatty acids.

IT'S IN THE EYES

If you're buying fresh fish whole, look at the eyes, which should be clear, and the gills, which should be transparent and bright red in color. Don't be afraid to ask the fishmonger to show you the fish close up – they might give you a fresher fish if they think you know what you're looking for!

ALWAYS REST THE ROAST

Let a roast stand for about 15 minutes before you carve it. This gives the juices time to be reabsorbed and get evenly distributed. When you cook a roast, the juices tend to be forced to the center as those near the surface gets evaporated by the heat. Resting the roast also allows the meat to firm up a bit, making it easier to carve thinner slices.

ADDING SOUP BONES TO STOCK

One mistake people frequently make when preparing stock is to place the animal bone in the water after it has come to a boil. This tends to seal the bone and prevent all the flavor and nutrients from being released into the stock. The bone should be added to the cold water when the pot is first placed on the stove. This will allow the maximum release of flavors, nutrients, and especially the gelatinous thickening agents that add body to the stock. Store soup bones in the freezer.

WHAT IS AMERICA'S FAVORITE PIZZA TOPPING?

Pepperoni—Americans consume 300 million pounds of it on pizza every year. If you placed all the pepperoni pizzas eaten in the United States in one year next to one another, they would take up an area the size of 13,000 football fields.

FLAKE YOUR FISH

For added crunch with fewer calories, use cornflakes instead of breadcrumbs to coat fish fillets. Not only do cornflakes contain fewer calories than breadcrumbs, they are less absorbent and give a lighter covering, so will absorb less oil.

FISH FINGERS

If you've been preparing fish and want to remove the smell from your hands, wash them with toothpaste. Lemon juice and a little salt also work well – the salt sloughs away dead skin and softens your hands.

CAREFUL HERE

Recent studies have shown that a typical piece of pork found in the supermarket may have only a few hundred bacteria per square centimeter, compared with more than 100,000 bacteria in the same measure of a piece of chicken. This is one of the reasons it is so important to clean up thoroughly after handling raw poultry.

KEEP A TIGHT LID ON IT

The best way to store biscuits or other foods that you want to keep really dry is in jars with screw top lids, or press-top storage jars that keep the air out more effectively than other lids. Tins don't generally tend to be airtight once they've been used for a few months.

A TASTY TREAT

If you are going to bake fish, try wrapping it in foil or parchment paper with a sprig of dill and a little chopped onion. This helps to retain moisture and adds flavor.

CONSUME IT OR FREEZE IT

Small cuts of meat will spoil more quickly than larger cuts and should not be kept in the refrigerator for more than a day or two. Liver, sweetbreads, and cubed meats should be cooked within one day, or else need to be kept frozen.

STOP 'SMELLING FISH'!

Fresh fish is a summertime treat, but fresh fish smell in your microwave is not. Get rid of the scent by putting a quartered lemon and a small bowl of vanilla in your microwave for a minute or two on high.

LEMON-AID

Grilling fish is always a drag because the skin inevitably gets stuck to the grate—particularly when cooking salmon. Avoid this by placing a few thin slices on lemon or lime on the grill, and then the fish on top. Not only will your cleanup be easier, but also the citrus flavor is great for just about any seafood.

IS THERE ANYTHING IT CAN'T DO?

Marinate the meat for your chili in beer. It's a great tenderizer for tough, inexpensive cuts of beef, and all you need to do is soak it for an hour before cooking. (You can also marinate it overnight in the refrigerator.)

MONDAY BLUES

Never buy meat from the supermarket on Monday morning. It's likely that those for sale were not sold on the weekend, and most shipments of fresh meat arrive on Monday afternoon or on Tuesday.

THE SALT OF THE SEA

You can reduce the saltiness of anchovies by soaking them in ice water for about 15 minutes. Because of their high salt content, anchovies will keep about two months under refrigeration after the can is opened, and up to a year without refrigeration in a sealed can. Once opened, they should be kept covered with olive oil.

GRILL AND BEER IT!

If you're grilling a steak on a closed barbeque, consider opening a can of beer and placing it on the hottest part of the grill. It will boil and keep the meat moist, while adding flavor, too.

TENDER HOOKS

For an exotic treat, add a ripe, unpeeled banana or two to the pan next time you fear your roast will be tough.

BAD BEHAVIOR

Some of the shrimp that is sold already breaded may have been over breaded to increase the total weight of the package. The FDA has taken action against some unscrupulous companies for this practice.

AND YOU'LL STAY UP ALL NIGHT, TOO

Adding some black coffee to the liquid when cooking lamb stew gives it a beautiful dark color and adds great flavor.

FISH FACTS

- More fish than ever are now raised in aquaculture fish farms, and more varieties are now available to consumers.
- The fats in fish are high in polyunsaturates and contain the omega-3 fatty acids that may protect us from heart attacks by keeping the blood from coagulating too easily. Studies show that even canned or frozen fish retains most of its omega-3 fatty acids.
- Many fish and shellfish harbor certain bacteria and parasites. To avoid food poisoning, always cook fish and shellfish; don't eat them raw. Also, one should never consume the skin or visible fat, which is where most of the contaminants are located.
- Fish should never smell of ammonia.

IS A PRAWN A SHRIMP?

Biologically, a prawn is different from a shrimp in that it has pincer claws similar to those of a lobster. A relative of the prawn is the scampi, which is the Italian name for the tail portion of several varieties of lobsterettes. When restaurants have prawns on the menu, they are usually just jumbo shrimp, which cost less than true giant prawns and are not as tasty.

"GONE FISHING" COULD BE OUR TWO FAVORITE WORDS OF THE SUMMER

Next time you get the chance to indulge, mix some coffee grounds into the soil in your bait box before adding the worms. They'll live longer that way.

IT'S GREAT WITH MELON

Prosciutto is an Italian ham that is never smoked and is prepared by a salt-curing process, seasoned, and then air-dried. *Prosciutto cotto* means that the ham has been cooked and is common delicatessen terminology.

BECAUSE NO ONE WANTS TO STINK

Before handling fish, rub your hands with lemon juice. Chances are, you won't smell fish on them afterward. After frying fish, put a little white vinegar into the frying pan to help get rid of the odor on the surface.

THE FRESH CATCH

- The skin should be shiny; when pressed with a finger, the flesh should spring back to its original shape. Never buy fish whose skin is bruised.
- The meat should be firm to the touch, with no visible blemishes.
- The eyes should be bulging, not sunken into the head, which is a sign that the fish is dried out. The eyes should also be clear, not cloudy.
- The scales should be intact, with a bright and shiny appearance. If you notice loose scales, don't buy the fish.
- The gills must look clean, not slimy. Their healthy color is bright red. Gray gills indicate an old fish.
- A fresh fish never smells fishy. If the fish does have a strong odor, it is probably because the flesh is decomposing and releasing the chemical compound trimethylamine. Seafood should be as fresh as possible—no more than two or three days out of water.

WHO KNEW?

We all know that odor from cooking fish can be nasty. By simply placing a bowl of white vinegar on the counter near the stove while cooking, most of the odor will disappear.

PINING FOR FRESH FISH BUT STUCK WITH FROZEN?

Try this: Cover the frozen fish in milk until it thaws, then cook. It will taste fresher and your family will never know it was frozen.

FAT SIDE DOWN

When roasting a pork loin, cook it with the fat-side down for the first 20 minutes. This will cause the fat to begin to liquefy. Then turn the roast over for the balance of the cooking time, and the fat will baste the meat.

REDUCE STRESS WITH FISH

Eating oily fish has been shown to reduce stress hormones by almost a quarter as well as boosting anti-stress hormones in the body – making it the perfect choice for a working lunch to set you up for a productive afternoon.

STEAMY FISH TALE

To steam fish fillets in the microwave, place them in a shallow microwavable dish (a glass pie plate is ideal) with the thinner parts overlapping at the center of the dish. Sprinkle with lemon juice or herbs, if you like, and then cover the dish with plastic wrap (making sure it doesn't touch the fish) and cook for 3 minutes per pound. If your microwave doesn't have a turntable, rotate the dish about halfway through the cooking time.

MILK? REALLY?

When fish is frozen, it tends to lose some of its flavor. If you thaw the frozen fish in low-fat milk, some of the original flavor will return. Frozen fish should be thawed in the refrigerator and cooked as quickly as possible. If your fish is frozen, skin it before you thaw it, because a frozen fish is easier to skin.

Fat Content of Common Fish (% of Total Fat)			
Cod	0.66	Striped bass	2.3
Haddock	0.71	Oysters	2.4
Pollack	0.8	Salmon, Pacific	3.4
Tuna, yellowfin	1.0	Bass	3.7
Grouper	1.0	Mullet	3.8
Crab	1.1	Swordfish	4.0
Flounder	1.2	Tuna, bluefin	4.9
Sole	1.2	Salmon, Atlantic	6.3
Hake	1.3	Lake Trout	9.4
Red snapper	1.3	Pompano	9.5
Ocean perch	1.6	Mackerel	13.8
Shrimp	1.8	Herring	18.0
Halibut	2.3		

WHO KNEW?

When grilling shrimp on skewers, always thread the shrimp onto the skewers lengthwise, so they won't curl on the grill. They're also less likely to fall into the fire. And remember—always soak wooden skewers for 30 minutes before grilling!

LOOK FOR PUFI

Seafood labels should read "Packed Under Federal Inspection" or PUFI. This signifies that federal inspectors of the Department of Commerce inspected, graded, and certified the fish as having met all the requirements of the inspection regulations, and that the product has been produced in accordance with official standards and specifications.

YES, THERE REALLY IS A FISH HOT LINE

The majority of fish caught in the oceans are safe to eat. If you are fishing in warmer waters, however, call the fish hot line to be sure that the type of fish you are going after is not infected with ciguatera, which has caused a number of cases of food poisoning. The toll-free number for the fish and shellfish hot line, sponsored by the U.S. government, is 800-332-4010, extension 3.

COMMON FORMS OF FISH

Cured Fish
Smoked, pickled, or salted fish. If the fish is sold as "cold smoked," it was only partially dried and will have a very short shelf life. If the label reads "hot smoked," the fish is fully cooked and should be consumed within a few days or kept frozen until used.

Dressed Fish
Scaled and gutted, with head, tail, and fins removed.

Dried Fish
Fish that has been processed with dry heat, and then salted to preserve it.

Fish Fillets
Sides of dressed fish, cut lengthwise away from the backbones. May be any size; seldom have bones.

Fish Steaks
Slices of larger dressed fish, cut across the body. May have bones.

Whole Fish
Comes complete with entrails and needs to be prepared soon after it is caught. It is almost never available at supermarkets.

JUST HUM HALF OF "THE MINUTE WALTZ"
Never cook abalone for more than 30 seconds on each side, or it may toughen. Before cooking, cut slashes about an inch apart to avoid curling.

YOU'RE DEAD TO ME

The shells of healthy clams should be closed when you buy them. The shells will open gradually as the clams cook. If you keep the clams on ice, they will also probably relax and open their shells. To make sure the clam is alive, tap its shell. If the shell doesn't close, the clam is sick or dead and should be discarded. Similarly, if a clam's shell doesn't open by itself when the clam is cooked, it should be discarded.

It's easy to overcook shrimp; they cook in as little as 3 minutes. When they're pink, they're done. Always plunge shrimp into cold water to stop the cooking process.

DON'T FORGET TO BE CAREFUL

To open shellfish, wash the shells thoroughly. Hold the clam or oyster in your palm and slip the tip of an oyster knife between the upper and lower shells. Run the knife around the edge of the shell and pry until you hear a pop at the hinge. Loosen the clam or oyster from the shell and remove any shell fragments.

AND CHECK FOR CUTICLES WHILE YOU'RE THERE

When purchasing abalone, make sure the foot muscle moves when touched. Never buy shellfish that is dead.

CLAMS

The most popular clam is the hard-shell clam. The soft-shelled geoduck (pronounced gooey-duck) clam is unable to close its shell because its neck sticks out too far and is too big. It weighs three pounds on average and has juicy meat with a rich flavor.

THE SWEETEST

For the most part, shellfish are sweeter than fish. They have a higher percentage of glycogen, a carbohydrate that converts to glucose. The amino acid glycine also provides some sweetness. Crayfish and lobsters are the sweetest, followed by crab and shrimp. However, if they are stored for more than a day or two, all shellfish will lose some of their sweetness.

THE KNIFE TEST

To test fish for doneness, insert a thin-bladed knife into the flesh at the thickest part. It should be just barely translucent in the center. Even though it might look not quite done, the fish will continue to cook after you remove it from the heat, and it will be fine by the time you serve it.

THE TRUTH ABOUT CLAM CHOWDER

Chefs always add clams to their chowder during the last 15 to 20 minutes of cooking. If they are added too early in the cooking, clams can become either tough or too soft.

CRAB

Different species of crabs are found in different oceans. Blue crabs are caught in the Gulf of Mexico or the Atlantic Ocean. Crabs caught in the Pacific Ocean are known as Dungeness crabs. The most prized crabs—and the largest—are king crabs, which are caught off the coast of Alaska and northern Canada. The smaller stone crab is found in the waters off the coast of Florida; only its claws are harvested (it's illegal to take the whole crab).

Crabs should be purchased only if they are active and heavy for their size. Refrigerate all crabs on ice as soon as possible, and cover them with a damp towel. Live crabs should be cooked the day they are purchased.

Soft-shell crabs are blue crabs; they can be found in a variety of sizes. The smallest are "spiders" and measure only about 3 ½ inches across, which is barely legal. "Hotel primes" measure about 4 ½ inches across; "primes" are 5 ½ inches. "Jumbo" crabs measure 6 to 7 inches across.

If canned crabmeat has a metallic taste, soak it in ice water 5 to 8 minutes, and then drain and blot it dry with paper towels.

YUCK

Fish that feed on the bottom of lakes, such as carp and bass, are the most likely to be contaminated.

Avoid shrimp that has been peeled and deveined before freezing. It causes a loss of texture and flavor.

THAT MUST REALLY HURT

Stone crabs are able to regenerate a new claw when one is broken off. In Florida, commercial crab companies now catch crabs, break off one of its claws, and then release the crab to grow another one. The crab is able to protect itself and forage for food as long as it has one claw.

REMOVING THE MEAT FROM CRAYFISH

Like lobsters and crabs, crayfish are always cooked live. Also known as crawfish or sometimes crawdads, they have a much sweeter flavor than either lobsters or crabs, and all its meat is found in its tail. To remove the meat easily, gently twist the tail away from the body, and then unwrap the first three sections of the shell to expose the meat. Next, pinch the end of the meat in one hand while holding the tail in the other, and pull the meat out in one piece. You can also suck out the flavorful juices from the head.

COLOR CHECK

Cooking blue crabs? If the shells of blue crab are orange after they are cooked, the crabs may not have the best flavor. The crabs' shells should be a bright red or bright pink after cooking.

AND THAT MAKES IT SPECIAL?

Blue crab is the only crab you can buy that isn't already cooked—Dungeness, snow, king, and stone crabs are only available cooked.

CRAYFISH

These are related to, and look like, shrimp. The largest supplier in the world is the state of Louisiana, which produces between 75 and 105 million pounds each year.

GOES NICELY WITH A FAKE BEER

Hundreds of years ago, the Japanese invented a way to make imitation shellfish called surimi. In recent years, this has become a booming industry in the United States. At present, we are producing imitation crab meat, lobster, shrimp, and scallops, most of which are made from a deep ocean whitefish called pollack (or pollock).

Surimi is lower in cholesterol than shellfish, contains very little fat, is high in good-quality protein, and is comparable with other forms of shellfish in sodium content. The processing lowers the level of other nutrients that would ordinarily be found in fresh pollack.

LANGOSTINOS

Langostinos are miniature lobsters; they are usually found frozen in the market and are used mainly for salads, soups, or stews. This small crustacean is also called rock shrimp, Dublin Bay prawn, and *langoustine* (in France; *langostinos* is Spanish).

WHO KNEW?

Be careful not to over-marinate fish. Never let fresh fish sit in acidic marinades for more than 30 minutes, or it will be mushy when cooked.

OR WEAR ONE OF THOSE EMBARRASSING BIBS

If you're eating whole lobster, cover it with a napkin or towel before twisting off the legs and claws. This will keep the juices from squirting about and causing a mess.

THE TWO LOBSTERS

The two most common species of lobster consumed in the United States are Maine and spiny. Maine lobsters are the most prized, and are harvested off the northeastern seaboard. These have excellent flavor, and their meat, when cooked, is snow-white. The spiny lobster is only sold live where it is harvested—the Gulf states and California. It is smaller than Maine lobster and can be identified by its smaller claws. Never purchase a lobster unless you see movement in the claws or its tail turns under when carefully touched.

BUT THEY ALL USE THEIR RIGHT CLAW WHEN SHAKING HANDS

Believe it or not, Maine lobsters are either right- or left-handed. They are not symmetrical. Rather, the two claws are very different and are used for different purposes. One is larger, with very coarse teeth for crushing, while the other has fine teeth for ripping or tearing. The flesh in the smaller, fine-toothed claw is sweeter and tenderer.

COOK WITH CARE

To retain its flavor, lobster meat should not be added to dishes until just before serving. Overcooking will destroy its taste.

NEWS ON NEWBERG

In 1876, a businessman named Ben Wenberg brought a recipe for a lobster dish to the chef at New York City's famed Delmonico's restaurant. The chef called the dish Lobster Wenberg. The chef and Wenberg had a falling out, and the chef took the dish off the menu. His customers, however, raised such a fuss that he returned it to the menu, but reversed the first three letters of Wenberg's name. It has remained a popular way of serving lobster ever since. Most restaurants purchase spiny lobster for this dish; it's less expensive than Maine lobster.

WELL, IS THERE A "POOR MAN'S MONKFISH?"

Monkfish is sometimes called "poor man's lobster."

MICROWAVE THAT LOBSTER!

I know it sounds crazy, but the taste, texture, and color of microwaved lobster is far superior to boiled or steamed, and microwaving produces an evenly cooked, tender lobster. A problem, however, is that you can only cook one lobster at a time.

To microwave a lobster, place it in a large microwavable plastic bag with ¼ cup water, and knot the bag loosely. A 1 ½ pound lobster should take 5 or 6 minutes on High, providing you have a 600–700-watt oven. If you have a lower wattage oven, allow about 8 minutes. To be sure the lobster is fully cooked, separate the tail from the body. The tail meat should be creamy white, not translucent.

Even when microwaved, the lobster must still be cooked live because of the enzymatic breakdown that occurs immediately upon its death. If you are bothered by the lobster's movements, which are just reflex actions, put it in the freezer for 10 minutes before cooking to dull its senses; the movement will be reduced to about 20 seconds.

I THOUGHT THEY WERE JUST REALLY, REALLY EMBARRASSED

Live lobsters always have a red coloring, but it is not visible until the lobster is cooked. Lobsters (like other shellfish and some insects) have an external skeleton that is made up of chitin. Chitin contains a bright red pigment called astaxanthin, which is bonded to several proteins. While the chitin is bonded, it remains a brownish-red color; however, when the protein is heated, the bonds are broken, releasing the astaxanthin and turning the exoskeleton bright red.

YUCK

Shellfish lovers seem to think it is a special treat is to consume the green tomalley, or liver, found in lobsters and the mustard found in crabs. These organs are similar to our livers and are involved in detoxifying and filtering toxins out of the shellfish. Many of these organs retain a percentage of those toxins and possibly even some PCBs or heavy metal contaminants. Because you can't be certain of a lobster's exposure to these substances, you should never eat these organs. However, the roe or coral found in female lobsters is safe to eat. Lobster roe is a delicacy in many countries.

SO KEEP THEM FROZEN

Shucked oysters will stay fresh, frozen in their liquid, for up to three months, but they will keep only a day or two in the refrigerator.

DEATH BY BEER

Lobsters and crabs have very potent digestive enzymes that start to decompose as soon as they die. The complexity and location of their digestive organs make it too difficult to remove them before cooking. Both lobsters and crabs should, therefore, be kept alive until they are cooked. If you are uncertain as to whether a lobster is alive or dead, pick it up. If the tail curls under, the lobster is alive. Most fish cookbooks and experts recommend plunging lobsters directly into boiling water in order to kill them. If you're squeamish, you can also kill them by severing the spinal cord at the base of the neck with the tip of a knife before boiling them. Some cooks immerse the lobster in beer for a few minutes to get it drunk before placing it in the boiling water.

KEEP 'EM COOL

Store live oysters in the refrigerator in a single layer with the larger shell down, covered with a damp towel. Eat them within two days of purchase.

DON'T LET THEM GET TOUGH

Oysters are easy to overcook, which will make them tough. If you are poaching oysters, take them out as soon as their edges start to curl.

MUSSEL MADNESS

Mussels are raised on rope ladders that keep them away from any debris on the bottom of the bed. This produces cleaner, healthier mussels and reduces the likelihood of disease. Mussels cultivated in this manner are also much larger.

Mussels are cooked when their shells open. Discard any mussel whose shell does not open during cooking.

When purchasing mussels, be sure they are alive. Tap their shells; if they are open, they should snap closed. Any mussels that don't close their shells they have probably gone to their reward and should not be eaten. When mussels are shucked, the liquid that comes out should be clear.

ANOTHER REASON MUSSELS DON'T LIKE TO SHAVE

Mussels should be cleaned with a stiff brush under cold running water and their visible "beard" removed just before cooking. Once they have been debearded, mussels will die.

I'LL BET YOU DIDN'T KNOW THAT

Live mussels will keep in the refrigerator for two to three days if placed on a tray and covered with a damp towel. Spread them out; never pile the mussels on top of one another.

SCALLOPS

Scallops have a very short life span once they are out of the water, and they become tough very easily if overcooked. Three types of scallop are available retail: the sea scallop, which is about two inches wide; the bay scallop, which is about ½-inch wide; and the calico, which is slightly larger than the bay scallop. Bay scallops are the most tender of the three. Scallops should be moist and should never have a strong odor.

COOL THEM FIRST

Shrimp will always cook up nice and tender if you cool them down before cooking. Either place them in the freezer for 10 to 15 minutes, or set them in a bowl of ice water for about 5 minutes. If you're boiling them, drop them into hot seasoned broth or court bouillon and boil for a minute, and then turn off the heat and let stand about 10 minutes. Sautéed shrimp are done when they are firm and pink, which takes 3 to 5 minutes. Grilled shrimp are cooked in about 7 minutes.

OFF WITH THEIR HEADS!

Shrimp with heads are more perishable than those without heads. In fact, the shrimp's head contains almost all its vital organs and the majority of the digestive system.

SHRIMP

Shrimp are sold in a variety of sizes, and to make matters confusing, the quantity of shrimp per pound can vary from store to store—and even from shrimp at shrimp at the same store!

The most common sizes are the jumbo shrimp, which average 21 to 25 per pound; large shrimp, which average 31 to 35 per pound; medium shrimp, which average 43 to 50 per pound; and tiny shrimp, which average more than 70 per pound. If you're lucky, you may find colossal shrimp (10 to 15 per pound) or even extra-colossal (less than 10 per pound). The size is not an indication of their quality.

Shrimp have a high water content and will reduce from 1 pound to about ¾ of a pound or less after cooking. Worldwide there are more than 250 species of shrimp, including prawns. Shrimp can be found in a variety of colors, from white (the most desirable) to brown, depending on where they feed and where they are caught. Brown shrimp feed mainly on algae and have a stronger flavor than white.

FROZEN FISH SMARTS

- If frozen fish has an odor, it has probably thawed and been refrozen. Thawed fish should have hardly any odor.
- Be sure the skin and flesh are frozen solid, with no discoloration or soft spots. The skin should be totally intact, with no areas missing.
- The wrapping should be intact, with no tears or ice crystals.

SQUID

Squid is a member of the shellfish family and is sold as calamari. It tends to become tough very easily and should be cooked for no more than 3 minutes for the best results. Conversely, it can also become tender if braised or stewed for at least an hour. Squid is the only shellfish that has more cholesterol than shrimp. With the exception of the beak, head, and innards, the entire squid is edible.

SO DON'T FREEZE SHRIMP

If shrimp develops an ammonia-like odor, it has started to deteriorate and should be discarded. Shrimp cannot be refrozen, and remember, almost all the shrimp you buy has already been frozen. This means that if you don't eat the shrimp the day you buy it, or possibly the next day, it should be thrown out.

A DIFFERENT "HAM-STRING"

If ham is on the menu for Easter this year, ask your butcher to slice it when you buy it. When it's time to cook, just secure the ham with dental floss, and bake as usual, and when you serve it…all the slices look perfect.

SALTWATER FISH

Anchovies

Surprisingly, anchovies are a popular poultry feed. Most of the more than 200 million pounds caught annually are ground up and used for feed. Anchovies used for canning range in size from 4 to 6 inches, they are commonly used as a pizza topping and in Caesar salad; anchovy paste, sold in tubes, is convenient because it gives the flavor without the mess.

FISH FOR PURITY

Oily fish show fairly high levels of pesticide and chemical residue. However, many of the fish tested are probably farmed and if you buy organic farmed or wild-caught versions, the residues are much lower.

OYSTERS AND "R" MONTHS

The old saying that you should eat oysters only in months whose names include the letter "r" may have been true in the decades prior to refrigeration—as long as they are cooked. With the exception of oysters harvested from the Gulf of Mexico, there is really no medical evidence to indicate that it is dangerous to eat oysters in any month of the year. However, oysters tend to be less flavorful and less meaty during the summer months, because that is when they spawn.

Anglerfish

This is also known as monkfish or by its French name, *lotte*. It has a relatively firm texture and is low in fat. Anglerfish can weigh from as little as three pounds to as much as 25 pounds. They are more popular in France than in the United States, but monkfish is becoming more popular on restaurant menus and is mainly used as a substitute for lobster because its tail is comparable in taste with lobster tail.

Barracuda

The barracuda can weight up to 10 pounds, but it is most commonly found at five pounds. It is a moderately fatty fish, usually caught in the Pacific Ocean. Pacific barracuda is the only edible variety, as most other barracuda have very toxic flesh as a result of ciguatera, a naturally occurring toxin found in the algaelike organisms barracuda eat.

Bluefish

This fish tends to deteriorate very rapidly and does not freeze well. Bluefish usually weigh three to six pounds and have a thin strip of dark flesh running down the middle that should be removed before cooking, because it may contain higher concentrations of PCBs than other parts of the fish.

Cod

Cod is a low-fat fish and has a very firm texture. The two varieties found in the fish market are Atlantic cod and Pacific cod; scrod is the term for young cod. As a substitute for cod, you might try the similar-tasting cuskfish, which is excellent in soups or chowders.

Hake

A relatively low-fat Atlantic fish with firm texture, hake has a mild flavor and usually weighs between one and eight pounds.

Halibut

Similar to flounder, low in fat and firm of texture, the halibut normally weighs anywhere between 10 and 60 pounds and is marketed as steaks or fillets.

Mackerel

This a high-fat, relatively oily fish similar to tuna. You may find it under a variety of names, such as Atlantic mackerel, wahoo, Pacific jack, kingfish, or Spanish mackerel. There is a red meat variety sold in cans that has an excellent level of omega-3 fatty acids. Mackerel is best cooked in an acid marinade that includes lemon juice or tomato.

Mahi Mahi

Even though mahi mahi is sometimes called dolphin fish, the two are not related. There is a slight resemblance between the two, but mahi mahi's bluish-green skin is unique. They may weigh up to 40 pounds and are considered one of the better eating fishes. They are usually sold as steaks or fillets, or whole.

Mullet

Most mullet is caught off the Florida coast. It has a very firm texture and a relatively strong flavor. The flesh is somewhat oily and good for smoking.

Croaker

All varieties are low in fat. This is a small fish, usually weighing ½ to two pounds, unless you are lucky enough to catch a redfish, which may weigh more than 30 pounds (redfish fishing is prohibited in some waters). The croaker is a popular chowder fish.

Eel

More popular in Japan and some European countries than in the United States, eel is a firm-textured, tasty fish that can grow to be three to four feet long. The tough skin must be removed before cooking.

Flounder

This is the most popular fish sold in the markets and may appear as "sole." There are more than 100 varieties, all of which have a mild flavor and a light texture. Flounder is one of the lowest-fat fishes and weighs anywhere from one to 10 pounds. Dover sole, which may be found on restaurant menus, is imported from England.

Grouper

A member of the sea bass family, grouper typically weighs four to six pounds but can get up to 15 pounds in the Gulf. Be sure to remove the skin before cooking. It is similar to the skin of the eel and is very tough. Grouper has a firm texture and is an easy fish to prepare either baked, grilled, or fried.

Haddock

Related to the cod, haddock is caught only in the North Atlantic. A common smoked form of this fish, called finnan haddie, is sold in markets. The flesh of haddock is somewhat softer than that of cod.

Orange Roughy

Almost all orange roughy is imported from New Zealand, usually as frozen fillets. It is a low-fat fish with a slightly sweet taste and a texture similar to that of sole. It may be cooked in many ways.

Pollack

Pollack is mainly used for making fish sticks and surimi. It has a flaky texture and rich flavor. The darker layer of flesh is not as mild as the lighter layer. Pollack is also a very common chowder fish. Atlantic pollack is sometimes called Boston bluefish, though it's not related to the bluefish.

Pompano

Found mainly off the coast of Florida, pompano has recently been affected by over fishing, upping its cost. It is oily and firm-textured.

Sablefish

Commonly called black cod, sablefish has a high fat content but a light texture. Usually found smoked, it can also be baked, poached, or fried.

Salmon

The fattiest salmon is the Chinook, or king, salmon; it is also one of the hardest and accounts for only 10 percent of the total Alaskan catch. The Coho salmon has less fat and is smaller than the Chinook. Other varieties include sockeye, whose flavor rivals king; and pink salmon, which has a dry, sometimes bitter flesh. Coho salmon deposit between 2,000 and 17,000 eggs each year during their five days of spawning.

WHO KNEW?

Don't store fresh fish for more than a day or two in the refrigerator, because it's very perishable. If you want to store it longer, wrap it tightly in freezer paper and freeze.

KEEP IT WARM

Fish tends to cool very quickly. It's best served on warm plates or a warmed platter.

Sardines

Sardines with bones are an excellent source of calcium. A 3-ounce serving contains more calcium than an 8-ounce glass of milk. Milk has vitamin D added to help metabolize the calcium, but sardines also supply vitamin D and phosphorus. Ounce-for-ounce, sardines can also supply you with more protein than a steak.

A member of the herring family, sardines are normally sold pickled or smoked and served as an appetizer. They are high in fat with a very fine texture. When caught, they weigh only about ¾ pound. The best quality sardine is the Norwegian bristling. Norwegian sardines are an excellent source of omega-3 fatty acids.

Sea Trout

These trout are usually caught along the Atlantic coast from Florida to Massachusetts. They are somewhat fatty but have a solid texture and are good for baking or broiling.

Shad

This is one of the fattiest fishes and is excellent baked, broiled, or fried. It is usually cooked whole, with just the entrails removed, because it is very hard to fillet. Shad roe (the eggs) is one of the more highly prized caviars.

Shark

Shark is becoming more and more popular. It is a tasty, low-fat fish with an excellent level of nutrients. More than 300 species of shark have been identified to date. The most popular, however, is mako shark, which is similar in texture to swordfish. Other common varieties include sand shark, dusky shark, sharpnose, bonnethead, and blacktip.

THEY ALSO LOOK BETTER IN A BATHING SUIT

River fish have more flavor than lake fish because they must swim against currents and thus get more exercise. This is one reason trout is so delicious. Fish from cooler waters also have a higher fat content and, therefore, more flavor.

Skate

A relative of the shark family, the skate has rays or wings that are the most edible part of the fish. The taste is similar to that of the scallop, and the meat looks like crab meat because of its striations.

Sturgeon

Sturgeon roe is one of the finest caviars. These fish can weigh several hundred pounds and are the largest of all freshwater fish. They are high in fat and excellent for grilling. About 52 percent of the calories in sturgeon caviar comes from fat.

Swordfish

Because its flesh was found to contain high levels of mercury, many people are still reluctant to eat swordfish unless they know it was caught well offshore. Usually sold as steaks, it is excellent for grilling. Swordfish has good flavor and fairly firm texture.

Tuna

The best kind of tuna is blue fin, but yellow fin is more readily available, costs less, and is nearly as delicious. Blue fin tuna may weigh up to 1,000 pounds. The meat of both blue fin and yellow fin is deep red; albacore is pale pink. Tuna has a very meaty, steak like texture. The fish swim almost constantly—up to 75,000 miles per year—at speeds up to 55 miles per hour; they are well muscled and have superb flavor. Tuna is quite low in fat and can be grilled, pan-seared, or broiled.

Albacore is the best quality of canned tuna, which may also be labeled light, dark, or blended. These tuna varieties are also very oily and usually higher in calories, even if water-packed. When tuna is packed in olive oil, it is sometimes called tonno, which is the Italian word for tuna.

GUT IT QUICKLY

The sooner a fish is gutted the better, because enzymes in the fish's gut tend to break down the flesh very quickly. These enzymes are very aggressive and powerful, which is one reason why fish is easier to digest than beef or chicken. When storing fish, remember that the muscle tissue is high in glycogen, which was the fish's energy source. When the fish is killed, this carbohydrate is converted into lactic acid, which is usually an excellent preservative; however, the fish tends to use up too much of its energy source thrashing around and trying to escape when it is caught. Another reason fish does not keep well is that certain bacteria are located outside digestive tract and remain active even below the freezing point.

THE FAT IN TUNA

Amazingly, the fat content of an albacore tuna may vary by as much as 500 percent. Tuna manufacturers typically use fish with about 1 gram of fat per serving. However, when the demand for tuna is extremely high, they resort to packaging higher-fat albacore, which may contain 4 to 5 grams of fat per serving. Always check labels.

Turbot

This is a mild, white-fleshed fish. European turbot is superior to American turbot, with a firmer texture and better flavor. It's easy to tell the difference: European turbot is more expensive.

TUNA FACTS

Solid-pack tuna is made from the loins, with the addition of a few flakes of meat. Chunk tuna may include parts of the tougher muscles, while flake tuna is composed mostly of muscle structure and smaller bits of meat.

QUICK-TRICK

If you're grilling or broiling thick fish steaks, marinate them for 15 minutes in lemon or lime juice before cooking. The acid from the juice 'cooks' the flesh on the fish a bit, cutting down on the time it needs to stay on the heat—so your fish is less likely to dry out.

BECAUSE NOBODY WANTS TO EAT SAND

Once clams are dug up, they must be cleansed of sand and debris. To accomplish this, the clams should be allowed to soak in the refrigerator in a solution of one part salt to 10 parts water for several hours or overnight. If you're pressed for time, rinse them in several changes of fresh water until no sand remains.

WHO KNEW?

Albacore tuna is richer than light tuna in omega-3 essential fatty acids, but it also contains more mercury. Light tuna is a safer choice.

DON'T BE AFRAID OF LOX

Good news for lox lovers! Smoked salmon, lox, or Nova that are commercially processed poses virtually no health risk. Lox is heavily salted during processing. According to the FDA, no case of contamination from parasites has ever been reported in lox. Most lox sold in the United States is made from farm-raised salmon. Cold-smoked salmon is always kept frozen, which will kill any parasites.

FRESHWATER FISH

Buffalo Fish

This is a common fish caught in the Mississippi River and the Great Lakes area of the United States. It has a fairly firm texture and enough fat to make it good for grilling. The average weight is eight to 10 pounds.

Carp

Used to make gefilte fish, this scavenger fish may carry some contamination. Carp should be purchased only if it is farm-raised, and only as fillets because it is extremely difficult to skin.

Catfish

One of the more popular and tasty fish. Because catfish are scavengers, 85 percent of those we eat in the United States are currently farm-raised. Catfish are a low-fat fish with a relatively firm texture and are not very good for grilling. Instead, fry, roast, or broil them.

DON'T OVERCOOK

If you overcook shellfish, it will become tough. Clams should steam 5 to 10 minutes, crab for 15 to 20 minutes, and lobster about 20 minutes. Crayfish and mussels need only 4 to 8 minutes. Grilling an 8-ounce lobster tail takes no more than 10 to 12 minutes.

Perch

A true perch is caught only in fresh water; ocean perch is really rockfish. Perch is relatively low in fat, with a fairly firm texture. The majority of perch sold in the United States comes from the Great Lakes. They weigh about one to two pounds and are available fresh or frozen.

Pike

Pike is a member of the perch family; it averages one to three pounds and is delicious pan-fried. If you can find walleyed pike, it is an excellent eating fish, though it has plenty of tiny bones and must be filleted carefully.

Smelt

One of the smallest fish, smelts are usually eaten whole, with just the entrails and head removed. Best prepared pan-fried, they are a high-fat fish with a firm texture.

Trout

Next to catfish, trout is one of the most common fish caught in the United States. The most popular variety is the rainbow trout, which is one of the tastiest. Almost all trout sold has been raised on fish farms.

Whitefish

A relative of the trout, whitefish is also one of the best eating fish. It is high fat and good barbecued, broiled, or baked. They are found in abundance in the Great Lakes.

A CANNY SOLUTION

If canned shrimp tastes metallic, soak the shrimp in 2 tablespoons vinegar and 1 teaspoon dry sherry for 15 minutes, or soak them the same length of time in a mixture of lemon juice and cold water.

CAVIAR

If the Russian word *malossol* is on a caviar container, it means that only a small amount of salt was used in processing. This caviar will not have a long shelf life. Caviar loses much of its flavor and texture when cooked and is best eaten cold. It should be stored in the refrigerator and will last for two months if the temperature remains at 35°F.

Beluga

Comes from the Caspian Sea's beluga sturgeon. The eggs (roe) vary in size but are usually pea-size and silver-gray to black. This is the most prized variety of caviar in the United States.

Osetra

This caviar is somewhat smaller than the beluga. Its color is gray to brownish-gray.

Sevruga

Even smaller than the osetra and gray in color.

Whitefish, Lumpfish, and Salmon

These are the least expensive caviars. Whitefish caviar is yellow-gold; lumpfish is tiny and black; and salmon, sometimes called red caviar, ranges in color from pale orange to deep red.

THICK IS THE TRICK

If you plan to broil or grill fish, be sure to purchase steaks that are at least 1-inch thick. Fish dries out very quickly on the grill, and the thicker it is the better. The skin should be left on fillets while grilling and removed after they are cooked. When frying, be sure the surface of the fish is dry before putting it in the oil.

WE SHOULD ALL BE AS THIN

Fillets are so thin that they cook through in a very short period. The meat of the fillet is also so delicate that it has a tendency to flake apart when overcooked, or if it is even turned. To be sure the fillet does not stick to the pan, use a nonstick cooking spray.

WHO KNEW?

Trout and salmon have double rib cages, so the fillets often have small pin bones. Remove them by pressing the flesh with your fingers or using tweezers.

RED SPOTS ON YOUR FISH

Red spots on fish fillets indicate that the fish has been handled roughly and is bruised. This may result from throwing them around when it is caught or from poor filleting technique. Too many bruises can affect the flavor of the fillet.

TRY THE HIGH-OCTANE TROUT

Fishermen in the know will never fish from a highway bridge because auto-exhaust pollution as well as the garbage thrown off the bridge affects the water.

MAYBE CALCIUM COULD HELP

For the most part, saltwater fish have thicker, denser bones than do freshwater fish, which have thinner bones.

SO LEAVE THE HEAD ON

Fish and shellfish do not have the extensive connective tissue found in land animals, so they gelatinize quickly when cooked with moist heat. If you overcook fish, the muscle fibers will toughen. Cooking fish with the head and tail on makes them moister because more of the liquid is retained during the cooking process.

Fat and Calories in Meat (per 3.5 Ounces)			
	FAT (g)	% FAT (CAL)	TOTAL (CAL)
BEEF			
Bottom round, roasted	6.0	31	117
Sirloin roast	5.6	28	180
Top round, broiled	4.0	19	190
Chuck arm, braised	6.3	29	198
Flank steak, broiled	10.1	44	207
Club steak, broiled	29.0	36	242
Chuck blade, braised	25.8	67	248
Ground beef (lean), broiled	18.5	61	272
Ground beef (reg.), broiled	20.7	64	289
T-Bone, broiled	23.3	68	309
Porterhouse, broiled	25.6	70	327
Rump roast	27.0	71	344
Sirloin steak, broiled	32.0	75	384
PORK			
Tenderloin, roasted	4.8	26	164
Ham leg (butt), roasted	8.1	35	206
Loin, roasted	9.6	41	209
Ham leg (shank), roasted	10.5	44	215
Shoulder, roasted	13.5	53	230
LAMB			
Foreshank, braised	6.0	29	187
Leg (sirloin half), roasted	9.2	41	204
Arm (or shoulder) chop, broiled	10.5	45	210
Loin chop, broiled	11.3	48	211
Rib chop, broiled	12.9	49	235
VEAL			
Sirloin chop, roasted	6.2	33	168
Blade steak, roasted	6.9	36	171
Loin chop, roasted	6.9	35	175
Rib roast	7.4	37	177

TURKEY TIPS AND CHICKEN FACTS

11

WHO KNEW?

When breading chicken cutlets, always use one hand for wet ingredients and the other for the breadcrumbs.

A GOOD THING

Look for stuffing bags, designed to be placed in the cavity of the bird before stuffing it. This is an excellent idea because the stuffing can be removed all at once. If you don't find stuffing bags at your market, lining the cavity with cheesecloth will accomplish the same thing.

SERIOUS STUFF

Stuffed or cooked poultry should never remain at room temperature for more than 40 minutes. Salmonella, which may be present in the meat, thrives at temperatures of 40°F to 145°F. All stuffing should be removed when the bird is ready for carving. Hot stuffing will keep the interior temperature just right for the growth of bacteria. Stuffing should always be cooked to a temperature of 165°F.

CHICKEN SALAD SMARTS

When you make a chicken or turkey salad, be sure the meat has been cooked to 185°F, and then allow it to cool in the refrigerator before adding salad dressing or mayonnaise.

HOW REVOLTING

Production chickens are raised in large coop farms, each of which houses more than 10,000 birds. The chickens are placed in holding boxes and fed around the clock to fatten them up. Poultry in other countries is never subjected to the conditions we allow in the United States, and the flavor of birds from foreign countries is much better.

FOR CHEAPER CHICKEN

To save money, buy chickens whole, cut them up with poultry shears, and freeze in portion-size packages. When you purchase whole birds, remember that larger birds are older, and therefore tougher. Younger chickens and turkeys have less fat.

FOR THE BEST CHICKEN

Lemon is a natural tenderizer for chicken and gives it a lovely flavor. Also, try basting chicken with a small amount of white Zinfandel; wine helps crisp the skin, and the sugar in the wine imparts a brown color and glaze to the outside of the meat. A chicken cooked at a constant 375°F will be juicier because more fat and moisture will be retained.

TICK TOCK

Chicken parts or cut-up chicken should be used within 24 hours. Do not keep uncooked whole poultry in the fridge for more than two days.

WHO KNEW?

Cooking chicken breasts with the ribs intact tends to keep the meat moister.

DON'T FENCE ME IN

A free-range chicken has an average of 14 percent fat compared with 18 to 20 percent fat in a standard cooped-up chicken.

JUST DON'T PUT THEM IN YOUR COCKTAIL

Make do-it-yourself bouillon cubes by freezing leftover chicken broth in ice-cube trays. The cubes can be kept frozen in zip-close plastic bags until needed. They are easily defrosted in the microwave—or just toss them into a soup or sauce, and they'll melt quickly enough.

FRESH CAN BE FROZEN

When you see a chicken labeled "fresh," ask the butcher whether it was previously frozen. Chickens can be stored at 26°F and still be called fresh, even though they will freeze at this temperature. If a chicken has been frozen, it would be best not to refreeze it.

THE UPSIDE DOWN SOLUTION

Try cooking your next turkey breast-side down on a V-rack for the first hour. The juices will flow to the breast and make the meat moist and tender. Remove the V-rack after the first hour. After trying this, you will never buy another commercially prepared self-basting bird.

REWRAP YOR CHICKEN

To store chicken in the refrigerator, wrap it in clean plastic wrap or waxed paper. The supermarket wrapping often contains bloody residues.

FOR A HAPPY TURKEY

Brush or apply a thin layer of white vermouth to the skin of a turkey about 15 minutes before you are ready to remove it from the oven. The sugars in the wine will give the skin a rich brown color.

FOUL FOWL TALK

Never stuff a turkey or other fowl and leave it overnight, even in the refrigerator. The inside of the bird acts like an incubator, promoting rapid bacterial growth. Cooking the bird may not kill all the bacteria. Hundreds of cases of food poisoning occur every year because birds are stuffed and then left for too long before roasting.

A PERFECT TIME FOR THE COOK TO HAVE A COCKTAIL

Once a turkey has finished cooking, it should be allowed to rest for about 20 minutes before carving. As with other roasts, this standing time allows the proteins in the meat to reabsorb the juices, so they stay in the meat rather than spilling onto the cutting board.

THE BIRD RULE

Always refrigerate chicken breasts after flouring, but before cooking. The coating will adhere better that way. Also, try adding a teaspoon of baking powder to your batter, and using club soda instead of water for a delicate coating.

BUY FREE-RANGE BIRDS

Always buy free-range chickens, which will have been reared with enough space to move around freely and develop muscle tone. The meat will be leaner and better for you than the meat from less-mobile birds.

SO YOU KNOW

Poultry, whether whole or parts, thaws at the rate of approximately 1 pound every five hours in the refrigerator.

LIVER COMES LATER

When cooking giblets, do not add the liver until the last five minutes. If added too soon, it will impart its flavor to all the rest of the ingredients.

A CHICKEN BY ANY OTHER NAME

You may find chicken labeled with any number of terms, some of which have only recently been regulated by the government. Here are some:

Broilers and Fryers

These are 2½ month-old birds that weigh up to 3½ pounds.

Capons

These are castrated roosters that are less than 10 weeks old and weigh 4 to 10 pounds. They usually have abundant breast meat.

Cornish Hens

A special breed of chicken that typically weighs less than 2 pounds. They are best grilled or roasted.

?·?
?

WHO KNEW?

The best way to thaw turkey is on a shallow baking sheet in the refrigerator, in it's original packaging. Allow 24 hours for every 5 pounds of bird.

Free-Range

According to USDA regulations, chickens' cage doors must be kept open, and the exercise they get as a result provides better flavor. The meat is a better quality, and they have a higher proportion of meat to bone. These chickens are usually sold whole.

Kosher

Are slaughtered and cleaned in compliance with Jewish dietary laws.

Mass-Produced

These are commercially raised in crowded coops and are never allowed to run free. They are marketed in exact sizes and always at the same age.

Organic

Not yet defined by the government, so each producer is free to set its own definition. Reputable chicken farmers will adhere to certain standards, such as raising chickens on land that has not been treated with any chemical fertilizer or pesticide in at least three years, feeding the birds chemical-free grains, and letting them range freely.

Poussins

The French term that refers to very young, small chickens. Poussins are best when grilled.

Roasting Chickens

These are usually hens that weigh 2½ to 5 pounds and contain more fat than broilers.

WHO KNEW?

If your roasted chicken tends to be too dry, try stuffing a whole apple inside the bird before roasting. Just toss the apple before serving.

Stewing Hens

Usually weigh 3 to 6 pounds and are 10 to 18 months old. Basically, these are retired laying hens. They are tough old birds that need to be cooked slowly, but they are very flavorful.

BE SAFE

If a piece of chicken that has 10,000 bacteria per square centimeter (sadly, not so unusual) gets to the supermarket, that number will increase 10,000 times after the bird is left in the refrigerator for six days. The Centers for Disease Control and Prevention estimates that 5,200 people die each year from food-borne illnesses, with as many as 76 million others becoming ill from bacterial, chemical, fertilizer, and pesticide residues left on poultry and other foods. According to the USDA, 40 percent of all chickens can be contaminated with salmonella, and even if contaminated, they can still pass USDA inspection.

DID YOU EVER PLUCK A DUCK?

To pluck a duck, dip it in water that is at least 155°F; it is easier to pluck the feathers if they are hot and wet. To pluck a goose, pheasant, or quail, the water should be at least 135°F. However, hot-soaking the birds breaks down fatty tissues in the skin, and should only be done if the birds are to be cooked immediately after plucking. If you plan to freeze the game birds or plan to hold them before cooking, pluck them dry.

DO THE MATH

A three-pound chicken will yield about 2½ cups of meat, or five servings.

GRANDMA ALWAYS DID IT THIS WAY

Do you find that stuffing spills out when you stuff a bird? Next time, seal the opening with a slice of raw potato.

CHECK FOR LIQUID

When choosing meat or poultry in the supermarket, make sure that there is no liquid on the bottom of the package. If there is, it means the food has been frozen and thawed; the cells have ruptured, releasing some of their fluids. Never refreeze poultry that has thawed.

AND NOBODY LIKES A STICKY RACK

When grilling chicken, always grease the rack well. Why? Because as the bird cooks, the collagen in the skin turns into a sticky gelatin, which will cause it to stick to the rack. Another way to solve the problem is to sear the chicken on the grill, and then finish it in a preheated oven 15 to 20 minutes, breast-side up.

CHECK THE LABEL!

It is best to compare nutrition labels when purchasing ground turkey or chicken. In most instances, their meats will be as high in fat as lean ground beef. Look for labels that say "ground turkey breast" or "ground chicken breast"—otherwise the poultry has probably been ground with the high-fat skin. If you can't find it at your supermarket, ask the butcher to grind boneless skinless chicken or turkey breast for you, or grind it yourself in a food processor.

SQUAB

Squabs are domesticated pigeons that have never flown; they are no more than a month old and weigh less than 1 pound. They are specially bred to be plump and are usually sold frozen. Look for birds with pale skin; the plumper the better. Squab can be stored frozen for about six months at 0°F.

THAT'S BEFORE WASHING THEM DOWN WITH BEER

Chicken wings, alias Buffalo wings, can supply up to 25 grams of fat per 3-wing serving.

SECRETS OF BARBECUED CHICKEN

Remember that barbecue sauces contain sugar, and high heat can burn the sugar as well as some of the spices in the sauce. Never apply the sauce to the bird until about five minutes before it is fully cooked. Another secret is to use low heat and leave the bird on the grill for a longer period. Never place the bird too close to the coals.

SCRUB YOUR CHICKEN

Chickens must be thoroughly cleaned inside and out before cooking in order to remove any residues that may be left from the slaughtering process. If you detect a slight off odor when you open the package, rinse the bird under cool water, and then put it in a solution of 1 tablespoon lemon juice or vinegar and 1 teaspoon salt per cup of water (use enough water to cover the bird). Refrigerate one to four hours before cooking.

GO NAKED

If you're used to eating roast chicken with the skin on, removing the skin will reduce the calorie count from 220 to 155 for an average portion, as most of the fat is in the skin. Trim the calories further by removing any excess fat before cooking.

ANYONE?

If your family picks at the turkey and trimmings before the meal is served, try this. Make more stuffing than you need. Fill some buttered muffin pans with the stuffing and bake in a very hot oven, and you'll have a crunchy treat that's moist on the inside. When folks come in for a taste of the feast, offer them a platter of stuffing muffins (*stuffins?*) instead.

GO STUFF A DUCK

Or better yet, don't. Duck is not a good candidate for stuffing, because its fat content is so high that it is absorbed into the stuffing during cooking.

THIS REALLY SAVES TIME

The easiest way to skin a chicken is to partially freeze it first. The skin will come right off the bird with almost no effort.

GIVE IT A TRY

Brushing chicken skin with reduced-sodium soy sauce during the last 30 minutes of roasting will produce a beautiful brown color.

THE ALL IMPORTANT POULTRY BATH

The safest method of thawing frozen poultry is to place it—still wrapped in plastic—in a bowl of cold water. Change the water as it warms up.

TRASH TO TREAT

Don't throw away excess chicken stock, wine, bacon grease, or anything else you use for your favorite recipes. Just freeze in ice cube trays, then store in airtight plastic bags. When a recipe calls for the frozen ingredient, just pop in a cube. Each ice cube is about one heaping tablespoon. Chopped parsley (when added to a bit of water) can also be stored this way as well.

DARK VERSUS WHITE

When you're cooking chicken parts, remember that dark meat takes longer to cook than white does because of its higher fat content. Start the dark meat a few minutes before the white. Assuming the parts are about the same size, smaller pieces of chicken will cook faster than larger ones. The white meat might be too dry if it is cooked as long as the dark.

STUFFING SAVER

If you plan to cook your stuffing in the turkey, consider this tip: Pack it into a piece of cheesecloth before placing it in the bird. When you're ready to remove the stuffing, simply pull the cheesecloth out, and none of the stuffing will be stuck inside the turkey.

STORE-AGE

If you're cooking less than a full package of bacon, how do you store the extra slices? In the refrigerator, the slices will go rancid in a little time, so the freezer is your best bet. Just roll each slice into a tight cylinder, place in an airtight plastic bag, and freeze. Simply thaw and unroll when you're ready to cook!

GOBBLE A HEALTHY FEAST

Turkey is a great source of protein because it's very low in fat. It's also high in B vitamins, which help boost your body's health, and in the amino acid tryptophan, which aids restful sleep – making it a great late-night snack.

FOR A TASTE TREAT

Chefs tenderize and improve the taste of chicken by submerging them in buttermilk and refrigerating for two to three hours before cooking.

GRADE INFLATION

Chickens in the United States are sold as Grade A, Grade B, or Grade C. Grades B and C are usually blemished and are used only for canning, frozen foods, and TV dinners; they are not available at the retail level. Grade A chickens are sold in supermarket meat departments.

CHEF'S SECRETS

chapter **12**

VEGETABLE COOKING

Baking or Roasting

Root vegetables—carrots, potatoes, winter squash, jicama, and beets—are well suited to baking and roasting. Make sure that the vegetable has high enough water content, or it will dry out quickly when cooked. Leave the skins on to preserve most of the vegetables' nutrients. Roast softer vegetables, like broccoli florets and asparagus, for 10 to 15 minutes.

Pressure Cooking

It can be difficult to pressure-cook vegetables; overcooking is common. Follow the directions that come with your appliance.

Stir-Frying

This is a fast method, provided the wok or skillet is well heated first. Because foods cook so rapidly, you're more likely to retain heat-sensitive vitamins, such as A and E.

WHO KNEW?

Before filling your measuring cup with honey or molasses the next time you make cookies, line it with flour. The ingredients then pour out easily, and make cleanup a breeze.

Waterless Cooking

Best for cooking green leafy vegetables. By using only the water that clings to their leaves after washing, it just takes only three to five minutes for it to get cooked thoroughly.

Boiling

When you boil vegetables, follow these guidelines:

- Vegetables should always be added to water that is already boiling.
- The shorter the time in the water, the more nutrients will be retained.
- Vitamin C is lost very quickly.
- The water should boil for two minutes before the vegetables are added to release some of the oxygen. Oxygen causes nutrient loss.
- If possible, cook the vegetables whole and unpeeled. The more surface that is exposed, the more nutrients will be lost.

Slow-Cooking

Avoid slow-cookers for vegetables. During prolonged cooking, most of the nutrients will be lost because of the heat.

Microwaving

Vegetables cook rapidly, so nutrients are retained. The water content of the vegetables will determine just how well they will cook. Microwave ovens should have a turntable so that the food will cook evenly. Foods cooked in a microwave may need to be rotated or stirred to ensure that they are cooked thoroughly and properly.

Measurement Facts
60 drops = 5 ml. = 1 teaspoon
3 teaspoons = 1 tablespoon
2 tablespoons = 30 ml. = 1 fl. oz.
8 tablespoons = ½ cup
5 large eggs = 1 cup
1 oz. = 28 g.

Steaming

This method cooks vegetables in a short period and retains most of the nutrients. Start with denser vegetables such as carrots or Brussels sprouts, and then add the softer ones, like broccoli florets, later.

Are You Steaming?			
VEGETABLE	TIME	VEGETABLE	TIME
Artichokes	20–25 minutes	Carrots	6–8 minutes
Green beans	10–20 minutes	Cauliflower	5 minutes
Beets	30 minutes	Corn on the cob	7 minutes
Broccoli florets	3–5 minutes	Green peas	5 minutes
Brussels sprouts	6–8 minutes	Pearl onions	20–30 minutes
Cabbage	10 minutes	Potatoes (all)	20–25 minutes

THERMOMETERS

To check the accuracy of a food thermometer, place it in boiling water for three to four minutes. The temperature should read 212°F.

Deep-Fat/Candy

The bulb should be fully immersed in the candy or fat and should never touch the bottom of the cooking container.

Instant-Read

These thin, pointed thermometers have many applications and advantages. Use them to measure water temperature for baking or internal temperatures of many cuts of meat or baked-egg dishes. They register temperatures almost immediately; their small shafts and sharp points mean that little of a meat's juices will escape. Just be sure you don't put these thermometers in the oven!

Meat

Insert the thermometer into the center or thickest part of the meat, making sure that it is not touching bone or a pocket of fat or connective tissue. These thermometers can go into the oven. If you have an instant-read thermometer, you don't need a meat thermometer.

Freezer/Refrigerator

These thermometers read from -20°F to 80°F. Frozen foods should always be stored at 0°F or below to slow nutrient loss and to maintain the quality of the food for a long time.

?? WHO KNEW?

When sautéing or frying, always heat your pan before adding butter or oil to ensure that nothing sticks.

Oven

These thermometers check the accuracy of your oven. If the temperature is not accurate, it can affect the results of the food being prepared, especially baked goods. The thermometer should be placed in the middle of the center rack. If the thermostat and the thermometer give different readings, you can either adjust the thermostat when you bake or roast, or have your oven's thermostat recalibrated.

Cooking Temperatures	
FOOD	TEMPERATURE
BEEF, LAMB, VEAL	
Rare	140°F (not recommended)
Medium-rare	145°F
Medium	160°F
Medium-well	165°F
Well-done	170°F
PORK AND HAM	
Medium	160°F
Well-done	170°F
Precooked (ham)	140°F
GROUND BEEF, PORK, LAMB	160°F
POULTRY	
Ground	165°F
Whole	180°F
Parts	170°F
Stuffing (alone or in bird)	165°F
Egg dishes	160°F
Leftovers	165°F.

GRANDMA WAS RIGHT

To keep a pot from boiling over, stick a toothpick between the lid and the pot. Other tricks include placing a wooden spoon across the top of the uncovered pot or rubbing butter around the inside lip of the pot.

VINEGAR TO THE RESCUE

To help control unpleasant cooking aromas, dampen a cloth with a 50-50 mixture of vinegar and water. Drape it over the cooking pot, taking care that the edges are far from the flame or intense heat.

CANOLA TO THE RESCUE

To sauté or fry with butter, margarine, or lard, add a small amount of canola oil to raise the smoke point. This will keep the solid fat from breaking down at lower temperatures.

PUDDING PROBLEMS?

Laying a sheet of wax paper directly onto a custard or pudding while it is still hot will keep a layer of skin from developing.

DON'T FORGET TO BLAME YOUR HUSBAND

If a child accidentally turns on the microwave when it's empty, it can be damaging to the oven. To avoid any problems, just keep a cup of water in the microwave when it is not in use.

WHO KNEW?

Always sprinkle a little salt in your pan before frying—it keeps hot oil from splattering and makes cleanup that much easier.

DON'T BE AN EGG POPPER

Never try to hard cook eggs in the microwave—whole eggs may explode. When cooking an egg with a whole yolk, prick a small hole in the yolk with a pin. The yolk won't break, but you'll allow for its expansion.

DEEP-FRYING SECRET

Sometimes food sticks together when you're deep-frying. To prevent this, lift the basket out of the fat several times before allowing it to stay in the fat. And don't try to fry too much at once—the fat may bubble over from the temperature difference of the cold food and the hot fat. And speaking of hot fat, be sure it's 300°F to 375°F before you add the food.

BETTER BREADING BLEND (SAY THAT THREE TIMES FAST)

The following breading blend can make any food taste better and enhance its flavor. Mix the ingredients together and refrigerate the mixture until needed. Use about ½ cup at a time, and let the breaded food stand at room temperature for 20 minutes before cooking.

2 cups whole-wheat pastry flour	1 teaspoon ground black pepper
½ tablespoon paprika	1 teaspoon dried basil
1 tablespoon dry mustard	1 teaspoon dried marjoram
¾ teaspoon finely ground celery seed	¼ teaspoon dried thyme

WHO KNEW?

Try adding a cup of water to the bottom of the broiling pan before cooking a roast. It'll make the roast more tender, and absorb smoke and grease.

NO BONE IS BEST

To brown meats in the microwave, you'll have to use a special dish. The dish should always be preheated for the best results. If you don't have a browning dish, brush the meat with soy or teriyaki sauce.

If the meat has a bone, more energy will go to the bone than to the meat, and the meat may not cook evenly. If possible, remove the bone.

AND LESS OIL IS ALWAYS BETTER THAN MORE OIL

To coat food with a very thin layer of oil, use a spray bottle with oil in it (there are special misters that can accommodate the viscosity of oil). This beats using a brush and reduces the amount of oil used.

AND WHO DOESN'T WANT LESS FAT?

Frying meat in oil does not lower the fat content—any fat that renders out will be replaced by oil that is absorbed. However, all other methods of cooking will lower the fat content.

STEAM RELEASE

When baking potatoes, pierce the skin with a fork to allow the steam to escape. Your reward will be a wonderfully fluffy texture.

75:25

Keep a shaker filled with a ratio of 75 percent salt and 25 percent pepper next to the range or food-preparation area.

WHO KNEW?

To crush ginger easily, peel it and put it through a garlic press.

BUT YOU KNEW THIS ALREADY, RIGHT?

Your market has only canned whole tomatoes and you need chopped? Not a problem. Simply insert a pair of scissors into the can and snip.

SO NEVER RUN OUT OF PAPER TOWELS

Use paper towels to blot dry any foods that will be fried or sautéed before cooking which prevents spatters. Also, set fried foods on paper towels for a few minutes before serving to allow the excess oil to drain off.

AND WHO WANTS TO EAT GRAY FOOD?

Don't add baking soda to foods while they are cooking. It may destroy certain B vitamins, and it turns some vegetables a grayish color.

IT'S GOOD TO BE SHALLOW

Always use a shallow pot for cooking roasts. This will allow air to circulate more efficiently. Elevating the meat by cooking it atop celery ribs, carrot sticks, or ¼ to ½-inch-thick onion slices also helps.

POP! GOES THE CONTAINER

A microwave oven is just as safe as a conventional oven. However, make sure you never place a sealed container in a microwave. The pressure can build up, and the container can explode (this is also why you should prick egg yolks and potatoes before microwaving them).

CRISPIER TOP

If you would like a crisp topping on your casserole, leave it uncovered for the last 15 minutes of baking.

RUST IS BUST

Cast iron and other pans with high iron content may rust. To prevent this, wash and dry the pan thoroughly, then wipe the inner surface with a thin layer of vegetable oil after each use.

KEEP THE VITAMINS

Cooking vegetables whole slows down nutrient loss. For example, carrots that are boiled whole will retain up to 90 percent of their vitamin C and most of their minerals. Sliced carrots will lose almost all of their vitamin C and niacin content when boiled.

CURDLING CAUSES

Acid, heat, and salt are the three main causes of curdling. Older dairy products have higher levels of lactic acid, so use fresh milk and cream in sauces.

WHO KNEW?

Put garlic cloves in the microwave for 15 seconds, and the skins will slide right off.

CURDLE CURE

Dairy products can curdle if cooked over a high heat. Take care to keep the heat low—no higher than 180°F—so that the food doesn't boil.

FRUIT AND VEGETABLE PREPARATION

Washing and Soaking

Water-soluble vitamins are very delicate and can be lost if vegetables or fruits are left to soak for too long. Dieters often store carrots or celery in a bowl of water in the refrigerator for easy access, but the natural sugars, most of the B vitamins, vitamin C, and vitamin D—not to mention all minerals except calcium—may be lost. It's best to wash vegetables just before you use them.

Slicing and Shredding

When you shred vegetables for salads you will lose 20 percent of the vitamin C content. Then, if you allow a salad to stand for one hour before serving it, you will lose another 20 percent.

POSITION IS EVERYTHING

When microwaving foods that are not uniform in shape or thickness, be sure to arrange the larger, thicker, or tougher areas toward the outside of the pan.

WHO KNEW?

Dip scissors often in hot water when cutting dried fruits, gumdrops, or anything sticky.

COOKWARE ALTERNATIVES

Aluminum

The majority of cookware sold in the United States is aluminum, which is an excellent heat conductor. Recent studies report that there is no risk from using this type of cookware unless your pans are deeply scratched, which allows aluminum to be released into the food.

Iron

Iron cookware will impart a fair amount of dietary iron. It can react with acidic foods such as tomato sauce or citrus fruit to produce off flavors. Iron pots and pans absorb and retain heat very well.

Stainless Steel

This metal is a poor heat conductor unless made with a copper or aluminum bottom. Stainless steel does not react with acidic foods.

Nonstick Cookware

These are made of a type of fluorocarbon resin that may react with acidic foods. If you do chip off a small piece and it gets into the food, don't be concerned; it will pass harmlessly through the body if you swallow it.

Never allow any brand of pan with a nonstick-cooking surface to boil dry. The pan may release fumes that are fatally toxic to pet birds like parakeets if heated above 530°F for long periods.

Glass, Copper, Enameled Cookware

Copper is one of the best heat conductors and is preferred by many chefs. Copper pans, however, should be purchased only if they have a liner of tin or stainless steel for safety; otherwise they may leach metals into the food. Glass and enameled cast iron are nonreactive. Glass heats up very slowly, but retains heat very well. When you bake or roast food in glassware, remember to reduce the oven temperature by 25°F.

Clay Pots

Always soak both the top and bottom of clay pots in lukewarm water for at least 15 minutes before using them. Don't preheat the oven when using a clay pot—put it into a cold oven, then turn on the heat; if sudden temperature changes occur, the cookware may be cracked. Never place a clay cooker on top of the range.

A Note on Convection Ovens

This appliance utilizes a fan that continuously circulates hot air. As a result, food cooks more evenly, and up to 25 percent faster than in a conventional oven. Convection ovens are great for baked goods and roasts, but be sure to follow the manufacturer's recommendations to the letter, especially concerning temperature. Baked goods are easily browned and need to be watched closely.

COAL TRUTH

- To add flavor to barbecued foods, place herbs on the hot coals. The best are savory rosemary, or dried basil.
- If the coals become too hot or flare up, spray them with water from a mister, or squirt them with water from a bulb baster.
- Store charcoal briquettes in airtight plastic bags, because they absorb moisture very easily.

PARCOOKING, DEFINED

Parcooking means to cook a food partially. You can parcook by boiling, blanching, steaming, or microwaving.

GREAT GRILLING

Coat your grill with a spray vegetable oil before starting the fire, and then clean it shortly after you are through. Never spray the oil on the grill after the fire has started—it may cause a flare-up.

Spray window cleaner on a grill that's still warm to make cleanup easier.

SAUTÉING

- When sautéing, make sure you only use a small amount of oil, and heat it to a high temperature before adding the food. To test the temperature of the oil, drop a small piece of food into the pan, if it sizzles, it is hot enough for sautéing.
- Food will brown faster and cook more evenly if it is not just out of the refrigerator. Cold foods tend to stick to the pan. But for food safety, never keep raw eggs, meat, fish, or poultry at room temperature for more than 20 minutes. During the sautéing process, the food should be stirred constantly to ensure that the browning will be even.
- Before sautéing carrots, potatoes, or any dense food, parcook it first. This ensures that the inside will be cooked before the exterior burns. Foods that are to be sautéed should be dry. Too much moisture on the surface can cause oil to spatter, and it can prevent the surface of the food from browning.
- Before sautéing meats, sprinkle a tiny amount of sugar on the surface of the meat. The sugar will react with the juices and then caramelize, causing a deeper browning as well as improving the flavor.
- Never crowd a pan with food. Overcrowding causes poor heat distribution, which will result in food that is not evenly browned.
- If the foods render too much fat, remove the excess with a bulb baster.
- Never cover a pan when sautéing. Steam tends to build up and the food may become mushy.

TRY A LITTLE TENDERNESS

Less tender cuts of meat that contain a large percentage of connective tissue, or have a tough fibrous structure such as those found in certain vegetables, should be cooked using moist heat. This method helps to break down the fibers of the food, which will tenderize it. There are, of course, exceptions to the rule, two of which are if the meat is heavily marbled or frequently basted. In these cases, dry heat is acceptable.

CHEMISTRY LESSON

When you heat food, you are increasing the speed of the molecules in that food. The faster the molecules move, the more they collide—and the more heat is generated, the hotter the food gets. This changes the texture, flavor, and even the color of the food. As a matter of fact, for every 20°F you raise the temperature over the normal cooking temperature, you increase the molecular activity by 100 percent.

ANOTHER REASON TO CUT BACK ON SALT

Salt draws moisture from foods. If a food is salted before it goes into the fryer, the salt will draw moisture to the surface and cause the food to spatter when it is placed into the heated oil.

AND THIS TO YOU IS A SURPRISE?

When it comes to slaving over a hot grill, it's Dad who gets the chore 60 percent of the time. However, Mom chooses what goes on the grill almost 100 percent of the time. Her most frequent choices: burgers, chicken, hot dogs, and corn on the cob.

COVER UP

When you boil water, cover the pot and the water will come to a boil faster—once it reaches 150°F. At this point, the water is generating steam, which when trapped, heats the water faster. Raising 1 gallon of water from 60°F to 212°F (the boiling point) on a gas range top takes 23 minutes with the lid on; without the lid it takes about 35 minutes.

A SLOW BOIL

When water boils, the temperature is 212°F (give or take one degree), whether it's boiling gently or rapidly. Food cooks more evenly and retains more nutrients if the water is at a slower boil. Hard water, due to its high mineral content, will reach boiling 1°F to 2°F above soft water.

SHUT IT

If you worry about the amount of heat escaping when you open the oven door when something's cooking, relax. When the door is opened or left ajar for a few minutes it usually takes 40 to 50 seconds for the oven to return to the preset temperature.

FRESH IS BEST

When oil is used for frying, the temperature is raised to such a high level that a percentage of the oil breaks down (which happens as the oil begins smoking) and decomposes into free fatty acids. Even the oil from a brand-new bottle can break down in a matter of minutes. As a result, it's always best to use fresh oil each time you fry.

THE HOT PAN TEST

Cooking pans should be made of a material that will distribute the heat evenly throughout the bottom of the pan, yet not all pans conduct heat evenly. To see whether a pan has hot spots, mix about 4 to 5 tablespoons of sugar with 2 tablespoons of water and pour it into the pan, swirling or spreading to cover the bottom in an even layer. Set the pan over medium heat. The syrup over the hot spots will caramelize and turn brown, creating a visible pattern. Ideally, you won't see a pattern of hot spots, and the sugar will caramelize at the same time. If you do see a pattern, use a heat diffuser under the pan or try the same test using a lower heat setting.

FUN WITH DEEP FRYING

When you add food to hot oil, the temperature of the oil will be lowered. The more food you add, the more the temperature will drop, and the longer it will take to return to normal frying temperature. When this happens, the food will absorb oil and become greasy. There are two steps to preventing this. First, never add too much food to the oil at one time: Not only does it lower the temperature of the oil, but the overcrowding will also prevent the food from frying evenly. Second, be sure the food is close to room temperature before placing it in the fryer: If the food is too cold the oil may drop down to the greasy range of about 300°F to 325°F and may never get back to the proper temperature.

BUT IT SURE LOOKS GOOD

Copper cookware can be pricey, and requires care to look its best. A paste of lemon juice and coarse salt makes an inexpensive copper cleaner.

SMOKE, FLASH, AND FIRE POINTS OF OILS

The so-called smoke point of an oil is the point at which the oil starts deteriorating—that is, the oil starts to convert into free fatty acids. All oils have different smoke points; those with the highest are best for frying. Most neutral-flavored cooking oils have the highest smoke points; oils from nuts or fruits, such as walnut oil, hazelnut oil, or olive oil, tend to have lower smoke points.

The flash point is the temperature at which a small amount of flame starts to emanate from the surface of the oil. This usually occurs at about 600°F and is a clear signal that the oil temperature has reached a dangerous level. The fire point is about 700°F. If oil gets this hot, it will ignite. Remember, never use water to put out a grease fire. Cover the pan with a lid, dump in a box of baking soda, or use a fire extinguisher.

Smoke Points of Fats	
FAT	SMOKE POINT
Safflower oil	450°F
Peanut oil	450°F
Soybean oil	450°F
Canola oil	435°F
Corn oil	410°F
Sesame oil	410°F
Sunflower oil	390°F
Olive oil	375°F
Lard	361–401°F
Vegetable shortening	356–370°F
Unclarified butter	350°F

COOKING STUFFED TURKEY

The best temperature for cooking stuffed turkey is 325°F. At lower temperatures, the stuffing doesn't get out of the danger zone of 40°F to 140°F, giving bacteria more time to multiply. Higher temperatures bring the turkey and stuffing to safer temperatures sooner, but may shorten the cooking time so that not all bacteria are killed. Slow overnight cooking with the dressing in the bird causes numerous cases of food poisoning.

WE LIKE GAS

Gas ranges for home kitchens burn hotter than electric ranges, and professional gas ranges burn the hottest of all. Gas heat is also easily controlled, and this is why most chefs prefer it. With electric ranges, it's more difficult to make small changes in temperature.

SWEET SECRET

Candy makers know that keeping the sugar from crystallizing during cooking is a big problem. There's a simple solution to this: Heat the sugar over low heat, without stirring, until the sugar is completely dissolved. To dissolve any sugar crystals that cling to the sides of the pan, cover the pan with a tight-fitting lid and continue cooking the syrup for three to four minutes. The steam that is generated will melt the sugar crystals.

WHO KNEW?

When you put the rolls in the oven to bake, put a ceramic tile in, too. When the rolls are done, the tile is hot. Place it in the basket and put your rolls on top. The tile will keep them warm.

KEEP 'EM RED

To keep beets, um, beet red when cooking, cook them whole with at least two inches of stem still attached, and add a few tablespoons of white vinegar to the water.

HEAVY METAL FACTS

There are a number of materials that are used to manufacture pots and pans, many of which are better for some tasks than for others. Remember, the thicker the gauge of the metal the more uniformly it distributes heat. The finish on the metal will also affect the efficiency of the cookware.

Aluminum

Aluminum cookware stains very easily, especially if you are cooking with hard water. Certain foods, such as potatoes, will also cause the pans to stain easily. Cooking high-acid foods such as tomatoes, onions, wine, or lemon juice, will probably remove some of the stain. However, if the pan is stained when the acidic food is cooked, the stain may transfer to the food and turn it a brownish color. Aluminum pans also tend to warp if they are subjected to rapid temperature changes, especially if they are made of thin-gauge aluminum. Heavy-gauge pans are excellent heat conductors and will not rust.

Cast Iron and Carbon Steel

These are both nonstainless-steel, iron-based metals that have a somewhat porous, jagged surface. These pots need to be seasoned. To accomplish this, you need to rub the cooking surface with canola oil and heat it in the oven to 300°F for 40 to 50 minutes, and then allow it to cool to room temperature before using it. The oil seals the pores and provides a somewhat nonstick surface. Once the pan is seasoned, the oil forms a barrier that keeps water out and rust at bay. These pots should be washed right after each use using mild soap (heavy scrubbing can remove the seasoning), and then dried immediately. Never use salt to clean the pot, since this may cause rusting. If a cleaner is needed, be sure it is a mild one.

Copper

Copper cookware provides excellent, even heat. It is difficult to keep clean, since black carbon deposits will affect the heat distribution significantly. Copper pots are usually lined with tin, and must be relined if the tin becomes worn; otherwise excess copper may leach into the food.

Copper is reactive, which means that acidic foods may develop off flavors or colors; if the food is high in vitamin C, copper may interfere with it. If you're thinking about purchasing a stainless-steel pan with a copper bottom, be careful—you get what you pay for. Inexpensive pans often have as little as $1/_{50}$-inch-thick copper coating, which is much too thin to distribute heat efficiently and uniformly.

Enamel-Coated

These pans are metal coated with a thin layer of enamel. The coating is produced by fusing powdered glass into the metal surface, which is in most instances cast iron. The cookware resists corrosion, but the enamel can chip easily if hit against another object or dropped, and can even shatter if removed from a very hot range and placed into cold water.

Glass Cookware

Rapid temperature changes may cause glass to crack or break. Glass has a very low "heat-flow" efficiency rating, so the heat that is transferred from the bottom of the cookware will travel slowly to the top of the pot. Because of this, the bottom of the pot will swell and the top of the pot does not expand, creating a structural type of stress where a crack is very likely. Although some glass pots are obviously intended for use on top of the stove, most glass will shatter when exposed to direct heat and should not be used on the stove or under the broiler. Check the product literature and heed the manufacturer's directions.

LUNCH DELIGHT

Hot dogs can be school day lunch treats. Just wrap a cooked dog in a sealed plastic bag and place in a thermos filled with hot water, pack a fresh bun, and send the kids to school. At lunchtime, they can assemble their favorite meal.

DON'T DISCARD THE RINDS OF LIMES, LEMONS OR ORANGES

Grate them and store in tightly covered glass jars in the fridge. They make excellent flavoring for cakes, and can be sprinkled over chicken and fish as well.

Multi-Ply

The bottoms of these pans usually have three layers. They are constructed with a layer of aluminum between two layers of stainless steel. Stainless steel does not have a hot-spot problem, and the heat will be more evenly diffused by the aluminum.

Teflon and Silverstone

These nonstick surfaces are the result of a chemically inert fluorocarbon plastic material baked onto the inside of the cookware or other type of cooking utensil. The surface is commercially seasoned, which produces the final slick coating. The food is actually cooked on jagged peaks that protrude from the pan, which keep the food from sticking. The major benefits of nonstick cookware are that you can use less fat, and cleanup is frequently much easier. Less expensive nonstick cookware usually has a very thin coating and will not last very long with everyday use. With frequent use and cleaning, the coating will eventually wear thin.

CRUCIFEROUS COOKING

When you cook cruciferous vegetables such as broccoli, cabbage, or cauliflower, never use an aluminum or iron pot. The sulfur compounds in the vegetable will react with the metal. For instance, cauliflower will turn yellow if cooked in aluminum, and brown if cooked in iron.

THE PRESSURE COOKING PLUSES

Pressure-cooking is especially beneficial for people who live in higher altitudes. At 5,000 feet above sea level, water boils at 204°F, so foods take longer to cook at higher elevations. A pressure cooker allows the water to reach 250°F by increasing the atmospheric pressure in the pot and using the steam to cook the food faster. Steam conducts heat better than air and forces the heat into the food.

HMMM! TURKEY AND CHEMICALS!

You may remember your mom or grandmother cooking turkey in a brown bag, but don't do it today! Most supermarket brown bags are produced from recycled paper containing a number of harmful chemicals. When heated, these chemicals can be released into the foods and may produce toxic free radicals.

HIC

The boiling point of alcohol is 173°F, much lower than the boiling point for water (212°F). When alcohol is added to a recipe it will lower the boiling point until it evaporates.

THE GOODS ON GRAVY

Home cooks often use flour to thicken gravy. Because flour thickens somewhat slowly, the temptation is to use too much. Since gravy thickens as it cools, it can become unappealing by the time you're ready for seconds. It can also taste "floury" rather than having the flavor of the meat juices it's made with. Chefs rarely use flour, but deglaze the roasting pan with water, and then add a small amount of butter before reducing the mixture over high heat, stirring frequently, until it is the right consistency.

BBQ TRICK

Impress your guests by barbecuing fresh corn to perfection this way: Before grilling, peel all but the innermost layer of husk from the corn, and trim the excess 'hair' as well. Place on the grill and as soon as the husk darkens enough that the outline of the kernels are visible through it, remove the corn. It will be perfectly cooked with a wonderful, smoky flavor.

BOILING POINT VERSUS ALTITUDE

As the altitude increases, the atmospheric pressure decreases. This places less pressure on water that is trying to boil. When this occurs it makes it easier for the water to boil and the water molecules are released more easily.

Altitude (feet)	Fahrenheit	Celsius
0	212°	100°
1,000	210°	99°
2,000	208°	98°
3,000	206°	97°
4,000	205°	96°
5,000	204°	95°
10,000	194°	90°

ENAMEL ENHANCERS

Remove stains from enamel with a paste of bicarbonate of soda and hydrogen peroxide (gentle bleach). Rub in and leave to dry, then rinse off. Or try a mix of borax and a cut lemon. Do not use scourers or bleach on enamel.

JUST DON'T TRY GLUE

Keeping breading on foods can be a challenge, but there are a few tricks to try. First, make sure that the food that is to be breaded is very dry. Use eggs at room temperature, and beat them lightly. If you have time, refrigerate the breaded food for an hour, then let the food sit at room temperature for 20 minutes before cooking. Homemade breadcrumbs are better than store-bought because of their uneven texture.

WHY PANS WARP

Metal pans have two advantages over other materials: they have a higher heat-flow efficiency rating and they have a tougher internal structure. However, metal pans will warp if exposed to sudden changes in temperature. Thinner pans are less able to withstand the structural stress than thicker ones, so are more likely to warp.

THE EFFICIENT OVEN

Standard and convection ovens are quite similar; the notable difference is that convection ovens have a fan that increases the distribution of the heat molecules, providing heat to all areas more evenly and rapidly. Because of the efficiency of the heat circulation, convection ovens usually require a lower temperature, thereby conserving energy. Roasts especially do well in a convection oven—because of the lower heat, the meat tends to be juicier.

FRYING TONIGHT

The lids of most deep-fat fryers are detachable and some are dishwasher-proof. Clean inside each time you change the oil with a plastic scouring pad and dishwashing liquid, avoiding damage to the non-stick coating. Outside, wipe over with a damp cloth and non-abrasive cleaner.

FOR THE STUBBORN LID

When you cook a food in a covered pot, the air inside the pot increases in pressure, raising the lid ever so slightly so heated air can escape. When you turn off the heat, the air pressure decreases along with the temperature and may become lower than the air pressure outside the pot. This decrease in pressure, along with the water from the steam, creates a vacuum around the lid and seals it tight. The longer the lid is left on, the tighter the seal. If this occurs, just try setting the pot over moderate heat for a minute or two. Why? Because the heat will increase the air pressure in the pot, loosening the lid's seal.

WHO KNEW?

A sharp knife is actually safer than a dull one. Dull knives are more likely to slip off foods, resulting in cut fingers.

ONE FROM COLUMN A, ONE FROM COLUMN B

Some appliance manufacturers are making ranges with gas cooktops and electric ovens, so home cooks can have the best of both worlds.

MICROWAVE SECRETS

Microwave cooking is less expensive than most other methods. However, it is desirable only for certain types of foods. Meats, for instance, seem to end up a little mushy and don't attain the brown color we find appealing. Frozen foods will take longer to cook, because it is difficult to agitate the water molecules until they have thawed considerably.

IF ONLY THE HOUSE WAS THAT EASY TO CLEAN

Electric ovens are capable of much higher temperatures than gas ovens, and self-cleaning ones can get as hot as 1000°F during the self-cleaning phase. In self-cleaning ovens, any food or grease particles disintegrate into dust that only needs to be wiped away.

WOK THIS WAY

Stir-frying foods in woks dates back 2,000 years to the Han dynasty in China. It was developed due to a lack of cooking oil. The stir-fry technique cooks food rapidly in a minimum of oil. Following are some pointers to ensure success when cooking with a wok:

- Freeze beef, pork, or chicken for about 20 to 30 minutes so it will be easy to cut thin, even-size pieces.
- For great flavor, marinate the sliced meat briefly while you are preparing the vegetables. Adding a small amount of cornstarch to the marinade will protect the meat from the high heat and make the meat more tender and juicy.
- Vegetables should be cut into uniform bite-size pieces so they will cook evenly. Denser vegetables like carrots and peppers will need to cook longer than vegetables like broccoli florets and snow peas.

- Use oil very sparingly. One tablespoon (enough for four servings) is just enough to coat the bottom of the wok.
- For the best results, never stir-fry more than ½ pound of food at a time.

THE QUICHE DILEMMA

Quiches, especially those made with onions and mushrooms, should not be allowed to cool. Both of these vegetables have a high water content, which will be released into the quiche as it cools. The result: a soggy crust and runny filling. Let onion or mushroom quiches stand about 10 minutes before cutting them, though, or like any quiche, they'll ooze.

SLOW COOKER SAFETY

Rival invented the slow cooker, which it markets as the Crock Pot, in 1971. Many people question whether the pot is safe or a breeding ground for bacteria because it uses low temperatures to cook foods. Most slow-cookers have settings that range from 170°F to 280°F; most bacteria die at 140°F. However, if the lid is left off, the food may not cook fully, so it could potentially harbor bacteria. To minimize the risk of food poisoning:

- Do not attempt to cook frozen or partially thawed foods. Foods at refrigerator temperature are safe.
- Cook only cut up pieces of meat, not whole roasts or fowl, to allow the heat to penetrate fully.
- Make sure that the cooker is at least half to two-thirds full or the food may not absorb enough heat to kill any bacteria.
- Cover the food with enough liquid to generate sufficient steam.
- Always use the original lid, and be sure it fits tightly.
- When possible, cook on the high setting for the first hour, then reduce it to low if necessary.
- Never use the cooker to reheat leftovers.
- Always follow the manufacturer's directions for temperature settings.

KNIFE BASICS

The four basic knives to own are a chef's knife (also called a French knife) for chopping and julienning, a paring knife, a slicer, and a boning knife. Additional knives you might want include a serrated knife for slicing bread, a cleaver, a fish-filleting knife, and a pair of kitchen scissors.

THE CUTTING EDGE

One of the most important utensils in a kitchen is the knife. There are a number of different materials used to make knife blades, which vary widely in price, durability, and weight, among other factors. Make sure the handle is secured with at least three rivets. Always test a knife before you purchase it by making sure it feels comfortable in your hand.

Carbon Steel

This is by far the best metal for having the sharpest edge. However, if the blade is not constantly kept dry, it will rust. Acids in foods may also take their toll and turn the blade black, and the flavor may be passed to foods.

A sharp knife is actually safer than a dull one. Dull knives are more likely to slip off foods, resulting in cut fingers.

Stainless Steel

This metal has the ability to resist rust and acid from foods. It is much stronger than carbon steel, but it is very difficult to get an extremely sharp edge on a stainless steel blade.

High-Carbon Stainless Steel

This is the most expensive and the one most chefs and serious cooks prefer. It will not rust or stain. It does not have to be washed and dried continually when in use. High-carbon stainless steel can be sharpened to a sharper edge than either of the other steel knives.

SHARP IS BEST

The preferred equipment for sharpening knives is a whetstone, which takes some practice to master. A grinding wheel or electric sharpener can restore the edge, and a sharpening steel keeps the edges in alignment.

If you have a problem keeping an edge on your knife it may mean that you are not using the steel as frequently as you should; you may have to use a grinding tool, such as a wheel or an electric sharpener, to restore the edge. Once your knife is sharp, run both sides of your knife along the sharpening steel at a 20-degree angle before each and every use; wipe off the blade on a clean towel to remove any metal fragments.

POTS AND PANS AND PURCHASING

When shopping for pots and pans, always look for a thick, heavy bottom so that the heat will be evenly distributed. To test for heaviness, simply pick up the pot to see how heavy it feels. Another piece of advice: Buy the biggest size pot or pan you need, since you can cook small quantities in a large pan, but not the other way around.

THE KINDEST CUT

A top-quality knife is a worthwhile investment for any cook. Purchase either stainless steel or high-carbon stainless steel knives that have good name-brand recognition (ask a knowledgeable salesperson or an accomplished cook for recommendations). Be sure the blade and the handle are forged from one piece of steel. Always hold a knife in your hand before you buy it to be sure it's comfortable. Chefs sometimes insist you need an 8-inch knife, but you might prefer one with a 6-inch blade.

SO YOU WANT TO CHECK YOUR OVEN TEMPERATURE WITHOUT A THERMOMETER?

Put about 1 tablespoon flour on a baking sheet and set it into a preheated 350°F oven for five minutes. If the flour turns light tan, the temperature is 250°F to 325°F. If the flour turns golden brown, the oven is 325°F to 400°F. If it turns dark brown, the temperature is 400°F to 450°F. An almost a black color means the oven is 450°F to 525°F.

TO STORE A KNIFE

Two of the best places to store knives are on a magnetic rack or in a wooden countertop knife block. Never store knives in a drawer with other utensils. Not only do you risk injury, but the knife blades may become nicked and dented.

PASTA AL STORMY

When the weather is bad and stormy, the atmospheric pressure goes down. The lower the pressure, the lower the boiling temperature of water. It only decreases by one or two degrees, but you may notice that it takes a little longer to cook pasta.

BAG THE PLASTIC WRAP

When heated, plastic wrap can release chemicals that migrate into the food. ("Microwave-safe" food wrap won't melt when it comes into contact with hot foods, but it may release fumes.) The wrap may also stick to the foods, especially fatty or sugary ones. Waxed paper, paper towels, or paper plates are good substitutes.

GOOD GRILLING

Cut a red onion in half, pierce it with a fork and dip in water. Use one onion half to wipe down the grill rack. This also helps reduce smoke and improves the flavor of food.

NON-STICK SEASONING

Wash, rinse, and dry new non-stick pans prior to use. Lightly season the coating by brushing a thin layer of vegetable oil inside. Re-season after dishwashing. Use a scourer designed for non-stick surfaces (never a metal or abrasive one) to remove burnt-on food.

VIBRANT VEGETABLES

Refresh green vegetables such as French beans and mangetouts in ice-cold water. This stops them from getting overcooked and helps maintain their color. Reheat quickly before serving.

LOW ON ODOR

Freshen up you kid's lunchbox with bread. Just moisten a slice of bread with white vinegar and letting it sit in the closed lunchbox over night. In the morning, any funky smells should be gone.

EASIER DONE THAN SAID!

When cooking lentils (do it, because they're great for you) add a few teaspoons of oil. It prevents the pot from spilling over and actually helps in the cooking process.

AVOID BUILD-UP

To keep your waste disposal working efficiently, grind small amounts of food at a time. After you've finished, run a steady, rapid flow of cold (not hot) water for up to 30 seconds. Hot water will solidify fat and greasy waste.

A TOUCH OF ZEST

One quick and easy way to deodorize your waste disposal unit is to grind orange or lemon peel inside it every so often.

REDUCE LAST-MINUTE PANICS

Stock up with essentials so you'll always have something in the house. Tinned tomatoes, olive oil, pasta, sea salt and peppercorns, Parmesan, wine vinegar, garlic, stock, and rice can all form the basis of a delicious supper.

RHUBARB, RHUBARB

Wash uncoated aluminum by hand, never in a dishwasher. Remove black tarnish by boiling up acidic foods such as rhubarb or a cut lemon with water. Wash thoroughly afterwards. Clean hard-anodized aluminum in hot soapy water. Brownish film may be removed with an abrasive cleaner.

COOK'S HANDS

Remove strong food smells from your hands by rubbing them under cold running water while holding a stainless steel spoon in the same way as soap. Rinse with soap and water. Or try the perfumer's trick: dunk your hands in coffee grounds then wash with soap and water.

WHO KNEW?

There's no need to throw out crystallized honey. Just heat the opened jar in a microwave in 15-second increments, stirring often, until it has liquefied.

HONEY

LEMON JUICE TO THE RESCUE

If your rice keeps sticking together, next time add a teaspoon of lemon juice to the water when boiling and your sticky problem will be gone.

YOUR GUIDE TO USE THE GUIDE

To keep a cookbook open and easy to read while preparing your meal, just place it under a glass pie plate. You'll be able to read it easily and the page stays clean too.

USE THE RIGHT SETTING

If you're defrosting meat or fish in the microwave, choose the defrost setting or use low power to stop the outer edges of the food cooking before the middle defrosts. Arrange loose pieces of fish or meat in a single layer with thickest parts or largest pieces toward the outside.

PAPER CAPERS

When braising or stewing meat or poultry, always place a piece of waxed paper under the lid. It will collect the moisture that otherwise would dilute your dish.

WAFFLES AND FRENCH TOAST ARE GREAT SUNDAY MORNING TREATS, RIGHT?

Always make more than you need, and freeze the extra in airtight plastic bags. It's really easy to pop them into the toaster on rushed weekday mornings.

ODOR EATER

Boil 3½ fl. oz. vinegar with 1¾ pints of water. The rising heat carries vinegar particles to surfaces on which cooking grease and smoke have landed and neutralizes their effect.

AUGH...DID YOU BURN THE RICE AGAIN?

Fear not—white bread to the rescue. Get rid of the scorched taste by placing a slice of fresh white bread on top of the rice, while it's still hot, and covering it for a few minutes. That's all it takes.

KEEP TRASH CANS SMELLING SWEET

Wash and deodorize trash cans with a solution of 1 teaspoon lemon juice to 1¾ pints water. Sprinkling baking soda into the base of every garbage bag will also keep smells at bay.

NOT EVERYONE LOOKS GOOD WITH A TAN

When making guacamole, cut the avocados with a silver or stainless steel knife, and leave the pit in the dip (until serving) to prevent it from browning. Sprinkle lemon juice on the surface of the dip, and cover tightly with plastic wrap.

ACRYLIC BRIGHTENER

Watermarks may be removed from an acrylic sink with white vinegar. Never use an abrasive cleanser or scourer on acrylic or you risk scratches.

WHO KNEW?

You don't have to avoid baked beans because you fear they'll make you a little, um, gassy. Instead, just add a dash or two of baking soda to the beans when they're cooking, and their gas-producing properties will be dramatically reduced.

TO FOIL OR NOT TO FOIL

You should never line the bottom of your oven with aluminum foil, as it could cause a fire. However, you can save a lot of time in clean up if while cooking a messy lasagna or roast, you line the rack below with foil.

PRESERVE YOUR HEALTH

Food that is labeled 'no preservatives' means exactly what it says, but don't confuse it with the label 'no preservatives added' – this is used to label food that could contain natural preservatives such as salt and essential oils.

SALAD NAYS

Never wrap foods with natural acids—like tomatoes, lemons, or onions—in aluminum foil. The combination of the foil and the acid in the foods produce a chemical reaction, which affects the taste of the food.

WHO NEEDS A SPOON REST WHEN YOU'RE AT THE STOVE COOKING?

Just rest your spoon on a piece of bread, which will catch all the juices and bits of food. Toss the bread when you're done cooking.

COMMON SUBSTITUTIONS

Unless otherwise noted, use the substitution in equal measure to the ingredient called for in the recipe.

IF THE RECIPE CALLS FOR	SUBSTITUTE
ACTIVE DRY YEAST (one ¼-ounce envelope)	1 cake compressed yeast
ALLSPICE	1 part ground cinnamon + 2 parts ground cloves or ground nutmeg (for baking only)
ANISE SEED	Fennel seed (use equivalent amount)
APPLES (1 cup chopped)	1 cup firm chopped pears + 1 tablespoon lemon juice.
ARROWROOT	Use 2 tablespoons flour for every 4 teaspoons arrowroot
BAKING POWDER (one teaspoon, double-acting)	⅝ teaspoon cream of tartar + ¼ teaspoon baking soda or ¼ teaspoon baking soda + ¼ cup sour milk or buttermilk. (Must take the place of other liquid.)
BASIL (dried)	Tarragon, summer savory, thyme, or oregano
BAY LEAF	Thyme
BLACK PEPPER	Cayenne pepper (use much less; start with a pinch)
BRANDY	Cognac or rum
BULGUR	Cracked wheat, kasha, brown rice, couscous, millet, or quinoa
BUTTER (in baking)	Hard margarine or shortening. Do not use oil in baked goods.
BUTTERMILK (1 cup)	1 cup milk + 1¾ tablespoons cream of tartar or 1 tablespoon lemon juice + milk to make 1 cup (let stand 5 minutes) or sour cream
CAKE FLOUR (1 cup)	1 cup minus 2 tablespoons unsifted all-purpose flour
CAPERS	Chopped green olives
CARAWAY SEED	Fennel seed or cumin seed
CARDAMOM	Cinnamon or mace
CHERVIL	Parsley, tarragon, or ground anise seed (use less)
CHIVES	Onion powder (small amount) or finely chopped leeks or shallots (small amount) or scallion greens
CHOCOLATE, BAKING, UNSWEETENED	3 tablespoons unsweetened cocoa powder + 1 tablespoon (one ounce or square) butter or 3 tablespoons carob powder + 2 tablespoons water
CHOCOLATE, SEMISWEET	6 ounces chips = 9 tablespoons unsweetened cocoa powder or squares + 7 tablespoons sugar + 3 tablespoons butter

IF THE RECIPE CALLS FOR	SUBSTITUTE
CILANTRO	Parsley and lemon juice
CINNAMON	Allspice (use less) or cardamom
CLOVES (ground)	Allspice, nutmeg or mace
CLUB SODA	Sparkling mineral water or seltzer
CORNMEAL	Polenta
CORNSTARCH	Flour, as thickener
CORN SYRUP (1 cup, light)	1¾ cup granulated sugar + ¼ cup more of the liquid called for in recipe
CRÈME FRAÎCHE	Sour cream in a most recipes or ½ sour cream + ½ heavy cream in sauces. Note that crème fraîche can be boiled but sour cream cannot.
CUMIN	1 part anise + 2 parts caraway or fennel
DILL SEED	Caraway or celery seed
EDIBLE FLOWERS (garnish)	Bachelor buttons, blue borage, calendula petals, chive blossoms, mini carnations, nasturtiums, pansies, rose petals, snapdragons, or violets
EGGS, WHOLE	2 yolks + 1 tablespoon water
EVAPORATED MILK	Light cream or half-and-half or heavy cream
FLOUR	Baking mix, quick-cooking tapioca, cornstarch, arrowroot (use small amount), potato starch, instant potato flakes, or pancake mix
GARLIC (1 medium clove)	¼ teaspoon minced dried garlic or ⅛ teaspoon garlic powder or ½ teaspoon garlic juice or ½ teaspoon garlic salt (omit ½ teaspoon salt from recipe)
GHEE	Clarified butter
HONEY (1 cup, in baked goods)	1 ¼ cups granulated sugar + ¼ cup more of the liquid called for in recipe
LEMONGRASS	Lemon juice or lemon zest or finely chopped lemon verbena or lime zest
LOVAGE	Celery leaves
MARJORAM	Oregano (use small amount), thyme, or savory
MASA HARINA	Cornmeal
MASCARPONE	8 ounces cream cheese whipped with 3 tablespoons sour cream and 2 tablespoons milk
MILK (in baked goods)	Fruit juice + ½ teaspoon baking soda mixed in with the flour
MILK (1 cup)	½ cup evaporated milk + ½ cup water or ¼ cup powdered milk + ⅞ cup of water. (If whole milk is called for, add 2 ½ teaspoons melted and cooled butter.)

IF THE RECIPE CALLS FOR	SUBSTITUTE
MILK, EVAPORATED	Light cream or half-and-half or heavy cream
MOLASSES	Honey
NUTMEG	Allspice or cloves or mace
OREGANO	Marjoram or thyme
PANCETTA	Lean bacon (cooked) or very thin sliced ham
POLENTA	Cornmeal or grits (corn)
POULTRY SEASONING	Sage + a blend of any of these: thyme, marjoram, savory, black pepper, and rosemary
ROSEMARY	Thyme
SAFFRON (⅛ teaspoon)	1 teaspoon dried yellow marigold petals or 1 teaspoon safflower petals or ½–1 teaspoon turmeric (adds color)
SAGE	Poultry seasoning or savory or marjoram
SELF-RISING FLOUR (1 cup)	1 cup all-purpose flour + 1 ½ teaspoons baking powder + ⅛ teaspoon salt
SHALLOTS	Small scallions or leeks or yellow onions
SHORTENING (1 cup, in baked goods only)	1 cup butter or 1 cup stick margarine
SOUR CREAM (1 cup)	1 tablespoon white vinegar + milk (let stand 5 minutes before using); or 1 tablespoon lemon juice + evaporated milk; or 1 cup plain yogurt if it is being used in a dip or cold soup; or 6 ounces cream cheese + 3 tablespoons milk; or ⅓ cup melted butter + ¾ cup buttermilk; or ⅓ cup melted butter + ¾ cup plain yogurt
TAHINI	Peanut butter
TARRAGON	Anise (use small amount) or chervil (use larger amount) or parsley (use larger amount) or a pinch of fennel seed
TOMATO PASTE (1 tablespoon)	1 tablespoon ketchup or ½ cup tomato sauce providing you reduce some of the liquid in recipe
TURMERIC	Mustard powder
VANILLA EXTRACT (in baked goods only)	Almond extract or other extracts that will enhance the flavor of the dish
VINEGAR	Lemon juice in cooking and salads only, grapefruit juice in salads, or wine in marinades
YOGURT	Sour cream or crème fraîche or butter milk or mayonnaise (use in small amounts)

FOR THE BAKER
chapter

FLOUR FACTS

Flour is most often ground from grains, but fruits, vegetables, beans, nuts, herbs, and seeds can also be used. Primarily, flour is used in breads, muffins, pies, cakes, cookies, and other baked goods. It is also used to thicken soups, stews, gravies, and sauces. Many foods are floured before they are breaded to help the breading adhere better. Most commercial flour is milled by the roller process. High-speed rollers and sifters crack grain, separate it from the bran and germ, and then grind it to a fine consistency.

Wheat flours are more popular than other types because they contain gluten. This protein gives wheat its strength and elasticity, which is important in the production of breads.

TYPES OF FLOUR

All-Purpose Flour

A blend of hard- and soft-wheat flour. It has a balanced protein and starch content, which makes it an excellent choice for breads, rolls, and pastries. It may be used for cakes when cake flour is unavailable (use $7/8$ cup all-purpose for every cup of cake flour). Presifted all-purpose flour has been milled to a fine texture, is aerated, and is best for biscuits, waffles, and pancakes. However, it can settle during shipping so it should be sifted before use if called for in the recipe.

Bleached Flour

A type of all-purpose flour.

Bran Flour

A whole-wheat flour that can have a drying effect on baked products.

Bread Flour

Made from hard wheat. It has a very high protein, or gluten, content and is used to make breads.

Brown Rice Flour

Contains rice bran as well as the germ and has a nutty flavor.

Cake Flour

A very fine white flour, made entirely of soft wheat. It is best for baking cakes and soft cookies. Produces soft-textured, moist baked goods.

Corn Flour

A very starchy flour used to thicken sauces; it has a slightly sweet flavor. It is not the same thing as cornstarch.

Gluten Flour

A very strong white flour that has twice the strength of standard bread flour. Used as an additive with other flours.

Instant Flour

A very finely milled white flour that pours and blends easily with liquids. It is used mainly as a thickener for sauces, gravies, and stews. It is rarely used for baking due to its fine, powdery texture.

Pastry Flour

Has gluten content between cake flour and all-purpose white flour; it is best for light pastries and biscuits.

Potato Flour

Used mainly to thicken stews, soups, and sauces. Because it produces a moist crumb, it is used in some baked goods.

BAKING PAN SMARTS

Choose your baking pans carefully—they're an important part of the baking process. The pans should be thick or insulated (heavy-duty pans don't warp) and light in color. Dark or nonstick pans absorb heat, and can result in cookies, cakes, breads, and pastries that are burnt, tough, or dry. Lighter pans reflect heat. The bottoms of cookies will be more likely to remain golden if you bake them on a shiny metal pan.

Rice Flour

Excellent for making delicately textured cakes.

Self-Rising Flour

A soft-wheat, white flour that should not be used in yeast-leavened baked goods. Contains a leavening agent that tends to cause deterioration. The flour should be used within one to two months of purchase.

Semolina

A somewhat coarsely ground flour made from durum wheat. Used mainly in commercial pasta and bread. Has high protein content.

Soy Flour

A gluten-free flour produced from lightly toasted soybeans, which have a somewhat sweet flavor. Baked goods made from soy flour tend to stay fresh longer than those made with other flours.

Whole-Wheat Flour

Ground from the entire wheat berry, including the bran and germ. It is sometimes sold as graham flour and has small specks of brown. Because it is slightly higher in fat than other flours, it should be stored in the freezer or refrigerator to retard spoilage.

WHICH IS IT?

Not sure whether the flour in the canister is self-rising or all-purpose? Taste it. Self-rising flour will taste salty because it contains baking powder.

UM, OFFICER, I HAD A POPPY BAGEL THIS MORNING

Poppy seeds are commonly derived from the same poppies used to make morphine and codeine, so they can cause a positive urine test for opiates.

WHO KNEW?

When a recipe calls for vegetable oil, try substituting half of the oil with applesauce. It's an easy way to reduce the fat content.

BECAUSE BUSY MORNINGS MAKE FOR UNHAPPY PARENTS

Take advantage of leisurely weekend mornings. If you're making French toast, waffles, or pancakes, cook some extras and freeze them. On harried weekday mornings, just pop them in the toaster for an easy breakfast.

GIVE ME SPACE

Never set pans next to each other on the same oven rack. Air space between pans is important, so the hot air can circulate.

SO SPEED IT UP!

Remember, on humid or very hot days, yeast dough can rise faster than you expect and can become very hard to knead. When this occurs, there is a loss of elasticity.

BAKING CAKES VERSUS PASTRIES

The ingredients for baking cakes and cookies should always be warm, never cold, to start. For pastry it is just the opposite: The ingredients should be cold.

DRY BEFORE WET

Never put a wet measuring spoon into a baking powder tin. Use 1 teaspoon of baking powder for each cup of flour.

THE BEST WAY TO STORE COOKIES

Rinse out coffee cans and store cookies in them. Use the original lids, or stretch plastic wrap across the top and seal with a rubber band.

WHO KNEW?

If you want sugar cookies to remain a little soft, try rolling the dough out in granulated sugar instead of flour.

A CAKEY COOKIE

If you're making biscuits or cookies, choose the soft drop, more cakey version rather than the rolled variety – they generally contain more air per serving and therefore fewer calories.

WHO KNEW?

Don't throw away unused garlic bread. Freeze it and later use as tasty bread crumbs for chicken or chops.

THE PASTRY CHEF'S SECRET

Here's a pastry chef's trick to add flavor to a lemon tart or pie: Rub a few sugar cubes over an orange or lemon, then include the cubes in the recipe as part of the total sugar. The sugar tends to extract just enough of the natural oils from the peels of the fruits to add some flavor.

THE NEED TO KNEAD

Electric stand mixers are a boon for bakers, because the dough hook attachment reduces or eliminates the need to knead. To keep the dough from climbing up the hook, spray the dough hook with nonstick cooking spray or vegetable oil before turning the mixer on.

BATTER UP

When mixing batter, spray the beaters with a vegetable oil spray before using them and the batter won't climb up the beaters.

BREAD BASICS

Don't be fooled by bread labels—be sure to read ingredient lists to be sure you're buying what you really want.

- If the package reads wheat flour or wheat bread it is probably made from white flour. Most flour is made from wheat, so "100 percent wheat" does not mean the same as "100 percent whole-wheat."
- Rye bread typically contains mostly white flour and very little rye flour. A bread made only from rye flour would be heavy and dense—almost inedibly so. But read labels and avoid those with artificial coloring.
- To purchase the highest quality white bread, make sure the list of ingredients reads "unbleached flour" or "enriched flour."

GROSS BUT TRUE

It is almost impossible to purchase any flour without some sort of bug infestation. In fact, it is so unavoidable that the FDA allows an average of 75 insect fragments per 50 grams (about 2 cups) of grain. At this level, your health is not in danger. Insects and their eggs may set up residence when the grain is warehoused, during transit, or even in your home. To reduce the risk of infestation, store your grains and flour in the freezer to prevent eggs from hatching.

SIMPLE BAKING TIP

For best results, preheat the oven for at least 20 minutes before baking. Another tip: In most instances, it is best to bake the food on the center of the rack so heat can circulate evenly.

OR HAVE MIKE TYSON DO IT

You can freeze bread dough. Let it rise once, and then punch it down, wrap well, and freeze. Don't forget to label it!

TIMING IS EVERYTHING

Make sure you turn pancakes as soon as air bubbles appear on the top. Why? Because if you wait until the bubbles break, gas escapes, and your pancakes won't be as light or fluffy.

FLAVOR ENHANCER

You can add flavor to piecrust by adding a little ground spice or minced herbs to the flour. Use cinnamon or ginger with an apple pie, and try finely chopped parsley with a meat pie.

VITAMIN C TO THE RESCUE

Adding a bit of ascorbic acid (vitamin C) to flour when baking bread can help to strengthen weak flour. For every 6 cups flour, add a pinch of powdered ascorbic acid to the yeast.

LEMON IN THE DOUGH

To speed whole-wheat bread dough's rising time, add one tablespoon of lemon juice to the dough as you are mixing it.

WHO KNEW?

It's easy to get a spoonful of cookie dough to drop to your baking pan, if you first dip the spoon in milk.

FOILED AGAIN

Serving fresh-from-the-oven rolls or bread for dinner? Here's a trick to keep them warm: Tuck a small piece of aluminum foil under the cloth in the breadbasket. It helps the food retain the heat.

WANNA DIP?

Pies with graham cracker crusts can be difficult to remove from the pan. However, if you dip the pan in warm water for 5 to 10 seconds, the pie will come right out without any damage.

JUST LIKE GRANDMA USED TO DO

If you find icing too sweet or too rich, try this cake topping: Set a paper lace doily on the cake, and then dust lightly with confectioners' sugar. Carefully lift the doily off the cake. Try colored confectioners' sugar or a mixture of confectioners' sugar and cocoa powder.

KEEP IT LIGHT

If you want to try something different, enhance cake flour by adding 2 tablespoons of cornstarch to every cup of cake flour, sifting them together. This will produce a light, moist cake.

WHERE SHOULD YOU STORE YEAST, YOU ASK?

Always store yeast in the refrigerator. The cold slows down deterioration. Bringing the yeast to room temperature will help it dissolve faster.

HOW TO CUT A PIE

Spray a small amount of vegetable oil on your knife before cutting a pie with a cream filling. This will stop the filling from sticking to the knife.

GOING UP

A little heat does wonders when it comes to cutting down on rising time. Set the dough (either in a bowl or a loaf pan) on a heating pad set on medium, or over the pilot light on a gas stove.

A COOL TRICK

If you are going to cut an unfrosted cake to arrange it into different configurations, try freezing the cake first. This will make it much easier to slice. Fresh cakes, especially those made from a mix, often crumble easily.

FLOUR THE FRUIT

Dried fruits sink to the bottom of cakes, muffins, and the like because they lose some moisture and become more solid during baking. If you coat them with a little flour, though, they will stay put.

TRY A LITTLE FLOUR

If you dip a biscuit cutter in flour, the dough won't stick to it. And when you cut biscuits out, don't twist the cutter. The motion seals the edges of the biscuits, keeping them from rising high.

SECRETS OF SOFTER BISCUITS

For soft biscuits, brush them with milk or melted unsalted butter, and then arrange them in a cake pan so the sides touch one another.

GREASING IS THE WORD

When you need to grease a baking pan, be sure you always use vegetable shortening. Butter has a low smoke point and burns easily, and salted butter can cause food to stick to the pan.

WHERE SHOULD YOU KEEP BREAD?

Keeping bread in the fridge can prevent mold developing, but the refrigerator's dry air draws moisture from the bread, so it will go stale faster. Freezing maintains the freshness, but when the bread thaws, ice crystals rupture and the texture of the bread suffers. The best place to store bread? That depends on how long it will take you to use it. For up to five or six days, wrap it in waxed paper or a paper bag; if you have a bread box, perfect—otherwise leave it on the counter. Avoid plastic bags, which can make the crust soggy. If it will take you more than six days to use the bread, it should go into the freezer.

SCISSORS SOLUTION

One of easiest ways to cut a pizza is to use scissors with long blades—you can cut from top and bottom, and you can cut through the pizza quickly. Make sure they are sharp and only used for food. Pizza cutters do work fairly well, provided they are always kept very sharp. However, most tend to dull quickly because they are made of poor-quality metal.

BEADING BE GONE

Occasionally meringue will develop small droplets of water on its surface shortly after it is removed from the oven. Beading is caused by overcooking. To prevent this, bake meringue at a high temperature (between 400°F and 425°F) for a short time—4 to 5 minutes.

THE SECRET TO CRISPY CRUST

If you prefer bread with a crispy crust, here's a secret: Put some ice cubes in a shallow pan and put this in the oven when you put in the bread. This will produce a dense steam, and as the water evaporates, the crust becomes hard and crispy. The steam also will allow the bread to rise more evenly, giving you a nice firm, chewy inside.

ANGEL IN DISTRESS

The best way to cool an angel food cake is to turn it upside down on an ice-cube tray or set it upside down in the freezer for just a few minutes.

TO SALT OR NOT TO SALT

Salt makes bread crust a little crisper and is essential for flavor, but it also slows down the growth of yeast, which prevents the dough from rising too fast. If this happens, the air pockets will be larger and your bread will have a coarser texture.

HOW TO BROWN COOKIES

When cookies do not brown enough, bake them on a higher rack in the oven. Other techniques to boost the browning of cookies: substitute a tablespoon or two of corn syrup for the sugar, use egg for the liquid, or use unbleached or bread flour in the recipe.

SUGAR GETS IT DONE

Add some sugar to your pastry recipe to help tenderize the dough. Pastry dough should look like coarse crumbs after you cut in the fat.

THE SLASHER

You can keep the top of your bread from cracking if you slash it first. Use a single-edge razor blade to make two or three shallow diagonal cuts across the top.

AND THE KIDS WILL LOVE IT

For a different type of toast, lightly butter a slice of bread on both sides and cook it in a waffle iron.

HOW TO REVIVE STALE BREAD

When bread is baked, water accumulates in its starch. As bread ages, water is released from the starch and evaporates, so the texture of the bread becomes more crumbly and firm. The longer bread lasts, the more water is released from the cells—resulting in an increasingly dry, hard loaf. Reheating bread allows the moisture that remains to be redistributed into the starch. The trick to reheating bread is to warm it just enough to move the water back into the cells—if it is heated too much, the water will evaporate. Keep the moisture in by heating the bread in a sealed container or in foil, and don't let the temperature go above 140°F.

LIGHTEN UP

Substitute buttermilk for milk in a muffin or quick-bread recipe. You'll be amazed at how light they are.

MASTERING MUFFINS

Muffins will come out of the baking pan more easily if you place the hot pan on a cool, wet towel for about 30 seconds.

TAP TAPIOCA FOR FRUIT PIES

The best thickener for fruit pies is 3 to 4 tablespoons of minute tapioca. Just mix it with the sugar before adding to the fruit.

WHO KNEW?

Store your rolling pin in the freezer. It's much easier to roll out pastry dough and piecrusts with a frozen rolling pin.

THE BAKING POWDER TEST

Baking powder loses potency over time. If you can't remember when you bought it, you should test it before using it. Put ½ teaspoon of baking powder in a small bowl, then pour in ¼ cup of hot tap water. The more vigorously it bubbles, the fresher the baking powder. Try this test on a fresh box of baking powder so you will be familiar with the activity level of the fresh powder. Be sure to check the expiration date on the box when you first purchase it to be sure it's fresh. Once opened, baking powder will remain fresh for up to a year.

BECAUSE ENQUIRING MINDS NEED TO KNOW

How does baking powder work, you ask? Well, baking powder is a mixture of leavening agents, including calcium acid phosphate (also known as cream of tartar), which act quickly at low temperatures; sodium aluminum sulfate, which reacts at high temperatures; and sodium bicarbonate. When this mixture of acids and alkalis come into contact with water, it produces carbon dioxide. This gas either enters air pockets that already exist in the batter or dough, or it creates minute air pockets.

When the dough or batter is heated, the baking powder releases even more carbon dioxide, and the trapped carbon dioxide expands, creating steam. This pressure swells the dough or batter, and it expands or rises.

TOO HARD

The high mineral content of hard water may retard yeast fermentation by causing the gluten in the flour to become tough. The minerals prevent the protein in the flour from absorbing water the way it normally would. There are a number of solutions: using bottled or unchlorinated water, adding a small amount of vinegar to reduce the pH, or adding more yeast. Water that is too soft can cause the dough to be sticky.

REDUCING THE CALORIES IN CAKES

Although there are a few substitutions you can use to replace fat in baked goods—and there are many excellent cookbooks outlining the fine points of this—it is important to realize that fat performs several important functions. It extends shelf life, adds tenderness and flavor, and contributes to the texture of baked goods. When fat is replaced, baked goods may be altered to an unacceptable degree. Replacements include: skim milk, egg whites, pureed cooked fruits such as applesauce or prune puree, and syrups; professional bakeries may use certain starches and gums. These can rarely replace all the fat, but they do help to retain moisture and may reduce the total calories.

BAKING WITH BUTTERMILK

Don't substitute buttermilk for milk measure for measure in baking recipes. Chemically, the two are quite different. Buttermilk is much more acidic than regular milk and will interfere with the leavening agent, reducing the amount of carbon dioxide.

To offset the additional acid, reduce the amount of baking powder by 2 teaspoons and replace it with ½ teaspoon of baking soda for every cup of buttermilk you use in place of milk.

WHO NEEDS BAKING POWDER?

No baking powder? No problem. Here's the formula to mix the equivalent of 1 teaspoon: use ⅝ teaspoon of cream of tartar and ¼ teaspoon of baking soda. If you plan to store a quantity of this mixture for a few days, add ¼ teaspoon of cornstarch to absorb moisture from the air. This formula tends to work more rapidly than do commercial baking powders. When you use homemade baking powder, plan to get the food in the oven as quickly as you can.

PICK A LARGE EGG

If your cookbook doesn't specify what size egg to use, go with large eggs. The volume difference in a small egg compared with a large egg can be enough to change the consistency and the quality of the item.

CAKE PROBLEMS BE GONE

Shortened Cakes

These are made by creaming shortening (usually butter) and sugar together. Eggs are then beaten into the mixture, and then dry and liquid ingredients are added alternately in increments.

If your cake is coarse-textured, heavy, and dense, you most likely didn't cream the sugar and fat long enough. These ingredients need to be mixed together very thoroughly for best results. Be sure the butter is at room temperature. Over baking can cause cakes to become dry; be sure to check the doneness after the minimum baking time. Elongated holes mean you may have over mixed the batter when you added the flour.

Angel Food, Chiffon, and Sponge Cakes

These are foam cakes—that is, they are made by beating egg whites just until the peaks bend over. If your cake isn't high, you may not have beaten the egg whites long enough, or you may have over mixed the batter when you add the flour. The ingredients should be gently folded in and combined until the batter is just smooth.

If an angel food cake falls, it's probably because you opened the oven door to test the cake for doneness before the proteins coagulated enough for it to hold its shape when the temperature changed. Other causes may be over beaten egg whites, or you may have forgotten to cool the cake upside down (this lets the steam dissipate throughout the cake, so it's lighter and fluffier).

Tough cakes result from over mixing when you add the dry ingredients. Ingredients should be blended only until they are mixed.

If your sponge cake has an uneven texture, you didn't beat the egg yolks long enough. They should be beaten until thick and lemon colored.

If your chiffon cake has yellow streaks, you probably added the yolks directly into the dry ingredients instead of making a well in the center of the dry ingredients and then adding the oil and egg yolks.

If your chiffon cake is uneven, you may have either over beaten or under beaten the egg whites. Beat the egg whites only until peaks bend over.

PANCAKE SECRETS

Short-order cooks and chefs have a host of tricks to make the lightest pancakes; here are a few:

- Replace the liquid in the recipe with an equal amount of club soda. This increases the amount of air in the pancakes and make them fluffier. But take note: batter with club soda won't keep, so you'll need to use it all after you mix it.
- Don't overmix the batter—leave a few lumps—so the gluten doesn't overdevelop and so the carbon dioxide doesn't escape.
- Refrigerate the batter for up to 30 minutes. This further slows the development of the gluten and the leavening action.
- Always, always, stir the batter before you pour it onto the griddle. The ingredients can settle; stirring recombines them and aerates the batter.
- If you like brown-on-the-outside pancakes, add a little extra sugar. The sugar caramelizes, giving a browner color to the pancakes.

DOUBLE DECKER

If you don't have an insulated or a thick baking sheet, there's a simple solution: Try baking the cookies on two sheets, stacked one on top of the other. It will eliminate burned bottoms.

USE THE RIGHT FLOUR

Low-gluten flour such as pastry flour is the best choice when you're making piecrusts. Cake flour is too soft and won't give the crust the body it needs, and bread flour contains too much gluten content to make a tender crust. As a substitute for pastry flour, combine 2 parts all-purpose flour and 1 part cake flour or instant flour.

MORE THAN YOU EVER, EVER WANTED TO KNOW ABOUT YEAST

A cake of yeast is composed of millions of one-celled organisms. Put yeast in a warm (ideally 110°F to 115°F), moist environment and feed them sugar or starch, and they'll multiply like crazy. Yeast causes carbohydrates to convert into a simple sugar, glucose, which then ferments into alcohol and carbon dioxide. It is the carbon dioxide that leavens, or raises, the baked goods by expanding the air and creating steam. There is no risk from the production of alcohol, because the heat from the baking evaporates the alcohol as well as kills the live yeast cells.

THE KEY IS EVEN BLENDING

If your biscuits are heavy and dense, check your baking powder for freshness and make sure that you sift all the dry ingredients together. If you don't have a sifter, put the dry ingredients into a large sieve and shake them into the mixing bowl, or whisk them. It's the even blending of the ingredients that's key. Shortening is also the preferred fat for biscuits. Butter makes for a more solid biscuit, and oil makes them greasy.

WHO KNEW?

Honey always sticks to your spoon when added to a recipe, correct? Not if you first rub the spoon with margarine.

THE MICROWAVE SOLUTION

Bread bakers take note: You can cut the rising time by one-third if you use your microwave oven. Here's how to do it for one standard loaf: Set ½ cup of hot water in the back corner of the microwave. Place the dough in a well-greased microwavable bowl and cover it with plastic wrap, and then cover the plastic wrap with a damp towel. With the power level set at 10 percent, cook the dough for 6 minutes, and then let it rest for 4 to 5 minutes. Repeat the procedure if the dough has not doubled its size. Do not heat the dough at higher than 10 percent power setting—the dough will turn into a half-baked glob. The only downside to this quick-rising trick is that the flavor of the bread may not be as full. When bread rises slowly, the flavor has more time to develop and permeate the dough.

Another quick-rising method is to heat the dough at 100 percent power for 1 minute, and then leave the oven door closed and let the dough stand 15 minutes. If you don't have a turntable, rotate the dough a quarter turn, and then repeat the process.

OF COURSE UNBLEACHED IS BEST

Unbleached flour is the best choice for most baking projects. It has a more natural taste because it lacks the chemical additives and bleaching agents used in bleached flour. Bleached flour is less expensive to produce because it doesn't require aging. Aging, however, strengthens the bonds among the gluten of unbleached flour. Don't skimp when buying unbleached flour; not all companies allow the flour to age adequately.

DEAD YEAST?

Yeast should always be tested, or proofed, before using it. To proof yeast, dissolve a little sugar in warm water; sprinkle in the yeast. The mixture should begin bubbling within about 5 to 7 minutes. If it doesn't, the yeast is either dead or too inactive to provide the leavening function.

SO YOU DON'T KNOW WHAT FONDANT ICING IS?

Now you do: fondant icing is made from corn syrup, granulated sugar, and water that is cooked to 238°F, then quickly cooled to 140°F and rapidly worked until it is white, creamy, and very smooth. It is then cured for as little as a day to as long as a week; it is reheated over a double boiler before using.

THREE CURES FOR DOMED CAKES

If your cakes "dome" when baked, it may be caused by one of three things: The oven temperature was too high (use an oven thermometer and adjust the temperature accordingly), your pan was too small (be sure to use the exact size specified in the recipe), or the balance of liquid, egg, flour, and fat was off (always measure accurately).

"BAKER'S MAGIC" REVEALED

Recipes for baked goods often call for greased and floured pans. The standard method is to grease the pan with oil and then sprinkle flour in and tap or shake the pan to distribute the flour as evenly as possible (don't forget the sides). Some recipes call for baking pans to be lined with a piece of waxed paper or parchment paper.

If you bake a lot, take a tip from professional bakers and mix up a batch of "baker's magic": Mix ½ cup of room temperature vegetable shortening, ½ cup of vegetable oil, and ½ cup of all-purpose flour. Blend the mixture well and use it to grease pans. The mixture can be stored in an airtight container in the refrigerator for up to six months.

EVEN MORE FUN FACTS ABOUT YEAST!

Compressed yeast has a higher level of moisture, about 72 percent compared with the standard dry yeast at 8 percent. Compressed yeast should be stored in the refrigerator and lasts for only about two weeks before losing its effectiveness. Dry yeast should always be stored in an airtight container because it absorbs water rather easily. The yeasts are interchangeable, with 1 packet of the active dry yeast equaling the leavening power of 1 cake of the compressed yeast.

FOR FLUFFY BISCUITS

When you cut out biscuits from the dough, be sure to press the cutter straight down—don't twist it even slightly. Doing so seals the edges of the biscuits and they won't rise as high.

THE BAKING SODA TEST

If you are not sure how old your baking soda is, test its activity level. Stir ¼ teaspoon into about 2 teaspoons of white vinegar; it should bubble vigorously If it doesn't, throw it out.

IF YOUR DOUGH WON'T RISE

One of the most frequent problems bread bakers encounter is yeast dough that doesn't rise adequately. There are a number of reasons for this.

- The dough may be too cool, which reduces the level of yeast activity. Dough can rise at lower temperatures—even in the refrigerator—but it takes several hours or overnight to attain the same volume that it can at 80°F to 90°F in an hour or two.
- The yeast may have been prepared with water that was too hot, which can kill it. The water must be around 115°F for optimum results.
- The yeast may have been too old. Proof the yeast before using it to be sure it's not ready for retirement.

KNEADING MAKES ALL THE DIFFERENCE

Don't skimp when kneading bread—it's what distributes the yeast and other ingredients evenly throughout the dough. If dough isn't kneaded properly, it won't rise evenly. Electric bread machines, stand mixers, and food processors, however, can make short work of this important task; many recipes are written specifically for these appliances.

ALWAYS USE THE STICK

When making cookies with margarine, the firmness of the dough will depend on the type of margarine used. Be sure to use stick margarine, not one in a tub. Margarine made from 100 percent corn oil will make the dough softer.

When using margarine you may need to adjust the chilling time and may have to place the dough in the freezer instead of the refrigerator. If you're making cutout cookies, the chilling time should be at least one hour in the refrigerator. Dough for drop cookies and bars does not have to be chilled.

BAKING POWDER AND CHOCOLATE ARE NOT FRIENDS

Chocolate is acidic enough to upset the balance between the acid (cream of tartar) and the alkali of baking powder. Baking soda (sodium bicarbonate) can make a chocolate cake too alkaline, so most recipes also call for a sour-milk product such as yogurt, sour cream, or buttermilk to ensure that the batter will not be too alkaline. If the batter becomes too alkaline, the cake will be red instead of brown, and it will taste bitter.

SALT STRENGTHENS

Never omit the salt from your bread recipe—salt strengthens and tightens the gluten, keeping bread from becoming crumbly.

SO YOU DON'T KNOW WHAT A ONE-BOWL CAKE IS?

Um, it's a cake made by mixing the batter in one bowl. When this is done you omit the step of creaming the shortening or butter and the sugar. Using the one-bowl method, you add the shortening, liquid, and the flavorings to the dry ingredients and beat. The eggs are then added and the batter beaten again. What you gain in simplification and easier cleanup, you lose in texture—one-bowl cakes tend to be coarser.

GET THE AIR CIRCULATING

When breads and cakes are baked, steam builds up inside, which needs to be released after they are removed from the oven. If the steam cannot escape, it will revert to water as it cools and will be absorbed back into the baked good, which will become soggy. To avoid this problem, remove the pan from the oven and cool the food in the pan for a few minutes. Then transfer the baked good to a cooling rack so air can circulate on all sides, evaporating the steam.

FOIL HELPS

To reheat biscuits or rolls, sprinkle them lightly with water and wrap them in foil. It should take about 5 minutes in a preheated 350°F oven.

PUFF PASTRY TIPS

Puff pastry dough is made from flour, butter, and water. A small amount of butter is layered between dough that is folded several times to form as many as 700 layers. When you cut puff pastry dough, be sure to use a very sharp knife and cut straight down; never pull the knife through the dough or cut the dough at an angle. Doing so will cause the ends to puff up unevenly as the pastry bakes.

THE DULLER, THE BETTER

For the best results, never use a shiny bread pan. It is best to bake bread in a dull aluminum pan. A dark pan may cook the bread too quickly, resulting in burned bottoms. A shiny pan reflects heat to such a degree that the bread may not bake evenly.

SUGAR TO THE RESCUE

If your bread rises too high, or rises and then collapses, you may have added too much yeast or water. Remember, a small amount of sugar will feed the yeast and make the dough rise faster. If you use too much sugar, though, it can actually inhibit the rising.

THE GLASS BAKING DISH RULE

Baked goods should always be baked at the temperature specified in the recipe, with one notable exception: If you are using a glass baking dish, reduce the specified oven temperature by 25°F. Glass heats slowly but it retains heat well; failing to lower the temperature can result in burned bottoms. Oven thermometers are inexpensive and are available at most supermarkets and hardware stores—if you are at all unsure how accurate your oven is, they're an easy way to tell.

WHICH LIQUID?

Different liquids tend to impart different characteristics to bread. Water, for instance, will cause the top of the bread to be crisp, and it significantly intensifies the flavor of the wheat. Potato water (saved after you've boiled potatoes) adds a unique flavor, makes the crust smooth, and causes the bread to rise faster due to the high starch content. A liquid dairy product imparts a rich, creamy color and leaves the bread with a fine texture and a soft, brown crust. Eggs provide a moist crust.

A liquid sweetener such as molasses, maple syrup, or honey will cause the crust to be dark brown and will keep it moist. Vegetable or meat broth will give the bread a special flavor and provide you with a light, crisp crust. Alcohol of any type will give the bread a smooth crust with a flavor that may be similar to the alcohol used, especially beer; just don't use too much or you'll kill the yeast. Coffee and tea are commonly used to provide a dark, rich color and a crisp crust.

THE FOUR TYPES OF BREAD

Batter Breads

These breads are leavened with yeast. They are always beaten instead of kneaded.

Quick Breads

These are leavened with baking powder or baking soda instead of yeast. They require no rising time, and in fact should be put into the oven almost immediately after mixing dry and wet ingredients.

Unleavened Breads

These have no leavening whatsoever and are easily identifiable because they are flat.

Yeast Breads

These are leavened with yeast and are always kneaded to stretch the gluten in the flour.

CHECK IT OUT

Always check cake or bread at least 10 to 15 minutes before the baking time is completed. If your oven temperature is inaccurate, it can be done before (or after) the baking time stated in the recipe.

HOW TO FREEZE BREAD CORRECTLY

If you are going to freeze a loaf of bread, make sure you include a paper towel in the package to absorb moisture. This will keep the bread from becoming mushy when thawed.

THE DAMP TOWEL TRICK

To remove muffins or rolls from a pan, set the pan on a damp towel for about 30 seconds. Use an old towel, because the pan might stick.

HOW REVOLTING

If you see the slightest sign of mold on baked goods, throw the item out. Mold often sends out "feelers" that cannot be seen in most instances.

WHO KNEW?

Next time you make chocolate icing, add one teaspoon of unsalted butter to the chocolate while it is melting to improve the consistency.

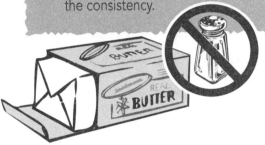

WEIRD BUT IT WORKS!

One of the best methods of keeping the insides of a cake from drying out is to place a piece of fresh white bread next to the exposed surface. The bread can be affixed with a toothpick or a short piece of spaghetti.

HOW DISGUSTING

Sucking on hard candy or lollipops causes a greater risk of tooth decay than consuming large quantities of cake, ice cream, or doughnuts. Hard candy dissolves slowly and surrounds each tooth with a layer of sugar for a longer period. Sticky foods like raisins have a similar effect.

BEAT IT

When your recipe calls for cream cheese, be sure it is at room temperature before you start, and make sure you beat it so it's light and fluffy before adding any other ingredients, especially eggs.

SLOW DOWN

If you would like to slow down the rising time, put your bread dough in a cool place—even in the refrigerator. The yeast will still be active (assuming it's alive in the first place), but it will be much more sluggish.

PUNCTURE POPOVERS

If you want the lightest popovers every time, puncture them with a fork when you remove them from the oven to release the air inside.

NOT EXACTLY A HEALTH FOOD TIP, BUT BOY IT TASTES GOOD

If you don't have to worry about your cholesterol count, substitute two egg yolks for one whole egg. The cake will be very rich—but it will also be a little denser, because the yolks won't hold as much air as the whites.

AND YOU WON'T STINK THE NEXT DAY

You can make lightly scented garlic bread by adding 1 teaspoon of garlic powder to the flour when you're making white bread.

HOW TO STAY SOFT

To keep icing from hardening, just add a very small amount of white vinegar to the icing after it is whipped.

KEEPING IT TOGETHER

If you have problems keeping a layer cake together when you are icing it, stick a few bamboo skewers into the cake through both layers; remove them as you're frosting the top.

IT MAKES SENSE

Cake flour is made from soft wheat; because of its low gluten content, it will make a lighter cake. If you don't have any cake flour, use all-purpose flour, but use $^7/_8$ cup all-purpose flour (1 cup minus 2 tablespoons) for each cup of cake flour.

GLAZING OVER

Before you put rolls in the oven, glaze their tops: Lightly beat an egg white with a tablespoon of milk and brush on. To glaze a baked cake, dissolve a little brown sugar in 1 tablespoon of milk and brush on.

WHAT'S YOUR POISON?

Most people think fruit and vegetables are higher in pesticide residues than other foods but according to a report by the FDA in the USA, the highest residues are actually found in bread, flour and potatoes. Buying organic versions of these foods will dramatically reduce residues, although there may still be some traces.

To keep the frosting from sticking to your knife as you cut the cake, dip your knife into a glass of cold water between each cut.

HOW TO POP BUBBLES

If you have bubbles in your cake batter, hold the pan an inch or two above the counter and tap it two or three times. Be careful—the batter might spatter.

FOR A RICH COLOR

If you like biscuits and rolls to be a rich golden color, add a teaspoon of sugar to the dry ingredients. It helps the crust caramelize, and it only adds 16 calories to the whole batch.

SAY CHEESECAKE

When preparing a cheesecake, go exactly by the recipe and don't make any substitutions. You'll have a better chance at success if you follow the recipe to the letter. Here are some other pointers.

- Be sure that the cheese is at room temperature before using it.
- When you bake a cheesecake at a lower temperature, there's less chance of it shrinking from the sides of the pan.
- Don't open the oven for the first 25 to 30 minutes when baking cheesecake; the cheesecake may develop cracks or partially collapse.
- Cheesecakes crack because they overcook. They're done when the center of the cake is still wobbly and shaky—it will look underdone.
- Flourless cheesecakes need to be baked in a pan of water (called a water bath or bain marie). The water keeps the eggs from coagulating.
- Cheesecake cracks can be repaired with creamed cream cheese or sweetened sour cream, but you'll be able to see the repair. It's better to top the cheesecake with berries.
- Never substitute a different size pan for a cheesecake recipe, use the exact size recommended.

TRY A COLD, WET TOWEL

When baked foods stick to the bottom of the pan, wrap the pan in a towel while it is still hot. You can also set the pan on a cold, wet towel for a few minutes.

REPLACE THE MOISTURE

When bread dries out, it hardens. To replace the moisture, wrap the loaf tightly in a damp paper towel for two to three minutes, and then remove the towel and heat the bread in a 350° oven for 15 to 20 minutes. When French or Italian bread hardens, sprinkle the crust with cold water and heat at 350°F for 8 to 10 minutes.

STOP ICING FROM RUNNING OVER

If you sprinkle a thin layer of cornstarch on top of a cake before you ice it, the icing won't run down the sides.

WHIPPING SECRETS

When you whip cream, add a small amount of lemon juice or salt to the cream to make the job easier. For a unique flavor, add just a small amount of honey at the very end of whipping.

ALWAYS BEAT IT PROPERLY

When your recipe calls for creaming butter or shortening with sugar, be sure you beat it for the entire time specified in the recipe. Shortening the time may yield a coarse-textured or heavy cake.

YOU KNEAD VEGETABLE OIL TO HELP

If your dough is thick and difficult to knead, rub a small amount of vegetable oil on your hands.

TWO-THIRDS IS ENOUGH

Remember, never fill a baking pan more than half to two-thirds full. Cakes, muffins, and other baked goods need room to expand.

BANANA FUN

A great and healthy summer treat for kids is to cut a banana in half (across the equator, not lengthwise), put a popsicle stick in the flat end and freeze for a few hours on waxed paper. Take it out, dip in chocolate, and your kids will love you. At least for a little while.

ANGEL FOOD FACT

An angel food cake can be left in the pan and covered tightly with foil for up to 24 hours or until you are ready to frost it.

THERE GOES THE CAKE

Hold off checking your cake until about 15 minutes before the time specified in the recipe—the cake may fall from the sudden change in temperature. But always check a few minutes early, just in case your oven temperature is too high and the cake is baking faster than you expect.

DON'T THROW IT OUT

When you boil potatoes, save the cooking water. It contains just the right amount of starch to use in a bread recipe. It will also help keep the bread fresher for a longer period.

FLAKY PIE CRUST TIPS

- Add a teaspoon of vinegar to the pie dough with the ice water.
- Substitute sour cream or whipping cream for any water.
- Replace the shortening or butter with lard. Lard has larger fat crystals and three times the polyunsaturates as butter.

NEVER COLD

To keep cookies or butter cakes from becoming too heavy, be sure the butter is at room temperature before you cream it with the sugar. Shortening of any type does not cream when it is cold.

WE HEART CAKES

A heart-shaped cake is easier to make than you might think. Simply divide your cake batter between one round pan and one square one. When the cakes are cool, cut the round cake in half. Turn the square cake so it looks like a diamond and set the half-rounds on the two top sides.

FAT MATTERS

Reduced-fat margarine, margarine spreads, and whipped butter should not be used for baking. They have too much water and air, which can cause cakes or cookies to collapse or flatten out. Always use the type of fat called for in the recipe.

BUT IT'S HEALTHIER

Whole-wheat bread dough will not rise as high as bread dough made from all-purpose or bread flour. Whole-wheat flour is denser because it's not as refined. This is why most whole-wheat bread recipes blend whole-wheat flour with either bread or all-purpose flour.

THE TENDER CAKE TRICK

The texture of a cake depends on the type of sweetener and fat used. These ingredients affect how tender the cake will be, so be sure you use the right ones. Never substitute granulated sugar for confectioners' sugar; granulated sugar is recommended for baking most cakes. Cakes made with oil are very tender and moist—oil doesn't hold air as well as butter or shortening, so eggs and other thick ingredients must trap the air.

THE BEST BOARD

A wooden board is your best bet for kneading bread, but other surfaces will work. Just be sure to flour the board and your hands adequately.

A COOL CRUST

When making piecrust, be sure the kitchen and all your ingredients and equipment are cool. A hot kitchen will affect the results. All pie ingredients should be cold when preparing a crust.

HOT WATER ONLY

If you add water to a candy recipe, always add very hot water for a clearer candy. Most homemade candy will remain fresh for two to three weeks.

SOFTENED, NOT MELTED

Don't melt butter unless your recipe directs you to do so. Most recipes, especially cake recipes, will have a better texture if the butter is just softened.

GET THEM DANCING

Pancakes should be cooked on a 325°F griddle. But how do you know when it's that hot? Flick a few drops of water on the heated griddle. The droplets should skitter and dance—steam causes the drops to rise, but gravity brings them back down. If the griddle is too hot the water drops will be propelled off the griddle; this usually occurs at about 425°F.

A DRY BOTTOM

If you have a problem with fruit or fruit juices soaking the bottom of your piecrust and making it soggy, brush the bottom crust with egg white before adding the filling. This will seal the piecrust and solve the problem. Other solutions include prebaking the piecrust, partially cooking the filling, or brushing the crust with jelly before you fill it.

When using a cream filling in a pie, sprinkle the crust with granulated sugar before adding the filling. This usually eliminates a soggy crust.

THE COLLAPSIBLE SOUFFLÉ

When you beat egg whites, you incorporate air into them. The air bubbles are trapped, and when a soufflé is placed in the oven, the air expands, causing the soufflé to rise. If the soufflé is punctured or shaken, the air will be released too early and the soufflé will collapse.

FLAKY CRUST SUGGESTION

Be sure the liquid going into your piecrust is ice cold. Ice-cold sour cream instead of ice water will result in a flakier crust.

BEST CROUTONS EVER

After cutting you leftover bread into cubes, fry in olive oil and a little garlic powder (not garlic salt), a pinch of parmesan cheese, and parsley. Fry until they're brown for a tasty treat. And they freeze well, too!

NICE RACK

Cookies should be transferred to a wire rack to cool completely, not left in the pan. Just be sure the cookies are fully cooled before you store them; otherwise, they risk becoming soggy.

TIMING IS EVERYTHING

Cookies can go from just right to burned in no time. To lessen the chance of this happening, take the cookies out of the oven when they are not quite done, but don't transfer them to the cooling rack right away. Let them sit on the hot pan for a minute or two to finish baking.

TOUGH COOKIES

When you mix cookie dough, don't overstir. Overstirring can cause the cookies to become tough.

AND IT TASTES GREAT, TOO

You can make pancake syrup by mixing ⅓ cup butter, ⅓ cup sugar, and ½ cup frozen orange juice concentrate. Heat, stirring constantly, until the sugar has dissolved and the mixture is syrupy.

BURNED BOTTOMS?

If you have a problem with burning the bottoms of cookies when baking a number of batches, let the baking sheets cool between batches; when you start with too hot a surface the cookies may burn. Two to three minutes cooling time is usually long enough. Another alternative is to line the baking sheets with parchment paper—simply lift the cookies, still on the parchment paper, onto the cooling rack.

TYPES OF COOKIES

Bar Cookies

Made by pressing dough into a shallow pan and then cutting into small bars after baking.

Drop Cookies

Made by dropping small mounds of dough onto a baking sheet.

Hand-Formed Cookies

Made by shaping cookie dough into balls or other shapes by hand.

Pressed Cookies

Made by pressing the cookie dough through a cookie press or pastry bag with a decorative tip to make fancy designs or shapes.

Refrigerator Cookies

Made by shaping cookie dough into logs, then refrigerating until firm. The logs are sliced before baking.

Rolled Cookies

The cookie dough is rolled to a thickness of about ¼ inch. Cookie cutters are then used to make different shapes.

I DARE YOU NOT TO EAT IT RAW

Unbaked cookie dough may be frozen for up to one month. Wrap as airtight as possible in a freezer bag.

KEEPING COOKIES SOFT

If you prefer chewy cookies, they'll stay soft if you add a half an apple or a slice of white bread to the jar. This will provide just enough moisture to keep the cookies from becoming hard.

FOR MOISTER CAKE

Never bake an angel food cake on the top or middle rack of the oven. It will retain moisture better if baked in the lower third and always at the temperature specified in the recipe. The best tool to cut the cake? An electric knife or unwaxed dental floss.

HIGH PEAKS

Here are hints for making world-class meringue and high peaks.

- Make sure that your egg whites are at room temperature. As you beat, add 2 to 3 tablespoons of superfine or granulated sugar for each egg used. Keep beating until the peaks stand up without drooping.
- To keep the peaks firmer for a longer period, add $\frac{1}{8}$ teaspoon of white vinegar per egg white while beating.
- Remember, if the weather is bad, rainy, or even damp out, the meringue peaks will not remain upright.

THE BEST OATMEAL COOKIES

When you make oatmeal cookies, boost the oatmeal's flavor by toasting it lightly on a baking sheet before adding it to the batter. Sprinkle the oatmeal on a baking sheet and heat it in a 300°F oven for about 10 minutes. The oats should turn a golden-brown.

OF COURSE, YOU CAN SAVE MORE BY HAVING A PIECE OF FRUIT INSTEAD

People who love pies can save about 150 calories per serving simply by eating single-crust fruit cobblers instead of two-crust pies.

WHO KNEW?

If you need to store a cake more than a day or two, put half an apple in the cake saver. The apple will provide just enough moisture to keep the cake from drying out too soon.

WHEN MOVIE NIGHT GOES WRONG

If you've ever burnt popcorn in your microwave, you know that it stinks, and the smell won't quit! Make it smell fresh again by stuffing the microwave with crumpled newspaper for a few hours. Remove the paper, and boil water and baking soda in a glass bowl for five minutes, and the smell should be gone.

DIDN'T CONFUSIUS SAY THAT?

Never stretch pie dough when you are placing it in the pan. Stretched dough usually shrinks from the sides.

JUST A PINCH WILL DO

If you are having a problem with icing drying out or stiffening before you're done frosting the cake, just add a pinch of baking soda to the confectioners' sugar. This will help the icing retain some moisture and it will not dry out as fast.

KNOW YOUR YEAST

Most bread machines are timed for the use of dry yeast. Compressed fresh yeast should never be used in bread-baking machines. If you have a bread machine, look for special bread-machine yeast.

COLD COLD DOUGH

Most recipes tell you to be sure pie dough is chilled before putting it in the pie plate. Why? Cold will help to firm up the fat and relax the gluten in the flour. This helps it to retain its shape and reduce shrinkage.

THE MICROWAVED SANDWICH

When heating a sandwich in the microwave, you'll get the best results using firm textured bread such as French or sourdough. The filling should be heated separately. If the filling is heated in the sandwich, be sure to spread it evenly over the bread and very close to the edges. Wait a few minutes before eating the sandwich, as the filling may remain very hot even if the bread is cool to the touch.

BLENDING BASICS

When baking, it is important that all the ingredients be blended well, without being blended too much. If you need to sift flour, add the other dry ingredients (such as leavening and salt) to the flour before you sift.

OR JUST DON'T MAKE THEM

You've heard it before, and it's true: A soufflé must be served as soon as it is removed from the oven. Soufflés begin to collapse as soon as they start to cool down. So it's best to serve them in the baking dish.

A CLEAN GRIDDLE IS THE KEY

Pancakes will never stick to the griddle if you clean it after every batch with coarse salt wrapped in a piece of cheesecloth. The salt will provide a light abrasive cleaning and won't harm the surface if you're gentle.

BUTTER IS BETTER

If you are using 100 percent whole-wheat flour and want the crunchiest cookies ever, try using butter instead of another shortening. Never use oil, as it will make the cookies spread too fast when baked.

PURE MAPLE SYRUP GETS IT DONE

Vermonters can tell you that a tablespoon of pure—and only pure—maple syrup added to your pancake batter will really improve the taste.

ALWAYS USE GLASS

The acid in fruits may react with metal pans and discolor a pie or tart. Always use a glass dish when baking a fruit pie or tart; remember to lower the temperature of the oven by 25°F.

THE MARSHMALLOW TRICK

For a unique pumpkin pie, put small marshmallows on the bottom of the pie. As the pie bakes, the air in the marshmallows expands and the marshmallows rise to the top.

GET A SCALE

A cup of flour can vary by several grams by weight depending on how much it has settled. For this reason, professional pastry chefs never use measuring cups—they weigh ingredients, especially flour, because accuracy is so important.

TRY THIS!

Keep soft cookies moist and maintain the moisture in cakes and pancakes by adding a teaspoon of jelly to the batter.

LOWER THE FAT AND RAISE THE PRICE

A reduced-fat Oreo contains 47 calories and 1.67 grams of fat. The original Oreo has 53 calories and 2.33 grams of fat. Not a big savings calorie-wise, and because reduced-fat foods often cost more than their original counterparts, your pocketbook may be the only thing that's lighter.

SLOWER IS BETTER

If you make bread with 100 percent whole-wheat flour, it will be moister if you add the flour to the water slowly and mix gently. Whole-wheat flour absorbs water at a slower rate than do other types of flour. Reserve ¼ cup of flour and knead in a tablespoon or so at a time as needed.

CHILL OUT

After you've removed bread from the oven, always cool it on a wire rack. This will allow air to circulate around the bread and should eliminate any soggy areas in the loaf.

CRISPY COOKIES

If you want crisp cookies, be sure your cookie jar has a loose-fitting lid. This allows air to circulate and evaporates any moisture.

CUTTING TIP

To get a sharp edge on your cookies when using cutters, dip the cutter in flour or warm oil occasionally during the cutting.

CHILLY DOUGH

Cold cookie dough will not stick to the rolling pin. Refrigerate the dough for 20 minutes for the best results.

IF YOU MUST CURL YOUR CHOCOLATE...

If you like the look of chocolate curls, all you have to do is run your vegetable peeler on a chocolate bar.

CONTINUE TO STIR

When you make pancakes, waffles, or latkes, always stir the batter between batches. This keeps the ingredients from settling and keeps the batter aerated.

EAT IT FAST

Authentic French bread is made without fat. Fat coats the strands of gluten in the flour, retarding their development, and tends to slow down moisture loss in bread. As a result, French bread can get stale in as little as six hours.

KEEP YOU WAFFLE IRON FROM STICKING

Here's a trick to keep waffles from sticking to the waffle iron: Beat a teaspoon of white wine into the batter. You'll never taste the wine.

WHO KNEW?

Another way to prevent sugar syrup from crystallizing: Once the sugar melts, cover the pan. The condensation that forms on the pot lid will melt the crystals.

BAD SUGAR BLUES

We all know it's bad for us, but new research has conclusively proved that too much white sugar will cause premature aging, particularly around the eye area where skin is fragile and prone to wrinkles.

YOU'RE WARPED

Warped baking pans should be discarded. The uneven surface will spoil the quality of the baked goods.

EASY DOES IT

One secret to light biscuits: Handle the dough gently. Overworking the dough and rerolling the scraps makes for tough biscuits.

LARGER HOLES ARE BEST

Fill a salt shaker with confectioners' or colored sugar for dusting candy or cookies. Choose one with large holes for best results.

THE SOUFFLE SOLUTION

When preparing a soufflé, be sure to use a soufflé dish with straight sides. This will force the soufflé to expand upward. Also, always use the exact size dish called for in the recipe.

HOW TO UNMOLD

A gelatin salad will be easy to unmold if you spray the mold with nonstick cooking spray before making the gelatin.

DOES YOUR CAKE STICK TO THE PLATE?

Sprinkle a thin layer of sugar on a plate before you put a cake on it. This keeps the cake from sticking, and makes the bottom crunchy.

WHO KNEW?

Most people believe brown sugar is a healthier option than white sugar but, in reality, the majority of brown sugar is simply refined white sugar with molasses added to change its color. For healthier options, demerara and muscovado are good choices. Both are unrefined and suitable to be added to hot drinks or for cooking, and also have reasonably good shelf lives.

BUT "FATTY LITTLE STICKS" REALLY ISN'T A GOOD NAME

It's always a good idea to read the list of ingredients and nutrition labels to check the fat content before you purchase bread sticks. They can contain up to 40 percent fat.

IT'S NOT THE HEAT

If you are having a problem with bread browning too fast, set a dish of water on the oven rack just above the bread. The added humidity in the oven will slow down the browning. This will work with cakes as well.

SUGAR SHOCK

Around the 1880s, Americans consumed just less than nine pounds of sugar per person per year. Today, we consume, on average, more than 20 teaspoons of sugar every day—which comes to 153 pounds per year.

The only health problem sugar causes in and of itself is dental cavities. However, it supplies no nutrients other than calories (in the form of simple carbohydrates). Consuming too much sugar can mean that you don't eat enough nutrient-rich foods, and it can lead to obesity—which can lead to a significant number of very serious health problems.

CORN SYRUP

Because corn syrup is very inexpensive to produce, it's one of the most common sweeteners. It is made from a mixture of starch granules derived from corn, which are then processed with acids or enzymes that convert it into heavy, sweet syrup. The syrup is then artificially flavored and used in literally thousands of foods, from pancake syrup to applesauce. The fact that corn syrup tends to retard crystallization makes it a good choice for candies, preserves, and frostings.

WHO KNEW?

You'll find sugar in the strangest places:

Baby foods	Lipstick	Soup mixes
Bacon	Lip gloss	Soy sauce
Canned fish	Peanut butter	Stamp adhesives
Cough drops	Pickle relish	Vitamins
Laxatives	Pickles	Waffle mixes

KEEP AN EYE OUT

Sugar has many names; here are a few of the more common ones:

Beet sugar	Hexatol	Mannitol
Cane sugar	High-fructose corn syrup	Molasses
Corn syrup	Honey	Sorghum
Dextrose	Lactose	Sucrose
Fructose	Levulose	Turbinado
Glucose	Maltose	Xylitol

JUST DON'T WRITE, 'HIPPY BIRTHDAY'

A baker's trick to make it easier to decorate the top of a cake: With a toothpick, trace the pattern, picture, or lettering before you pipe the icing.

AND SAVE A FEW CALORIES

Substituting light cream or reduced-fat sour cream for the liquid in a packaged mix will yield the same results in most instances.

AND WHO WANTS MOLDY BREAD?

If you don't plan to use a loaf of bread within a week, wrap it in waxed paper and store it in the refrigerator. The bread will not get moldy as fast as it would on the counter.

HEAT TREATMENT

Honey should be stored in as airtight a container as possible since the sugars attract moisture and absorb water from the air easily, especially if the relative humidity is more than 60 percent. Honey tends to crystallize easily, which releases the glucose from the sugars. Heating the honey slightly will force the glucose back into the sugar molecules and return the honey to a liquid. Microwaving it for about 30 seconds can liquefy crystallized honey. Never allow honey to boil or get too hot, because it will break down and then must be discarded.

NO SUBSTITUTIONS ALLOWED

Maple syrup has a very pronounced flavor. Use it only when called for in recipes—never substitute it for honey, brown sugar, or any other sweetener.

AND YOU THOUGHT YOU WORKED HARD

Bees gather honey by drawing the flower nectar into their proboscis (a tube extending from their heads). The nectar then passes through their esophagus into a honey sac (storage pod) located just before the intestine. The nectar is stored until the bee returns to the hive. While the nectar is in the sac, the bee secretes enzymes that begin to break down the starch into simple sugars and fructose. The hive contains one mature queen, about 100 male drones, and 20,000 female workers. The bees utilize eight pounds of honey for daily activities for every pound that reaches the market. For every gallon of honey the bees consume, they travel 7 million miles, or 7 million miles to the gallon if you prefer. When a worker returns to the hive, it pumps and mixes the nectar in and out of its proboscis until the carbohydrate concentration is about 50 to 60 percent, and then it is deposited into the honeycomb.

AIN'T NOTHING LIKE THE REAL THING

Maple syrup is best stored in the refrigerator after it is opened to retain its flavor and retard the growth of mold. If it granulates, just warm it up slightly. It should last about one year from the time it is opened, and is best used at room temperature or slightly heated.

Read the label well! Make sure it doesn't read "maple-flavored," "maple-blended," or "imitation." The real thing is expensive and contains nutrients such as iron and calcium. Typical pancake syrup is almost always pure corn syrup and artificial maple flavoring.

Maple sugar must contain a minimum of 35 percent pure maple syrup. Look for pale maple sugar. The lighter the color, the higher the quality.

ALL ABOUT THE SAP RUN

The sap run is one of the mysteries of nature. Pure maple syrup is the product of the rock maple tree, which is the only tree that produces high-quality syrup. The amount of sap available depends on whether the leaves are able to convert the right proportions of sunlight, water, and carbon dioxide into sugar. Sap is collected only between the first major spring thaw and the time the leaf buds begin to burst. If the sap collection is not discontinued at this point, the syrup will have a bitter flavor.

Conditions must be nearly perfect to have a good sap run. The winter must be severe enough to freeze the trees' roots, the snow cover must extend into the spring to keep the roots very cold, the temperature swings must be extreme from day to night, and the tree must have excellent exposure to sunlight.

Maple sap is about 3 percent sucrose, and each tree produces 10 to 12 gallons of sap on average per spring season. Early in the season, it takes 20 gallons of sap to produce one gallon of pure maple syrup; as the season progresses, it can take as many as 50 gallons. Pure maple syrup is composed of 62 percent sucrose, 35 percent water, 1 percent glucose, 1 percent fructose, and 1 percent malic acid. The longer the syrup is boiled during processing, the darker the syrup becomes; this is due to a reaction between the sugars and proteins.

RAW SUGAR (TURBINADO)

Despite its name, this is almost exactly like refined white sugar—it's partially processed, so a little molasses is left on the surface for color, and its grains are often larger than granulated. It has no advantage over granulated sugar, and its price is higher. As with all sugar, it can be labeled "natural" to make you think that it is more healthful than it really is.

MOLASSES

When sugar cane is processed to make white sugar, it undergoes a complex process that removes virtually all nutrients except calories. The residue that remains after processing is molasses. Whether a molasses is sulfured or unsulfured depends on whether sulfur was used during processing. Unsulfured molasses is lighter in color and has a cleaner flavor than either sulfured or blackstrap molasses. Blackstrap molasses is the result of the third boiling and is the dregs of sugar production. It is only slightly richer in iron, calcium, and potassium than its more refined cousins.

If a recipe calls for dark molasses, you can use light molasses without a problem. If you use molasses in place of another sweetener in baked goods, be sure and reduce the heat about 25°F, or the food may over-brown. Molasses has a degree of acidity that can be neutralized by adding 1 teaspoon of baking soda to the dry ingredients for every cup of molasses the recipe calls for. Molasses is best used in gingerbread, gingersnaps, and baked beans, where its robust flavor can really shine.

If you need to measure molasses, coat the measuring utensil with nonstick spray so it will flow better and have a more accurate measurement.

ARTIFICIAL SWEETENERS

Sucralose (Splenda)

Best known by the trade name Splenda, sucralose is a concentrated form of granulated sugar that has been approved by the FDA, is 600 times sweeter than regular sugar, and has no calories. It is very stable in foods and carbonated beverages. Currently it is used to sweeten over 3500 products.

A SOUR TASTE

Along with refined sugar and white potatoes, over-processed white bread is one of the worst foods for blood-sugar control. If you want white bread without the sugar, choose sourdough bread. It contains lactic acid, which slows down digestion and gives sourdough its tangy flavor.

A TRICK TO STOP SYRUP FROM CRYSTALLIZING

When boiling syrup, one of the more frequent and annoying problems is that it crystallizes. The easiest way to avoid this is to put a pinch of cream of tartar in the syrup while it's cooking. This adds a small amount of acidity—just enough to prevent crystals from forming.

Aspartame

Best known by its trade names Nutrasweet and Equal. This sweetener is produced from two amino acids—phenylalanine and aspartic—and methanol. When aspartame was approved in 1981, the FDA set a maximum recommended amount of 50 milligrams per kilogram of body weight per day. This equates to a 140-pound person drinking 20 diet drinks per day or the equivalent in food. The World Health Organization recommended a maximum of 40 milligrams per kilogram of body weight for adults. A child who consumes artificially sweetened gum, candy, puddings, and beverages could easily exceed the adult maximum amounts.

It has been implicated in animal laboratory testing in contributing to nerve disease. However, testing is not conclusive and the studies were conducted using high dosages, which may have skewed the outcome. Recent negative study results by leading universities and the Arizona Department of Health Sciences were regarded by the FDA as "unfounded fears." Future testing may prove more conclusive.

Caution must be taken when aspartame is heated, because a percentage may turn into methyl alcohol. It is not recommended for use in baked goods or any drink that requires a liquid being brought to a boil.

Cyclamates

Banned by the FDA.

L-Sugars

These contain no calories or aftertaste. Can be substituted cup for cup for granulated sugar in recipes.

Saccharine

Has been around since 1879 and is 300 times sweeter than sugar. It is used in many common products such as mouthwashes and lipsticks. Saccharine has long been suspected of causing cancers. Recently, however, it was determined that the cancers developed by laboratory animals are not the type developed by humans. In fact, no tumors or cancers in humans were linked to saccharine in more than 20 years of study.

Stevia

Native to Paraguay, stevia has been used in South America and Japan for years as a calorie-free sweetener. Stevia is an extract from a member of the chrysanthemum family that is sold in health-food stores as a dietary supplement. Because it is a natural herbal product, the Dietary Supplement Act of 1994 applies, and stevia was allowed into the country. It is unapproved as a food additive—stevia cannot be promoted for use as a sweetener, but can be sold as a dietary supplement. However, the FDA is still not sure of any potential problems that might arise since testing is not yet conclusive. Research from Japan says it is safe and may even prevent yeast infections, boost energy levels, and doesn't promote tooth decay. The extract is concentrated and is 200 to 300 times sweeter than table sugar. It is being used for cooking and may leave a licorice-flavored aftertaste.

STIR YOUR FUDGE

Fudge should be stirred vigorously or beaten with a wooden spoon from its glossy, thin consistency to a slightly thick consistency; depending on the recipe, this can take a good 20 minutes. If the fudge doesn't set when cooked, add a few tablespoons of water and cook it again.

MAKE SURE YOU BRUSH

Starchy foods like soda crackers and graham crackers can be bad news for oral hygiene. They stick to your teeth, and then the starch changes to sugar, which bacteria thrive on.

OR JUST PULL OUT YOUR SWEET TOOTH

There are two ways to eliminate the craving for sweets. One way is to place a small amount of salt on your tongue. The second: Dissolve about a teaspoon of baking soda in a glass of warm tap water, then rinse your mouth out and don't swallow. The salt or baking soda tends to stimulate the production of saliva, which eliminates the craving for sweets.

TEMPERAMENTAL CANDY?

If you're making candy, be sure to follow recipe directions to the letter. Candy recipes are very exacting and variances can compromise quality. Candy must be cooked at the recommended temperature—never try to speed up the process by increasing the heat. The lower the final temperature of the candy after it is cooked will determine the softness of the final product. In fact, most candy-making cookbooks stress the importance of waiting for a cool, dry day.

A GOOD SWEETENER?

Fruit is high in the sugar fructose. However, all studies show that there is no risk factor involved with this sugar and consumption of fruit does not have to be—in fact, should not be—limited. Fructose breaks down at a slower rate than most sugars, giving the body more time to utilize it before it is completely broken down to glucose.

- Milk chocolate must contain at least 10 percent chocolate liquor and a minimum of 12 percent milk solids.
- Unsweetened chocolate, sometimes called baking chocolate, must contain at least 50 percent cocoa butter.

BRRRR

Freezing has a negative effect on many candies. Their flavors can change and the candies may even lose their consistency: Hard candies may crumble, jellies become granular, and the rest lose their original consistencies due to the expansion of the liquid in their cells.

IT MAKES SENSE

If you must satisfy a sugar craving, don't opt for a high-fat candy bar or cookie. Instead, eat a sugar cube. One provides a mere 10 calories and contains no fat or preservatives.

READ FIRST

Jams and jellies can be produced from a number of artificial ingredients, so it's best to read labels and purchase those made from real fruit. If they are and are labeled "light," so much the better—that's an indication that the sugar content has been reduced.

IN CASE YOU'VE ALWAYS WONDERED WHERE TO STORE MARSHMELLOWS

Store marshmallows in the freezer. Just cut them with a scissors that have been dipped in very hot water to get them apart.

IS YOUR BROWN SUGAR LUMPY?

Brown sugar loses moisture rather quickly and develops lumps easily. To soften it, put the sugar in the microwave with a slice of fresh white bread or half an apple, cover the dish tightly and heat for 15 to 20 seconds; let it stand five minutes before using. The moisture from the bread or apple will produce enough steam to soften the sugar without melting it. Store brown sugar in the freezer to keep it from getting lumpy in the first place.

SHAPE UP!

You can make perfectly shaped pancakes by filling a meat baster with the batter, and squeezing it on to the griddle that way.

STOP THAT SYRUP

Frustrated with syrup running down the sides of the bottle? Try this trick: Rub the threads at the neck of the bottle with a small amount of vegetable oil.

KIND OF SCARY, ISN'T IT?

The percentage of sugar in some common foods:			
Candy corn	89.6	Oreo cookie	39.4
3 Musketeers	76.8	Ketchup	22.3
Milky Way	71.6	Flavored gelatin	18
Breakfast cereals	up to 46		

IT'S NOT THE REAL THING

Despite its name, white chocolate does not include any chocolate liquor and thus is not really chocolate. It is produced from sugar, milk solids, cocoa butter, lecithin, and vanilla.

IN CASE YOU'VE ALWAYS WONDERED HOW TO SOFTEN MARSHMELLOWS

Add a slice of very fresh white bread or half an apple to a bag of marshmallows to soften them. Just leave them alone for one to two days until the marshmallows absorb the moisture.

ODOR CONTROL

Candies stored in the refrigerator can pick up odors from other foods. Keep them in an airtight container.

GET RID OF THE LUMPS

Granulated sugar clumps less than brown sugar, but it can still become lumpy. Keep this from happening by sticking a few salt-free crackers in the canister to absorb the moisture; replace the crackers every week.

NOT TOO HOT

If the weather is hot and humid, don't try to make candy, especially chocolates, unless your kitchen is air-conditioned. The best temperature for making most candies, including chocolate truffles, divinity, hard candy, and fudge, is between 62°F and 68°F, with low humidity. These candies absorb moisture from the air very easily.

CARPE CHOCOLATE

When you melt chocolate, water droplets, condensation, and high temperatures may cause the chocolate to seize or stiffen. To alleviate this problem, add 1 teaspoon vegetable shortening per ounce of chocolate and stir. More oil can be added if needed to ensure proper consistency.

JUST SAY LESS

You can often reduce the amount of sugar in a recipe for cookies, cakes, pies, and other baked goods by up to one-third without having a negative affect on the results of the recipe.

DUMP BAD FOODS

Refined carbohydrates like cakes, cookies and candy, as well as processed ready-made meals, all cause havoc with the healthy working of the mind and body. Our bodies become lethargic and sluggish when processed foods are filled with additives and chemical preservatives.

SWEET LITTLE LIES

If you're not a great baker, but love the smell of fresh baked goods, try this trick: Dab a few drops of vanilla extract on a cool light bulb, then turn it on. When it heats up, your kitchen should be filled with a wonderful smell.

WHO KNEW?

The easiest way to separate eggs when baking is to crack them into a funnel. The whites slide out, leaving the yolk behind.

SWEET AS HONEY

Renowned for its medicinal properties since the time of the ancient Egyptians, dark-colored honeys such as buckwheat possess more antioxidants than the lighter varieties, and also provides nutrients for the growth of new tissue, helping skin rejuvenate itself and stay young-looking.

BE A CHOCOHOLIC

Flavanoids are super nutrients that help protect the body from potentially dangerous free radical cells. They are found in good-quality dark chocolate that contains at least 70 percent cocoa solids.

RUST REMOVER

To treat rust on metal baking dishes and cookware, sprinkle powdered detergent on the spot. Scour with the cut side of half a raw potato. Alternatively, pour Coca-cola over the rust and leave it to work overnight. Wash it off in the morning. Rust on iron or steel can be removed with steel wool.

MILK IS MORE

If you have a daily chocolate addiction, choose dark chocolate as it contains less fat than milk chocolate and is higher in cocoa solids, which makes it richer and which means you're most likely to eat less. However, it does have double the caffeine of milk chocolate, at up to 50 mg a bar.

THE FLOSS TOSS

If your freshly baked cookies are stuck to the baking tray, fear not. Simply hold a length of dental floss taut and slip it underneath the cookie. It works better than a spatula…or your hands.

SPREAD AWAY SUGAR

Instead of jam, which can be packed with sugar, try no-sugar jam or make your very own healthy apple spread. Cook sliced sweet eating apples with a dash of cinnamon in little water (it can be stored for two months in an airtight container).

HAVE YOU NOTICED HOW THE FROSTING ON BAKERY CAKES ALWAYS HAS A WAVY, SILKY LOOK?

Yours can too if you gently blow-dry the frosting, until it melts slightly and appears smooth and wavy.

FOR A POST-HALLOWEEN CHOCOLATE EXTRAVAGANZA

Melt chocolate in a fondue pot with some milk, and dip in some cut up fruit. It is not only a great way to use up some of your kids' chocolate, but also lets you get them to eat fruits.

OR GET A BAT

Your brown sugar's hard but you don't have a microwave? Wrap the entire box tightly in a towel and hit it on the counter a few good whacks.

LEAVE A MARK

For your next bake sale, write out the recipe on an index card and tape it to the plate or box. That way, if buyers find your goody to their liking, they'll know they can make it themselves in the future.

SHOPPING SPREE

Look for after–Valentine's Day sales on red candles, pillows and other decorative items, which can double as Christmas items. Also, don't forget to buy plenty of solid chocolate hearts packs available on discount rates—freeze them and use for baking all year long.

Happy Valentine's Day.

HERE'S A NEW TWIST ON TRANSPORTING FROSTED CAKES

Don't just insert toothpicks and cover in plastic, because the sharp ends can puncture the plastic and result in a gooey mess. Instead, attach miniature marshmallows to the toothpicks before covering. Stands of spaghetti can also be used instead of toothpicks.

FOR THE SAKE OF THE CAKE

If a cake recipe calls for flouring the baking pan, use some of the dry cake mix instead, and you won't have a floury mess on the outside when the cake is done.

STRANGE BUT TRUE

Kids nauseous from eating too much candy? Don't worry, just try these home remedies: Have your child drink a little ginger ale, then chew a handful of crushed ice, and finally sniff a black and white newspaper. Really, it works.

MAKING GRAHAM CRACKER PIE CRUST IS A MESS

Particularly when pressing the crumbs into the pie plate with greasy, buttered hands. Stop the crumbs from sticking by putting your hands into a plastic bag before the pressing begins!

CLEAN-UP TIPS

If you've spilled sugar, just glide a lint roller over the mess. And when you're done baking, sprinkle your messy countertop with salt, and the doughy, floury mess that it leaves behind can be easily wiped away with a damp sponge.

YOU KNEW THEY HAD A SECRET

Do you want your pies to glisten like those in the bakery? It's easy with this trick: Just beat an egg white and brush it over the crust before baking.

STOP STICKING

Before replacing the lid on gooey molasses, syrup, or honey, try this: Coat the threads of the jar with vegetable oil. The oil will prevent the lid from sticking next time you open it.

BEST FOR LAST

Keep your ice cream cones leak-free with this simple tip: Just put a miniature marshmallow or chocolate kiss in the bottom of the cone before adding the ice cream. Either of them can help prevent to tip of the cone from leaking.

SIMPLY PERFECT!

Save your store-bought bread bags for times when you bake bread. They are perfectly sized bag for homemade breads.

FRESHNESS TEST

Here's how to test to see if you're baking powder is still fresh: Just put a small amount in some hot water. If it bubbles, it's still fresh; if not, toss it.

CELERY TRICK

Bread stays fresh for a longer time if you add a stalk of celery and place it in an airtight bag.

VANITY SANITY

Consider keeping a clean powder puff in your flour container. It's a great way to dust flour onto rolling pins or pastry boards. And remember, always store your flour in the freezer to prevent any sort of bug infestation.

CANDIED CANDLES

Use lifesavers, or other round candy with holes in them, to hold candles on your kid's birthday cake. More sugar means more fun for the little ones, of course.

POTATOES, PASTAS, AND GRAINS

14

THE GOODNESS OF GRAINS

Familiar with the Food Pyramid? Then you know you should be eating 3 ounces of whole grains every day. Eating an adequate amount of nutrient-rich whole grains can be difficult.

The typical American diet includes only 25 percent complex carbohydrates; in comparison, a typical Japanese person's diet is 65 percent. In recent years, Americans have begun to realize the importance diet plays in overall health; unfortunately it took an increase in cancer and heart diseases to bring this realization about.

Grains are composed of three parts: the bran, the endosperm, and the germ. The outer covering, or bran, contains most of the grain's nutrients and almost all the dietary fiber. The endosperm is the heaviest part of the grain; it contains most of the protein and carbohydrates. It is this portion that is used to make white flour. The germ contains polyunsaturated fat and is rich in vitamin E and the B complex vitamins. Because it is so high in fat, it is usually removed to avoid rancidity.

GRAIN VARIETIES

Amaranth

Was first grown by the Aztecs. The seeds are incredibly small—there are about 700,000 in one pound. Amaranth is the only grain that contains adequate amounts of the amino acid lysine. When this grain is consumed with rice, wheat, or barley it provides a biologically complete protein containing all the essential amino acids.

Barley

An excellent source of B vitamins and soluble fiber. Half the barley grown in this country is used as animal fodder; 30 percent is used in brewing beer or distilling liquor. Of the remaining 20 percent, most is sold pearled or whole, but some is available as barley grits. Malted barley can be purchased in health-food stores.

Buckwheat

Actually the seed of a leafy plant related to rhubarb. It has a strong nutlike flavor and is especially high in the amino acid arginine. Considered a minor crop in the United States, it is primarily prepared as kasha. Kasha, or buckwheat groats, is buckwheat kernels that are hulled and crushed. It can be prepared the same as rice, and it has a high nutritional value.

Millet

The only grain higher in B vitamins than whole wheat or brown rice. It is also an excellent source of copper and iron. People with wheat allergies can usually eat millet without a problem. Millet is popular in North Africa, China, India, and Ethiopia, where it is used to make flatbread.

Oats

Were first grown in the United States in the 1600s. By the 1880s, they were packaged and sold, with oatmeal being the most popular breakfast food of that time. Oat bran is known to contribute to lowering cholesterol levels. It is high in a number of vitamins and minerals, and is an excellent source of soluble fiber, which can reduce the risk of heart disease. Besides oatmeal, oats are used in granola and muesli cereals.

CORN

A grain native to the Americas, corn is high in fiber and yellow varieties are a fairly good source of vitamin A. Corn is popular in many forms, from fresh on the cob and kernels to ground preparations like grits and corn-bread—even distilled into bourbon.

Quinoa

This grain is s related to chard and spinach; its leaves can be cooked similarly for a nutritious green. The grain has a delicate flavor and can be substituted for most other grains. It quadruples in volume when cooked and is usually found in natural foods stores. Quinoa is high in potassium, iron, and riboflavin and has good levels of zinc, copper, and manganese.

Rye

This grain is higher in protein (75 percent higher than brown rice), iron, and the B vitamins than whole wheat. Most rye breads are usually made from a combination of rye and wheat flour because rye has no gluten—a loaf made just of rye flour will be too dense and strongly flavored. Only 25 percent of the rye crop goes into human food production; the balance is used for whisky and animal fodder.

RICE

Comes in more varieties than nearly any other food. There are hundreds of types of long-, medium-, or short-grain rice grown around the world. Rice is popular in the United States; Americans consume about 25 pounds per person, annually. In Japan, annual consumption is about 30 pounds per person. Rice was first cultivated in Thailand around 3,500 B.C., however, China produces almost 90 percent of all the rice grown worldwide.

Rice is an excellent source of the B complex vitamins and a number of minerals. Long-grain rice is just slightly more nutritious than short- and medium-grain rice. Brown rice is more nutritious and higher in B vitamins and fiber than white rice. Of all rices, only brown has vitamin E.

Quick-cooking brown rice is available, and though its texture isn't quite as chewy, it cooks in 15 minutes. If you soak brown rice 8 to 10 hours or overnight before cooking, it will cook in about 22 minutes. White rice has had the outer husk and bran removed. Because the bran portion is higher in fat, brown rice may go rancid if not used quickly.

Triticale

A hybrid of wheat and rye that is high in protein and B vitamins. It may be used in breads due to its excellent gluten content. Triticale can be found in most natural-food stores.

Wheat

The number-one grain crop in the world and used mainly in breads and pastas. The majority of wheat is processed into white flour; whole wheat is very high in the B vitamins and numerous minerals, including iron. Researchers are currently studying the effects wheat fiber might have in decreasing the risk of colon cancers.

BROWN IS BEST

When the bran is removed to make white rice, nutrients are not added back to fortify the grain. Even though rice may be sold as "enriched," the number of nutrients replaced is minimal. When the rice is cooked, most of those additional nutrients are lost. In terms of nutrition, instant rice is your worst bet.

TYPES OF OAT PRODUCTS

Instant Oats

These oats are sliced into very small pieces, and then cooked and dried. Some varieties "cook" when mixed with hot water, others require brief cooking. Instant oats cannot be used in recipes that call for rolled or quick-cooking oats. They lack the texture we find so appealing in cookies, for example.

BREAD TO THE RESCUE

If your rice burns, spoon the unburned rice into a clean pot and set a slice of white bread on top for 5 minutes, then remove and discard. The white bread will absorb the burnt odor.

QUICK-COOKING OATS

Sliced into smallish pieces, and then steamed and flattened, these oats take only five minutes to cook.

Oat Bran

The ground outer casing of the grain. It is very high in soluble fiber and can help to lower cholesterol levels.

Oat Flour

Very finely ground oats. It must be mixed with wheat flour when baking breads, as it does not contain gluten and will not rise if used alone.

Rolled Oats

Steamed, flattened, and flaked, these oats take about 15 minutes to cook. Both quick-cooking and rolled oats can be used interchangeably with no problem in recipes.

Steel-Cut Oats

Cut instead of rolled. They are not steamed and take about 30 minutes to cook. They have a very chewy texture.

RINSE THE RICE?

Unless the instructions explicitly direct you to rinse rice before cooking, don't—most rice sold in the United States is coated with a fine powder that contains the B vitamins thiamine and niacin. If you rinse the rice, you wash these nutrients down the drain.

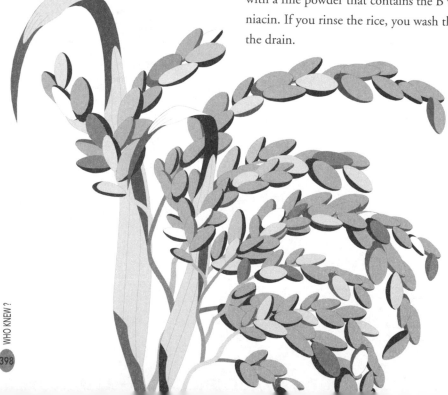

THE FLUFFY GUARANTEE

Converted rice is actually parboiled rice—that is, it has been soaked, steamed, and dried in such a way as to ensure it cooks up fluffy every time. Despite the fact that it is partially cooked, it does take slightly longer to cook than does regular rice.

I STILL PREFER RAISINETS AT THE MOVIES

Jasmine rice smells and tastes something like popcorn. Try it as a side dish for a different treat. It pairs nicely with simple grilled chicken or fish.

THE RICE THAT ISN'T

Wild rice is not a grain, but actually a seed of a shallow water grass. It was a staple food of the Chippewa and Dakota. Wild rice has one-third more protein than does long-grain white rice and is high in B vitamins when cooked. Wild rice has fairly high moisture content and can become moldy in high humidity; it should be stored in the refrigerator.

FIRST, YOU TOAST

Toast oatmeal before using it in cookies and breads: Spread it in a thin layer in a baking pan and bake at 350°F for about 10 minutes, shaking the pan once or twice.

THE RICE FORMULA

If you're cooking long grain-white rice, here's an easy formula to determine how much water you need—twice as much water as you have rice. Once the water comes to a boil, add the rice, and then reduce the heat to a simmer and cook for 15 minutes. If you like dry, fluffy rice, once the rice is cooked, wrap the lid with a cotton dishtowel and set it on the pot for about 15 minutes. The cloth will absorb the steam.

WHEAT INCLUDED

Many people are allergic to wheat or have celiac disease, a condition where ingesting gluten and similar proteins in rye, oats, barley, and triticale damages the lining of the small intestine. Wheat can lurk in a surprising number of foods that you might not suspect:

Beer	Sanka	Graham flour	Bouillon cubes
Malt liquor	Whisky	Rye flour	Gravy
Malted milk	Candy bars	Gluten flour	Soy sauce
Gin	Pudding	Patent flour	
Postum	Corn flour	Lima-bean flour	

WHO KNEW?

When you make pasta, don't rinse it after it's cooked. Sauce will cling better, and you'll retain more nutrients.

DOPEY NAME, GOOD CHOICE

Cracked wheat can be a nutritious substitute for rice in many dishes. It is prepared by toasting whole-wheat berries (the bran and germ are kept intact), which are then broken into coarse, medium, and fine fragments.

AU NATURAL

If you're a fan of peanut butter, but not of the high levels of unhealthy Trans-fats (which can't be properly digested by the body) it contains, switch to a natural product. While not being lower in calories, these are free of hydrogenated oils. They make a better choice as spreads on crackers or oatcakes and can be eaten with an apple as a mid-morning snack.

MAKE IT LIGHTER

If you want the nutrients of whole-wheat flour but want a lighter texture for your baked goods, use whole-wheat pastry flour.

THE GOOD GERM

Wheat germ is high in nutrients and fiber. Because wheat germ can go rancid quickly, once you've opened the vacuum-sealed jar, store it in the refrigerator. It will stay fresh for six months. It's easy to tell if the jar of wheat germ in your fridge has gone rancid: If it tastes bitter, toss it. Fresh wheat germ should taste sweet.

NUTS TO YOU

Nuts are full of vital nutrients like protein, potassium, vitamin E, B vitamins, and iron. The only drawback to nuts is their fat content: Most nuts range between 50 and 70 percent fat. At 72 percent fat, macadamia nuts are the highest, with coconut and Brazil nuts not too far behind. Coconut gets nearly all its fat in the form of saturated fats. Peanuts, which are really a member of the legume family, and pine nuts are good sources of protein. Shelled nuts go rancid more quickly than do nuts that are in the shells, because the shells protect the oils from oxidizing.

Seeds of many plants are edible and contain an excellent level of nutrients, especially trace minerals that can be difficult to obtain from other foods. The most popular seeds for eating are pumpkin, sesame, and sunflower. Poppy seeds come from a plant related to opium poppies, so eating two poppy seed bread rolls (or about 1.5 grams of seeds) can cause urinalysis to be positive for opiates.

ALWAYS READ THE LABEL

When you buy bread, be sure to read the list of ingredients. White flour is made from wheat, so any bread made from white flour is a wheat bread—but it won't be as nutritious as whole-wheat bread. If you want whole-wheat bread, look for labels that read "whole wheat" or "whole grain" flour. Whole-wheat flour can be stored only for about two months at room temperature before it goes rancid. Under refrigeration, it can be stored for about five months. If you freeze it, whole-wheat flour should last one year; just be sure to bring it to room temperature before you use it.

WHICH IS WHY GRANDMA ALWAYS ADDED MEATBALLS

When eating pasta, try to balance the meal with some protein. This will allow the blood-sugar levels to be normalized.

NOT A TYPO

Have you heard of beanut butter? It is made from soybeans and, like regular peanut butter, provides high-quality protein. It contains sufficient quantities of estrogen-like substances called isoflavones, which may be effective in reducing the symptoms of menopause such as hot flashes; lowering cholesterol levels; boosting bone density, thus reducing the risk of osteoporosis; and may provide antioxidant properties, possibly protecting against cancers of the bladder, prostate, colon, and breast. The fat content of beanut butter is 11 grams per 2 tablespoons compared with 16 grams in regular peanut butter and has two-thirds the saturated fat. The fat tends to separate as in natural peanut butter and can be poured off to reduce the fat content even more.

TYPES OF NUTS

Defatted ("Lite") Peanuts

These are processed to reduce their fat content, but don't be fooled—they are still not a low-fat nibble.

Dry-Roasted

These are never cooked in oil. All nuts, however, are naturally high in fat. Most dry-roasted nuts are high in salt.

ALMOND PASTE VERSUS MARZIPAN

Both of these are made from blanched ground almonds and are used in pastries and confections. They are not the same, however. Marzipan is almond paste with sugar and unbeaten egg whites; it is stiffer and lighter in color. Almond paste contains more blanched almonds, and it costs more.

Raw Nuts

Commonly packaged in cans (which keep them fresh longer), because they tend to go rancid very easily. Raw nuts should be stored in the refrigerator or freezer to slow down deterioration.

Roasted Nuts

Often thought to be higher in fat than dry-roasted nuts, but are only slightly so. They are dipped into and out of the oil so rapidly that they actually absorb very little, and the excess oil is drained off after roasting.

A SIMPLE WAY TO SAVE

Can't quite see your way to buying bread crumbs? Set aside a special jar and pour in the crumbs from the bottom of cracker boxes or low-sugar cereal boxes. Make low-in-sodium seasoned breadcrumbs by adding dried herbs to suit the flavors of your dish.

AND YOU CAN'T DUNK COOKIES INTO THEM, EITHER

Almonds are a good source of calcium—but they're no substitute for milk. One ounce of dry-roasted almonds provides 80 milligrams of calcium but has 166 calories. A half-cup of fat-free milk provides 228 milligrams of calcium and has about 45 calories.

WHO KNEW?

When chopping nuts in a blender, try adding a small amount of sugar. It will keep the nuts from sticking together.

It's easy to shell pecans if you first soak them in boiling water for 15 minutes.

STORE IT UPSIDE DOWN

Once natural peanut butter is opened, it spoils much more rapidly than highly processed commercial brands. It will stay fresh for one year if unopened. Once opened, natural peanut butter will stay fresh for up to four months, stored in the refrigerator upside down. The oil in natural peanut butter separates because there are no chemical stabilizers.

NUTS IN A PINCH

When a chicken recipe calls for a coating of bread crumbs and you don't have any (or if you just want to try something new), substitute your favorite unsalted nut. Chop it as finely as possible.

BUT YOU KNEW THAT ALREADY, RIGHT?

Peanuts are commonly grown in the southern United States; almost 50 percent of the country's crop is used to make peanut butter.

PEANUTS IN THE FRIDGE

Botanically, peanuts are more like beans than nuts; they are members of the legume family. The two most popular varieties of peanuts are Spanish and Virginia. Unshelled peanuts will last for six months if you wrap them in a plastic bag and keep them in the refrigerator.

CHUCK IT

Nuts, beans, whole grains, corn, and peanut butter should be discarded if there is even the slightest sign of mold or unusual odor. They may contain the dangerous carcinogen aflatoxin.

IS YOUR GRAIN FRESH? TRY THIS TEST

Always test grains for freshness before cooking them. Just pour a small amount of water into a pan and add a small amount of grains. Fresh grains sink to the bottom, and older grains float to the top.

A GREAT SOURCE OF PROTEIN

Lentils are small dried members of the legume family called pulses that are a good source of protein. They do not need to be soaked before cooking and can be on the table in about half hour, though they will take longer if cooked with highly acidic foods such as tomatoes.

STICK WITH RICE AND BEANS

A 12-ounce broiled sirloin steak provides 104 grams of protein—almost double the daily requirement—and tips the scales at 684 calories, 28 grams of fat (12 of them saturated), and not a shred of fiber. A meal of white rice and black beans—one cup of each—provides 21 grams of protein (about one third of the daily requirement), a mere 494 calories, 2 grams of fat—zero of which are saturated—and 11 grams of dietary fiber.

A TOUGH NUT TO CRACK

If you're having problems shelling nuts, put them in the freezer for about an hour. You'll find the nuts much easier to crack.

RICE ON TOAST

Rice can be stored in fridge for a longer time if you store a slice of toast on top of it. The toast will absorb excess moisture and keep the rice fluffy and fresh.

GO FIGURE

Unlike rice, which triples when cooked, there's no simple formula for converting a measure of uncooked pasta to cooked—a cup of tiny pastina or alphabet shapes will cook up quite differently than a cup of the large, irregularly-shaped bow ties, for example, and how would you measure a cup of uncooked spaghetti? What is constant is this: A cup of cooked pasta provides you with about 7 grams of protein.

BUT NO ONE HAS A SUNFLOWER SEED AFTER NOOKIE

Sunflower seeds produce a similar reaction on the body as smoking a cigarette: Both cause the body to produce adrenaline, which goes to the brain, resulting in a pleasant feeling. The seeds, however, must be raw, not roasted, for this to take effect.

WHO KNEW?

One ounce of sunflower seeds contains 160 calories and 14 grams of fat. They're a good source of magnesium, folate, and zinc. Although they may be considered a health food, they're not a diet food!

LOOK FOR THE SUN

Making pasta from scratch? Don't make it if it's rainy or very humid. Like bread dough, the pasta dough will be very difficult to knead.

THE ILLUSION OF SPINACH

Spinach and other vegetable pastas contain very little of the vegetable: A cup of spinach pasta contains less than one tablespoon of spinach. Vegetable pastas are barely higher in nutrients than unflavored pasta.

AND TIMING IS EVERYTHING

Always follow the cooking directions on the pasta box, especially regarding cooking times. They can vary considerably from brand to brand.

THE KEYS TO TASTY PASTA

Cook pasta only until it is slightly chewy (what the Italians call *al dente*, or "to the tooth"). The longer you cook pasta, the less nutrients it will retain and the mushier it will become. Always use plenty of water, and keep the water at a rapid boil—the pasta needs to move around as it cooks, to keep it from sticking together. And never salt the water when cooking pasta, because it tends to toughen the food. Use sugar instead, and salt just before serving.

PASTA FOR EVERYONE

Most pasta is easily digested and has fairly low fiber content, making it a good food for children, the elderly, and those with digestive problems. Most pastas are salt- and fat-free. Just be careful with your sauce and you'll have a healthy dinner.

IT'S NOT JUST TURKEY THAT MAKES YOU SLEEPY

A large pasta meal may help you relax by increasing a chemical in your brain called serotonin.

PASTA IN A PINCH

Capellini and capelli d'angelo, or angel hair pasta, cooks up in as little as two minutes. Keep either on hand for times when you need a speedy dinner. Just top these delicate strands with a light sauce.

PASTA LIKES IT DARK

Pasta is fortified with vitamins that are light sensitive. If you transfer pasta from the cardboard cartons to decorative glass jars, use it within one or two months. To store it longer, keep it in airtight containers in the dark. Pasta will keep for about 18 months.

Pasta Shapes	
THIN STRANDS	**WHAT THE NAME MEANS**
Bavette	"Little dribbles." Another name for linguine.
Capelli d'angelo	"Angel's hair." Very thin pasta strands.
Capellini	"Very fine hair." Slightly thicker than capelli d'angelo.
Capelveneri	Flat, medium-width noodles.
Fedelini	Another name for capellini.
Linguine	"Little tongues." Flat, narrow ribbons.
Spaghetti	"Little strings." Long, thin strands.
Spaghettini	Very thin spaghetti.
Vermicelli	"Little worms." Between spaghettini and capellini in thickness.
THICK STRANDS	**WHAT THE NAME MEANS**
Bucatini	"Pierced." Hollow thin strands.
Fettuccine	Flat ribbons, sometimes made with eggs.
Fusilli	Corkscrew-shaped pasta.
Gemelli	"Twins." Pasta strand folded in half and twisted together.
Lasagna	Very long, broad noodles.
Mafalda	Ripple-edged flat, broad noodles.
Pappardelle	"Gulp down." Wide noodles with rippled sides.
Perciatelli	Thin, hollow tubes, about twice as thick as spaghetti.
Tagliarini	Pasta shaped like ribbons, usually paper thin.
Tagliatelle	Very long, flat egg noodles.

Pasta Shapes

TUBES	WHAT THE NAME MEANS
Cannelloni	"Large tubes." Up to 4 inches long.
Magliette	Short, curved pasta tubes.
Manicotti	Tubes between 4 and 5 inches long.
Mostaccioli	"Little mustaches." Tubes about 2 inches long with a slight curve.
Penne	"Quills." Tubes that are diagonally cut, about 2 inches long.
Rigatoni	"Ribbed." Larger than penne, with grooved sides.
Tubetti	Very tiny hollow tubes.
Ziti	"Bridegrooms." A very short tubular-shaped pasta.

OTHER SHAPES	WHAT THE NAME MEANS
Anellini	"Small rings."
Cavatappi	"Corkscrews." Short spiral-shaped macaroni.
Cavatelli	"Little plugs." Short, shells with a rippled edge.
Conchiglie	"Shells" Available in a variety of sizes.
Ditalini	"Little toes." Used in soup.
Farfalle	"Butterflies." Shaped like a bowtie. Sold in two sizes, large and small.
Orecchiette	"Little ears." Small dimpled circles.
Orzo	Small pasta slightly larger than rice.
Pastina	Very, very small pasta, usually used in soups.
Radiatore	"Radiators." Short and thick, with several ridges.
Ruote	"Wheels." Round pasta with spokes, sometimes called rotelle.

THE HOME FOR POTATOES

Sweet potatoes are a root, whereas yams and white potatoes are enlarged stems called tubers that extend underground. The tuber is where the plant stores excess carbohydrates. If white potatoes are stored below 40°F., they tend to release more sugar and turn sweet. Potatoes will last longer and remain solid longer if they are stored in a cool, dry spot, preferably at 45° to 50°F. Air must circulate around potatoes; otherwise, moisture will cause them to decay.

SWEET POTATOES AND YAMS

Sweet potatoes are usually available around Thanksgiving; yams are available year-round. Sweet potato skins are normally a light copper color, while yam skins range from reddish brown to a dirty white.

Don't buy either sweet potatoes or yams if you see any soft spots, mold, or white areas on the skins. Sweet potatoes and yams tend to decay faster than white potatoes due to their high sugar content.

Sweet potatoes tend to become sweeter the more you cook them because some of the starch converts to sugar when the potato is heated. The cells in a sweet potato are not as strong as those in a white potato; when boiled, the sweet potato readily absorbs water and swells.

Sweet potatoes contain the same number of calories as white potatoes; however, they contain more vitamin C and three times the beta-carotene.

??? WHO KNEW?

To peel sweet potatoes easily, boil them 15 to 35 minutes, depending on their size, then immediately immerse them in a bowl of ice-cold water for 20 to 30 seconds. The skins should fall off almost by themselves.

POTATOES AND PANTY HOSE?

Have you ever seen both of those words in a sentence before? Well, check it out: Potatoes prefer to be stored in panty hose (so do onions). Just cut a leg off and drop the potatoes in, tying a knot between them. Hang in a cool, dry spot, cutting just below the knot to get to the potatoes. They'll keep longer that way.

CAN YOU FREEEZE POTATOES?

White potatoes do not freeze well because a large majority of the cells will burst, causing the potato to become mushy and watery when thawed. Commercial frozen potatoes are specially processed to avoid this.

Cooked, peeled sweet potatoes can be frozen without becoming mushy. Store them in a tightly sealed plastic container with as little air as possible (use the smallest container they'll fit in), and then put the container into a tight-sealing plastic freezer bag. They will keep for 10 to 12 months.

THE GENERATION GAP

A new potato has more moisture than an older one does, and each has its strengths. Use new potatoes in dishes such as potato salad; they absorb less water when boiled and less mayonnaise when prepared (your salad will have better flavor and less fat) and they're less likely to break when you mix the salad. Older potatoes are better for baking and making French fries. They are drier, meatier, and starchier, so they have a lighter texture when baked. Their lower water content means the oil will spatter less when you fry them. When baking a potato, make sure you pierce it so steam can escape; otherwise, it may become soggy.

OIL NOT FOIL

Many people wrap a potato in foil thinking that it will speed up the baking time. A faster method is to rub the skin lightly with vegetable oil.

AND WHO DOESN'T?

If you would like a richer color to your potato salad, try adding a small amount of mustard when you are mixing it.

POTATO TRICKS

To keep peeled potatoes from discoloring, place them in a bowl of cold water, add a few drops of white vinegar, then refrigerate. Drain before cooking. Add a small amount of sugar to the cooking water to revive some of the lost flavor.

YEAH, BUT SOMETIMES IT COMES WITH A TOY

If you have a stuffed baked potato at a fast-food restaurant, don't do it for your health—you're better off ordering a specialty burger. One chain's bacon-and-cheese baked potato packs 730 calories and 43 grams of fat, 15 of which are saturated. By comparison, a Burger King Whopper has 630 calories and 38 grams of fat, 11 of which are saturated.

IT CONVERTS

Potatoes should be stored at cool room temperature away from light. Never refrigerate potatoes, because that tends to turn potato starch to sugar. However, if the potato is removed from the refrigerator and left at room temperature for a few days, the sugar will convert back to starch.

APPLES AND GINGER HELP

It is best to purchase potatoes in bulk bins—not in bags, which make it hard to determine which are bruised. If you store fresh ginger with potatoes it will help keep them fresh longer. Half an apple stored with potatoes will stop the sprouting by absorbing moisture before the potato does.

WHO KNEW?

If your potato chips are stale, simply heat them in a microwave for 30 to 60 seconds, and let them stand for a minute or two. They'll be crispy again.

THEY TASTE BETTER, TOO

Cooked potatoes are easier to digest, and because cooking breaks down the cell walls of the potatoes, the body is better able to use the nutrients. Potatoes should never be cooked in aluminum or iron pots—they will turn yellowish—nor should they be sliced with a carbon-steel knife. Cook potatoes in a stainless steel, glass, or enamel pot for a nice pale color.

ALWAYS SOAK FRIES IN WATER

The surface of a cut potato deteriorates very quickly when exposed to air, forming a layer of sticky starch on the potatoes when they're placed into the frying vat. The potatoes may stick to one another as well as the pan and will be almost impossible to serve. Soaking the potatoes in ice water for five to seven minutes before frying will wash off a lot of the surface starch and the sticking problem will be avoided. Just be sure to pat them dry thoroughly with paper towels before you put them in the hot oil to prevent spatters.

JUST IMAGINE IF YOU COOKED THEM THREE TIMES

Many cooks swear the best fries are twice fried, once at a lower temperature to cook them through, then at a higher temperature to make them crispy.

A POTATO MESS

It is not unusual for a potato to pop open during baking if the skin is not pierced. It doesn't really explode; however, it may crack open and make a mess because potatoes build up a good head of steam as they bake. It is best to prick the skin with a fork before baking.

CHEF'S SECRETS FOR GREAT MASHED POTATOES

- Never pour cold milk into cooked potatoes. It will change the taste of the starch, giving it an unpleasant flavor, not unlike cardboard. The milk should be warmed in a pan with a small amount of chives for flavor before being added.
- Buttermilk will give the potatoes a great flavor. If you're watching your weight, save some of the cooking water from the potatoes and use that instead of butter or cream.
- A pinch or two of baking powder will give mashed potatoes extra fluff. Never put baking soda in potatoes; it will turn them black.
- Never overmix or overcook potatoes. The cell walls will rupture, releasing an excess of starch and resulting in soggy, sticky potatoes. Potatoes should be mashed with a vertical motion, not stirred in a circular motion, to minimize the damage that occurs by crushing the cells on the wall of the bowl.
- Try adding powdered milk or instant potato flakes for extra fluffy mashed potatoes.

ONIONS HATE POTATOES

Onions should never be stored with potatoes because moisture from the onions can cause potatoes to sprout. Onions also release gases that will alter the flavor of a potato.

BOIL IT FAST

When boiling potatoes, put them into a mesh-frying basket so you can remove and drain faster; they soften quickly after cooking.

IT'S NOT EASY BEING GREEN

Avoid potatoes with a greenish cast to them, unless you peel or cut away the green part. Overexposure to light causes a chemical reaction that increases a chlorophyll buildup (which is not harmful) and encourages the production of an alkaloid called solanine. Solanine imparts a bitter taste to the potato, and ingesting high levels can actually cause abdominal discomfort, nausea, and diarrhea. Store potatoes in a dark location to avoid solanine buildup.

THE SKINNY ON SKIN

Cooking a potato in its skin will retain of most of its nutrients. This is true whether you bake or boil the spud.

THERE GOES THE VITAMINS

Attention hosts and hostesses: Mashed potatoes that sit out on a buffet will lose significant amounts of their vitamins after one hour. The loss is due to the constant heat, lights, mashing, exposing more of the surface to oxidation, and cooking in boiling water.

POTATO PANIC NO MORE

Uh-oh—you've reached the bottom of the potato barrel and what's left is a little soft. Don't despair (or run out to the store). Just soak them in ice water for about a half hour or until they become hard.

SHORTER IS BETTER

If you store a boiled or baked potato in the refrigerator for three to four days it will lose approximately 90 percent of its nutrient value. Potatoes should only be stored for one to two days.

ROAST POTATOES

Instead of using your deep-fat fryer to make French fries, create a healthy version by roasting thick slices of sweet potato in olive oil – leave the skins on for added goodness.

IF YOU WANT POTATOES PEELED AND WHITE

The best way to peel a boiled potato is to drop it into a bowl of ice water for a few seconds to loosen the skin. To keep peeled potatoes white during cooking, add a small amount of white vinegar to the water.

AND YOU THOUGHT YOU KNEW EVERYTHING ABOUT VICHYSSOISE

The cold potato soup called vichyssoise was actually invented in New York City. Chef Louis Diat of the Ritz-Carlton Hotel adapted his mother's recipe of *soupe bonne femme* to make a chilled soup of the white part of leeks and potatoes in a base of cream and milk. The name of the soup comes from Vichy, the spa near Diat's home in Bourbon.

FRENCH FRIES

WHO KNEW?

Did you know potatoes can remove some stains from your hands? Just rub raw potato slices against the stain under water.

JUICE YOUR MASH

It might not sound a likely combination, but try squeezing some fresh lemon juice into your mashed potatoes instead of butter or oil. Season it with freshly ground black pepper for a no-added-fat mash that is flavorful and goes fantastically well with roast chicken.

SPRINKLE SOME SEEDS

Seeds are packed with nutrients and beneficial oils and won't add too many calories to your diet. Sprinkle seeds on cereal and salad, or, if you don't like their hard texture, grind a mixture of pumpkin, sunflower, sesame and linseed in a coffee grinder, and use whenever you can.

THE BEST POTATO CHIPS YOU CAN MAKE

To make a wonderful potato chip, cut potatoes in half crosswise, exposing two flat surfaces. Use a vegetable peeler to cut paper-thin slices. Spray them lightly with vegetable oil and arrange in a single layer on a baking sheet. Bake at 450°F for about 10 to 12 minutes or until they are a light golden brown. Finally, place the chips in a brown paper bag with a small amount of sea salt (¼ teaspoon per potato) and shake. This seasons them lightly and also removes some of the fat.

STAY STRONG WITH VITAMIN D

An essential vitamin that requires synthesis from sunlight to turn it into an active form, vitamin D can help with back pain and aching joints, and slow the progression of osteoporosis. It is found in milk and fish such as salmon and sardines so include plenty of these in your diet.

WHY ARE CASHEWS ONLY SOLD UNSHELLED?

Cashews are among the most popular nuts worldwide. The cashew is related to poison ivy, which is one reason you never see cashews in the shell. The shell contains an oil that is a skin irritant. The oil is driven off by heat processing before the cashew nut can be extracted without becoming contaminated. The extraction process is a delicate operation, because no oil residue can come into contact with the nut. The oil is then used in paints and as a rocket lubricant base.

BEANS ARE BEST

Beans – particularly kidney beans, black beans and chickpeas – are great carbohydrate choices if you're trying to regulate blood sugar, because they provide lots of fiber but are low in calories.

ISN'T BULGUR CRACKED WHEAT?

Nope. Cracked wheat is uncooked wheat that is dried and coarsely milled, which cracks it apart. Bulgur wheat is steamed, dried, and then crushed into three different sizes. The coarsest wheat is used for bulgur pilaf and stuffings, the finest in breads or desserts, and the medium granulation for tabbouleh and other side dishes, and for cereals.

MAX YOUR MONOS

Try to maximize your intake of monounsaturated fats (like olive oil, avocados, walnuts, almonds and sesame seeds) and omega-3 fatty acids (from cold water fish, hemp and flax seeds), which have health benefits for all the organs of the body, including the brain and heart.

EAT NUTS FOR HEALTHY HAIR

Calcium, magnesium and potassium are all essential for the growth of thick, healthy hair. Snack regularly on almonds that are packed with these nutrients and contain more calcium than any other nut.

GREEN IS GROSS

Potatoes can turn green if exposed to light. It's best to avoid the green parts, which can be toxic in large amounts.

BUT THEY TASTE SO DAMN GOOD

Potato chips are cooked in 75-foot-long vats of oil; the oil is filtered but rarely changed. Present day production is about 200 pounds an hour. The high temperature (375°F) causes the oil to deteriorate, so it contains a high proportion of free fatty acids, which are potentially unhealthy. Potato chips, corn chips, and tortilla chips contain 10 times more fat than pretzels or air-popped popcorn; in fact, most potato chips get 61 percent of their calories from fat.

THE METTLE OF THE METAL

Peeling potatoes can be a time-consuming drag, but can be made much easier if you scour them with a clean, metal sponge instead. It's the quickest and easiest way to peel potatoes.

WHO KNEW?

Salt homemade potato chips by putting them in a paper bag with salt and shaking. This way, the salt is distributed—and the paper absorbs the excess grease. Save calories wherever you can!

THE STARCH FEED

Your houseplants need nourishment, particularly in the dead of winter when the sunlight is limited, yet there's no need to buy expensive plant food. Just remember to save the water in which you boil potatoes or pasta, let it cool, and use it to water your plants. They love the starchy water.

PASTA SMARTS

When cooking pasta for your family, it's a good idea to heat the serving bowl first. Try this: Put the colander in the bowl, then pour the pasta in, and let the hot water sit in the bowl for a few minutes. Then empty the bowl of water, add the pasta and you're ready for dinner.

NUTS TO YOU

The easiest way to shell pecans and other nuts? Freeze them first. It shrinks the nut away from the shell, and makes the job a breeze.

CHEW UP ON ALMOND SKINS

Research has shown that almond skins alone contain 20 potent antioxidants to protect against heart disease. They are also rich in vitamin E which is thought to help slow down the aging process.

A REAL TREAT

For the greatest French fries, soak cut potatoes in ice-cold water in the refrigerator for an hour; this will harden them so that they absorb less fat. Dry them thoroughly, then fry them twice. First cook them for six to seven minutes, drain them well, and then sprinkle them lightly with flour (this step makes them extra crispy and crunchy). Then fry them one to two minutes, until they are golden brown.

SOUPS, STEWS AND SEASONINGS

chapter 15

AND WHAT IS WORSE THAN CLOUDY SOUP?

To make a clear noodle soup, cook the noodles, then drain and rinse before adding them to the soup. When noodles are cooked in the soup, the excess starch will turn the soup cloudy. Use this trick for any soup with pasta or dumplings, from wonton soup to tortellini in brodo to chicken noodle soup.

THE THREE MAJOR TYPES OF FATS

Polyunsaturated Fatty Acids (PUFA)

This type of fat always remains in a liquid state, whether at room temperature or in the refrigerator. Examples are safflower, corn, and peanut oil.

Monounsaturated Fatty Acids (MUFA)

These tend to thicken when refrigerated but are still liquid at room temperature. Examples are olive and canola oil. Recent studies show that MUFA oils may be more effective in lowering harmful blood cholesterol levels than PUFA oils.

Saturated Fatty Acids (SFA)

Normally, these are either solid or semisolid at room temperature. Examples are butter, lard, shortening, and stick margarine. The exceptions to the rule are tropical oils like coconut and palm, which are sludge-like at room temperature. SFAs tend to raise cholesterol levels, even though they may not actually contain cholesterol.

DISPOSING OF OIL

Never pour used oil down the drain; it may solidify and cause clogging. Pour the oil in a metal can. When it cools, cover it and throw away.

GET YOUR MONEY'S WORTH

If you really want to get all the shortening out of a can, pour 2 cups boiling water into the container and swirl it gently until the fat melts. Refrigerate the container until the shortening solidifies on the water's surface, then just lift or skim it off with a knife blade or a sharp-edged spoon.

AND MAYONNAISE FACTS, TOO!

Mayonnaise must contain at least 65 percent oil by weight; any less and it must be called salad dressing. Most fat-free mayonnaise contains more sodium than full-fat mayonnaise. A tablespoon of mayonnaise contains only 5 to 10 milligrams of cholesterol, because very little egg yolk is used.

KNOW THE SMOKE POINT

Never allow oil to heat to the smoke point, as it may ignite. It can make the food taste bitter and may even irritate your eyes. The oils with the highest smoke points are canola, safflower, peanut, and soybean oil.

TRY BUTTERMILK IN PASTRIES

Buttermilk can be substituted for 2 percent or whole milk in most pastry or bread recipes. Buttermilk is less than 1 percent fat, almost equal to skim milk, but it has a thicker consistency.

REALLY EFFECTIVE

If you're broiling steaks or chops, save a few slices of stale, dried bread and set them in the bottom of the broiler pan to absorb fat drippings. This will eliminate smoking fat, and it should also reduce any danger of a grease fire.

THERE'S ALWAYS A CATCH

Olive oil is one of the more healthful fats, but that doesn't give you license to overindulge. It still packs in 119 calories per tablespoon.

HMMM, HMMM FAT!

Some of the highest-fat content crackers are butter-flavored (either round or oval shaped) and small ones shaped like fish. Both types contain about 6 grams of fat per ounce.

YOU MEAN YOU DON'T GRADE YOUR BUTTER?

The highest quality butter in the United States is U.S. Grade AA, which is produced from fresh sweet cream. U.S. Grade A is almost as good but has a lower-quality rating (the ratings are based on flavor, body, texture, color, and salt content). U.S. Grade B is usually produced from sour cream. The milk-fat content of butter must be at least 80 percent.

A LIGHTER COAT

When making a batter for foods for deep-frying, try adding ½ teaspoon of baking powder for every ½ cup of flour. The coating will be lighter.

LARD FACTS TO IMPRESS YOUR FRIENDS

Lard can be refrigerated for six to eight months. It can become rancid quickly and should never be stored at room temperature. If you substitute lard for butter or shortening, reduce the amount you use by 25 percent.

OIL BE GONE

Oil should never be reused. "Cleaning" the oil with a few slices of raw potato before storing is an old wives' tales—it doesn't work.

OLIVE OIL PRIMER

Expect to pay top dollar for extra-virgin cold-pressed olive oil. It is made from plump, Grade A olives, has the best flavor, and is processed by pressing the oil from the olives with as little heat and friction as possible. The next best is virgin olive oil, which is also from the first pressing and has an acidity of 3 to 4 percent. Pure olive oil is rougher oil, or a blend of refined and virgin oils. Beware of labels touting "cold-processed"—unlike cold-pressing, cold processing may mean the oil is extracted from the olives with a chemical solvent.

FOR BETTER BUTTER, TERRA COTTA

If you would like to have your butter ready and spreadable at all times, try a butter dish made from terra cotta. The top of the dish needs to be soaked in cold water every day for butter to be kept spreadable.

BECAUSE EVERTHING THAT TASTES GOOD IS BAD FOR YOU

Pigs in blankets (sausages wrapped in biscuits) are 60 percent fat, almost all of which is saturated.

WHIP IT GOOD

Butter will go further and have fewer calories per serving if you beat it well, increasing the volume with air. Unless you happen to churn your own butter, look for whipped butter—but use it only as a spread, not in recipes for cooking or baking.

THE OLIVE OIL MIX

Olive oil is healthful as oils go, but it has a low smoke point, which means that it will break down rapidly when exposed to heat. You can increase the smoke point of olive oil by adding a small amount of canola oil, which has a very high smoke point. If your recipe calls for you to sauté in a tablespoon of olive oil, use 2 ½ teaspoons olive and ½ teaspoon canola oil.

IT'S WHAT THE KIDS CALL 'NEW MATH'

When changing the yield of a recipe, do not increase the seasonings proportionately. If, for example, you are doubling the recipe, increase the seasonings only by one-and-a-half; if you are tripling the recipe, double the amount of seasoning.

AND WHO WANTS INSOMNIA?

Most fat should be consumed either at breakfast or lunch. High-fat meals late in the day may cause the digestive system to overwork while you are sleeping, disturbing your sleep patterns.

OIL QUALITY TEST

Test the quality of your olive oil by frying a few drops in a pan – really good quality oil which has the most health benefits will stay green and light. If it turns dark and loses its shine, it's not a good quality oil.

ANOTHER REVOLTING FACT

A 6- to 7-ounce bag of potato chips contains a little less than the equivalent of 1/3 cup of oil—more than half a stick of butter!

OR USE OLD KETCHUP BOTTLES

Purchase plastic-squeeze condiment bottles to use for storing your cooking oils. They are opaque, which will prevent deterioration of the oil, and the narrow opening makes it easy to pour when you're preparing a dish. Label the bottles with a permanent felt-tip marker.

FAT VS. CARBS

Every ounce of fat contains two and a quarter times more calories than an ounce of carbohydrate or protein.

SHORTENING VS. OIL

Shortening is a fat that is always a solid at room temperature. The term "pure shortening" means that the product contains vegetable or animal fat, or a combination of the two. If it is labeled "pure vegetable shortening" it must be made from only vegetables sources. If the shortening does not have the word "pure" on the label, then it contains a number of additives to increase its shelf life; however, these additives frequently lower the smoke points, and such products should be avoided. Shortenings that are made from vegetable sources are hydrogenated, which means that hydrogen is added to a liquid fat until it becomes a semisolid.

OIL YOUR VEGETABLES

Instead of adding cholesterol-building butter to your steamed vegetables, make them even healthier by using a low-fat dressing or a dash of olive or flaxseed oil.

IT TASTES BETTER, TOO

To make a creamy salad dressing without the cream, put all the dressing ingredients except the oil into a blender and turn it on. Then, very slowly, pour in cold-pressed olive oil.

SWEET AND HOT

If you eat a lot of stir-fried food, try substituting soy sauce, which is very high in salt, with sweet and sour sauce or hot mustard. Do this every other meal to help keep your sodium intake down.

DO THE MATH

The stomach can digest approximately 10 grams of fat per hour. Two scrambled eggs, toast (with 1 tablespoon of butter), coffee, and milk contain about 42 grams of fat—which means that you'll probably start on lunch before you've digested just the fat from your breakfast!

FRYING TEMPERATURES ARE CRITICAL

Oil needs to be at the proper temperature whether you're sautéing or deep-frying. If the temperature is too low, the food will absorb too much oil and become greasy, not crispy. If the oil is too hot, the food may burn on the outside and not cook through. Most breaded foods are normally fried at 375°F, but check the recipe. Chicken should be fried at 365°F for 15 to 20 minutes for white meat, 20 to 25 minutes for dark.

Fat Calories in Common Foods	
FOODS	% OF CALORIES FROM FAT
Bacon, butter, margarine, lard, mayonnaise, solid shortenings, cooking oils, olives, baking chocolate, cream cheese	90–100
Macadamia nuts, salad dressings, pecans, walnuts, avocados, sausages, corned beef, coconut	80–90
Hot dogs, peanuts, most chips, blue cheese, cashews, lunch meats, peanut butter, prime rib, oil-packed canned tuna, Swiss cheese, sunflower seeds	65–80
Hamburger, rib steak, chicken with skin, canned ham, salmon, trout, bass, veal cutlet, eggs, ice cream	50–65
Most baked goods, lean hamburger, ground turkey, Canadian bacon, ham, steak, whole milk, round steak	35–50
Low-fat yogurt, 2 percent milk, veal chops, loin and rump cuts of beef, sweet breads	20–35
Crab, baked chicken without skin, most shellfish, water-packed canned tuna, low-fat cottage cheese, low-fat broiled fish	10–20
Buttermilk, skim milk, beans, rice, cereals, potatoes, pasta, fruits, vegetables, egg whites	Very small amount

FLAVOR SAVER

Crushing dried herbs before using them will boost their flavor, as will soaking them for a few seconds in hot water. This also works well if they have lost their flavor.

HERBS AND AROMATICS THAT IMPROVE THE TASTE OF MEATS

Beef
Garlic, onion, basil, thyme, summer savory, and rosemary

Buffalo
Rosemary, basil, garlic, and sage

Fish
Sage, fennel, parsley, dill, basil, and chives

Lamb
Mint, ginger, rosemary, garlic, and basil

Pork
Sweet marjoram, sage, garlic, thyme, rosemary, and basil

Poultry
Sage, basil, sweet marjoram, chervil, onion, and summer savory

Veal
Rosemary, garlic, thyme, tarragon, and basil

LARGE DOSE

If a food is labeled 'High in…,' it will contain at least 20 percent of the recommended daily amount of that nutrient. Check the label carefully to find out exactly how much each serving provides.

BUSTED!

Don't be duped by reduced-fat peanut butter. It has the same number of calories per serving as does regular peanut butter (about 190 per serving). The fat was replaced with sweeteners.

WHO KNEW?

Put garlic cloves in the microwave for 15 seconds, and the skins will slide right off.

A GREAT GARLIC TIP

Here's a great tip when cooking with whole garlic cloves that you plan to remove before the dish is served: stick a toothpick firmly in the garlic so it will be easy to take out. Put herbs that fall apart during cooking in a tea infuser to make them easy to remove.

BUT SAVE THE EGG WHITES

To cut fat and cholesterol in a recipe, replace the egg yolks with an equal amount of egg substitute, or just reduce the number of yolks.

FIND A COOL, DRY SPOT FOR HERBS AND SPICES

Herbs and spices contain volatile oils that oxidize easily. It is best to store dried seasonings in a cool, dry spot away from heat and out of direct sunlight, where they'll maintain optimal flavor for up to six months. Two of the worst locations are near a microwave exhaust fan and over the stove. If you store herbs and spices in the refrigerator, remove them at least 30 minutes before you plan to use them to release their flavor and aroma.

THAT'S INTENSE

Drying intensifies the flavor of herbs, so fresh herbs are milder than dried.

ALL ABOUT ALLSPICE

The flavor of this spice has hints of cinnamon, cloves, and nutmeg. Jamaica is the largest producer of allspice, but it also comes from Central and South America, and it is sold both whole and in ground form. It is used in pickling and to flavor meats, fish, baked goods, relishes, puddings, and fruit preserves. Allspice is commonly used in a number of ready-to-serve foods such as hot dogs, soups, and baked beans.

SPICE SAVERS

Both cayenne pepper and paprika are affected by light and heat, and have a shorter shelf life than just about anything else on your spice rack. In fact, take them off your spice rack—store them both in the refrigerator.

BAY LEAVES, LIKE A MOUTHFUL OF STRAW

Bay leaves are usually sold whole rather than ground and are commonly used in stews, sauces, soups, dill pickles, meat dishes, veal, and poultry. They are also used in numerous ready-to-serve foods.

Remember to remove bay leaves from foods before you serve them. If someone eats a piece, it will be like eating a mouthful of straw. Never crumble a bay leaf when using it in a recipe and stir the dish gently so as not to break the leaf up.

The Turkish variety of bay leaf has a milder flavor and is wider and shorter than the California variety.

BASIL BASICS

There are more than 60 varieties of this herb found worldwide; these include lemon basil, cinnamon basil, and opal basil, which has purple leaves. The basil we're most familiar with is sweet basil, which is grown primarily in California. It is a common seasoning for fish, meat, tomato dishes, soups, stews, pizza sauce, and salad dressings.

A member of the mint family, basil should be stored in the refrigerator wrapped in a damp paper towel and sealed in a plastic bag. It should retain its flavor and aroma for about five days. Basil tends to lose most of its flavor after about 15 minutes of cooking, so it should be added no more than 10 minutes before the food is done.

CARDAMOM

A member of the ginger family with a pungent aroma and slight lemon flavor, cardamom is used in pickling, pastries, pumpkin dishes, and sweet potatoes. Available as pods or ground, cardamom is often imported from India and is popular in Scandinavian cooking as well as Indian. If you are making a stew or curry, the shells of cardamom pods will disintegrate during cooking. Cardamom is an effective cover for bad breath.

CARAWAY

With a flavor somewhat similar to anise, caraway seeds are harvested at night before the dew evaporates. The majority sold in the United States are imported from the Netherlands. Caraway seeds are commonly used in rye bread, cookies, organ meat dishes, dips, cabbage, sauerkraut, soft cheese spreads, sweet pickles, and sauerbraten.

CAYENNE PEPPER

A common spice, also called ground red pepper, cayenne is sold crushed, ground, or whole. It is used in curries, relishes, salsas, chili powders, many Mexican dishes, Italian and Indian foods, sausages, and dressings.

CAPERS

These are the buds of a shrub native to the Mediterranean. Capers are almost always sold pickled in brine; some gourmet markets sell them packed in salt. The tiny capers called nonpareils are from France; larger capers are from Italy. If you are on a sodium-restricted diet, be sure to rinse capers before you use them. Capers are commonly used in smoked fish, chicken, eggs, or veal dishes.

WHO KNEW?

To keep herbs fresh longer, loosely wrap them in a damp paper towel, store in a plastic bag, and keep in the vegetable crisper of the refrigerator.

CHILI POWDER

Chili powder is often blended from cumin seed, dried hot chili peppers, oregano, coriander, cloves, and garlic. It is available in a variety of heat levels, from mild to hot. Some gourmet shops sell pure chili powder, which is made from ground chili peppers with no other spices included.

CHIVES

Chives have a light oniony flavor and are used to flavor dips, sauces, soups, and baked potatoes, or to replace the flavor of onion in a recipe.

CHERVIL

This herb is a member of the parsley family; it is more common in France than in the United States. It can be used in salad dressings or any dish that would also be flavored with parsley.

CELERY SEED

This is used for pickling, and in soups, stews, salad dressings, fish dishes, salads such as cole slaw, and many vegetable dishes. Celery salt is a blend of ground celery seed and salt.

CELERY FLAKES

Celery flakes are made from the dehydrated leaves and ribs of the celery plant and are used in the same dishes as celery seed.

CHILI PEPPERS

To prepare chili peppers for cooking, spear them with a long-handled fork and singe them over a gas-stove burner (if you don't have a gas stove, broil the chilies) until the skin blisters. Wrap the singed peppers in a cloth towel or foil and let them steam. The skin will relax and pull away, making it easy to peel the chilies and to remove the seeds and veins. (Always wear gloves when you do this, as a compound in hot chilies can irritate skin.) The pulp will be very spicy, but the seeds and veins are even hotter. Don't use too many of the seeds unless you want a really fiery dish.

CLOVES

Tanzania is the largest producer of cloves, which are usually sold whole or ground. This is a strong spice and should be used only in small amounts. Cloves are often used in baked beans, pickling, ham, sweet potatoes, baked goods, puddings, mustards, soups, hot dogs, sausages, and barbecue sauces.

CILANTRO

The leaf of the coriander plant, cilantro looks very much like flat-leaf, or Italian, parsley. It is used in certain Mexican and Thai dishes, to flavor salad dressings, and in salsa.

CUMIN

This is used mainly in its ground form in curry, chili powder, soups, deviled eggs, fruit pies, stews, soft cheeses, and chili con carne.

CINNAMON

Real cinnamon is not common in the United States. Imported from China and Indonesia, it is harvested from the bark of the laurel tree. The color is the giveaway. True cinnamon is actually a light tan color. Most cinnamon sold in the United States is actually cassia, which is usually imported from Vietnam; it is a dark reddish-brown.

It is used in its whole form for preserving; to flavor spiced beverages, such as cider or hot wine drinks; in meat or chicken dishes; in puddings; and for pickling. The ground form is used in baked goods, ketchup, vegetables, apple butter, mustards, and spiced peaches.

WHO KNEW?

Don't throw away celery leaves. Set them on a paper plate, let them dry, and throw in stuffing, salads, and soups for great extra flavor.

POPPY SEED

With their rich, nutlike flavor, poppy seeds are used in Indian dishes, salads, cookies, pastry fillings, muffins, and other baked goods.

CORIANDER

A relative of the carrot family, coriander has a sweet, musky flavor. The seed or ground form is used in gingerbread, cookies, cakes, biscuits, poultry stuffing, pork dishes, pea soup, and cheese dishes.

DILL

Sold either as dill seed, dried dill, or as a fresh herb, dill comes into its own as a flavoring for cottage cheese, chowders, soups, sauerkraut, salads, fish, meat sauces, potato salad, and spiced vinegar, and for pickling. It's also great for livening up egg salad.

CURRY POWDER

Curry powder is a blend of up to 20 spices and herbs. The ingredients may include chili peppers, cloves, coriander, fennel seed, nutmeg, mace, cayenne, black pepper, sesame seed, saffron, and turmeric; this last spice gives curry its distinctive yellow color. Curry powder is common in Indian cooking, poultry, stews, soups, sauces, and meat dishes.

FENUGREEK

Sometimes used in curry powder, fenugreek is used as a component of imitation maple syrup and in tea form as a digestive aid.

HOT OR SWEET?

Hot paprika is always labeled such; sweet paprika is often just labeled "paprika."

GARLIC

This member of the Allium (lily) family is sold fresh, chopped and packed in jars, or processed into garlic salt or garlic powder. Garlic is used in thousands of dishes in all cuisines and has been used throughout history as a medication. There are hundreds of varieties of garlic grown worldwide. Most of the garlic used in the United States is grown in Gilroy, California, the "Garlic Capital of the World."

- Elephant garlic is another member of the Allium family. As you might surmise from the name, elephant garlic is much larger than common garlic. Also, its flavor is milder.

- To make garlic easy to peel, soak it in very hot water for two to three minutes, or rinse the garlic under hot water to loosen its skin.

- For special flavor, rub a clove of crushed garlic on the sides of your salad bowl before mixing your salad.

- A head of garlic should keep for eight to 10 weeks in a cool (as close to 50°F as possible), dark, dry location. It will lose its flavor more quickly if stored in the refrigerator. When garlic sprouts, some of the flavor will go into the sprouts; however, the sprouts can then be used for salads. If a garlic clove is damaged or nicked with a knife it must be used or it will develop mold very quickly. Garlic should not be frozen.

Garlic has little aroma until the tissues are disturbed and the sulfurcontaining amino acid cysteine is released. Make garlic vinegar by mincing two to three cloves and combining with a pint of white-wine vinegar in a sterilized jar. Let this stand for for at least two weeks before using. If you make garlic oil, be sure to use it at once. If stored for more than a day or so, garlic oil can develop botulin spores.

FENNEL

The flavor of fennel is similar to that of anise, but it is somewhat sweeter. It is usually used in pork dishes, squash, Italian sausage, sweet pickles, fish dishes, candies, cabbage, pastries, oxtail soup, and pizza sauce.

When you buy fresh fennel, make sure you choose clean, crisp bulbs that are not browning. The stalks and green fronds should be removed, but you can use the fronds as you would dill. The bulb, also known as finocchio, can be used raw in salads, or it can be braised.

JUST A LITTLE RUB

To tell flat-leaf parsley from cilantro, rub a leaf between your fingers. This will release the herb's fragrance—and if it's cilantro, you'll know at once.

TOO MUCH GARLIC? TRY THIS TRICK

If you have added too much garlic to your soup or stew, add a small quantity of parsley and simmer for about 10 minutes. To remove the odor of garlic from your hands, sprinkle salt on a slice of lemon, and then rub this on your hands.

GARLIC FROLIC

Mincing garlic used to be a sticky mess, but no more, if you sprinkle the garlic with a few drops of olive oil beforehand. The oil prevents the garlic from sticking from your hands or the knife.

GINGER

Grown in Jamaica, India, West Africa, and China, ginger has a pungent, spicy flavor. It is available fresh or ground and is used in pickling spices, conserves, fruit compotes, gingerbread, and pumpkin pie.

WHO KNEW?

Fragrance is the best indicator of potency in dried herbs: the greater the smell, the better the seasoning. If you're not hit with a wonderful fragrance when opening a jar of dried herbs, throw it out.

MINT

Mint grows in Europe and the United States and is used to flavor lamb, fish, stews, soups, peas, sauces, desserts, and jellies. For an instant breath freshener, try chewing a few fresh mint leaves. Mint flakes, the dried leaves of peppermint and spearmint plants, have a strong, sweet flavor.

MARJORAM

Marjoram is part of the oregano family and has a sweet flavor. It can be purchased in leaves and is imported primarily from the Nile Valley. It is usually combined with other herbs and used in soups and sauces, salad, potato dishes, stews, fish dishes, and as poultry seasoning.

OREGANO

Oregano is a member of the mint family. It is commonly sold in both leaf and ground forms. Oregano is found in many Italian dishes, including pizza and spaghetti sauces.

MUSTARD

- Yellow or white seeds will produce a mild mustard, while brown seeds produce the more spicy variety. Mustard oil, which is pressed from brown mustard seeds, is extremely hot and sometimes used in Chinese or other Asian dishes. Mustard powder has almost no aroma until it is mixed with a liquid.
- Mustard has hundreds of uses and is one of the most popular spices around the world. Mustard seeds will keep for up to one year. Store mustard powder for up to six months in a dry, dark place.
- If a recipe calls for a particular mustard, it is best not to substitute another variety. When you use a different mustard, you risk altering the taste of the finished dish.

TYPES OF PREPARED MUSTARD

American Mustard

The typical hot-dog mustard, this variety is produced from mild yellow mustard seeds combined with a sweetener and vinegar; it gets its vivid yellow color from turmeric. It has a very smooth texture.

Chinese Mustard

This is made from brown mustard seeds, mustard powder, water, and strong vinegar. Because there is no sweetener, it packs quite a wallop. In fact, Chinese mustard is the most pungent of all prepared mustards.

Dijon Mustard

Originally from Dijon, France, this is produced from brown mustard seeds, white wine, unfermented grape juice, and a variety of seasonings. It typically has a smooth texture and is usually a dull yellow color; when made with whole mustard seeds, Dijon mustard is called coarse-ground or country-style.

English Mustard

This mustard is produced from both white and black mustard seeds, a small amount of flour, and turmeric for coloring. It is one of the hottest mustards on the market.

German Mustard

Produced from a variety of mustard seeds, German mustard can range from sweet and mild to quite hot. It is usually made with a small amount of sugar, which tempers its bite. German mustards vary in color but are most often a brownish-yellow.

SAGE

A very pungent herb that is a member of the mint family, sage is available in whole leaves or ground form. It is commonly used in veal dishes, pork dishes, stuffings, salads, fish dishes, and pizza sauces.

SAFFRON

This is one of the more difficult herbs to harvest and, not surprisingly, also one of the most expensive. It is extracted from the stigma of the flowering crocus. The best saffron is imported from Spain. It is used in moderation in poultry, baked goods, and rice dishes.

PEPPER

- Pepper, one of the most popular spices in the world, comes from India and Indonesia. It is harvested at various stages of ripeness and is sold whole, cracked, or ground.
- After pepper is ground, it loses its flavor rather quickly. Use a pepper mill so your pepper will always be fresh and flavorful.
- White pepper has had the black shell removed. Use it in light-colored dishes, such as cream sauces, if you don't want little black flecks. Its flavor is milder than that of black pepper.
- Szechuan pepper berries, harvested from the prickly ash tree, have very tiny seeds and a mildly hot taste.
- Pink peppercorns, harvested from the Baies rose, have a very pungent odor and a somewhat sweet flavor.

NUTMEG

A relatively sweet spice imported from the West Indies, nutmeg is available whole and ground. It is commonly used in sauces, puddings, custards, creamed foods, eggnog, whipped cream, sausages, frankfurters, and ravioli. Freshly grated nutmeg is more aromatic and flavorful than that which is sold ground. Special nutmeg graters are sold in specialty kitchenware shops.

PAPRIKA

Paprika is made by grinding sweet red pepper pods. The best paprika is imported from Hungary; but Spain, South America, and California are also producers. This spice is used in a wide variety of dishes, including cream sauces, vegetables, mustards, salad dressings, ketchup, sausages, and fish preparations. It also makes an excellent garnish. Hot paprika is indeed hot—if it's all you have, use it sparingly.

MACE

Mace is the dried husk of the nutmeg shell. In its ground form, it is used in cakes, beverages, chocolate dishes, jellies, pickling spices, ketchup, baked beans, soups, deviled chicken, and ham spreads.

ROSEMARY

A sweet, fragrant, spicy herb with a pungent aroma, rosemary is used in stews, meat dishes, salad dressings, and meat and poultry stuffings. It is common in many southern European and Mediterranean cuisines, including Italian, Greek, Spanish, Portuguese, and Provençal.

PARSLEY

There are more than thirty varieties of parsley, but the two most common are curly and flat-leaf, which is also called Italian parsley. Of these two, flat-leaf has better flavor. This variety is grown in the United States and Southern Europe and is used in countless dishes, including cheese sauces, marinades, salads, soups, vegetable dishes, chicken potpies, and herb dressings. It is high in nutrients, especially vitamins A and C, though you would have to eat it as more than a garnish to get the effects. Curly parsley, which has much less flavor, is used mainly as a garnish to decorate serving platters. Parsley will alleviate bad breath.

POULTRY SEASONING

Composed primarily of sage, thyme, marjoram, and savory, this seasoning is commonly used to flavor poultry stuffings and soups.

PEPPERMINT

Peppermint contains the oil menthol. Menthol is used in cigarettes, candies, liquors, toothpaste, mouthwash, and many other products. In low concentrations, menthol will increase the temperature of skin, paradoxically making a warm area feel cool. It has also been used as an anesthetic.

If you have a problem with mice, try this: Saturate cotton balls with a small amount of oil of peppermint, and set them as near as you can to their hole. It will rid the area of pests. This also works for underground rodents.

TYPES OF SALT

The majority of salt used in the United States is mined from deposits that were laid down thousands of years ago and are readily accessible.

Rock Salt

A poorly refined salt that is grayish in color, with very large crystals. It is rarely used in cooking—one of its few culinary uses is to make the ice melt faster in old-fashioned ice-cream makers.

Kosher Salt

This salt is additive-free and has excellent flavor and texture. Kosher salt has larger crystals with a more jagged shape than table salt, which means they will cling to food better. Because of these characteristics, kosher salt has the ability to draw more blood from meats; kosher meats must be as free of blood as possible to meet strict dietary laws.

Pickling Salt

A fine-grained salt that is additive-free and used in the preparation of pickles and sauerkraut.

Sea Salt

Sea salt has a fresh flavor and is available fine or coarse-grained. It is usually imported and is preferred by many chefs and serious cooks for its pure flavor. Sea salt, as its name implies, is acquired by allowing salt water to accumulate in pools where the sun evaporates the water, leaving a stronger-flavored salt with a few more trace minerals than regular table salt. It can be quite a bit more expensive than table salt.

Table Salt

A highly refined, fine-grained salt that contains additives to make it flow freely but has not been fortified with iodine.

Iodized Salt

Standard table salt with iodine (sodium iodide) added. Iodine is the nutrient that prevents hypothyroidism. However, some people find it adds an unpleasant taste to salt.

GREEN, BLACK, AND WHITE PEPPERCORNS

These are the same item, harvested at different times of maturity and processed differently. Green peppercorns are picked before they are fully ripe. They are preserved in brine and used mainly for pickling and in dishes that do not require a strong pepper flavor. Black peppercorns are picked when they are almost fully ripe. White peppercorns are picked when fully ripe, and the pungent black shell is removed. Their flavor is somewhat milder, and they have a smooth surface. Use them when black pepper would detract from the color of the dish.

SAVORY

A member of the mint family with a slightly peppery flavor, savory is commonly sold in both leaf and ground forms. There are two varieties: Summer savory is milder than winter savory, but both can be quite strong and are best used judiciously. Dried savory is typically made from summer savory. This herb marries well with eggs, meats, poultry, and fish.

SESAME SEEDS

These seeds have a rich, nutlike flavor and high oil content. They are also high in many nutrients—by weight, sesame seeds have more iron than liver does; they are also high in calcium. However, we seldom eat enough sesame seeds to provide nutritional benefits.

Sesame seeds are commonly used to flavor many Chinese dishes, and in Middle Eastern dishes like halvah (a dessert made with ground sesame seeds and honey), hummus (a spread made from ground chickpeas), and tahini, which is ground sesame seeds. It is also used as a topping for many baked goods.

THE MICROBE INHIBITOR

For thousands of years, salt has been used to preserve foods because of its ability to inhibit microbial growth. It does this by drawing water out of bacterial and mold cells.

- Hundreds of years ago, the English preserved meats by covering them with large grains of salt known as "corn," hence the name corned beef.

- Fast food restaurants may use high levels of salt to hide the unpleasant flavor of low-quality foods.

SALT

While salt is a seasoning containing important minerals that are beneficial to the body, in excess it may be detrimental to your health. Here's an easy test to see whether you might be eating too much salt: Eat a piece of bacon. If it doesn't taste salty, take a look at your diet—you may need to lower your sodium intake.

The distribution of fluids in the body depends on the location and concentrations of sodium and potassium ions. Our kidneys regulate blood sodium levels and provide the bloodstream with the exact amount required. When blood levels rise due to excess sodium ingestion, the body's thirst receptors are stimulated and our fluid intake increases to balance the sodium-to-water ratio. The kidneys then excrete the excess sodium and water. When this balance cannot be maintained, the result might be high blood pressure and increased deposits of atherosclerotic plaque material. (When excess sodium builds up in the bloodstream, the kidneys are unable to clear the excess water. An increase in blood volume occurs, and the heart has to work harder, causing higher blood pressure.)

The American Heart Association estimates that more than 50 million Americans have some degree of high blood pressure. Because sodium is found in thousands of food items, it is recommended that added salt be avoided to help control one's total sodium intake. Regular table salt contains 40 percent sodium while "lite" salt contains 20 percent.

Kelp can be ground up and used in a shaker to replace salt. It only contains 4 percent sodium and the taste is very similar.

When salt is processed commercially, certain natural minerals are stripped away. The salt may then be enriched with iodine; dextrose is added to stabilize it, sodium bicarbonate to keep it white, and anticaking agents to keep it free flowing. Kosher salt and pickling salt contain no additives. Fine-grained pickling salt dissolves quickly, but kosher salt rarely dissolves completely.

WHO KNEW?

A great way to mix and crush spices is to place them in a pan and press with the bottom of a smaller pan. A coffee grinder works great, too.

CHINESE FIVE-SPICE POWDER

This fragrant spice mixture is common in Chinese cooking. It is a blend of cinnamon, star anise, fennel seed, Szechuan peppercorns, and cloves. To make your own, grind the spices and combine in equal measure. You can also purchase it in supermarkets.

THYME

There are nearly as many varieties of fresh thyme as there are of basil. Available in both leaf and ground forms, thyme has a strong, nicely spicy flavor and is used to flavor tomato-based soups, stews, sauces, chipped beef (an old army favorite), mushrooms, sausages, clam chowder, herb dressings, and mock turtle soup. If you live near a specialty greengrocer or farmer's market, keep an eye out for lemon thyme. This herb has a pleasantly astringent flavor and can perfume a simple broth or sautéed vegetables with an appetizing lemon fragrance.

TARRAGON

Although this herb is native to Siberia, Arabs were the first to use it in cooking. Most tarragon sold in the United States is grown in California. Tarragon has a strong flavor similar to licorice and is used in béarnaise sauce, meat dishes, salads, herb dressings, and tomato casseroles.

TURMERIC

Imported from India and the Caribbean, turmeric is ground from the root of a tropical plant similar to ginger. Turmeric is used in chicken and meat dishes, pickles, salads dressings, curry powder, Spanish rice, relishes, and mustards. It imparts a vivid yellow color to the foods it is used in and is, therefore, sometimes substituted for the more expensive saffron (although their flavors are nothing alike).

Sodium Content of Common Foods (in milligrams)		
	SERVING SIZE	SODIUM
Macaroni & cheese (frozen)	1 cup	1,290
Turkey dinner (frozen)	1 large	990
Dill pickle	1 large	833
Tomato soup	1 cup	730
Bologna	2 slices	620
Pancakes (mix)	Three 4" cakes	560
Pretzels	1 ounce	486
Beef frankfurters	1 regular	458
Cottage cheese (creamed)	½ cup	457
Cheese pizza (frozen)	1 medium slice	412
American cheese (processed)	1 ounces	406
Mashed potatoes (instant)	½ cup	380
Corn flakes	1 cup	305
Tuna (oil-packed)	3 ounces	301
Angel food cake (mix)	½ cake	255
Peanuts (roasted in oil)	2 ounces	246
Doughnut (packaged)	1 medium	205
Carrots (canned)	½ cup	177
Whole milk	1 cup	120
Margarine (salted)	1 tablespoon	102
Mayonnaise	1 tablespoon	80
Turkey (roasted)	3 ounces	70
Egg	1 medium	62
Fruit cocktail	½ cup	8
Orange juice	½ cup	2
Fruit (canned)	½ Cup	1
Oatmeal (cooked)	3 ounces	1
Macaroni (cooked)	1 cup	1

SALT OF THE EARTH

The average person consumes about six to 15 grams of salt daily, which amounts to about 2 teaspoons. The body requires only 500 milligrams, or half a gram, daily unless you are perspiring heavily. The American Heart Association recommends no more than 2.4 grams, or 2,400 milligrams.

It is necessary to read labels and be aware of the many ingredients in packaged foods that contain sodium. MSG is one of the leading ones, and many commercial spice blends also contain sodium. On page 450 is a list of some spices and flavorings that are sodium-free:

Sodium-Free Seasonings	
Allspice	Nutmeg
Almond extract	Paprika
Bay leaves	Parsley
Caraway seeds	Pepper
Cinnamon	Pimiento
Curry powder	Rosemary
Garlic	Peppermint extract
Ginger	Sage
Lemon extract	Sesame seeds
Mace	Thyme
Maple extract	Turmeric
Marjoram	Vanilla extract
Mustard powder	Vinegar

A GREAT TIP FOR ADDING HERBS

Herbs provide both aroma and flavor. Chefs know how to appeal to your sense of smell when preparing a dish and will add either some or all of the herbs just before the dish is served, because the flavor and aroma can dissipate during the cooking process.

VANILLA

Vanilla beans grow on trees that are a member of the orchid family. The reason real vanilla is so expensive is that the plants are hand-pollinated when grown commercially; in the wild they are pollinated by only one species of hummingbird. More than 75 percent of all vanilla beans are grown in Madagascar, where the pods are actually marked with the grower's brand to prevent vanilla bean rustlers from stealing the crops.

Soaking chopped beans in a solution of alcohol and water makes pure vanilla extract. Imitation vanilla is produced from the chemical vanillin, which is a by-product of the wood-pulp industry.

TYPES OF VANILLA

Imitation Extract

Imitation vanilla extract is produced from artificial flavorings and has a stronger, harsher taste than pure vanilla. Imitation extract should be used only in dishes where the vanilla flavor will not predominate.

Mexican Extract

Some Mexican extract has been found to contain the blood thinner coumarin, which is banned in the United States. There is no way to tell which Mexican vanilla contains coumarin and which does not, so it's best to avoid this entirely.

Pure Extract

If the label says "pure vanilla extract" it must be made with vanilla beans; however, the taste will be less intense than that of the bean itself. Still, pure vanilla extract has an excellent flavor.

Vanilla Beans

These are long, thin, dark brown beans. They are expensive and not as easy to use as vanilla extract. To use the bean, you must split it and scrape out the seeds. Vanilla beans will keep up to six months when stored in plastic wrap, sealed in an airtight jar, and refrigerated. Put a vanilla bean in your sugar bowl to impart a subtle flavor to the sugar.

VINEGAR

Despite the literal translation of its French root *vinaigre* and contrary to popular belief, vinegar is not sour wine. Vinegar is produced from wine, beer, or cider fermented with the bacteria acetobacter, which feeds on the alcohol, converting it into acetic acid (vinegar). Vinegar is a stimulant to the palate, making the taste buds more receptive to other flavors.

YUCK

Pesto sauce tends to turn brown in a very short time. Enzymes in the stems and leaves of the basil plant cause this browning. When nuts, such as walnuts, sunflower seeds, or pine nuts are added to the sauce, it will turn almost black. There is little to be done to keep pesto green, so it's best to serve the pesto immediately after it is prepared.

TYPES OF VINEGAR

Apple Cider Vinegar

This is produced from apple juice and is a good, all-purpose vinegar. It has a mild, somewhat sweet, fruity flavor.

Balsamic Vinegar

This is made from white Trebbiano grape juice. Balsamic vinegar is aged in wooden barrels for three to 12 years before being sold. (The real thing, from Modena in Italy, can be aged for decades.) The aging produces dark brown vinegar with a mellow, very sweet flavor. Most balsamic vinegar sold in supermarkets is red wine vinegar that has flavorings and colorings added to it. It is best used in salad dressings and will bring out the flavor of many vegetables. Sprinkle it on fresh fruit to perk up their flavors.

Distilled White Vinegar

This is produced from grain alcohol and is too harsh for most cooking, but is excellent for pickling.

Flavored Wine Vinegar

Made by steeping herbs or other flavorings in white-wine vinegar. Chefs commonly use tarragon wine vinegar for flavoring shellfish and poultry dishes. Rosemary wine vinegar is excellent with lamb dishes. Garlic vinegar adds a pleasant bite to salad dressings.

Malt Vinegar

Produced from malted barley. Used in chutneys, fish dishes, sauces, pickling, and as a condiment with French fries.

Raspberry Vinegar

This vinegar, made by soaking raspberries in white-wine vinegar, has a pleasant fruity flavor. Use it in sauces, salad dressings, and on fruits.

IT'S TIME TO GO

Dried herbs and spices lose their potency over time; most retain peak flavor for about six months. When you open a new jar, write the date on it so you'll know when it's time to replace it.

Rice Vinegar

Produced from fermented rice, this has a slightly sweet flavor and is used in fish marinades, Asian sauces, sushi, and pickles.

Sherry Vinegar

A product of sherry fermentation. Its flavor is somewhat nutty, and sherry vinegar is used mainly in vegetable dishes.

Wine Vinegar

Produced from red or white wine. The red is used for meat dishes and the white for poultry and fish dishes. It is also frequently used in marinades and salad dressings.

WHAT IS HERBES DE PROVENCE?

This blend of dried herbs is original to the south of France, hence its name. Most typically made of basil, fennel, lavender, marjoram, rosemary, sage, summer savory, and thyme, herbes de Provençe is available in gourmet markets and better supermarkets. Sprinkle the mixture on cooked vegetables, rub it into pork chops before cooking, or stuff it under the skin of poultry before roasting.

DON'T SUBSTITUTE OIL FOR A SPICE

Although you might think it's a good idea, it's difficult to make this substitution. Oils are so concentrated that it is almost impossible to calculate the amount needed to replace the spice and obtain the same degree of flavor. A good example is cinnamon, whose oil is 50 times stronger than the ground spice. If you did want to use cinnamon oil to replace ground cinnamon, you would need only 1 to 2 drops of oil to replace ½ teaspoon of ground cinnamon in candy or frostings.

Substituting Herbs and Spices	
HERB OR SPICE	SUBSTITUTE
Allspice	Cinnamon, plus a dash of cloves
Aniseed	Fennel seed
Basil	Oregano
Caraway seed	Aniseed
Chives	Scallion tops
Cinnamon	Nutmeg
Cloves	Allspice
Cumin	Chili powder
Dillweed	Fennel tops
Ginger	Cardamom
Mace	Allspice
Parsley	Tarragon
Thyme	Rosemary

USE CAUTION

You might think of storing herbs or garlic in olive oil to prolong their shelf life or to flavor your oil, but don't do it. Serious health hazards may result from this practice. Flavored oils may contain the deadly *Clostridium botulinum* bacteria, which is present in the environment and may be present on some herbs. The bacteria does not thrive well in oxygen but loves an anaerobic environment such as that provided by the oil.

When you put an herb or garlic in oil, the bacteria has a perfect oxygen-free place to multiply. The FDA has warned that a number of people have become ill from putting chopped garlic in oil. Ideally, any flavored oil should be used immediately. Any leftovers should be refrigerated and used within three days to be considered safe.

When an herb and olive oil mixture is sold in the market, the label must state that the product has to be refrigerated, and the mixture will also contain a preservative, probably phosphoric acid or citric acid.

WHO KNEW?

Canned peas have 100 times the sodium of raw peas.

WATER AND PLASTIC DOES THE TRICK

To keep fresh herbs at their best, put them in a glass of water (as though you were putting flowers in a vase) and cover the glass with a plastic bag. Stash in the refrigerator and use within a week. Or wrap fresh herbs in damp paper towels and put this bundle in a plastic bag.

MAKE THEM AT HOME

If you have more fresh herbs than you can use, hang them upside down to dry. (Tie them together and hang them from a peg.) In about a week, you'll be able to crumble off the leaves. The flavor won't be quite as wonderful as that of fresh herbs, but it will still be much better than commercial dried herbs.

ROAST YOUR BERRIES

Allspice berries and peppercorns should be roasted before use to intensify their flavor. Roast them in a 325°F oven on a small cookie sheet for 10 to 15 minutes and you will be surprised at the difference in their flavor and aroma. They can also be pan-roasted over medium-high heat for about five minutes. Other whole spices can be pan-roasted as well.

UNSAFE HERBS

The herbs on the following pages, many of which have been used medicinally, are classified as unsafe for human consumption and should not be used in any food or beverage. This is only a partial listing of the hundreds of unsafe herbs.

THE LOW FAT WAY

To make a lower-fat cream soup, try adding a little flour to milk instead of using cream. The flour adds a little body and results in a thicker soup without additional fat. It even works with 1 percent milk.

NAME	SCIENTIFIC NAME	DANGER
Bittersweet, woody nightshade, climbing nightshade	*Solanum dulcamara*	Contains the toxin glycoalkaloid solanine as well as solanidine and dulcamarine.
Bloodroot, red puccoon	*Sanguinaria canadensis*	Contains the poisonous alkaloid sanguinarine as well as other alkaloids.
Buckeye, horse chestnut	*Aesculus hippocastanum*	Contains the family of toxins saponin glycoside, of which aesculin is one.
Burning bush, wahoo	*Euonymus atropurparens*	Contains evomonoside, a digitalis-like *cardioactive* glycoside. Also contains peptide and sesquiterpene alkaloids.
Belladonna, deadly nightshade	*Atropa belladona*	Contains the toxic tropane alkaloids hyoscyamine, atropine, and hyoscine.
European mandrake	*Mandragora officinarium*	Contains a substance similar to belladonna as well as the alkaloids hyoscyamine, scopolamine, and mandragorine. Considered very dangerous for internal use.
Heliotrope	*Heliotropium spp.*	Contains alkaloids that may cause liver damage.
Hemlock, spotted hemlock, California or Nebraska fern	*Conium maculatum*	Contains the poisonous alkaloid coniine. Slows the heartbeat leading eventually to coma and death.
Henbane, hog's bean, devil's eye	*Hyoscyamus niger*	Contains the alkaloid hyoscyamine as well as atropine.
Indian tobacco, asthma weed, emetic weed	*Lobelia inflata*	Contains the alkaloid lobeline.
Jalap root, High John root, St. John the Conqueror root	*Ipomoea purga*	Usually found in Mexico, this plant's resin contains a powerful poison.
Jimson weed, thornapple, tolguacha	*Datura stramonium*	Contains the alkaloid scopolamine.
Lily of the valley, May lily	*Convallaria majalis*	Contains the toxic cardiac glycoside convallotoxin.
American mandrake, mayapple, wild lemon	*Podophyllum peltatum*	A poisonous plant containing more than 15 biologically active compounds, including a violently purgative substance.

NAME	SCIENTIFIC NAME	DANGER
Mistletoe	*Viscum album*	Contains toxic polypeptides, toxic amines, and toxalbumins that inhibit protein synthesis in the intestinal wall.
Morning glory	*Ipomoea tricolor*	Plant contains a purgative resin. Seeds contain lysergeic acid.
Periwinkle	*Vinca major, Vinca minor*	Contains toxic alkaloids that can injure the liver and kidneys. The entire plant is considered very dangerous for herbal use.
Pokeweed, pigeonberry, skoke	*Phytolacca americana*	Contains phytolaccigenin, phytolaccin, and phytolaccatoxin, which cause abdominal cramps, vomiting, and in severe cases, convulsions and death.
Broom, scotch broom	*Cytisus scoparius*	Contains the toxin sparteine and other alkaloids.
Spindle tree	*Euonymus europaeus*	Produces violent purges.
Sweet flag, sweet cane, sweet root	*Acorus calamus*	Asarone, a volatile oil from the root, is potentially harmful and has been implicated as a tumor-causing agent.
Tonka bean	*Dipteryx odorata*	Seeds contain coumarin. Can cause serious liver damage.
Water hemlock, poison parsnip, spotted cowbane, wild carrot	*Cicuta douglasii* *Cicuta maculata* *Cicuta virosa*	Holds the distinction of being the most violently poisonous plant in the North Temperate zone. Contains an unsaturated alcohol called cicutoxin.
White snakeroot, snakeroot, richweed	*Eupatorium rugosum*	Contains a toxic alcohol called tremetol.
Leopard's bane, Mountain tobacco, Wolfsbane	*Arnica montana*	Contains helenalin, which causes dermatitis in some people. Also a potent cardiotoxic agent. The entire plant is considered unsafe for internal use.
Wormwood, madderwort	*Artemisia absinthium*	Contains oil of wormwood, a psychotropic drug or hallucinogen. The liquor absinthe contains wormwood and is banned in the United States and many parts of the world.
Yohimbine	*Cornynanthe yohimbe*	Contains toxic alkaloids.

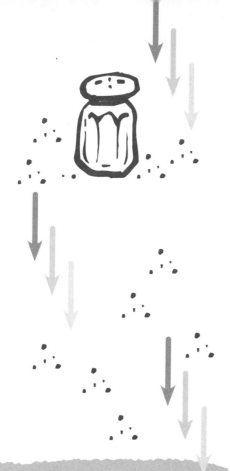

REDUCE YOUR SALT

If you're on a reduced-sodium diet, you probably already rely on herbs and spices to perk up flavors—but beware of commercially prepared seasoning blends. Many are loaded with sodium. You're better off reading the ingredient lists and concocting your own, with less—or no—added salt. Here are some to try.

Poultry Seasoning

Mix 2 teaspoons dried crumbled rosemary leaves, 2 teaspoons dried crumbled sage leaves, ½ teaspoon ground ginger, ½ teaspoon dried thyme leaves, and ¼ teaspoon freshly ground black pepper.

Cajun Seasoning

Mix 2 crumbled bay leaves, 1 teaspoon filé powder, ½ teaspoon salt, ½ teaspoon freshly ground black pepper, ½ teaspoon ground white pepper, ½ teaspoon dried thyme leaves, ¼ teaspoon cayenne pepper, ¼ teaspoon dried crumbled sage leaves, and ¼ teaspoon dry mustard.

Italian Seasoning

Mix 1 tablespoon dried oregano, 4 teaspoons parsley flakes, 4 teaspoons dried basil, and 1 ½ teaspoons dried crumbled sage leaves.

Mexican Seasoning

Mix 1 teaspoon chili powder, ½ teaspoon salt, ¼ teaspoon ground cumin, ¼ teaspoon dried oregano, and, depending on how hot your chili powder is, ¼ teaspoon freshly ground black pepper and a pinch or two of cayenne pepper.

GOOD FAT?

Medium-chain triglycerides are sold in health-food stores for people who have digestive disorders and problems absorbing fats. These are produced primarily from coconut oil, have a very low smoke point, and do not produce free fatty acids when heated.

SUPER SOUPS

The varieties of soup are endless, but the most common types listed here.

Bisque

A thick, smooth, creamy soup, prepared from shellfish or fish, tomatoes, and seasonings. Can be served as a main dish.

Bouillon

A clarified, concentrated broth made from meat, fish, or poultry (and/or the bones from each), and/or vegetables.

Broth

A clear liquid made from simmering meats, fish, or vegetables in water.

Chowder

A relatively thick, creamy soup often made with a fish or clam base, and which contains vegetables, especially potatoes.

Consommé

A very strong, clarified soup made from brown meat or fish stock.

Cream Soup

Usually made with the addition of milk, cream, or butter, or sometimes all three. Make sure you never boil a cream soup; if you do, it will develop a film on the surface.

A BUNCH OF HERBS WITH A FANCY NAME

In classical French cooking, a bouquet garni (traditionally parsley, thyme, and bay leaf) is tied in a bundle or wrapped in cheesecloth and used to flavor broths, soups, and stews. The bouquet is removed before the dish is served. If you don't have cheesecloth, put the herbs in a tea ball.

WHO KNEW?

Wine corks (not plastic) have a natural chemical that, when heated, tenderize beef stew. Just throw in 3 or 4 corks while cooking your stew!

PEANUT BUTTER TO THE RESCUE

Use your blender to smooth lumpy gravy, or add a pinch of salt to the flour before adding any liquid. If your gravy burns, just stir in a teaspoon of peanut butter to cover up the burnt flavor without altering the taste.

WHERE'S THE BEEF?

Commercial spaghetti sauces packaged as "containing meat" may have very little. By law, companies need to include only 6 percent actual meat. Add your own meat to a marinara sauce, and you will know what you are eating.

SNACK ON SEEDS

When an attack of the munchies hit you, a small handful of sunflower seeds are much better for you than a bar of chocolate. Rich in natural compounds that lower cholesterol, they are also full of vitamins and minerals that are good for healthy hair and skin.

A SOUP DIET

You can de-fat soup and gravy easily even if you don't have time to refrigerate it. Remove it from the heat for five to 10 minutes. Put four or five ice cubes in a piece of cheesecloth and swirl it around in the soup or gravy. Alternatively, stir a few lettuce leaves into the soup for a few minutes, and then discard them. Fat is attracted to the cold and to the lettuce leaves. A third method is to make a mop from a few paper towels (crumple, then hold the corners together), and swish it over the soup.

WHO *DOES* THIS RESEARCH?

Research shows that if you hold a spoonful of very hot soup at room temperature before consuming it, it will take 103 seconds to cool down to a temperature that will not burn your mouth. If you blow on that same spoonful to speed up the cooling process, it will cool down to the same temperature in just 66 seconds. Blowing speeds up the air moving over the soup. This faster air carries away the heat more efficiently than cooler air does, because it forces evaporation from the surface of the soup.

YES—YOU CAN STOP CURDLING

Whenever you prepare a cream soup or sauce, there's always the risk it will curdle. One easy way to avoid the problem is to thicken the mixture with flour or cornstarch before adding any acidic ingredients, such as wine, citrus, or tomatoes. Remember, too, that the heavier the cream the less likely it is to curdle.

TOO SALTY? TRY ONE OF THESE REDUCTIONS

If your soup or stew is too salty, pick one of these methods based on the flavors you prefer: Add a can of peeled tomatoes; add a small amount of brown sugar; or stir in a slice or two of apple or raw potato, let simmer a few minutes, then discard the apple or potato.

HMMMMM

Whenever possible, make your own sauces and gravies. Packaged items, whether from bottles or mixes, typically contain numerous additives, preservatives, and coloring agents.

SUPER SOUP SECRETS

Always make soup at least a day ahead of time, so the flavors have time to blend. Wait to season with salt or pepper until the soup is almost done; both of these seasonings will intensify and may give the soup too strong a flavor. Always cook soup with the lid on to help the flavors become better absorbed. When you make a cold soup, remember that it needs more seasoning than a hot soup; cool temperatures mute flavors.

CHECK YOUR FATS

'Cholesterol Free' or 'Low Cholesterol' means that the product does not contain any or only small amounts of animal fat or saturated fat, but it does not necessarily mean the product is low fat. Vegetable oils are cholesterol-free but made entirely of fat.

BACK IN THE DAY

Nineteenth century cooks added onion skins to the gravy while it cooked to give it a brown color. If you try the trick at home, just make sure you remove the skins after a few minutes and discard.

WHO KNEW?

A healthy and tasty addition to soup is leftover cooked broccoli. It also works great in chili.

BUY SMALL

If you don't use spices and dried herbs very often in your cooking, buy the smallest quantities you can. Ground, blended and chopped spices last around six months in your cupboard before they start to lose their potency, while whole spices can retain their taste for up to a year.

SHAKE IT FIRST

To help a semisolid or condensed soup slide right out of the can, shake the can first, and then open it from the bottom.

NEVER BOIL

For the best results and to keep the flavors intact, soups and stews should simmer, never boil.

SOUP REVAMPED

To make soup go further, just add cooked pasta, rice, or barley to it.

USE HERBS WISELY

Instead of seasoning with flavored salt such as garlic, celery, or onion salt, try using herb-only seasonings to reduce your sodium intake. Try garlic powder, finely chopped garlic or onion or celery seeds instead.

FASTEST DIPS

To make dips and sauces, look for dry soup mixes made with dried vegetables and seasonings and few, if any, additives. Keep in mind that these mixes are usually high in salt.

WHO KNEW?

Old bay seasoning is not just for summertime crab boils. Try it in crab cakes, tuna salad—even shrimp cocktail.

BUY SMALLER SIZES

Have some of the dried herbs and spices in your spice rack been there since the 1980's? Throw them out. Spices and herbs loose their potency quickly; so only buy small jars if you can.

BOTTLE NECK

When sauce refuses to come out of the bottle, push a drinking straw right to the bottom and then take it out again. This adds enough air to get it flowing.

SI, SENOR PABLO

To enhance stew, stack a few corn tortillas and cut into thin strips. Add them to the stew during the last 15 minutes of cooking.

COOL TRICK

Freeze homemade beef, chicken, or fish stock in an ice-cube tray, and then use the cubes in soups and stews at another time. If you have leftover soup, put it in zip-close freezer bags. Squeeze out as much air as you can, and then stack the bags in your freezer.

QUICK THICKENERS

An easy method of thickening stews is to add a small amount of quick-cooking oats, a grated potato, or some instant mashed potatoes.

THERE'S MORE SALT IN COMMERICAL BRANDS, TOO

Spaghetti sauce is really best if it is homemade. Commercial sauces are almost always much higher in fat and calories. One brand's extra chunky with sausage and green peppers is 47 percent calories from fat, and another brand's marinara is 40 percent calories from fat. Read labels and choose those that are low in fat and additives, and high in vegetables.

A READY THICKENER

Mix a stick of softened butter and ½ cup of flour in a covered bowl, and keep it in the fridge. When you want to thicken creamed vegetables or soups, just add some of the mixture. It melts easily and will thicken without lumps.

WITHOUT ORDER, WE HAVE CHAOS

Cream-of-tomato soup can be tricky to make from scratch. To keep it from curdling, the order in which you add the ingredients matters: add the tomato base to the milk instead of the milk to the tomato. Stirring a small amount of flour into the milk first also helps.

REMEMBER THIS EQUATION

If a recipe calls for fresh herbs and all you have are the dried variety, use one third the amount specified in the recipe.

GARLIC LOVES PARSLEY

When you overdo the garlic in a soup or sauce, place a few parsley flakes in a tea ball to soak up the excess garlic. Garlic is attracted to parsley.

WHO KNEW?

Herbs are often used in soups and stews, but tend to lose much of their flavor after about 15 minutes of cooking. For maximum flavor, always add herbs, whether fresh or dried, during the last 10 minutes of cooking.

HANDY CONTAINERS

Empty plastic ketchup and mustard containers are great for holding icings and oils. Allow a mixture of warm water and baking soda to sit overnight in the containers, and then rinse thoroughly with hot water.

JUST A LITTLE SAUTÉING SECRET

If you sauté with butter, be sure you use the unsalted kind. When salted butter melts, the salt can separate from the butter and may consequently impart a bitter taste to the dish.

TAPIOCA

A thickener, tapioca is usually sold as a pudding mix, and is actually a starch that is extracted from the cassava root. It is found in three forms:

Pearl Tapioca

This usually has to be soaked for a number of hours before it is soft enough to use.

Quick-Cooking Tapioca

This is the type used for puddings. It is normally sold in granular form, needs no presoaking, and is popular for use as a thickening agent.

Tapioca should be mixed with water until it forms a thin paste before adding it to the food that needs thickening. Adding undiluted tapioca directly to the food will cause it to become lumpy. Try not to over-stir tapioca when it is cooking, or it may turn into a thick, unpalatable paste.

Tapioca Flour

Normally found only in health food stores, this is also very popular as a thickening agent for soups and stews.

WHO KNEW?

The rind of Parmigiano-Reggiano cheese is a great flavor enhancer for soups. Add a 3-inch square to your next pot of soup, and when you're serving the soup, break up the rind and include it in each bowl. It's completely edible.

YOU CAN'T SPELL TENDER WITHOUT "T"

The tannic acid in strong black tea can tenderize meat in a stew, as well as reduce the cooking time. Just add ½ cup of strong tea to the stew when you add the other liquid.

KEEP IT TOGETHER

Emulsification is the process of combining two liquids that do not normally blend: Oil and water is one example. Oil and vinegar is another, and if you've ever made a salad dressing, you know that it takes a bit of doing to combine them. When the oil and vinegar solution is whisked vigorously or shaken, the oil breaks into small droplets for a short period of time, resulting in a temporary emulsion. There are a number of emulsifiers that will help keep the oil suspended in the vinegar. Prepared mustard is one, which is one reason why Dijon mustard is often added to a vinaigrette (flavor, of course, is another reason).

USE IT AS A THICKENER

Arrowroot is derived from the rootstalks of a South American tuber; it is finely powdered and used as a thickener. Its thickening power is about one to two times that of all-purpose flour, and like cornstarch, it should be mixed into a paste with adequate cold water before it's added to a hot mixture. Unlike some thickeners, arrowroot will not impart a chalky taste if it is overcooked, and it does not become cloudy—your sauce will remain clear. It's best not to over-stir a mixture that contains arrowroot or it will become thin again. If your recipe calls for arrowroot and you don't have any, you can substitute 1 tablespoon of cornstarch or 2 tablespoons of all-purpose flour for every tablespoon of arrowroot.

GELATIN FACTS AND TIPS

Gelatin is pure protein, derived from animal hooves, muscle, bones, and connective tissue. (Agar, made from seaweed, and carrageenan, made from Irish moss, are vegetable-based thickeners.)

Gelatin granules have the capability of trapping water molecules and then expanding to 10 times their original size. The firmness of a food will depend on the ratio of gelatin to water. Fresh figs, kiwi, papaya, and pineapple contain enzymes that break down protein, which keeps gelatin from setting. Bromelain, the enzyme in pineapple, can be neutralized by simmering the fruit for a few minutes.

When using gelatin for a dish, be sure to moisten the gelatin first with a small amount of cold water, and then use hot water to dissolve it completely. If you combine the gelatin with hot water, some of the granules will clump together so they won't all dissolve, and the finished dish may be somewhat grainy. If your recipe calls for an equal amount of sugar and gelatin, the cold-water step is not required, since the sugar will stop the clumping. However, never pour hot water into the gelatin; instead, sprinkle the gelatin into the water.

IT'S PECTIN FOR JELLY

Pectin, a carbohydrate, is the only thickener for jellies. If your jelly doesn't set, it's probably because you used too little pectin or the wrong proportions of other ingredients. Jelly requires a number of ingredients to set properly, and pectin is only one of the most important. The acid and sugar content will both affect the setting properties of the jelly, and cooking the jelly for too long will destroy the pectin.

Certain types of fruit jellies need only a small amount of pectin, because most fruits are relatively high in pectin. Higher-pectin fruits include apples, cranberries, and all citrus. Those with less pectin include peaches, cherries, raspberries, apricots, and strawberries. To make the most of the fruit's natural pectin, the fruit should be very fresh.

STARBUCKS GRAVY

Here's a trick to give your gravy to have a rich, dark-brown color. Spread the flour in a dry skillet and cook over low heat, stirring frequently, until it browns. Add a bit of coffee to the gravy during the last few minutes of cooking.

OIL DOESN'T GET IT DONE

Because of its liquid nature, oil tends to collect instead of distributing evenly through a dough. This may cause baked goods to become grainy. When a solid fat is used, baked items tend to be flakier and retain their moisture better. Bottom line: Use the fat your recipe calls for (some will specify vegetable oil).

STOP SEPARATION ANXIETY

Does your gravy separate? When it does, simply add a pinch or two of baking soda to emulsify the fat globules in a matter of seconds.

ONE WAY TO ELIMINATE FAT

When fat floats to the top of gravies, soups, or stews, it can be easily removed by placing a slice of fresh white bread on top of the fat for a few seconds. After the bread absorbs the fat, it should be disposed of—if you leave the bread on the soup too long, it will fall apart.

SIP ON A LEMON

Lemon is a very good oil for detoxifying and stimulating a sluggish system, which can help with weight loss. Rosemary is also recommended as it can help promote clarity of thought and improve concentration.

OIL YOUR JOINTS

We all know that fish oils help fight arthritis, but olive oil can also help protect against this inflammatory disease. It is said that those who eat it every day reduce their risk by 2.5 times, possibly because of its high levels of antioxidants.

SPICE IT UP

Hot spicy foods can help the body burn up calories. Using spices like cayenne pepper and chili powder elevates the body temperature which makes the heart beat faster and requires more energy.

USE DRY MARINADES

Instead of marinating meats in oil and your favorite spices, rub the dried spices into the meat instead. That way, you won't be adding any extra fat to the meat and you'll get the same yummy taste.

DON'T FORGET TO STIR GENTLY

To thicken a stew or to make a sauce of medium consistency, dissolve either 1 ½ tablespoons of cornstarch, 2 ½ teaspoons of potato starch, or 2 teaspoons of arrowroot in 3 tablespoons of water for every cup of liquid, then add this mixture to the food. Let it simmer for three to five minutes.

SAY YES TO SAFFLOWER

Increasingly, cosmetic companies are waking up to the benefits of safflower oil to create and purify emulsions. The product increases the skin's absorption of oils without making it oily, so is a great choice for anti-aging creams.

HERBILICIOUS!

Grow herbs in a window box outside your kitchen or buy pots from supermarkets to keep indoors and you'll always be able to cook something interesting. Start your collection with basil, thyme, parsley, sage, tarragon and rosemary.

OFFER AN OLIVE

Olives are a great snack for children as they are healthy snacks–filling and without sugar or fat. They can be salty, though, if stored in brine, so wash before eating or offer water alongside when served.

OLIVES ARE OK

If you need an early evening snack with your glass of wine choose olives instead of potato chips, which are calorie-laden. There are loads of different varieties to choose from, and they are all full of great essential fatty acids (EFAs), and contain relatively few calories.

OILS HATE SUN

Always purchase oils in opaque containers, never clear bottles. Oil is very sensitive to light and will deteriorate more rapidly when exposed to it. If you can't find it in an opaque container, transfer it to one at home.

HOLLANDAISE SAUCE, REDEEMED

The secret to saving curdled hollandaise sauce is to catch the problem as it starts. As soon as the sauce begins to curdle, vigorously beat in 1 to 2 tablespoons of cold water for every ¾ cup sauce until the sauce is smooth. Repeat this for the balance of the sauce, never adding more than 1 or 2 tablespoons at time. If the sauce has already curdled, beat 1 tablespoon of cold water into the sauce to help bring back the smooth texture.

SEND FOR THE SALSA

Instead of buying commercially prepared tomato ketchup, choose fresh salsa – or buy tomatoes, red peppers and chilies and make your own. Chop them up and mix together to make it a great alternative to ketchup for meat, eggs and burgers.

GARLIC HEAD

Garlic tastes best when the heads are firm and plump with no green shoots. Green shoots coming out of the bulbs means the garlic has been in storage for too long and will taste less fresh and may be slightly bitter. The bulbs can still be used for cooking, although they won't taste as good, but discard the green bits.

ADD FLAVOR LATER

For dishes that take a longer time to cook, beware of over flavoring with herbs and spices, which often develop stronger flavor the longer they are cooked. Add very few herbs and spices at the beginning. An hour before serving, add more if you think the dish needs it.

KITCHEN COLOR CORRECTOR

If blonde hair turns a strange shade of 'green' after a summer spent swimming in chlorinated pools, comb tomato ketchup through your hair and leave for 20 minutes to neutralize color. Afterwards wash and condition in the usual way.

IN CASE YOU WERE WONDERING

If you wear eyeglasses when frying, you may have noticed that the oil droplets collect on the inner surface of the lens as well as the outer surface. The reason? Minute droplets of oil become airborne when heated. If you are bending over while you work, the oil droplets can land on the inside of the lenses as gravity pulls them back to earth.

FAST, EASY, DELICIOUS

Easiest-ever pot pies: Put leftover stew into individual baking dishes or small casseroles, cover with prepared pie crust or biscuits, or dumplings made from a mix, and bake until the topping is golden brown.

READ IT. LEARN IT. LIVE IT.

- Never increase the sugar in tomato-sauce dishes.
- Never increase salt in a recipe by more than a pinch or two at a time.

HERB CUBES

One of the reasons so many people like shop-bought sauces is that they never have the right ingredients ready at hand. Stock up with herbs that won't last in the refrigerator, like basil or parsley, by finely chopping and freezing with a small amount of water in ice-cube trays. When you need herbs for a recipe, just toss in a cube.

A SWEET SOLUTION

To sweeten a soup or stew, stir in a small amount of pureed carrots. Use one of the sweeter carrot varieties.

ANISE IS ANISEED

Anise is found in licorice candy (as a substitute for real licorice), and in cookies, pickling spices, and soft drinks. It is also used to make anisette (the anise-flavored liqueur) and can be used as a substitute for ginger in some recipes. It is commonly available as the spice aniseed.

NO MUSS, NO FUSS

Next time you make stock, put all the ingredients in a metal pasta insert or basket. Set the insert into your pot and cook. When the stock is done, remove the insert—and all the veggies, meat, or bones—easily.

THE PROTECTORS

If you plant basil, parsley or garlic among your flower beds, it will deter bugs from bothering your flowers. Use the herbs as an edging around your garden for best results.

A BONY BASE

Hearty soups start with good beef or chicken stock, so don't throw away roast, chicken or steak bones. Wrap in airtight plastic bags, and freeze. When it's time to make soup, defrost the bones and brown under a broiler, about six inches from the heat, and use as the basis for your soup stock.

IT BEATS USING YOUR FINGERS

Wire whisks work better than any other kitchen tool for removing lumps in soups and sauces.

TO GAIN MORE TASTE...MAKE IT A DAY BEFORE SERVING

When cooking a hearty winter soup, it's a good idea to make it a day before you plan to serve it, so the seasonings have time to really meld. Also, always cook soup with the pot covered to help the flavors become better absorbed.

MORE THAN A REPELLENT FOR VAMPIRES

Studies have shown that garlic inhibits blood coagulation, reduces the level of LDL (bad cholesterol), and raises the level of HDL (good cholesterol) in the blood.

A SMOOTHER FINISH

When serving creamed soups, beat or whisk for a few seconds before heating and your soup will be silky smooth.

CHEESE, EGG AND DAIRY

A CHEESE PRIMER

Cheeses come in a wide variety of flavors and colors, few of which are natural. Surprisingly, most cheeses are naturally white—not yellow. Nor are most naturally pink, green, or burgundy.

Be more aware of the types of cheese you buy and try to buy cheeses without the added chemicals. If you buy low-fat and nonfat cheeses, you're in a bit of a bind, because these rely heavily on chemical stabilizers and thickeners. Even if the label reads "all-natural," you should still look for the phrase "no preservatives or coloring agents." Consumers need to read labels more than ever these days.

SOMETIMES IT REFUSES TO MELT

One frequent error when melting cheese is heating it at too high a temperature for too long a time. When this occurs, the protein is separated from the fat, and the cheese becomes tough and rubbery, and the cheese is ruined. Remember to keep the heat low, and use a double boiler if the recipe says to do so. Don't try to melt large pieces; cut the cheese into small chunks before melting. Grating it will also make it easier to melt, and is the best method for making sauces. The most popular soft cheeses that don't need to be grated are ricotta, Camembert, and Brie, which have a higher water content and lower fat content than hard cheeses. Cheese should be the last item added to most recipes.

Reduced-fat cheeses melt less successfully than their full-fat counterparts; the more fat that is removed, the less likely the cheese is to melt well.

WHO KNEW?

Goat cheese is heat sensitive and becomes grainy when overheated. When using in recipes, heat just until it's melted.

CHEESE CULTURES

One teaspoon of cheese-starter culture can contain 5 trillion living organisms. In the past, cheese producers were never sure of the activity of their culture, which came from milk-souring lactic acid bacteria. Today, there are companies that specialize in producing cultures of bacteria in whey (a protein) that actually separate the curd in the cheese-making process. These companies use lactobacillus and lactococcus bacteria to ferment milk sugar (lactose) into lactic acid. The acid is necessary to prevent unwanted microbes from growing in the cheese.

BUYING BRIE AND CAMEMBERT

Both of these very popular soft cheeses are sprayed with special mold to form a very thin, white, flexible rind. These cheeses ripen from the outside in and turn creamier, with a more intense flavor, as they age. These cheeses should never smell of ammonia. Ideally, they should be somewhat springy when prodded and should never have a hard core. These cheeses will continue to ripen for a day or two even when refrigerated, and should be eaten within five days of purchase.

Soft cheeses can become too ripe, at which point they may harden in texture until they are cut. Once soft cheese is cut, the ripening process stops. If the cheese appears runny, it has been overaged and may be bitter.

THE CASE FOR STRONG CHEESE

Many low-fat cheeses are made with low-fat or fat-free milk; examples include part-skim mozzarella and ricotta, and farmer cheese. Many cookbooks advise using a strongly flavored cheese, such as extra-sharp Cheddar or Parmesan; their richer flavors mean you can use less cheese. Use low-fat and fat-free cheeses in dishes that don't require heat, such as salads or sandwiches, because they don't melt well.

GREAT GRATING TIP

When grating cheese, try spraying a liquid vegetable oil or nonstick cooking spray on the grater to make cleanup easier.

oil spray

ALL THE VELVEETA FACTS YOU COULD EVER POSSIBLY NEED

Elmer E. Eldridge, a chemist at Cornell University, was hired by the Phenix Cheese Company and developed a Velveeta-like product in 1915. The intention was to try to duplicate the consistency of a processed Swiss cheese. Eldridge separated the whey (liquid protein) from the cheese and mixed it with cheese and a small amount of sodium citrate as an antioxidant. The original name of the cheese was Phen-ett, after the Phenix Company. At the same time, Kraft scientists developed a similar product called NuKraft; the two companies agreed to share patent rights.

Velveeta is now called "cheese spread" and contains about 60 percent moisture, not less than 20 percent butterfat, a few gums to hold it all together, and, of course, sweeteners. Velveeta was first marketed in 1928 when Kraft patented a method of packaging the cheese spread in foil-lined wooden boxes. The challenge had been to make the foil stick to the cheese, not the box, creating a hermetic seal that would keep the cheese fresh for long periods.

Velveeta melts beautifully, so it is used in casseroles, on burgers and sandwiches, and in soups. Its mild flavor makes it especially popular with children, as well as with cooks who know that a more assertive cheese would overpower the other flavors in their dish.

CHOOSING CHEDDAR

One of the first things to look for when purchasing Cheddar cheese is uniform color. White spots or streaks are a sign that the cheese has been stored too long. The texture should always be relatively smooth, although it is not uncommon to find Cheddars that are grainy and crumbly. If the Cheddar has a rind, be sure the rind is not cracked or bulging, which might mean the cheese will be bitter as the result of poor manufacturing practices. Cheddar will continue to age in the refrigerator for months, and should be stored wrapped in plastic.

Cheddar originated in England, but in the United States it is the most widely produced variety of cheese, with Wisconsin, New York, and Vermont as the major manufacturers.

CHEESE RIPENING CLASSIFICATIONS

Blue-Veined

These cheeses are cured with bacteria and specific mold cultures that grow throughout the inside of the cheese, producing their familiar blue-veined appearance and unique flavor. They are typically quite pungent and include Roquefort, Gorgonzola, Maytag, and Stilton.

Firm

These cheeses are ripened by use of a bacterial culture and continue to ripen as long as the temperature is favorable. Firm cheeses have lower moisture content than the softer cheeses and usually take longer to cure. Parmesan, Parmigiano-Reggiano, and pecorino Romano are the most popular firm cheeses.

WHO KNEW?

Always bring cheese to room temperature one hour before serving it; the flavor will be much better.

Semisoft

When cheese ripens from the inside as well as the exterior, the curing continues as long as the temperature is warm. These cheeses have higher moisture content than do firm ripened cheeses. Semisoft cheeses include Gouda, Monterey Jack, and Tilsit.

Soft

These cheeses are cured from the outside, or rind, toward the center. The process involves using particular molds or bacterial cultures that are allowed to grow on the surface of the cheese, creating the specific flavor, body, and texture of that cheese. These cheeses usually contain more moisture than semisoft ripened cheeses. Examples include Brie, Camembert, and triple-cream cheeses like Boursin.

Unripened

These are normally consumed shortly after manufacture and include cottage cheese, a high-moisture soft cheese. Examples of other unripened cheeses are ricotta, cream cheese, farmer cheese, and mascarpone.

COMMON CHEESES YOU SHOULD KNOW ABOUT

American

Pasteurized processed cheese made from shredded Cheddar mixed with dyes and emulsifiers to make a mild, meltable cheese. More than half of all cheese consumed in the United States is, fittingly, American.

Beer

This is a smooth cheese that has been compared with Limburger but is milder. It originated in Germany as Bierkäse.

Bel Paese

Originating in Italy, this semi soft cheese has a mild flavor. It is usually eaten with fruit for dessert.

Blue (Bleu)

Easily identified by the blue streaks throughout its interior, blue cheese crumbles easily and has a somewhat soft texture. In the United States and Britain, it is often sold in wheels; in France, it is sold in wheels or small medallions. It is also available crumbled.

Brick

A somewhat soft, yellow cheese with a medium-soft texture. It is from the American Midwest.

Brie

Originating in the south of France, this cheese is produced with an edible white coating. It has a mild flavor and a creamy texture. Brie is available in wheels and occasionally in wedges cut from the wheels.

Boursault

A French cheese that is soft, delicate, and mild. It is usually served as part of a cheese board, or in soup, fondue, or sauces.

Camembert

This cheese has a soft, yellowish interior with a thin, dull white, edible coating. It ripens in four to eight weeks and was named by Napoleon, after the Norman village where a farmer's wife first served it to him.

Store cheese near the bottom of the refrigerator, where temperature fluctuations are minimal.

Cheddar

The natural color of Cheddar is white, not yellow. The yellow color is produced by natural dye called annatto, which is derived from achiote seeds. (Manufacturers believe that yellow cheese is more marketable.) Cheddar has a mild to very sharp taste and a fairly firm texture. It is sold in numerous shapes as well as sliced. Cheddar originated in the village of Cheddar, England, and was first imported to the United States in the nineteenth century. Because of its low moisture content, Cheddar will last for years, with its flavor becoming sharper as it ages. Cheddar gets about 70 percent of its calories from fat, of which 40 percent is saturated.

Cheshire

Produced in England, this is a hard cheese with a rich, mellow flavor similar to that of Cheddar.

Colby

Usually sold as a light yellow cheese, Colby originated in Wisconsin and has a somewhat mild flavor with a texture similar to that of cheddar. It is normally sold in wedges cut from a large round.

Coldpack

This cheese is a mixture of natural cheese, typically Cheddar, and other ingredients like spices, artificial flavorings, and port wine. A soft, spreadable cheese, it is available in a variety of colors and flavors.

Edam

This Dutch cheese is commonly available in large spheres with red wax coating. The interior is a creamy yellow-orange color, the consistency is semi soft, and the cheese has a light, nutlike flavor. Edam has a lower milk-fat content than Gouda, which is a similar cheese.

Feta

A soft to semidry Greek cheese usually produced from goat's milk. The taste of feta is somewhat salty and sharp.

Farmer Cheese (Pot Cheese)

A close relative to cottage cheese, farmer cheese is usually pressed into a block shape and is sold mostly in delicatessens.

Fontina

One of the finest semi soft cheeses from Italy, it has a mild, somewhat nutty flavor and a light brown rind. It is often used for fondue.

Gjetost

From Norway, this is a relatively mellow, semi soft cheese that is sold in cubes or rectangles. It is usually a pleasant golden color and is made from a combination of cow's- and goat's-milk whey; the milk is cooked until it is caramelized, and thus the cheese is sweet. Similar to Myost.

Gorgonzola

Mold plays a significant role in the coloring of this Italian cheese. It is always found with blue-green veins and has a soft texture with an off-white exterior. The flavor is tangy and somewhat peppery, and the cheese is quite creamy. It is usually made with whey or cow's milk.

Cream Cheese

Usually made with whole cow's milk before the cream has been skimmed off, cream cheese gets 90 percent of its calories from fat. It is semi soft and usually white, although flavorings are sometimes added. Some cream cheeses are made with propylene glycol alginate, which is derived from seaweed and is used as a stabilizer.

Gouda

Usually sold in a wheel or wedge with a red wax coating, this Dutch cheese has an inside that is semi soft and creamy yellow, with a nut-like flavor. The cheese contains irregular or round holes.

Gruyère

Made in Switzerland and similar to Swiss cheese, Gruyère is usually sold with mold inhibitors added. Check the label.

Limburger

Originally from Belgium, and once among the most popular cheeses in America, Limburger has fallen on hard times and is now produced by only one plant in the United States, the Chalet Cheese Co-op in Monroe, Wisconsin, which manufactures a million pounds per year. It is a smooth, creamy, soft, aged cheese with a pronounced aroma. Limburger will continue to age after it is purchased and will actually develop more flavor. It will last five to six months and should be stored in a well-sealed glass container. (Make that *extra*-well sealed.)

Mozzarella

Produced from either part-skim or whole milk, mozzarella has a firm texture and is sold in rounds, shredded, or sliced. If you live in or near an Italian neighborhood, seek out fresh mozzarella, which is infinitely superior to the stuff in supermarket dairy cases.

Muenster

Usually sold in wedges or blocks, Muenster, from Alsace, is moister than brick cheese. It has a creamy-white interior with a yellowish exterior and possibly small holes throughout. Flavor is mild, and texture is semi soft.

Myost

Sold in pie-shape wedges or in cubes, this Scandinavian cheese is similar to Gjetost. It is light brown in color and has a sweet, caramel flavor.

Neufchâtel

With a soft texture and a mildly acidic flavor, Neufchâtel is lower in fat than cream cheese. It is from France.

Parmesan

Although Parmesan is often sold pregrated, it is best bought in a block and grated as needed. In bulk it is a creamy-white cheese with a hard, granular texture. It is usually produced from partially skimmed milk.

Pasteurized Processed Cheese

This product is a blend of cheeses that varies in consistency from brand to brand. The flavor is relatively mild. This cheese has a low melting point.

Pasteurized Process Cheese Food

Similar to processed cheese, except that milk or whey is added to make the cheese spreadable. These cheeses are softer, with a lower fat content and a milder flavor, than pasteurized processed cheese.

Port du Salut

Creamy yellow with a buttery texture and mild, savory flavor, this French cheese has small holes throughout. It comes in thick cylinders.

HEE HAW

While almost all butter sold in the United States is produced from cow's milk, butter may be produced from the milk of many other animals. In other countries, butter is made from the milk of donkeys, horses, goats, sheep, buffalo, camels, and even yaks when cow's milk is not available.

Provolone

This Italian cheese has an off-white interior with a somewhat yellowish exterior. It is unsalted, with a mild flavor; the texture is fairly smooth.

Quark

This is a soft, unripened cheese with the texture of sour cream. The flavor is richer than that of yogurt. From Germany.

Ricotta

Produced from either whole or skim milk, ricotta has a somewhat nut-like flavor and looks like small-curd cottage cheese. From Italy.

Romano

A yellow-white cheese with a greenish-black exterior and a sharp flavor, Romano is sold both in wedges and pregrated. It can be made with whole cows, sheep's, or goat's milk. *From Italy.*

Roquefort

Mold is introduced to create marbling and blue veins throughout the cheese. It has a white interior and is usually produced from sheep's milk. The flavor is somewhat peppery, and the texture is always crumbly. Sold mostly in wedges or packaged already crumbled. From France.

Stilton

Similar to Roquefort, this English cheese has a pale yellow interior with blue mold streaks. Unlike Roquefort, it is normally produced from cow's milk. Stilton has a crumbly texture and is usually sold in logs or wedges.

THE TRUTH ABOUT SWISS CHEESE AND ITS HOLES

When Swiss cheese is cured, microorganisms produce a gas that causes pockets of air to form, and these remain after the cheese ripens. The holes should, however, be relatively uniform in size and not too large. The borders of the holes should have a moist, shiny appearance.

Tilsit

The inside of this cheese is usually a light yellow color and the texture is semisoft. This German cheese is produced from pasteurized milk and takes about five months to ripen. The fat content runs about 40 percent.

Swiss

Usually produced from whole milk, this cheese has a light yellow interior; Swiss cheese has a somewhat sweet, nutty flavor. The texture is firm and the characteristic holes may vary in size. It is usually sold in rectangular blocks or sliced. Do not buy Swiss cheese that has a grayish rind. The flavor will become stronger when the cheese is wrapped in plastic wrap and refrigerated. Cut wedges should last for one or two months.

CHEESE FACTS

- An ounce of cream cheese may contain as many as 110 calories. As advertised, it does have fewer calories than butter by comparable weight, but then again, we tend to use more of it.
- Look for cheeses that are low-sodium, low-fat, or reduced-fat. There are new varieties appearing in supermarkets and health-food stores.
- Be sure to read the label. If it is not a chemical concoction, the name of the cheese must be preceded by the word "natural."
- Most cheese substitutes are produced from soybean or vegetable fats. Many low-fat cheeses substitute water for the fat.
- It takes 8 pounds of milk to produce 1 pound of cheese. An average slice of American cheese contains 8 ounces of milk.
- The wax coating protects the interior of a cheese. If there is an exposed edge, cover it with plastic wrap or butter to keep it moist and fresh.

ALWAYS STORE COTTAGE CHEESE UPSIDE DOWN

Cottage cheese is a United States original. It is made from nonfat milk and is either plain-cured or plain-cured with cream. Its texture is always soft, with curds of varying size. If the label says, "curd by acidification," it was made with rennet. After processing, cottage cheese retains only 25 to 50 percent of the calcium from the milk it is made from. Because of its high water content, cottage cheese will last only until the expiration date on the container unless it is stored in the container upside down.

EGG CHEMISTRY

Despite all the negative publicity, the fact is that eggs are still about the best and most complete sources of protein. Most of this publicity revolves around the high levels of cholesterol (approximately 213 milligrams) found in the egg yolk.

Some significant studies have recently shown that consuming egg yolks does not, in fact, appreciably elevate blood cholesterol levels. (Consuming saturated fat, not cholesterol, is more likely to raise blood cholesterol levels—though dietary cholesterol still plays a part.) Nevertheless, it is wise to heed the recommendation of the American Heart Association, not to mention most cardiologists and nutritionists, and strive to limit your cholesterol to 300 milligrams per day.

Egg-Quivalents

CALORIES	MEASURING EGGS
1 large egg = 80 calories	1 large egg (2 oz) = ¼ cup
1 egg white = 20 calories	1 medium egg (1 ¾ oz) = ⅕ cup
1 egg yolk = 60 calories	1 small egg (1½ oz) = ⅙ cup

NO MORE ALUMINUM BOWLS—EVER!

Aluminum bowls and cookware tend to darken an egg. The reason? The aluminum's chemical reaction with the egg protein.

THE GRADING SYSTEM

There are three grades of eggs: U.S. Grade AA, U.S. Grade A, and U.S. Grade B. Grade B eggs are used by bakeries and commercial food processors. Eggs marked "A" or "AA" on the carton are not officially graded unless they show the USDA shield as well as the letter grade.

JUST THINK OF J. LO

To increase the volume of beaten eggs, use a bowl that's about 10 inches in diameter and five to six inches deep, and that has a rounded bottom. A balloon whisk is the ideal tool for incorporating air into the eggs.

IT BEATS THROWING THEM OUT

If you have used egg whites in a recipe and want to save the yolks for another use, slide them into a bowl of water, cover with plastic wrap, and store in the refrigerator for a day or two.

POACH TO PERFECTION

Salt, lemon juice, or vinegar will make the egg white coagulate faster; add it to the water when you're poaching eggs to help them keep their shape.

AND WHO WANTS DEVILED EGGS THAT AREN'T CENTERED?

To keep yolks centered when boiling eggs for deviled eggs, stir the water while they are cooking. When storing deviled eggs, stick toothpicks into the eggs around the edge of the plate, then cover with plastic wrap. The toothpicks keep the plastic off the eggs.

ANATOMY OF AN EGG

The yolk of an egg is 50 percent water; 34 percent lipids, or fats; and 16 percent protein. The yolk contains most of the cholesterol, three-fourths of the calories, and most of the vitamin A, thiamine, and iron in an egg—the yolk is the source of nutrients for a chick before it hatches. The egg white is mostly water; about 10 percent of it is protein, with traces of minerals, glucose, and lipids. The white's primary purpose is as a barrier against bacteria for the developing chick.

VINEGAR AND SUGAR WILL HELP

To keep cheese longer without mold forming, place a piece of paper towel that has been dampened with white vinegar in the bottom of a plastic container with a tight-fitting lid. Add three or four sugar cubes, which will attract the mold if some has formed.

IT'S SIMPLE GEOMETRY

To keep deviled eggs from wobbling on the platter, cut a thin slice off two sides of the egg before you halve it lengthwise.

FREEZING FACTS

Freezing hard-cooked eggs causes the whites to become tough. When freezing fresh eggs, always break the yolk. The whites and yolks can be frozen separately unless you plan on using them at the same time.

SPIN IT

It's easy to tell whether an egg is hard-cooked: Spin it. If it wobbles it's raw—the yolk sloshes from one end of the egg to the other; a hard-cooked eggs spins evenly, because the yolk is held in place by the cooked egg white.

TRY USING LEMON

You can prevent boiled eggs from cracking by rubbing a cut lemon on the shells before cooking them.

COLD WORKS BETTER

Cold water cleans egg off utensils better than hot water. Hot water tends to cause the protein to bind to surfaces and harden.

TIMING IS EVERYTHING

Add sour cream to hot dishes just before serving. Dishes containing sour cream must be reheated slowly to prevent the cream from separating.

COOL YOUR EGGS

Always cool a hard-cooked egg before you try to slice it; it will slice more easily and will not fall apart. Using unwaxed dental floss makes slicing hard-cooked eggs easy.

ADDED AIR

Air is whipped into all commercial ice cream. If the air were not added, the ice cream would be as solid as a brick and you would be unable to scoop it out. The air improves the texture and is not listed among the ingredients. However, a gallon of ice cream must weigh 4½ pounds.

BUT YOU KNEW THAT ALREADY

When preparing scrambled eggs, allow 3 per person. Most people eat more eggs when they are scrambled. If other ingredients are added, such as cheese or vegetables, 2 eggs per person will be sufficient.

IT'S CALLED TEMPERING

When adding raw eggs or yolks to a hot mixture, be sure to mix part of the hot mixture into the eggs, and then gradually add this new mixture to the hot mixture. It's extra work, but it makes the eggs less likely to curdle and separate.

WHO KNEW?

How do you know if beaten egg whites are stiff enough? Just run a knife through the middle of the bowl—if they whites stay separated, they're ready.

ASSUMING YOU WANT A WHITE FILM

To guarantee a white film over the yolks of cooked eggs, place a few drops of water in the pan just before they are done and cover the pan.

HOLLANDAISE HELL

Eggs have been found to contain the salmonella bacteria even when the shells were not cracked. Because of this, be sure not to use eggs in sauces that are not cooked thoroughly. When preparing a hollandaise or béarnaise sauce, it might be best to microwave the eggs briefly before adding them to the sauce. Use a 600-watt microwave oven and no more than 2 large Grade A egg yolks at a time.

First, separate the egg yolks completely from the whites. Second, place the yolks in a glass bowl and beat them until they are well combined. Third, add 2 teaspoons of lemon juice and mix thoroughly again. Fourth, cover the bowl, place in the microwave on High, and observe the mixture until the surface begins to move.

Cook for 10 seconds past this point, remove the bowl, and beat the mixture with a clean whisk until it appears smooth. Return the bowl to the microwave and cook again until the surface starts to move. Allow it to remain another 10 seconds, remove, and whisk again until smooth. Finally, allow the bowl to stand for about 1 minute. The yolks should be free of salmonella and still will be usable in your sauce.

WHO KNEW?

To get more meringue from egg whites, add 2 teaspoons cold water for each egg white before beating.

MISCELLANEOUS FACTS AND TIPS TO IMPRESS YOUR FRIENDS

- Egg whites contain more than half of the protein of the egg and only 33 percent of the calories.

- When frying an egg, the butter or margarine should be very hot before the eggs are added—a drop of water should sizzle. However, the heat should be reduced just before the eggs are added to the pan. Cook the eggs over low heat until the whites are completely set.

- If you are storing hard-cooked eggs with raw eggs, add a small amount of food coloring to the boiling water so that it will be easy to tell which eggs have been cooked.

- White or brown eggs are identical in nutritional value and taste.

- Egg whites begin to coagulate at 145°F; at 150°F, the yolks begin to set. The entire egg white will be firm yet still tender at 160°F. Be sure to cook eggs over low heat to guarantee a tender white and smooth yolk.

- When beating egg whites, remove all traces of yolk with a Q-tip or the edge of a paper towel before trying to beat the whites. The slightest trace of yolk will prevent the whites from beating properly, as will any trace of fat on the beaters or bowl.

- When preparing a number of omelets or batches of scrambled eggs, always wipe the pan clean with a piece of paper towel after every two to three batches to prevent the eggs from sticking to the pan.

- The fresher the egg, the better it is for poaching. The white will be firmer and will help to keep the yolk from breaking. Bring the water to a boil and then reduce it to a simmer before adding the egg.

- For best results, start scrambled eggs in a hot pan, but immediately lower the heat and cook them slowly over low heat.

- Did you know? It takes about four hours to digest a whole egg because of its high fat content.
- To remove an unbroken egg that has stuck to the carton, just wet the carton. If the egg is broken, throw it out.

I LIKE IT SPIKED

- In many dessert recipes that call for whole milk, eggnog makes a delicious substitute, but it adds lots of cholesterol and calories.
- If you freeze eggnog and find upon thawing that it has separated, whir it in a blender before using it.
- Eggnog has a short shelf life; use it within five days of purchase.

SAFETY FIRST

USDA regulations state that eggs must be refrigerated during all phases of shipping and in supermarkets. In many instances, however, they are left on pallets in supermarkets without refrigeration. Do not to purchase eggs you suspect have been unrefrigerated, because the temperature of an egg should never rise above 40°F. Unfortunately, there's no way to tell whether eggs have been stored improperly.

YOU MEAN YOU DON'T HAVE AN EGG FUNNEL?

To separate eggs easily, break the egg into a small funnel placed over a measuring cup. The white will drain through the funnel; just be sure not to break the yolk when cracking the egg. Never separate eggs by passing the yolk back and forth from one half of the shell to the other, because there may be bacteria on the shell that could contaminate the egg.

THE UPSIDE-DOWN EGG

Eggs should be stored with the tapered end down to maximize the distance between the yolk and the air pocket, which may contain bacteria. The yolk is more perishable than the white, or albumen, and even though it is more or less centered in the egg, the yolk can shift slightly and will move away from possible contamination.

HARD AND SOFT

Soft-boiled eggs should be cooked at least four minutes to kill any bacteria that may be present. The whites of fried eggs should be hard, although the yolks may be soft. Eggs are considered safe at 160°F. Some eggshells contain cracks that allow harmful bacteria to enter. If you find a cracked egg in the carton, throw it out; it is probably contaminated.

DON'T THROW THEM OUT

Make an excellent mineral plant fertilizer by drying eggshells and pulverizing them in a blender.

CRAZY, BUT IT WORKS

If an egg cracks during boiling, remove it from the water and, while it is still wet, pour a generous amount of salt over the crack. Let the egg stand for 20 seconds, then put it back into the boiling water.

SUBSTITUTIONS

- Substitute 2 egg yolks for 1 whole egg when making custards, cream pie filling, and salad dressings.
- If you come up 1 egg short when baking a cake, substitute 2 tablespoons of mayonnaise, but don't substitute for more than 1 egg.

WHO KNEW?

Eggshells are great for cleaning bottles: just break the shells and drop them in the bottle with a few drops of detergent and a bit of water, shake, and voila!

OR TRY
KRAZY GLUE

If you dampen your fingers a little before handling an egg, it will stick to your fingers and won't slip away.

JUST IN CASE SOME ONE ASKS YOU, "WHAT ARE CHALAZAE CORDS?"

The twisted strands of egg white that you find in eggs are called chalazae cords. They hold the yolk in place, and are more prominent in very fresh eggs.

TAKE THAT, MARTHA

To serve the family something different, try frying eggs in metal cookie cutters of various shapes. Just place the cutter in the pan and break the egg into it. Spray the cutter with nonfat cooking spray after placing it in the pan so the egg will be easy to remove.

NOT EXACTLY THE DA VINCI CODE, BUT PRETTY COOL

Before eggs are graded they are "candled." This means that the egg is viewed by passing it in front of an intense light that allows the inspector to see through the shell. If a cloud of white obscures the yolk, the egg is very fresh. If the air pocket at the base of the egg is about the size of a dime, this is also an indication the egg is fresh. Grade AA eggs are the highest quality, and grade A are just a bit lower. Grade B eggs are seldom available in stores; they are used in egg products.

Grading is voluntary. All graded eggs have an expiration date on the carton. The date is 30 days or less from the day the eggs were packed. If there is no date, there may be a three-digit code that indicates the day the egg was packaged. The code refers to the day of the year when the egg was packaged. For example, eggs packaged on January 1 would be coded 001; those packaged on February 1 would be coded 032, because there are 31 days in January. Use eggs within five weeks of purchase.

THIS IS PROGRESS?

In 2006 the chicken population in the United States totaled about 289 million, which means that there are more chickens than people. In 1800, chickens only laid 15 to 20 eggs a year, while they strolled around the barnyard pecking and scratching and generally living a natural chicken lifestyle. Now the fowl are cooped up in temperature-controlled warehouses, fed a special diet, not allowed to move about, and forced to lay egg after egg to produce 300 to 325 eggs per year. Each breeder house holds 50,000 to 125,000 chickens and 900 roosters to keep the chickens productive. The record number of eggs laid by a cooped up chicken in a single year is 371, established by the University of Missouri College of Agriculture. The larger chicken farms produce 250,000 eggs per day. Americans consumed about 260 eggs per person in 2005, down from 332 in 1944, as a result of all the negative information about cholesterol disseminated by the medical community.

HOW OLD IS THAT EGG?

Fill a small, deep bowl about three-quarters full with cold water. Gently drop in an egg. If it sinks to the bottom and lies on its side, it's fresh. If the egg stays on the bottom at a 45-degree angle, it is three to five days old. If it stays on the bottom and stands straight up, it is 10 to 12 days old. But if the egg floats to the top, it is bad and should be thrown away. Older eggs are more buoyant because the yolk and white have lost moisture and the air pocket gets larger. Eggshells are porous, and moisture evaporates through them.

WHO KNEW?

When poaching eggs, try adding a bit of white vinegar to the water. It helps the eggs set and prevents the 'streamers' of egg white from moving.

THE SHELF LIFE OF AN EGG

The refrigerator shelf life of eggs is about five weeks from the time you buy them. For longest life, and to avoid the absorption of refrigerator odors, always store eggs in their original carton on an inside shelf of the refrigerator. Never store them on the door.

COOL DOWN

Boiled eggs should be cooled at room temperature before refrigerating them in an open bowl.

THE BEST EVER OMELET

To make a great omelet, be sure the eggs are at room temperature (take them out of the fridge 30 minutes beforehand). Cold eggs are too stiff to make a fluffy omelet. Also, try adding a pinch of water instead of milk. The water increases the volume of the eggs at least three times more than would the milk. The coagulated proteins hold in the liquid, resulting in a moist omelet.

HARMLESS BUT KIND OF GROSS

When eggs are overheated or overcooked, they undergo a chemical change that causes the sulfur in the egg to combine with the iron in the yolk and form the harmless chemical ferrous sulfide, which forms a green ring around the yolk. This reaction is more prevalent in older eggs, in which the elements are more easily released. To avoid this reaction, do not cook eggs for more than 12 to 15 minutes, put the cooked eggs immediately cold water, and peel them as soon as possible.

WHO KNEW?

The fastest way to chop eggs is to peel them, place in a bowl, and chop with a pizza cutter.

WHY EGGS CRACK WHEN BOILED

A newly laid egg is very warm. As it cools down, the yolk and white cool and shrink, resulting in an air pocket at the large (nontapered) end. This air pocket tends to expand as the egg is heated during boiling, and the gas has no place to go except out of the shell, which can crack. When this occurs, the albumen escapes and solidifies almost immediately in the boiling water. To avoid cracks, bring eggs to a gentle—not vigorous—boil.

JUST WHAT IS AN EGG WASH?

It's a mixture of an egg or egg white beaten with milk, cream, or water. The egg wash is then brushed over baked goods before they are baked to help the tops brown more evenly and give them a shiny, crisp finish. It is also used to hold toppings on rolls and other baked goods.

USE A COPPER BOWL

Always use a copper bowl to beat egg whites. The copper will release ions during the beating process that cause the protein in the whites to become more stable. The next best material to use is stainless steel; however, you will need to add a pinch of cream of tartar to stabilize the whites. Whatever bowl you choose, make sure it has a rounded bottom to ensure that all the mixture comes into contact with the mixing blades. Also, be sure there is not even a trace of egg yolk in your whites. The slightest hint of fat will prevent the whites from beating properly.

SKIN SECRETS

When milk is heated, water on the surface evaporates, which causes the proteins there to concentrate and form a skin. When the skin forms, a number of valuable nutrients, protein among them, are lost. To minimize skin formation, cover the pan or stir the mixture rapidly for a few seconds to create a small amount of foam. Both these actions will slow the evaporation and reduce the amount of skin formation.

LOW-FAT WHIPPED CREAM?

Evaporated milk, sold in cans, is available in whole, low-fat, and nonfat varieties. It is sterilized with heat and can be stored unopened at room temperature for five or six months. Partially frozen, evaporated low-fat milk can be whipped to make a low-fat substitute for whipped cream—just remove it from the can before you freeze it. For higher peaks, add a bit of unflavored gelatin softened in water.

IN CASE YOU WONDERED

The fat in milk contains carotene, which gives the milk its yellowish color. This is why nonfat milk is whiter than whole milk.

EATING YOUR CURDS AND WHEY

Curds and whey are two proteins found in milk and milk products. The curd is actually casein and tends to be solid in form. The whey may be composed of several proteins (the most predominant being lactoglobulin), all of which are suspended in liquid. The liquid that you see on the top of yogurt or sour cream and other natural dairy products is not water but the protein whey, which should be stirred back into the product.

THEN WHY DON'T MORE OF US DRINK IT?

Goat's milk is actually more healthful than cow's milk for humans, especially infants. The protein and mineral ratio is closer to that of human milk, and goat's milk contains higher levels of niacin and thiamine (B vitamins) than cow's milk. Even the protein is of a better quality and is less likely to cause an allergic reaction.

WHO KNEW?

Store your ice cream container in a sealed plastic bag in the freezer. It will stop ice crystals from forming.

THE BIG CHEESE FACT

To soften a piece of hardened (but not moldy) cheese, submerge it in a bowl of buttermilk for one minute.

AS IF YOU'D EVER RUN OUT OF BUTTERMILK

If a baking recipe calls for buttermilk and you don't have any, you can make sour milk as a substitute. Simply put 1 tablespoon of white vinegar or lemon juice in a measuring cup, then pour in enough milk to make 1 cup. Stir a few times and let stand 5 minutes before using.

WHIP IT GOOD

Light cream can be whipped to a firm, mousse-like consistency—and will not weep—if you add 1 tablespoon of unflavored gelatin that has been dissolved in 1 tablespoon of hot water for every 2 cups of cream. After whipping, refrigerate it for two hours. Heavy cream will set up faster if you add 7 drops of lemon juice for each pint of cream.

JUST DON'T DRINK OUT OF THE CARTON

When you freeze milk, be sure to pour off a small amount from the container first to allow for some expansion.

WHO KNEW?

Never buy milk in clear containers. When exposed to light, low fat or skim milk can lose up to 70 percent of its vitamin A. Tinted or opaque containers will protect the vitamin A.

NEVER THROW MILK OUT AGAIN

Adding a teaspoon of baking soda or a pinch of salt to a carton of milk will keep it fresh for a week or so past it's expiration date. However, leaving milk at room temperature for more than 30 or 40 minutes will reduce its life span.

REMOVING...

To remove the shell from a hard-cooked egg, exert gentle pressure while rolling it around on the counter, then insert a teaspoon between the shell and the egg white and rotate it.

GOT MILK FACTS?

Milk from dairy animals was first consumed by humans about 4000 BC. Human milk is easier to digest than cow's milk, which tends to be higher in protein. Both cow and human milk protein curdles when it combines with stomach acid, but less of the protein in human milk curdles. The percentage of protein by weight in human milk is about 1 percent compared with 3.5 percent in cow's milk. Heating causes animal milk to form a looser curd, improving its digestibility.

TRY PARMALAT TO SAVE REFRIGERATOR SPACE

Europeans have been drinking milk processed at ultra-high-temperatures for years; it's now available in the United States. The processing preserves milk's nutritional value and makes it possible to store milk for two to three months without refrigeration. It's sold in boxes, often near canned milk, in many supermarkets.

YUCK

Avoid any ice cream listing ethyl vanillin on the label. This is a flavoring agent that has caused organ damage in multiple laboratory animals.

THERE'S REALLY NOTHING BETTER THAN HOMEMADE

Use these tips to achieve the best results when using an ice cream maker:

- Before you start the freezing process, chill the mixture in the refrigerator to 40°F. This will reduce the freezing time.
- If you prefer a fluffy ice cream, fill the canister only two-thirds full to allow room for expansion as air is beaten into the ice cream.

THE ICE CREAM FORMERLY KNOWN AS ICE MILK

Reduced-fat ice cream used to be called ice milk. All of a company's ice-cream products containing at least 25 percent less fat than the brand's regular ice cream may use this labeling. By law, any food labeled "low-fat" must have no more than 3 grams of fat per 4-ounce serving.

SO WATCH OUT

Never place peeled hard-boiled eggs in cool water. Eggs have a thin protective membrane that may be removed or damaged when they are peeled. If the eggs are then placed in water or in a sealed container, bacteria may begin to form.

A QUESTION TO PONDER FOR THE AGES

Have you ever wondered why cream whips and milk doesn't? The reason is that cream has a higher fat content than milk. Heavy cream must contain at least 36 percent fat, while whole milk is only 3.25 percent fat. When the cream is whipped, the fat globules cluster together in the bubble walls, forming a network that holds air.

BETTER YET, AVOID THE MICROWAVE

When you soften butter in a microwave, it often becomes a runny mess. This is because microwaves cook food from the inside out. It is best to cut the butter into pieces, put it in a glass measuring cup, heat it at 100 percent power for 30 seconds, and then stir it. It should have the consistency of whipped butter. Of course, you can expect to lose 40 percent of the flavor and aroma from microwaving. It's best just to soften butter at room temperature.

PROVING PEOPLE WILL STUDY ANYTHING

Years ago, people were told not to drink milk when they were sick because it would increase mucus production. In the last several years, the connection between milk and mucus has been studied, with interesting results. In Australia, 125 people were given chocolate-peppermint-flavored cow's milk or identically flavored nondairy soymilk, so they could not taste the difference. The people who believed that milk produced mucus reported that both beverages produced a coating on their tongue and in their mouth. They also reported that they had trouble swallowing because their saliva had thickened.

In another study, the same researchers infected a group of healthy people with a cold virus, and then tracked their dietary habits and cold symptoms. Their finding was that was that those who drank milk produced no more mucus than those who did not drink milk. The researchers concluded that milk did not produce any excess mucus, but that the sensation of excess mucus resulted from the consistency and texture of the milk.

MAKE SURE IT DOESN'T GO BAD

Every half-gallon of Grade A pasteurized milk contains tens of millions of bacteria and if left unrefrigerated, it will sour in a matter of hours. Ideally, milk should be stored at 34°F rather than at the average refrigerator temperature of 40°F. Milk should never be exposed to light, which can diminish flavor and vitamin A content in about four hours. The light actually energizes oxygen atoms that invade the carbon and hydrogen atoms in the fat through a process known as autoxidation.

DID YOU EVER WANT TO SOFTEN CHEESE?

Buttermilk can be used to soften cheese that has become too dry. Place the cheese in a shallow dish with a 1-inch layer of buttermilk, cover the dish, and refrigerate overnight.

LOW-FAT WORKS BEST

If you are low on sour cream and need to make a dip, try creaming cottage cheese in your blender.

PAY ATTENTION. THERE'S GOING TO BE A TEST ON MONDAY

Is low fat milk really low fat? Not always. If that sounds confusing, it's because the milk producers mean it to be. Here's a good example: Two-percent milk, which most people think of as low-fat, gets approximately 34 percent of its calories from fat (thus making it not a low-fat product). Whole milk is actually 3.3 percent fat by weight, or about 50 percent, while 1 percent milk gets about 23 percent of its calories from fat.

If fat content is important to you, it's best to use nonfat milk or buttermilk, which is now made from a culture of nonfat milk.

YOUR VERY OWN NONSTICK SURFACE

Before heating milk in a saucepan, spread a thin layer of unsalted butter on the bottom of the pan to keep the milk from sticking. Remember to use unsalted, since salted butter may cause the milk to stick.

I LOVE PAYING FOR AIR

Unless a recipe specifies whipped butter, it should not be used in cooking. Whipping incorporates air into butter. Whipped butter is 50 percent air by volume and is better to use on toast than in recipes because it will spread more easily.

SOUR CREAM KNOW HOW

It's easy to make sour cream. Combine 1 tablespoon lemon juice with enough evaporated whole milk to make 1 cup, and then let the mixture stand at room temperature for about 40 minutes. You can also mix ¾ cup sour milk or buttermilk with 5 tablespoons melted and cooled butter.

USE UNSALTED BUTTER IN RECIPES

The salt content of salted butter can vary from 1 to 1½ percent. If you use salted butter, taste the dish before you add salt—it may not need any. Unsalted butter tends to taste fresher than salted butter. But salt acts as a preservative, meaning that salted butter can be stored longer.

ACIDOPHILUS WHEN YOU'RE ILL

Acidophilus milk is low-fat or nonfat milk to which a bacterial culture has been added. As the milk is digested, the bacteria are released and become active, helping to maintain the balance of beneficial microorganisms in the intestinal tract. It is especially useful when taking antibiotics, as it replenishes the bacteria—especially those that produce B vitamins—which are destroyed by the medication. Other products with a similar bacteria-building effect are yogurt, buttermilk, and kefir. You can also take acidophilus in capsule form; it's available in the vitamin sections of drugstores, health food stores, and natural products stores.

A YOGURT BOOST

Live yogurts contain high levels of bone-boosting calcium and also probiotics, which improve balance in the digestive system. Low fat and natural yogurt is best.

IT MIGHT BE BEST NOT TO KNOW

Butter-flavored sprays are made from water, a small amount of soybean oil, salt, sweet cream buttermilk, gums, and flavorings. A three-second spray has 20 calories, 3 grams of fat, and no sodium.

CHEESE AWAY

Instead of throwing moldy cheese away, take a knife or cheese grater, dip it in vinegar and slice the mold off. Dip the knife in vinegar after each slice—it kills the mold and prevents it from coming back.

ALERT THE MEDIA: WE CAN STOP SCALDING

Scalding—heating milk just to the point where wisps of steam rise off before it starts to boil—destroys certain enzymes and it kills certain bacteria. However, any contemporary recipe that calls for scalded milk has been reproduced in its original form from an earlier source. Scalding is now unnecessary because pasteurization accomplishes the same thing.

CONDENSED OR EVAPORATED?

Condensed milk is not sterilized because its high (40 percent) sugar content acts as a preservative, retarding bacterial growth. The milk itself is not very appetizing and is only used as a dessert ingredient. Evaporated milk is sterilized by heating it in the can to 241°F to 244°F. The milk tends to taste burnt and can taste metallic if stored too long.

MAKE YOUR OWN MILK

You can make your own healthy low-fat buttermilk for recipes by mixing one cup (235 ml or ½ pint) of plain yogurt with either one teaspoon cream of tartar or one cup of milk and a tablespoon of vinegar.

BUT BREAST IS STILL BEST

If there is any formula left in the baby's bottle, it is best to dispose of it, because it is possible for bacteria from the baby's mouth to enter the formula through the nipple. Once the bacteria have been introduced, they will multiply to high levels.

Even if the formula is refrigerated and reheated, there may still be enough bacteria left to cause illness, especially because infants have immature immune and digestive systems. So remember: Formula bottles should be filled with just enough formula for a single feeding.

IS THAT WATER IN MY YOGURT?

Um, no. It really isn't water that collects on the top of the yogurt, it's whey—a protein that tends to liquefy easily and should be stirred back in. Use the separation to your advantage to make dips and spreads. Line a strainer with cheesecloth or a coffee filter, set it over a bowl, spoon in plain yogurt, cover with plastic, and refrigerate. The longer it stands, the thicker the yogurt becomes—after six hours it will be like sour cream; if it drains overnight it will be more like cream cheese.

WHIPPED CREAM 101

Cream whips because of the high number of fat globules it contains. As the cream is whipped, the fat globules are encompassed by air bubbles. This action produces the foam and causes the mixture to become stable. The fat globules actually cluster together within the bubble walls. The colder the ingredients and utensils, the more easily the cream will whip. Fat globules are more active and tend to cluster more rapidly at lower temperatures. The cream should actually be placed in the freezer for 10 to 15 minutes before whipping.

Adding a small amount of dissolved gelatin to the mixture will help stabilize the bubble walls so the mixture will hold up better. Sugar should never be added at the start of the whipping process; it will interfere with the clumping of the proteins and will decrease the total volume of the final product. Always stop beating at the point when the cream becomes stiffest. If small lumps appear in your whipping cream, you have over-beaten, and the cream is turning to butter. At that point, there is really nothing you can do to save the situation except to spread the butter on your toast and start with a new batch of cream.

CAN BUTTER GO RANCID?

You bet. Oxidation will take its toll on butter just as it does on any other fat. Oxygen reacts with unsaturated fats, causing rancidity. To maintain its freshness as long as possible, butter should always be kept tightly wrapped in the refrigerator or freezer.

BETTER BUTTER

Where you store butter will affect how long it lasts. Butter tends to absorb odors and flavors more rapidly than any other food. If you store it near onions, it will have an onion smell. If it's around fish, it will smell fishy, and so on. If butter is refrigerated, it will retain its flavor for about three weeks, after which time it starts losing flavor fairly fast. Date the package to be sure you're getting the most flavor from your butter. To freeze butter, wrap it in two layers of plastic, and then in foil to keep it from absorbing freezer odors. It will last for six months if fresh, when frozen; it must be kept at 0°F.

CANOLA OIL OR CLARIFIED BUTTER: YOU MAKE THE CALL

When butter is heated, the protein in the milk solids goes through a change that causes the butter to burn and scorch easily. A small amount of canola oil added to the butter will raise the smoke point and slow down this process. However, if you use clarified butter—butter from which the protein and water have been removed—you can cook foods at higher temperatures. You can also store it longer than standard butter.

IS 'DECURDLE' A WORD?

If your milk-based sauce curdles, whirl the sauce in a blender for a few seconds.

HOW TO GUARANTEE CREAMY CUSTARD

The formula for basic custard calls for 1 egg, 1 cup of milk, and 2 tablespoons of granulated sugar. For richer custard, add 2 to 3 egg yolks (which will increase the fat and cholesterol significantly). For a custard that is creamy rather than solid, stir the mixture continuously over low heat to keep the protein from setting too quickly.

The milk is not the main protein source in custard, but it contributes fats that separate the egg proteins from one another, allowing the custard to coagulate at a higher temperature, thus reducing the possibility of curdling. Never replace the milk with water, because your custard will not set. The milk and sugar also impede the bonding of the egg proteins, thus promoting tenderness. Never try to speed up the cooking process by increasing the heat. Making the perfect custard takes time and patience.

STORING DAIRY PRODUCTS

All dairy products are very perishable. The optimal refrigeration is actually just over 32°F; however, few refrigerators are ever set that low or hold that low a temperature. Most home refrigerators remain around 40°F, and the temperature rises every time the door is opened. Store milk on an inside shelf—never on the door—toward the back of the refrigerator.

CREAM OF THE CROP

Cream comes from the fat that rises to the surface of nonhomogenized milk. The larger supermarkets generally carry four varieties of cream: half-and-half, which is the lightest and contains between 10.5 to 18 percent milk fat; light cream, with between 18 and 30 percent milk fat; then light whipping cream, which is between 30 and 36 percent milk fat; and finally, heavy whipping cream, with at least 36 percent milk fat. By contrast, whole milk contains only 3.25 percent milk fat.

HOW TO SAVE YOUR CREAM

If cream begins to develop an odor, try mixing in $^1/_8$ teaspoon of baking soda. The baking soda will neutralize the lactic acid that is causing the souring in the cream. Before you use the cream, however, taste it to be sure the flavor is still acceptable.

THE BUTTER GRADING SYSTEM

The butterfat content of any product labeled "butter" must be 80 percent. A natural coloring agent called annatto is added to some butter to give it a deep yellow color. The USDA grades butter by taste, color, aroma, texture, and body. Grading is done on a point system, with 100 being the best. Grade AA must have received at least 93 points, Grade A at least 92, and Grade B a minimum of 90 points. Salt is added to some butter to increase its shelf life.

THINK OF IT AS A NICE STICK OF FAT

Stick margarine must contain no less than 80 percent fat, along with water, milk solids, salt, preservatives, emulsifiers, artificial colors, and flavorings. The fat may be composed of tropical oils, which are high in saturated fat, or polyunsaturated oils. Better-quality margarines use corn or safflower oil. Tub margarines are the same formulation as stick margarines, but they have had air mechanically incorporated into them. They still contain salt as well as artificial flavorings and preservatives. Liquid margarines are composed entirely of polyunsaturated fat and will not harden in the refrigerator. Light or diet margarines vary from 40 to 60 percent fat content and have more air and water added along with the preservatives, salt, and flavorings.

SKIM ON THE MILK

Each time you swap 1 cup of skimmed milk for one of whole milk, you'll save 70 calories. Based on one serving a day, at the end of the year you will save more than 25,000 calories and potentially lose 7 lb.

HEALTHY INSIDE AND OUT

Low-fat organic yogurt is not only rich in vitamin A which is needed to boost cell regeneration, but also contains acidophilus, the 'live' bacteria that is good for the gut. A boost of vitamin A accompanied by a healthy digestive system will surely be reflected in a fabulous skin tone.

BE A GOOD EGG

Vegetarians who don't eat meat or fish should try to include eggs in their diet as a regular feature as these are the only other source of the amino acid L-Lysine, which has been shown to work with vitamin C to reduce damage to arteries.

HOW TO IMPRESS AND ANNOY YOUR FRIENDS

It's easy to make butter at home, especially if you have a food processor. Freeze the bowl and metal blade for 20 minutes. Measure 2 cups of cold heavy whipping cream (try to use pasteurized, not ultra pasteurized) into the bowl and process three to five minutes, scraping down the sides to make sure all the cream is incorporated. Continue processing until all the solids are separated from the liquid. Then pour off the liquid, which is the whey. (Save the whey and use it in place of milk in bread, biscuit, or pancake recipes.) The butter must be refrigerated and used within three to four days. Two cups of cream will make about 6 to 7 ounces of butter.

A FRESH FEEL FOR EGGS

'Country-fresh' eggs, accompanied by a nice picture of hens running around in the sunshine, could come from caged battery-farmed hens that have never seen natural daylight. The same applies to eggs labeled as 'farmhouse', 'farm fresh', 'selected' and 'traditional'. The only way you can be sure is to choose free range and/or organic.

GRATE, FINE

It's the fat in cheese that helps it melt uniformly – low-fat varieties often melt in patches or take much longer. To make sure your low-fat cheese melts properly, grate it first using the fine side of your grater.

EGG ON

When poaching eggs, always add a tablespoon or two of white vinegar to the water, to keep the egg whites from spreading.

SAY CHEESE

If you swap 1 oz reduced-fat cheese (90 calories) for 1 oz regular cheese (115 calories), you'll save 25 calories. And if you swap it for fat-free cheese you'll save 75 calories per ounce – perfect for sauces or pizza where the taste of the cheese isn't paramount.

COOK UP AN OMELETTE

If you've only got a few minutes for supper, an omelette with vegetables like spinach, onion and broccoli makes a quick healthy meal. Use lots of vegetables and just enough egg to hold it together, then add salad for an extra health boost.

NEVER EAT A SOFT-BOILED EGG WITH A SILVER SPOON

Not only will the spoon tarnish quickly, but the reaction of the egg and the silver can leave a foul taste in your mouth.

THE MIGHTY EGG

Don't throw out the water when you're done boiling your Easter eggs—it's full of minerals. After the water has cooled, feed it to your houseplants instead of buying expensive plant foods.

CRACK-FREE

To prevent eggshells from cracking, add a pinch of salt to the water before hard-boiling the eggs.

SWALLOW SOME SOY

If you're worried about cholesterol, add some soy to your diet. It's been shown in some tests that it boosts omega-3 fatty acids and strengthens the immune system, as well as reduces cholesterol in the bloodstream.

ADD THE FLUFF

For the fluffiest egg whites, add a pinch of salt before whipping, and always use a copper bowl. Also, bring the eggs to room temperature before whipping.

LIKE CLOUDS

For the fluffiest omelets ever, add ½ teaspoon baking soda for every three eggs.

"CHEESY" CLEANING

The easiest way to clean a cheese grater (usually a nasty job) is to spray it with vegetable oil beforehand. Afterwards, rub the crusty heel from a stale loaf of French bread over the dirty end, and your cleanup will be a snap.

REFRIGERATE BEFORE YOU GRATE

It's easier to grate Cheddar cheese if you place it in the freezer for ten to fifteen minutes before grating. And don't even use a grater on soft cheese. Just push them through a colander with a potato masher.

HOT ALERT!

Always use low heat when cooking cheese, and remember, when it's melted, it's cooked and needs to be removed from the heat. Too much heat makes cheese stringy.

EGGS-TRA SAFE

Eggs don't have to be stored in the fridge. A cool place will do, especially as most recipes assume that the required eggs will be at room temperature. They should be stored, small-side down, away from strong smells because the shells are porous and can absorb strong flavors.

HOW TO PEEL AN EGG

To make the eggs easier to peel, add a small amount of salt to the water to toughen the shell. Another trick is to add a teaspoon of white vinegar to the water, which may also prevent cracking. The vinegar tends to soften the shell, allowing the interior more room for expansion.

WHAT'S THE EASIEST WAY TO MAKE A CLEAN CUT IN A CHEESECAKE?

Forget dipping the knife in hot water—just get a piece of unwaxed, unflavored dental floss, and use it to make a perfect slice. It works on all kind of cakes and soft cheese, too.

FRUITS AND VEGGIES

chapter 17

SOFT TOUCH FOR SOFT SKINS

Because they have soft skins, most fruits and vegetables easily lose their nutrients. It takes very little to bruise them or to damage their flesh—even air, light, and heat have their effects. When cooking or preparing produce, it is best to leave it in the largest possible pieces until you are ready to serve it. Exposing the surface of any fruit or vegetable will cause nutrients to be lost immediately, and the longer the surfaces are exposed, the greater the nutritional loss. Surprisingly, the vitamin C in some fruits can be completely lost in less than one hour of exposure to air.

PICKING FRUIT

When selecting fruits, try (if possible) to check the box the fruit originally was shipped in to see whether it was graded U.S. Grade No.1, or at least had a USDA stamp. To preserve the nutritional quality of frozen fruits, leave them in their original packaging material. This will reduce the risk of exposure to air, which might result in a loss of flavor and cause discoloration.

Bruised areas on fruits mean that the sensitive inner flesh has been exposed to air, oxidation has taken place, and vitamin C content has been lost. Brown discoloration of the flesh can be reduced if you slice bananas, apples, plums, and peaches with a stainless-steel knife and then either combine them with any citrus fruit or sprinkle them with lemon or pineapple juice. The citric acid from the lemon or pineapple neutralizes the effects of the oxidation.

SO BAG THE BAKING SODA

Baking soda added to the cooking water will help vegetables retain their color, but it will also cause them to lose texture and vitamins. To keep their color, cook vegetables for no more than 5 to 7 minutes.

??? WHO KNEW?

Never throw out another overripe banana! Rather, mash and freeze it, and you can use it for baking at a later date.

PECTIN, A.K.A. SOLUBLE FIBER

One of the nutritional buzzwords these days is pectin. Studies report that pectin, also called soluble fiber, has the ability to lower LDL (bad cholesterol) levels and is being used to treat bowel diseases. These studies may well be valid, and pectin supplement sales are on the rise. However, there are many natural sources for pectin. Here are a few of the better ones.

Pectin Levels in Certain Foods (in grams)		
FOOD	QUANTITY	PECTIN
Soybeans	1 cup, cooked	2.6
Figs	5 fruits, dried	2.3
Orange	1 medium	2.2
Chestnuts	1 ounce, dried	2.1
Pear	1 medium	1.8
Potato	1 medium	1.8
Sweet potato	½ cup, mashed	1.3
Brussels sprouts	½ cup, cooked	1.1
Apple	1 medium	1.1
Papaya	½ fruit	1.1
Broccoli	½ cup	1.0
Banana	1 medium	1.0
Strawberries	1 cup	0.9
Tomato	1 medium	0.9
Lima beans	½ cup, cooked	0.9
Hazelnuts	1 ounce, raw	0.9
Carrot	1 medium	0.8
Pistachios	1 ounce	0.8
Peach	1 medium	0.7
Peas	½ cup, cooked	0.6
Almonds	1 ounce	0.6
Walnuts	1 ounce	0.6
Green beans	½ cup, boiled	0.5
Summer squash	½ cup, boiled	0.5
Grapefruit	½ medium	0.3
Spinach	½ cup, raw	0.2

GO BANANAS

For an energy boost to help you through a late-afternoon dip in energy, choose a banana. They're packed with potassium for extra energy.

DON'T THROW OUT OVERRIPE BANANAS

Mash and freeze them in one-cup portions for the next time you make banana bread.

FOR A QUICK RIPE

To ripen avocados and bananas quickly, close them in a brown paper bag with an apple for a few days.

THEY'RE JUST NOT AS GOOD

Some varieties of vegetable seeds sold in garden catalogs were developed for commercial growers, not home gardeners. Avoid varieties that stress "firm" or "long shelf life."

TO REFRIGERATE OR NOT?

The majority of fruits and vegetables handle cold fairly well. Naturally enough, the exceptions are tropical fruits, whose cells are just not used to the cold. Bananas will suffer cell damage and release a skin-browning chemical, avocados don't ripen when stored below 45°F, and oranges will develop brown-spotted skin. These fruits (bananas, avocados, and all citrus), as well as squash, tomatoes, cucumbers, melons, bell peppers, and pineapples, are best stored at 50°F. Most other vegetables, including lettuce, carrots, and cabbage, prefer 32°F. Humidity is also an important factor, and most fruits and vegetables should be stored in the refrigerator crisper bins, which will prevent them from drying out.

ICE HELPS

Any salad that has a dairy product in a dressing should be kept cold. The easiest method is to place a larger bowl with ice or dry ice under the food dish. This will keep the salad cold enough so bacteria growth will be slowed while it is out of the refrigerator.

ALWAYS STORE YOUR APPLES IN THE REFRIGERATOR

They'll last five times as long than if you leave them at room temperature. Keep them in a plastic bag, or they can speed up the ripening process of the other items in the your produce drawer.

KEEP TOMATOES OUT

Don't put tomatoes in the fridge, which stops the ripening process. Keep them stem-side down in a cool place, spaced so that they're not touching.

HOW TO STOP FRUIT FROM BROWNING

Fruits contain a phenolic compound that turns the exposed flesh brown when the fruit's skin is broken by cutting or biting into it. This happens fairly rapidly, especially to apples, bananas, pears, potatoes, and avocados. The browning is caused by the enzyme polyphenoloxidase, which causes the phenolic compound in the cells to oxidize. This is similar to the action that occurs when your skin is exposed to the sun's rays. (Citrus fruits and melons lack the enzyme, but if these fruits are allowed to sit out with their flesh exposed to oxygen for any length of time, they will turn brown through normal oxidation.)

The browning can be slowed down by refrigerating the fruit at 40°F. Salt will also slow down the enzyme but will negatively affect the flavor. Placing the fruit in cold water will slow the process by keeping the surface from the air. Brushing lemon juice on the cut surface or dipping the fruit in acidulated water (water mixed with lemon juice or vinegar) also works.

THE BROWN BAG TRICK

Fruit normally gives off ethylene gas, which hastens ripening. Some fruits give off more gas than others and ripen faster. Other fruits are picked before they are ripe and need a bit of help. If an unripe fruit is placed in a brown paper bag, the ethylene gas it gives off does not dissipate into the air but is trapped and concentrated, causing the fruit to ripen faster.

?? WHO KNEW?

The easiest way to peel tomatoes? Place them in a bowl of boiling water for a minute and the skins practically fall off.

SHAVE THIS FRUIT

The rambutan is oval, about three to four inches long, crimson red—and is covered with what looks like hair. The name of the fruit comes from the Malayan word for hairy. The skin, however, is harmless and peels off easily, and the fruit is usually sold in cans; look for it in Asian markets. Its taste is slightly acidic, like a grape.

GLASS BOTTLES ARE BEST

The methods of preparation and packaging will determine the level of vitamin C that remains in a commercial juice. Frozen orange juice loses only about 2 percent of its vitamin C over three months of home-freezer storage. If the juice is sold in glass bottles, it will retain almost 100 percent of its vitamin C; however, if it is stored in plastic or waxed cardboard containers, oxygen will pass through the container and reduce the potency of the vitamin C over time. Your best bet is to buy fresh-squeezed orange juice, if possible.

PRUNES: YOU BET THEY WORK

Do prunes really help relieve constipation? Uh-huh. Prunes contain the organic chemical dihydroxyphenyl istatin, which is a relative of another compound, bisacodyl, that is the active ingredient in some over-the-counter laxatives. Bisacodyl tends to increase the secretion of fluids in the bowel and will stimulate contractions of the intestines, thereby pushing waste material on its way. Prunes are also a good source of minerals, and a natural laxative is almost always better for you than a laboratory-produced chemical concoction.

TRY BABÁCO AS A MEAT TENDERIZER

A recent arrival in supermarkets is the tropical fruit babáco, which is indigenous to Ecuador. A relative of papaya, it has a golden-yellow skin when ripe and pale yellow flesh. Unlike papaya, the babáco has no pips, and the skin is edible. Babáco is high in vitamin C, has low sugar content, and contains the enzyme papain that is used as a meat tenderizer.

IT'LL FRIGHTEN THE KIDS

The largest fruit known to exist is the jackfruit. It can measure up to three feet long and 20 inches across and can weigh up to 100 pounds. It has a hard, green-colored skin with pointed warts and large seeds that can be roasted and taste similar to chestnuts. The seeds are high in calcium and contain protein. Jackfruit is indigenous to India and East Africa.

YOUR 'GEE WHIZ' FACT OF THE DAY

The largest watermelon that has ever been grown weighed in at 262 pounds. The world's longest zucchini grew to almost 70 inches. The world's largest squash was 654 pounds. The largest cabbage was 123 pounds. The world's largest lemon was 5 pounds, 13 ounces, and the world's largest tomato tipped the scales at 4 pounds, 4 ounces.

COVERT VEGETABLES

If your kids won't eat their vegetables, try pureeing carrots, corn, or broccoli into your spaghetti sauce before serving, and they might just go for it. That's assuming they eat spaghetti at all, and are not on a strict chicken fingers and French fries diet.

MAKING A FRUIT SALAD FOR TOMORROW'S PICNIC?

Fill a spray bottle with water and a few dissolved vitamin C tablets and spray on the cut fruit. The salad will turn brown much more slowly once it's sprayed.

As more and more produce is being imported to the U.S., more outbreaks of food-borne illnesses are reported, especially those relating to the strain of bacteria called E. coli 0157:H7. This often deadly strain of bacteria usually results from the fecal contamination of meat during slaughtering and processing, but is now showing up on vegetables and fruits. Salmonella has also been found on melons and tomatoes, and other dangerous bacteria have been found on cabbage and mushrooms. In one instance, more than 245 people in 30 states became ill from eating cantaloupe. Seventy percent of all produce is now imported from developing nations.

When buying fresh produce, make sure you purchase only as much as you need for a short period. If bacteria are present in or on the fruit, the longer you store the produce, the more the bacteria will multiply. Always wash your hands before handling produce, and then wash the produce thoroughly using a clean vegetable brush before cutting it with a knife. Alternatively, use an organic produce cleaner, which can be found in many supermarkets.

?•?? WHO KNEW?

Wrap celery in aluminum foil, and store it in the fridge: it will last for weeks and weeks.

ALWAYS ADD SUGAR

To avoid mushy fruit when cooking, always add sugar to the cooking syrup. The sugar will draw some of the fluid back into the cells to maintain equilibrium in the sugar concentration. The fruit will retain a more desirable and appealing texture.

JUST THINK OF IT AS NATURE'S CEMENT

Many a cook still believes that preserves acquire their smooth, semi-solid consistency from the amount of sugar added to the fruit. Actually, the consistency is also controlled by the level of pectin extracted from the cell walls of the fruit. Pectin is similar to cement in that it holds the cell walls together and forms a string-like network that traps liquids and converts them into solids. A number of fruits, such as grapes and a few varieties of berries, contain enough pectin to gel on their own. Other fruits, including apricots, peaches, and cherries, need additional pectin to gel.

Commercial pectin used for home preserving is derived from apples or the white layer just under the skin of citrus fruits. In making preserves, the balance between sugar and pectin is very delicate. The optimum pH is between 2.8 and 3.4. Pectin concentration should be no more than 0.5 to 1.0 percent, with a sugar concentration of no more than 60 to 65 percent. Because of these exacting percentages, it is best to follow your recipe to the letter. Reduced-calorie preserves are made with a special pectin that contains calcium ions and gels, and they use very little sugar.

YUCK

Never wrap acidic fruits such as lemons, oranges, tomatoes, and grapefruits in aluminum foil. A chemical reaction may take place that will corrode the foil. A common method of preparing meat loaf is to place tomato sauce on top while the meat is cooking and then cover it with foil, but tomato sauce or paste can eat right through the foil.

SEPARATE BUT EQUAL

Whether you or a clerk bags your groceries, be sure that produce and meats (including poultry and fish) are in separate bags. Meat packaging can leak and might contaminate the produce.

THE EASIEST WAY TO PEEL

Peeling thin-skinned fruits like peaches, tomatoes, plums, or nectarines will be easier if you first place them in a bowl, cover them with boiling water, and allow them to stand for 1 to 2 minutes. You'll be able to remove the skin with a sharp paring knife. You can also spear the food with a fork and hold it about 6 inches above a gas flame until the skin cracks.

Peeling thick-skinned fruits or vegetables is much easier. Simply cut a small portion of the peel from the top and bottom, set the food on an acrylic cutting board, and then remove the balance of the peel in strips, working from top to bottom.

ZESTY FRUIT

The rind of a citrus fruit is made of bitter white pith and a thin zest, which is the outermost layer. The zest contains flavorful aromatic oils and is often called for in recipes. The tool used to remove that outer rind without any of the bitter white pith is called a zester. It has tiny holes that peel off the zest in thin strips.

AND THE KIDS WILL LOVE IT

Grate the zest from an orange and mix it with orange juice and light sour cream to create a tasty dressing for fruits.

COLOR ME RED

It's easy to ripen fresh-picked green tomatoes in a hurry. Just store them with a ripe apple in a closed brown paper bag for a few days, and the tomatoes will turn red.

STEM SECRET

Always store your tomatoes stem side down. They'll last longer that way.

AND WHO HASN'T HAD THIS PROBLEM?

If you have problems getting fruit jelly to set, pour the jelly back into the pot and cook it again until it reaches 220°F. Be sure to resterilize the jars and use new lids.

DRIED FRUIT FACTS TO KNOW AND LOVE

- Vitamin C is lost when fruits are dried or dehydrated. However, most other vitamins and minerals are retained.
- The sulfites commonly used to preserve dried fruits may cause an allergic reaction in susceptible individuals.
- Dried fruits are graded Extra Fancy, Fancy, Extra Choice, Choice, and Standard, based on size, color, and water content.
- If frozen in a liquid, dried fruits should be thawed in the same liquid to retain their flavor.
- If you store dried fruits in airtight containers they will keep for up to one month at room temperature. If placed in a cool, dry location or refrigerated, they will last for about one year.
- Refrigeration places the cells of dried fruits in a state of suspended animation, which helps preserve their flavor. For best taste, allow cold fruit to stand at room temperature for about 30 minutes before eating it.

BUTTER IN JELLY?

If you add a small pat of butter when cooking fruits for preserves and jellies, there will be no foam to skim off the top. The fat acts as a sealant and prevents the air from rising and accumulating on top as foam. For safety's sake, always make jellies and preserves in a large pot. Boiling-hot, sugary fruit can be a dangerous mess if it boils over a too-small pan.

??? **WHO KNEW?**
Avocados contain cholesterol-lowering sterols.

ACKEE

The ackee is grown in Jamaica and is very popular throughout the Caribbean. When mature, the fruit splits open, exposing the edible white aril—the outer covering of the seed.

APPLES—ALL YOU NEED TO KNOW

- Certain varieties of apple may have a different taste at different times of year. If you buy apples in large quantities, it would be best to taste a few first. They should be firm, with no holes and no bruises, and they should have a good, even color.
- If an apple is not ripe, leave it at room temperature for a day or two, but not in direct sunlight.
- Apples will ripen very quickly at room temperature. If you are not sure of their level of ripeness, leave them out for two to three days before refrigerating them.
- Apples should be stored in the refrigerator to stop the ripening process. Wash them, dry, and place in a plastic bag. When refrigerated, apples will stay fresh for two to four weeks but risk becoming mealy.
- The ideal way to store apples is in a barrel with sawdust, in a cool, dry location. Stored this way, they will last four to six months. The apples should never touch one another.
- Apples to be frozen must first be cored, peeled, washed, and sliced. Spray them with a solution of ½ teaspoon ascorbic acid (vitamin C) mixed with 3 tablespoons of cold water and place the apple slices in a container with ½ inch of space at the top.

APPLE VARIETIES

Akane

These should be used shortly after purchasing. They have
a sweet-tart flavor, and their skin is thin and usually tender
enough so it doesn't need peeling. Akanes retain their tartness
when they are cooked. Good for eating and making applesauce.

Braeburn

These store exceptionally well. The skin is tender, and the flavor
is moderately tart. Good for eating raw, applesauce, and pie.

Cortland

Cortlands are very fragile and must be separated when
transported and stored to avoid bruising. They resist browning
better than most other apples. Normally very thin-skinned, with
a tart-sweet taste, Cortlands keep their shape well when baked.

Criterion

These should be a nice yellow color. They are very fragile,
and are difficult to handle without bruising. They resist
browning. The skin is tender, and their flavor is so sweet
they are sometimes called "candy apples." Criterions are
good for baking.

Fuji

These store well when firm. They have a tangy-sweet flavor and
retain their shape when baked. The shape is similar to that of an
Asian pear.

Gala

These apples have a tender yellow skin with light reddish stripes. They are sweet, with a hint of tartness. They hold their shape well when baked; however, they tend to lose flavor when heated. Best eaten as a snack.

Granny Smith

Grannies should be a light green color, perhaps with a slight yellow tint, but they shouldn't be intensely green. The flesh resists browning. A good all-purpose apple, they hold their shape when cooked.

Idared

This apple stores exceptionally well and becomes sweeter during storage. Idareds resemble Jonathans and have tender skin. They bake well and will retain their full flavor. A good all-purpose apple.

Jonagold

A hybrid of Jonathan and Golden Delicious, Jonagold tends to have a good sweet-tart balance and is very juicy with tender skin.

ALL YOU NEED TO KNOW ABOUT GOLDEN DELICIOUS APPLES

These will store fairly well for three to four months in a very cool location, but they spoil fast at room temperature. They should be light yellow, not greenish. Their skin is tender and the flavor is sweet. They resist browning, and they retain their shape well when baked. There are more than 150 varieties of Red and Golden Delicious apples grown worldwide, more than any other apple.

Jonathan

Grown mostly in California and harvested around mid-August, they tend to become soft and mealy very quickly. Thin-skinned, Jonathans cook tender and make a good applesauce. They do not bake well.

McIntosh

Most McIntosh are grown in British Columbia. Early harvests are mostly green with a red blush. Later harvests are good for cooking, especially applesauce, and for eating out of hand. Should be peeled before cooking, as their skin is quite tough. Good for baking.

Melrose

Grown mainly in the Pacific Northwest, these apples tend to store very well, and their flavor actually improves after one to two months of storage. They have a well-balanced, sweet but somewhat tart flavor and retain their shape well when cooked.

Mutsu

These may be sold as Crispin. They resemble a Golden Delicious but are greener and more irregular in shape. Mutsus store well and have a sweet but spicy taste with a firm, fine texture. Good for applesauce.

Newton Pippin

The color should be yellowish-green; wait until you find them a light green for the sweetest flavor. They keep their shape well when baked or used in pies and make a nice, thick applesauce.

Northern Spy

These are tart, green apples that are especially good for pies. They are excellent in all kinds of cooking and baking.

WHO KNEW?

Don't wash strawberries and until you're ready to use them. They keep better dry.

Red Delicious

May range in color from pure red to red-striped. They will store in the fridge for up to 12 months but will not last long at room temperature; the longer they are stored, the mealier they become. They are normally sweet and mellow, with just a hint of tartness. Unlike their Golden counterparts, Red Delicious apples do not cook or bake well. Good eaten out of hand.

Rhode Island Greening

These are among the best pie apples, but they are rarely available. They can be found only in October and November on the East Coast.

Rome Beauty

These do not store for long periods and become bland and mealy quickly. They are very mild and have a low acid level, which means that they brown easily. The skin is fairly thick but tender, and they are excellent for baking because they hold their shape well.

Spartan

Cannot be stored for long periods without getting mushy and mealy. They are sweet and very aromatic, but their flavor dissipates with cooking, so they are not recommended for baking.

Stayman Winesap

These tend to store well. They are crisp, with a spicy-tart flavor and a thick skin that separates easily from the flesh. Good cooking apples that retain their flavor well, they are excellent for baking and pies.

WHO KNEW?

Always submerge lemons in hot water for 15 minutes and roll them under your palm before squeezing. You'll yield twice the amount of juice that way.

FINALLY! THE DIFFERENCES BETWEEN APPLE JUICE AND CIDER REVEALED

In both products the apples are pressed and the juice extracted. Apple juice is strained, clarified, and usually pasteurized. Cider is pasteurized less frequently. Apple cider sold at roadside stands is often without the protection of pasteurization. Pasteurized cider will be slightly less flavorful, but because of potential health risks, it should be your cider of choice. Cider must be labeled as such; if it isn't, it's just apple juice in a jug.

THOSE GASSY APPLES

Never store an apple near a banana unless you wish to ripen the banana very fast. Apples tend to give off more ethylene gas than most other fruits (except green tomatoes) and will hasten the ripening of many other fruits and vegetables. Ethylene is a natural gas that all fruits and vegetables release as they ripen. In fact, it has been used for centuries to hasten the ripening of fruits and vegetables.

Ethylene increases cell membrane permeability, allowing the cell to breathe more and use the oxygen it takes in to produce carbon dioxide up to five times faster than it would ordinarily. This increased cellular activity causes the fruit or vegetable to ripen faster.

AN APPLE A DAY

Apples have been used for hundreds of years as a folk remedy for diarrhea. Raw apples contain a high level of pectin, which is one of the main ingredients in over-the-counter antidiarrheal medications.

OK, SO IT'S KIND OF A CHEAT, BUT TASTES GOOD

If apples are dry or bland, slice them and put them in a dish, and then pour cold apple juice over them and refrigerate for 30 minutes.

HOW ABOUT THEM APPLES?

If you place a whole apple in the oven and bake it, the peel will withstand the heat and retain its shape for some length of time. The peel contains insoluble cellulose, which reinforces it and keeps it intact. The flesh of the apple, however, will partially disintegrate as the water being released from the cells dissolves the pectin in its cell walls. The cells then rupture, and the apple turns to applesauce. The reason apples stay relatively firm in commercial apple pies is because of the acid sulfite bath they are given before they are frozen.

AND UNSWEETENED TASTES BETTER

Commercially prepared sweetened applesauce can contain up to 97 calories per half-cup serving; the same amount of unsweetened applesauce contains a mere 52 calories.

THINK OF IT AS BOTOX FOR APPLES

To prevent baked apples from wrinkling, peel the top third or cut a few slits in the skin to allow for expansion.

IT BEATS BOBBING FOR FRENCH FRIES

If you've ever wondered why we bob for apples and not for other fruits, here's why: Apples float because 25 percent of their volume is made up of air pockets between the cells.

IT'S THE SAME THING

Nutritionally, there is no difference between natural (unfiltered) and regular apple juice; even the fiber content is the same. However, apple juice is not high on the nutritional scale. Most varieties of apple juice contain only a small amount of natural vitamin C.

I LOVE THE TASTE OF PESTICIDES IN THE MORNING

Americans consume approximately 19 pounds of fresh apples per person annually, and another 28.2 pounds of processed apples. But take note: As many as 43 different pesticides were discovered to be present in 33 percent of all apples tested by the USDA.

AND YOU DON'T EVEN NEED A PRESCRIPTION

Researchers at Yale University recently discovered that sniffing apple spice fragrance has a calming effect on human beings. Smelling mulled cider or baked apple actually reduced anxiety attacks.

WHO KNEW?

If a recipe calls for just a few drops of lemon juice, just poke a fork in a whole lemon, and squeeze out what you need. If you then store the lemon in the refrigerator, you can use it again and again.

WHICH IS WHY MOMMA ALWAYS WANTED YOU TO EAT APPLES

Studies have shown that apples stimulate body secretions. Apples contain malic and tartaric acids, which may help to relieve disturbances of the liver and aid general digestion. Kidney stones are very rare among populations that drink unsweetened apple juice on a regular basis. The low acidity level in apples tends to stimulate gum tissue and salivary flow. Studies also indicate that consuming apples daily will reduce the severity of arthritis and asthma. The skin of the apple contains a high level of pectin, which is active in raising HDL (good cholesterol) levels.

POISON APPLES?

Apple seeds contain cyanogen, which is converted to cyanide when the seeds are damaged and an enzyme in the seeds that liberates the cyanide comes into contact with the cyanogen. Fortunately, apple seeds will pass through the digestive tract undigested. Even if a seed were to split open, the amount of cyanide released would not place you at any risk. Other fruit seeds, such as those of apricots and peaches, also contain cyanogen. Although these seeds split more easily than apple seeds do, they still do not pose any risk to a healthy person.

WHO KNEW?

The best way to keep lettuce fresh is to wrap the head in paper towels and place in a plastic zip lock bag or airtight container.

HAVE YOU EVER HAD A FRESH APRICOT?

In the United States, apricots are grown mainly on 17,000 acres in California's Santa Clara Valley. Because they are so fragile and bruise so easily, they do not travel well or last very long once they ripen. For these reasons, and because they are so difficult to transport, many people in this country have never tasted a fresh, ripe apricot.

BATTERED FRUIT

Avoid all bruised fruit, and never place a bruised piece of fruit next to an unbruised one.

WHAT A BUMMER

Dried apricots are more than 40 percent sugar. When buying dried apricots, look for the unsulfured variety if you are allergic to sulfur.

APRICOTS

- The apricot, a relative of the peach, is usually the first fruit of the summer season.
- Three fresh apricots contain enough beta-carotene to supply 25 percent of your daily requirement of vitamin A.
- Apricots were originally grown in China more than 4,000 years ago and were brought to California by the Spanish in the late 18th century.
- California is still the largest producer of apricots, with more than half the crop being canned because of their short growing season.
- Unripe apricots will ripen quickly at room temperature. Once ripe, they should be refrigerated.

WHAT'S AN ATEMOYA?

This unusual fruit is grown in Florida and is available in markets from August through October. The atemoya is pale green and should not be purchased if it is cracked. This fruit looks like an artichoke and has a cream-colored flesh that is sweet and almost fat- and sodium-free. The atemoya is an excellent source of potassium.

KIDS, DON'T TRY THIS AT HOME

To remove an avocado pit, thrust the blade of a sharp knife into the pit, twist slightly, and the pit will come right out.

AVOCADOS, FILLED WITH GOOD FAT

- Originally from Central America, avocados were first grown in the United States in the 1800s in Florida and California. California produces 90 percent of all avocados now sold. The most popular varieties are the Fuerte and Hass.
- Approximately 71 to 88 percent of the calories in avocados come from fat. However, most of the fat is monounsaturated, the same type found in olive oil and canola oil.
- Avocados are available year-round. They range in color from bright-green to purple-black. They should feel heavy for their size and be slightly firm. Avoid those with soft spots and discolorations.
- Avocados will ripen quicky if placed in a brown-paper bag and set in a warm location. They will ripen even faster if you place them in a wool sock. Refrigerate them once they are ripe, and they will keep 10 to 14 days. Pureed, they can be frozen for three to six months.

IS THAT WHAT SHARON STONE USES?

Apricots have been used topically as a folk remedy to smooth out wrinkles and lighten age spots.

IT'S NOT EASY STAYING GREEN

Do you think that leaving the avocado pit in the guacamole will prevent it from turning black? Think again. Only by wrapping the guacamole in plastic wrap can you prevent the fruit from oxidizing. Guacamole (with lemon juice) will oxidize on the surface in about 60 to 90 minutes if it is left uncovered.

BANANA FACTS YOU CAN USE

- Bananas are available year-round because they grow in a climate with no winter. They should be plump, and their skins should be free of bruises as well as brown or black spots.

- As soon as a banana ripens at room temperature, it should be stored in the refrigerator to slow down the ripening process. The skin will turn black, but this will not affect the flesh for a number of days.

- Bananas can be frozen up to six or seven months if left in their skins, but they will be a bit mushy when thawed (wait to peel them until they've thawed). Then again, a frozen banana makes a delicious treat.

- The new miniature bananas have more taste than many of the larger ones and can be used for cooking in the same manner as the full-size ones. Cinnamon and nutmeg are delicious with bananas.

- Bananas chips are not a healthful snack food because they are usually fried in oil derived from saturated fat. One ounce of fried banana chips can contain 150 calories and up to 10 grams of fat, most of which is saturated. It would be best to eat air-dried chips, if you can find them.

- Americans consume 11 billion bananas annually. The majority of the bananas being exported to the United States today are from Latin America. Uganda is the leading producer of bananas in the world.

- Although bananas are a tropical fruit, they are also grown in Iceland, in soil heated by volcanic steam vents.

WHO KNEW?

If your hands smell of garlic or onion, rub them on any stainless steel bowl, under water, and the smell will disappear. Go figure.

REPORTED HEALTH BENEFITS FROM BANANAS

Historically, potassium-rich bananas have been reported to improve conditions such as stomach ulcers, colitis, diarrhea, hemorrhoids, and even to increase energy levels. The inner surface of the banana's skin has antibacterial properties and has been used to heal burns and boils.

WHAT DO BROWN SPOTS INDICATE?

Bananas are always picked when they are green. If they are allowed to ripen on the tree they tend to lose their taste and become mealy. The sugar content starts to go up as soon as the banana is picked and increases from 2 percent to 20 percent as it ripens. The yellowier the skin becomes, the sweeter the banana. Brown spots indicate the sugar level has increased to more than 25 percent. The more brown spots, the higher the sugar.

THE RIPENING TRICK

If an avocado is too hard and you want to use it right away, try placing it in the microwave on High for 40 to 70 seconds. Prick the skin before cooking it, and flip it over halfway through. This won't ripen the avocado, but it will soften it.

REPORTED HEALTH BENEFITS FROM AVOCADOS

Avocados contain significant amounts of protein and beneficial fats, which stimulate tissue growth and regeneration.

RIPENING 101

If you wish to ripen bananas quickly, wrap them in a wet paper towel and place them in a brown-paper bag. Or place a ripe banana next to the green ones. If you keep apples and bananas in a fruit bowl on the counter, the bananas will ripen very quickly, because apples give off more ethylene gas than other fruits.

I DARE YOU TO COOK AN AVOCADO

It would be a rare event to see a recipe calling for cooked avocado. The heat will cause a reaction that releases a bitter chemical compound. When restaurants do serve avocado in a hot dish, they add it just before serving or cook it just briefly. Simply slicing an avocado releases the enzyme polyphenoloxidase, which causes it to turn brown. Ascorbic acid will neutralize or slow this reaction.

BANANA VARIETIES

Cavendish

The standard curved banana that is widely available, these are imported mainly from South America.

Manzano

Known as the finger banana, this variety tends to turn black when ripe.

Plantain

Very large, green bananas with a high starch content. These are more palatable when prepared as a vegetable. In South America, plantains are used as a starchy vegetable, much as potatoes are used in North America.

Red Banana

Usually straight instead of curved like the standard banana, these tend to turn a purplish color when ripe, and they have a sweet flavor.

WHO KNEW?

You can de-gas beans by soaking them overnight with fennel seeds. Use one teaspoon of fennel per pound of beans.

TOOTHPICK TEST

If you are not sure whether a banana is ripe, insert a toothpick in the stem end. If it comes out clean and with ease, the banana is ripe. Alternatively, look to see whether it has brown spots.

REPORTED HEALTH BENEFITS FROM BERRIES

Blackberry leaves have been used to relieve the symptoms of arthritis, weak kidneys, anemia, gout, and minor skin irritations; as a blood cleanser and antidiarrhetic; to reduce inflammations; and to alleviate menstrual disorders. Strawberries have been used effectively to cleanse the skin and blood, as well as to relieve the symptoms of asthma, gout, and arthritis, and to benefit the cardiovascular system.

BERRY IMPORTANT FACTS

All berries should be firm and brightly colored. They do not ripen after picking, should be refrigerated, and should never be allowed to dry out. For best flavor and nutritional value, berries should be used within two to three days of purchase.

- Choose only bright red strawberries and plump, firm blueberries that are light to dark blue.
- Always check the bottom of the container to be sure it is not stained from rotting or moldy berries. Mold tends to spread quickly, and you should never leave a moldy berry next to a good one.
- Never hull strawberries until after they are washed, or they will absorb too much water and become mushy and waterlogged.
- Frozen berries can be defrosted by placing them in a plastic bag and immersing them in cold water for 10 to 12 minutes.

BATTER BETTER BE THICK

If you're making a cake with a recipe that calls for berries, be sure the batter is thick enough to hold the berries in suspension. Berries added to thin batters just sink to the bottom.

HEALTHY BERRIES

Blueberries and strawberries are higher in vitamin A than most berries. Strawberries are one of the more nutritious berries, with just one cup containing only 45 calories and considerably more calcium, phosphorus, vitamin C, and potassium than blueberries and raspberries.

EASY FREEZY

Blueberries are easy to freeze. Just wash, lay them on a cookie sheet, and put in the freezer. Store them in plastic bags once they're frozen, and you'll have blueberries all year long.

CRANBERRIES

- Cranberries are usually too tart to eat raw, and are, therefore, used in making sauces, relishes, and preserves.
- Only 10 percent of the commercial crop in the United States is sold in supermarkets; the balance is made into cranberry sauce or juice.
- Canned cranberry sauce has only 14 percent of the vitamin C found in fresh berries and three times the calories.
- Cranberries contain ellagic acid, a tannin that contributes the tart, astringent taste to raw cranberries.
- When purchasing fresh cranberries, try to see whether one will bounce (another name for cranberries is bounceberries). Cranberries should be hard, bright light- to dark-red, and sealed in plastic bags. If frozen, they will keep for up to one year.

POP GOES THE CRANBERRY

Cranberries will not absorb much heat before the water inside produces enough steam to burst the berry. When a cranberry bursts, it is best to stop the cooking process; otherwise, the berries will become bitter and very tart. A teaspoon of unsalted butter added to the water for each pound of cranberries prevents boiling over by reducing the amount of foam that develops. Adding lemon juice and sugar to the cooking water will help to preserve the color.

WATER ROBBERS

When cleaning strawberries, remember to rinse them only— never soak them. They'll absorb water if you soak them for more than a few minutes.

BREADFRUIT

This fruit looks like a large melon and may weigh from two to 10 pounds. It is high in starch and vitamins and is a staple food for the Pacific Islanders. It has a greenish, scaly skin and pale-yellow flesh. When ripe, it is very sweet. Make sure you choose a relatively hard breadfruit and allow it to ripen at room temperature until it has some give when pressed. It is usually cooked and eaten as a vegetable.

OF COURSE, IT WORKS BEST IF YOU DON'T MIX IT WITH VODKA

Recently, Israeli researchers found that a substance in cranberries may interfere with the ability of bacteria to adhere to the surface of the bladder and the urinary tract. In addition, a study conducted in Boston found that people who drank 12 ounces of cranberry juice cocktail every day for six weeks had fewer bacteria and white blood cells in their urine.

REPORTED HEALTH BENEFITS FROM CRANBERRIES

In folk medicine, cranberries have been used to alleviate numerous skin disorders and liver and kidney disorders, as well as to reduce high blood pressure. They have been used extensively for more than 150 years to reduce the symptoms of urinary tract infections.

REPORTED HEALTH BENEFITS FROM CANTALOUPE

Cantaloupes have been used to lower fevers, reduce blood pressure, relieve the symptoms of arthritis, alleviate bladder problems, and maintain bowel regularity. They also can alleviate jaundice, inflammation, sunburn, and other burns.

CANTALOUPE

- Cantaloupes are at their prime between June and September. They should be round, smooth, and have a depressed scar at the stem end. Be aware that if the scar appears rough or the stem is still attached, the melon was picked too early and will not ripen well.
- The stem spot should be somewhat soft, but make sure that the melon is not soft all over.
- Cantaloupes are best if the netting of the skin is an even, yellow color with little or no green.
- Melons can be left at room temperature to ripen, but they do not ripen under refrigeration. The aroma will usually indicate if a cantaloupe is ripe and sweet. Once it reaches this point, it should be refrigerated as soon as possible.
- Whole melons will last for a week if kept refrigerated. Cut melons, wrapped in plastic and refrigerated with the seeds left in place, are best eaten within two to three days.
- One average cantaloupe will produce about 45 to 50 melon balls, or about 4 cups of diced fruit.

CARAMBOLA

The color of the skin of a ripe carambola should be golden-yellow. When sliced, the fruit yields perfect star-shaped sections. It has a sweet but somewhat tart flavor and may be purchased green and allowed to ripen at room temperature. It is an excellent source of vitamin C.

WHO KNEW?

Broccoli stalks are great when making soups. And what were you going to do with them anyway?

CHERRIES

Cherries should be stored in the refrigerator with as much humidity as possible. Under these conditions, they will keep for about four days.

For best flavor, place cherries unwashed in a plastic bag and allow them to stand at room temperature for 30 minutes before eating. If you freeze cherries, they must be pitted first and sealed airtight in a plastic bag; otherwise they will taste like almonds.

CHERRY VARIETIES

Bing

A sweet cherry that is usually very large and heart-shaped, with flesh that ranges in color from deep red to almost black. The skin is usually smooth and glossy.

Chapman

A sweet cherry. Large, round, with purplish-black flesh. Produced from a seedling of the Tartarian variety. The fruit matures early in the season.

Early Richmond

A sour cherry. Round, medium-red in color, with tender flesh and a tough, thin skin. Grown in the Midwest and eastern United States.

YOU KNOW HOW WHITE WINE TAKES OUT RED WINE STAINS?

Well, berry juice stains can usually be removed from your hands with lemon juice.

Lambert

A very large, usually round cherry with dark to very dark red flesh. Very firm and meaty.

Montmorency

A sour cherry, usually round but slightly compressed. Very juicy, with a clear, medium-red color. Excellent for pies, tarts, and jams. This is the most widely grown sour cherry in the United States.

Morello

A sour cherry. Round in shape and very deep red in color, becoming almost black. The flesh is red, tender, and somewhat tart. This variety is not grown commercially in large quantities in the United States.

Republican (Lewellan)

A sweet cherry. Small to medium-sized, heart-shaped, with crisp flesh ranging from very red to purplish-black. The juice is very dark and sweet.

Royal Ann (Napoleon or Emperor Francis)

A sweet cherry. These are heart-shaped and light golden in color. The flesh may be pink to light red. Usually firm and juicy, with excellent flavor. The light-fleshed variety is used commercially in canning.

Schmidt

Similar to a Bing cherry.

Tartarian

A sweet cherry. Very large, heart-shaped, with purplish to black flesh. Very tender and sweet, thin-skinned, and one of the most popular cherries of the mid season.

REPORTED HEALTH BENEFITS FROM CHERRIES

Cherries are very high in magnesium, iron, and silicon, making them valuable for treating arthritis and gout; cherries are also considered effective in lowering the risk of cancer, stroke and heart disease. They tend to stimulate the secretion of digestive enzymes. Numerous people have reported that consuming eight to 10 Bing cherries per day relieved their symptoms of arthritis, but this claim has not been scientifically substantiated.

PIERCING THE EYES

Coconut juice, or water (the clear liquid inside the fruit), should be removed before you crack open the fruit. First, pierce two of the three eyes with an ice pick. One hole will allow air to enter as the coconut juice comes out the other one.

To separate the outer shell from the inner meat, bake the coconut for about 15 minutes at 400°F, and then tap the shell lightly with a hammer. The moisture from the meat will try to escape in the form of steam and will establish a narrow space between the meat and the shell, separating them.

COCONUTS

Coconuts are available in many markets year-round. When choosing one, be sure that it's heavy for its size and that you can hear the sound of liquid when you shake it. If the eyes are damp, do not buy it. Coconuts can be refrigerated for up to one month, depending on how fresh they are when purchased. If you are going to grate coconut for a recipe, make sure you first place the meat in the freezer for at least 30 minutes. This will harden the meat and make it easier to grate.

DATES

- Dates contain more sugar than any other fruit; some varieties get 70 percent of their dry weight from sugar. Dates are a concentrated source of calories and should not be considered a diet food.
- Dates are classified as either soft, semisoft, or dry. Semisoft dates are the most common ones sold in the United States, and Deglet Noor is the most common semisoft variety. Two of the other popular date varieties are Zahidi and Medjool.
- A date cluster can hold between 600 and 1,700 dates and can weigh up to 25 pounds.
- Ounce for ounce, dates supply 1,144 percent more potassium than an orange and 165 percent more than a banana.
- Medjool dates will last for up to one year if refrigerated.

REPORTED HEALTH BENEFITS FROM DATES

Dates have been used in cases of anemia, to raise low blood pressure, to cure colitis, to relieve constipation and aid digestion, and to improve sexual potency. Crushed dates have been made into syrup for coughs and sore throats.

CHEF'S SECRET

When preparing onion rings, make sure you fry only a few at a time. This prevents them from sticking together and ensures even cooking.

WHO KNEW?

If your uncooked celery, carrots, or potatoes get soft and limp, put them in a bowl of water with ice cubes and set them in the refrigerator for 45 minutes. Sometimes adding a small amount of lemon juice also helps.

FIGS

Figs, one of the oldest commonly eaten fruits, are native to Asia Minor. The majority of the figs grown now are sold dried, with less than 10 percent reaching markets in their fresh form. They were brought to California by the Spaniards, and most are still grown in California. The most common variety found in supermarkets is the Calimyrna. Other varieties include Black Mission, Kadota, Brown Turkey, and Smyrna. Dried figs are very high in calories relative to their size. Figs are pollinated by a small fig wasp.

Fig concentrate is sold in health-food stores and some specialty stores. It is a syrupy, seedless puree of figs that is used as a topping for ice cream and to flavor cakes and other desserts.

AN EXCELLENT MEAT TENDERIZER

Fresh figs contain the chemical ficin, which is a proteolytic enzyme, one that is capable of breaking down proteins with an action similar to that of papain (found in papayas) or bromelain (found in pineapples).

Ficin is effective in heat ranges of 140°F to 160°F, which is the temperature range for simmering stews. If fresh figs are added to the stew, they will help tenderize the meat and will impart excellent flavor. Canned figs will not work because they are heated to very high temperatures during the sterilization process.

REPORTED HEALTH BENEFITS FROM FIGS

Figs are beneficial for curing constipation, anemia, asthma, gout, and a number of skin irritations. They also help to lower blood pressure, control cholesterol, and prevent colon cancer. Fig juice makes an excellent natural laxative and can be made into a poultice for boils.

GRAPEFRUIT

The heavier the grapefruit, the juicier it will be. Florida grapefruits are usually juicier than those from the West; however, those grown in the western United States have thicker skins, which makes them easier to peel. When refrigerated, grapefruits should last for up to two weeks. When you buy them, they should be firm and their skin should be unblemished, with no discoloration. Fruits that are somewhat pointed at the end tend to be thick-skinned and have less meat and juice.

White grapefruit has a stronger flavor than the pink variety. Grapefruits from Arizona and California are at their peak from January through August; the Florida and Texas crops are best from October to June.

REPORTED HEALTH BENEFITS FROM GRAPEFRUIT

Grapefruit has been used to dissolve the inorganic calcium found in the cartilage of the joints of people with arthritis. Fresh grapefruit contains organic salicylic acid, which is the active agent in aspirin. Grapefruit also relieves cold symptoms, helps prevent cancer, reduces bruising, and helps prevent heart disease and stroke. Recent studies have shown grapefruit pectin to be effective in lowering the LDL cholesterol levels.

THE SALT SOLUTION

A small amount of salt will make a grapefruit taste sweeter.

WHO KNEW?

Always store unripe plum tomatoes at room temperature, and only use when they are deep red.

GRAPES

- The grape industry—growing table, raisin, wine, and juice grapes—is reported to be the largest single food industry in the world.
- All varieties of grapes are really berries and are native to Asia Minor, where they have been cultivated for 6,000 years. Grapes are now grown on six continents. The growing of grapes is known as viticulture. Of all the European varieties grown in the United States, California produces 97 percent and Arizona 3 percent.
- Grapes should be plump and firm and attached to a green stem. They should have good color and should never appear faded.
- Grapes do not ripen off the vine—so if possible, try and taste a grape from the bunch you have selected before you buy. But be aware that this can get you arrested in some stores.
- Grapes will stay fresh only for three to five days, even if refrigerated. They should be stored, unwashed, in a plastic bag in the coldest part of the refrigerator, but they must be washed very well before eating.
- Grapes do not freeze well because they have a high water content and would become mushy when thawed. They can, however, be eaten frozen (they're especially tasty treats), and frozen grapes can be used in cooking. They will keep in the freezer for about one year.

GRAPE VARIETIES

Black Beauty
A seedless black grape.

Calmeria
A green grape with a thick skin and a rich, tangy flavor.

Champagne

These are wonderfully sweet, tiny grapes. You're more likely to find them in gourmet food markets.

Concord

A common variety of American grape. Concords are usually blue-black with a sweet but somewhat tart flavor.

Delaware

A small pink grape with a tender skin.

Emperor

A very popular small grape. They are reddish-purple with small seeds.

Exotic

A blue-black grape with seeds.

Flame Seedless

These are deep red, seedless, and about the same size as the Emperor variety, but somewhat more tart.

Italia

Green-gold, with a sweet, full-bodied flavor. Has seeds.

Niagara

These large, amber-colored grapes may be somewhat egg-shaped and are not as sweet as most other varieties.

Perlette Seedless

A green grape grown in desert areas of California.

Queen

A large red grape that has a mild, sweet flavor.

Red Globe

A very large grape with seeds and a delicate flavor.

Red Malaga

A thick-skinned, reddish grape that is usually fairly sweet.

Ribier

One of the larger grapes. It is blue-black, with tender skin.

Ruby Seedless

A very sweet, deep-red grape.

Steuben

A blue-black grape that resembles the Concord variety.

Thompson Seedless

The most common grape sold in the U.S. and the one most commonly used to make raisins. This is a small, green grape with a sweet flavor.

Tokay

A much sweeter version of the Flame Seedless grape.

THE DRIED GRAPE

Raisins are just dried grapes and can be dried either artificially or naturally. They are sold in a number of varieties, such as:

Golden Seedless

These are produced from Thompson Seedless grapes but are somewhat tart. Sulfur dioxide is used to bleach them.

Muscat

These raisins are made from Muscat grapes and are always sun-dried. They are larger than Thompson Seedless, darker in color, and naturally very sweet.

Natural Seedless

Sun-dried, always dark brown in color, and very sweet, these are produced from Thompson Seedless grapes and are the most common variety of raisin.

Sultana

The British word for golden raisin.

Zante Currants

Produced from the black Corinth grape, these are always sun-dried and are smaller than most other grapes. They are dark and somewhat tart. Because of their size, zante currants are used mainly for baking.

PUFF THEM UP

To plump raisins, place in a small baking dish with a little water, cover, and bake in a preheated 325°F oven for 6 to 8 minutes. Or, pour boiling water over the raisins and let them stand for 10 to 15 minutes.

WATCH OUT

In Latin America, marinating raw fish in lime juice is common. The dish called ceviche is made from raw fish or shellfish marinated in lime juice. Don't believe that the acid in lime juice is strong enough to kill bacteria. Lime juice will not kill E.coli, nor will it kill any parasites that are in the fish's flesh.

HONEYDEW MELON

The best honeydews have creamy white or pale yellow skin with a slightly silky finish. They are at their prime between July and September. A faint smell usually indicates ripeness. The blossom end (opposite from the stem) should be slightly soft. Like most melons, honeydews taste better if left unrefrigerated for a few days; whole ones will keep in the refrigerator for up to five days. Store cut half-melons with their seeds intact in plastic bags and eat them within two days. Do not purchase half-melons whose seeds have been removed unless you intend to eat them the same day.

UNSTICK THOSE RAISINS

Raisins will not stick to knives and such if they are first soaked in cold water for 10 minutes.

REPORTED HEALTH BENEFITS FROM HONEYDEWS

Honeydews have been used to lower the risk of birth defects and heart disease (because of their high levels of folate) and to help keep blood pressure low (because of their potassium).

THEY LAST A LONG TIME

Raisins will last for several months if they are wrapped tightly in plastic wrap or a plastic bag and kept at room temperature. They will last for up to a year in the refrigerator if kept in a tightly sealed plastic bag.

WORKS LIKE A CHARM

Kiwi, which contains the enzyme actinidin, is an excellent meat tenderizer. Pureed fresh kiwis can be used as a marinade for any type of meat or poultry. Rub it on the meat and refrigerate it for about 30 minutes before cooking. The meat will not pick up the kiwi flavor.

Actinidin will also prevent gelatin from setting, so kiwis should not be added to gelatin dishes until just before serving; they should preferably sit on the top. Cooking the fruit, however, will inactivate the enzyme.

KIWI

- Although it is now closely connected with New Zealand, the kiwi actually originated in China and was formerly called the Chinese gooseberry. It was brought to New Zealand in 1906 and renamed for the New Zealand bird. It is also grown commercially in California, and because California and New Zealand have opposite seasons, kiwis are available year-round.

- Kiwis are two to three inches long, with a furry brown skin and lime-green flesh. They are easily peeled with a vegetable peeler.

- Firm kiwis, left at room temperature, soften and sweeten in three to five days. To ripen them more quickly, place them in a brown paper bag with an apple or a banana.

- Ripe kiwis feel like ripe peaches. Refrigerated, they stay fresh for weeks.

- Two kiwis contain as much fiber as a half cup of bran flakes, and they are an excellent source of vitamin C.

REPORTED HEALTH BENEFITS FROM LEMONS

The flesh—but not the skin—of lemons and limes is an astringent. It can be used as a diuretic, an antioxidant, and to heal cuts and bruises. It is used as a natural antiseptic to destroy harmful bacteria and as a topical agent for relief of acne and other skin irritations.

SPRAY AWAY THE BROWNS

To keep cut avocados, apples, pears or bananas from browning, just squirt on a little lemon or lime juice. The acid in the juice inhibits the growth of the enzyme that turns the fruit brown.

LEMONS AND LIMES

- Lemons and limes were probably brought to this country by one of the early explorers and were first grown in Florida in about the 16th century. The commercial lemon-growing industry was started in about 1880, and limes were first grown commercially in about 1912. California is now the largest producer of lemons in the United States.

- There are two types of lemons, the very tart and the sweet. We are more used to the tart because sweet lemons are cultivated mostly by home gardeners.

- If refrigerated in plastic bags, lemons and limes will last for 10 days. Frozen, both their juice and grated peel will last about four months.

- Look for lemons and limes with the smoothest skin and the smallest points on each end. These will have more juice and a better flavor. Also, submerging a lemon or lime in hot water for 15 minutes before squeezing it will produce almost twice as much juice. Warming a lemon in the oven for a few minutes will also work.

- If you only need a few drops of juice, puncture one end of a lemon or lime with a skewer, squeeze out the desired amount of juice, and return the fruit to the refrigerator. The hole will seal itself and the rest of the fruit will still be usable.

- Lemons and limes will keep longer in the refrigerator if you place them in a clean jar and seal the jar well. After using half of a fruit, store the other half in the freezer in a plastic bag. This reduces the loss of moisture. The texture will suffer, but you'll be able to use the juice.

- Using lemon as a flavoring tends to eliminate the craving for additional salt. Lemon and lime skins contain the oil limonene, which may cause skin irritations in susceptible people.

LAY OFF THE JUICE

Fruit juice contains 100% pure fruit juice (although it may be made from concentrate), but a 'juice drink' only has to contain 5% pure fruit juice to get its name. That's a tiny dribble in every bottle and the remainder can be water, artificial sweeteners, sugar, colors, flavorings and even thickeners.

MAMEY

Sometimes called the national fruit of Cuba, the mamey resembles a small coconut. It has a brown, suede-like skin and bright yellow flesh. The pulp is scooped out and eaten or added to milk and made into a shake.

MANGOES

- Mangoes originated in India, which is still the largest producer. Mangoes come in hundreds of varieties and a number of shapes and sizes. The majority of the mangoes sold in the United States are imported from Mexico, Central America, and Hawaii. Only about 10 percent of the commercially sold fruit is grown in Florida.
- The flavor of mangoes is somewhat of a combination of peach and pineapple, with a flowery aroma.
- Mangoes are at their peak from May to September and are an excellent source of vitamins A and C. They are also one of the best sources of beta-carotene, containing 36 percent more per serving than cantaloupes and 66 percent more per serving than apricots.
- Mangoes will last for a couple of days if refrigerated in a plastic bag. Underripe fruit can be placed in a paper bag and ripened at room temperature for a few days.

REPORTED HEALTH BENEFITS FROM MANGOES

Mangoes may help to alleviate the symptoms of kidney diseases as well as to reduce acidity and aid digestion. They are also used for reducing fevers and asthmatic symptoms, and they prevent heart disease and cancer. When crushed and made into a paste, they help to cleanse the pores of the skin.

REPORTED HEALTH BENEFITS FROM NECTARINES

Nectarines are used as a digestive aid and to relieve flatulence. They have been used to lower blood pressure and to alleviate the symptoms of arthritis.

NECTARINES

- Nectarines have been around for hundreds of years. The Greeks gave them the name nectar, from which nectarine is derived.
- There are more than 150 varieties worldwide, and California grows 98 percent of all nectarines sold in the United States. Their peak season is July and August.
- Nectarines are related to peaches. Their color should be brilliant yellow, blushed with red.
- Avoid very hard, dull-looking nectarines. If they are too hard, allow them to ripen at room temperature for a few days; the fruits will not ripen in the refrigerator.

ORANGES

- Oranges were first grown commercially in St. Augustine, Florida, in 1820. Florida now grows more citrus than any other state and still produces 70 percent of the Unites States' orange crop.
- The color of an orange does not necessarily indicate its quality, because oranges are sometimes dyed to improve their appearance. Brown spots on the skin, in fact, indicate a good-quality orange.
- Pick a sweet orange by examining the navel; those with the largest navel will usually be the best. If you place an orange in a hot oven for two to three minutes before peeling it, the pectin will melt into the flesh and no white fibers will be visible.
- Mandarins are a very close relative to the orange. They peel more easily, have more pronounced sections, and come in a number of varieties.
- The zests of citrus fruits should be stored in a tightly sealed jar and refrigerated. They may be grated and used for flavoring cakes, frostings, and cookies. However, you should remove the zest before you cut the fruit; it is very difficult to zest a citrus fruit after it has been sliced or halved.

WATCH OUT WITH ANTACIDS

If you take antacid that contains aluminum, avoid any kind of citrus juice for at least three hours. A half cup of orange juice can cause a ten-fold increase in the absorption of the aluminum from antacids. Aluminum can collect in tissues, and at high levels, it may affect your health.

THE ORANGE JUICE FIZZ RECIPE

Add ¼ teaspoon of baking soda to eight to 10 ounces of orange juice, lemonade, or any other acidic fruit drink. Stir the drink well, and it will do a great deal of fizzing. Kids love it. It will also reduce the acidity level of the drink.

GREEN IS GOOD

Oranges that look green have undergone a natural process called regreening, which occurs when a ripe orange absorbs chlorophyll pigment from the leaves. Such oranges are usually very sweet. Florida oranges are normally greener than oranges from California or Arizona because the warm Florida days and nights allow the orange to retain more of the chlorophyll. A number of companies that sell Florida oranges dye them because we tend to think they are not ripe. When oranges are dyed they must be labeled "Color Added" on the shipping container. The cooler nights in California and Arizona remove the green; however, both states have laws prohibiting adding any color to citrus fruits.

UM, AND THIS IS GOOD NEWS?

The orange-juice industry uses every bit of every orange it processes. Everything, including the pulp, seeds, and peel, is used in food products such as candy, cake mixes, and soft drinks.

REPORTED HEALTH BENEFIT FROM ORANGES

Oranges are recommended for relief of asthma, bronchitis, arthritis, and to reduce high blood pressure. They can lower the risk of heart disease and stroke, stop inflammation, and fight cancer. Drinking orange juice reduces the desire for alcohol.

FLORIDA ORANGE JUICE

ORANGE VARIETIES

Blood

Has blood-red flesh derived from anthocyanin pigments and is sweet and juicy. Blood oranges are grown in California.

Hamlin

Grown primarily in Florida and best used for juicing. The Hamlin averages 46 milligrams of vitamin C per 3.5-ounce serving.

Jaffa

Imported from Israel and similar to the Valencia, but sweeter.

Navel

A large, thick-skinned orange that is easily identified by its "belly button," located at the blossom end. It is seedless and sweet, easily peeled, and a favorite in the United States.

Parson Brown

A good juice orange from Florida. This variety averages 50 milligrams of vitamin C per 3.5-ounce serving.

Pineapple

These oranges were named for their aroma, which is similar to that of a pineapple. They are very flavorful and juicy, and average 55 milligrams of vitamin C per 3.5-ounce serving.

Temple

A sweet-tasting juice orange that averages 50 milligrams of vitamin C per 3.5-ounce serving.

Valencia

The most widely grown of any orange, Valencias are used mostly for juice. They average 50 milligrams of vitamin C per 3.5-ounce serving.

PAPAYAS

- The papaya is sometimes called the pawpaw, but they are two different fruits. Papayas are native to North America and are now grown extensively in Hawaii, the continental United States, and Mexico.
- The fruit can weigh from one-half pound to as much as 20 pounds and comes in a variety of shapes, from pear to oblong.
- Papaya seeds are edible and can be used as a garnish for fruit salads or to make salad dressings. They may also be dried, ground, and used as you would pepper.
- Hawaiian papayas are the sweetest and those most commonly found in markets. Mexican papayas are much larger and not as sweet.
- Papayas contain the enzyme papain, which is an excellent meat tenderizer. Only papayas that are not fully ripe contain sufficient papain to be useful for tenderizing; the riper the papaya, the less papain it contains. The leaves also contain this enzyme, and in Hawaii meat is commonly wrapped in papaya leaves for cooking.
- When ripe, papayas are completely yellow. They will take three to five days to ripen at room temperature.

REPORTED HEALTH BENEFITS FROM PAPAYAS

Papayas are used to reduce the risk of heart disease and cancer, and to aid digestion because the enzyme papain is also an intestinal cleanser. The juice has been used to relieve infections of the colon and has a tendency to break down mucus.

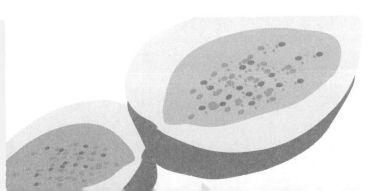

PEACHES

- Peaches are native to China. They were brought to the United States in the 1600s and planted along the eastern seaboard. They have been grown commercially in the States since the 1800s. Although the first commercial peach plantings were in Virginia, it is Georgia that has become known as the Peach State.

- To ripen peaches, place them in a box covered with newspaper or in a paper bag. The gasses they give off will be sealed in and the peaches will ripen in two to three days.

- Peaches rarely get sweeter after they are picked; they will just become softer and more edible.

- Peach skins are easily removed with a vegetable peeler. Also, you can put them in boiling water for a few seconds and the skins will peel off.

- There are two main varieties of peaches: clingstone and freestone. The clingstones are best for canning, making preserves, and general cooking. The freestones are the best for eating because the meat separates easily from the pit.

- Peaches are an excellent source of vitamin C and are available in many varieties, the favorite being the Alberta.

- Never cook peaches with the pit in, because it may impart a bitter taste to the finished dish. The reddish area around the pit may also be bitter and should be removed as well.

PEARS

- Pear trees, which were brought to the Americas by early European settlers, will live and produce for approximately 90 years.

- Pears are actually a member of the rose family.

- Pears are an excellent source of fiber.

- One medium-sized pear provides about 10 percent of the daily requirement for vitamin C—but because most of this nutrient is concentrated in the skin, pears should not be peeled before eating.

- Ripen pears by placing them in a brown-paper bag with a ripe apple for two to three days. Punch a few holes in the bag and leave it in a cool, dry spot. Apples give off ethylene gas, which will help speed the ripening of most fruits. As pears ripen, their starch content turns to sugar and they may become somewhat mealy.

PEAR VARIETIES

Anjou

A winter pear with a smooth, yellow-green skin, the Anjou is not as sweet as most other pears.

Bartlett

A summer pear and one of the most popular in the United States, accounting for 65 percent of all commercial production. The Bartlett pear is large and juicy and is best when purchased golden-yellow or allowed to ripen to that stage.

Bosc

Has a brown skin and long, tapering neck. Excellent for baking.

Comice

This is the sweetest pear and a favorite for dessert recipes. This is the pear that is usually found in gift baskets. Other pear varieties include Red Bartlett, Seckel, Asian pear, and Clapp.

REPORTED HEALTH BENEFITS FROM PEARS

Pears are excellent for constipation and as a digestive aid. They are thought to lower cholesterol, improve memory and alertness, and keep bones strong, and have also been used to cure skin irritations.

RIPEN PEACHES & PEARS

Place pears in a paper bag with a ripe apple to ripen them. Quickly ripen peaches by placing them in a box and cover them with several sheets of newspaper.

PERSIMMONS

The persimmon is a native of Japan, and is widely grown there. Persimmons are high in vitamins and minerals. The Japanese persimmons sold in the United States are Hachiya and Fuyu. The Fuyu is the smaller of the two and is shaped like a tomato. Persimmons are available in markets from October through February. They have a smooth, shiny, bright-orange skin, which is very sour and should be removed before eating.

PUCKERLESS PERSIMMONS

Persimmons are high in tannins and, therefore, very astringent. That astringency is somewhat dissipated when the fruit ripens, and the Fuyu in particular is not at all astringent when ripe. Persimmons should be very soft, almost liquid, when fully ripe. They smell luscious and sweet.

REPORTED HEALTH BENEFITS FROM PERSIMMONS

Persimmons are used to increase energy, as well as to treat stomach ulcers, intestinal worms, diarrhea, and colitis. They have also been used to treat pleurisy, sore throats, and yeast infections.

PINEAPPLE

- Pineapples originated in South America and were brought to the Hawaiian Islands for cultivation in the 1700s. The pineapple became the main crop of Hawaii and was canned there for the first time.
- Pineapples are similar to melons in that the starch, which converts to sugar as a fruit ripens, is found only in the stem until just before the fruit reaches maturity. The starch then converts to sugar and enters the fruit.
- The fruit will not become any sweeter after it is picked.
- To check for ripeness, gently pull out a leaf anywhere on the stem. If the leaf comes out easily the pineapple is ripe. It should also smell sweet.
- Pineapples are available year-round, but are best from March through July. Buy ones that are as large and heavy as possible, and be sure the leaves are deep green. Do not purchase pineapples with soft spots, and refrigerate them as soon as possible.
- Fresh pineapple contains the enzyme bromelain, which will prevent gelatin from setting. This enzyme may also be used as a meat tenderizer. Future studies may also show that bromelain is effective in reducing arterial plaque.
- Keeping a pineapple at room temperature for a few days will reduce the acidity, though the fruit will not become any sweeter.

FRUIT JUICE TO RESCUE

Take the fresh juice of an orange, sweet lime, watermelon or papaya and apply on the face as a mask. It cleanses the skin, close pores and stimulates blood circulation. And it's relaxing too!

DRIED PINEAPPLE FROM TAIWAN

Most of the dried pineapple sold in the United States is imported from Taiwan and is saturated with refined sugar. The sugar-sweetened dried pineapple will be very plump and will have a coating of sugar crystals, while the naturally sweetened dried pineapple will look somewhat mottled and fibrous, and will lack the surface crystals.

A DOUBLE BAGGER

It's likely that a watermelon is going to be the biggest food item you try to squeeze into the fridge. If you're pressed for refrigerator space, a chilled watermelon will stay cold in a double brown-paper bag for up to one hour.

REPORTED HEALTH BENEFITS FROM PINEAPPLES

Pineapples have been used to keep bones strong, to aid digestion, and to relieve symptoms of arthritis and colds, as well as to reduce the risk of heart disease and cancer.

PLUMS

- There are hundreds of varieties of plums grown worldwide. The majority of the United States' crop is the Santa Rosa variety, which was developed by Luther Burbank in 1907.
- Dried plums are prunes.
- Plums are available from May through October. Buy only firm to slightly soft plums; hard plums will not ripen well.
- The flavor of plums ranges from sweet to tart.
- To ripen plums, allow them to stand at room temperature until fairly soft. Do not place them in a window where they will be in direct sunlight, as this will dissipate what little vitamin C they have.
- Plums should be refrigerated after ripening and last for only two to three days.

REPORTED HEALTH BENEFITS FROM PLUMS

Plums are used for liver disorders and constipation, as well as to relieve flatulence and bronchitis and to heal cold sores.

ALERT THE MEDIA

The traditional English plum pudding no longer contains plums. Today this tasty steamed cake is filled with currants and raisins.

POMEGRANATE

This has always been a difficult fruit to eat. The seeds and pulp are edible (though the pulp is quite bitter), but it is best to juice the fruit to obtain its vitamins and minerals. Pomegranate juice is used to flavor grenadine syrup. Pomegranates are an excellent source of potassium and are available from October through November.

REPORTED HEALTH BENEFITS FROM POMEGRANATES

Pomegranates are used as a blood purifier and for worm infestations, especially tapeworm. They may also have some benefit for alleviating the symptoms of arthritis.

PRICKLY PEAR

The prickly pear is a type of cactus fruit. It has a green to purple-red skin and light yellow to deep-golden flesh, and is covered with spines. It has a sweet, somewhat bland taste, similar to that of watermelon, and a melon-like aroma. Other names it may go by are Indian fig and barberry fig.

SAPOTE

Also called chayote or custard apple (and, in Louisiana, mirliton), these fruits have a greenish-yellow, scaly skin and creamy, white pulp. They are a good source of vitamin A and potassium.

STAR APPLE

Also called caimito, this fruit has a skin that is usually dull purple or light green. A cross section reveals a star shape. The star apple is used in jellies and is eaten like an apple.

TANGELO

These were produced by crossing a grapefruit with a tangerine. They have pinkish-orange flesh, are nearly seedless, and are sweeter than grapefruits. Sometimes called Ugli fruit, the tangelo originated in Jamaica and is now grown in Florida. Choose a fruit that is heavy in the hand. It has a yellow, pebbly skin with green blotches that turns orange when the fruit ripens. They make excellent eating and are high in vitamin C.

WATERMELON

- The exterior of a ripe watermelon should be a smooth, waxy green, with or without stripes.
- If the watermelon has been cut, choose one with a bright, crisp, even-colored flesh. Whole melons will keep in the refrigerator for no longer than one week. Once cut, they should be kept refrigerated and covered with plastic wrap.
- A good test for ripeness is to snap your thumb and third finger against the melon; if you hear a sound like "pink" in a high tone, the melon is not ripe. If you hear "punk" in a deep, low tone, the melon is more likely to be ready to eat and should be sweet.

YUM YUM

Chow-chow is a relish made from chopped vegetables—usually cabbage, peppers, cucumbers, and onions. It is packed in a sugar-and-vinegar solution and seasoned with pickling spices. It is typically served with meats and sausages.

THE EGGPLANT OF THE MUSHROOM WORLD

Puffball mushrooms can be found dried or can be picked from the forest floor during the hot, humid, summer months. They are called the eggplant of the mushroom world because they are very large, and their flesh is similar to the eggplant's.

WHAT ARE THE BEST GREENS?

The following vegetables are listed in descending order of the nutritional value provided by a half cup cooked portion.

How Greens Rate	
VITAMIN A (IU)	
Spinach	7,371
Dandelion Greens	6,084
Kale	4,810
Turnip greens	3,959
Beet greens	3,672
Mustard greens	2,122
Arugula (raw)	237
VITAMIN C (milligrams)	
Kale	27
Turnip greens	20
Mustard greens	18
Dandelion greens	10
Spinach	9
Arugula (raw)	2
CALCIUM (milligrams)	
Turnip greens	99
Dandelion greens	73
Swiss chard	51
Kale	47
Arugula (raw)	16
IRON (milligrams)	
Spinach	3.21
Beet greens	1.37
Dandelion greens	0.94
FIBER (grams)	
Turnip greens	2.5
Spinach	2.2
Mustard greens	1.4
Kale	1.3

SOGGY SALAD DAYS ARE GONE

Avoid soggy salads by placing an inverted saucer in the bottom of the salad bowl. The excess water that is left after washing the vegetables and greens will drain under the saucer and leave the greens high and dry.

VEGGIE STORAGE SUGGESTIONS

The best way to store cooked vegetables is in tightly sealed plastic containers in the refrigerator, where they will last three to five days. To freeze cooked vegetables, seal them in an airtight freezer bag or in a container from which most of the air has been removed.

Because cells will burst when vegetables thaw, releasing some of their liquid, they will be a bit soggy when thawed, but they can be used in soups and stews. Vegetables frozen this way will last for 10 to 12 months.

REDUCE THE RISK OF STROKE

A recent study of 800 middle-aged men found that those who ate three servings of vegetables a day reduced their risk of stroke by 22 percent.

ALL IN THE FAMILY

The carrot family includes more than 3,000 species, many of which—including coriander, anise, cumin, dill, caraway, fennel, and parsley—have strongly scented, oil-rich seeds.

CHOOSING THE MOST NUTRITIOUS GREENS

Arugula

Has a slightly peppery flavor. Often used in salad blends.

Beet

Small, young leaves are best.

Dandelion

Young leaves are the best. Buy them from a reputable source to be sure they have not been exposed to weed killers.

Endive

A type of chicory that grows in a smaller, cone-shaped head. Very pale leaves, somewhat bitter flavor.

Kale

Young leaves are the best. Look for thin stems and small, frilly leaves. Best in winter.

Romaine

One of the best lettuces.

Spinach

High in nutrients, but contains oxalates.

FIDDLEHEAD FERN FACTS

The young fronds of the fiddlehead fern (also known as ostrich fern) are shaped like the scroll at the end of a violin. Fiddleheads are about two inches long and about 1½ inch in diameter. Their texture is similar to that of green beans, with a flavor somewhere between asparagus and green beans. Fiddleheads are safe to eat if cooked; they can be stir-fried or steamed, but they should never be eaten raw. Cook fiddleheads for no more than 5 minutes for best flavor and texture.

BETTER TO BE SAFE

Certain vegetables—including cabbage, cauliflower, lettuce, beets, celery, eggplant, radishes, spinach, and collard and turnip greens—contain nitrites that, when they enter the stomach, may convert to nitrosamines, which are known carcinogens. An adult with a healthy immune system will not have a problem with these foods, although they may not be recommended for infants whose intestinal tracts do not yet contain the acid-producing bacteria necessary to inhibit nitrite formation.

KALE POWER

Curly kale is a neglected super food that is full of glucosinolates that help to fight cancer. It also contains more vitamin C than oranges (vital for healthy skin and hair), along with a healthy dose of fiber.

GRADING VEGETABLES

All canned, frozen, and dried fruits and vegetables are sold in three grades: U.S. Grade A Fancy; U.S. Grade B, or Extra Standard; and U.S. Grade C Standard. Grades B and C are just as nutritious as Grade A but have more blemishes.

JUST DON'T CALL IT HEALTH FOOD

Lots of snack chips made from vegetables other than potatoes have come onto the market in the last few years, but many are no more healthful than everyday potato chips—most are fried in oil. Any fried chip will be high in calories and fat and almost devoid of nutritional value. If the chip is baked, it will have fewer calories; however, because of the high heat used in baking, the nutritional value will be significantly reduced.

STEAMING PRESERVES COLOR IN VEGETABLES

The acid that is released in vegetables during the cooking process causes a chemical reaction that results in a loss of pigment. After a while, the cooking liquid may deplete the acid and turn alkaline, changing the color of the vegetable again. In green vegetables, the acid that is released reacts with the chlorophyll, lightening the color. In red cabbage the pigment anthocyanin may change from red to purple, depending on the acid or alkaline nature of the liquid. Adding baking soda to the water will help reduce and neutralize the effects of the acid and keep some vegetables close to their natural color, but it will also destroy a number of vitamins, especially C and thiamine. The best way to make sure vegetables keep their original color is to steam them.

THINK OF THE ALTERNATIVE

When washing vegetables, place a small amount of salt in a sink full of cold water to draw out any sand and insects.

AVOID THE FROST

Frost might belong on pumpkins, but keep it off of packages of frozen vegetables. It's a sign that the food has thawed and refrozen, and a percentage of moisture has already been lost. The fact that one package of a particular product is damaged indicates there's a good chance the rest of the shipment has also deteriorated.

FRESH PRODUCE GRADING

Fresh fruits and vegetables can also be found in three grades: U.S. Fancy, U.S. Fancy #1, and U.S. Fancy #2. These grades are determined by the product's size, color, shape, maturity, and the number of visible defects.

THE JURY'S OUT

To salt the cooking water or not? Some feel that salting the water when cooking a vegetable will draw out some of the liquid; this may change the consistency, and the food may not cook evenly. Others, however, believe that salting improves the flavor of the vegetables, and that the vegetables absorb a minimal amount of salt—the sodium content will not be appreciably affected. If you do decide to cook vegetables in salted water, the proper ratio is 1 ½ tablespoons salt to 4 quarts water.

PECANS CAN HELP

Unless you really like the smell, try placing a few unshelled pecans in your saucepan when cooking kale, cabbage, or collard greens to reduce the odor. When cooking onions or cabbage, boil a small amount of vinegar in another pan to eliminate the odor. Take care you don't overcook the vegetables so they won't get odoriferous.

TODAY'S USELESS ARTICHOKE FACT

Artichokes contain the chemical cyanarin, which stimulates the taste buds that are linked to sweetness and keeps them stimulated for three to four minutes—but only in people who have a genetic predisposition to be sensitive to cyanarin. Any food that these people consume immediately after eating an artichoke will taste sweet.

MOLD HEARTS MOISTURE

It is always a good idea to line the crisper bins of your refrigerator with a few paper towels to absorb excess moisture. Mold spores love moisture.

IT MIGHT HAVE CHOKED ARTIE, BUT IT AIN'T GONNA CHOKE ME

When you eat an artichoke, remember that the part to eat is the flesh at the base of the leaf. The rest of the leaf is bitter and tough. Place the leaf in your mouth upside-down and draw it through your front teeth, removing the tender meat. After eating all the leaves, you will be left with the choke and the heart of the artichoke. Scrape way the hairy choke and eat the succulent heart with a fork.

SWEETENS THEM UP, TOO

Caramelizing vegetables will make the flavors and colors more intense. If you toss them in extra virgin olive oil and roast them in a 400°F oven for 10 to 30 minutes, they should turn a nice golden brown. The plus of caramelizing: great flavor. The minus: A big loss of nutrients.

STILL BREATHING

Wrap all produce loosely; air circulating around fruits and vegetables reduces spoilage. A sealed perforated plastic bag is ideal.

FOR A FIRMER SALAD

To crisp cut-up greens, soak them in cold water for 15 to 20 minutes.

ARTICHOKES

- The artichoke originated in Italy and was brought to the United States in the 1800s. Almost all of the artichokes sold in the United States are grown in California.

- The artichoke is actually the unopened flower bud of a thistle-like plant. The most tender and edible part is the heart or center of the plant. Artichokes tend to vary in size, but size does not indicate quality.

- There are 50 varieties, and it is best to purchase them from March through May. Choose those with compact, tightly closed heads and green, clean-looking leaves. Avoid ones that have brown leaves or show signs of mold. Leaves that are separated indicate that the artichoke is old and will be tough and bitter.

- Wear rubber gloves when working with artichokes to avoid being pricked by the sharp ends of their leaves. Artichokes should never be cooked in an aluminum pot as the metal can turn them gray.

- Artichokes should be steamed or cooked in boiling salted water; however, they are also easy to overcook. Use stainless steel knives to cut them; carbon blades tend to react with the chemicals in the artichoke and darken the flesh.

- For best flavor, add a small amount of salt to the cooking water. The artichokes will be sweeter and will retain their color better.

- Artichokes can be refrigerated in a plastic bag for up to one week.

REPORTED HEALTH BENEFITS FROM ARTICHOKES

The juice of artichoke leaves has been used as a powerful diuretic as well as to treat liver disorders and to relieve bad breath. Other uses include relieving arthritis, atherosclerosis, liver problems, memory loss, neuritis, and glandular disorders.

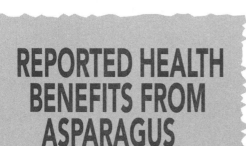

REPORTED HEALTH BENEFITS FROM ASPARAGUS

Asparagus juice has been used to break up oxalic acid crystals in the kidneys. It has also been used to alleviate symptoms of arthritis and hypertension, and as a cure for lip sores, blackheads, and constipation.

KEEP IT GREEN

When an artichoke is cooked, the chlorophyll in the leaves reacts with the acids in the artichoke and forms the compound pheophytin, which turns the leaves olive-brown. This is why many cooked artichokes have a bronze tint. Much research has been conducted to preserve the green color, but nothing has been found that really does the trick.

A few methods to try include rubbing the leaves with the cut side of a lemon after they have been trimmed, or soaking the artichokes for 20 to 30 minutes in a quart of water with 1½ tablespoons of white vinegar. The vinegar will stabilize the chemical that produces the color—and not only that, it will also improve their taste.

ASPARAGUS

- Asparagus can be traced back to ancient Greece and has been referred to as the aristocrat of vegetables. A member of the lily family, it is excellent source of vitamins and minerals.
- There are two types of asparagus: white and green. White asparagus is planted under a mound of soil that prevents the sun from reaching the vegetable, so photosynthesis cannot take place.
- Canned asparagus contains less vitamin C than fresh because the nutrient is dissipated by the heat used in the canning process and by the water in the can. If you use the water in the can in other dishes, you can retrieve some of the heat-sensitive and water-soluble nutrients.
- The stalks of large asparagus spears may be fibrous and should be peeled. Asparagus loses approximately 50 percent of its vitamin C content along with some of its sugars within two days of picking. Fresh asparagus should be eaten within a day of purchase.

- Put asparagus in a pitcher of water, then refrigerate. Refrigeration will help to retain the nutrients. As the natural sugars are lost, the asparagus becomes tougher.
- When choosing asparagus, look for stalks that are green, with compact, closed tips. Avoid flat stalks or those that contain white streaks.
- The best time of year to purchase asparagus is March through June.
- To freeze asparagus, remove the bottom 2 inches of the stalk and blanch the vegetable in boiling water for 2 to 4 minutes or steam it for 3 to 5 minutes, depending on the thickness of the stalks. Freeze it first on a tray or baking sheet before transferring it to a plastic bag to keep the tips in good condition.
- The greener—or whiter—the asparagus, the more tender it will be.
- Asparagus contains a sulfur compound that develops an unpleasant odor during the digestive process. Everyone who eats asparagus excretes this compound in their urine, but the ability to smell this odor varies from one person to the next.

THERE'S THAT ICE BATH AGAIN

Soaking them in cold water with ice cubes for 30 to 45 minutes can revive raw asparagus spears that are too limp.

ASPARAGUS S.O.S.

Asparagus is usually canned upside down; it would be wise to read the top of the can before opening it.

CHOP IT

If you've overcooked asparagus, try cutting it into small pieces and adding it to a can of creamed soup.

FOR A DIFFERENT ASPARAGUS TREAT

The flavor of fresh asparagus is one of the pleasures of spring. But if you ever want to doctor the taste, try adding a bouillon cube or a small amount of soy sauce to the cooking water.

JUST BOIL THEM

Almost all legumes, including beans, peas, and lentils, contain a substance called lectin, which can cause abdominal pain, nausea, diarrhea, and severe indigestion. To destroy the lectin, legumes must be cooked at a rolling boil for 10 minutes before lowering the heat to a simmer. Peas and lentils need to boil for only 2 to 3 minutes.

EDIBLE-POD BEANS

- Edible-pod beans are picked before they are fully ripe, as the inner seed (bean) is just starting to form. These immature seeds contain high levels of beta-carotene and vitamin C. The dried seeds are high in protein and carbohydrates.
- Bean pods may be green, purple, or yellow; the best for eating will have no scars or discolorations.
- When broken open, beans should have a crisp snap. Beans are available year-round, but are best from May through August.
- Refrigerate beans whole to retain their nutrient content. Never leave beans soaking in water.

THAT'S RIGHT, BLAME THE BEANS

After eating beans, there's often the problem of flatulence. Gas is produced by the fermentation of complex sugars called raffinose sugars, which are found in beans and some other vegetables. The small intestine does not have the proper enzyme to break down this sugar, so it passes into the large intestine, where bacteria break it down and ferment it, producing hydrogen, methane, and carbon dioxide gases.

Flatulence was first studied when it became a problem for pilots (the higher the altitude, the more gas expands). At 35,000 feet, it will expand to 5.4 times more than at sea level, causing pain and discomfort. Almost 50 percent of the gas is nitrogen, about 40 percent is carbon dioxide produced by aerobic bacteria in the intestinal tract, and the rest is a combination of methane, hydrogen sulfide, hydrogen, ammonia, and the real odor makers—indoles and skatoles. Believe it or not, in the late 1960s one of the criteria for selecting astronauts was whether they produced large amounts of gas after eating beans.

There are now gas-free lima beans, which contain less of the hard-to-digest complex sugar that causes the problem.

HOW MANY LEGUMES ARE ROASTED?

Only two legumes—soybeans and peanuts—are commonly roasted. This is because their high oil content compensates for the dryness that occurs during roasting. When roasted, both legumes change flavor and texture. The low water content and high temperature used for roasting are responsible for the browning of the outer coating.

Soak the beans for 12 hours, and then drain the water and roast slowly at 250°F until soft, stirring occasionally to avoid burning the surface before the inside is done.

THE BEST CHILI BEGINS HERE

The first secret to making chili is to soften any beans you add without having them fall apart. The cell walls have to be weakened and the starch granules have to be gelatinized. Initially, the beans are soaked in water for three to four hours. The beans are then cooked in boiling water with $\frac{1}{8}$ teaspoon of baking soda (per cup of dried beans) until they are tender but not too mushy. The texture of the beans will remain more stable if the cooking is performed in a somewhat alkaline solution. That is why you add the baking soda to the cooking water. Chili sauce is acidic, and the beans will not continue to soften after they are added to the sauce. Many cooks who try to save time rely on the acidic chili sauce to complete the cooking of the beans and end up with hard beans.

REPORTED HEALTH BENEFITS FROM POD BEANS

Pod beans have been used to alleviate hemorrhoids and to offset anemia.

POD BEAN VARIETIES

Chinese Long

These mild-tasting beans can grow as long as three feet and are sometimes called yard-long beans. They are best when young and tender.

Haricots Verts

A slender variety of snap bean originally developed in France, haricots verts is French for green beans.

Italian Green

Also known as Romano beans, these have a broad, flat, bright green pod and are among the most popular for freezing.

Purple Wax

Has a dark purple pod that changes to green when cooked. Looks similar to a small, yellow wax bean.

Scarlet Runner

Has broad, flat, green pods and black-and-red speckled seeds. The blossom is also edible.

Snap

These beans have tender, crisp pods that snap in half easily. The ends are usually snapped rather than cut off. These are the familiar green beans or yellow wax beans formerly known as string beans. The string has been bred out and their name has been changed.

SHELL BEANS

These are actually mature fresh seeds that are in the development stage between fresh seeds and dried seeds. Dried beans are higher in protein, potassium, and iron. Shell beans should have a bulging, tightly closed pod. If the pods are sealed, they should last for two to three days.

SHELL BEAN VARIETIES

Cranberry

These beans have red markings on the white pods and the bean.

Fava

Similar to lima beans in taste and texture, but with longer pods. These have also been called broad beans and are popular in salads. Individual beans must be peeled.

Lima

The most common shell bean in the United States, limas originated in Peru. Almost the entire U.S. crop is used for canning or freezing. Limas are very perishable and should be used as soon as purchased. A tiny bit of salt added to the cooking water will help to bring out their flavor.

HOW LONG CAN YOU STORE THEM FOR?

Cooked pod beans have a refrigerator life of approximately three to four days. If you boil the beans whole without even removing the ends, you will retain 50 percent more of their nutrients. A very small amount of salt added to the cooking water will bring out the flavor. Baking soda added to the water will reduce the nutrient content of the beans. Acidic foods, such as tomatoes, will turn the beans a drab olive color.

HAVE YOU HAD YOUR CYANIDE TODAY?

Lima beans produce an enzyme called cyanogen, which is a form of cyanide. Some countries have laws that restrict the growing of certain varieties. European and American farmers have developed new varieties of lima beans that do not produce as much of the toxin and are safer to eat. These potentially harmful toxins may be removed by boiling the beans in a pot without a lid, allowing the hydrogen cyanide gas to escape with the steam. Neither lima beans nor their sprouts should be eaten raw.

SOYBEANS

- Usually sold dried in the United States, fresh soybeans are more popular in Asia. They are high in protein and mild in flavor. Soybeans contain the highest quality protein of all the legumes and approach meat in their amino acid balance.
- Soybeans are now the third largest crop in the United States, after wheat and corn, and are the largest source of protein meal for livestock. They are also used to make vegetable oil.
- Soybeans originated in China, and the ancient Chinese considered them one of the five sacred grams necessary for life.
- The bean has a protein content of 40 percent protein and fat content of 20 percent. The oil derived from soybeans was originally used in paints, soaps, and varnishes but was not used in foods until the process of hydrogenation was invented, making its taste more acceptable. The food industry first used soybean oil to make margarine as a replacement for butter during World War II.

SOY FOODS

Is soy the miracle food it's claimed to be? The jury is still out, but what is not in dispute is soy's list of benefits: It is an excellent source of protein, is cholesterol-free and low in saturated fat, and provides calcium, folate, omega-3 fatty acids, and compounds called isoflavones. On page 585 are a few of the most common soy products.

Tofu

Tofu is prepared by boiling soybeans in water, and then grinding the beans into a paste and adding calcium sulfate to coagulate the curd; this makes it a better source of calcium than raw soybeans. In most Japanese and Chinese tofu, however, the curd is coagulated by the addition of an acid, such as lemon juice or vinegar, rather than calcium sulfate.

The coagulated curds are compressed into blocks and stored in water under refrigeration or vacuum-packed. If you do this, the tofu will last for up to one week, and possibly two weeks beyond its sell date if it was very fresh when purchased. If you are going to freeze tofu, do it immediately after purchase, and leave the tofu in its original water and container. It can be frozen for about two months at 0°F. After it is thawed, however, it will be a little bit more fragile and will disintegrate unless added to dishes just before serving.

The proteins in tofu are 90 percent digestible, which is close to the ratio one would get from milk. Reduced-fat tofu is now available in markets.

Miso

This is a fermented soybean paste. It is high in sodium, but it is also high in protein, isoflavones, and antioxidants. Miso is most commonly used as a flavoring for soups and stews.

Soy Milk

Extracted from soybeans and consumed by people who have an allergy to cow's milk. Soy milk is usually supplemented with vitamins D and B12 and calcium. It is available flavored with carob or vanilla.

TEMPEH

Made from whole cooked soybeans that have been infused with a starter bacteria and allowed to ferment. This produces a very dense and chewy food with a nutty flavor. Tempeh can be fried, grilled, or used to make veggie burgers. It is one of the only vegetable sources of vitamin B12.

DON'T OVERCOOK!

To get the best flavor from green beans, don't overcook them. Boil or steam them for 5 to 10 minutes in salted water; if you boil them, flush them with cold water to stop the cooking.

Textured Vegetable Protein (TVP)

Made from compressed soy flour, TVP is an excellent source of calcium, and, because of its consistency, it is used as a replacement for hamburger in many recipes. Try replacing 30 to 50 percent of the ground beef with TVP next time you make meatloaf, chili, or sloppy Joes.

REPORTED HEALTH BENEFITS FROM SOY PROTEIN

Soy protein has been linked to reducing the symptoms of menopause. Soybeans have been given to athletes because of their high-quality protein.

HOW TO STORE LEGUMES

If legumes are kept in a dry spot below 70°F they will last for up to one year and retain most of their nutrient content. They may be stored in their original bag or container or transferred to a sealed glass jar. Never mix old beans with new beans, as they will not cook evenly. It is not necessary to freeze dried beans, and freezing will not help to retain their nutrient content. Cooked dishes containing beans can be frozen for up to six months, but the beans might become mushy when thawed.

THE VEGETABLE OIL SOLUTION

When cooking dried beans, add 1 tablespoon of a pure vegetable oil to the water to help prevent boil overs. Or, cook the beans in a large pot.

DON'T WORRY ABOUT THE COOKING TIME

Many people worry that beans and legumes will lose their nutrients because they must soak and cook for such a long time. Studies performed by the USDA, however, have proved that legumes, even if they require more than 1 hour of cooking, will still retain 70 to 90 percent of their vitamin content and almost 95 percent of their mineral content. The most affected were the B vitamins, of which about 45 to 50 percent were lost.

COOKING TIPS FOR BEANS

- To tell whether a bean is fully cooked, squeeze it. There should be no hard core at the center.
- Cooking the beans with an acidic ingredient, such as with tomatoes, will slow down the cooking time, and testing for tenderness is a must.
- The taste of beans is improved by adding a small amount of brown sugar or molasses at the end of cooking.

YOUR PROTEIN WINNERS

Soybeans are about the best vegetable source of protein. Lentils come next in the protein stakes, followed by split peas, navy beans, kidney beans, chickpeas, and lima beans.

PINTO BEANS

Pinto beans are an excellent source of protein. Pinto beans contain about 22 percent protein, while beef has only 18 percent and eggs 13 percent. They are speckled or have streaks of reddish brown on a pale pink background; fading is a sign of aging or long storage. Try to purchase beans of uniform size; otherwise, the smaller ones might become mushy before the larger ones are cooked. If you think this might be a problem, try adding a small amount of baking soda to the water while the beans are cooking to soften the beans.

Bean Cooking Chart		
BEAN	PRESOAK	COOKING TIME
Adzuki beans	Yes	30–40 minutes
Black beans	Yes	30–60 minutes
Black-eyed peas	No	30–60 minutes
Chickpeas (garbanzos)	Yes	1½–2 hours
Great Northern beans	Yes	1½–2 hours
Kidney beans	Yes	1½–2 hours
Lentils (green and brown)	No	20–30 minutes
Lentils (red and yellow)	No	5–8 minutes
Lima beans	Yes	50–90 minutes
Mung beans	No	1½–2 hours
Navy beans	Yes	1½–2 hours
Split peas	No	30–60 minutes
Pinto beans	Yes	50–60 minutes
Soybeans	Yes	1¾–3 hours

OFF WITH THEIR HEADS

As with any vegetable that has a leafy top, beet greens should be removed after the beets are purchased and before they are stored. The leafy tops will leach moisture from the root or bulb and shorten the vegetable's shelf life. Beet greens can be prepared like chard.

BEETS

- Beets have one of the highest sugar contents of any vegetable, but they are low in calories and are an excellent source of vitamins and minerals.

- Both the roots and the leaves are edible. It is best to buy only small or medium-sized beets, as the larger ones are not very tender and may have a stronger flavor. Never purchase beets that are shriveled or flabby.

- Beet greens should be used as soon as they are purchased and the roots within seven to 10 days.

- Cook beets whole and unpeeled to retain their nutrients. Beets contain the chemical pigment betacyanin, which gives them their red color. Some 15 percent of the population can't metabolize this pigment; though it's harmless, it will turn their feces and urine red for a few days.

JUST LIKE THE MORNING CEREAL OUR KIDS EAT

A two-pound standard beet contains 14 teaspoons sugar. Sugar beets are 20 percent sucrose by weight and have twice the sugar content of standard beets. It takes 100 pounds of sugar beets to produce five pounds of sugar.

THEY'RE GREAT, BUT BOY DO THEY STAIN

Disposable rubber gloves are recommended when working with beets. Be aware that they will lose some of their color and turn the other foods red when cooked.

REPORTED HEALTH BENEFITS FROM BEETS

Beets have been used to relieve coughing, fever, glandular swelling, headaches, and toothaches. Two pounds of raw mashed beets consumed daily have been used to treat tumors and leukemia. Beet greens have higher iron content than spinach and have been used to treat anemia.

BROCCOLI

A member of the cruciferous family of vegetables that also includes cabbage and Brussels sprouts, broccoli was first grown in United States in the 1920s and is one of the more nutritious vegetables. It will have a higher nutrient content if eaten fresh.

- Cooked broccoli still contains 15 percent more vitamin C than an orange.

- Broccoli is available year-round, but is best from October through May. The stems should not be too thick and the leaves should not be wilted. The florets of broccoli should be closed and a good, solid green. If the buds are open or yellow, the broccoli is old and will have lost a significant amount of its nutrient content. The florets of broccoli contain eight times more beta-carotene than the stalks.

- One cup of broccoli contains 271 percent of the Daily Value of vitamin A, 193 percent of vitamin C, 5 percent of niacin, 9 percent of calcium, 73 percent of thiamine, 57 percent of phosphorus, and 9 percent of iron. It also provides 25 percent of your daily fiber needs and even has five grams of protein.

- Broccoli should be washed in a good organic cleanser. The EPA has registered more than 50 pesticides that can be used on broccoli, and 70 percent of these cannot be detected by the FDA after harvesting. In a recent study, it was reported that 13 percent of all broccoli still retained pesticide residues even after the initial processing. Try to buy organic broccoli, or consume broccoli in moderation.

- Prepare broccoli stems for cooking by peeling them, and then cutting them into small, even pieces.

- Broccoli should be cooked as quickly as possible to retain its green color. Broccoli's color is also very sensitive to acidic foods and will turn a drab olive color if cooked in the same pot with them.

THIS REALLY STINKS

Broccoli, as well as Brussels sprouts, cabbage, and cauliflower, contains the natural chemical called isothiocyanate that, when heated, breaks down into a foul-smelling compound of hydrogen sulfide and ammonia. And take note: You should never cook these vegetables in an aluminum pot or the reaction will cause an even more intense smell. The longer you cook the vegetables, the more chemicals are released and the smellier the kitchen. Cook florets 2 to 4 minutes, the whole head for 6 to 8 minutes.

If you keep a lid on the pot and place a piece of fresh bread on the top of the vegetable, the bread will absorb some of the odor—but it may disintegrate as well. If you cook broccoli too long, the compounds will react with the chlorophyll that is responsible for its green color, and the vegetable will turn brown. Cooking broccoli in only a small amount of water will slow down this reaction.

WHERE DOES IT GO?

Broccoli should be stored in a perforated plastic bag in the refrigerator, where it will keep for three to five days before the florets start opening and it begins to lose nutrients. To freeze broccoli, remove the leaves and peel the stalks, cut the broccoli into small lengthwise strips, and blanch it for 5 minutes. Chill it, drain it well, and place it in a sealed plastic bag. It can them be frozen for 10 to 12 months at 0°F.

REPORTED HEALTH BENEFITS FROM BROCCOLI

Broccoli has been used to treat constipation, to reduce high blood pressure, and as a digestive aid.

BRUSSELS SPROUTS

This vegetable was named after the Belgian capital, where it originated. A relative of the cabbage family, it even resembles small heads of cabbage. Brussels sprouts were brought to North America from England in the 1800s. They are an excellent source of vitamins A and C.

They are easily overcooked and will become mushy. Store them in the refrigerator to prevent the leaves from turning yellow.

GET OUT YOUR KNIFE

Cut an X on the stalk end of a Brussels sprout before cooking, and the sprout will cook evenly and quickly.

REPORTED HEALTH BENEFITS FROM BRUSSELS SPROUTS

Brussels sprouts are used as a general tonic for blood cleansing, as well as to cure headaches and constipation, and to reduce hardening of the arteries.

BROCCOFLOWER, THE ODDLY NAMED HYBRID

A cross between broccoli and cauliflower, this vegetable looks like a light-green cauliflower. Its flavor is milder than that of either of its relatives. To assure maximum nutrition, make sure the florets are tightly closed.

CABBAGE

- Cabbage originated in the eastern Mediterranean region and was popular among the ancient Greeks. It is available year-round in three main varieties; red, green, and savoy, which has crinkly leaves. Avoid cabbages with worm holes, and be sure to smell the core for sweetness. Green and red cabbage should have firm tight leaves with good color. Cabbage should be refrigerated in plastic bags, where it will keep for up to two weeks.

- Cabbages, like other cruciferous vegetables, are high in a phytochemical called indoles. Because of its indole content, cabbage is being studied for its ability to prevent cancer. Initial studies indicate that if you consume half a green cabbage daily you may prevent a number of cancers.

- When making stuffed cabbage, boil the whole head, removing the cabbage from the water and taking off the leaves as they become tender. The individual leaves will come apart without tearing.

- Flatulence problems related to the consumption of cabbage can be eliminated by boiling the vegetable for 5 to 6 minutes, draining the water, and continuing to boil it in fresh water. The chemical that causes the problem is released during the first few minutes of cooking.

- When preparing a recipe that calls for cabbage wedges, try steaming instead of boiling them; the wedges will retain their shape.

REPORTED HEALTH BENEFITS FROM CABBAGE

Cabbage has been used to control asthma, for blood cleansing, to promote healthier hair and nails, and to cure bladder disorders and skin irritations. It is also reputed to help prevent cancer and lower cholesterol, as well as reduce the symptoms of stomach ulcers and yeast infections such as candidiasis.

AND IT SOUNDS SO MUCH BETTER THAN "FERMENTED CABBAGE"

According to one legend, fermented cabbage was popularized by Genghis Khan, when his marauding hordes brought the recipe from China in the 12th century. The recipe traveled throughout Europe to Germany, where the cabbage was fermented with salt instead of wine and given the name "sauerkraut." In 1772, it took on heroic proportions when Captain James Cook, who had heard of the possible health benefits of sauerkraut, decided to take 25,000 pounds of it on his second journey of exploration to the Pacific Ocean. Because sauerkraut contains vitamin C, Captain Cook lost only one sailor to scurvy in more than 1,000 days at sea. The sauerkraut supply lasted one year without going bad.

CABBAGE VARIETIES

Bok Choy

Looks like a cross between celery and Swiss chard. When cooked, bok choy has a slightly sharp flavor, but the stalks are rarely bitter. Bok choy is an excellent source of calcium and vitamin A.

Green

Has smooth, darker green outer leaves, and paler green inner leaves.

Napa

Has a more delicate flavor than most cabbage and is high in nutrients.

Red

Has solid red-to-purple outer leaves, sometimes with white veins or streaks on the inside leaves.

Savoy

Has crinkled, ruffled, yellow-green leaves and is less compact than most cabbages.

CARROTS

With the exception of pumpkin and dandelion greens, carrots contain more beta-carotene than any other vegetable. Studies show that carrots may lower cholesterol levels, but drinking an excessive amount of carrot juice may turn your skin orange.

- Carrots are available year-round. They should be well formed, with a smooth skin and a solid orange color. Store them in the refrigerator and don't soak them in water for a length of time, especially if they are peeled. If carrots lose their crispness, refrigerating them in a bowl of ice cubes and water for no more than an hour will refresh them. If they are soaked for too long, the excess water will build up in the spaces between the cells and cause the carrots to become limp.

- To slip the skin off carrots, drop them in boiling water, let them stand for 5 minutes, and then place them in cold water for a few seconds. If you're in a hurry or only have a few carrots to peel, a standard vegetable peeler does the job speedily and easily.

- Blanch carrots before using them in a stir-fry because they take longer to cook than most other vegetables.

- To make carrot curls, peel off slices with a vegetable peeler and drop them into a bowl of ice water.

- Retain a portion of the green top to use as a handle while grating carrots. This will keep your fingers from becoming shorter.

- The body absorbs the iron in carrots more efficiently than that from most other vegetable sources.

CARROTS AND CHOLESTEROL

Studies show that eating 7 ounces of carrots every day for three weeks can lower cholesterol levels by 11 percent, probably because of the calcium pectate, a type of fiber found in carrots. Drinking carrot juice won't help though, because this fiber is usually lost during the juicing process.

COOKED CARROTS ARE BETTER FOR YOU

When carrots are cooked, a percentage of the hemicellulose (fiber) will become softer, making them easier to digest and allowing the digestive juices to reach inside the cells and release the nutrients in the vegetable so that the body can utilize them more easily. Also, cooking carrots causes almost no loss of vitamin A.

I LIKE 'EM YOUNG

As a general rule, young vegetables are best for freezing. Their nutrient content will be higher, and they will contain less starch. Freeze them as soon as possible. And remember: Freshly harvested produce has stronger cell walls and will handle freezing better.

KEEP THE TOPS

Don't discard the carrot tops after you cut them off. They are high in vitamins K and E, which are lacking in the carrot itself. You can snip the tops into salads.

STORING CARROTS

Remove the tops from carrots before they are stored. Otherwise, the tops will draw moisture from the carrots, cause them to become bitter, and will reduce their storage life. Carrots should be stored in sealed plastic bags. Carrots are very susceptible to a number of microbes that will cause them to decay. They freeze well with only minimal blanching.

REPORTED HEALTH BENEFITS FROM CARROTS

Carrot juice has been used for the treatment of asthma, allergies, anemia, insomnia, bad breath, constipation, diarrhea, fatigue, and colitis, as well as to improve eyesight and to promote healthy hair and nails. It is also an excellent antioxidant.

CAULIFLOWER

- A member of the cruciferous family of vegetables, cauliflower has a very compact head and grows on a single stalk. The head is surrounded by green leaves, which protect it from the sun and cause the cauliflower to remain white instead of producing chlorophyll.
- Cauliflower is best purchased from September through January but is available year-round. Do not purchase cauliflower whose clusters are open or if it has a speckled surface, which is a sign of insect injury, mold, or rot. A patch of gray on the surface, however, simply means that the sun has reached the surface of the cauliflower. Trim off the gray and the vegetable can be eaten.
- Cauliflower should be stored in a perforated plastic bag in the refrigerator.
- A small amount of lemon juice added to the water will keep cauliflower white during cooking. Overcooking darkens it and makes it tough.
- To reduce the odor of cooking cauliflower, replace the water after it has cooked for 5 to 7 minutes. Cauliflower cooks in 10 to 15 minutes.
- Do not cook it in an aluminum or iron pot because contact with these metals will turn cauliflower yellow, brown, or blue-green.

AREN'T YOU GLAD HE DIDN'T GRAB A PENCIL?

The idea of using a celery rib as a stirrer in a Bloody Mary was introduced in the 1960s.
A celebrity (whose name has been lost to history) enjoying a cocktail at the Ambassador East Hotel in Chicago needed to stir his drink and grabbed a rib of celery from a nearby relish tray.

REPORTED HEALTH BENEFITS FROM CAULIFLOWER

Cauliflower is used as a blood cleanser and to alleviate kidney and bladder disorders, as well as anxiety, poor circulation, and headaches. In some cases, it is also used to cure asthma, gout, end high blood pressure.

CELERY

- Celery was brought to North America from Europe in the 1800s. It was first grown in the United States in Kalamazoo, Michigan, in 1874 and, to popularize it, was given free to train passengers.
- Presently, 2 billion pounds are grown annually in this country.
- Celery has a very high water content and is low in calories. It is available year-round.
- The ribs should be solid, with no hint of softness, which would indicate the cottony texture that old vegetables acquire. If even one rib is wilted, do not purchase the celery.
- Celery will keep in the refrigerator for no more than seven to 10 days and should never be placed in water.
- Don't discard the celery leaves. Chop them and use as you would an herb to flavor soups, stews and stock; or add to meat loaf or stuffing.

CELERIAC

This root vegetable resembles a turnip and may be prepared like any other root vegetable. It has an ivory interior and a strong celery flavor with a dash of parsley. Celeriac should be firm and have a minimum of rootlets and knobs. It is excellent in salads and can be shredded like carrots. Celeriac comes into its own in the appetizer found on menus around the world: *céleri rémoulade*, from France.

CELERY STRINGS

Celery is easy to cook; the pectin in the cells breaks down easily in water. However, the strings, which are made of cellulose, are virtually indestructible and will not break down under normal cooking conditions. Even the body has a difficult time breaking the strings down, and many people cannot digest them at all. Be sure to remove the strings with a vegetable peeler before chopping or using the celery. When preparing stuffed celery stalks for a party, it's best to remove the strings first.

A CELERY RELATIVE

The herb lovage is a relative of celery. Its leaves are used in cooking, while its hollow stems (the herb grows 4 to 6 feet tall!) can be cut and used as straws or swizzle sticks in tomato juice or Bloody Marys.

REPORTED HEALTH BENEFITS FROM CELERY

Celery juice has been used as a tonic to reduce stress. Other uses include asthma relief, to control diabetes, as a diuretic, and to reduce the incidence of gallstones. It is also purported to reduce the symptoms of insect bites, nervousness, and, not surprisingly to millions of dieters, obesity.

GET OUT THE PLASTIC BAG

When handling cauliflower, avoid injuring the florets. This will cause the head to loosen and discolor. Put the unwashed head in a loosely closed plastic bag and store it in the vegetable crisper. It should keep for four to seven days. Wash the head well before eating to eliminate the chemicals that are often used to preserve its freshness. To freeze, cut the cauliflower into small pieces, wash it in cold, lightly salted water, and then blanch it in salt water for 3 minutes. Drain, chill, and freeze it in a plastic bag.

REPORTED HEALTH BENEFITS FROM POPCORN

Popcorn has been used to combat anemia and constipation.

CORN

- Corn was first grown in Mexico or Central America and was a staple of the Native Americans.
- When ground for tortillas, corn releases a high level of niacin. However, as a vegetable, it ranks low on the overall nutritional scale.
- Corn is 5 to 6 percent sugar, making it a taste favorite. Some hybrids of sweet corn are even higher.
- Corn is available from May through September, and the kernels should be evenly colored. Do not purchase husks that are straw colored; they should be green. The straw color indicates that the corn is dried and is fit only for animal fodder.
- Yellow corn kernels are higher in vitamin A than white kernels. Some corn lovers think yellow kernels have a more robust flavor, and that white kernels are sweeter.
- The easiest way to remove the kernels from an ear of corn is to stand the corn on end on a board and cut down the cob with a knife.
- When boiling corn on the cob, adding a little milk to the cooking water will bring out the sweetness of the corn.
- Never add salt to the water when cooking corn; table salt contains traces of calcium, which will toughen the kernels.
- Unused fresh corn should be cooked for a few minutes just to inactivate the enzymes. Store it in a sealed plastic bag for up to two days.
- To freeze corn, blanch the ears for a minute or two in boiling water, drain, and immediately flush with cold water to stop the cooking. Freeze the ears on a tray, leaving room between them so the kernels are not crushed and hold their shape. Once the corn is frozen, place the ears in a sealed plastic bag. Frozen corn will keep for one year.

THEY LIKE TO BE COOL AND DRY

Always store corn in a cool, dry location, and keep the ears separated in order to prevent them from becoming moldy. Remember that as it warms up, the sugar in corn converts to starch very quickly. In fact, when corn is piled high in supermarket bins, the ears on the bottom will be less sweet because of the heat generated by the weight of the ones on top.

CARPE CORN

Corn is one vegetable that is always better eaten when it is fresh, preferably on the day it was picked. As soon as corn is picked, its sugars start to convert to starch. The milky liquid in the kernel that makes corn sweet will turn pulpy and bland in as little as two to three days. If you've only eaten corn from a supermarket, stop at a farm stand one day and pick up some ears that have just been picked. You're sure to marvel at the difference in flavor and texture.

NO MORE RUBBERY CORN

When corn is cooked, the protein goes through a chemical change called denaturization, which simply means that the chains of amino acids (proteins) are broken apart and reformed into a network of protein molecules that squeeze the moisture out of the kernel, turning the corn rubbery. Heat also causes the starch granules to absorb water, thus swelling and rupturing the kernel, thereby releasing the nutrients.

Corn should be cooked for 30 seconds to three minutes, which prevents the protein from becoming tough. When corn is boiled in water, about 50 percent of the vitamin C is destroyed; however, if you cook it in a microwave without water, almost all of the vitamin C is retained.

TRY HERBS

When wrapping corn in aluminum foil for grilling, try placing a sprig of a fresh herb within each ear's foil wrap. Marjoram is the most popular choice, but almost any herb will do: try tarragon, Italian parsley, sage, chives, dill, chervil, oregano, and thyme.

IS IT WORTH THE PRICE?

Nutritionally, regular popcorn and gourmet popcorn are equals. The only difference is that gourmet popcorn pops into larger blossoms.

A TIP FOR PICKLES

If you add a small piece of grape leaf, scuppernong leaf, or cherry leaf to the pickle jar, it will keep the vinegar active while preventing the pickles from becoming soft.

FLUIDS AND FIBER

Popcorn is composed of a complex carbohydrate (starch), and includes insoluble fiber (cellulose), which may help prevent constipation. It is always best, however, to drink plenty of fluids when consuming a large amount of insoluble fiber, which tends to absorb water from the intestinal tract and add bulk.

TOO POOPED TO POP?

It happens to corn kernels all the time. These kernels usually have lost too much moisture—but they can be revived. Soak them in water for 5 minutes, then dry them off and try again. Or freeze them overnight and pop them when frozen.

THE ART OF PICKING CORN

Choosing fresh corn can be difficult unless you have some experience. If the corn still has its husk, peel back a small area and examine the kernels. The kernels should be close together with no gaps between rows. (Gaps between the rows indicate that the ear is over-mature.) If the tip has no kernels, the corn was picked too soon and was not allowed to mature. The kernels should always be plump and juicy and should spurt a milky, starchy liquid. If the center of the kernel is sinking inward, it is drying out and will not be as sweet. Always purchase corn with smaller kernels at the tip of the ear; larger kernels are usually a sign of over-maturity.

STEAM IT

Steaming corn for about 5 to 7 minutes is one of the preferred cooking methods. Roasting or grilling corn gives it an appealingly smoky flavor.

NOW, IF THEY COULD ONLY MAKE BETTER MOVIES

Americans consume 17.3 billion quarts of popcorn every year. After a huge brouhaha several years ago, movie houses and other venues stopped making popcorn in high-saturated fat coconut oil and switched to canola oil.

- One ounce of air-popped popcorn measures 3.5 cups and provides 107 calories.
- One ounce of oil-popped corn measures 2.6 cups and contains 140 calories.
- An ounce of potato chips (about 10 chips) contains 114 calories.

CUCUMBERS

- Cucumbers belong to the gourd family. They originated in Asia and were brought to the Americas by Columbus.
- Cukes are grown in all sizes, from one-inch gherkins to as much as 20 inches long. They have a very high water content and are an excellent source of fiber.
- The greenhouse, or English, cucumber is becoming more and more popular; however, the price of this thin-skinned, skinny cuke is considerably higher than that of the standard market cucumber.
- Cucumbers should be firm and either light or dark green—but never yellow. Purchase only firm cucumbers and store them in the refrigerator. As with some other vegetables, smaller cucumbers have better texture and flavor.
- Cucumbers are capable of holding 30 times their weight in water and, because of this high water content, have only 13 calories per 3.5-ounce serving.

SWEETER CUCUMBERS?

Cucumbers contain no starch and are therefore unable to produce sugar. They will, however, get softer as they age and absorb more moisture into the pectin. If a cucumber gets too soft, slice it, and soak the slices in lightly salted cold water to crisp them. The unsalted, lower-density water will be drawn from the cells and replaced by the higher-density, salted water.

WAXED CUCUMBERS ARE LONGER

Cucumbers tend to shrink during shipping and storage, and the wax coating (which is edible) prevents the shrinkage.

FORGET FREEZING

Cucumbers should be stored unwashed in the crisper drawer of your refrigerator in a perforated plastic bag to allow air to circulate. Cucumbers will keep for only four to five days and do best at around 40°F. They do not freeze well because their high water content causes too many cells to burst, making them mushy.

YOU MIGHT LOOK A LITTLE WEIRD, BUT IT WORKS

This is really surprising, and some think it is just another old wives' tale, but it works. Next time you purchase a standard cucumber (not the long, skinny English variety), cut about one inch off the end and rub the two exposed areas together in a circular motion while occasionally pulling them apart. This will cause enough suction to release a substance that causes some cucumbers to have a bitter taste. Then discard the small end you used to release the bitterness.

MUNCH ON NEGATIVE CALORIES

If you want to snack on something that won't pile on the weight try a stick of celery: it takes more energy to digest celery than it contains in calories.

DID YOU ALWAYS WANT TO KNOW HOW A PICKLE GETS PICKLED?

Then this is your lucky day. It all starts with a fresh cucumber arriving at the pickle factory. There are three types of processes to control fermentation. The first begins with a curing stage, during which the cucumbers are stored in large tanks filled with a salt-brine mixture. Next, they are washed and placed in a vat of fresh water, and then they are heated to remove any excess salt residues. After being cleaned and heated, they are packed in a final acid solution that turns them the dark green color we are familiar with.

The second type of processing is for fresh-pack pickles. This process eliminates the holding tanks and speeds the cucumbers into a flavored brine or syrup. These fresh-pack pickles are less salty than the cured pickles and are lighter green in color.

The third method of processing is done completely under refrigeration. These special pickles are known as *deli dills*. They are cleaned and graded and proceed directly to the flavored brine. They are never cooked or pasteurized and remain very cucumber-like in flavor and texture. These pickles must be stored under refrigeration.

Sour pickles are completed in a solution of vinegar and special spices. *Sweet pickles* are just sour pickles that have been drained of all brine and bathed in a mixture of vinegar, sugar, and spices. The most popular sweet pickles are small gherkins.

REPORTED HEALTH BENEFITS FROM CUCUMBERS

Cucumbers are used as a natural diuretic and to help lower high blood pressure. They have also been used to alleviate symptoms of allergies, diaper rash, insect bites, and eye and skin problems.

A LITTLE OFF THE TOP

When making pickles, slice about a quarter inch from the blossom end of the cucumber. The blossom end contains an enzyme that may cause the pickles to soften prematurely.

DO THE MATH

Dill pickles have five calories per ounce while sweet pickles have 40 calories per ounce—eight times more.

EGGPLANT

- Eggplant is a member of the nightshade family of vegetables, which also includes potatoes, tomatoes, and peppers. As vegetables go, it is not very high on the nutrient scale.
- Varieties include Chinese, Japanese, and Italian eggplants, with great variety in sizes and colors.
- Eggplant contains the toxin solanine, which is destroyed when the vegetable is cooked. It is best never to eat raw eggplant.
- Eggplants are available year-round, but they are at their best in August and September. Their purple-black skin should be smooth, glossy, and free of scars, and they should be firm. Soft eggplants are usually bitter. Keep them cool after purchase and use them within three to four days.
- Eggplant should never be cooked in an aluminum pot, as this will cause the vegetable to become discolored.

KIND OF GROSS

In a recent study, fried eggplant was found to absorb more fat than any other vegetable—even more than an equal portion of French fries.

SAVED BY SALT

Eggplant can be bitter, and the easiest way to eliminate the bitter taste is to slice it, salt the slices, and let them drain on a wire rack for 30 minutes. Then rinse them well and pat them dry. This procedure also reduces the amount of oil they absorb during frying.

FENNEL

Fennel is a member of the parsley family and looks somewhat like a very plump head of celery. It tastes like anise and has a sweet flavor. It is very low in calories, can easily be substituted for celery, and is high in vitamin A, calcium, and potassium. The bulbs should be firm and clean with fresh-looking leaves. Don't buy fennel that has visible brown spots. It tends to dry out quickly and should be wrapped in plastic wrap and used within three to four days.

BE AN OLD PRUNE

Dried plums – prunes – have been given the ultimate super food status, as they are thought to contain the highest level of antioxidants, which neutralize the dangerous free radicals associated with DNA degradation and accelerated aging.

AN APPLE A DAY

It's amazing, but true: sliced apples will remove the smell of cigarette smoke in an enclosed area. Try placing a bowl of apple slices on a table or mantelpiece.

IT'S NOT EASY BEING GREEN

- Among the most nutritious of all vegetables, leafy greens are packed with vitamins, minerals, and the plant-based substances called phytochemicals.
- Because some greens must be cooked to tame their bitterness and mellow their flavors, they are often called cooking greens to differentiate them from salad greens.
- Most dark greens are high in calcium, vitamins A and E, beta-carotene, folate, and iron.
- Greens can grow in sandy soil and thus should be washed thoroughly. If you sauté them, you don't need to dry them well but can add them to the pan still wet—watch out for splatters!
- Choose greens with richly colored leaves—avoid any with yellowing or slimy leaves or tired looking stems.
- Store greens in a perforated plastic bag in the crisper drawer for three to five days.

KINDS OF GREENS

Collards

Popular in the South, collards are loaded with the B vitamins; vitamins A, C, E, and K; beta-carotene; and trace minerals like iron, calcium, magnesium, potassium, and phosphorus. They have large, flat leaves.

Kale

Like collards, to which it is very closely related, kale is a nutritional powerhouse. It is high in vitamins A, C, and E, and is a good source of calcium, iron, and the B vitamins. Kale is at its best in the winter—not only does it survive frost handily, but its flavor improves after exposure to cold temperatures. It can be quite pungent, however, and older kale requires long cooking to tame its bitterness.

Swiss Chard

A relative of the beet, chard has been cultivated for thousands of years. Most frequently, it has white or red stems (don't discard them; use them as you would celery).

Turnip Greens

These have the highest calcium content of any green; turnip greens are also high in beta-carotene as well as vitamins C, E, and the B complex.

HORSERADISH

Horseradish can be found year-round and stores very well. Make sure you purchase firm roots with no soft spots or withering. If wrapped in a plastic bag and refrigerated, horseradish should last for a few weeks. After that, it may turn bitter and lose its hot bite.

DON'T BIN THE BANANAS

Don't throw away overripe bananas. Use them in cooking (for banana cake or loaf) or for smoothies with other fruits or yogurt. You can also freeze them and use as an alternative to fruit sorbet or ice cream (over-ripe bananas freeze better than ripe ones).

JERUSALEM ARTICHOKES

These are members of the sunflower family and are also known as sunchokes. They should be firm and look fresh and will keep under refrigeration for about a week. They are easily peeled with a vegetable peeler; however, they contain a fair amount of nutrition in the skin.

The Jerusalem artichoke has a nutty, sweet flavor and should be crunchy when served raw. It can be roasted, boiled, sautéed, or breaded and fried.

KEEP IT WHITE

Sunchokes are very high in iron, which may cause them to turn gray when cooked. Adding ¼ of a teaspoon of cream of tartar to the boiling water 5 minutes before they are done will prevent the discoloration. Adding 1 tablespoon of lemon juice to the boiling water when you first start cooking will keep the root crisp and also prevent the color change.

JICAMA

Jicama originated in Mexico and is now popular in the United States. It is a root vegetable that can weigh up to six pounds. The skin is brown and the flesh is white, with a crunchy texture similar to that of a water chestnut. It has a slightly sweet flavor and can be substituted for potatoes. It can also be used in salads either diced or cut into small sticks. Choose only unblemished jicama with no soft spots. It's excellent for stir-fries and is a good source of vitamin C.

LEEKS

Leeks are a close relative of the onion family but are milder and sweeter. They are also more nutritious, containing a wide variety of vitamins and minerals. They are best purchased between September and November. They should have green tops and white necks extending two to three inches from the roots. Do not purchase leeks with wilted tops or any signs of aging. Refrigerate and use them within five to seven days.

LETTUCE

- Lettuce can be traced back to ancient Rome and was originally named for the Romans—hence, romaine lettuce.
- In popularity of vegetables, lettuce is second only to potatoes in the United States. It is mainly used in salads and as a garnish.
- Lettuce is available in markets year-round. The darker the leaves of the lettuce you buy the higher the nutrient content.
- Never add salt to lettuce prior to serving, as this may cause it to wilt.
- Americans consume about 11 pounds of lettuce per person per year.

WASH IT GOOD

There are more than 60 chemical agents that may legally be applied to lettuce. Most of these chemicals can be removed by washing the lettuce with a good organic cleanser or by placing the head stem end up in a sink with six to eight inches of cold, lightly salted water. Shake and swirl the lettuce around for a minute.

TEAR IT OR CUT IT?

Some chefs tear lettuce while others cut it with a knife. Many of the chefs we know swear that their method prevents the lettuce from browning quickly. It actually makes no difference. Either way, it will oxidize and turn brown.

LETTUCE ABUSE

Before you store iceberg lettuce, you should remove the core by hitting it once against a hard surface and then twisting it out.

COLD IS BEST

All types of lettuce love the cold, and the closer the temperature gets to 32°F (without going below), the longer the lettuce will last and the crispier it will be. Most refrigerators range between 35°F and 40°F, which is good, but not ideal. The lettuce should be stored unwashed in a sealed plastic bag with a small hole or two for ventilation. Lettuce turns brown if stored near most other fruits or vegetables because of the ethylene gas they give off. Iceberg lettuce remains fresher than any other type because of its higher water content. Iceberg will store for seven to 14 days, whereas romaine lasts for six to 10 days, and butterhead for only three to four days. To crisp lettuce leaves, soak them in ice-cold water for 15 to 20 minutes, then dry them.

LETTUCE CATEGORIES

There are hundreds of varieties of lettuce, and each falls into one of these four categories.

Arugula

A solid green lettuce with a high beta-carotene and vitamin C content. Arugula has small, flat leaves on long stems and a somewhat peppery flavor. It is a close relative of the radish.

Butterhead

Is a loose head lettuce with a soft, buttery texture. Boston, limestone, and Bibb lettuce are examples. The leaves are dark- to grass-green.

Crisphead

Iceberg, the most popular lettuce in the United States, is the best known of this variety: It is also the least nutritious of all the lettuces and has a water content of 96 percent. Best to choose any other lettuce for nutrition.

GOJI GOOD FOR CELLULITE

One leading skin care expert has dubbed goji juice the 'cellulite assassin'. This energy-boosting drink contains more beta carotene than carrots and more iron than spinach.

Looseleaf

The leaves are loosely packed and joined at the stem. Varieties include red-leaf, oak, leaf, and green-leaf. These are crisp lettuces with mild and delicate flavor.

Romaine

Sometimes called cos, romaine has long, green leaves and is usually very crisp. It is used in Caesar salads. Romaine lettuce has seven times as much vitamin C and vitamin A as iceberg lettuce.

NON-LETTUCE SALAD CHOICES

Belgian Endive

A type of chicory, Belgian endives are bullet-shaped, tightly closed heads of creamy white and yellow leaves. Belgian endive is even lower in vitamins and minerals than iceberg lettuce.

Chicory

Has loosely bunched, very thin, ragged-edged leaves on long stems. The outer leaves are dark green, and their taste is somewhat bitter. The center leaves, however, are yellow and have a mild taste.

Escarole

Has broad, wavy leaves with smooth edges and a bitter flavor.

Mâche

Is very perishable, more expensive than most other lettuces, and is sold only in small bunches. The leaves are delicate green in color and have a fingerlike shape with a mild taste.

Radicchio

A member of the chicory family, radicchio looks like a very small head of red cabbage with variegated, red-and-white leaves.

Watercress

Has dark green leaves and a peppery, mustard-like flavor. It is commonly used in salads.

REPORTED HEALTH BENEFITS FROM ENDIVE

Endive has been used to treat asthma, gout, high blood pressure, arthritis, and liver ailments.

MUSHROOMS

- Mushrooms can be traced back to the time of the Egyptian pharaohs.
- Mushrooms are fungi and are an excellent source of nutrients.
- There are approximately 38,000 varieties of mushrooms, and unless you know what you are doing, it can be very difficult to tell the edible from the inedible. It is best never to pick and eat a wild mushroom.
- Mushrooms are available in markets year-round but are best from November through March. Be sure that the caps are closed around the stem and refrigerate them soon after purchase.
- Mushrooms can be kept white and firm during sautéing if you add ¼ teaspoon of lemon juice for every 2 tablespoons of butter or olive oil.

STORING MUSHROOMS

Fresh mushrooms have a shelf life of only two to three days and must be stored in the refrigerator in an open container. The original container or another paper product will work best. Never use plastic containers, which tend to keep the mushrooms too wet. Never wash mushrooms before storing them; they will retain the water and become soggy. If you must keep them for a few days, place a single layer of cheesecloth on top of the container. If they do become shriveled, they can still be sliced or chopped and used in cooking. To freeze mushrooms, wipe them off with a piece of damp paper towel, slice them, sauté them in a small amount of butter until they are almost done, allow them to cool, then place them in an airtight plastic bag and freeze. They should keep for 10 to 12 months.

MUSHROOM VARIETIES

Button

This common white mushroom is widely cultivated throughout the world. These are short and stubby with round caps and gills on the underside. They can vary in size from less than one to several inches in diameter. A large majority of the production is dried or goes into cans or jars.

Cèpe

Cèpes, also known as boletes or porcini, are stout, brown mushrooms with pores instead of gills on the underside. Cèpes range in size from one to 10 inches in diameter and are among the best-tasting mushrooms.

Chanterelle

These are shaped like trumpets. They are large with frilly caps and range in color from gold to yellow-orange.

THE FLAVOR OF MUSHROOMS

The unique flavor of fresh mushrooms is caused by glutamic acid, the natural form of the flavor enhancer monosodium glutamate (MSG). Mushrooms, however, do not have any sodium.

Enoki

These are sprout like, with very small caps on long, thin stems. Their color is a creamy white and they have a mild flavor. They are best served raw in salads or soups and are sometimes called enokitake mushrooms.

Italian Brown

Also known as cremini, these inexpensive mushrooms are similar in appearance to button mushrooms. They have more flavor but are not as tender as button mushrooms.

Morel

These are among the most highly priced mushrooms. They are dark brown and conical in shape, and their spongy caps have a honeycombed structure.

Oyster

This variety of mushroom can be wild or cultivated. These range in color from off-white to a gray-brown. They grow in clusters and have a very dense, chewy texture. They are more flavorful when cooked.

Portobello

These large mushrooms are overgrown Italian brown mushrooms. They have a hearty flavor, circular caps, and long, thick stems. Cut off the woody part of the stem before using them. They have a meaty texture and can, in fact, be marinated and prepared like steak.

Shiitake

At one time these dark brown mushrooms were grown only in Japan, but they are now cultivated and available in the United States. They are grown on logs and are umbrella shaped. They have a rich flavor and are an excellent addition to many dishes. Shiitakes are also known as golden oak, forest, oriental black, or Chinese black mushrooms. Remove the stems before using them.

Wood Ear

These may have anticoagulant properties, and health claims are presently showing up in the media. There are no conclusive studies at present in relation to their ability to prevent heart attacks. They are mostly sold dried and have ear-shaped caps that tend to vary in size, with a crunchy texture. They have also been known as tree ear and black tree fungus.

REPORTED HEALTH BENEFITS FROM MUSHROOMS

In Japan, a chemical compound extracted from shiitake mushrooms has been approved as an anticancer drug.

LUTEIN FOR HEALTHY EYES

Many people suffer from farsightedness, cataracts, glaucoma and other eye problems as they age. To keep your eyes healthy, increase your level of lutein – available in vegetables such as carrots, broccoli, spinach, Brussels sprouts and kale. Lutein can decrease the risk of cataracts and macular degeneration.

TRUFFLES

These fungi grow underground and can be found only by pigs and trained dogs. They have excellent flavor and are a very expensive delicacy. There are two types; the black truffles from France and Italy, and the white truffles from northern Italy. White truffles are even more expensive than black.

OKRA

- Okra originated in north Africa and was brought to the United States via the slave trade in the 1700s. It became a Southern favorite and is used in many Creole dishes, especially gumbos.
- Okra tastes like a cross between eggplant and asparagus and, because of its thick juice, is used mainly in soups and stews, or is sliced and fried. It is a good source of vitamins and minerals.
- Okra pods should always be green and tender and should never look dry or shriveled. Okra tends to spoil rapidly and should be refrigerated soon after purchase.
- It is usually best between May and October. Never wash okra until you are ready to use it; washing removes the protective coating that keeps the pods from becoming slimy.
- Try brushing okra with a bit of olive oil and grilling it.

REPORTED HEALTH BENEFITS FROM OKRA

Okra has been used as a treatment for stomach ulcers, burns, dermatitis, eczema, poison ivy, and psoriasis.

A GREAT THICKENER

Okra pods comprise many unripe seed capsules and are very high in carbohydrates, fiber, and starch. Because okra contains a significant amount of pectin and gums, it is an excellent thickener for soups and stews. As okra is heated, the starch granules absorb water and increase in size. They then rupture and release amylose and amylopectin molecules, as well as some of the gums and the pectin. These elements attract additional water molecules, increase in volume, and thicken the food.

ONIONS

- Onions probably originated in prehistoric times and were popular in ancient Egypt and Rome.
- The onion family includes more than 500 varieties. They are low in calories, and scallions—also called spring onions or green onions—are an excellent source of vitamin A.
- Onions should be purchased hard and dry. Avoid those with wet necks; they have begun to decay. Also avoid onions that have sprouted. They are still good to use as onion sprouts, but not as onions.
- Ideally, onions should be stored in hanging bags that allow the air to circulate around them. Never purchase an onion that has even the slightest hint of decay because the decay will quickly spread to the healthy onions with which it is stored.
- Onions will keep for two to three weeks in a cool, dry place, but if the weather is hot and humid, their storage time will be cut in half. Refrigerated, they will last for about two months, but they may pass on their aroma to other foods in the refrigerator, even eggs.
- Remove the smell of onions from your hands or a cutting board with very salty water or some white vinegar.
- Chives should be wrapped in paper towels, put in a plastic bag, and refrigerated. They will last about a week but should be used within three to four days of purchase to ensure the best flavor. If snipped or finely chopped and frozen, they can be added to food without thawing.

DON'T ASK WHY THEY'RE CALLED "SWEET"

Sweet onions actually have less sugar than regular onions. They also have less sulfur, which is what gives onions their pungency.

THE HEARTBREAK OF POPPED ONIONS

Have you ever cooked a whole onion only to have the insides pop out? Piercing the onion with a skewer once or twice will allow the steam to escape and prevent the onion from bursting. Another method, similar to that used to keep chestnuts from exploding, is to cut an X on the root end, which will allow the steam to escape without damaging the onion.

TO COOK AN ONION

Cooking will actually turn the sulfurs in onions into sugars, which is why cooked onions taste sweeter than raw ones. As onions brown, the sugars turn deep brown and caramelize, which intensifies the flavor.

GO FIGURE

If you need only half an onion, use the top half first, because the root half will store longer in the refrigerator (it won't sprout).

NO MORE TEARS

A sliced onion releases a substance that reacts with the fluid in your eyes to form sulfuric acid. The eyes protect themselves from the acid by tearing, which rids them of the irritant. Here are some ways to prevent tearing:

- Cut off the root end of the onion last.
- Freeze the onion for 10 minutes, or refrigerate it for 1 hour before slicing.
- Ball up a piece of white bread and impale it on the tip of the knife to absorb the fumes.
- Chewing gum while you chop onions may also help.

DON'T THROW IT OUT

If an onion becomes pithy and starts to sprout, place it in a pot on a windowsill and, as it continues to sprout, snip off pieces of the sprouts to use for salad seasoning.

THE SWEET TRUTH

There are several varieties of sweet onions, including the Maui, the Walla Walla, and the Vidalia, which is grown in Georgia. Sweet onions brown better in the microwave than other onions. Combine 2 cups of sliced sweet onions with 4 tablespoons of butter in an uncovered dish and microwave on High for about 30 minutes.

ONION VARIETIES

Bermuda

These are the most common variety of large onions and may be white or yellow. Their flavor is somewhat mild, and they are commonly used in salads.

Boiling

White onions, about one inch in diameter.

Pearl

These white onions are about the size of marbles.

Purple or Red

These are usually among the sweetest and have the strongest flavor. They are commonly used on hamburgers and in salads.

Spanish

These are light brown and larger than most other onions. They caramelize easily and become very sweet.

White

Smaller than most onions, these are usually used in soups, stews, or dishes that are creamed.

Yellow

The standard onion bought in bags in supermarkets, yellow onions are simply smaller Spanish or yellow Bermuda onions.

WHO KNEW?

When sautéing onions and garlic together, be sure to sauté the onions first for at least half of their cooking time. If you start the garlic at the same time as the onions, it will overcook and possibly burn, releasing a chemical that will make the dish bitter.

REPORTED HEALTH BENEFITS FROM ONIONS

Onions are used as a diuretic. They also have laxative effects, and have been used as an antiseptic. Over the ages, onions have been used to treat countless ailments, including arthritis, asthma, athlete's foot and other skin conditions.

PARSNIPS

Parsnips look like top-heavy, ivory-colored carrots. They have a celery-like, nutty flavor. Parsnips are more easily digested when cooked because they are very fibrous and have strong cell walls. They are often used to flavor soups and can be roasted like other root vegetables.

REPORTED HEALTH BENEFITS FROM PARSNIPS

Parsnip is used to alleviate the symptoms of gout, edema, fatigue, gallstone, and hypoglycemia, and as a diuretic.

PEAS

- Peas are actually legumes—plants that bear pods with interior seeds. Green peas are one of the best vegetable sources of protein and have been used as a food since ancient times.
- Only 5 percent of all green peas arrive at the market fresh; almost all are frozen or canned.
- Like fresh corn, fresh peas are best cooked as soon as possible after they are picked, before their sugars have the time to convert to starch.
- Always choose pods that are well-filled but not bulging. Never buy yellow, flabby, or spotted pods. Refrigerate and use peas within three days.
- When dried peas are placed in water, the good ones will sink to the bottom and the bad ones will float to the top for easy removal.

REPORTED HEALTH BENEFITS FROM PEAS

Peas contain nicotinic acid and may help to lower cholesterol levels. Peas have also been used to treat abscesses, constipation, and skin problems.

- The peas inside a snow pea pod are so tiny that these pods are never shelled. The pods themselves are quite tender. The easiest way to cook snow peas is to sauté them in a bit of butter, or add them to a stir-fry with scallions, red bell pepper strips, broccoli florets, and baby corn.
- Snow peas and snap peas can be served raw in salads or cooked and served in their pods, either whole or sliced in half diagonally. Be careful not to overcook them!
- When cooking shelled fresh peas, always add a few washed pods to the water; this will improve the flavor and give the peas a richer green color.
- The delicate flavor of peas marries well with many foods but can be overpowered by strong flavors like garlic. Cook them with pearl onions, mushrooms, or top them with minced, fresh mint leaves.

PEPPERS

- When purchasing peppers, be sure the sides are firm and the colors are bright. Refrigerate and use them within two to three days.
- They are a good source of vitamins A and C. In fact, red bell peppers contain more vitamin C than oranges.
- Nutritionally, sweet red peppers are superior to green ones. They are 11 times higher in beta-carotene and have 1 ½ times more vitamin C.
- Hot red peppers contain about 14 times more beta-carotene than hot green peppers; however, their vitamin C content is the same.
- Probably one of the earliest spices, chilies may have been used since 7000 B.C., according to archeological digs in Mexico.

OUCH

Peppers contain capsaicin—the compound that gives them heat—and can irritate tissues. The hotter the pepper, the more capsaicin it has. To prevent irritation, wear rubber gloves when working with hot peppers so your hands do not touch the pepper and then, accidentally, your eyes, lips, or other sensitive body parts. If you get hot pepper juice on soft tissues, you will remember the experience!

A recent study has shown that the anticoagulant chemicals in hot chili peppers may actually lower cholesterol levels and increase the amount of time it takes for blood to coagulate.

THESE COLORS DON'T RUN

Green peppers contain chlorophyll as the coloring agent. When the pepper is cooked it releases acids that react with the chlorophyll and cause discoloration. Red and yellow peppers, on the other hand, rely on carotenoid pigments for their color. These pigments are not affected by acids or the heat from cooking.

THE HOT TRUTH

- The color of a chili indicates only its ripeness. If the chili is picked before full maturity it will be green and contain more chlorophyll than a red chili, which has matured and lost its chlorophyll.
- The highest concentration of capsaicin is in the white ribs to which the seeds are attached. If you remove the ribs and seeds and rinse the pepper in cold water, you will reduce the heat by 70 to 80 percent.
- When a chili is fried or boiled, it will lose even more of its potency. It has also been found that people who consume chilies frequently become less susceptible to their heat.

SO FIRE IT UP

Studies have shown that eating hot peppers does not cause stomach ulcers and may even speed the healing process by increasing circulation.

PUTTING THE FIRE OUT

Capsaicin does not dissolve in water. In fact, if you've eaten a too-hot chili and your mouth is on fire, taking a drink of water or beer only makes it worse—the liquid spreads the capsaicin. Sour cream, yogurt, or even milk are the ideal remedies. A protein in dairy foods called casein breaks the bond between capsaicin and the pain receptors in your mouth.

HOW HOT IS TOO HOT?

The chemical capsaicin acts directly on the pain receptors in the mouth and throat. A single drop of this pure chemical diluted in 100,000 drops of water will still cause a blister to form on a person's tongue. Capsaicin is measured in parts per million, which are converted into heat units called Scoville units. This is how the hotness of a chili pepper is measured. One hundred and fifty thousand Scoville units is equivalent to 1 percent capsaicinoids. The hottest known pepper, the habanero, has a Scoville rating of 100,000 to 350,000; next is the Thai chiltepin at 50,000 to 100,000; followed by the Tecpin cayenne at 30,000; the de arbol at 15,000 to 30,000; the serrano at 5,000 to 15,000; the jalapeño at about 2,500 to 5,000; and the cascabel at 1,500 to 2,500.

PEPPER VARIETIES

Anaheim

A hot chili. One of the most common chilies, with a mild to moderately hot bite, anaheims are consumed in either the green or red stages of maturity. Dried red anaheims are available in long, decorative strings.

Ancho

Dried hot peppers that are flat, wrinkled, and usually heart-shaped. They are mild to moderately hot and are usually ground for use in sauces and salsa.

Banana

A sweet pepper with a mild flavor. They resemble bananas in both color and shape. They are available fresh or pickled.

Bell

A sweet pepper available in many colors, including green, red, orange, white, brown, and yellow. Bells are relatively sweet, but each color has a distinctive flavor. When different colors are mixed in a salad, it is a real taste treat. Bell peppers contain a recessive gene that neutralizes capsaicin, which is why they are not hot.

Bell peppers should be stored in the refrigerator in a plastic bag, where they will stay fresh two to three days. They can be frozen for 10 to 12 months and still retain a good portion of their nutrients.

To seed a bell pepper, hold it tightly and slam the stem end down on the counter. This will loosen the seed core, and it should pull out easily.

Cascabel

Moderately hot red chilies with seeds that tend to rattle inside them. When dried, their skins turn a brownish-red.

Cayenne

These are among the hottest chilies. They are three to four inches long, with sharply pointed, curled tips, and are usually dried and ground.

Cubanelle

A sweet pepper with a tapered shape. About four inches long, the cubanelle ranges in color from yellow to red.

Habanero

This lantern-shaped pepper ripens to yellow-orange in color and grows to about two inches in diameter. The habanero is the hottest pepper and is known for the lingering effect of its bite. Have milk handy when eating this one.

Hungarian Wax

A moderately hot, yellow-orange pepper. May be purchased fresh or pickled.

Pimiento

A sweet, heart-shaped pepper generally sold in jars and usually found in gourmet markets.

Serrano

Popular in Mexico, these chilies look like small torpedoes and are very hot.

STRONG COLORS COUNT MORE

All fresh fruits and vegetables contain powerful antioxidants but in general the deeper and more intense the color, the higher the content. Choose red and orange pepper, tomatoes, cranberries, pomegranates and broccoli.

RADISHES

- Radishes are native to the eastern Mediterranean.
- They are in the mustard family and contain phytochemicals that are being investigated for their possible use as a cancer preventative. Their green tops are edible and tend to have a peppery flavor.
- Radishes are available year-round. The larger ones can be cottony in texture while the smaller ones are usually more solid; squeeze them to be sure they are not mushy or pithy, and don't buy them if the tops are yellow or if there is any sign of decay.
- Varieties of radish include California Mammoth Whites, Daikons, Red Globe, and White Icicles, among others.

REPORTED HEALTH BENEFITS FROM RADISHES

Radishes have been thought to be effective as an appetite stimulant, to relieve body odor, burns, cancer, coughing, fever, indigestion, diarrhea, thyroid problems, nervousness, and constipation, and to dissolve kidney stones and gallstones.

SPINACH

First grown in the United States in the 1700s, spinach is high in vitamins and minerals and is one of the best vegetable sources of protein. Spinach, however, does contain the chemical oxalate, which binds with certain minerals such as calcium and limits their absorption by the body.

KEEP IT UNCOVERED

One trick chefs use to keep spinach green is to cook it in an uncovered pot. The steam that builds up when a pot is covered causes the plant's volatile acids to condense on the lid and fall back into the water.

THE RAW TRUTH ABOUT SPINACH

While most vegetables can be eaten raw, some—including spinach and carrots—have tough cellular walls that release their maximum nutrients only when cooked. If these vegetables are eaten raw, the digestive system cannot break them down sufficiently to obtain the most nutritional benefits from them. (Of course, uncooked spinach is still a viable source of many nutrients, so you needn't forego spinach salads!) Cook spinach in as little water as possible and as briefly as possible. Spinach boiled in 1 cup of water rather than 2 will retain twice as many of its nutrients.

STORING SPINACH

Spinach will keep in the refrigerator for two to three days, providing it is stored in a sealed plastic bag. Do not wash it or cut it before you are ready to prepare it. If you buy packaged spinach, open the bag when you get home and remove any brown or darkened leaves which, if left in the bag, may cause the rest of the spinach to deteriorate faster.

To freeze spinach, remove the stems, blanch the leaves for 2 minutes, and then drain and freeze. Removing the stems lets the leaves retain more of their moisture. The spinach should keep for 10 to 12 months at 0°F.

REPORTED HEALTH BENEFITS FROM SPINACH

Spinach has been used to fight blindness, diabetes, eye problems, anemia, tumors, arthritis, high blood pressure, and bronchitis.

JALAPEÑO

One of the most common hot peppers, Jalapeños are usually moderately to very hot and are sold at their green stage. At the red stage of full maturity, the jalapeño is super-hot. Canned jalapeños are usually milder because they are packed in liquid.

BUT HOW DO YOU GET FOREARMS LIKE POPEYE?

Spinach contains antioxidants that may be important in preventing an age-related disease of the eye called macular degeneration. This form of blindness is prevalent in people over 65 and is the leading cause of blindness in the elderly. Experts believe that overexposure to sunlight, pollution, and smog over a period of years may contribute to this problem. Regularly consuming foods that are high in these antioxidants, such as kale, collard greens, spinach, red bell peppers, mustard greens, and hot chili peppers, may lower the risk of contracting macular degeneration by as much as 75 percent.

DO LIKE POPEYE

Eat spinach – it's rich in vitamin C, calcium and beta carotene, boosts folic acid and helps keep blood and bones healthy. Steam lightly and add to sauces or wash and use instead of lettuce in salads.

SPROUTS

When seeds are moistened, they grow into edible sprouts or shoots. When this occurs, the seed utilizes its carbohydrates and fat and retains a good percentage of its vitamins, making sprouts a healthful food.

- When purchasing fresh sprouts, remember that they can be stored for only seven to 10 days.
- Sprouts should be left in their original container, lightly moistened, then placed in a plastic bag, sealed, and refrigerated.
- Storing sprouts in too much water will cause them to decay.
- Sprouts cannot be frozen successfully; they become mushy and bland when thawed.
- The shorter the tendril, the younger and more tender the sprout.

WHO KNEW?

One of the best sources of vitamin A and beta-carotene is pumpkin. An 8-ounce serving provides 40 calories and about 27,000 IU of vitamin A.

SPROUT VARIETIES

Adzuki Bean
Very sweet, with a nutty flavor, this variety looks like grass.

Alfalfa
Threadlike white sprouts with small, green tops and a mild, nutty flavor.

Clover
Looks like the alfalfa sprout, with tiny seeds that look like poppy seeds.

Daikon Radish
Has a silky stem and a leafy top. The taste is somewhat peppery and spicy-hot.

Mung Bean
These are larger than the alfalfa sprouts and have a blander taste. They are thick, white sprouts and are used in many Asian dishes.

Soybean
These sprouts have a rather strong flavor but are a good source of protein. They may contain salmonella and should not be eaten in large quantities. Cooking the sprouts for at least five minutes can kill the bacteria.

Sunflower
Crunchier than alfalfa, with a milder flavor.

CHERRY
Shaped like a cherry, this variety ranges from mild to moderately hot. Sold either fresh or in jars.

PUMPKIN PRESERVER

A problem every Halloween is that pumpkins get soft and mushy soon after they are carved. This occurs because air comes in contact with the inside flesh, allowing bacteria to grow. Spraying the inside of the hollowed-out pumpkin with an antiseptic spray will retard the bacterial growth and increase the time it takes for the pumpkin to deteriorate. Make sure you do not eat a pumpkin that has been sprayed.

SQUASH

- Squash is a fleshy vegetable with a solid, protective rind. It has been a staple for thousands of years.
- Squash is low in calories and contains excellent levels of vitamins and minerals, which may vary from one variety to another. It is available year-round. The soft-skinned types should be smooth and glossy. The hard-shelled types should have a firm rind. Refrigerate all soft-skinned varieties and use them within four to five days.
- Summer squash varieties include chayote, pattypan, yellow crookneck, yellow straightneck, and zucchini.
- Winter squash varieties include acorn, banana, buttercup, butternut, calabaza, delicata, golden nugget, Hubbard, spaghetti, sweet dumpling, turban, and pumpkin.
- Winter squash tend to develop beta-carotene. They contain more of this nutrient after they have been stored than they do immediately after being picked.
- The smaller the squash, the more flavorful it is.
- Squash blossoms are edible and delicious. They make a great garnish for many dishes and can even be battered and fried. Try stuffing them with cream cheese for a real treat.
- If you puree squash in the blender, the strings will be easy to remove because they will become wrapped around the blades.

TOMATOES

The question of whether the tomato is a fruit or a vegetable was settled by the United States Supreme Court in 1893 when it was officially declared a vegetable—but this was done for tariff purposes.

- Botanically, the tomato is a fruit—actually, a berry. It is a member of the nightshade family and is related to potatoes, bell peppers, and eggplant.
- Tomatoes are available year-round and should be well-formed and free of blemishes. Green tomatoes will eventually turn red, but will not have good tomato flavor. A vine-ripened tomato is always best.
- Never refrigerate tomatoes. Tomatoes can be frozen whole and used as needed for cooking; their texture suffers, though, and they should not be used in salads. When they thaw, the skins slip off easily.
- Tomatoes will keep longer if you store them stem end down. Don't let them ripen in direct sunlight, or they will lose most of their vitamin C.
- If you expect a frost and have tomatoes on the vine, pull them up by the roots and hang them upside down in a cool basement until the fruit ripens. Green tomatoes will ripen faster if you store them with apples.
- Storing tomatoes at temperatures below 50°F will keep them from ripening.
- To peel tomatoes, cut an X in the bottom of each tomato and drop them in boiling water, remove the pot from the heat, let them remain in the water for 15 seconds, and then plunge them into cold water. The skins around the X will curl away from the flesh and will become easy to peel away.
- Americans consume about 24 pounds of tomatoes per person, per year.

ONE AMAZING LITTLE BERRY

Known as one of the anti-aging super foods, the acai berry is indigenous to the Amazon rain-forests, and contains the same compounds called anthocyanins that makes red wine good for us. Try concentrated fruit drinks, or eat the berry itself, to help slow down the aging process.

EASY WAY TO LOWER THE ACIDITY IN TOMATOES

Some people are unable to eat spaghetti sauces and other tomato based foods because of their higher acidic content. Adding chopped carrots to any of these dishes will reduce the acidity without affecting the taste.

SO ACT FAST!

If you enjoy the aroma of fresh tomatoes in your salad, don't refrigerate them. Tomatoes should always be stored at room temperature. They should never be sliced or peeled until just before you are going to serve them. A chemical that is released when the tomato is sliced open produces the aroma. The chemical lasts at the maximum aroma level for only three minutes before it starts to evaporate.

A REAL MESS

Never put a whole tomato in the microwave: It will explode.

TOMATO VARIETIES

Beefsteak

Beefsteak refers to a specific variety of tomato, but it is also used in a general sense to describe any large tomato. Beefsteak tomatoes often weigh more than a pound each; those that tip the scales at two or three pounds are not unheard of. As their name suggests, these tomatoes have a meaty texture. Their flavor is sweet and aromatic, with just a hint of acidity.

WHO KNEW?

Celery is a super snack food – not only is it crunchy and refreshing, it genuinely does take your body the same amount of calories to eat and digest it as it gives you. Avoid smothering it with creamy dips and go for healthy versions instead, such as hummus made with olive oil or low-fat yogurt mixed with garlic and fresh herbs.

Cherry

These tomatoes can range in size from smaller than one inch in diameter to almost two inches. Typically, they are perfectly round, with smooth, thin skins that can be red or yellow. They are sweeter than other varieties.

Plum

Slightly elongated plum tomatoes have a firm flesh with little juice. Because they also contain few seeds and minimal gel, they are ideal for tomato sauce and paste.

HEIRLOOM TOMATOES

In the tomato world, growing heirloom varieties has become a popular pursuit with gardeners—and with discerning chefs who buy the green, gold, pink, orange, and yes, even black globes from them. Heirloom tomatoes add scrumptious taste and dazzling colors to summer dishes. If you're lucky, you may find a source at a local food stand or market—or grow your own. Unlike the smooth, round product of modern plant breeders, heirloom varieties often have pincushion shapes.

REPORTED HEALTH BENEFITS FROM TOMATOES

Tomatoes have been used as a natural antiseptic and may protect against infection. They have been used to improve skin tone and as a blood cleanser, as well as a preventive for diarrhea, fatigue, hypertension, sunburn, and wounds.

SUN-DRIED TOMATO SAVVY

Made from halved and dried plum tomatoes, these succulent little morsels have a concentrated flavor. Those packed in oil can be very high in calories and fat; buy them dry and you can reconstitute them in hot water or low-fat Italian salad dressing.

TOMATILLOS

Also called Mexican green tomatoes, tomatillos look like small, green tomatoes with a thin, parchment-like skin. They have a somewhat lemon-apple flavor and are popular in salads and salsas. Purchase only firm tomatillos. They are usually available year-round.

HOT WATER FOR VEGGIES

If you need to add more water to vegetables as they are cooking, make sure the added water is as hot as possible. Adding cold water may affect the cell walls and cause the vegetables to toughen.

TURNIPS

Turnips are a cruciferous vegetable, and are related to rutabaga and cabbage (rutabaga, in fact, evolved from a cross between the turnip and cabbage). They grow easily, even in poor soil conditions, and can weigh up to 50 pounds. Turnips are a good source of complex carbohydrates, vitamin C, and fiber, including soluble fiber.

If you find turnips with the tops, or greens, still attached, don't discard them! Turnip greens are highly nutritious. One cup of boiled greens provides vitamin C, vitamin A, calcium, potassium, and beta-carotene.

WATER CHESTNUTS

Water chestnuts grow in muddy water and are the tip of a tuber. They must be refrigerated or they will sprout. They are an excellent source of trace minerals, especially potassium, and also contain vitamin C.

BUY BROCCOLI

Broccoli is one of the richest sources of antioxidants and vitamin C known, and the fresher the better. If you can't get it really fresh, choose frozen as it keeps its goodness for longer.

EAT YOUR GREENS

Learn to love green foods like cabbage, leeks and broccoli, which are rich in sulphur, the 'beauty mineral' that promotes healthy skin and nails. They also contain high levels of antioxidants, which helps to prevent skin from aging.

WORLDLY WISE

More than 50% of papaya (paw paw) from Hawaii is genetically modified to resist a virus so choose papayas grown in Brazil, Mexico, or the Caribbean, where there are currently no GM varieties.

COOK UP PERFECT SKIN

If you want skin that's as smooth as a tomato, then eat one! Tomatoes contain lycopene, a skin-friendly antioxidant that is also thought to reduce the risk of cancer. Cooking tomatoes makes lycopene more readily absorbable by the body, so choose tomato sauces over the raw fruits in salads.

LEMON ZESTER

A morning cup of hot water and lemon juice is a great way to start the day. It kick-starts the metabolism after a night's sleep, aids digestion and provides a natural way to cleanse the liver and stomach. It also provides you with an excellent source of vitamin C.

PEAR TOMATOES

Like cherry tomatoes, pear tomatoes have red or yellow skins; they are about the same size as the cherries, but pears have a distinct neck. Pear tomatoes are still relatively rare at supermarkets, but you may find them at gourmet markets. Yellow pear tomatoes are a popular heirloom variety.

FORBIDDEN FRUIT

Choose foods labeled with the name of the fruit rather than 'fruit flavored'. For example, strawberry yogurt must contain strawberries, but strawberry-flavored yogurt probably doesn't contain any fruit and usually includes additives to create the flavor. Also, if there's an image of real strawberries on the packaging, the product's flavor must, by law, come wholly or mainly from strawberries.

TOP-SCORING ORAC FOODS

The high levels of antioxidants found in the ORAC (Oxygen Radical Absorbance Capacity) foods come from plant pigments called poly phenols, and it is thought to be the combination of vitamins, iron and folic acid that makes them so effective. Top-scoring ORAC foods are avocado, blueberries, broccoli, garlic, kale, plums, raisins, red grapes and spinach.

SMOOTH FINE EYE LINES

After a night out in a smoky atmosphere, eyes can become tired and red. Soothe them by grating cucumber onto a muslin cloth. Wrap it up like a tortilla wrap and hold it gently against your eyes. The enzymes in the cucumber will help to reduce swelling and smooth out fine lines.

ZING WITH GINGER

A great herbal infusion to choose for an after-lunch energy boost, without caffeine, is ginger root (Zingiber officinale), a pungent herb that's not only good for digestion but also relieves nausea, improves circulation, warms the body, and has antiseptic and anti-inflammatory properties.

PEEL AWAY PESTICIDES

An apple a day is supposed to keep the doctor away, but the average eating apple – the most pesticide-heavy fruit – has been sprayed 18 times with many different chemicals. Most of the residues of chemical fertilizers and pesticides stay on the skin. If you buy non-organic apples, make sure you peel them or at least wash them thoroughly. This will also remove dirt and bacteria.

WATER RETENTION

Chemicals such as pesticides and fertilizers sprayed on foods during the growing process are thought to be held for longer in watery fruit and vegetables such as cucumber and watermelons.

BEST OF THE BUNCH

Among the foods found to be least contaminated with pesticide residues worldwide are asparagus, avocados, bananas and broccoli, so you can generally eat these without worrying, although it's still safest to wash before use. Other good choices are corn on the cob, cauliflower, marrow, squash and swede.

CUT UP A CABBAGE

In order to protect yourself against cancers, it's important to increase your intake of plant phyto-chemicals, which contain tumor-busting enzymes. They are present in all fruits and vegetables but cabbage, broccoli, cauliflower, brussels sprouts and tomatoes contain the highest quantities.

CHECK OUT ORAC FOODS

Oxygen Radical Absorbance Capacity (ORAC) is an American test tube analysis that has pinpointed the highest levels of antioxidants in fruit and vegetables. Early findings by the US Department of Agriculture suggest ORAC foods may help slow the aging process in the brain as well as the body, and young and middle-aged people may be able to reduce risk of diseases of aging, including senility, by adding high-ORAC foods to their diets.

SMELL YOUR BERRIES

The best way to check if berries are fresh is to smell them. They should smell fresh and fruity. If you're buying in cartons, make sure the carton is still dry and that no juices are in the bottom. Store them on kitchen paper towels in the fridge.

ENERGY-BOOSTING BERRY

Freshly juiced black-currants contain a host of antioxidants that can protect cells from premature aging, as well as lower cholesterol levels and guard against cancer.

COOKING WITH YOGURT

Preserve the benefits of the active cultures in your yogurt by not heating it above 50°C (120°F). High temperatures can kill the beneficial bacteria in yogurts so if you want to use it in cooking, try adding it at the end.

KEEP IT LEMON FRESH

When preparing ripe avocados, to avoid the flesh from turning brown and looking unattractive when exposed to air, immediately place the cut fruit (flesh side down) in lemon juice until ready for use. Covering the cut surface tightly with cling film (plastic wrap) and putting it in the fridge will also stop it from changing color. Use within a couple of days.

GET WITH THE BEET

For beet root, the key to flavor is in appearance – look for smooth round uniform bunches with small to medium roots. Avoid beet roots that are blocky or angular in shape, rough-skinned or oversized. Freshness of tops or leaves is not an indication of quality.

DON'T SUPER SIZE YOUR RADISHES

Choose radishes with medium-sized firm crisp roots. Avoid wilted or soft roots, which is a sign of them being too old, or oversized roots, which will taste pithy. And choose smoother skins, because those with growth or cracks retain fewer nutrients.

WHO KNEW?

Watercress is being hailed as the new super food because the chemical compounds it contains have been shown to help stop cancers developing by slowing down the degradation of cells. Use it in salads, sandwiches, soups and pasta.

GO MAN-GO

Mango is packed with vitamin C. When buying, don't worry if the mango is almost all green or red, as color doesn't make any difference to how ripe it is – it's simply down to a difference in varieties. Put a little pressure on the fruit and if the flesh gives way a little bit, the mango is ripe.

CHOOSE TIGHT BUNCHES

If you want to make sure you're choosing the best broccoli, Brussels sprouts or cauliflower, choose tightly compacted flower clusters on broccoli and cauliflower, and compact, uniform sprouts. Avoid wilted, yellow, or dirty heads, and avoid loose, open sprouts or those that are yellow or pale green.

SWALLOW SOME SOY

If you're worried about cholesterol, add some soy to your diet. It's been shown in some tests to boost omega-3 fatty acids and strengthen the immune system as well as reducing cholesterol in the bloodstream.

DON'T THROW AWAY THE OUTER LEAVES FROM A HEAD OF LETTUCE!

They come in handy when you need to cover foods in the microwave-and the leaves even add extra moisture, too.

IT CHANGES THE TASTE

Never store strawberries, melons or oranges near your butter. The aroma from the fruit is easily picked up by the butter, altering its taste.

WHO KNEW?

The vitamin-C content of fruit juices halves after a few days in the fridge, so if you're drinking juices at home, it's best to drink them as freshly squeezed as possible to make the most of the nutrients.

AT THE SUPERMARKET OR RESTAURANT

chapter

18

GET A GOOD PIZZA

Your best bet for flavorful, nutritious pizza is a local pizzeria, not a national (or even regional) chain. A mom-and-pop place is more likely to make the crust and sauce every day and use top-quality ingredients.

CHECK THE TEMPERATURE BEFORE YOU BUY

The meat freezer cases should have a thermometer in plain sight, which should read 0°F or below. Dairy should be stored at 40°F or below. Frozen foods should be between 0°F and 10°F. If you see ice crystals, don't buy the item; it means moisture has crept in.

LETTUCE TAKE THE LETTUCE TEST

Want to see whether lettuce is fresh? Look at the bottom. Check to be sure that the stem ring is white, not brown.

SUPERMARKET KNOW HOW

- Shop when the store is not crowded so you can see the specials.
- Never buy food in a sticky jar or a dented can.
- Most weekend specials start midweek.
- Foods on the lowest shelves are usually the least expensive. The most commonly purchased items are always found at eye level on the shelves.
- Processed hams should be kept refrigerated.
- If the market has a sale, buy by the case whenever possible.
- Don't be afraid to return poor-quality goods.

CARBO OVERLOAD

From the bread basket, choose breadsticks, hard rolls, French and Italian bread, pita bread, wafers, and melba toast. These don't have as much butter or sugar as soft rolls, biscuits, croissants, and muffins.

OY VEY

Although kosher foods do not contain any edible offal or animal-based additives such as lard, they still may contain tropical oils (palm and coconut), which are high in saturated fats. Kosher meats usually have higher sodium content than other meats due to the heavy salting during processing. For the most part, kosher products are no more healthful than others are, and the additional cost is not worth it—unless, of course, you adhere to the dietary restrictions.

HO HO HURL

Be careful around the holidays. Many stores place foods in chest freezers, piling the food higher than the freezer line. Chickens and turkeys over the line have probably thawed and refrozen a number of times. When you are ready to use them, they may have gone bad.

AND YOU WONDER WHY WE'RE FAT

In 2005, the average American consumed:

- 152 pounds of refined sugar
- 61 pounds of fats and oils
- 339 cans of soft drinks
- 195 sticks of chewing gum
- 21 pounds of candy
- 15 pounds of potato chips, corn chips, popcorn, and pretzels
- 79 doughnuts
- 52 pounds of cakes and cookies
- 22 gallons of ice cream
- 105 tablespoons of peanut butter
- 7 pounds of carrots
- 5 pounds of bell peppers
- 5 pounds of broccoli

SODIUM IS NOT YOUR FRIEND

If you are on a low-sodium diet, be aware that relish trays and antipastos are extremely salty. Avoid pickled vegetables, relishes, and cured meats. Also watch out for mustard, Worcestershire sauce, steak sauce, salsa, barbecue sauce, and ketchup—all very high in sodium.

GO AHEAD, GIVE IT A SQUEEZE

Give bags of frozen foods a quick squeeze before putting them in your cart. If the food is solid, it has thawed and refrozen. Choose another package.

CARDBOARD IS BEST

If you can, avoid milk in clear plastic containers. When they are exposed to light for four hours, low-fat and nonfat milk lose 44 percent of vitamin A. Supermarkets in some areas of the country now package milk in yellow containers to shield it from light, and some markets have even installed "light shields" or store the milk under counters to protect them.

Light can also affect the nutrients in juices, especially vitamin C. Avoid juice in clear containers.

SO THAT'S WHY THE MILK AISLE IS SO FAR AWAY!

Almost 50 percent of a supermarket's profits come from the perimeter of the store: produce, meats, dairy, and the salad bar. The produce department is the showcase of most stores, and they want to stimulate your appetite by making you walk past the great-looking fruits and vegetables first. Meats are often at the back of the store so you notice them at the end of every aisle. Since many people run in for milk mid-week, dairy is usually as far from the entrance as possible to get you to walk past other food. Anchor displays are placed at the end of each aisle. These are products the market needs to rid its inventory or are higher profit-items. Breakfast cereals make more money than any interior store product and are given a large amount of space.

SORRY TO BE A BUZZKILL

Think that a salad is a better choice? Add one packet of ranch dressing to a McDonald's Chef's Salad, and it will have more fat than a Big Mac.

READ IT AND WEEP

For every $100 spent on food, almost $18 goes for meat, seafood, or poultry. Produce takes almost $10, snack foods take just more than $5, and beans, rice, and dried vegetables take $1. More than 80 percent of households buy potato chips every two weeks. In 2008, $49 million worth of Twinkies were sold.

EATING OUT

When it comes to healthful eating, fast food restaurants are one thing, and restaurants with table service are another. At the latter, you have more control over the amounts of fat, sodium, and sugar that end up on your plate. There are more items to choose from, of course, and you can ask that rich sauces or dressings be served on the side or not at all.

PETS AND FOOD

In 2005, people in the United States spent almost over $8.8 billion on dog and cat food.

- The higher-quality pet foods contain more protein and less sugar, as well as fewer artificial dyes and additives.
- Veterinarians estimate that about 30 percent of cats and dogs are overweight. One study linked overweight pets to overweight owners.
- Feeding cats a saucer of milk may not be a healthful treat. Some cats are lactose intolerant and a treat with less lactose, like cottage cheese or yogurt, would be better for them.
- Chocolate is toxic to dogs, but cats won't even touch it because they can't taste sweets.

WHY PRICES KEEP GOING UP

Shoplifting is a real problem in supermarkets, with losses estimated to be $5 billion per year. The most common stolen items are cigarettes, health-and-beauty aids, meats, fish, and batteries. Two of the most common problems are internal: stock staff who steal and cashiers who don't ring up items for friends or family.

IMITATION

A food substitute, usually nutritionally inferior, and may contain the same calories and fat as nonimitation. Any new food with less protein or lesser amount of any essential vitamin or mineral must be labeled imitation.

WHO KNEW?

When you arrive home from the supermarket, always put newer foods in the back of the fridge so older food gets used first.

WHO KNEW?

The average serving of General Tso's chicken in a Chinese restaurant contains 1600 calories and 59 grams of fat. Kung Pao chicken has the same amount of calories—and 76 grams of fat.

IT MAKES A DIFFERENCE

If you prefer fruits and veggies with the peels, try to buy organic produce. You'll still need to wash it, but there will be less need to worry about pesticide residues.

READ THE LABEL: DEFINITIONS

Diet or Dietetic

The product may be lower in calories, sodium, or sugar than a comparable product. The FDA has not defined this term.

Enriched

A processed product that is sometimes fortified with a percentage of the nutrients that was originally there.

Extra-Lean

Meat and poultry must have no more than 5 grams of total fat, less than 2 grams of saturated fat, and less than 95 milligrams of cholesterol per serving amount.

Lean

Meat and poultry must have no more than 10 grams of total fat, 4.5 grams or less saturated fat, and less than 95 milligrams of cholesterol per serving amount.

Lite or Light

This is one of the more confusing terms. If 50 percent or more of the calories are from fat, the fat must be reduced by at least 50 percent from the original food. If less than 50 percent of the calories are from fat, the fat must be reduced at least by 50 percent, or the calories must be at least one-third of the original food. For main dishes or meals, the item must also meet the definition for low-calorie or low fat.

Low-Calorie

Meats and main dishes are allowed to contain 120 calories per serving; all other foods can contain 40 calories per serving.

Low-Cholesterol

Cannot contain more than 20 milligrams of cholesterol per serving.

Low-Fat

The food must contain no more than 3 grams of fat per serving and no more than 30 percent of calories from fat per serving size.

Low-Sodium

Must contain 140 milligrams or less per serving.

Natural

May mean anything. No regulations apply, and the word may be seen on foods that have no additives and preservatives.

No Cholesterol

This means that the item has less than 2 milligrams per serving amount. But it still may be high in saturated fat.

No Salt Added

Salt cannot be added during processing, though the food may have other ingredients that contain sodium. If so, the label must state, "This is not a sodium-free food."

Organic

A food that is produced without the use of genetic engineering, growth hormones, antibiotics, or fertilizer made from sewage. Organic foods are not necessarily more healthy or nutritious.

WHO KNEW?

The United States cans more than 1,500 different kinds of foods, with billions of cans being sold annually. There are more than 40 varieties of beans alone, 75 varieties of juices, and more than 100 different types of soups. A can of food will last for about two years and still retain a reasonable level of nutrients if stored in a cool, dry location.

LEAVE A THIRD

Portion sizes in restaurants are usually at least double what a person would normally eat, especially as you usually have more than one course, so it is important to keep that in mind when ordering and eating. If your portion is too large, a good rule of thumb is to leave a third of each serving.

Reduced-Calorie

Must have at least 25 percent fewer calories than the original product.

Reduced-Sodium

The sodium content in the food has been reduced by at least 25 percent.

Sodium-Free

Must contain less than 5 milligrams of sodium per serving.

Sugar-Free

Must contain less than 0.5 gram of sugars per serving.

Very Low-Sodium

Must contain 35 milligrams or less of sodium per serving.

FUNNY, IT FEELS LIKE PRISON, TOO

The produce area usually has the most influence on where you choose to shop. Produce is the second highest profit for the market (meat is first). In supermarket terms, the aisles (as opposed to the perimeter) are called the prison, because once you enter you cannot get out until you reach the other end. The prison, however, in most instances is where the least profitable foods are found.

SOUNDS DELICIOUS!

One nationwide fast food chain reports that its "roast beef" is just processed ground beef, water, salt, and sodium phosphate. But it is lower in cholesterol and fat than real roast beef or the average hamburger, so it's a healthful choice when it comes to fast-food fare.

REMOVE POULTRY SKINS

If you order chicken or turkey, remove the skin before you eat it and you'll end up with less fat. (As for duck, it's fat through and through.)

ROASTED CHICKEN FACTS

Roasted chicken chains provide some healthful choices, but they can also have artery-busting food. A roasted half chicken with skin can contain between 650 and 750 calories and about 3 tablespoons of fat. Choose skinless chicken, and stick with lower-fat side dishes.

THE BETTER CHOICE

Nutritionally, pizza is a reasonably good choice. The tomato sauce provides vitamins A and C, the cheese provides calcium, and if you have veggie toppings instead of sausage or pepperoni, you'll get additional nutrients without much fat.

TIME TO EAT THE DOUGHNUTS

In 2008, Americans ate more than 14 billion doughnuts.

THEY CAN EVEN RUIN FISH

Fish is healthful, right? Not if you order a fried-fish sandwich. Otherwise low in fat, fish gets 50 percent of its calories from fat when it's fried.

TOO BAD IT'S SERVED WITH A BILLION-CALORIE BURGER

Some fast-food restaurants offer multigrain buns, which are an excellent source of fiber.

WOULD YOU LIKE FAT ON THAT ICE CREAM?

Steer clear of soft-serve ice cream dipped in chocolate coating. There's very little chocolate—it's actually a high-fat product made from fats that have a very low melting point.

??? WHO KNEW?

A "Bloomin' Onion" with dipping sauce contains 2310 calories and 134 grams of fat!

OR JUST DRIVE ON BY

If you think you are getting a low-fat meal by ordering a fast food chicken sandwich, think again. Most chicken sandwiches contain 20 to 29 grams of fat, but some contain more than 40 grams—which is like eating a pint of regular ice cream in one sitting.

IT AIN'T HEALTH FOOD

Just because it's chicken doesn't mean it's healthful. If it's fried, if the skin is still on, and if there are special coatings, a chicken sandwich has, in most cases, more calories and fat than a regular burger.

CHECK OUT THEIR SITES

Most fast-food restaurants have Web sites where they post the nutrient analysis of their food.

A BETTER CHOICE

Some seafood chains offer baked fish, which provides about 200 calories less than fried fish; it also clocks in with about one-half as much sodium.

BUT IT SOUNDS BETTER THAN "NOW WITH BONE AND GRISTLE"

Beware of claims of "100 percent pure beef." Legally, this label can be given to any processed meat that contains ground bone, gristle, fat, and almost any other part of the animal.

Common Fast-Food Meals				
	CALORIES	CHOLESTEROL	SODIUM	FAT
Hamburger on a bun	550	80 mg	800 mg	57%
Regular fries	250	0 mg	115 mg	52%
Thick shake	350	31 mg	210 mg	8%
Apple pie	260	6 mg	427 mg	21%
TOTAL	1,410	117 mg	1,552 mg	NA

SPECIAL ORDERS DON'T UPSET THEM

Always order fast food as a special order so that you can specify that you do not want the special sauce (loaded with fat), ketchup (sugar), mayonnaise (fat), and pickles (salt).

IS IT REALLY A DIET PLATE?

A lot of so-called diet plates feature a ground beef patty, cottage cheese, and some kind of salad. But a 3-ounce patty can have as much as 19 grams of fat, and even cottage cheese has 5 grams of fat per half-cup.

MAYBE THEY CAN SERVE IT WITH AN ANGIOPLASTY

If you really want a high-fat meal, try Hardee's Monster Thickburger. This one is on top of all charts with 1,417 calories and 107 grams of fat, half of which is saturated. Double the fat by adding a thick shake and a large order of fries.

BLAME IT ON THE DEEP-FRIED BOWL

One of the worst meals for calories and fat is the Taco Salad from Taco Bell. It can tip the scales with as many as 905 calories and 61 grams of fat, 16 grams of which are saturated.

OK IN MODERATION, BUT REALLY KIND OF GROSS

Many fast-food chains advertise that they do not use any animal fats for frying. What many neglect to mention is that they have switched to tropical oils like coconut and palm—both of which are high in saturated fat. Another thing you should know: Some chains precook their fries at a central location to reduce cooking time on-site. This prefrying is typically done in high-saturated fat vegetable oils.

IT'S BETTER THAN BURGERS

Pizza is the most popular fast food in the United States, and pepperoni is the number one topping. In Japan, the favorite pizza toppings are tuna and scallops—maybe one reason the Japanese have fewer heart problems.

BLAME IT ON THE DEEP-FRIED BOWL

One of the worst meals for calories and fat is the Taco Salad from Taco Bell. It can tip the scales with as many as 905 calories and 61 grams of fat, 16 grams of which are saturated.

BECAUSE DIRT IS GROSS

The cleanliness of a supermarket is critical. This includes the floors, counters, and even the employees. Check the bathrooms, too.

UM, HOW IS THE FAT PREPARED?

In restaurants, avoid fried appetizers such as breaded jalapeños stuffed with cheese, breaded zucchini sticks, and any appetizers that mention cream or butter in the menu description. On salads, avoid creamy and cheese-based dressings—especially blue cheese and thousand island—and choose a simple oil-and-vinegar dressing instead. Good alternatives to fatty appetizers are a clear soup or a shrimp cocktail.

SURPRISING AND REVOLTING

Most thick shakes contain so many additives that are derived from sodium that one serving can contain more sodium than an order of French fries.

DO YOU REALLY NEED TO STUFF YOUR CRUSTS?

As tasty as they are, stuffed pizza crusts add about 4 grams of fat to the pizza and at least 150 to 160 more calories.

HOW REVOLTING

The three biggest national burger chains sell almost 4 million pounds of French fries daily—that's a total of 1 million pounds of saturated fat.

??? WHO KNEW?

Skinless fried chicken has almost as much fat as the regular variety.

CHINESE

Soup Choices: Wonton or hot-and-sour soup

Main Courses: Stir-fried vegetable dishes, white or brown rice, chow mien dishes, and most vegetable-based dishes

Stay Clear of: Anything bread or fried, especially egg rolls, sweet-and-sour dishes (very high calorie), and any dish sautéed in large amounts of oil

ITALIAN

Soup Choice: Minestrone

Main Courses: Any grilled lean meat or seafood, vegetable dishes without cream, pasta with marinara sauce

Stay Clear of: Antipasto, garlic bread, cream sauces, dishes topped with cheeses, breaded and fried foods

FRENCH

Soup Choices: Broth or vegetable soups

Main Courses: Any grilled lean meat or seafood, stews with a tomato base, vegetable dishes without cream sauces

Stay Clear of: French onion soup topped with cheese, pâté, anything in butter or cream sauce, croissants, au fromage or au gratin dishes

MEXICAN

Soup Choice: Corn-tortilla soup

Main Courses: Bean-and-rice dishes without cheese, chicken fajitas without cheese, corn tortilla, or tacos

Stay Clear of: Flour tortillas and chips, cheese sauces, guacamole, beef dishes, fried tortilla dishes, enchiladas, and burritos

FAST-FOOD CHAINS

Breakfast: Scrambled eggs, English muffin with no butter, orange juice

Lunch: Small burger with no cheese or sauce, grilled chicken sandwiches without sauce, salads with low-cal dressing, small single layer cheese pizza with vegetable toppings, Wendy's chili, Jack-In-The-Box Club Pita

Stay Clear of: Everything else

IMPORTANT
SAFETY TIPS

chapter

19

THE CUTTING BOARD CONTROVERSY

Studies continue regarding the safety of cutting boards. Plastic cutting boards were thought to be the better than wood because they are less porous. Then, a study commissioned by the Food Research Institute reported that bacterial levels on wooden cutting boards were low after only a few minutes. A subsequent study, however, indicated that bacteria burrowed deeper into the wood, not that the wood was inhospitable to them.

While the jury is still out on which is safer—plastic or wood—here are some critically important rules to follow:

- Reserve one cutting board only for raw meats, poultry, and fish; use other cutting boards for prepping vegetables, cheeses, and cooked meat, poultry, and fish.
- Wash all cutting boards immediately after use in very hot soapy water. Run them through the dishwasher to sterilize them (hint: plastic withstands the higher temperatures better than wood does), or wash them with a weak bleach solution.
- Remember that it's harder to scrub bacteria out of nooks and crannies; discard cutting boards whose surfaces have deep knife marks.
- Avoid setting hot pans on wood cutting boards or butcher-block countertops. Bacteria love heat, and the hot pan may serve to activate them or draw them to the surface of the wood.

AVOID THE GERMS

Dishcloths and sponges should be washed or run through the dishwasher every day. Paper towels are safer to use in most instances. Can openers also have the potential to spread germs; wipe them clean after each use.

WHO KNEW?

To disinfect a plastic cutting board, wash it throughly, rub half a cut lemon over it, and microwave for a minute.

KNOW THE SYMPTOMS

Symptoms of food poisoning will vary depending on the amount and type of the bacteria or virus ingested. Symptoms usually include chills, stomachache, nausea, muscle aches, and diarrhea. If diarrhea occurs shortly after a meal, it is usually a sign of food poisoning. If you experience any symptom or even suspect that you have eaten a contaminated food, contact your doctor immediately.

PARTY ON

Many food poisonings are linked to potluck parties. When protein-based dishes—meat, poultry, egg, or dairy—are left at room temperature for more than two hours, bacteria multiply rapidly.

KIDS, DON'T TRY THIS AT HOME

Avoid using paraffin or wax of any kind to seal jars of preserves. Wax seals fail more frequently than do the two-piece caps of rings and seals. The result: Mold can grow.

BACTERIAL SAUNA

Some of cooks insist on roasting their turkeys on low heat overnight. Although this results in a juicy bird, it also gives the bacteria plenty of time to multiply, because it takes longer to get to a temperature that's high enough to kill all the bacteria. If the bird is not heated to 180°F, food poisoning is a possibility.

HOW REVOLTING

Every day in the United States, more than 220,000 people get sick from eating foods that are contaminated. This explains why there are so many telephone hotlines devoted to food safety, including the Consumer Nutrition Safety Hotline: 1-(800) 366-1655.

CHECK WITH THE DOC

If you're given antibiotics, ask your doctor or pharmacist whether you should take them on an empty stomach. Food tends to slow down the absorption of the medication, and this may reduce its potency.

THERE GO THE NUTRIENTS

As long as the seal is intact, canned foods can last for years. The nutrient content will diminish, however, the longer the food stays on your shelf.

HEALTHY TIPS

Never purchase a can or jar if there is a bulge or any sign of damage. When you open a can or jar always smell the contents and check for mold. Never put a utensil that's been in your mouth into a container. This includes fingers, for those who love peanut butter or to nibble olives.

IT'S WHY WE HAVE CELLARS

Canned foods need to be stored in a cool, dark place. Heat causes dormant bacteria to become active and multiply.

UM, JUST WHAT ARE THE INSPECTORS INSPECTING?

Food-borne illnesses sicken more than 81 million Americans every year. The majority of these cases are relatively mild, and most people get over the illness in two to three days. However, about 10,000 of these cases are fatal, with 75 percent of the fatalities caused by salmonella and campylobacter, primarily found in meat and poultry.

HIGH & DRY

Keep medicines in a cool, dry place – heat and humidity can affect potency so a steamy bathroom is not ideal. Store on high shelves in cupboards or a dedicated cabinet out of sight and reach of children. Anything beyond the expiry date should be thrown away.

USE VINEGAR FOR CANNING

Any vinegar with 4 to 6 percent acetic acid is acceptable for canning. But pick your vinegar wisely: Some have distinctive flavors that might not be suitable for all pickling recipes.

HOT OR COLD, BUT NOT WARM

When you're setting out a buffet, keep foods either warm or cold—not lukewarm. Cold foods should be kept at 40°F at the most, while hot foods should stay at 140°F in a Crock-Pot or chafing dish.

IT ALWAYS EXPANDS

Foods high in starch, such as corn, peas, and lima beans, should be packed loosely because they expand during and after processing; leave 1 inch of head space in their jars. Fruits and berries should be packed with about ½ inch of head space because of shrinkage and because their texture does not stop the heat penetration.

CHILLY CHILI IS NOT A GOOD THING

If you make chili with beef or poultry, be sure and heat it to a temperature of 165°F before serving it. Follow this rule whether the chili is being served for the first time or you're reheating leftovers.

DON'T KISS THE COOK

If you ever spy a restaurant cook with a cigarette, consider taking your business elsewhere. Saliva cross-contamination when smokers touch a cigarette then food is quite common.

BUY 'EM WHOLE

Cutting fruits and vegetables, especially those like citrus fruits and melons that are high in vitamin C, can speed nutrient loss. It's best to buy them whole and cut them yourself, rather than purchase tubs of cubed fruits at supermarkets or salad bars.

HOW ABOUT A BAG O' SALAD?

Have you thought that the plastic bags of salads, broccoli florets, spinach, and other vegetables available at the market are inferior to bulk produce? Be reassured: Studies have demonstrated nutrient content is excellent, even to the point of surpassing those sold loose. (Of course, you pay a premium for the quality.) Two caveats: Wash packaged produce before eating it, and heed the "use by" dates.

ALWAYS, ALWAYS, ALWAYS

When canning anything by any method, sterilizing is an important part of the process. Be sure to sterilize the jars and lids, as well as utensils like spoons or ladles, by boiling them for 10 minutes before you fill the jars.

WELL-LIT SPACES

You'll feel safer if you can see who is at your door. Have enough light outside your front door and fit a peephole to a door or window so you can see without being seen.

LOOK FOR THE SEAL

As long as the seal is intact, freezer-preserved foods are still safe to eat. However, as with all frozen foods, the taste and texture may be different.

RESCUE ANGEL

Once poison ivy season is in full bloom, make sure you carry moist towelettes with you. If you are exposed to the poisonous leaves, wipe the affected area right away (within thirty minutes of exposure) and it will really help lessen the effects of the poison. And remember, the best way to relieve itching from poison ivy is to soak the affected area in hot salt water.

BECAUSE NOBODY WANTS A SOFT PICKLE

Keep the crunch in your pickles when you make them. Be sure that your vinegar is adequately acidic and that you use enough. Other causes of soft pickles include not covering the cucumbers completely with brine during fermentation; not sealing the jars so they're airtight; using moldy garlic or spices; or processing the jars for too long—or too short—a time. Storing the pickles in the refrigerator will help keep them firm.

BUT YOU KNEW THIS ALREADY, RIGHT?

When grilling, never put cooked meat or poultry back onto the same plate that held the raw food. This form of cross-contamination has been the cause of many cases of food poisoning.

UH-OH

If you see a black deposit on the lid after you open a canned food, it is not a good sign. Throw the food out.

DON'T BE A BUTTERFINGER

How many times have you hit your fingers while hammering in a nail? Next time you're hanging pictures, put the nail between the tines of a fork before hammering. Your fingers will thank you, and your kids won't hear you swear.

HEAT TREATMENT

If you refrigerate leftovers for more than 36 hours, reheat to 165°F before serving. Refrigerator temperatures are usually not cold enough to slow bacterial growth for much longer than a day and a half.

WHO KNEW?

If the liquid in a food jar is cloudy, the food inside is probably spoiled. Dispose of the jar without even opening it, or harmful spores may be released into the air.

GROSS, WHEN YOU THINK ABOUT IT

If smoking in bars is still allowed in your state, avoid drinking from a glass that has been stored upside down over the bar. Smoke and other contaminants get into the glass and remain there.

ALWAYS LEAVE ENOUGH SPACE

After canning food, tap the lid of the jar. You should hear a clear, ringing note, unless the food is touching the top. Be sure to leave the proper amount of space.

SWEETER IS BETTER

Always thaw frozen fruits in the refrigerator. The fruit will have time to reabsorb the sugar as it thaws.

YOUR MOTHER WAS RIGHT

You should always wash your hands before preparing food. Bacteria that cause food-borne illness can't be smelled or tasted, but are probably on your hands nevertheless.

AVOIDING LEAD

Imported lead crystal decanters, as well as some imported ceramics and pottery, are best used as decoration rather than for storage. A number of liquids—especially vinegar and wine—can leach the lead out of crystal over time.

DON'T LET YOUR OIL SPOIL

Oils break down and become rancid over time, especially if exposed to light. If you buy large containers of oil, look for dark containers and store them in the refrigerator if the oil will not be used within 30 days.

BEFORE YOU DIG IN

If you order a dish made from custard or whipped cream, or one that has a cream filling, be sure it is served cool to the touch. These are all supposed to be refrigerated desserts.

GO FREE RANGE

If you're using raw eggs in a recipe, such as chocolate mousse or mayonnaise, use free-range eggs. Almost no salmonella has been found in free-range eggs.

OUCH!

Pizza party crisis: Your kid has burned his tongue or roof of his mouth with the first piping-hot bite. (That's just bad parenting, folks). Fix the situations by quickly giving him a sip of milk, then coat the affected area in sugar, and the pain should soon be gone.

IT'S ENOUGH TO MAKE STAY IN BED AND PULL THE COVERS OVER YOUR HEAD

There are 1,800 strains of salmonella, most of which cause food poisoning. The Centers for Disease Control and Prevention estimates there are 2 to 4 million cases of salmonella poisonings every year, with 200,000 serious enough to warrant medical care and 1,000 to 2,000 resulting in death. Most cases are caused by human error and many have been associated with restaurant uncleanliness.

RAINDROPS ...

Rainwater is considered to be mineral water and may have a number of impurities. (We have all heard of acid rain, after all.) The purest water is distilled water.

LEAKING GAS

Never ignore the smell of gas – it is always a warning. Learn where the gas mains are located in your house and how to close the valve in case of a leak. If you can smell gas, contact your supplier immediately – never use an open flame to look for a gas leak.

BECAUSE BACTERIA IS NEVER INVITED TO A PARTY

Instead of setting out the food for a buffet all at once, keep most of it in the fridge. Then, before replacing a food, either wash the platter or get a new one before adding fresh food. Put out larger servings of foods that are going quickly and smaller servings of foods that are less in demand.

BURGLAR DETERRENTS

Don't let people see inside your home as this is a good way to spot anything worth stealing; draw curtains or blinds whenever you put the lights on. If you are selling your home, have the estate agent call you about every viewer and make sure they accompany potential purchasers.

IT MAKES SENSE

Preservatives, additives, or artificial colorings should never be added to home-canned foods. Clean all food residue off the jar exteriors by wiping them with white vinegar before storing.

DEEP-FAT DRAMA

Avoid filling a deep-fat fryer so the oil is more than a third of the way up the pan. If fat catches fire while you are cooking meat, sprinkle both the fat and the meat with bicarbonate of soda to put out the flames.

RADIATION: YES OR NO?

Many scientists and doctors believe that foods exposed to radiation are as safe to eat as foods that have not been irradiated. According to the Centers for Disease Control and Prevention, researchers have noted that levels of thiamine in food are slightly reduced, but not enough to result in a deficiency. In addition, there are no significant changes in levels of amino acids, fatty acids, or the vitamin contents of foods.

In well-controlled studies, irradiated foods have been fed to animals and people. Some of these animal studies have lasted for several generations in several species, including mice, rats, and dogs. Researchers have found no evidence of adverse health effects in these studies. Nevertheless, many people prefer to avoid irradiated foods. If you have any questions, call the Consumer Nutrition Safety Hotline: 1-(800) 366-1655.

PUT IT OUT WITH SODA

Humble baking soda is the best defense against small kitchen fires – simply throw baking soda at the base of the flames. But don't use this method if the fire is caused by fat or grease, as splashing could result in severe burns.

RX, VINEGAR

White vinegar stops nosebleeds. Just dampen a cotton ball and plug the nostril. The acetic acid in the vinegar cauterizes the wound.

RASH SOOTHERS

An effective and natural way to soothe diaper rash is by adding a cup of baking soda to your baby's bathwater.

SUFFERING WITH BAD SUNBURN?

You big dope—don't you know too much sun is bad for you? The good news is you don't need an expensive after-sun lotion. Just cut an apple in half, remove the core, and rub over the affected area for three to four minutes. That should keep your skin from blistering or peeling.

FREE STUFF! ^{chapter} **20**

FREE

DISCOUNTS

WHO KNEW?

If you go to Google, the Internet search engine, and type in "free stuff," you will be directed to more than one billion links.

HEATING HELP

The Low Income Home Energy Assistance Program helps pay the winter heating bills or summer cooling bills of low-income and elderly people. Check out www.liheap.org for details.

THE BEST THINGS IN LIFE ARE FREE...

...And you can get them from the Internet, in the mail, and from the government. There are lots of incredible offers available, and in this chapter, we focus on some of the best. Many of the best free offers today come from the Internet, but you need to use caution when claiming them. Always, always, set up a new email address before you start responding to free offers, because once you start, you'll be inundated with email (trust us). Also, some of the offers change frequently, so don't be disappointed if the specific freebie you're after is no longer available. Just hunt around using the addresses listed below. There are plenty of others! Finally, never give out your social security number to anyone on the Internet, and never give out your credit card information unless you are 100% sure the site is trustworthy. Be careful...and enjoy the freebies!

WE LOVE MOM

Perhaps our all time favorite site for savings is www.couponmom.com, where you can save time and money by matching your store's weekly sales items with coupons available from the Sunday newspaper or online websites. What's so unique about this site is that it provides a list of best grocery deals and coupons by state. So, if you're interested in what's on sale at, say, Shop Rite in New Jersey, for example, each week's offerings are noted here. In addition, the site provides a "Virtual Coupon Organizer," which really helps organize website coupons. Check it out!

FOR YOUR FURRY COMPANIONS

Is your pet one of those organic types? Get a free all-natural sample of dry food for your cat or dog at www.highestqualitypetfood.com.

THE SKYPE IS THE LIMIT

Make free phone calls to practically anywhere in the world with Skype—a software you download, then use to talk to people through your computer speakers and microphone. You can also call cell phones and land lines for as low as 2 cents a minute. Visit www.skype.com to start chatting.

I CAN SEE CLEARLY NOW

You can get a certificate for a free pair of contact lenses, plus a $30-off coupon, at www.acuvue.com/specialoffers.htm. (Of course, you'll need to see an eye doctor to fill the prescription and there may be a cost for that.)

PAMPER YOURSELF

Keep your skin soft and smooth with free samples and coupons from Oil of Olay (www.olay.com/samplesandoffers) and Dove (www.dove.us/#/offers/freesamples). You can also sign up for email newsletters that will keep you apprised of deals and special offers.

KEEP YOUR CREDIT CLEAN

Did you know that you are entitled to one free credit report per year? Visit AnnualCreditReport.com to keep an eye on your rating and to make sure there are no errors on your report. Tip: don't be fooled by other "free credit report" sites, which may charge you a membership fee.

FREE MEDICINE

It's out there. Patient assistance programs provide free prescription medicines to more than 6.2 million Americans, and many more could benefit from these programs but don't know about them. Log on to www.freemedicineprogram.com to find out if you qualify for free medicine.

JAVA AND NO JIVE

Yes, there is a site named www.freecoffeesite.com, and their reason for being is to provide free coffee samples. All you have to do is complete a short survey and the coffee is yours. No strings attached at all.

BECAUSE WE ALL WANT TO BE HEALTHIER

Check out www.qualityhealth.com for free samples of everything from sleeping pills to tissues. Just click on "Special Offers and Savings" on the bottom right.

BE HIP

HIP Mommy's Place.com is just that—a fun site run by a hip mom who is good at finding deals on the internet. Get links to free samples of food, household cleaning products, and much more. Best of all, they are all tested out by the Hip Mommy herself, so you know exactly what you're getting! Just visit hipmommysplace.com and click on "Hip Free Stuff."

TURKEY TIPS

For year round answers to any questions about how to cook turkey, call 1-800-BUTTERBALL. Also, for recipes and free coupons, try www.butterball.com.

EAT ON THE CHEAP

Get great deals on dining at www.retailmenot.com/coupons/food, where you'll find printable coupons and discount codes for dozens of restaurants. Never feel bad about ordering seconds again!

UH, HE DOESN'T LIVE HERE ANYMORE

Never have to lie about who you are to a telemarketer again. Put your name on the official "do not call list" for free by calling 1-888-382-1222 or going to www.donotcall.gov.

MORE FREE COUPONS

Some of the easiest coupons to print out can be found at www.coolsavings.com, in addition to some great offers on diapers, detergents, and more.

OUR TAX DOLLARS AT WORK

The government has myriad programs offering financial assistance, awards, loan repayment and other benefits. There are simply too many for us to list here. The best way to see what is available is to go to www.govbenefits.gov and fill out a simple questionnaire, which will give you a complete list of the programs for which you're eligible. You'll be amazed at what is available.

HOW DO YOU SAY "FREE" IN ITALIAN?

Take lessons in Spanish, French, Italian, and German absolutely free at www.bbc.co.uk/languages and you can travel internationally more easily (or just impress your friends). The site also offers quickie lessons in Chinese, Japanese, and even more exotic languages like Kudu.

FOR THE ONLINE SHOPPER

At www.gogoshopper.com, they offer coupon codes, promotion codes and coupon savings to the most popular online shopping destinations, such as Target, JC Penney, and Dell. It's much easier to get the coupon codes here than to search through a merchant's website. The site also has an impressive array of links for free samples as well.

WHO KNEW?

Jonathan Winters once said, "I couldn't wait for success, so I went ahead without it." You can get a free wisecrack like this emailed to you each day by joining www.fakecrap.com.

YOUR HOME (PAGE) AWAY FROM HOME

Tons of coffee shops, restaurants, hotels, and public buildings offer wireless internet service for free or free-with-purchase. Find local "hot spots" at WiFiFreeSpot.com, and don't forget to submit any WiFi zones you find for others on-the-go.

KEEPING IT CLEAN

Visit www.colgate.com click on "special offers" for coupons and free samples of toothpaste, dish soap, and other household goods. Or go to www.marksdailyapple.com/natural-cleaners for all-natural cleaners you can make out of ingredients you already own!

FOR THE BUNDLE OF JOY

There are plenty of websites featuring free stuff for newborns. At www.babiesonline.com, you can get everything from free diapers and diaper bags to magazine subscriptions as well. If you type "Enfamil Family Beginnings" into a search engine, you can find sites where you can get $60 in free formula checks, a diaper bag and formula samples, and be automatically entered for a chance to win a $2500 baby registry.

WARNING: YOU MIGHT GET HOOKED!

Boss disabled your solitaire game at work? Try out www.idiotsdelight.net, where you can choose from more than two dozen solitaire card games you can play online. Click on "Klondike" to play "regular" solitaire.

SOMETHING FOR EVERYONE

Whether you work in education, IT, retail, or dozens of other industries, you can get magazines relating to your profession absolutely free at www.mercurymagazines.com.

WHO NEEDS SIMPLICITY AND BUTTERICK?

Get free patterns for sewing, quilting, knitting, crochet, and even paper crafts at freepatterns.com. Just download and print out!

GREAT GROCERY OFFERS

At www.eversave.com, each week they offer about $80.00 worth of printable coupons to redeem and save. In addition, if you click on the "free stuff" icon on their home page, it will take you to some great free offers. You can also try www.dealpass.com. You'll love scanning to the bottom of your receipt to see how much you saved!

BECAUSE GRANDMA DIDN'T HAVE A RECIPE FOR MOJITOS

Our favorite site for free recipes is epicurious.com, where you can browse recipes by type (appetizers, drinks, entrees), or type in key words to search for specific recipes. Since their recipes are pulled from publications like *Bon Appétit* and *Gourmet*, you know they're going to be good, but if you're not sure, you can read reader reviews. You can also start a "recipe box" of your favorite recipes from the site—make sure to include one of their more than 400 recipes for chocolate cake.

BUT WHO'S JUDY?

Another great site for local deals is Judysbook.com, which will show you current sales of neighborhood businesses, as well as providing coupon codes for online stores. On a recent visit we found out that a nearby bike shop was offering 30% off, printed out a coupon for discounted dry cleaning, and checked out links to sales at an online candle store.

WHO DOESN'T LOVE SAMPLES?

Startsampling.com pulls together the best online offers for free samples, from magazine subscriptions to vitamins. The site also offers some valuable coupons that you can print out and take with you to the store.

YOUR SECRET WEAPON

Never miss a birthday again! Get free email and text message reminders about birthdays (or any other important event) at www.birthday-reminders.com.

BUY SOME GAS, SAVE FOR COLLEGE

At Upromise.com, you can earn money toward your children's college educations—or help pay off student loan debt already accrued—through your everyday purchases. Register your credit/debit cards along with cards from grocery and drug store reward programs, and then earn points for every purchase you make at thousands of retailers nationwide.

WHO KNEW?

According to government studies, there are over 6 million children who are eligible for financial assistance and don't receive it—because their families don't know it's available.

BECAUSE A CLEAN HOME IS A HAPPY HOME

Great recipes, cleaning and decorating tips and a free newsletter are available from www.cleanhomejournal.com. Our favorite "gee whiz" cleaning tip? A slice of white bread rolled into a ball will clean scuffs and stains from wallpaper or painted walls. Who knew?

YOUR COMPUTER WILL THANK YOU

At download.com, you can download free screensavers, anti-virus software, games, and more. Just type what you're looking for in the Search bar, then click "Free" under "Narrow Your Search" on the left.

AND FOR THE REALLY NICE STUFF...

Like most cosmetic counters, you can get free samples simply by asking at the counter of Kiehl's, a "high end" carrier of soaps, lotions, and haircare products (even shampoos for pets!). But you can also call 1-800-543-4572 and request up to three free samples of their products to be mailed to your home.

FREE DOWN PAYMENTS FOR YOUR HOME?

It's true. The Genesis Program is a non-profit organization established to help honest, hard-working people achieve the dream of home ownership buy giving gifts of up to $22,500 for a down payment. Yep, it's a gift, and you don't have to pay it back. Their goal is to help those of us who have good jobs and credit histories but have unable to save enough for a down payment. Check out their site at www.thegenesisprogram.org for details.

MORE HELP FOR HOMEOWNERS
(AND WOULD-BE HOMEOWNERS)

Like The Genesis Program, the Home Down Payment Gift Foundation (www.homedownpayment.org) provides gifts of up to $30,000 for down payments. In addition, they have a "Rainy Day Program," in which they offer financial help for homeowners who find themselves in unexpected trouble.

ALL KIDS NEED MEDICAL INSURANCE

Every state in the nation has a health insurance programs for children under 18 years old. It's available for children in working families, and provides (at little or no cost) insurance to pay for doctor's visits, prescriptions, and much more. To see if you qualify go to www.insurekidsnow.gov, then click on "Your State's Program" or call 1-877-KIDS-NOW.

FREE LIFE INSURANCE

Mass Mutual offers free premiums for a life insurance policy with a $50,000 death benefit if you quality. You must be between 19–42, and be the parent or legal guardian of one or more children under the age of 18, and also meet specific financial criteria. For details go to www.massmutual.com, search "LifeBridge" or call 1-800-272-2216.

WHEN TIMES ARE TOUGH

The Health Resources and Services Administration (www.hrsa.gov) can direct you to a health center which will provide health and dental care to people of all ages, whether or not they have health insurance or the money to play for help care. Just go to their web site, and then click on the "find help" icon.

WHAT IF YOU STILL WANT MORE FREE STUFF?

Just go to www.bigcoupons.com. They've got some interesting offers, but also links for countless other sites offering an array of coupons and free things. Just click on the icons marked "Other Coupon Sites" or "Other Freebie Sites."

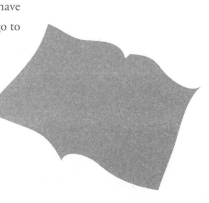

BEST WAY TO LOWER YOUR DRUG COSTS

Get a discount drug card from United Networks of America, at www.freedrugcard.com. It's free, open to everyone, and offers discounts of up to 75% on many prescriptions that might not be covered by health plans.

THE FIRST DAY OF THE REST OF YOUR LIFE

Get all kinds of free, professional advice on your career (or desired career) at www.careeronestop.com (or call 1-877-348-0502), which will give you tutorials on résumés and cover letters, give you salary information, help you find free classes in your area, and more.

READ A MAGAZINE ONLINE, SAVE A TREE

If you don't mind reading them on the computer, at zinio.com you can download a free "digital" issue of many magazines, including *Reader's Digest*, *Hello!*, and *Women's Health*.

IF YOU'RE STARTING A BUSINESS

The Association for Enterprise Opportunity is an association of organizations committed to small businesses. On their site you'll find plenty of information about the grants and other resources that are available for the budding entrepreneur. You can find it all at www.microenterpriseworks.org.

JUST DON'T TRADE THIS BOOK!

Exchange books (not just paperbacks) at paperbackswap.com. Featured on the *Today Show* and in *Real Simple*, *Wired*, and *Good Housekeeping*, the site allows you list books you don't want any more. Once you send them to other users, you'll get credits you can use towards a new (to you) book of your own.

AND MORE FREE BOOKS

You can get a book or pamphlet on virtually any subject, free of charge, by logging onto www.pueblo.gsa.gov or calling 1-888-878-3256. The Federal Citizen Information Center offers free publications on cars, employment, housing, travel, money—the list goes on. Sometimes there is a small fee for shipping and handling; in all cases, you can download the text for free. It's really worth your time to check this out.

ANOTHER REASON NOT TO HAVE CHILDREN

The US Department of Education has created a "one-stop shop" site for up-to-date and accurate data on aid available to help you pay for college. This year, over $82 billion in grants, loans and other assistance will be given out. Claim yours at www.studentaid.ed.gov.

FOR THE MORE ADVENTUROUS

Massachusetts Institute of Technology—one of the United States' most preeminent technological universities—offers free course materials online. Get reading lists, homework assignments, and audio and/or video lectures for hundreds of classes including SCUBA diving, Chinese, TV theory, and more. Want to really impress your friends? Try some classes on nanotechnology, brain structure, bioengineering, even "Wheelchair Design in the Developing World." Visit the site at www.ocw.mit.edu and click on "Audio/Video Courses" on the upper left-hand side.

EVERYONE LOVES IRONING

Ever wanted to know the perfect way to get all the wrinkles out? Find out now with this free DVD called "The Art of Ironing." Just enter your information at www.artofironing. com/free_dvd.php.

THE BEST COFFEE-MAKER YOU'LL EVER HAVE

Sick of buying cheap coffee makers that can't handle your raging coffee addiction? Visit Gevalia.com and sign up for their coffee delivery service to receive a free state-of-the-art coffee maker, a pound of gourmet coffee, and a coffee scoop. You'll have to pay $14.95—and make sure to call and cancel your membership right away—but for a coffee maker valued at more than $100 (and won't scorch your coffee!), it's worth it!

WHO KNEW?

Over $35 billion worth of grants were given out in the United States in 2005.

WATCH YOUR MONEY

With IRAs, 401(k)s, stocks, and other investments, it's hard to keep everything straight. Sign up for a free portfolio tracker at Kiplingers.com or Smartmoney. com and you won't sweat so much around tax time.

BILLIONS OF DOLLARS HAVE BEEN LOST. IS SOME OF IT YOURS?

There is over $24 billion worth of unclaimed property in the US, and www.unclaimed.org is the official government site where you can get information about it all. You can search by name or state, and they also provide access to databases maintained by each state. Just click on the "missing money" icon on their home page.

GET FREE ADD-ONS FOR YOUR ELECTRONICS

Looking for a good offer when purchasing a Macintosh computer, iPod, camcorder, plasma TV, or other electronics? Macmall.com offers all kinds of special promotions, from free printers to ipod covers to hundreds of dollars off. Just make sure to send in the mail-in rebates before it's too late—many offers expire in less than 30 days.

THE SURVEY SAYS

The folks at surveyspot.com not only want your opinion, they'll pay for it. Sometimes. If you qualify. The truth is, if you join this site (it's free) you'll receive 5 to 7 surveys a week. Each takes between 10 to 45 minutes to complete, and each time you complete a survey, you're entered into a sweepstakes where you can win $10,000 and some other great prizes. In addition, in some case they'll pay $2–$10 for a completed survey, and enter you into their sweepstakes! Go to the site for details.

IF YOU HAVE LOTS OF FRIENDS

…who don't mind getting email spam, check out www.notebooksforfree.com, where you can get a free laptop computer. The catch? You not only have to complete at least one promotion (which often require you to make a purchase), but sign up 18 to 24 friends who all must complete an offer as well.

MISSING MEDALS

If you or a deceased family member received service medals from the army, navy, air force, marines, or other service and they have been lost, you can obtain free replacements by writing to the military branch they were awarded by. To see a list of addresses to write to, visit www.archives.gov/veterans/military-service-records/replacement-medals.html.

SAY GOODBYE TO PESKY CATALOGS

We used to get catalogs for everything from girls' clothes (we only have boys) to farm equipment (we *do* have a couple of pigs…). Not anymore. Go to www.catalogchoice.org and get your name off all those weirdo mailing lists.

AND DON'T FORGET TO INVITE HIM OVER FOR CAKE

The White House will send a greeting from the President to you or a loved one for your birthday (if you're at least 80), anniversary (if you're married at least 50 years) or to commemorate a wedding, birth of a child, or other special occasions. For details, go to www.whitehouse.gov/greeting or write to: The White House, Attn: Greetings Office, Washington, DC 20502-0039.

PAY 10, GET 25

Paying for a gift certificate isn't much of a bargain, unless you're only paying $10 for $25 off! That's the name of the game at Restaurant.com. Type in your zip code to find dozens of local restaurants offering gift certificates for less than they're worth. Though most come with requirements, they're usually pretty easy, like using the certificate on a weekday or spending a minimum of $35.

TUTORING FOR KIDS

At www.tutorsforkids.org, you can find out if your child is eligible to receive free tutoring. It's available in every state, for virtually every subject.

FREE ATMS!

Did you know there are about 37,000 free ATMs in the U.S.? That's right---you never have to pay a fee again. Just go to www.allpointnetwork.com, enter your zip code, and start saving!

WHO KNEW?

Many of your favorite brands offer coupons on their websites. You can usually find the web address printed on their labels!

A GOOD, FREE MAGAZINE

Food & Family magazine contains over 60 pages of recipes for making deliciously simple entrees, desserts, and more (all with Kraft products). Claim your free subscription at www.kraftfoods.com by clicking on the "Sign up" icon.

FREE: PRETTY MUCH EVERYTHING

Craig's List is a site that connects people who live nearby—the ultimate online classifieds. Visit www.craigslist.org, find your city, and browse thousands of listings for jobs, roommates, garage sales, personal ads, classes, volunteer opportunities, and pretty much anything else you can think of. Click on "free" under "for sale" to find tons of people giving away all sorts of stuff—you normally just need to go pick it up.

DO YOU WANT $1000 WORTH OF FREE GASOLINE? FREE AIRLINE TICKETS? A $500 GIFT CARD? A FREE PLASMA TV?

Of course you do. Who doesn't? All of these offers exist at sites that operate as incentive promotion programs, where advertisers pay to get users to their websites, or to receive their solicitations. You'll receive your gift after fulfilling the participation requirements. Sounds easy? It's not. At most of these sites, you typically have to complete 4–6 offers from advertisers in order to collect, and navigate through a maze of offers to boot. They may require you to sign up for free trial offers, or for credit cards, and some require a small purchase. Still up for it? Great. It's a good idea to read the small type when you get on a site offering these types of gifts. Typically, they have a link to either "Terms and Conditions" or "Participation Requirements." That's where you'll find out exactly how many offers you need to complete to claim your gift. Good Luck! Some of the incentive promotion sites you might want to try are www.mycoolrewards.com, www.bigwin.com, www.freegiftworld.com, www.internetopiniongroup.com, www.incentiveleader.com, www2.i-dealrewards.com, and www.e-researchgroup.com. You can also go to an Internet engine and type in "free stuff."

FREE INFO

Never pay for directory assistance again. When you would normally call 411, dial 1-800-FREE-411 instead. You can use this service from a cell phone or a land line, and after listening to a brief advertisement, you can have an operator look up telephone numbers and addresses for free.

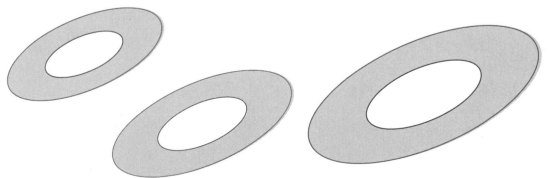

BILL-PAYING MADE EASY

It's hard to get free cable, gas, electricity, and other services, but it's easy to pay the bills without having to pay for stamps, envelopes, or checks. Go online or call the number on your bill to sign up for direct debit, which will automatically deduct the money from an account of your choosing each month. Most banks also offer free online bill payment, where you can consolidate your bills and pay them all at once online. Check your bank's site for more details.

NEVER SIT THROUGH A RERUN AGAIN

If you have a fast internet connection and a fairly new computer, you can watch TV and movies online for free! At hulu.com, you can watch TV right on your monitor. Play the most recent episodes of shows from FOX, NBC, Bravo, and other networks; or classics like *Alfred Hitchcock Presents* and *The A-Team.* They even have a good selection of movies, whether you're looking for something to entertain the kids or something R-rated for date night.

JUNK MAIL BE GONE!

Sick of getting a million credit card offers every time you open your mail box? You can opt out for free by calling 1-888-567-8688 or visiting optoutprescreen.com. Signing up will eliminate all of those "pre-approved" offers.

JUST TAKE US WITH YOU

If you're planning a vacation in the US, you can get free travel guides from 24-7vacation.com.

JUST LIKE NEW

You can find hundreds of items—from furniture to exercise equipment—at freecycle.org, a non-profit website whose goal is to decrease landfill waste. Users join up and post about items they are giving away or need, and connect with other users who want the items or have what they're looking for. Just be careful—some free things are hard to resist, but do you really need that bedazzled couch cover?

Do you have a great hint or tip to help save money or time? Share it with us! If we feature it in our next revision of Who Knew? or our next book, we'll be sure to include your name next to the hint.

Just email us at **hintsandtips@castlepointpub.com**, and please include your contact information so we can reach you if we decide to include your submission.

To reach us by mail, just send your hint to:
Hints and Tips
Castle Point Publishing
PO Box 1090
Hoboken, NJ 07030

Don't forget to include your return address or email address.

And thanks for your help!

INDEX

A

Abalone, 262
Acidophilus, 506, 511
Ackee, 528
Aflatoxin, 405
Air freshener, 130, 207
Alcohol
  in beer, 189
  boiling point, 323, 324
  cardiovascular disease and, 188
  champagne, 181, 182
  congeners in, 181
  freezing food with, 229
  igniting, 184
  immune system and, 190
  magnesium and, 180
  motion sickness and, 180
  proof, 180
  soot marks and, 108
  for stain removal, 23
  thirst and, 169
  vitamin absorption and, 180
  zinc and, 180
Alka Seltzer, 82
Alpha hydroxy acids AHAs, 69
Ammonia, 32, 36, 48, 112, 139, 162
Anchovies, 271
Anglerfish, 272
Anise, 472
Apples, 528–536
  baking, 534
  health benefits, 534, 535, 536
  juice/cider, 533, 534, 535
  pectin in, 519, 533
  pesticides and, 535
  varieties, 529–532
Applesauce, 534
  substitute for oil, 342
Apricots, 537
Aquaculture, 257
Arrowroot, 466
Artichokes, 567, 568, 569
  health benefits, 578
  steamed, 302
Arugula, 571, 572, 612
Ascorbic acid, 210
Asparagus, 578–579
  health benefits, 578

reviving, 579
Aspartame, 382
Atemoyas, 537
Automobiles
  tire cleaning, 120
  vegetable oil, 151, 57
  wheels, 135
  windshield cleaning, 100
  windshield deicing, 46
  windshield wipers, 120
Autoxidation, 504
Avocados, 527, 538, 540, 640
  health benefits, 540
  skin care and, 70

B

Babáco, 523
Baby powder, 35, 56, 136, 138, 165
Bacon
  brine-cured, 244, 245
  choosing, 239
  cooking, 238, 239
  nitrites in, 239, 245
  splatters from, 245
Bag
  vinyl shoe bag, 125
Bain marie, 364
Bakery products
  freezing, 223
Baking, 340–391
  air circulation and, 358
  "baker's magic" and, 356
  baking powder, 350, 354, 357, 391
  bake sale, 389
  baking soda, 350
  biscuits, 347, 364, 376
  blending ingredients, 344, 373
  bread, 344, 345, 346, 347, 348, 349, 355, 357, 358 359, 360, 361, 362, 363, 365–368, 370, 372, 374, 375, 377, 378, 381, 391
  with buttermilk, 349, 351, 425
  cakes, 322, 340, 343, 347, 352, 356, 358, 366, 367 374, 389, 515
  checking before completion

time, 361
  chilled dough, 372
  cookies, 341, 343, 348, 353, 357, 366, 369, 370, 371, 373–375, 387, 388, 399
  croutons, 368
  cupcakes
    eggs and, 351, 362
    fats and, 367
    flour, 372, 373, 374, 375, 390
    fondue, 389, 483
    fruit pies in glass, 373
    glass dishes and, 359
    graham cracker pies, 346, 390
    greasing pans, 347
    meringue, 348
    muffins, 294, 347, 349, 361, 644
    pans, 341
    pastries, 340, 341, 402, 425
    pies, 192, 346, 390, 471
    popovers, 362
    rolls, 363, 364, 499
    sticking to pan problems, 364
    vegetable oil and, 365
    vegetables, 300
    weighing ingredients, 374
    yeast and, 343, 348, 350, 354, 355, 356, 357, 359, 360, 361, 362, 372
Baking powder
  chocolate and, 357
  in self rising flour, 342
  substitutions for, 351
  testing for potency, 350
  cooking and, 308
  for icing, 372
  testing, 356
Bananas, 519, 520, 521, 539, 540
  health benefits, 540
  overripe, 609
  pectin in, 519
  ripening, 520, 533, 539, 540
  varieties, 541
Barbecuing
  chicken, 294
  herbs in, 313

Barley, 462
nutritional value, 395
Barracuda, 272
Basil, 154, 160, 433, 451
Bath
bathroom, 48, 55, 104, 126,
139, 143, 145, 203, 205,
660
body scrub, 67, 86
bubble bath, 71
bubble solution, 147
epsom bath salts, 86, 140
loofah, 86
scented bath oil, 204
Bay leaves, 160, 433, 458
Beans
black, 242, 405
chickpeas, 419, 446, 587
cooking, 581, 583, 586,
587, 588
edible-pod, 580
flatulence and, 580
green, 582, 586
health benefits, 582
kidney, 587
lectin in, 580
lima, 580, 583, 584, 587,
661
nutritional value, 405
pectin in, 519
pinto, 587
shell, 583
soybeans, 402, 581, 584,
585, 586, 587
steamed, 302
storage, 583, 586
varieties, 582, 583, 588
Beanut butter, 402
Beef
brisket, 233
chuck, 233, 236
color, 240
cooking temperatures, 304
fat/calories in, 283
flank, 233
freezing, 236, 247, 249, 251,
252
french beans and
mangetouts, 330
hamburger, 195, 243, 246,
251, 586, 621

kobe, 249
loin, 47, 259, 278
manganese absorption and,
241
meatballs, 248
meat loaf, 238, 525
refrigeration and flavor, 248
rib, 233, 234, 238, 624
roasts, 236, 237, 240, 242,
250, 253, 308
round, 234
steaks, 234, 425
stir frying, 326
tenderness, 156, 234, 249
Beer, 186–191
age of, 190
alcohol in, 189, 190
ale, 190
bock, 190
british cellar temperature,
187
calories in, 190
chili in beer, 256
chilling, 188, 189
cleaning, 131
cooking with, 188
draft, 187
fruit, 191
head, 187, 188
lager, 189, 191
light, 188, 187, 190
pilsner, 191
porter, 190, 191
slugs and, 165
storage, 187, 188, 189, 190
stout, 191
wheat, 191, 400
Beer cheese, 480
Beets, 588–589
greens, 588, 589
nutritional value, 589
steamed, 302
Bel paese cheese, 481
Berries
in bakery goods, 364, 542
choosing, 542
freezing, 542
nutritional value, 542
Beverages, 168–192
alcoholic, 174, 179–191
blue color and kids, 179

body temperature and, 176
cooling, 192
soft drinks, 179
summer, 170, 172, 179,
192, 198
tea, 172–174
water, 172, 174, 176, 195,
196, 199
Biscuits
color and, 364
cutters, 347, 356
even blending of, 354
reheating, 358
softer, 347
Blinds
cleaning, 33, 37
Bluefish, 272
Bock beer, 190
Bolognese, 228
Botox, 68
black magic marker, 58
Bouquet garni
Boursault cheese, 481
Boursin cheese, 480
Brass, 47, 49, 53
Bread
air circulation and, 358
batter, 360
browning, 377
coffee/tea and, 360
cooling, 374, 356
crispy crust, 348, 360
crumbs, 115, 254, 324, 341,
354, 403, 404
dairy liquid and, 360
enriched, 344
freezing, 361
french, 193
garlic, 362, 368
hard, 365
kneading, 357
kneading boards, 367
labels, 401
liquids for, 360
micro waving to rise, 355
mold and, 347, 378
pans, 359
potato water and, 366
quick, 359
quick, rising, 355, 357
reading labels, 401

reviving stale, 349
rising dough, 367
salt and, 358
salted crust, 348
slashing crust, 349
slowing rising time, 362
starch in, 407
sticks, 377
storage, 378, 391
sugar and rising, 359
sweetener and, 360
toast, 349
unleavened, 360
Vitamin C in, 345
whole wheat, 374
yeast and, 372, 386
Breadfruit, 544
Breading, 306, 324
    chicken cutlets, 286
    with crushed nuts, 404
    shrimp, 257
Brie, 477, 480, 481
Broccoflower, 592
Broccoli, 322, 590–591, 623,
    628, 636
    cooking, 513, 523
    pectin in, 519
    steamed, 302
    storage, 222
Brussels sprouts, 590, 591, 592
    pectin in, 519
    steamed, 302
Buckwheat
    nutritional value, 388, 395
Buffalo fish, 279
Bulgur, 419
Butter
    absorption of odors and
      balls, 199
    clarified, 509
    in cookies, 366, 373
    creaming, 352, 358, 365
    fancy pats, 196
    fat in, 426, 490
    grading system, 426, 511
    making, 512
    melting chocolate and, 361
    microwaving, 504
    from other than cow's milk,
      485
    oxidation of, 509

    rancid, 509
    room temperature for
      baking, 366
    softening, 367
    sprays, 506
    storage, 509
    terra cotta dish for, 427
    unsalted, 347
    whipped, 367, 427, 508
Buttermilk, 501
    baking with, 351
    in pastry, 425
    for softening cheese, 504
    substitute for milk, 349
    for tenderizing chicken, 297
Bungee cord
    secure the, 127
Buttons, 119

C

Cabbage, 593–595
    health benefits, 593
    steamed, 302
    varieties, 594–595
Cabinet, 46, 100, 137, 144, 660
Cables, 44, 58, 146
Caffeine
    calcium and, 175
    contents, 178
    heartburn and, 178
    in soft drinks, 169, 179, 181
    sources of, 178
    in tea, 172, 173, 174
    thirst and, 169
    withdrawal, 181
Cajun seasoning, 458
Cakes
    air circulation and, 358
    angel food, 352, 366
    baking, 341
    berries in, 542
    bubbles in batter, 364
    checking before done, 366
    chiffon, 352
    cooling, 355
    cutting, 347, 515
    cutting shapes in, 347
    domed, 356
    dry middles, 361
    eggs in, 362
    falling, 366

    flour, 340, 341
    heart shaped, 366
    icing, 346, 355, 363, 365,
      372, 378, 465
    ingredient temperature, 343
    moist, 367, 374
    one bowl, 358
    oven temperature and, 366
    problems with, 352–353
    reducing calories in, 351
    replacing fats in, 351
    shortened, 352
    sponge, 352, 366
    sticking to plates, 376
    storing, 356
    tenderness of, 367
    transporting cakes, 390
Calamari, 271
Camembert, 477, 480, 481
Candy
    freezing, 384
    fudge, 383
    humidity and, 387
    making, 319, 367, 384
    shelf life, 367
    storage, 387
    temperature and, 384, 387
    tooth decay and, 362
Can opener, 107, 118, 135, 658
    cleaning, 658
Candle, 43, 47, 57, 103, 117,
    120, 126, 131, 143, 148,
    156, 199, 389, 391, 675
Cantaloupe, 524, 545, 559
    health benefits, 545
Capers, 434
Caraway, 434, 572
Carbohydrates, 428
    refined, 387
Carbonation, 171
Carcinogens, 222, 242, 245,
    405, 573
Cardamom, 434
Carnation, 124
Carotene, 411, 500, 537, 559,
    580, 590, 595, 609, 612,
    623, 632
Carp, 263, 279
Carrots, 595–597
    cooking, 309, 314, 326,
      472, 523

health benefits, 597
pectin in, 519
steamed, 302
storage, 310, 520
Casein, 109, 500, 625
Casseroles, 478
crispy tops, 309
Catfish, 279, 280
Catnip leaves, 155, 164
Cauliflower, 322, 573, 591, 592,
597, 639, 641
health benefits, 598
steamed, 302
storage, 597, 599
Caviar, 276, 277, 281
Cayenne pepper, 161, 211, 433,
434, 437, 458, 468, 625,
627
Celeriac, 598
Celery, 237, 250, 308, 391, 594
flakes, 435
health benefits, 599
leaves, 436
seed, 306, 435
Chair caning
tightening, 104
Champagne, 98, 181, 182, 553
storage, 182
type, 182
Cheese
American, 480
beer, 480
bel paese, 481
blue-veined, 479
boursault, 481
Boursin, 480
Brie, 477, 481
camembert, 477, 480, 481
cheddar, 479, 480, 482, 514
cheshire, 482
colby, 482
cold pack, 482
color, 194
cultures, 477
Edam, 482
farmer, 483
feta, 483
firm, 479
fontina, 483
Gjetost, 483
goat, 476

gorgonzola, 483
Gouda, 484
graters, 478
grating, 478
Gruyère, 484
Limburger, 484
melting, 479
mold, 477, 479, 480, 483,
484, 486, 489, 501, 507
mold and, 477
monterey Jack, 480
mozzarella, 484
muenster, 484
myost, 485
Neufchâtel, 485
NuKraft, 478
parmesan, 368
for parties, 192
pecorino Romano, 479
port du salut, 485
pot, 483
provolone, 486
quark, 486
reduced-fat, 477
ricotta, 486
ripening, 477, 479
romano, 486
roquefort, 486
semisoft, 480, 481
soft, 436, 477, 480
softening, 504
spread, 478
stilton, 486
swiss, 487
tilsit, 487
unripened, 479
velveeta, 478
Cheesecake
cracks in, 364
tips for, 364, 515
Cheesecloth, 286, 296, 373, 460
Cherries, 546–547
health benefits, 598
varieties, 546–547
Chervil, 431, 601
Cheshire cheese, 482
Chicken
bacteria and, 218, 251, 254,
292
barbecued, 294
broilers/fryers, 239, 290

buying in bulk, 291
Calories, 651, 652
capons, 290
cleaning before cooking, 294
cooking temperature, 286,
287, 293, 296
cornish hens, 290
cutlets, 286
dark meat, 296
fat/calories in, 243, 294,
651, 652
free-range, 288
freezing, 243, 251, 295, 463
frozen bouillon cubes from,
288
grading, 297
grilling, 293
ground, 293
kosher, 291, 645
lemon tenderized, 287
moist, 288
organic, 291
poussins, 291
previously frozen, 288
production, 287, 497
raising, 287
refreezing, 645
refrigerating, 288, 289
roast, 291, 294
salad, 286
serving size, 292
skinning, 651
with soy sauce, 295
stewing, 292
frying, 326
storing, 287
tenderizing, 297
whole, 287
with wine, 287, 289
wings, 293
Chicory, 572, 613, 614
Chili
peppers, 623–627
powder, 623–627
reheating, 661
China
stacking, 221
Chinese five
spice powder, 448
Chives, 415, 431, 435, 619
Chocolate, 198, 647, 651, 389

baking powder and, 357
curls, 375
icing, 361
melting, 387, 389
stains, 22
white, 386
Cholesterol, 460
   carrots and, 595
   in liver, 243
Chow chow, 570
Ciguatera, 260, 272
Cilantro, 436, 439
Coca-cola, 146, 178, 179, 388
Cinnamon, 107, 112, 146, 389,
   432, 436, 448, 453, 539
Clams, 261, 262, 279
   buying, 261
Chowder, 263
   cleaning, 49, 278
   hard shell, 262
   opening, 261
   soaking, 278
Cleaning
   car battery, 110
   car's wheels, 57, 151
   ceiling fan, 207
   ceramic floors, 140, 145
   chinaware, 130
   clean up tips, 390
   copper cookware, 318
Correction fluid, 45
   creases, 44, 203
   crystal or fine china, 130
   dashboard plastic, 149
   doors and windows, 17, 43,
     56, 107, 120, 132, 140,
     151, 202, 203, 205
   drains, 52, 206
   dryer, 13, 23, 28, 36, 51,
     136, 142, 144
   dryer lint, 133
   dust, 27, 37, 43, 109, 117,
     118, 121, 123, 137, 146,
     151, 228, 326
   fireplace, 92
   grill, 16, 45, 139, 158, 313,
     330
   lampshades, 48, 142
   lid, 45, 117, 118, 137, 325,
     391, 527, 662, 663
   mattress, 147

mineral deposits, 202
newspaper, 13, 33, 45, 132,
   140, 199, 206, 372
   ovens, 326
oven fan, 46
porcelain, 36, 204
rubbing alcohol, 49
satin and gloss finishes, 125
sink, 33, 52
silver, 119, 121, 122, 146
stone floors, 49
taps, 72, 202, 203, 204, 205
tarnished, 122
thermos bottles, 50
toilets, 205, 206
vacuum, 30, 33, 39, 50, 53,
   109, 146, 155
vinyl tile, 17, 51, 96, 149
wallpaper, 104
water rings, 150, 188
Clothes
   A-line skirt, 75
   back, 74
   bed sheets, 134
   bra, 75, 76
   bust-line, 76
   combat pants, 75
   detergents, 12, 15, 23
   double and single breasted
     jackets, 74
   drying, 23, 141
   flat-fronted, 74
   G-string, 76
   jeans, 27, 39, 75
   legs, 75
   lycra, 76
   panty hose, 71
   T-shirt bras, 76
   towels, 127, 206
   trousers, 74, 75
   tulip skirt, 75
   undies, 76
   upper arms, 74
   washing, 26, 27, 28, 30
   winter, 128
   woolen, 130
Cloves, 107, 146, 155, 159,
   436, 438, 454
Club soda
   for stain removal, 15, 33, 128
instead of, 289

Cobblers, 371
Coconuts, 401, 458, 559, 603
Cod, 212, 252, 260, 272, 275
Coffee, 175, 177
   acidity in, 176
   bean storage, 174
   temperature, 177
   espresso, 180
   filters, 98, 175
   grinding, 174
   grind size, 180
   kona, 175
   stains, 26, 31, 32, 35, 54,
     56, 78
   in stews, 257
   turkish, 180
Colby cheese, 482
Cold pack cheese, 482
Collard greens, 608, 575, 630
Convection ovens, 308, 312
Cookies
   bar, 357, 370
   browning, 348
   burned bottoms, 341, 353,
     369
   chilled dough, 375
   cooling rack for, 369
Crispy, 373, 374
Cutting, 195, 357, 375, 496
   drop, 343, 357, 370
   freezing dough, 357, 370
   hand formed, 370
   margarine and, 357, 367
   moist, 370, 374
   oatmeal, 371, 399
   over stirring, 369
   pressed, 370
   reduced fat, 374
   refrigerator, 370
   rolled, 370
   soft, 341
   storage, 343, 369
   sugar, 343, 371
   timing, 357
   tough, 341
   using butter in, 367, 373
   bacon, 226, 239, 245, 295,
     296
   beans, 175, 194, 242, 302,
     330, 381, 405, 436, 580,
     581, 583–588

with beer, 188, 256, 268, 360
broccoli, 300, 302, 322, 326, 513, 590, 591, 662
Carrots, 300, 302, 309, 314, 326, 472, 595, 596, 634
Corn, 302, 323, 326, 341, 346, 348, 355, 365, 377, 378, 379, 400, 466, 600
fish, 251, 252, 254, 255, 258, 259, 260, 262, 264, 268, 658
with gas, 316, 319, 435
measurements, 302
moist heat, 156
odors, 575
onions, 620
pasta, 330, 406, 407, 408, 421, 424
rice, 42, 221, 332, 333, 396, 397, 398, 399, 405, 453
roasts, 325, 327, 236, 237, 240, 242, 250, 253, 308
stuffed turkey, 319
substitutions, 335–337
temperatures, 304
turkey, 286, 288, 289, 294, 296, 323, 645, 651, 659
vegetables, 322, 326, 327, 330, 429, 452, 453, 464, 513, 518, 570 572, 574, 575, 576
vitamins and, 309
waterless, 301
with wine, 185
Cookware. See Pots and pans
Coriander, 436, 437
Corn
cooking, 600
grilling, 323
nutritional value, 600
picking, 602
reviving, 602
steaming, 302, 602
storage, 601
Cornish hens, 290
Corn syrup, 348, 355, 377– 379
Cottage cheese
storage, 487
Crabs, 263–264
blue, 264

claws, 263
cooked shell color, 264
dungeness, 264
king, 264
sizes, 263
shell, 263
stone, 264
Cranberries
health benefits, 544
Crayfish, 279
removing meat from, 264
Cream
heavy, 501, 503
light, 427
reviving, 510
sour, 366, 368, 378, 426, 486, 491, 505
varieties, 510
weeping when whipped, 501
whipping, 365, 500
Cream cheese, 362, 364, 483
temperature for beating, 362
Croaker, 273
Croutons, 368
Cucumbers, 603–606
eye freshener, 69, 71, 638
health benefits, 606
pickles from, 605
Cumin, 435, 436
Curry powder, 437
Curtains
slipping, 125
stealing, 666
Custard, 510
Cutting boards, 117, 658
Cyclamates, 382

D

Dairy products
See also Cheese
allergies to, 500
autoxidation in, 504
butter, 347, 361, 366, 367, 426, 490, 509, 511, 512
buttermilk, 501, 506, 507, 351, 425
casein in, 109
condensed milk, 507
cottage cheese, 487
cream, 366, 368, 427, 500, 503, 505, 510

curdling, 221, 309, 464, 510
evaporated milk, 337, 500, 505, 507
fat in, 500
goat's milk, 483, 500
ice- cream, 503
ice milk, 503
milk, 215, 503, 504, 505, 506, 507, 509, 511, 585, 646
sour cream, 366, 368, 378, 426, 486, 491, 505
storage, 510, 644
whey in, 500
yogurt, 477, 500, 508
Dandelion greens, 571
Dates, 549, 662
Deer, 155, 157
Deglazing, 323
Degreaser
for stain removal, 16
dehumidifier, 139
Dehydration, 174
dental floss, 22, 55, 57, 271, 388, 491, 515
Denture tablet, 18, 31, 32, 35, 50, 56, 110
Detergent, laundry, 17
Dextrose, 378, 447
Diaper pails
deodorizing, 95
Dietary Supplement Act (1994), 383
Dill, 255, 437, 439, 606
Dips, 462, 508
Dishcloths / sponges, 658
Doughnuts, 651
Drawers, 57, 103, 127, 137, 139
Dublin Bay prawns, 265
Duck
plucking, 292
stuffing, 295
drinking straw, 114, 143, 165, 463, 599

E

E. coli, 232, 242, 524, 555
Eating out, 197, 647, 650, 655
Edam cheese, 482
Eels, 273
Eggnog, 442, 494

Eggplant, 224, 606, 607, 618
Eggs
    aluminum cookware and,
        488
    boiling, 503, 513
    broken, 494
    calories, 488
    candling, 496
    chalazae cords in, 496
    cholesterol and, 488
    chopping, 498
    cleaning utensils of, 490
    cooking temperatures, 498,
        510
    copper bowls and, 499, 514
    cracked, 490, 499, 513
    deviled, 489, 490
    egg cartons, 131
    egg white, 108, 243, 371,
        489, 514
    eggshells, 95, 140
    freezing, 490
    freshness, 493, 496, 512
    glazing baked goods and,
        363
    grading, 488
    green, 498
    handling, 496
    in baking, beating, 324
    in cakes, 366
    in Hollandaise
    in souffles, 368
    laying, 497
    measuring, 488
    microwaving, 302, 306, 308
    nutritional values, 489
    omelets, 493, 498, 513
    peeling, 498, 515
    poaching, 489, 493, 512
    safety with, 494
    saving yolks, 489
    scrambled, 491, 493
    seedlings, 140
    separating, 494
    shelf life, 496, 497, 498
    shells, 95, 140
    size, 351
    slicing, 491
    storage, 219, 493, 498, 515
    substitutes, 336, 348
    temperature and, 304, 324

    tempering, 491
    vegetarians, 512
    wash, 499
Eldridge, Elmer, 478
Emulsification, 466
Endive, 572, 614
    belgian, 613
    health benefits, 614
Energy
    save, 147, 325
    waster, 129
Equal sweetener, 382
Escarole, 613
Eyes
    browline, 84
    contact lens, 79, 671
    crow's feet, 68, 87
    eye brows, 63, 69, 81, 84
    eye glasses, 57, 58, 136, 471
    eye shadows, 63
    hollow eyes, 62
    puffy eyes, 71
    wrinkles, 63, 68, 79, 81,
        211, 375, 538
Ethylene, 224, 521, 533, 540,
    565, 612

F

Fabric softener, 17, 26, 27, 37,
    38, 56, 120, 127, 138, 206
Facial treatments, 84
Farmer cheese, 477, 483
Fast foods, 413, 446, 647, 650,
    651, 652, 653
Fats
    in baking, 367
    in bread sticks, 377
    in cakes, 351
    calories in, 430
    in commercial sauces, 463
    considerations for freezing,
        243
    in crackers, 426
    in dairy products, 500
    in fish, 251, 252, 257, 260,
        272–275, 278–279
    good, 458
    in margarine, 511
    in mayonnaise, 425
    in meats, 234, 236
    mono unsaturated, 419, 424

    in peanut butter, 431
    polyunsaturated, 424
    reduced in cookies, 374
    for rose bushes, 101
    saturated, 424
    shortening, 354, 429
    sleep patterns and, 428
    trans-fat in calories, 400
Flavanoids, 388
Fennel, 214, 439, 607
Fenugreek, 437
Fertilizer
    house plant, 95, 140
Feta cheese, 483
Figs
    health benefits, 550
    pectin in, 519
Fish
    bait box, 257
    cod liver oil, 212
    ammonia smell, 271
    anchovies, 256, 271
    anglerfish, 272
    aquaculture, 257
    bacteria, 257, 277, 555, 658
    baking, 222
    barracuda, 272
    bluefish, 272
    bones, 282
    bottom feeding, 263, 269
    bruising, 258, 282
    buffalo fish, 279
    carp, 279
    catfish, 263, 279
    ciguatera and, 260, 272
    cod, 210, 252, 260, 272
    cooking, 261, 262, 263,
        265, 269, 279, 282
    croaker, 273
    cured, 261
    dressed, 261
    dried, 261
    eel, 273
    eliminating smell, 254, 255,
        258
    eyes, 253, 258
    fat content, 251, 252, 257,
        260, 272–275, 278, 279
    fillets, 254, 259, 261, 274–
        276, 279–282, 327, 328
    fishy smell, 258

flavor, 255, 258, 262, 264, 266, 270, 271, 272, 273, 274

flounder, 273 freezing, 267, 270, 271, 272, 275, 463

freshwater, 277, 279, 282

frozen, 257, 259, 261, 265, 268, 270, 271, 275, 279

gills, 253, 258, 274, 615

government hot line, 260

grouper, 273

gutting, 277

haddock, 252, 273

hake, 274

halibut, 274

heads, 270

inspections, 253, 258, 260

mackerel, 274

mahi mahi, 274

marinating, 274

microwaving, 267

monkfish, 267, 272

mullet, 274

orange roughy, 275

parasites, 257, 279, 555

perch, 280

pike, 280

pollack, 264, 265, 275

pompano, 275

refrigerating, 275

sablefish, 275

salmon, 215, 251, 255, 273, 275

saltwater, 271–278, 282

sardines, 215, 276

scales, 258

seatrout, 276

shad, 276

shark, 276

skate, 277

skin signs

smelt, 280

steaks, 261, 272

steamed, 267

sturgeon, 277

swordfish, 277

thawing, 259, 270

trout, 280

tuna, 277

turbot, 278

whitefish, 280

whole, 261, 263, 265, 274, 276, 280

Flounder, 273

Flour

adding vitamin C, 345

aging, 355

all purpose, 340

cake, 341

insects in, 345

oat, 398

pastry, 341

self rising, 342

tapioca, 350, 465

types, 340–342

unbleached, 344, 355

whole wheat, 342

as wood patch, 103

finger paints, 150

Flowers

cutting, 96, 145

prolonging life of, 123

Fontina cheese, 483

Food borne illness

from fish, 260

Food borne illness, 292, 524, 660, 664

E. coli, 232, 242, 524, 555

salmonella, 218, 524

Foods. See also individual fooand groups

freezing, 218, 219

preservation, 218, 222

refreezing, 223

salt-cured, 222

smoked, 222

storage, 221, 223

Free items, 670–683

Freezers

chest, 52, 224

filling, 222

power failures and, 39, 172

temperature, 218

upright, 224

Freezing

bakery products, 223

berries, 229, 543, 552

bread, 361

candy, 384

chicken, 243, 287

chicken broth cubes, 288, 295, 463

cookie dough, 370

cranberries, 543

eggs, 490, 498

food with alcohol, 229

freezer burn and, 219, 225

intensification of flavors and, 221

juice boxes, 229

meats, 252

milk, 501 negative effects of, 220

oysters, 269

panty hose, 71

plastic wrap and, 249

potatoes, 221

raw meat, 251

sandwiches, 220

sauces, 221

shrimp, 271

soup bones, 253

soups, 463

vegetables, 520, 572, 575, 579, 596

wild rice, 226

Fructose, 378, 379, 384

Fruit beer, 191

ackee, 528

apples, 528–536

apricots, 536.537

atemoyas, 537

avocados, 538

babaco, 523

bananas, 539, 540, 541

berries, 543–544

black currants, 639

blueberries, 542

breadfruit, 544

browning of, 87, 523, 526, 529, 530, 538, 539, 557, 640

bruising, 517, 528, 536, 539

cantaloupe, 545

cherries, 547

choosing, 518

cranberries, 543, 544

dates, 549

dried, 347, 527, 574

figs, 551

fruit salad, 523, 563

grading system, 574, 575

grapefruit, 551

grapes, 552–556
honey dew melon, 556
jackfruit, 523
kiwi, 556, 557
lemon, 557, 558
limes, 558
mangoes, 559
nectarines, 560 oranges,
 560–562
oxidation, 518, 521
papayas, 563
peaches, 564
pears, 564–565
pectin in, 519
peeling, 526, 529, 560
persimmons, 566
pineapple, 567–568
plums, 568
pomegranates, 569
preparation, 310
prickly pears, 569
prunes, 568, 607
rambutan, 522
refrigerating, 520
rinds, 195, 322
ripening, 520, 521, 526,
 528, 533, 536, 537, 538,
 539, 540, 542, 556, 557,
 565
sapote, 569
star apples, 570
storage, 525
sugar in, 384
tangelos, 570
vitamins and, 527
watermelon, 570
Frying
 deep, 306, 426, 430
 meats, 307
 paper towels for, 308
Fudge, 383
Furniture
 clay pots on, 37
 cabinet space, 144
 counter space, 135
 outdoor, 97
 polish, 17, 109, 124, 179
 scratches in, 56
 sofa, 50, 136
 cover nicks, 45
 water rings, 150

white rings on
 wicker, 134, 150
 wooden, wooden97, 124,
 131, 150

G

Gardens
 grass, 23, 97
 planting, 140
Garlic, 438
 bread, 344, 362
 capsule, 160
 cooking, 432, 621
 excess, 439
 microwaving, 309
 mincing garlic, 439
 nutritional value, 638
Gas leak, 666
Gelatin, 466, 467
 unmolding, 376
 in whipped cream, 500
Giblets
 cooking with liver, 290
Gifting
 bride, 138
 get well card, 146
Ginsenocide, 212
Ginger, 413, 439
 crushing, 308
Ginger ale, 390
 for desalting ham, 239
Ginger root, 638
Ginseng, 212
Gjetost cheese, 483
Glass cleaner, 17
Glucose, 262, 354
Gorgonzola cheese, 483
Gouda cheese, 484
Grains
 amaranth, 394
 barley, 394
 buckwheat, 388
 bulgur, 419
 corn, 248, 446
 daily requirement, 394
 freshness, 405
 millet, 335
 oats, 371, 397
 quinoa, 396
 rice, 396
 rye, 396

triticale, 397
Grapefruit, 101
 pectin in, 519
Grapes, 525, 552
 dried, 554
 varieties, 552, 554
Gravy
 coffee in, 467
 de-fatting, 460
 lumpy, 460
 separation in, 468
 thickening, 323
Greens, 225
 beet, 571, 588–589
 crisping, 576
 health benefits, 573
 nutritional value, 571, 573
 spinach, 571
Varieties, 571
 ginkgo bilboa, 215
Grilling
 chicken, 293
 corn, 323, 602
 for a crowd, 246
 fish, 255
 greasing the rack, 293
 shrimp, 257
 spraying with oil, 313
 steak, 256
Grouper, 260
Grout
 cleaning, 49
Gruyere cheese, 484

H

Haddock, 252, 260, 273
 blow-dryers, 80
 coloring, 80
 copper peptides, 88
 dandruff, 65
 feathered cut, 87
 fine hair, 69
 greasy hair, 64
 hair color, 62, 471
 hair damage 88
 hair length, 88
 hair loss, 210
 hair mask, 214
 hair products, 89
 hair thins out, 80
 haircut, 86, 87, 88

hairstyle, 79, 88, 89
halloween, 115, 632
highlights, 214
perms, 80
scalp massage, 68
scalp, 64, 68, 210, 212
shiny hair, 64, 69
shorter layers, 86
split ends, 88
wet hair, 88
Hair care
alcohol in hair products, 64
beer, 190
brittle hair, 89, 210
brushes, 147
conditioner, 34, 64, 68, 80
finishing spray, 163
honey for, 64
leave-in conditioners, 69, 78,
80
wash-out conditioners, 69
Hake, 260, 274
Halibut, 260, 274, 252
Ham
boning, 238
brine, 238, 244, 245
canned, 240
coloration, 244, 249
country, 244
desalting, 239
gelatin content, 238, 240
pigmentation changes, 249
salt-cured, 238, 244
slicing, 239, 271
water weight, 238
Hamburger, 223, 243
additions to, 621
cholesterol in, 650, 652
doneness, 242
prebaking, 246
Hands
cleaning, 28, 85, 87, 104,
254, 331, 439, 664
Headaches, 589, 592
Herbes de Provence, 453
Health
arthritis, 468
bedtime schedule, 72
blood-sugar control, 381
brain function, 252
cellulite, 215

chemical reaction, 334, 416
fitter body, 197
gum disease, 73
hammertoes and bone spurs,
85
height, 72
improve balance in, 506
improve concentration, 468
improve moods, 211
liver and stomach, 637
natural acid balance, 70
neutralize the110
regenerative sleep, 87
regulate blood sugar, 419
relieve nausea, 390
serotonin, 211
sleeping posture, 81
sore throat, 549
stress hormones, 259
toxins, 222
vitamin supplements, 190
weight loss, 468
wrinkles on neck, 73, 84
Herbs and spices 226, 233,
432
adding, 432
cooking, 407
dried, 403, 431, 462
for meats, fish, poultry, 431
freshness, 432, 452, 454
grow herbs, 469
in barbecuing, 323
in oil, 454
potency, 462
rubs, 233
safety of, 658
short shelf-life, cayenne
pepper and, 161
stock up, 331, 471
storage, 454
substitutes, 454
timing, 407
unsafe, 455
varieties, 469
when to add
Heterocyclic aromatic amine
(HAA), 242
Hexatol, 378
Hollandaise sauce, 470
Honey, 64
for hair care, 64

production of, 379
storage, 379
whipped cream and, 500
Honey dew melon, 556
Hormones
in meat, 259
Horseradish, 609
Horse chestnuts, 162
Hot dogs, 195
cooking, 238
ingredients, 237
protein in, 237

I

Ice, 171
clean, 171
for coffee/tea, 172
sharpens, 132
Ice cream
air in, 491, 503
fat in, 430
harmful ingredients in, 502
homemade, 503
fat, 503
ice cream cones, 391
storage, 223
Icing
chocolate, 346
of, 346
fondant, 355
lettering on, 378
running over, 365
sticking, 363
stiffening, 363
Ingredients
substitutions, 335, 337
Insects
in flour, 391
repellant
Italian seasoning, 458
Itch, 662

J

Jackfruit, 523
Jam and jelly
ingredients, 385
making, 385, 527
pectin in, 519
setting, 527
no-sugar jam, 389

Jerusalem
artichokes, 609
Jewelry
chokers, 74
cleaning amber, 82
cup hook, 147
diamond, 128
earrings, 119, 133, 136
emeralds, 83, 110
gems, 110
gold, 110
Jicama, 300, 610
marcasite, 83
necklace, 74, 140, 143
organiser, 143
pearls, 82, 110
platinum, 82
polishing, 82
stones, 82, 110

K

Kale, 571, 573, 575, 608, 617, 630, 638
Kasha, 335, 395
Kettle, 37
Kidneys, 447, 457, 578, 168, 236,
Kiwi, 235, 467, 556, 557
Knives, 577, 328, 329, 556
Knives
basic, 328
carbon steel, 328
carbon stainless steel, 328
choosing, 329
safety, 328
sharpening, 328
stainless steel, 328
storing, 329
chicken, 645

L

Lactobacillus, 477
Lactose, 647, 378
Lager, 189, 190, 191
Lamb,
cooking temperatures, 304
fat / calories, 283
fell, 235
grades, 235
shanks, 241
sweetbread, 236

kidneys, 236
components, 245
black coffee, 257
herbs, 431
mint, 440
flavoured wine vinegar, 452
corduroy, 24,
dark clothing, 28
ironing, 23, 24, 26, 29, 38, 679
shrinkage, 39,
facbric softener, 26
sorting socks,
wool, 24,
Lavender, 53, 72, 87, 155, 157, 159, 453
Laxatives
natural, 522
Lead
in crystal, 664
in dinnerware, 106
Leather
reviving, 108
lease of life to, 122
Leeks, 335, 417
Lemon, 418
on fish, 254
polish, 179
health benefits, 468, 557
juicing, 558
to prevent cracked eggs, 490
rust stain removal, 12
for shoe polishing, 13
for skin blemishes, 518
Lentils, 331
nutritional value, 587
Lettuce, 611
freshness, 644
romaine, 613
storage, 612
varieties, 612
Levulose, 378
Light bulbs
broken, 92
Limburger cheese, 480
Limes
for headaches, 557
Lin seed oil
wood,
Lipstick
broken, 20

stains, 20
Liver,
cholesterol in, 237, 243
toxins in, 268
Lobster
claws, 266
color, 267
cooking, 264, 267, 279
handedness, 266
maine, 266
miniature, 265
roe, 268
spiny, 266
Lox, 279

M

Mace, 443, 450
Mache, 613
Mackerel, 229, 260, 274
magnetic strip, 46
Mahi mahi, 274
Malt liquor, 189, 191, 400,
Maltose, 378,
magnesium sulfate, 86
Manganese, 241, 396
absorption of, 241
Mangoes, 559
Manila envelope, 137
Milk thistle, 214
Mannitol, 378
Maple syrup, 373, 379, 380, 437
in pancakes, 373
storage, 379
Margarine, 28, 223, 357, 367, 449, 493, 511, 584
in cookies, 357
fat in, 367, 430
stick, 511
storage, 223
Marinades, 246, 247
Marinating
fish, 555
meats, 469
poultry, 556
ribs, 234
Marjoram, 431, 443
Marshmallows,
as candle holders, 117
in pumpkin pie, 374
Marzipan, 402

Mayonnaise, 109, 412, 425, 430, 449
Maytag cheese,
Mouse, 154
  mousetrap, 163
Measuring cups, 374
Meatballs, 248
  moist, 248
Meat loaf, 525, 238
Moist, 238
Meats, See also specific meats
  ageing, 236
  blood in, 444
  color, 240, 246
  contaminated, 246, 526
  cost per pound, 236
  fat/calorie counts, 430, 649,
  freezing, 220, 223, 249
  internal temperature, 246
  less tender cuts, 255
  marinating, 469
  microwaving, 307, 326
  preparation for storage, 526
  refreezing, 240
  rubs, 233
  storage, 646
  storing cooked, 240
  sweetbreads, 255
  tenderness, 246
  thawing, 240
Medicine, 53, 544, 671
Meringue, 223
  beading, 348
Mexican seasoning, 458
Microorganisms
  bacteria, 506
  E. coli, 232, 242, 524
Mold, 246, 361, 477, 483
  yeast, 218, 335, 346, 354, 355, 356
Microwave oven, 302, 308
  defrosting in, 247
Microwaving, 302, 310
  brown sugar, 385
  butter, 504
  eggs, 306
  fish, 332
  lobster, 267
Meats, 307, 326
  vegetables, 302
Mildewed pages, 123

bacteria in, 507
breast, 507
in clear containers, 646
condensed, 507
consumption,
curdling, 184
evaporated, 336, 500
fat in, 500
goat's, 500
heating, 502
Low-fat, 503, 506
  processed, 502
  scalding, 507
  soy, 585
  soy proteins, 67
Millet, 395
  milk thistle, 214
Mint, 440
Mirrors
  cleaning, 57
Miso, 585
Molasses, 381
Money
  save, 22, 30, 34, 117, 141, 146, 675
  vouchers, 670
  online bill payment, 683
Monkfish, 267, 272
Monterey Jack cheese, 480
Mosquitoes, 106, 156, 159, 161
Moths, 128, 156, 161
Mozzarella, 484
Muenster cheese, 484
Muffins
  removal from pan, 349
  removing from pan, 361
Mullet, 274
Mushrooms, 614
  health benefits, 617
  puffball, 570
  storage, 615
  varieties, 615–617
Mussels, 269
  debearding, 269
  refrigerating, 269
Mustard, 440
  prepared, 441
Myost cheese, 485

N

Nail

hammering,105
Nails
  emery board,108
  over-buffing,85
  nail polish bottles,118
Nectarines, 526
  health benefits, 560
Neufchatel cheese, 485
  threading,56
  sewing machine needle,93
NuKraft cheese, 478
Nutmeg, 539
Nutrasweet, 382
Nuts, 135,401
  almonds, 402
  cracking, 419
  roasted, 402, 403
  nutritional value, 419
  pillows, 141
  peanuts, 581
  pecans, 421
  roasted, 581

O

Oatmeal, 371
  for arthritis pain
  cookies, 371
Oats
  bran, 395
  flour, 396
  instant, 397
  nutritional value, 396
  cooking, 397
  rolled, 397
Oils, 424–429
  in baked goods, 468
  canola, 318, 320, 424,425
  catches fire, 666
  citronella, 156
  "cleaning," 426
  coconut, 458
  corn, 430
  disposing of, 424
  frying temperatures, 430
  in grilling, 601
  herbs and spices in, 432
  in mayonnaise, 449
  mineral, 460
  olive, 538
  sweet almond oil, 82
  birch oil, 81

in opaque containers, 470
palm, 645
peanut, 645
in potato chips, 418, 420
for remove glue residue, 110
safflower, 318, 337
salad dressings, 430
soybean, 506
frying, 233
types of, 424
vegetable, 429
Okra, 618
    health benefits, 618
Olive, 47, 618
    quality of, 428
Omega-3
    fatty acids, 513
Onions, 575
    cooking, 575, 620
    health benefits, 619, 622
    pearl, 621
    storage, 619
    sweet, 619, 621
    tears from, 620
    varieties, 621
    vidalia, 621
    red onion, 621
Orange roughy, 275
Oranges, 322, 560
    antacids and
    health benefits, 561
    juice containers, 561
    varieties, 562
Orange peels, 56
Oregano, 335–337
Oven cleaners, 52
Ovens
    baking pan arrangement in,
        302
    self-cleaning model, 35
    checking temperature
    convection, 312
    eletric, 319
    gas, 319
    self cleaning, 326
Oysters, 260
    cooking, 263
    freezing, 16, 268
    opening, 93
    refrigerating, 269
    season for, 272

P

Painting
    brushes,
    cleaning brushes,
    door hinges, 92
    keeping paint fresh,
    paint liners, 148
    keeping track of colors, 103
    low areas, 108
    lumpy paint,
    paint removal, 21
    primer, 52
    rollers, 103
    steps, 95
    tinting spackle,
    using varnish, 102
Pancakes,
    cooking, 345, 368
    making syrup,
    maple syrup in batter, 373
    secrets for, 353
    sticking, 373
Panty hose
    for plant bulbs, 98
    for plant ties, 100
    sanding wood and, 102
Papayas, 563
    health benefits, 563
    pectin in,
Paprika, 433, 437, 442
Parasites
    in fish, 257
Parcooking, 313
Parmesan cheese, 368
Parsley, 435, 439, 443
Parsnips, 622
Parties,
    buffets, 197
    dips, 462
    holiday, 59
    invitations, 194, 197
    planning, 197
    serving sizes and amounts,
    party invitations, 194
    vacation, 683
    restaurants, 446, 647
    movies, 399, 683
    picnics,
    petroleum jelly, 53, 54, 63,
        70
Pasta

adding protein, 402, 406
cooking, 330, 400, 407, 421
making, 407
nutritional value, 408
rinsing, 400
serotonin and, 408
shapes, 409, 410
in soup, 424, 462
spinach, 407
storage, 165, 408
timing, 407
Pastries 341
    baking, 343
    buttermilk in, 425
    crust, 348
    ingredient temperature, 343
    puff, 358
    sugar in, 376
Peaches, 564
    health benefits, 564, 565
    pectin in, 519
Peanut butter 460
    fats in, 318
    lumpy gravy and, 460
    for mice, 158
    to remove gum from hair,
    storage, 565
Peanuts 581
    uses, 401
Pears, 325, 564
    health benefits, 565
    pectin in, 519
    varieties, 565
Peas, 302, 622
    canned, 622
    health benefit, 564
    pectin in, 519
    shelling, 623
    sodium in, 575
Pecorino Romano cheese, 479
Pectin, 467, 599, 603
Peeling, 122
    potato peeler, 59, 198
    piercing, 620
    reviving,
    skin, 221
    soup, 243
    stain removal and, 320
    steamed, 302
    storage, 411
    stuffed, 413

sweet, 411, 519
twice cooked, 414, 421
yams, 411
Peephole, 662
pencil, 598
Pepper, 335
cayenne, 335, 433
chili, 434
timing in use of, 623
Peppercorns, 331
Peppermint, 440, 444
digestive, 196
Pepperoni, 253
Peppers, 435, 623
capsaicin in, 624, 625
varieties, 211
Perch, 260
Perfume, 21, 72
fading, 70
stains, 21
in steam irons, 114
storage, 70
Persimmons, 566
health benefits, 566
Pesticides, 535
Pesto, 451
Pests and bugs
ants, 162
bees, 165
bugs, 244
carpenter ants, 162
chiggers,
deer, 155
fleas, 155
fly spray and, 160
fruit flies, 156
hair spray and,
herbs and, 209
on house plants,
lavender oil and, 157
meal worms,
mice, 158
mosquitoes, 160
moths, 161
mothballs, 96
peppermint and,
roaches, 161
rotten eggs and, 155
silverfish, 159
slugs, 157
snails, 156 165

squirrels, 161
wasps, 160
Pets
aquarium, 123
bird bath, 161
cat, 647
dog, 647
food, 156
fish bowl, 160
hair, 676
on furniture, 162
hairballs,
health tips, 156, 676
vitamin C for pregnancy,
154
Pies
cold ingredients for crust,
644
flaky crust, 346
flour for, 340
graham cracker crust, 346
meringue, 223
Pike, 280
Pilaf
bulgur, 419
Pillow
stress, 81, 121
Pilsner, 189, 191
Pineapple, 520, 567
dried, 567
health benefits, 568
Pizza
cutting, 348
toppings, 271
Plants
bringing inside,
care while away, 98
repotting, 100
ties for, 98
transplanting, 97
watering, 92
Plastic
bag, 576
wrap, 570
Plums, 568
health benefits, 568
Poison ivy, 419
Pollack, 260
powder puff, 391
polyphenols, 173
Pompano, 260

Popcorn, 420, 600, 601
Poppy seeds, 401
Pork
cooking temperatures, 304
fat/calories in, 245, 283
freezing, 223
ham, 304
roasts, 259
sausage, 223
stir / frying, 326
Port du Salut cheese, 485
Porter, 190
Posters, 51
Potato chips, 418
Potatoes, 393
baking, 300, 307
boiling, 366
chips, 420
freezing, 219
french fried,
green color, 420
mashed, 223
moisture in,
nutritional value,
pectin in, 519
Pot cheese, 483
Pot pie, 471
Potpourri 121
Pots and pans
aluminum, 359
baking, 365
boiling over,
bread, 334
cast iron, 311, 312
clay, 97
copper, 311, 312
enameled, 312
glass, 312
grease fire in, 107
heat distribution in, 314
heating first,
hot spots, 317
lid knob replacement,
lids, 325
nonstick, 341
oven arrangement, 312
purchasing, 329
roasting,
salting, 575
shallow, 348
stainless steel, 414

Poultry, 292
  cooking temperatures, 304
  marinating, 247
  plucking, 292
  purchasing, 293
  seasoning, 337, 443
  stuffing, 443
  thawing, 293, 295
Poussins, 291
Prawns, 257
Pressure cooking, 300
  altitude and, 322
Pears, 564
Provolone cheese, 486
Prozac, 211
Prunes, 568, 607
Pudding
  plum, 568, 607,
Pumpkin, 213

Q

Quark cheese, 486
Quiche
  cooling, 327
  crust, 514
Quinoa
  nutritional value, 396

R

Rabbit, 223, 244
Radicchio, 614
Radishes, 628, 640
Raisins, 362, 554, 556
Rambutan, 522
Ranges
  filters, 92
  gas, 319, 326
  reservatrol, 196
  rubber plunges, 145
  radiators, 81, 147
Refrigeration, 256, 570
  changing flavors, 384
  chicken, 243, 251
  food to be kept from, 219
  fruits/vegetables, 222
  of leftovers, 304, 327, 454
  mold in, 576
  mussels, 269
  shellfish, 257
  defrosting, 228, 247
  odors in fridge, 498, 509

Ribs
  marinating in refrigerator, 238
Rice
  brown, 341, 395
  burned, 333
  cooking, 221
  fluffy, 399
  freezing, 406
  in soup, 655
  jasmine, 399
  nutritional value, 395, 396,
    430
  quick cooking, 396
  rinsing, 398
  wild, 399
Ricotta, 477
Ring
  slip off, 127
Roasting, vegetables, 300
Roasts
  beef, 223, 242
  choosing, 242
  dry/moist heat for, 233, 327
  elevating, 308
  internal temperature, 312
  pork, 326
  removing fat from
  resting before carving, 289
  storage, 223
  timing, 242
Rolls, dinner, 346
  glazing, 363
  keeping warm, 346
  removal from pan, 361
Romano cheese, 479
Roquefort, cheese, 479, 486
Rosemary, 431, 443
  rubber bands, 118
Rubs
Rust, 12
  metal dishes, 328
  mothballs, 128, 135
  mower, 134
  on tools, 96, 135
  onions, 55
  preventing, 135
Rye
  nutritional value, 396

S

Saccharine, 383

Safety tips, 657, 658
  bills, 129, 683
  buffets, 197
  bulging tin cans, 660
  canned food, 660
  canning, 564, 661
  childproof cabinets,188
  cooking oils, 318
  cubed fruits and vegetables,
    662
  cutting boards, 658
  dishcloths/sponges 658
  grilling, 278, 293, 313, 663
  hand' 524,664,15,18
  identity theft, 129
  irradiated foods, 667
  ladders, 269
  lead crystal, 664
  saucepans, 505, 575
  washing, 49, 130
Saws
  sunglasses, 136
  swimming pool, 106
  thawing food, 240, 247
  water, 211
St John's Wort, 211
Safflower, 469
Saffron, 442
Sage, 431, 441
Salmon, 215
  lox, 279
Salmonella, 218, 524
  salsa, 470
Salt, 649
  bread and, 192, 620
  eggplant and, 607
  food content, 649
  freshening coffee with
  in ham, 238–239, 244
  preserving and, 49, 218
  reducing
  rice in for humidity, 115
  sedation, 95
  timing in use of, 250
  types, 444
Sandwiches, 477
  freezing, 347
  microwaving, 302 , 372
Sapote, 569
Sardines, 276
Sauces'34

commercial, 179
decurdling, 509
with dry soup mix, 462
fats in, 257
freezing, 471
hollandaise, 470
lumpy
Sausage' 235
shrinkage
Splitting
sausage patties, 235
Sauteing, 314, 430
Savory, 313, 443, 446
summer, 446
Scallops, 653
Scissors, 208, 328
sharpening, 328
Seafood, 220, 646
bacteria, 223
ciguatera and, 260
fat content, 260, 276
grilling, 277
parasites, 257
Sea kelp, 212
sealing
spirulina, 213
Seasonings. 428, *See* Herbs and
spices
Sea trout, 276
Serotonin, 408, 211
Sesame seeds, 446
Shad, 276
Shark, 276
Shellfish, 265, 268
abalone, 261
clams, 261
crabs, 263
crayfish, 265
imitation, 265, 647
langoustines, 265
liver, 268
lobsters, 266
mussels, 269
mustard, 440
opening, 428
overcooking, 266
oysters, 268, 269
prawns, 257, 270
refrigerating, 268
scallops, 265
shrimp, 264

shucking, 268, 269
soaking, 256
squid, 271
sweetness in
tomalley, 268
Shoes, 108
boots, 144
laces, 29
odors in, 54, 56
polish, 108
Shrimp, 265
breaded, 430
canned, 660
freezing, 220
grilling, 275
heads, 270
overcooking, 262, 270
rock, 265,
sizes, 270
Sidewalks and patio, 125
Skate, 277
Skin, 67
anti-ageing effects, 67
antioxidants, 639
avocados, 639
body brushing, 86
detoxifying, 213, 468
double chin, 73
dry and chapped hands
dull and sallow, 65
essential oils, 334
facial muscles, 81
finelines, 68
freckles, 87
frownies, 81
hands, 85
lymphatic drainage-based
treatment, 198
massage, 86
mild soap, 85
pollution, 630
skin's absorption, 469
T zone area, 81
wider nose, 81
SPF 20, 87
photo ageing and liver spots,
81
melanoma, 87
sunbathing, 72
Self-tan, 80
blemishes, 87

bruises, 87
calluses, 85
dry skin, 70
facial treatment, 66, 80
fresh baby wipe, 35
liquid soap, 84
premature ageing, 375
pumice stone, 17
rough lips, 64
skin products, 67
skin tone, 62, 198, 511, 635
soft feet, 89
UV lights, 72
Skin-boosting, 213
baby oil, 127
foundation, 73, 78, 80
fresh for longer [make up],
66
fuller lips, 64
Make-up brushes, 84
Make-up pencil, 69
make-up, 66, 69, 78
minerals, 213
rejuvenating skin, 210
Skin care, 67, 213, 612
aloe vera and
baby oil and, 13, 127
cleanser, 66
exfoliating cream, 66
moisturizer, 62, 84, 102
night cream, 65, 73
over cleansing, 66
oxygen to, 65
tomatoes, 635
vinegar for, 205
water, 665
Sleeping, 81
induce a, 95
Slow cooking, 250
safety, 314, 327
tenderness and, 351
Social Security card, 138
Slugs, 158
beer, 165
Smells
smoke smell, 49
holiday smell, 146
coffee grounds, 54, 177, 331
Smelt, 280
Snacks, 190
Soap

dish, 674
Soda bicarbonate
Soft drinks, 169
   solar power, 145
Solvents
   for stain removal, 15
   selenium, 213
Sorghum, 378
Souffles 373
   collapsing, 373
Soups
   adding herbs, 450
   bones, 472
   bouillon, 579
   broth, 655
   chowder, 263
   cloudy, 424
   cold, 460
   cooling, 226, 460
   cream, 460, 464
   curdling, 464
   de-fatting, 460
   low fat, 236, 243, 259
   mixes, 461, 462
   simmering, 550
   stock, 471, 472
   thickening, 461, 463
   too salty, 461
Soybeans, 581
   pectin in, 467
Soy products, 584
   peanut butter, 645
   health benefits, 660
Soy sauce 579
   for basting
Spices.
   See Herbs and spices
Spinach, 407
Splenda, 381
Splinter removal
Squab, 293
Squash
   summer, 519
Squid, 271
Stains
   adhesive, 19
   alcohol, 19
   bacon grease, 18
   bath stains, 203
   black stains, 205
   blinds, 33

blood, 15
blueberry, 35
bumper sticker, 144
chewing gum, 19
chocolate, 22
cigarette burns
coffee and tea, 19, 31, 32
concrete, 36
cooking oil, 25
cosmetic, 19
crayon, 19
deodorant, 19
fruit, 20
gasoline, 35
grass, 20
grease, 20
gum, 20
ink, 13, 20
iodine, 20
lavatory cleaners, 206
lipstick, 20
mildew, 20
milk, 20
mustard, 20
nail polish, 21
oil-based, 25
oven rings, 30
paint, 21
painted walls, 676
pen marks
perfume, 21
perspiration, 21
red stains, 18
remove burned food
rust, 151, 309, 320, 328
scorch marks, 13, 21
scuffmarks, 13, 54
silver, 146
soot stained brick, 124
streaks, 140
tar, 21
thermos, 38, 50
toilet bowl, 18
tomato, 19, 22
tree sap, 28
tupperware stains'
water-based'
wax, 19, 22
wine, 21, 38
yellow, 26
Star apples, 570

Steaks, 425
   grilling, 246, 256, 278
   internal temperature, 245
   marbling in, 248
   rare, 304
   seasoning, 330
Steamed, 302
   corn, 601
   fish, 255, 261, 278
   vegetables, 302
Stevia, 383
Stews 223
   adding coffee, 257
   de-fatting, 460
   pot pie from, 471
   simmering, 550
   sweetening, 472
   thickening, 463
   too salty, 461
   tortillas in, 463, 655
Stilton cheese, 486
Stir
   frying, 326
   vegetables, 326
Storage
   bacon, 35
   baseball cap, 149
   beans, 587
   beer, 187
   bread, 226
   butter, 424
   cakes, 560
   candy, 319, 362
   carrots, 596
   cauliflower, 592
   champagne, 181
   containers, 118
   cookies, 343
   corn, 424
   cottage cheese, 243
   dairy products, 219
   decoration, 144, 664
   eggs, 226
   electrical cord, 96
   food, 218
   fruit, 530
   heavy mirror, 144
   herbs and spices, 226
   honey, 379
   ice cream, 223, 651
   lettuce, 460, 520

maple syrup, 379
margarine, 223
meat, 256
mushrooms, 327
newspaper clippings, 223
oils, 454
onions, 226, 619
paper towels, 245
pasta, 472
peanut butter
perfume, 522
potatoes, 219, 223
recipes, 295
socks, 98, 151
solvents, 14
spices, 226
steel wool pads, 130
store breads, 255
storing foods, 118, 218
storing sauces and
    gravies, 135
storing wild rice, 399
storing wraps, 42
vegetables, 470, 572 , 604
wine, 185
yeast, 346
Stout, 615
Strawberries, 638
pectin in, 467, 534
Stuffing
bags, 286
duck, 292, 295
keeping in bird, 304
poultry, 287, 290
temperature and, 286
turkey, 296, 449
Sturgeon, 277
Substitutions, ingredient,
    335–337, 453, 454
Sucralose, 381
Sugar, 381
beet, 589
brown, 381, 385
cane, 381
cravings, 385
creaming with butter, 508
in fruit, 527
health problems from, 549
lumpy, 385
as major ingredient, 385
names for, 377

nutrients in, 377
in products, 377
reducing, 387
thirst and, 169
turbinado, 380
Sunburn, 667
relief, 557
Sunchokes. 609
    (See Jerusalem)
artichokes, 577
Sunflower seeds, 406
nutritional value, 406, 430
sunlight, 215
Supermarket tips, 254
buy chocolates
buying fattier meat, 244
buying fresh fish, 253
free range chickens, 290
Surimi, 265, 275
Sweetbreads, 236
SweetOne sweetener, 381
Sweets and sweeteners, 378, 385
artificial, 118, 385, 558
aspartame, 382
candy, 385
corn syrup, 378
cyclamates, 382
dextrose, 378
fructose, 378
glucose, 378
hexatol, 378
honey, 378
jams and jellies, 378
lactose, 378
levulose, 378
maltose, 378
mannitol, 378
maple syrup, 379
marshmallow, 385
molasses, 378, 391, 587
saccharine, 383
sorghum, 378, 381
stevia, 383
sucralose, 381
sucrose, 378
sugar, 378
tooth decay and, 362
turbinado, 378, 380
xylitol, 378
Swiss cheese, 430, 487
Swordfish, 251, 260, 276, 277

T

Tabbouleh, 419, 478
Tables, picnic, 93
Tangelos, 570
Tape
scotch-tape, 81
Tapioca, 336, 350
for thickening, 465
Tarragon, 335, 337
talcum powder, 59, 123
Tea, 172, 173
black, 466
brewing temperature, 174
caffeine in, 175, 178
cloudiness in, 173
green, 212
oolong, 173
stains, 32, 37
herbal teas, 211
green tea compress, 68
astragalus tea, 214
sachets of black tea
telephone, 58, 659, 682
Tempeh, 585
tweezers, 46
tryptophan, 296
Temperature
butter cream, 505, 508, 509
cream cheese, 479, 480
drinking water, 168, 170
eggs and, 494
fish, 229
for ageing beef, 236
for banana, 539
for beer, 187–190
for bread, 544
for brewing tea, coffee, 173,
    174, 177
for buffets, 197
for cakes, 352, 364
for candymaking, 387
for custard, 510
for milk, 502
for stuffing, 286, 319
for wine, 182, 185
for yogurt, 640
freezer, 218
meat, 245, 246, 250
poultry, 659
Tenderizing
chicken, 287, 297

meats, 248, 256, 550
with lemon, 287
with tea, 466
with wine corks
Thermometers, 304, 359
Thirst, 447
altitude and, 170
Thyme, 335, 448
Tilsit cheese, 480
Toads, 157
Tofu, 585
Toilet
cleaning, 18, 42
paper, 45
Tomatillos, 635
Tomatoes, 331, 334, 521, 633
acidity in, 583, 587
chopping, 224
dried, 635
freshness, 224
health benefits, 635
heirloom, 635
microwaving, 634
pectin in, 519
peeling, 526
refrigerating, 521
sun'
varieties, 634, 635
Tongs, 139
for turning grilled meat
Toothpaste, 23, 444
Triglycerides, 458
Triticale, 397, 400
nutritional value
Trout, 260, 276, 280, 282
Tuna, 430, 449
mercury intake, 251
Turbinado, 378
Turbot, 278
Turkey, 296, 449
brown bag cooking, 323
cooking upside down, 288
cooking, 289
ground, 430
rack for cooking, 288
resting before carving, 289
salad, 430
stuffing, 296
thawing, 247, 295
wine basted, 287
Turmeric, 437, 448

Turnips, 636
greens, 225

V

Valerian, 215
Vanilla, 450, 451
Vaseline, 53
Veal, 241
cooking temperatures, 304
fat/calories in, 283
milk fed, 241
production of, 241
Vegetables, 171
See also individual types
artichokes, 302
asparagus, 573, 578
baking, 300, 307, 309, 329
beans, 587
beets, 588
blanching, 596
broccoflower, 592
broccoli, 617, 636
brussels sprouts, 617
cabbage, 636
caramelizing, 576
carrots, 595
cauliflower, 597
celeriac, 598
celery, 598
commercial, 50
cooking, 300, 322
corn, 302, 315, 323
cruciferous, 590, 593,
597, 636
cucumbers, 520, 570, 603,
604-606, 663
eggplant, 224, 570, 606–607
fennel, 214
freezing, 218–222
grading system, 574
green, 225, 246
jerusalem artichokes, 609
frying, 610, 623, 655
jicama, 610
leeks, 417, 610
lentils, 331
lettuce, 460, 520
mushrooms, 524, 570,
614–617
okra, 618
onions, 226, 302, 327

parsnips, 622
peas, 580, 587, 622–623,
661
peppers, 326, 435, 463
preparation, 395
radishes, 628, 640
refrigerating, 173, 297, 595
relish, 570, 598
root, 212, 300, 411, 448,
451
spinach, 513, 589, 612, 628,
629
steaming, 593, 602
storage, 470, 572, 587, 596,
604, 619
tomatoes, 637
turnips, 636
Vichyssoise, 417
Vinegar, 451–453
for sting, 159
for sunburn, 71
laundry rinse, 15, 27
types, 452
unclog iron, 24
Vitamins, 209, 211, 214
cooking and, 310, 587
in fruit, 117
water soluble, 310
preserving, 310
in Millet, 395
VCR tapes, 134

W

Waffles, 223
sticking to iron, 375
Wallpaper
grease spots and, 104
hanging, 94
removal, 104
Water, 168, 171
altitude and, 169, 170
and stomach irritation, 43
carbonated, 171, 182
dehydration and, 170
distilled, 665
filtered, 168
hangovers and, 174
in umbrella stands, 118
need for, 169
temperature, 168
wasting, 171

Water chestnuts, 636
Watercress, 614
Watermelon, 567, 570, 639
   windburn, 63
WD–40, 36
   for crayon stains, 36
Wheat
   age and, 185
   beer, 400
   cracked, 398, 400
   germ, 398, 401
   wheat grass, 214
   whole, 397, 400, 401
Whitefish, 265, 280, 281
Windows
   cleaning, 14, 132, 140
   frosting, 104
   washing, 107
   wind shield, 120
Wine
   age and, 184
   aroma, 183, 185
   blush, 183
   composition, 185
   coolers, 193
   cork removal, 133, 197
   food guidelines, 185
   fortified, 183
   in cooking, 186
   nonvintage, 183
   pour size, 185
   stains, 38, 109
   storage, 183
   temperature and
   vintage, 183
Wrap
   foil, 225
   plastic, 355, 433, 451, 455,
      479, 489, 538, 545
   sticking to self, 114
   supermarket, 448, 452
   waxed paper, 134

proofing, 355, 357
storage, 346
workings of, 354
Yogurt, 506, 508
   whey in, 500

X

Xylitol, 378

Y

Yeast
   dry, 335, 356, 372
   hard water, 350
   in bread machines, 372